Writing in the Workplace

Jo Allen

East Carolina University

Allyn and Bacon

Boston ■ London ■ Toronto ■ Sydney ■ Tokyo ■ Singapore

In unwavering and loving memory of my father, Bob Allen

To Mom, Kay, Doug, and Sarah Beth
who convinced me from my first breath that I could do anything
I wanted to do . . .

and to Mike
who convinced me I should do this

Vice President, Humanities: Joseph Opiela
Developmental Editor: Allen Workman
Marketing Manager: Lisa Kimball
Senior Editorial Production Administrator: Susan McIntyre
Editorial Production Service: Andrea Cava

Composition Buyer: Linda Cox
Manufacturing Buyer: Suzanne Lareau
Cover Administrator: Linda Knowles
Text Design and Electronic Composition: Denise Hoffman

 Copyright © 1998 by Allyn and Bacon
A Viacom Company
160 Gould Street
Needham Heights, MA 02194

Internet: www.abacon.com
America Online: keyword: College Online

Library of Congress Cataloging-in-Publication Data
Allen, Jo.
    Writing in the workplace / Jo Allen.
      p.   cm.
    Includes index.
    ISBN 0-205-17373-X (alk. paper)
    1. English language—Rhetoric.   2. English language—Business
English.   3. English language—Technical English.   4. Technical
writing.   5. Business writing.   I. Title.
PE1479.B87A47   1997
808'.06665—dc21   97-40070
                                                     CIP

Printed in the United States of America
10 9 8 7 6 5 4 3 2 1   RRD 04 03 02 01 00 99 98 97

Contents

9 *Designing and Formatting Your Workplace Document*   291

PART II LETTERS, MEMOS, AND REPORTS

10 *Letters and Memos*   321

Preface to the Instructor

At the heart of this book is a desire for students to discover that on-the-job writing matters: to the organization that sponsors it, to the writer who creates it, and to the reader who relies on it. The processes and products of successful workplace writing reflect a critical balance between the writer's options for expressing what seems important and the reader's need to get clear, usable information. This book aims to address the realities of a contemporary course in workplace writing and to reflect my own experience and that of many students.

This writing course provides the best opportunity for students to learn these important workplace communication skills:

- How to be realistic about what a writer can accomplish within the parameters of any workplace setting and situation and how to choose the best writing resources and strategies for accomplishing the goal

- How to approach writing projects with a realistic awareness of the needs of workplace audiences, including supervisors, coworkers, and those who must do their own work based on the information that writers communicate

- How to think critically and ethically about the writer's responsibility to readers and the writing situation

- How to respond creatively to the challenges of today's changing workplace: the growing globalization of business, the rapid technological changes in electronic communication affecting every organization, the increasing diversity of the workforce, and the realities of collaborative involvement in almost every workplace situation

For the student approaching workplace writing, these considerations usually boil down to making practical decisions about good writing form—choosing the best structure, tone, and content for reports, letters, or other documents—and choosing the best writing process and strategy in order to accommodate a workplace occasion, social and technical setting, and audience.

Writing in the Workplace combines a product and process approach for instructors who want students to understand the routine realities as well as the special sensitivities of the workplace and the writing that sustains it. The book strives to develop a balance between these concerns and to offer specific strategies that help students accept these challenges—how to recognize and prune wordiness, how to decide which graphic form to use and how to create it with clarity and flair, and how to incorporate tactfulness into their documents. With clear advice about writing and annotated examples of documents and their revisions, this text helps students understand the available writing options and their results.

ix

Special Features

Writing in the Workplace uses distinctive instructional features to help students find a sense of balance about writing and gives clear, practical advice and examples that show why choices matter. Here are some features that students will find useful:

- *Strategy Review:* This integrated box feature recurring in all but two of the chapters helps students see the link between effective processes and good forms—two elements of workplace writing that are often hard to merge and reconcile. With explanations and frequent cross-references, this feature repeatedly reminds readers that the best writers adopt specific tactics in various phases of the writing process. The tactics of invention (topic focus and prewriting strategies), drafting (content selection, organization, and expressive choices), and revision (for clarity, accuracy, and conciseness) lead to appropriate communication. Strategy Review boxes provide connections and tactical issues in workplace writing: special tips, reminders, and important links between writing processes and document forms.

- *Annotated examples:* A generous sampling of realistic workplace writing documents provides concrete illustrations for writing principles. Each sample document is linked to the text and annotated with careful explanatory comments that pinpoint why a given choice makes a difference in effective communication. Many of the examples illustrate an ongoing workplace writing situation or occasion, demonstrating the importance of context in making careful selections and decisions about a writing situation.

- *Applications:* Most chapters include a continuous applied exercise situation that runs parallel with the text. The Application is a boxed feature that presents a real-world writing project or situation and offers an optional opportunity for an immediate application or for a class discussion of text concepts.

- *The World of Workplace Writing:* The technical and business environment is the focus of this special feature that shows real-world issues confronting writers. The World of Workplace Writing boxes highlight ethical issues, writing career issues, or the technical and economic concerns underlying the creation of workplace documents.

- *In-depth coverage on the forms and tools of electronic communication:* This book emphasizes learning about and adopting the benefits of the electronic workplace. Research on the Internet, E-mail and electronic communication, computer graphics, and graphics features in word processing programs are shown as integral to the basic patterns of researching and formatting typical workplace documents. The value of electronic media and methods is emphasized in the instruction in electronic processes (writing, research on the Internet) and in creating formats (the design and graphics of Web pages and E-mail communications) in the contemporary workplace writing environment. The influences of electronic processes appear throughout the book in the examples of workplace writing: letters and memos, job application documents, and report writing for informational, instructional, analytical, and persuasive purposes.

■ *Collaboration in workplace writing:* In a unique separate chapter (Chapter 7) and integrated throughout the discussions, examples, and exercises in the book, the role of collaboration receives special attention as preparation for the realities of information gathering and multiple authorship. Collaborative relationships with subject matter experts, other writers, editors, and graphics specialists are described, along with keys to enhancing the collaborative process. Collaborative work is also the focus of the Collaborative Exercises at the end of each chapter.

■ *Special emphasis on oral communications:* A separate chapter on oral presentations (Chapter 16) offers techniques for communicating material to live audiences in workplace situations. Focusing on small group and large group settings, Chapter 16 describes methods for creating and structuring a successful presentation, delivering the presentation, and selecting and incorporating appropriate graphics to support the content of the presentation.

■ *Chapter Checklists:* Distinctive lists at the ends of the chapters summarize the processes or features of each chapter in the form of suggestions or cautions to students who are beginning their own writing projects. The checklist also serves as a practical review of key concepts covered in each chapter.

■ *Class-tested exercises:* Both individual exercises and collaborative exercises appear at the ends of chapters to offer extra opportunities for students to apply what they have learned. An Ongoing Assignment is also offered as a project for students to develop as they move through the course from one chapter to the next.

■ *Instructor's Resource Manual:* To give instructors additional support with the instructional goals of this book, the *Instructor's Resource Manual* provides insights from the author on useful points and teaching strategies. Included are additional writing samples suitable for overhead transparencies or handouts. Sample responses for in-chapter exercises provide additional guidance for expectations of students' work. Finally, a resource listing of additional readings, professional organizations, and professional conventions offers support to new teachers of workplace writing.

Acknowledgments

Innumerable people have helped me refine a sense of my work and the discipline of workplace writing. My colleagues in professional communication organizations throughout the nation have taught me a tremendous amount about communication, learning, and intellectual exploration. I have always contended that professional communicators are the friendliest and warmest group of professionals on earth and their invaluable teachings—and friendships—throughout the years have been indescribably rewarding. On a more personal note: To all my writing teachers—especially Bertie Fearing, Keats Sparrow, and Thomas Warren—I give my gratitude. To other special professors whose unique approaches taught me to value learning and whose classroom performances inspired me to teach—Betty Webb, Susan Gilbert, Tom Parramore, and Ed Walkiewicz—I note equal appreciation. To Sherry Southard, I thank you for your constant teaching about writing, work, and friendship. And to all my students who have been enthusiastic guinea pigs for this ongoing project, I appreciate your willingness to teach as well as to learn.

The help I have received from Allyn & Bacon has been profound. Thanks to Joe Opiela, who saw potential in my work, and to the production editors, Susan McIntyre and, especially, Andrea Cava, who tried to make the book more approachable. A very special thanks to an outstanding editor and friend, Allen Workman. His phone calls and encouragement were exceedingly well timed.

I would also like to thank the following reviewers for their helpful comments: Jane Allen, New Mexico State University; Carolyn Boiarsky, Purdue University at Calumet; Darrell E. Costa, DeVry Institute at Pomona; Sam Dragga, Texas Technical University; Joseph F. Dunne, St. Louis Community College at Meramac; Allison Fernley, Salt Lake Community College; John Ferstel, University of Southwestern Louisiana; Laurie Fitzgerald, Madison Area Technical College; Eddye Gallagher, Tarrant County Junior College; Lawrence Milbourn, El Paso Community College; John Olson, ECPI College of Technology; Diana Reep, University of Akron; Samantha Segale, Heald Institute of Technology, San Francisco; Katherine Staples, Austin Community College; Emily Thrush, University of Tennessee at Memphis; and Tom Warren, Oklahoma State University.

I owe special thanks to three graduate students—Katie Cole, Amy Natale, and, especially, Alexa Thompson—who compensated for my lack of artistic sophistication. Thanks, friends.

Jim Badenhop (Sauder Woodworking), Rocky Willett (Uniden), and Don Rabon (The Justice Academy) were especially kind in negotiating permissions for use of their organizations' graphics. And Mark Lambecht (Black & Decker) opened his graphics files for me, which, on a tight deadline, meant the world.

Finally, a special thanks to my family who have exhibited unflagging pride in my work and in me over the years, who have graciously forgiven my absences from family gatherings when deadlines encroached, and who have heard about "the book" more than anyone should have to. And to Mike, always.

CHAPTER 1

Understanding the World of Workplace Writing

Organizational Images, Cultures, and You

- ■ **Your Experience as a Writer**
- ■ **Your Role as a Workplace Writer**
- ■ **Organizational Image**
- ■ **Organizational Culture**
- ■ **Changes in Organizational Culture**
- ■ **Organizational Image, Culture, and Communication**
- ■ **Ethics and Communication**
- ■ **Changes in Workplace Communication**
  - *Technology*
  - *Workplace Diversity*
  - *Globalization*
  - *Collaboration*
- ■ **Summary**
- ■ **Exercises**

One of the most common complaints among workers is the sea of paperwork that fills each workday and, for the most ambitious and overworked employees, each night and weekend as well. On any given day, workers must read numerous memos, letters, and reports and are frequently expected to respond—in writing—to these communications, thereby adding to the sea of paperwork that must be processed. To make matters worse, some of the writing may be irrelevant to the reader's particular position; or it may be garbled with jargon and technicalities or overblown with pomposity and wordiness.

As unnecessary, poorly written, and inconsequential as some paperwork may be, however, no one seriously argues that all on-the-job writing can be dismissed. In fact, memos, letters, reports, proposals, manuals, summaries, and numerous other forms of communication are essential because they

- *communicate objectives:* What do we, as an organization, want to do (in terms of hiring, expanding, problem solving, diversifying, downsizing, etc.)?
- *outline strategies, procedures, and policies:* What steps should we follow to meet these objectives?
- *summarize progress:* How much have we accomplished so far?
- *highlight problems:* What unexpected costs, legal rulings, shipping and delivery delays, and other problems are we encountering?
- *establish goodwill:* How should we communicate our plans and decisions to project a positive image of our organization and maintain the goodwill of our customers or clients?
- *substantiate or eliminate fears and rumors:* How can we make sure our employees and clients know enough about our plans and decisions to prevent panic or to prepare them for some bad news?
- *articulate specific plans for future decisions and activities:* Where do we go from here?

Whether you own your own business, work in a service or artistic organization, or work for a major international conglomerate, these roles of communication will be essential to the health of your organization. The more practice you have communicating these kinds of issues to readers who need the information, the more likely you will overcome communication pitfalls and succeed as a workplace writer/thinker.

In this chapter, you will begin to see how your role as a workplace writer will coincide with any career you have already chosen, whether a teacher's aide, nurse, lab technician, auto mechanic, safety inspector, or CEO of your own organization. First, you will see how your writing experience in college will serve as a basis for the writing you will do in the workplace. Next, you will understand your role as a workplace writer and how writing (and writers) fit into every organization's mission. Discussions of an organization's external image and internal culture—features that are unique to every organization—provide a basis for discovering the best means of communicating and recognizing changes within your organization. Finally, the chapter highlights elements (technology, workforce diversity, globalization, and collaboration) that are most likely to create ongoing changes for all organizations.

Your Experience as a Writer

The writing you have already produced in college is a good foundation for this course, but the writing in this course will be quite different from your earlier class experiences. Table 1.1 on page 4 shows some of those differences.

If you already have a job, you may know that much communication frequently goes on behind the scenes. As you take on more responsibilities or are promoted within your organization, you will learn that communication is necessary for

- documenting your work and the work of others,
- describing events and policies with which you are involved, and
- articulating changes and revised ideas that will more clearly direct the goals and activities of your organization.

From the memo that announces changes in retirement policies to the proposal for expanding a service area, on-the-job writing serves a distinct purpose in the U.S. workplace: it provides authenticity, stability, goodwill, and direction for conducting each organization's daily work, while setting a course for its future.

Your Role as a Workplace Writer

Essentially, there are two types of workplace writers: (1) professional writers (technical writers, legal writers, advertising copywriters) and (2) professionals who write (accountants, managers, technicians, and even company presidents). If you intend to become a professional writer, you will certainly take many more writing courses that will hone your skills; nevertheless, the strategies you learn from this text will provide a solid foundation for your remaining coursework.

The second group—professionals who write—will command the most attention throughout this text. If you aspire to a career as an agricultural adviser, medical technician, engineer, or even social worker, the quality of the on-the-job writing you produce will make a tremendous difference in how knowledgeable, insightful, and promotable you are judged to be. And if you work for a small company, start your own company, or work for a charitable or philanthropic organization, you may have to take on some of the writing that larger organizations assign to their professional writing staff.

T A B L E 1.1   College Writing versus Workplace Writing

	College Writing	*Workplace Writing*
Readers	■ teachers ■ classmates	■ boss/supervisor ■ coworkers ■ subordinates ■ clients/customers ■ suppliers/vendors ■ accountants ■ lawyers ■ technicians ■ sales/marketing representatives ■ government workers ■ stockholders/investors ■ general public
Readers' Qualities	■ know as much or more about your topic than you ■ have at least as much education as you	■ know less than you do about your topic ■ need to know about topic and, thus, need to read your work ■ may have significantly more or less education than you
Purpose(s) for Writing	■ to prove mastery of the information	■ to inform ■ to persuade ■ to explain/clarify ■ to propose ideas ■ to solve problems ■ to instruct or teach
Forms	■ essays ■ term papers/research papers ■ examinations ■ notes	■ letters/memos/E-mail ■ reports (informational or analytical) ■ proposals ■ notes ■ manuals (employee, policy, instruction, etc.) ■ job descriptions ■ performance evaluations ■ brochures/fliers ■ financial analyses

Depending on an organization's particular products or services, workers may have to produce different forms of communication to conduct their daily work. Thus, the forms, tones, and purposes for communicating at a software development company may be very different from those of a retail clothing chain. For example, if you work for a software company, you might have to write

- *software documentation* that describes how to use a particular software package,
- *reports* that chart corporate growth over the past six months,
- *letters* that answer questions for confused software users,
- *proposals* that recommend developing a new graphics software package, or
- *summaries* that explain to government officials or legislators the financial dangers of software copyright infringements (pirating).

In contrast, at a retail clothing outlet, you might have to write

- *documentation* that describes how to use the new cash registers,
- *sales reports* that highlight successful sales strategies or explain why current sales figures are down,
- *letters* to customers urging them to use company credit cards (or pay their credit card bills),
- *proposals* that argue for the restructuring of middle-level management, or
- *policy statements* that define the company's guidelines for returning or exchanging merchandise.

And if you work for a charitable organization, you might have to write

- *letters* requesting donations,
- *memos* organizing fund-raising events,
- *reports* to the national headquarters about your fund-raising successes, or
- *policy statements* that tell volunteers the appropriate ways to solicit funds.

Further, you might be asked to respond to customers' letters about rude clerks, demonstrate the feasibility of opening a new store in a rural location, and answer inquiries from other entrepreneurs who want to start a business similar to yours in another part of the country. Clearly, these differences in types of workplace communication are based on the particular organization, its product or service, and the purpose and readers of the particular communication.

Similarly, if you have worked in different departments of a single organization, you have probably noticed that they use different forms of communication. In some departments, for instance, employees may spend a great deal of time writing proposals—documents designed to entice other businesses or groups to buy a product or service. Employees in other departments may write numerous reports—lengthier documents that address a number of routine and complex issues (such as outlining the plans for upgrading the technology in a certain part of the organization, describing procedures for diversifying the organization, summarizing its financial achievements, and even detailing its structural weaknesses). Still other employees may write manuals—instructions that tell readers how to use a new piece of equipment, the procedures for applying for retirement benefits, or how to interpret the results of a test, survey, or experiment. Because the different departments exist for different purposes, their workers are likely to write quite different kinds of communications.

Whenever you write on the job, you need to consider your organization's primary role and responsibilities—whether its purpose is to generate sales for its products, organize a special event, develop new products, or some other primary task. Making sure your writing promotes the purpose of your division and your organization is critical to everyone's success.

Throughout the remainder of this chapter, we will consider how communication can determine the success or failure of any organization. All workplace communications—from form letters to personal replies, from employee handbooks to operational policies, from memos to reports, and from explanations to descriptions—reflect the personality of the organization and its role as a community citizen.

Additionally, each writer's own personality and integrity are also evident in the writing produced on the job. Throughout this text, you will see samples of writing that send positive messages about the writer and some that send negative messages. Remember that as a worker and as a writer, you will be constantly sending messages about yourself—your attitudes, work habits, values, character, and ambitions. You will want to make sure that *whatever* you write sends the right message about you.

Organizational Image

Just as different organizations communicate about different topics, the message and tone of their communications may also differ. Some companies, for example, are known for their generous accommodation of their customers, and their communications reflect those policies by sounding reassuring, apologetic, or friendly. Other companies evidently believe that their customers are dishonest, untrustworthy, and ignorant, and, again, their communications reflect that assessment by sounding arrogant, accusatory, and unyielding. Some charitable organizations imply that you are bad and uncaring if you don't donate to their cause, whereas others focus on making you feel good about whatever contribution you can make.

Consider the tone of two responses to a complaint about a defective toaster that the customer, though she does not admit it in her letter of complaint, has splattered with water (see Figure 1.1 on page 7 and Figure 1.2 on page 8). What assessments can you make about the company and about the writer? It is pretty easy to decide which version you would prefer to receive if you owned the toaster. The first writer sounds accusatory and makes the reader feel like a criminal. Her choice of words ("claim," "warned," and "refuse") and emphasis on "simply malfunctioned" sound snide. In the second version, the writer is much more upbeat and accommodating. She realizes, first, that the malfunctioning toaster (regardless of what caused the problem) can easily be fixed. So rather than risk losing the customer's goodwill, the writer agrees to have the service department repair the defective coil. Then, she omits all references to the owner's responsibility and reinforces the positive solution to the problem.

Synopsis Appliances
223 Dowdy Avenue
Las Cruces, NM 25002

14 January 1999

Ms. Patricia Arthur
108 Hunt Hill Place
Las Cruces, NM 25003

Dear Ms. Arthur:

1   **2**   **3**

Your claim that the MX820 toaster "simply malfunctioned" has been disproved in our laboratory tests. We are convinced, in fact, that you must have gotten water in the toaster.   **3**   **4**   **4**   **4**

5   **5**

Since we warned you not to wet the toaster, we refuse to replace it.

I am sure you understand that we cannot repair such problems or else we'd go out of business.

6

Sincerely,

Rosa Del Fuego

Rosa Del Fuego
Service Department

---

1. opening phrase suggests she's lying

2. quotation marks make the comment sound snide

3. implies that infallible tests "caught you"

4. states a categorical certainty

5. scolding tone, adamant position

6. implies customer could single-handedly bankrupt the company

FIGURE 1.1   Sample Letter 1: Communicating an Organizational Image

Of course, companies cannot always offer the perfect solution, and sound business practices often prevent the accommodation of the consumer's request. Nevertheless, an upbeat and courteous response, as in the third version (Figure 1.3 on page 9), can still retain the consumer's goodwill. The third version's writer sees the problem, recognizes that replacing or repairing the toaster is beyond the company's policy, but also deletes any references to the customer's liability. Then, she offers a token of goodwill to assuage the reader. Although the customer would certainly prefer to receive a free replacement toaster, the last version sustains the respectful relationship between the company and the consumer. Further, the writer has emphasized the company's commitment to safety as well as consumer convenience and goodwill. And, since the reader will have to buy a

---

Synopsis Appliances
223 Dowdy Avenue
Las Cruces, NM 25002

14 January 1999

Ms. Patricia Arthur
108 Hunt Hill Place
Las Cruces, NM 25003

Dear Ms. Arthur:

opens with good news · explanation

We have fixed your MX820 toaster and are returning it to you by overnight express mail. We replaced one of the coils (which might somehow have been splashed with water).

"you" orientation personalizes the message

At any rate, you should have the toaster back in time to make your breakfast toast on Monday morning—bon appétit!

Sincerely,

Rosa Del Fuego

Rosa Del Fuego
Service Department

FIGURE 1.2 Sample Letter 2: Communicating an Organizational Image

---

new toaster anyway, isn't she likely to buy it from Synopsis Appliances due to Ms. Del Fuego's courtesy and the discount coupon?

Organizational image, therefore, is an "outsider's view" of an organization. Typically, the image is established through the quality and cost of the products/ services the organization offers; its advertising; the spokesperson, actors, or scenery in the advertisements; the display or arrangement of the organization's stores; the kind of music it plays in the workplace; and even the kinds of customers it attracts. Many organizations spend thousands and even millions of dollars on their images. Their advertising strategies signal how they want to be perceived in the marketplace. Think of some of your favorite advertisements, for example, and see how the organization is trying to establish itself as prosperous, fun, stylish, efficient, or cost-effective.

Synopsis Appliances
223 Dowdy Avenue
Las Cruces, NM 25002

14 January 1999

Ms. Patricia Arthur
108 Hunt Hill Place
Las Cruces, NM 25003

Dear Ms. Arthur:

opening reference
to letter sets
context
primary quality

As your letter reminds us, we at Synopsis Appliances know how much you count on your toaster for the convenience of your cooking. And as the world's leading manufacturer of toasters, we know you expect us to make those toasters with safety, as well as your convenience, in mind.

additional quality

offers reasons,
explanations,
consequences

Because of safety concerns, our toasters, such as your MX820, are designed to short out whenever water hits them rather than continue to transmit electricity. Such shortages, of course, are irreversible, which explains why we cannot repair your toaster, but are certainly preferable to the electrical shocks that can be caused by the toaster's continuing to conduct electricity.

bad news has
alternative

We don't want you to be without your MX820—or your morning toast—any longer than necessary, however. The enclosed coupon for a 10% discount will help toward your purchase of a new MX820. And we've added a free toaster cover to help keep water out of your new toaster.

goodwill closing

We hope you continue to enjoy our products, and we appreciate your business.

Sincerely,

Rosa Del Fuego
Rosa Del Fuego
Service Department

FIGURE 1.3   Sample Letter 3: Communicating an Organizational Image

Of course, advertising is just one way to establish an image. Many stores try to update their appearances or their logos to demonstrate that they are keeping up with what today's consumers want; J. C. Penney's stores, for instance, have undergone organization-wide facelifts that include more chrome and mirrors to create a sleeker, more modern, and appealing look. K-Mart added Jaclyn Smith fashions to appeal to working women on a budget. And a number of organizations, from makers of cereal to athletic shoes to underwear, have hired athletes such as Michael Jordan to enhance the image of their products. All of these strategies are designed to communicate a particular message about the organization and, consequently, to make you feel a certain way about it. If your impressions are positive, you are likely to be loyal to that organization; otherwise, you will probably look to a competing organization to meet your needs.

This text offers readers a chance to apply ideas from the chapter by working with a boxed exercise called an Application. The cues or situations in the Application will allow you to draw on your experiences in terms of chapter ideas and to develop your viewpoint in writing, through discussion, or through reading the exercise. The first Application, on page 11, lets you apply your experience to become more sensitive to organizational images.

Organizational Culture

You may know quite a bit about the images of many companies and organizations from personal experience, the experience of others, or the history, reputation, and advertising strategies of the organization itself. Whatever associations you have with the organization's image, however, are external and are different from its internal *culture*. The organization's culture is no whimsical matter, for it consists of the powerful expectations, attitudes, and behaviors workers and management in a particular organization hold. Organizational culture will occupy much of our attention throughout this text because—unlike images, which are largely determined by marketing consultants, public relations experts, and advertising agents—culture is more directly controlled or influenced by the decisions and communications of managers and the daily work habits of all the other employees and/or volunteers.

Organizational culture is an extremely complex mixture. It includes an organization's most visible decisions, such as its choice of company cars, its commitment to upgrading equipment and introducing new technology, the decor of its offices, and even the standard gift for retiring workers. Organizational culture also includes the organization's more subtle attitudes regarding such things as expectations about overtime work, the appropriate dress for employees at all levels, and the acceptability of socializing, joining a civic or country club, or even acknowledging an alternative lifestyle. Thus, an organization's culture may be conservative or progressive, innovative or predictable, stable or faltering, or it may lie somewhere between these extremes.

Most of us, in fact, know very little about an organization's culture unless we work for that organization (or unless it is featured in a special news report,

Consider the following groupings of competitors and evaluate each company's *image;* if you are unfamiliar with one of the companies listed, substitute a comparable business in your area:

1. IBM versus Apple versus Radio Shack
2. K-Mart versus The Gap versus The Limited
3. McDonald's versus Hardee's versus Burger King
4. Revlon versus Estée Lauder versus L'Oreal
5. MCI versus Sprint versus AT&T
6. Chrysler versus Mercedes versus Honda
7. Motel 6 versus Holiday Inn versus Hilton
8. Nike versus Adidas versus Converse
9. Harley Davidson versus Yamaha versus Honda
10. Chili's versus Chi Chi's versus Taco Bell

You probably assigned one company in each group a higher level of quality than the others. Think carefully about the basis for your evaluation of each company's image: Personal experience? Friends' or family members' experiences? Cost of products? Reputation? Advertising campaigns? Do you have any particular feelings (positive or negative) about the company's spokesperson or the music it uses in its advertisements?

Now, consider service agencies or philanthropic/artistic organizations such as the Peace Corps, the American Red Cross, or the United Way. Or consider a local hospital, symphony, or theater group. What kind of images do these organizations have? Where did you get your impressions about these groups?

such as *60 Minutes*). Beyond the typical information available in corporate annual reports about profits, losses, and standard business practices, several "hidden" factors also affect or establish the culture of any given organization:

- Its understood or stated dress code (suits? blue jeans? sports clothes?).
- Its policies regarding vacations, tardiness, hiring, retirement, and promotions.
- Its reliance on E-mail, videoconferencing, and other technologies to communicate and to get work done.

- Its inclusion of women, minorities, and various age and ethnic representatives in all levels of its workforce.
- Its encouragement or discouragement of music, pranks, and socializing in the office.
- Its expectations about overtime work, attendance at staff meetings, and community involvement.
- Its general attitude toward workers. Does it view them as innovative and enthusiastic if given appropriate and challenging tasks? Or does it consider them lazy slackers who will cheat, steal, and ruin the company unless watched by the managers?

Numerous other factors also affect an organization's culture, and many of them are very subtle. We find it relatively easy, for instance, to choose the proper clothes for our positions by looking around to see how other employees (clerical workers, delivery people, salesclerks, or managers) dress. Unfortunately, we may need months or even years to truly figure out other aspects of corporate culture, such as the importance of a college degree, the relationship between managers and assistants, and attitudes toward race, gender, and sexual orientation. Nevertheless, you can start by answering two questions about your organization:

1. How do people work with and relate to each other?
2. What is expected of me beyond my job description?

Because each organization has its own culture, you should also be aware that if you work with people from another company, such as subcontractors, they are likely to be part of a different set of expectations fostering a different organizational culture. Thus, these employees may dress more or less formally than you do, take their work more or less seriously than you do, and tend to pay more or less attention to deadlines, meeting times, and requests. Although you cannot *change* their culture, you should at least be aware of areas where your expectations may vary from theirs and adjust your communications so you can get along with them and get the job done.

Clearly, an organization's culture, like its image, is also largely a matter of communication. In some organizations, communication's role in establishing and promoting the culture is rather obvious, perhaps even stated either in an employee handbook or manual or during an interview. Most organizations, however, rarely communicate their more subtle expectations. Whether the culture is communicated explicitly or implicitly, however, it is unmistakably there, and astute workers are sure to pick up on it.

Use the list of cultural elements in the second Application on page 13 to evaluate the organizational culture with which you are most familiar—most likely, either your job or your college environment. Some of these issues, of course, involve general etiquette and sensitivity, making them critical no matter where you work; others depend more on the individual chemistry of an office or plant, making them acceptable in some organizations but unacceptable in others. And some,

APPLICATION

To help you determine how various behaviors and attitudes might help or hinder you in fitting into an organization's culture, consider the (often subtle) messages that lie beneath the following behaviors and attitudes. What do you think of people who behave or think in these ways? Then, put a check in the *yes* box or *no* box beside each activity/attitude to characterize your own behaviors and attitudes. In the final column, indicate the behaviors or attitudes you'd like to possibly adopt or change about yourself.

What does it mean when people . . .	Do I?		Should I change?	
	yes	no	yes	no
tell ethnic/offensive jokes on the job	☐	☐	☐	☐
wear casual clothes to work	☐	☐	☐	☐
wear suits to work	☐	☐	☐	☐
wear sexy/provocative clothes to work	☐	☐	☐	☐
talk about families/partners	☐	☐	☐	☐
talk about weekend activities	☐	☐	☐	☐
talk about politics or religion	☐	☐	☐	☐
talk about sex	☐	☐	☐	☐
wear unusual hairstyles	☐	☐	☐	☐
wear conspicuous jewelry	☐	☐	☐	☐
have decorated offices (pictures, plants, etc.)	☐	☐	☐	☐
socialize with peers after hours	☐	☐	☐	☐
socialize with supervisors after hours	☐	☐	☐	☐
criticize superiors	☐	☐	☐	☐
take on additional projects eagerly	☐	☐	☐	☐
acknowledge birthdays and other occasions	☐	☐	☐	☐
make coffee	☐	☐	☐	☐
take notes at committee/staff meetings	☐	☐	☐	☐
ask questions or contribute ideas	☐	☐	☐	☐
praise staff	☐	☐	☐	☐
show up on time for work	☐	☐	☐	☐
come in early, work on weekends, or stay late	☐	☐	☐	☐

Based on your assessment of the standard culture of your primary organization, write a list of do's and dont's for newcomers (perhaps newly hired employees or freshmen on your campus).

of course, reflect your own personal style and are neither "right" nor "wrong." Only you can determine which of these qualities are important in your primary organization and whether you should deviate from them or imitate what your peers and superiors do. At a minimum, though, you should consciously evaluate these and other aspects of an organization's culture to determine whether and how well you will fit in. The decision whether to accommodate the company's expectations, of course, is largely up to you, but failing to recognize critical expectations can certainly limit a career and may, in serious cases, even get you fired.

Throughout this text, your instructor may ask you (and, possibly, your collaborative partners) to return to this checklist for an ongoing, course-long series of assignments (including a letter series, short report, formal report, proposal, and orientation manual). If so, you should expect that some of your responses will change once you begin more serious investigations and writing assignments; you may be surprised to discover that some of the elements you now believe to be part of your organization's culture merely disguise other elements that will become clearer with more thinking, more observations, and more writing.

Changes in Organizational Culture

Organizational cultures typically develop over time, and many aspects are not established for years. Even so, just as images can change, so can cultures—becoming more or less formal, accessible, and responsive. Recognizing signs that an organization's culture is changing is just as critical as figuring out that culture in the first place, for again your place in the organization can be enhanced or threatened by your compliance with or deviation from those expectations.

Many developments or events can initiate a change in an organization's culture:

- A new CEO or supervisory group (especially one with a new management style)
- A new location (a move to a mall, a new building, or some other distinctive locale)
- A change in clientele (higher or lower class; more or less buying power)
- Diversification of the company's holdings (getting rid of some subsidiaries and investing in others, for example)
- Redesign of the store or office (to update the look of the workplace or make it look more traditional)
- A new philosophy in management (employees should or should not get raises every quarter)
- Recruitment of various ethnic/international workers (more Asian Americans, Muslims, etc.)
- Recruitment of younger or older workers (more energy? more experience?)

- Promotion of women and other workplace minorities into management positions (will different kinds of ideas be more welcome now?)
- Reorganization of management, departments, office staff, or any of their responsibilities (who is getting more/less power?)
- New economic or trade regulations (such as NAFTA or GATT)
- The aging of the workforce (socializing changes)
- A shift in the number of married versus single workers (socializing changes)
- Changes in local, state, or national political power (shift from emphasis on big business to emphasis on smaller employers)

You will want to pay particular attention to such changes in your workplace and be alert to which staff members signal whether the changes are welcome.

Organizational Image, Culture, and Communication

In progressive organizations that are astutely managed, images and cultures don't just happen; they are carefully crafted to send a particular message about the organization to clients and employees. In short, images and cultures are largely matters of *communication:* the organization sends a message about itself through its appearance, the variety and quality of its merchandise, its advertising, and its reputation as an organization and as an employer. Both employees and consumers respond to images and cultures through their behaviors, which may be *nonverbal,* such as spending or not spending money or working hard for that company, or *verbal,* such as writing letters or phoning in praise or complaints to management (see Figure 1.4 on page 16).

Both the nonverbal and verbal messages will eventually be clear to the organization and its leaders, for when enough consumers and employees send the same message back, the organization either succeeds or fails. Clearly, therefore, communicating an acceptable organizational image and culture is critical because success depends on maintaining the approval and goodwill of most of the organization's consumers and employees.

We have seen, broadly, how an organization's image and culture are communicated both externally and internally. And as the earlier toaster scenario demonstrates, written communication is a powerful means of communicating both these aspects of an organization's personality. In terms of image, culture, and workplace communication, all messages are crucial, but none may be more crucial than the written communication. A written message is concrete, and thus, for that particular document at least, it represents an unchangeable assertion of an organization's culture and image—its ways of doing business.

It's easy to understand, therefore, why an organization's leaders might be distraught over a message that is misinterpreted or, worse, intercepted by the

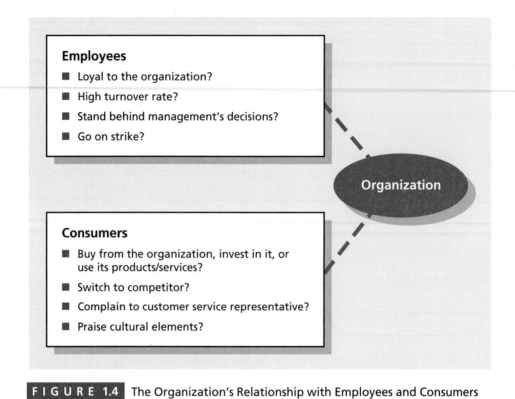

FIGURE 1.4   The Organization's Relationship with Employees and Consumers

wrong people. The memo detailing a slightly unethical, though still legal, attempt to discredit a competitor becomes a tremendous embarrassment in the wrong hands. Even if the organization's managers unanimously reject the ploy, the memo would still be damaging. A report that explains the organization's plans to reorganize a small subsidiary in the Midwest, exaggerates the contributions of a particular plan or employee to the company's overall worth, or suggests dismantling a department or division and laying off its workers can seriously affect the organization's culture and image and thus have numerous effects on its stock, profits, reputation, and future. Hence the workplace writer not only must ensure that all writings reflect the organization's culture and image but must also use discretion in handling written communications.

Ethics and Communication

As mentioned earlier, your future as an employee, your potential for promotion, and your work-based sense of ethics and self-esteem are tremendously affected by how you respond within the culture of your organization. Throughout this text, you will encounter numerous situations that may challenge your ethics—typically defined as your sense of right and wrong. Unlike legal issues, which are usually black and white (activities are either legal or illegal depending on the law), ethical issues often require you to determine whether an activity or a communication is acceptable, based on a number of questions:

1. Does anyone suffer from one choice over the other?
2. Are issues of morality at stake?
3. Does my conscience tell me that this is the right/wrong thing to do?
4. Would I be embarrassed if others knew I did/wrote this?

For example, slight shadings of meaning may not matter in some cases. Does it really matter whether you say that a toilet is "temporarily out of order" rather than

APPLICATION

Your style of communicating—both oral and written—is one of the most obvious indicators of your character and of your own ideas about work and working relationships. The words in the following list describe some of the more prevalent workplace communication styles. First look through the list and check off, item by item, which qualities you associate with the writers of the letters in Figures 1.1, 1.2, and 1.3. Then, determine which descriptions most closely coincide with your own style, circling the ones you believe you already have and those you'd like to develop:

☐ clear	☐ obtuse	☐ positive	☐ cynical
☐ offensive	☐ complimentary	☐ flowery	☐ stiff
☐ diplomatic	☐ arrogant	☐ colloquial	☐ tactful
☐ gracious	☐ flirtatious	☐ blunt	☐ prim
☐ objective	☐ fumbling	☐ critical	☐ hurried
☐ honest	☐ manipulative	☐ rational	☐ aloof

You'll note, of course, that there's a big difference between someone who chooses words carefully and someone who fumbles for words, between someone who is complimentary and someone who is flirtatious, and between someone who is objective and someone who is blunt. Of course, whether you have had an upbeat or a depressing day can certainly affect how you communicate on any given day, and different situations may require different responses. Overall, however, most of us want to project a positive image of ourselves (and our organizations) by being polite, clear, and gracious in our communications, as the writer of the letter in Figure 1.3 did.

saying that it is "broken"? Probably not, because reasonable people will know not to use it; thus, the different meanings produce the same result. But does it matter whether you say that a computer in your workplace is "temporarily down" rather than saying that it is "broken"? Suppose someone hangs around believing the computer will be back up in a few minutes, when actually the computer is broken and will be "down" until next week when someone can come to fix it. Thus, the difference between a computer being "broken" and being "down" might cost someone a sale, delay a crucial communication, or prevent the transfer of critical data.

Your consideration for your own values and ethics should be the primary concern in your work decisions. Though many might call you naive, if you are uncomfortable with the way your organization does business and the resulting responsibility placed on you to communicate in a particular way—to shade the truth, perhaps, or to overstate the gravity of a situation or to trivialize it—you may want to consider the possibility of changing that organization's culture or changing jobs. These decisions are hardly easy, but they do reflect the responsibilities you have as a workplace communicator and as a conscientious member of society.

Changes in Workplace Communication

Even subtle changes in the workplace can drastically affect communication and its need to change. Many of the more obvious changes in workplace communication, however, are caused by increasing technology, workplace diversity, globalization, and collaboration (see Figure 1.5).

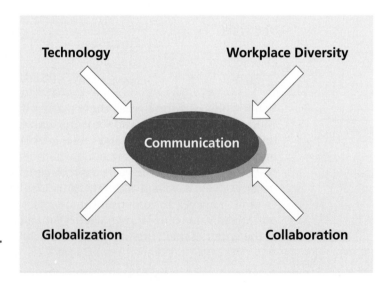

FIGURE 1.5

Influences Leading to Changes in Communication

Technology

Technology's increasing role in the workplace calls for different kinds of knowledge and different understandings of the workings of any given organization. Because information is generated and transferred more rapidly than ever before, an organization's planners can wait to order supplies, rather than tying up the organization's money to keep inventories well stocked. Information is available at a touch of the keyboard, and cellular telephones, fax machines, teleconferencing and videoconferencing technologies, and the Internet enable suppliers and consumers to "talk" more readily than ever before.

Consider, for instance, what the Internet means to workplace writers. First, as a system of rapid information exchange, the Internet offers an entire network of resources—in the office and around the world. Writers can place orders, in writing, without waiting for standard mail delivery. They can check credit histories and references in moments, tremendously reducing the number of bad investments or unqualified hirings. Using Gopher, Veronica, or other networked databases, they can find information about a number of research topics. Applicants can apply for jobs without investing in expensive mailings and can answer questions without having to make long-distance or overseas phone calls.

Workplace Diversity

Another change in workplace communication reflects the growing commitment to and appreciation of diversity—especially the hiring and promotion of women and minorities in U.S. organizations. These organizations typically understand

---

THE WORLD OF WORKPLACE WRITING

Technology and Changing Communications

As a good example of how technology changes communication, you might also consider the Internet's influence on proper grammar, punctuation, and letter format. Although the lack of proofreading, proper spacing, and punctuation disturbs many traditional English teachers, most Internet correspondents admit to being relatively unconcerned with such traditional worries in their writing and in their reading. Thus, they are less willing to "penalize" a writer for misspelled words that appear over the Internet than for those that appear in hard copy. In this case, technology is increasing the acceptability of informal formats, which would have been considered highly inappropriate and unprofessional before the Internet.

Some users, however, still consider proper grammar, spelling, punctuation, and spacing essential to professionalism. Therefore, you should take care to correct any errors when you are communicating with someone new or with someone who might not share your sense of Internet informality.

that women and people from non-Caucasian cultures add a different perspective to daily work; therefore, their needs and perspectives on what motivates others to buy certain products or services can be crucial to the organization.

Further, because women and African Americans are increasingly two of the most powerful buying groups in the nation, the organization's products and services—and the advertisements or promotional strategies for those products and services—frequently target these groups and their experiences. Think, for instance, how little sense it would make to have an all-male advertising team trying to figure out what sells women's suits with no input from women at all. That does not mean that men cannot sell women's suits—in fact, some of the greatest designers of women's clothes are men—but these men carefully solicit instructions, advice, opinions, and preferences from women who can explain where they want pockets, what length the skirt should be, and what kinds of fabrics they find most appealing.

The influx of women and minorities into the workplace has affected communication far beyond just developing or expanding strategies for a company's daily work. These other changes are related to the social nature of the workplace. Because men and women, people of various ages, and people of all ethnic groups are working side by side and collaborating on special projects, more attention is being focused on the ways we communicate: the language we use, the attitudes that language conveys (or betrays), and the expectations we hold about each other's capabilities, rights, and predispositions. Thus, whereas certain kinds of language (jokes, comments, and discussions) might have been tolerated before the influx of various groups into these organizations, such language is now so inappropriate that it might be grounds for legal action, as in the case of sexual harassment or racial discrimination. The court system, especially the Supreme Court, has ruled again and again that language and other forms of communication are so important in the workplace that organizations can take special steps to regulate its propriety.

Globalization

Closely related to the effects of the influx of women and minorities into the U.S. workforce is the influence of globalization. As the U.S. market becomes saturated, more and more organizations are expanding abroad to take advantage of markets that have had little or no access to their products or services.

In international situations, communication can present quite a challenge, for the traditional U.S. ways of doing business frequently conflict with other countries' business styles. In particular, our social customs, straight business talk, sense of humor, emphasis on profits, strict adherence to deadlines, and minutely detailed legal contracts often embarrass or offend businesspeople from other countries. Because all these cultural aspects depend on communication, organizational leaders are recognizing the importance of learning about the cultural habits and expectations of other nations and groups.

THE WORLD OF WORKPLACE WRITING

Globalization and Changing Communications

To understand how communication can vary internationally, consider the following true story. An executive for a major U.S. oil company was assigned to the Mexican office to coordinate the opening of trade relations through NAFTA (the North American Free Trade Agreement). Communicating with his counterparts through memos was standard procedure for this executive, yet he noticed increasing hostility from his Mexican colleagues. One Mexican coworker finally explained that the other workers felt that given their proximity—they were, after all, in the same building—information should be exchanged directly, not through memos. In fact, they perceived his memos as a sign that he was aloof and withdrawn and did not want to contact them personally.

This executive quickly modified his communication tactics: he visited or phoned his Mexican colleagues to communicate new information to them; then, he followed up those communications with memos to make sure everything was properly documented. As a result, he won the respect and friendship of his Mexican coworkers, while still guaranteeing that proper corporate procedures were being followed.

Collaboration

Workplace communication is also changing because of an increased emphasis on collaboration and teamwork. It used to be assumed that even when work was assigned as a project, the project workers divided the work and then each member went to a private office or cubicle to work—solo. Today, managers are learning the value of teamwork in ways rarely imagined twenty years ago. Having work groups brainstorm on a project or having team members share perceptions of a product's strengths and weaknesses has proved invaluable as a means of ensuring quality and building employee morale. Further, many organizations have teams of workers/writers who brainstorm about every element of the writing: from its content to the arrangement of that content and the final design. Many organizations are also experimenting with quality circles and emphasizing total quality management—strategies designed to encourage more input from employees at every level of the company hierarchy.

Although detailed discussion of collaboration in workplace writing will be reserved until Chapter 7, you probably already have some experience working in group settings. Draw on that experience in the collaborative exercises provided at the end of each chapter.

All these changes in the workplace—the increasing role of technology, the influx of women and minorities, the globalization of the economy, and the encouragement of collaboration—mean that workplace writers have to consider how these changes are affecting their communication. Further, each worker in each organization may be affected differently by these changes. As an important participant in your organization's culture, you need to evaluate these and other workplace changes that might affect how you will communicate on the job.

Summary

In this chapter, you've had a chance to place the importance of on-the-job communication in two crucial and interdependent contexts: your own career and the welfare of your company. Further, you have been challenged to think of the ways in which your communicative messages and style affect your own image, reflect your ethics, and, invariably, enhance or erode your self-esteem. Developing a more positive, clear, and considerate communicative style, therefore, can greatly enhance your worth to the company as well as your opportunities for advancement. Then you can either reinforce or make responsible changes in the organizational image and culture that you and your organization choose to project.

Being aware of the image you want to send about yourself and your organization transcends the traditionally limited concerns for profits because of the changing nature of work: the expanding role of technology, the influx of nontraditional groups into various roles (and often higher levels) in the workplace, the internationalization of commerce, and the encouragement of collaboration on the job. Your ability to see how work is changing—and, thus, how communication must also change—will mark you as an insightful, valuable employee whose potential and self-esteem are enhanced by such qualities.

EXERCISES

Individual Exercises

1. Describe in one paragraph the image of an organization that you patronize in your town; if you know anything about its culture, describe that in a second paragraph. In a third paragraph, explain what you think it would take to get ahead in that company. What kinds of behaviors and attitudes would be appropriate? What would be inappropriate? Finally, conclude your description with a paragraph explaining whether you think you could fit in at that company. Would you want to? Why or why not?

2. In a daily newspaper, perhaps the *Wall Street Journal*, follow the stories about a particular organization in the news for a few days. Summarize the stories; then, in a one-page overview, evaluate the image and culture of that organi-

zation, based on what you learned from the news articles and how the organization's spokespeople responded to questions. Are the news accounts strengthening or eroding the image of the organization? In what ways?

3. Schedule brief interviews with people who work for two organizations in your area. See if you can develop either (a) or (b).

   a. A profile of the organizations' cultures and images. How do these organizations differ from each other? Save your list of questions and compare it with those of your classmates. Did you ask the same questions? Are there questions you wish you had asked, but didn't?

   b. A summary, based on responses in your interview, of the workers' views and uses of communication on the job. What kinds of writing did they most often produce? Descriptions? Reports? Letters? Brochures? Other documents? For what reader or group of readers did they most often write? Was the primary purpose of their writing to convince or persuade? To explain? To summarize? To document time, money, or job activities? Some other purpose?

4. Describe in a brief paragraph an occasion when your dealings with a company were unpleasant. Perhaps you tried to return something, lodge a complaint, or offer a suggestion to the manager. In a second paragraph, explain how the company representative could have handled the situation better.

5. Think of some companies that have changed their images or expanded their product lines to better market themselves. In a one-page analysis, describe the kinds of changes that were made and the effect(s) of the change(s).

6. For each of the following sentences, describe the writer's style of communication. You may want to refer to the Application on page 17. Note the primary strengths and weaknesses and think of revisions that would make the sentence more positive, clearer, and more tactful. We'll discuss particular strategies for revising these kinds of statements in Chapter 6, but go ahead and see if you can add details, soften or clarify the language, and emphasize positives rather than negatives.

   a. Your work on the Mellon case lacked oomph.

   b. No one is going to tell me how to run my department.

   c. That reporter who is investigating our pricing strategies is just trying to make sure we don't make a profit on our merchandise.

   d. You always do such a brilliant job on these end-of-the-year sales figures. In fact, no one can match the clarity of your work and explanations. You're so bright, I'll bet you could do them in a day, if you had to. So how about it? Could you get the figures to me by noon tomorrow?

   e. Send these letters out.

   f. You're almost as intelligent as you are pretty.

   g. As per your request of 9 July 19__, I have the sales financial figures.

h. I really did want to get the company reports done this weekend, but my mother-in-law showed up unexpectedly and brought three of my wife's bratty little nephews. They climbed all over everything and broke stuff and whined and yelled all weekend. So then I had to take them to the park and let them yell and climb all over the playground. Of course, that wasn't enough and we had to go to the fast-food restaurant and get milk shakes, which they spilled all over the car—not that the car is that important, but they didn't even apologize. Anyway, as you can tell, there was no way I could get this work done.

i. I'll bet he didn't even try to get those company reports done. He probably went to the beach and hung out with his old college buddies all weekend.

j. Why in the world would you think I'd want to be on a 7:30 A.M. flight to Chicago? You know I always travel at night.

Collaborative Exercises

1. Cut out several advertisements in your newspaper or in a magazine you have bought. Try to determine what message the company is sending about itself. To what groups of people is the company trying to appeal? Who are the company's competitors? How are the competitors trying to attract similar or dissimilar audiences? Answer these questions in a brief description of the most unusual or outstanding advertisement you selected.

2. Save some of your "junk mail"—mail that you did not request—for a week. Describe your impression of the companies that have mailed letters to you. Then, select two items that exemplify the best and worst of the lot. For the best (or most convincing) sales appeal, explain why readers might tempted to buy the company's products. Did the product seem to fit your needs or be a wise investment? What particular wordings, graphics, or testimonials made the product appealing? For the worst appeal, explain why you were not tempted to invest in the product. What particular aspects of the communication turned you off?

Extended Collaborative Exercises

3. Identify several workers at various levels in an organization in your area. After guaranteeing their confidentiality and/or anonymity, ask about the organization's inclusion of women and minority workgroups. What roles do these workers typically play? Why? What perspectives have these people added to the company's vision? Interview some of the women and minorities who work for the organization: Do they feel welcome there? Why or why not? What do the interviewees' attitudes say about the organization? About the interviewees themselves? Report your findings in a two-page discussion and to the class, honoring your promises of confidentiality and/or anonymity.

4. Identify several workers at various levels in a company in your area. Ask for thirty-minute interviews to find out more about how changes in technology are affecting the company's routine operations. You will probably learn that different forms and uses of technology pervade different levels of the company. Describe these differences, along with any long-range plans the company has for increasing its reliance on technology, in a two-page discussion. Be sure to investigate how technology affects the ways people communicate with each other in the company (and with people outside the company). Report your findings to the class.

5. Identify several workers at various levels in a company in your area. Ask for interviews to find out about employee interaction either in on-the-job collaborative situations, such as quality circles or committees, or in off-the-job social situations, such as company picnics or social hours. How important are these interactions to the people you interview? In what ways? Report your findings to the class.

6. Go to the library and find a resource for handling international business relations with one particular country (for example, Germany, South Africa, or Japan); compare the kinds of information provided about that country's business and social practices to your own culture's standard practices. Note the kinds of behaviors and attitudes you would have to monitor carefully if you were doing business with members of that culture. Present your findings in a two-page discussion and then report to the class.

➡ ONGOING ASSIGNMENT

- Just as companies have corporate cultures and corporate images, so do colleges and universities. From a student's perspective, briefly describe your institution's culture and image. How do they conflict? Why do they conflict?

- In what ways do some students fit in while others do not? Write a brief list of do's and don'ts for fitting into your school's culture for incoming students (freshmen or transfer students). (See the Applications on pages 13 and 17.)

Planning Your Writing Strategy

If you have ever stared at a blank computer screen or a clean sheet of paper when you were trying to write, you have experienced a problem shared by millions of writers: the frustration of getting started. The real problem, however, may be that you are unsure about what your writing is supposed to accomplish. This chapter will help you focus on some critical elements of well-written messages *before* you start to compose. In short, the chapter offers you a way of planning your writing.

First, you will examine the way you receive your writing projects, then the means for clarifying the writing situation, and, finally, the techniques for putting your planning strategy to work. These ideas form a cohesive plan that helps you understand where you want to go with your writing and how to get there, especially when you have to respond quickly to on-the-job writing situations.

Throughout this chapter, you will follow a scenario involving the members of a boat design team at Brady Black Sailboats, who are working to design a new four-person sailboat. The problems the lead writer faces underscore the importance of considering the reader's needs and the purpose of the document as crucial planning elements for constructing a successful document; Applications appear throughout the chapter to give you some practice applying your new knowledge of critical thinking and planning that go on during this early stage of the writing process.

As in any other discussion of the writing process, you may modify any of the ideas in this chapter to suit your own writing situations, and you may address them in any order that makes you feel comfortable. Most important, however, is that you understand the subtleties of the complex process of writing before you begin taking blind shortcuts that can sabotage your efforts.

Getting On-the-Job Writing Projects

As part of the message you send about your organization's culture and your own reputation, you should be prepared to respond proactively to communication situations. On-the-job writing projects may be known well in advance of a deadline or may arise quickly as a result of a sudden change in the organization's environment, policies, or competition. In either situation, you should be prepared to respond appropriately, with thoughtful consideration for the best communication strategy.

You may not remember your first big writing project in high school or college, but you probably know how you got the project—your teacher announced that a paragraph or paper was due on a particular topic. Similarly, your first on-the-job writing project will probably come directly from your boss, but the means by which this project is assigned may vary.

Advanced Knowledge

First, *you may know well in advance that you will have to document some aspect of your work*. For instance, the members of the Brady Black team who are working on a new design for a four-person sailboat may know all along that they'll have to file a monthly report, known as a progress report, that details the work done on this design. Throughout the work process, the lead writer, Nicholas Petrokov, will probably keep notes or perhaps a work log (more about that in Chapter 3) that describes the successes and failures of various configurations they have tried, modifications they have made, and plans for the next attempt. Then, when it's time to write the progress report, he'll have the information he needs. (See Chapter 13 for more on progress reports.)

Impromptu Requests

Second, *you may be given a writing project at a moment's notice*. Perhaps your boss drops by your work area to ask informally how your work is coming along. She may listen for a while and then decide that, rather than take up more of your time (and her own), she would like you to put the details in writing, outlining where you are with the work. Although such a request may be made casually, the phrase "How about writing that up for me?" carries a lot of weight in the workplace and should never be regarded as unimportant. Certainly, she wouldn't have asked for the information if she weren't interested in the details. The problem for many workplace writers, however, is that they do not know *how much* information she wants (the big picture or lots of details?) or exactly how she might *use* the information (to determine whether to terminate the project or, on a brighter note, to give you more money for the project). Learning how to determine these factors is also part of your role as a writer, as discussed below, and is an aspect of constructing successful documents.

The Writer's Initiative

Third, *you may (although you may not believe it right now) give yourself a writing project through your own initiative*. Perhaps you find it difficult to articulate your ideas clearly in person or to get your boss's full attention when she comes to your work area. Putting your ideas or requests in writing can help you focus on exactly what you want from your boss and can give her a clearer picture of the importance of your requests. Although frivolous requests or whining (especially in writing!) can damage your reputation and future far more than just keeping quiet, a reasonable, persuasive memo explaining why your project needs an additional team member, more money, or a month's extension can, indeed, accomplish your goal.

When Nicholas plans a memo to his boss, telling her about the team's progress on the boat design project, he first decides to answer a series of questions that help him determine what to communicate (the content) and how to communicate it (the style). Essential to all these questions, of course, are decisions good writers make about their audience, their purpose, and their role as writers; you'll see these elements in some rather subtle places throughout the following list of Nicholas's concerns:

- *Status of project:* How is work truly progressing on this project? How close are we to our schedule? How close are we to our deadline?

- *Quality of work:* What is the quality of the work we have produced so far? Have we had to cut any corners? Were they good corners to cut? Will we have to cut any more? What will the consequences be?

- *Amount of detail:* How much detail does my boss want about our progress—just a quick summary assuring her that we'll meet our deadline or a more detailed overview explaining the challenges we have faced?

- *Bad news:* How will I tell her the bad news—that we're way behind schedule and need to revise our plans for completion? How does my boss respond to bad news? Can I balance the bad news with some good news—perhaps reassure her that, in spite of delays, the work is going to be top quality when it's completed? How will she respond to that sort of good news/bad news presentation?

- *Contributions from others:* How will I report the help that others have given us? Similarly, what input should I seek from the other team members in constructing this memo?

- *Graphics:* Should I include any graphics to clarify my information, make it more professional, or highlight specifics?

- *Design:* Should the memo be formatted in a special way to make it more readable, to draw out the most important facts, or to highlight details of the work we have accomplished?

- *My reputation:* Does my boss have faith in me? Does she believe that I do good work? How can I reinforce her good opinion or encourage her faith in me?

These concerns show the kinds of decisions that, like Nicholas, you will have to make about your own documents at their earliest phase, concerns that require you to understand the writing situation as a balance of the document's audience, purpose, and content, along with your role as a writer.

Planning the Strategy: An Overview of the Writing Situation

However you get your on-the-job writing project—whether it is assigned well in advance, given at a moment's notice, or taken up on your own initiative—it is crucial that you understand the document's audience, purpose, and content/

Throughout this chapter, you will have opportunities to put your new knowledge to work in Application exercises, which you may use as vehicles for class discussion or as actual writing assignments. A scenario is provided for you, but your instructor may substitute a different kind of problem for you to resolve.

Scenario

Consider the appearance and efficiency of the external lighting, landscaping, walkways, and pathways on your college campus or at your place of work. How efficient are these features? You may find, for instance, that students (or workers) often take alternative routes to classroom buildings, the library, or dormitories. What kinds of landscaping strategies might better serve these students? You might find that lighting along various walkways or parking lots is inadequate for night students. Or you might discover that much of your campus lacks reasonable accessibility for people with disabilities.

Building on the probability that you have given little thought to the layout of your campus, develop a series of questions that you would want to investigate, indicating the kind of information you would want to include in a written document that notes the strengths and weaknesses of your campus landscape. You might use the list of questions Nicholas developed about his writing project as a model of the topical matters you would want to address, as well as the smaller elements and more precise information you would want to uncover about those elements.

context, as well as your role as a writer; these four elements comprise the writing situation. Thus, the *writing situation* encompasses all factors that affect the tone, appearance, length, and every other characteristic of the written document.

Unfortunately, no concrete model exists to describe every writing situation because the writing situation has no universal shape; rather, it reflects the concerns that a good writer will work with to shape the writing for each particular situation. For example, when writing for the president of his corporation, Nicholas might make his audience his chief concern, parlaying all other elements of the writing situation into a "shape" that noticeably accommodates that reader (see Figure 2.1 on page 32).

In a different context, with a different writer, audience, and purpose, the writing situation might look completely different. For example, if the most important factor in a writing situation is the purpose—say, convincing Nicholas's immediate boss to reassign a technician from Section B, which is currently ahead of schedule on its windshield design project—then the writer may shape the writing situation as shown in Figure 2.2 on page 33.

APPLICATION

Based on the list of questions you generated in the first Application, determine whether the primary focus of your writing will be the audience, the purpose, or some other element. What alternative focus might be appropriate in a different situation or with different readers?

Draw two models that might be appropriate for your ideas.

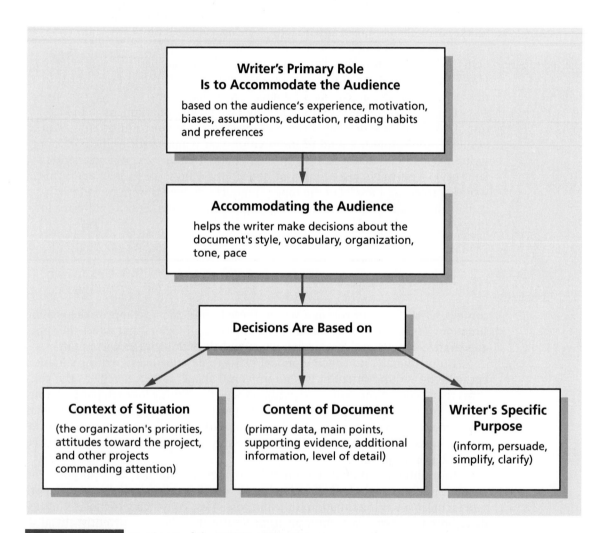

FIGURE 2.1 Version 1 of the Writing Situation

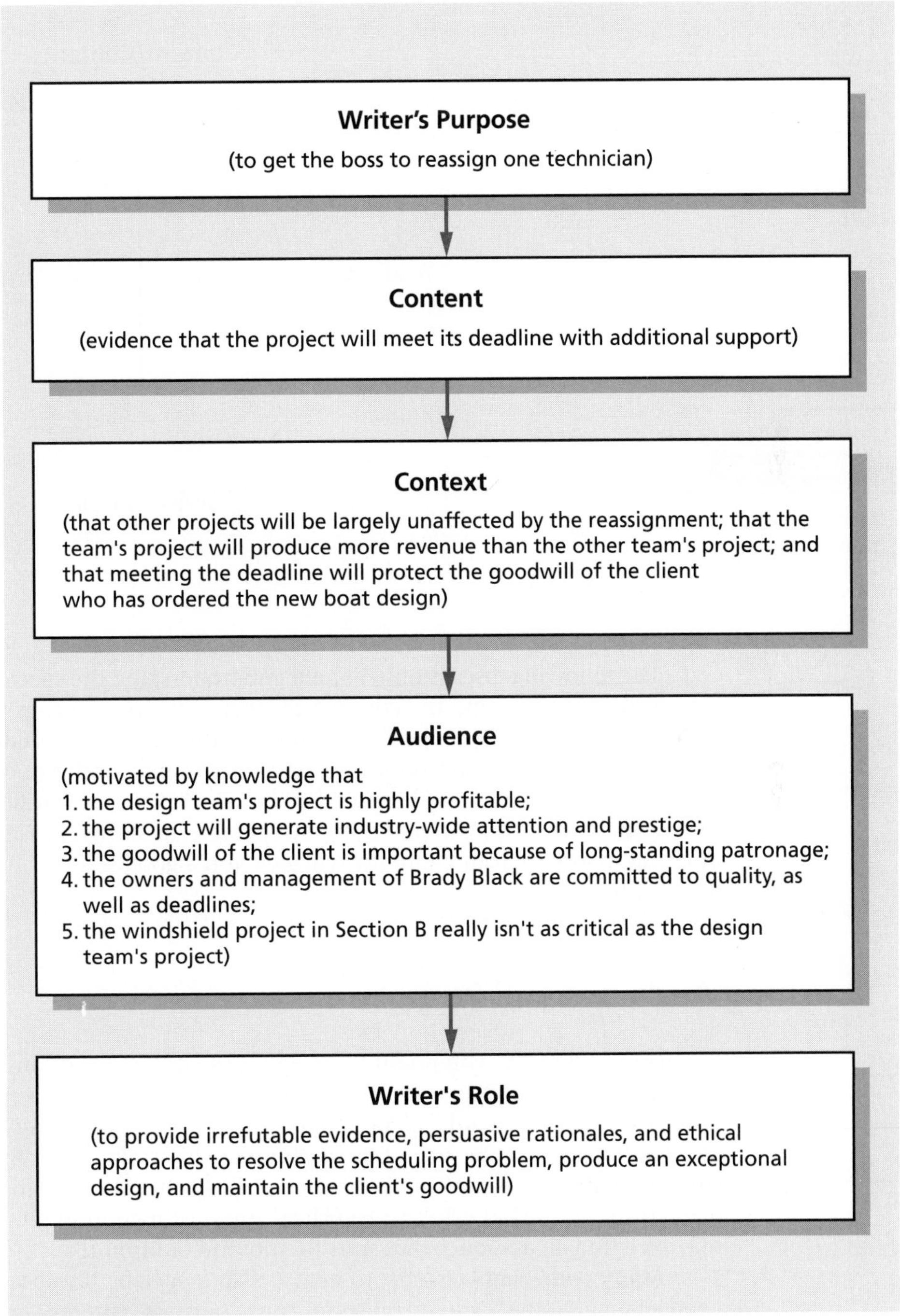

Writer's Purpose

(to get the boss to reassign one technician)

Content

(evidence that the project will meet its deadline with additional support)

Context

(that other projects will be largely unaffected by the reassignment; that the team's project will produce more revenue than the other team's project; and that meeting the deadline will protect the goodwill of the client who has ordered the new boat design)

Audience

(motivated by knowledge that
1. the design team's project is highly profitable;
2. the project will generate industry-wide attention and prestige;
3. the goodwill of the client is important because of long-standing patronage;
4. the owners and management of Brady Black are committed to quality, as well as deadlines;
5. the windshield project in Section B really isn't as critical as the design team's project)

Writer's Role

(to provide irrefutable evidence, persuasive rationales, and ethical approaches to resolve the scheduling problem, produce an exceptional design, and maintain the client's goodwill)

FIGURE 2.2 Version 2 of the Writing Situation

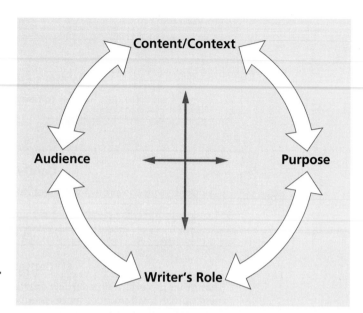

FIGURE 2.3

The Interrelationship of the Writing
Situation Elements

The following discussion will help you understand the special qualities of the
reader, the purpose, and the content/context of the message, as well as your role
as the writer, that will shape the writing situation and then guide your decisions
while planning your communication. Again, you may prefer to consider these elements in a different order from that in which they are presented here; ultimately, however, you will find them inseparable, as shown in Figure 2.3. You will
also find that these four elements will give you a good sense of how to succeed at
your writing task.

Matching Audience and Purpose

If you enjoy comedy, you might think about the difference in the humor and content of various comedians' shows. Whereas one comedian feels that certain kinds
of language (swear words, taboo language, racist or sexist terms) are inappropriate, another makes the use of such language his trademark. And, whereas the
content of one comedian's show might be highly objectionable to some audiences,
it might be hysterically funny to others. Interestingly enough, both comedians
may well find an audience that suits their brand of humor.

Many comedians also try to accomplish a specific purpose beyond making
people laugh. Some try to instill social consciousness, whereas others try to break
down barriers. Still others help us to laugh at ourselves and overcome the cyni-
cism that surrounds us. Just as successful comedians present the kind of humor

that is most likely to appeal to their audiences while achieving their goals of raising consciousness or smoothing the rough edges of society, successful workplace writers figure out the kind of information—along with its support, tone, and visual presentation, discussed in later chapters—that is most likely to appeal to their audiences and achieve the goal they have set for each document they write.

Understanding the Audience

Understanding readers and their needs is a key factor in creating useful workplace documents. In the boat design example, for instance, it would certainly help Nicholas to understand a few things about the reader and her need for information. Consider the difference it would make if she prefers an overview to lots of details, facts, and figures in every document. What if she likes graphics and simple charts instead of a lot of text? Or what if her background is marketing, not design—can you see how different the terminology might be in a report written for her versus a report written for another design engineer?

Although all elements of audience analysis or identification hinge on some basic stereotypes, and relying entirely on stereotypes for any purpose is dangerous, these four basic elements of audience analysis might, nevertheless, affect how you would write your document:

- *Use of information:* Most readers read workplace documents to help them perform their jobs and want to know rather quickly how any given document concerns them. Thus, you must determine whether your audience will use your document to make decisions, understand the history of an idea or position within your organization, gain insights about related matters, perform a task, fulfill a requirement, or accommodate a policy (see The Reader's Purpose later in the chapter). *Therefore, job-related factors that determine how the reader will use the information you provide will help you decide what kinds of content to include for your audience.*

  Remember, also, that readers may be external to your organization. In the context of their own jobs (and interests), members of government agencies, community groups, professional organizations, consumers, vendors, and the media may have to understand the kind and quality of work your organization performs. Accommodating their needs as readers is just as important as addressing your internal readers' needs.

- *Level of education:* Generally, the more education audience members have, the stronger their reasoning skills, the more advanced their vocabulary, the greater their familiarity with metaphors and other comparisons, and the greater their capacity for following complex and even theoretical arguments. *Thus, knowing your audience's level of education will allow you to make some decisions about the style of your writing and the appropriate sophistication of your argument or explanation.*

THE WORLD OF WORKPLACE WRITING

Taking a Wider View of Your Situation

Because personal experience is by definition limited, it provides a limited base for viewing a workplace writing situation. Writers gain a huge advantage when they look beyond themselves to observe, read, and talk to diverse others about new ideas. By going beyond their own world and that of people like themselves, writers can overcome the ingrown fears, obsessions, or limitations that restrict their view of what is important or possible in finding creative new opportunities. Looking for outside information helps writers see the big picture and the full context of their writing project's situation.

In the workplace as in daily life, a writer's experience or knowledge builds up gradually as layers of resources accumulate and eventually develop into a broader base of support for making decisions and taking action. The following diagram envisions this process as a series of layers of information available to writers. The most limiting resources are on the surface or top layer, while wider experiences expand beyond it to create an increasingly broad context for decisions and a solid basis for action.

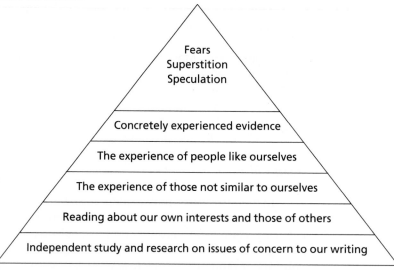

Writers who live and make decisions based entirely on superstition, mythology, and fear may not dare to venture into new territory; they may blindly worship the way things have always been done and make decisions solely in reaction to events, almost by a coin toss. Writers who are more likely to make meaningful decisions take advantage of every available source of information, from concretely experienced evidence to the evidence of diverse others and knowledge gained by reading and research.

■ *Audience motivations:* As mentioned earlier, most readers respond to workplace writing because the content of the message affects their jobs. Other readers, however, respond (believe, think, or act the way you have requested) because they believe their work lives or their personal lives will be somehow better as a result. These motivations are the bases for most persuasive messages, including sales pitches and political advertisements, and may include appeals to the following:

health	prestige	power	popularity
self-reliance	security	safety	wealth
ethics	humanity	fear	education

Thus, if the boat designer's progress memo is written to a reader who prides herself on her workers' safety record, the writer might get further by explaining that meeting the deadline could cause some slipups that could endanger workers and future boat owners. *Knowing what motivates your reader(s) can help you determine how to organize your message and structure your content.*

■ *Audience preferences:* Although it isn't always possible to know your readers' preferences about their reading material, you might consider some of the following elements:

size and style of type	types of support
length of sections	use of lists and headings
organization (big or bad news first?)	amount of details
amount and type of graphics	use of quotations or citations
level of formality	use of metaphors/comparisons
size of margins	density of paragraphs

If you know any of your readers' preferences about documents they read, you have a big advantage over the writer who knows nothing about such matters. *Accommodating reader preferences is another key to creating a successful document.*

Although it is difficult to know everything about your readers, the more you know about them and accommodate them, the better your chances for producing a useful document that accomplishes your goals. Sometimes, however, you may be writing to an unknown audience, consisting of anyone in the reading public who finds your message interesting, noteworthy, or useful. For example, suppose you work for a company that makes flashlights, and you are asked to draft the copy for a brochure that home safety inspectors will pass out to their clients. What assumptions can you make about the readers' job-related factors, levels of education, motivations, and preferences? Although the readers are obviously motivated by safety concerns, you have no information about the jobs they perform, their level of education, or their reading preferences. In such cases, you have to let your document "find" its own audience: write to a "typical," safety-conscious reader and allow your work to stand for itself.

APPLICATION

> List all the people (or groups of people) who might be affected by a communi-
> cation you write describing how to redesign the landscaping of your campus or
> workplace. What do you know about these readers' use for the information,
> their level of education, their motivations, and their preferences for reading?
>
> Why would they be interested in your project? How would they likely
> react to your findings about the efficiency of the campus layout? Why? What
> would their reactions likely be to your preliminary recommendations or ideas
> for modifying the layout? Why?

Understanding the Purpose

As you think about your audience, you should begin to consider what you want
the reader to do with the information you provide. In the boat design example,
the writer may want his boss to reassign a technician from another project. But
suppose Nicholas is writing to the team leader of that other project. What would
he want then? More than likely, he'd want the other team leader to go along with
the plan and agree to lend one of his technicians for a month or two. How will
Nicholas persuade him to go along with the plan? Could Nicholas barter with this
leader or offer him something useful in the meantime? Perhaps Nicholas's promise not to keep the technician permanently after the project is completed would be
enough to convince the other team leader to go along with the proposal. At any
rate, as you can see, the communication with this team leader is quite different
from the communication with the boss, again showing that audience considerations are inseparable from other elements that define the writing situation.

The Writer's Purpose

As you can see from the boat design example, "what you want the reader to do"
might be an action (reassign a technician) or an attitude change (go along with
the reassignment). In short, the writer's purpose changes with the audience and
the message itself.

The following are some of the most common purposes of on-the-job writing:

- To convey information, either background information or updated infor-
  mation
- To provide the basis for decision making
- To describe a process or procedure

- To propose solutions or alternatives
- To explain how to do something
- To explain, justify, or argue for a particular course of action
- To compare similarities
- To contrast differences
- To clarify a technical, scientific, or legal idea
- To describe something that happened
- To explain why something happened
- To present the results of a particular course of action
- To define technical/scientific/specialized terminology
- To describe a problem and/or solution
- To predict future trends or events

The Reader's Purpose

Once you have determined what you want the reader to do with the information you present, you have completed half of the purpose task. The other part requires you to work from a different angle: figuring out why your reader might *read* what you have written. Some of the most common purposes for reading on the job include the following:

- To gain information necessary for the reader's job performance
- To gain information to be used in a meeting, presentation, or written document
- To gain information for general knowledge (who's doing what? what's happening?)
- To determine the quality of the product, service, or course of action described
- To evaluate the progress on a project
- To determine the feasibility of the product, service, or course of action described
- To determine the costs of the product, service, or course of action described
- To understand a problem and its potential solutions
- To see how ideas fit together
- To understand how individual company projects contribute to corporate goals
- To understand the company's plans for the future

TABLE 2.1 Matching Purposes with Forms

Purpose	Possible Forms or Genres
to explain a situation or decision	letters/memos, progress reports, summaries, background reports, trip reports, abstracts, justification reports
to instruct	operator's or instruction manuals
to clarify information	memos, reports, brochures, job descriptions
to document information	employee evaluations, organizational evaluations, reports, memos/letters
to recommend solutions	letters/memos, reports, proposals
to suggest alternatives	letters/memos, reports, proposals, feasibility studies
to describe a process/procedure	reports, manuals, employee handbooks

One of the most frequent reasons for reading on the job combines a number of these purposes into the broad purpose of decision making. Organization leaders charged with making decisions rely on highly accurate, up-to-date, unbiased information. You will learn more about the extended forms that such analyses take in the discussion of analytical reports in Chapter 13.

In fact, a number of the purposes described here—from both the writer's and the reader's perspective—are so common in the workplace that they have evolved into special workplace document forms. Although these forms (or genres) of writing sometimes overlap, they are consistently recognized in the workplace for the purposes they most often seek to fulfill (see Table 2.1).

Multiple Purposes

Of course, you may have more than one reason for writing, just as your reader may have more than one reason for reading. With the boat design example, for instance, the primary purpose (the reason why the assignment was made) is to describe the team's progress on the design, but the secondary purpose is to convince the boss to reassign a technician from Section B. By combining the reasons for writing a particular piece of communication with the reader's reasons for reading that communication, Nicholas gets a clearer picture of what his writing must accomplish. In this case, his strategy would be reflected in Figure 2.4.

As Figure 2.4 shows, the writer's and the reader's primary purposes match quite nicely, but the secondary purposes do not. Nicholas can, however, make the secondary purposes match by presenting a convincing argument that if the boss reassigns Carlos, the work will be finished by the deadline. He will need to support

Writer's Primary Purpose	**=**	**Reader's Primary Purpose**
To report the progress of work on the boat design		To find out how work is progressing on the boat design

Writer's Secondary Purpose	**≠**	**Reader's Secondary Purpose**
To convince the boss to reassign Carlos, the technician from Section B, to our project for two months		To make sure the work will be finished by the deadline

FIGURE 2.4 Multiple Purposes: The Match Game

APPLICATION

Using Figure 2.4 and your proposal for the redesign of the campus layout as guides, match your primary and secondary purposes for writing with the primary and secondary purposes of the reader. Do the goals match? If not, determine what strategy you would use to align your and your reader's purposes more closely. What kinds of evidence, examples, details, or other options would you use to help match purposes?

that assertion, of course, by demonstrating why one more person would make such a difference in his team's performance and progress. But once he supplies that evidence, he will have made a very strong case for his request by bringing together his purpose as a writer with the reader's purpose for reading.

Negotiating the Content/Context

The subject matter about which you are writing, along with the other people and projects that may be affected by your communication, constitute the combined content/context of your document. You know, of course, that you must have thoroughly sound information about your project; your *content* must be accurate, complete, and well supported.

In addition to the specific message or content you have to convey to the reader, you also need to see the *context*, the bigger picture of how your project fits into the organization's overall plans. Thus, you will also need to know something about the other people and projects in your organization and forgo the tendency to overrate the importance of your own project. For example, if Nicholas decides to ask his boss for another technician to work on the boat design project, he must consider whether other projects are going to suffer if his request is granted. With good research, he might ask his boss whether the new windshield project in Section B could be delayed for a couple of months and one of those technicians reassigned to Nicholas's project until his team meets its deadline. If he can show, for example, that his project will bring in 22 percent more potential revenues than the windshield project or that the client's goodwill is at stake, he might convince the boss that the temporary reassignment is wise. If, however, he asks for another technician without considering where the technician might come from or what project(s) might be affected, he has made it remarkably easy for his boss simply to say, "We can't hire anybody else right now."

Parameters of the Message

In addition to considering the big picture, at this stage you also need to start making decisions about what is and is not relevant to your message, what you do and do not intend to cover in your writing. Although you will refine the content in the editing and revising stages (see Chapter 6), you should already consider the kinds of issues you should include or eliminate. Refining your sense of the information that truly belongs in your document requires a keen understanding of audience needs, your purpose, and the ethical power you wield as a workplace writer (see the discussion in the next section).

You can think of your writing as an enclosed geometric entity (a square, circle, or whatever) with definite boundaries. The *scope* of your writing is the information inside that entity—everything you need to include. The *limitations* of your writing constitute the information outside that entity—minor details or related ideas that serve no purpose in the particular communication you are creating. You should construct those boundaries carefully, including the information your reader needs to know (or has specifically asked for) and omitting the details that are likely to muddle the message, make you seem long-winded and unsure of your purpose, or annoy your reader.

In the boat design memo, for example, Nicholas's task is to report concisely the progress on his team's project. First, he brainstorms about the general topics that come to mind when he thinks of the boat design project. Strategy Review 2.1 shows a mapping strategy Nicholas uses to determine the boundaries for what should be included and excluded.

STRATEGY REVIEW 2.1

MAPPING THE PARAMETERS OF A PROJECT

In the boat design scenario, Nicholas begins to define the parameters of his project by brainstorming a list of ideas related to the boat design project:

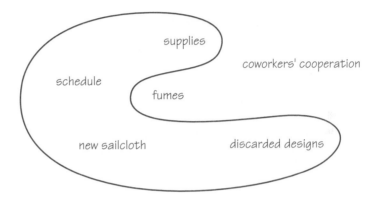

He may be tempted to complain that the fumes from the composition room are wafting through the ventilation system or that one team member is not really pulling her share of the weight, but careful consideration convinces him that none of that information is relevant in a progress report. (He may report the ventilation problem in a separate memo to the maintenance department; he may report the problem with his coworker in a separate team evaluation form, due at quarterly intervals in the project.) In fact, if he were to report either of these problems in the progress report, his boss might see the report as irrelevant ramblings or as "tattling" or grousing (see Assuming the Writer's Role later in this chapter). Thus, he uses a mapping technique to show that only four topics are truly relevant: supplies, new sailcloth, discarded designs, and schedule.

Keeping a clear sense of what should and should not be reported in any written assignment is crucial to your reader's understanding of your true message and, thus, to your success as an on-the-job writer.

Ethical Matters of Relevance

Your decisions about what does and does not need to be reported must reflect clear, ethical judgment. Unfortunately, some writers are unethical in their reporting by underreporting the facts or omitting damaging evidence or statistics, alternative points of view, or other types of information. At the same time, overreporting—giving too much information—can be every bit as problematic for readers as underreporting. In addition to betraying the writer's rhetorical ignorance (in this case, lack of knowledge of the audience and its needs), overreporting may also lead readers to assume that everything mentioned carries an equal amount of weight. As an ethical writer, you must include sufficient information and details to satisfy your purpose for writing and your reader's purpose for reading, while giving the keenest consideration to accuracy and the reader's needs.

Sources of Information

As you develop your sense of the appropriate content, you should also consider the means by which you will gather information for your document, a process discussed in detail in the next chapter. Some projects will require substantial research into library materials, corporate documents, work logs, and government specifications. Other projects will require you to interview your coworkers and colleagues from other departments. Still other projects will require you to test products or chemical compounds to obtain physical evidence that supports your decisions and work strategies. Then, you will describe those tests and their results in a report or in some other appropriate document.

Knowing how to get information, whether that information is already compiled for you (either on-line or in some document) or whether you have to generate it from tests or other people, is a crucial talent no matter what your job is. Ironically, it's also a talent that many people take for granted. But if you are ever in a situation where you do not have access to information, do not have the time or funds to carry out a valid test, or cannot get people to tell you about a project or a problem, you'll quickly learn that being able to find information and enlist the cooperation of others are two of the most important skills you can develop on the job. (These people skills should also remind you of the social nature of writing on the job, discussed especially in Chapters 1 and 7.) From the beginning of a writing assignment, you should be thinking about the kinds of information you will need to complete your assignment (Chapter 3 is devoted to strategies for finding information). Will you need to go through the company's records for background information? Will you need sales trends or personnel information? Will you need to conduct some tests or experiments? Will you need to talk with your coworkers or your boss? Will you have to talk to your colleagues in other parts of the company?

Nicholas may decide that most of his information for the boat design progress report will come from his own notes and from tests his coworkers have run on the new design. But he will also want to enlist the memories of his coworkers; he will need to check with suppliers about the delivery of some of the materials the team will need for the final model they are designing; and he will need to design visuals and handouts for a presentation to his boss and her supervisors. In short, he will need the help of others who can provide information about the "already-done" segments of the project, as well as those who can help with the "still-to-do" portions of the work.

All of these elements of the content of your document—primary message, context, parameters, and sources of information—are shaped by decisions you

> Brainstorm a list of ideas that might be associated with your writing project. The ideas may be related to the topic, the audience, the purpose of your writing, the factors affecting it, your reader's response, and the outcome of the changes you are trying to make. Further, you should consider your knowledge of your campus context: the bigger picture facing the ongoing concerns of your potential readers. For instance, if your college is currently trying to raise millions of dollars to upgrade your library's computers, that project may take precedence over matters of landscaping.
>
> Then, based on the matching of audience and purpose you achieved in the preceding Application and focusing on the content/context of your message, determine some boundaries for your writing. You might consider the appropriateness of the material to your topic, audience, and purpose as a means for limiting your discussion. You might also consider a reasonable length for your document and the time you have to investigate and write the document as other parameters of your message.
>
> Now, revise your list—or draw lines around appropriate topics—to show the ideas you would and would not have to accommodate in a discussion of your campus landscape.
>
> Finally, determine the most likely place to gather information for your project. For instance, list the areas you would want to physically observe, as well as the people with whom you would want to discuss your ideas and from whom you might gather more information about your observations.

have already made about your audience and your purpose; in turn, the decisions you make about content may help refine your sense of audience and purpose. Again, the interrelatedness of all elements of the writing situation is apparent.

Assuming the Writer's Role

Although you may have expected your role as a writer to have been addressed much earlier in this chapter, you probably now understand that having a broad sense of the other three elements of the writing situation—audience, purpose, and content/context—lays the foundation for the decisions you make about your role. Once you understand these elements, you can see that your role is determined by the relationship you have or establish with the audience, the blending of your purpose(s) for writing with your readers' purpose(s) for reading, and your understanding and presentation of the appropriate content/context of your message. Chapter 1 described the writer's role as representing the organization's culture and the writer's own philosophies about business, ethics, and human relations. That discussion merits more details now that you are ready to plan a particular writing task.

As a writer, you have the option of playing a number of roles that can fall along a continuum from good to bad qualities:

informer	to	tattler/gossiper
persuader	to	manipulator
negotiator	to	waffler
visionary	to	dreamer

Although no one wants to be at the negative end of the spectrum, good writers take special care to make sure their roles fall in an appropriate range. Understanding your role as a writer means determining what your relationship is to the information to be presented, the audience for that information, the purpose of providing the information, the organization that holds the information, and your own credibility and professionalism. Asking yourself a few questions can help; if your answers settle on the left-hand part of the continuum in Strategy Review 2.2, you are probably in an appropriate role.

STRATEGY REVIEW 2.2

THE WRITER'S ROLE

1. What is my relationship to the information in this document?

   A ——————————————— B ——————————————— C

   A. I base the information on my own work and observations. I have supported the information by surveying others to see if their work and observations bear out my findings.
   B. I have no firsthand knowledge of the information, but I obtained it from reliable sources.
   C. I heard the information around the workroom from unreliable sources.

2. What is my relationship to the reader(s) of this document?

   A ——————————————— B ——————————————— C

   A. Because I have more information about this topic than my readers do, I will take on an instructional role that will give them the information they need about this topic.
   B. I have more information about this topic than my readers do, and I'll tell them whatever occurs to me.
   C. I will present what I know; if the readers don't get it, tough.

3. What is my purpose in writing this document?

A ———————————————— B ———————————————— C

A. I want to give explanations to my readers or persuade them to act in ways that will allow them to make sound, ethical decisions.
B. I want to impress my readers with my knowledge and persuasive skills so that they will accept whatever I tell them.
C. My boss told me I have to write this document and have it on her desk before I go on vacation.

4. What is my relationship with the organization?

A ———————————————— B ———————————————— C

A. I am a reasonable advocate for the organization's products and services.
B. I am an indifferent representative of the organization's products and services.
C. I am either subversive, hoping to destroy the organization, or so blindly loyal that I cannot see any weaknesses at all.

5. What will this communication say about me and my professionalism?

A ———————————————— B ———————————————— C

A. I am professional in gauging my readers' needs and providing clear, accurate, and complete information. I recognize that communicating ethically, effectively, and efficiently sends a special message about my integrity and about my ability to think clearly and creatively.
B. I present the information I know, and I hope it will say the right things about me.
C. I send a message; as long as my reader knows what I mean, that's the end of my job.

Using the continuum in Strategy Review 2.2, Nicholas in the boat design example might describe his role as follows:

My relationship with the *subject/content* is thorough because my teammates and I participated in every aspect of the project. My *audience,* on the other hand, knows only the broadest generalities about this project. She does not need to know all the details, but she does need to get a sense of the problems we have encountered, the cooperation we have received from others in the company, and the vision we have for completing the work. She also needs to know that the high quality we are striving for is costing us time and money; consequently, we do not believe the project will meet its current deadline. Fortunately, I have an excellent relationship with my boss. She has reviewed my accomplishments annually and consistently gives me high ratings for innovative responses and high-quality work. She also knows that I rarely ask for extensions, nor do my

Using the worksheet in Strategy Review 2.2 and drawing on Nicholas's response as a model, determine your own role as a writer on the landscaping project. The paragraph should culminate in an acknowledgment of the primary responsibilities you feel you should meet within your role as a writer.

projects come in over budget. Thus, the *purpose* of this memo is not only to give her the necessary details about our progress, but also to encourage her to consider extending our deadline and "lending" us a technician from another project. I believe I can make a successful case that our project is likely to bring in more dollars than the windshield project that Section B is currently working on (and is ahead of schedule on); perhaps I can convince her that one of Section B's technicians should join our project temporarily. As a strong advocate for quality in our organization's designs, I believe my insights carry a great deal of weight with my colleagues. Thus, I see my role as the writer of this progress report as follows:

1. The advocate of an extended deadline and reassignment of a technician
2. The clarifier of details regarding delays and modifications (without making excuses)
3. The representative of the high quality my colleagues and I envision for this new boat design.

I anticipate my reader's reviewing our work and concluding that we have worked diligently, creatively, and honorably to design the new four-person boat.

Your decisions at this stage will have a noticeable impact later on in the writing you actually produce; they will affect the amount of detail, the tone, and even the length of your document (see Chapter 5, Drafting Your Workplace Documents). Remembering that each decision reflects the role you have chosen for yourself will help you make appropriate decisions.

Putting the Strategy to Work

Figuring out your own strategy for planning is useful only if you can put it into action. The remainder of this chapter offers some ideas that may be of use in that quest.

First, learning to see your work in steps or stages can be extremely valuable, especially if you tend to be overwhelmed by writing assignments or by big projects

THE WORLD OF WORKPLACE WRITING

Writing as the Basis for Your Workplace Evaluation

In addition to the standard uses of on-the-job information described in this chapter, your writing can also be used to evaluate you and your work and even your potential for promotion into higher managerial levels. Although few workplace documents are *consciously* used to evaluate workers outside the professional writing staff, you must remember that your writing reflects your attention to detail, your clear thinking, your vision for new projects, your consideration of other workers, and your commitment to a project.

Further, every aspect of your communication says something about you. Consider, for example, what your reader might think if you were to submit a handwritten request for $50,000 in new computer equipment. Rather dismayed? Now consider what that reader might think if the request were written on a sticky note. Design elements are discussed in detail in Chapter 9, but you should already be thinking about how the presentation of your information both reflects on you and shows consideration for your readers.

Ironically, perhaps, a really strong piece of communication may not draw attention to the writer at all. After reading anything you write, your reader should think, "Good, I can use this," or "Okay, I'm convinced," or "Good, I know more about this subject now." If your reader responds in these positive ways, no doubt you will look better—and reap the rewards—as a result. Above all, the writing should not send *bad* messages about the writer. If your reader is wondering what the point of your message is, where you learned to spell, or how your ideas relate to each other, your reader is likely to take a dim view of your work and your potential.

of any sort. For the progress memo on the boat design, Nicholas might want to think in terms of (1) what's already been accomplished, (2) what problems remain, and (3) what needs to be done. Having already decided that the memo will probably be no more than two pages, he's cut the work into three portions, making the task more manageable.

By dividing your work into stages and then *starting with the one you like best* (more about that in the section "Putting Prewriting Strategies to Work" in Chapter 5), you can often get through the entire process with surprising ease. At least the process is not so overwhelming as when you saw it as one monumental job. Taking a task step by step usually makes even the most unpleasant chore a bit more bearable.

When writing the boat design memo, Nicholas might break down his writing activities into the following plan:

1. Review notes from the past month.

2. Brainstorm with partners about the successes and failures we've encountered.

3. Determine which kinds of information are most important for my reader to gain a thorough sense of our progress (i.e., what's already been accomplished and what remains to be done)

4. Solicit additional information from coworkers in other departments, suppliers, illustrators, and others.

5. Draft an outline of major points for the document and the graphics to accompany those points.

6. Begin writing the "easiest" section and continue until the memo is completed.

7. Determine elements of layout and design that will make the memo more readable.

8. Revise, polishing the text, graphics, and layout.

9. Proofread.

Of course, another writer might take a different approach to planning these steps, but good writers agree that a well-planned approach will foster successful writing.

Second, a broad perspective of the planning phase can also help you apply your insights when planning a writing project. The worksheet presented in Strategy Review 2.3 documents Nicholas's view of his writing project and provides an outline of the concerns you have learned to consider so far in this chapter.

S T R A T E G Y   R E V I E W   2 . 3

OUTLINING THE WRITING PLAN

CONTENT: My assignment is to write about ___the four-person sailboat project.___

CONTEXT: This work is surrounded by other projects, such as ___the windshield___ project, the gearshift project, and the UX-1000 line.

The goal of *all* our work is to help the company accomplish [these objectives] ___safe, innovative designs___ and promote [this image] ___high-quality, prestigious boats___

AUDIENCE: Name ___LeMare Daniels___ [or] People who _____

PRIMARY PURPOSE: What I want my reader to do is ___see that the project is___ going well, but needs a deadline extension.

What I want my reader to think is ___that the deadline extension will___ ___promote quality and safety.___

SECONDARY PURPOSE: Further, my reader should ___consider reassigning a___ ___technician from Section B___ and should believe that I am ___competent, innovative, ethical.___

PARAMETERS OF THE TOPIC: My document will include these points:
___new sailcloth, discarded designs, supplies, schedule___

Although related, the following ideas are not relevant to this particular document because of its audience and purpose:
___coworkers' cooperation, fumes from other sections___

SOURCES: For the information I need to supply, I will investigate company or library materials: ___my notes, colleagues' logs, supply requisitions___;

interview ___coworkers___;

and/or test or survey ___—NA—___

SCHEDULE OF WORK: In order to complete this assignment by my (date) _____ deadline, I need to accomplish the following tasks by the following dates:

1. Review notes and interview coworkers by 12-30-98.

2. Outline plan and strategy for writing by 12-31-98.

3. Draft text and graphics by 1-2-99.

4. Revise and submit memo by 1-5-99.

Having seen the kinds of answers Nicholas provides for this worksheet, you should be prepared to complete a similar strategy for the next Application.

APPLICATION

Using the worksheet in Strategy Review 2.3 and Nicholas's responses for his project, construct your own overview of plans for your document. By now, you should have determined a specific audience and purpose, along with any secondary audiences and purposes, as well as the parameters of the project and your role as the writer.

Scheduling the Writing Project

Many people think of planning as a matter of scheduling—determining when to begin and complete a writing project—but this is a rather narrow interpretation that can sabotage some of the more critical elements you have learned about planning in this chapter. Nevertheless, once you have outlined the steps that will lead to the development and completion of your assignment, scheduling will help you complete the planning phase.

Although many good writers can just sit down and write, most writers don't work that way. Instead, most writers go through some of the steps you have already read about: making decisions about the audience, purpose, content/context, and writer's role. After making these decisions, the writers work on the more complex aspect of scheduling their writing, being careful to allow plenty of time to check and recheck their facts and the writing itself.

Coordinating the Research Strategy

Early in your writing process, you will have to consider what sources of information you will use for your assignment. Remember that just because you need statistics from a report filed a year ago or need to talk to the project engineer does not mean that this information or that colleague will be available to you whenever you are ready. For instance, what will happen if the project engineer goes on vacation just as you realize you need some information from her? What if the report you need is boxed up to be stored in the new corporate library and won't be unpacked for a week? Or what if the information you need is available only on-line and you have no idea how to access it? Asking for information as soon as you know you will need it is a critical part of scheduling your writing assignment.

Finding Time to Write

One of the most difficult scheduling problems for many workplace writers is actually finding the time to write. For most of us, the workplace is filled with interruptions—from phone calls to coworkers to our bosses—and pressures to attend to other projects. Good writing requires concentration that can all too easily be sabotaged by such distractions. That's why so many people write at night or on weekends. Learning to use your time wisely, however, can greatly reduce your off-hours work schedule or, better yet, free up some of your regular work hours for writing.

Quite early in your career, you will probably learn that *finding* time to write actually means *making* time to write. To help you make time to write, try following these tactics that many writers use when they have a writing project:

1. Let your coworkers know you have a writing assignment—and a deadline—that you'll be working on for a few hours. It is important that your fellow workers know what you are working on (in this case, at least) so they don't resent your unexplained absence from another project.

2. Find a low-traffic area where you can work or close your office door. In many organizations, conversations are going on in the workplace at almost any given time; coworkers regularly drop by each other's offices or work areas to brainstorm ideas, check on recent developments, or even chat briefly about outside events. Although it may seem antisocial to "hide" or close your office door, taking yourself out of the conversation loop can be critical to making time to write.

3. Learn to say no—politely—to other requests. Because so many workers want to get ahead, it is tempting to take on more work than anyone could possibly do. If you learn to temper your ambition with some reality, however, you will be able to devote quality time to the projects you do take on. Although taking on a lot of work may look impressive, getting a lot of work done in a shoddy manner impresses no one. Take on a reasonable number of tasks and then give them your undivided attention.

4. Ask for help. In addition to realizing early in a writing project the kinds of informational support you will need to complete your project, you should also be prepared to ask for help with illustrations, copying, and text reviews. Delegating certain portions of the text to subject matter experts may also be a useful strategy. As work increasingly becomes a collaborative effort, you will begin to understand how teams work together to produce successful documents (see Chapter 7 on collaboration).

Spending Time Wisely for Revisions

Although you may know many writers who procrastinate and therefore have no time to revise their writing, other writers are plagued by the opposite dilemma: overkill. These writers begin working on a writing project as soon as they get it—within the hour if at all possible. And they continue to work on that project on and off (mostly on) until it is due. The result may be exceptionally good writing, but they have also probably wasted valuable time that they could have spent on other tasks. In other words, they could probably have produced just as good a document by using their revising time more wisely. Furthermore, by spending so much time on an assignment, they lose their "critical eye."

Crucial to good revising is letting your writing "cool off," that is, putting your work aside for a day or two before returning to revise it. You might be surprised how different your words and ideas sound when you haven't seen them for a few days. By using this strategy, you can approach your writing much as your reader will—with a fresh perspective.

You may not always have the luxury of this "cooling-off" period, however, especially if you must produce a communication quickly. But having the experience of a slower-paced revision strategy will serve you well whenever you face such demands (see Chapter 6 for more on pacing your revisions).

Meeting Deadlines

Finally, you need to be aware of how important deadlines are in the workplace. Because other people's work probably depends on your work, meeting a deadline can smooth the process of filling work orders, help your organization win a new client or contract, demonstrate your ability to organize your work to get the job done, and, ultimately, mean success or failure—both for you and for your organization.

In school you may have occasionally asked for extensions on papers or projects due in your classes. Whether you were granted those extensions probably depended on your teacher's generosity. In the workplace, however, your boss will rarely be so generous, simply because deadlines are often crucial in an organization.

You can think of the situation this way: Suppose your company president wants your report about the budget for a new product line by noon on Tuesday. You may assume it doesn't matter whether she gets the report by noon or by, say, 2:00 P.M. on Tuesday or maybe even Wednesday morning. It does indeed matter, however, if she is getting on the company jet at 12:30 P.M. on Tuesday to fly to Tulsa to present the new product concept to the board of directors. You may think "Okay, so I'll just fax it to Tulsa and she'll have it when she lands at 2:00." That is not good enough. She intends to read your budget plan on the plane; if she gets the information in Tulsa, she has no time to go over your figures or prepare answers to questions about the budget you have incorporated into your report. Because you missed the deadline, your company president is unprepared and looks foolish, and sometimes people lose their jobs when they have made their company president look foolish. At the very least, she's likely to reconsider your potential for promotions, salary increases, and more challenging assignments.

Missing a deadline can have even more serious consequences for many organizations. At some time, either as a company employee or as a customer of some business, you have probably failed to receive promised merchandise, services, or materials by the guaranteed date. As inconvenient as it is to wait at home for hours for a promised service call, shipping or repair delays can be even more devastating to an organization because they can delay regular procedures, cost thousands of dollars in downtime, and even shut down the organization altogether. Because some organizations literally live or die by the calendar and the clock, deadlines are no small matter; even if your own organization is not so tied to the clock, it probably does business with others that are. Missing a deadline, submitting a proposal after the deadline, or failing to meet agreed-to shipping dates can disqualify organizations or ruin their reputations for future business with the contracting agency. In most workplace settings, therefore, you must meet your deadlines—even if the quality of your work has to suffer. On a brighter note, meeting your deadlines—especially with high-quality work—helps your organization and sends good messages about your professionalism, dependability, attention to detail, and overall competence.

Summary

In this chapter, we have discussed the primary considerations for planning to complete an on-the-job writing assignment. You may know that you will have to make periodic reports throughout your work cycle; such knowledge gives you plenty of time to plan your writing. With more impromptu writing assignments, you may not have the luxury of extensive planning, but having gone through the process of planning, as presented in this chapter, gives you an edge in understanding the elements of the writing situation that will control your writing decisions.

Four primary elements define the writing situation: the audience, the purpose, the content/context, and the writer's role. By understanding more about each of these elements, you begin to understand the powerful choices you have as a writer, as well as your responsibility to provide ethically balanced, complete, and accurate information that the appropriate audience can use.

Once you understand the broad aspects of the writing situation, you are ready to put your plan to work and can schedule your strategy and your time for moving on with the writing process. You can refine your strategy for writing by considering your information sources, finding time to write, allowing time to revise, and meeting your deadlines. The final worksheet in this chapter (in Strategy Review 2.3) can help you look at each phase more carefully and integrate all the aspects of planning described in this chapter. Such a strategy can help you take control of the writing situation, help you anticipate and overcome potential problems, and help you set a course for producing a truly good piece of writing that will communicate the message you intend—about your subject, your organization, and yourself.

✓ CHECKLIST

✓ Allow time to slow down your writing process whenever possible, but especially for critical communications when the slower pace can help you make better choices about your writing.

✓ Take advantage of scheduled writing assignments by planning them and working on them all along.

✓ Take impromptu writing assignments seriously, even if you have to cut some corners at the planning stage.

✔ Use complete planning strategies when you take on a writing assignment on your own initiative.

✔ Learn to recognize and thoroughly develop the four primary elements of the writing situation: the audience, the purpose, the content/context, and the writer's role.

✔ Identify, as much as possible, your audience's job requirements, level of education, motivation for reading, and preferences for reading.

✔ Determine your purpose(s) for writing, along with your audience's purpose(s) for reading, and try to make sure that your document fulfills each purpose.

✔ Determine the proper content for your document, considering the other elements of the writing situation, along with the context of your message, the parameters of your discussion, and your sources of information.

✔ Take responsibility for your role as the writer, determining how clear, accurate, concise, ethical, and accommodating you choose to be for this particular writing situation.

✔ Figure carefully the steps and amount of time you need to devote to a writing task.

✔ Complete the planning phase by coordinating your information sources, making time to write, allowing time for revisions, and meeting deadlines.

EXERCISES

Individual Exercises

1. Briefly list the rituals that you go through when you have a writing assignment for one of your classes. Compare your list (your process) with those of your classmates. What differences did you note? Could you work on your writing following someone else's processes and rituals?

2. Interview two workers in a local organization who have to write on the job. Then, write a brief paragraph on each worker describing the processes each follows when preparing to write. Be sure to include information about when and where the workers write. How do their processes compare or contrast with your own?

3. If you have a job already, think about parts of your work assignments that you dislike. If you are a full-time student, list some aspects of your campus

or your curriculum that you dislike. Then, briefly describe in a paragraph or two how your work or your environment could be restructured to make it more pleasant. If you proposed this restructuring to your boss or your teacher or the college president, what would the reaction likely be? Why? Write a final paragraph describing your audience and the anticipated reaction to your ideas.

4. Draft a list of questions you would want to answer in a progress report on your work toward a college degree. (You may use the questions on page 49 as a guideline.) What information would your memo include and what would its tone be if you were presenting your progress report to your parents, assuming that they are paying your tuition? If they are not paying your tuition? To a prospective or a current employer? To the newly reactivated military draft board? To your adviser? To your cousin (the Ph.D.) who has loudly predicted to other relatives that you'll never finish your degree?

5. If you have a job, prepare a brief description (three or four sentences) of the project you are currently working on. Then, describe (again, briefly) your coworkers' projects. Which projects require more personnel? More time? More of the budget? Which projects have short-term completion dates? How would you go about prioritizing these projects? Would the list differ if you were submitting it to the accounting department versus the human resources department? To the company president versus the stockholders?

6. Given the work you currently do—or expect to do when you graduate— make a list of at least ten reasons why you might have to write on the job. For each reason, provide a brief notation about who your readers might be and why they would want or need to read your communication.

7. To get a better idea of how motivations are matched to audiences, consider some recent automobile advertisements. Can you name a few cars/vehicles that appeal to a driver's preference for the following features?

luxury	safety	speed	ruggedness
hauling capacity	sportiness	prestige	economy
uniqueness	engineering	quality	styling

Collaborative Exercises

Choose a partner or a team to work with you on some of these exercises.

1. Briefly, describe the potential audiences for a report on improving the in-flight services of a major commercial airline. Which groups of airline workers might be interested in the suggestions? What particular aspects of the report would they be interested in? Make one group the primary reader for such a report and describe how you would structure the information for that group. Using the planning worksheet in Strategy Review 2.3, outline your strategy for writing to this group of readers.

2. List the qualities about your college that you believe attracted most of your student peers. Then, list the qualities you believe were not a consideration and explain why not. Next, list ideas you would want to include as the content of a brochure you are writing to encourage prospective students to attend your college or university. Now, consider how you might change the content if you were writing to the students' parents. Make a separate list of topics you would address. Why would you make these changes in the content?

3. Identify a place in your community that could use some cleanup—perhaps a park, river, or neighborhood. How would you try to motivate other citizens to help you with the cleanup project on a weekend? Would you use different strategies to motivate different groups of citizens? Why? Write a brief position paper, devoting one paragraph to each group you have targeted for this project, the motivations you recommend for them, and why.

4. Select two or three comedians who use similar formats for their comedy (either talk shows, sitcoms, or stand-up routines). Compare and contrast their styles. What sorts of topics do they discuss? What sorts of language do they use in their routines? Would you characterize their humor as mainstream or offbeat? Do they base their humor on the average person's ordinary routines or on uncommon situations found in politics, the movie industry, or city/country lifestyles? What do your insights about these comedians suggest about their sense of audience and purpose? How appropriate is each comedian's material for children or for tourists visiting from other countries? Write two or three pages describing these comedians for someone who wants to see a performance or show and is not sure which comedian to choose.

➡ *ONGOING ASSIGNMENT*

■ Using the information you learned in Chapter 1 on organizational cultures and images and the do's and don'ts you listed for newcomers into your primary organization (see the Ongoing Assignment in Chapter 1), what kinds of plans would you make for producing a useful collection of ideas for an appropriate group of readers? Use the strategies you have learned from this chapter to complete a planning worksheet (see Strategy Review 2.3).

CHAPTER 3

Researching and Gathering Information

Preliminaries, Sources, and Strategies

Throughout your career, you will write about products, services, and projects about which you know a great deal. In these cases, you will already have most of the necessary information through your project notes, your memory, and the additional information the rest of your team members can quickly provide. Research on these projects, therefore, may be a relatively simple task because of your familiarity and comfort with the topic.

On some occasions, however, you may be asked to write a report on a project on which you have only limited knowledge. Or you may feel that your own experience may be different from others' experiences, making it wise to verify your personal knowledge by asking others about their experiences. Thus, the level and quality of your expertise are important factors in determining how much and what kind of research you need to conduct.

Consider Sarah's situation as the transportation manager of a small (hundred-employee) company that sells specialty doors and windows to building supply dealers. Sarah's boss has asked her to investigate the feasibility of the company's purchasing company cars for its eight-person sales force. Because her duties as transportation manager have focused on the fleet of delivery trucks that transport the windows and doors to the supply houses, Sarah is not familiar with the advantages and disadvantages of company car fleets, nor with the kinds of deals she might get as a multivehicle buyer, nor with the specific type of car to recommend for purchase. Where should Sarah go for this information?

This chapter will use this company car scenario to discuss the research strategies that Sarah can use to support her eventual writing of a feasibility report (see Chapter 13 for more about the specifics of writing a feasibility report). The Application exercises interspersed throughout the chapter will give you some opportunities to apply what you are learning from Sarah's experience. You will probably find it useful to return to many of the planning elements described in Chapter 2 to clarify your experience and role as a writer, your knowledge (and how sound that knowledge is), your readers and their needs, and your purpose for writing. Paying attention to these details in these early stages will guide your research strategy for any reports or documents that you are required to write in the workplace.

Preliminaries in Gathering Information

Before gathering information about your subject (discussed later), you may first need to learn about the members of your audience and their environment and also obtain some additional information about your own environment. Although these steps are frequently omitted from the research process, they often contribute to a document's success; therefore, you would be wise to consider them in your own research process.

Learning More about Your Audience

Numerous well-meaning workplace writers have seen their efforts wasted when their audience turned out to be entirely different from the reader they had imagined would be reading their work. As you can see, pitching a new idea to a person who is predisposed to like your idea, versus someone who is likely to hate it, will require quite different strategies and, perhaps, even different kinds of information. As Chapter 2 pointed out, knowing how much your readers already know and need to know, as well as how they are likely to respond to your information, your requests, and your ideas, will determine what kinds of information and presentation strategies are best for your audience. You will be able to gather much of your information about your readers from working with them, but you can also talk with colleagues who frequently work with or write to these readers. Unfortunately, you may have to write to readers whom you cannot really research for many reasons, including the following:

- The reader is someone you don't know: a customer in Arkansas, a stockbroker in New York, or an executive in Brazil.
- The readers are actually a group of unrelated people, drawn together by some common element: users of an information network, such as Prodigy; people who buy a new Buick LeSabre; investors in XYZ Corporation's stock; alumnae from Meredith College; or men over fifty who have had hair transplants.
- The readers are from various groups, and each is looking for a different kind of information in your document: managers who want to know the basics of your idea, accountants who want to know the budget for your idea, or advertisers who want to know the potential buyers of the product or service you are describing.

In each of these cases, investigating your audience is difficult, but nevertheless important. Try to find representative readers in your own workplace—workers who have similar backgrounds, needs for information, and even confusions about your subject—to be "test" readers for your writing. For instance, if you are describing stock investments for people with little financial expertise, you might ask representative readers from the loading dock, the sales department, the clerical department, and the executive offices in your company to read your work and mark sections they find confusing.

Of course, you may not even have such representative readers nearby; in that case, you will sometimes have to make assumptions about your reader. Be sure that any assumptions you make have a clear rationale and are not based on oversimplified (and often offensive) stereotypes.

In the company car scenario, Sarah may have to write a report that both the company president and the sales team members will read. She makes the following assumptions about both groups:

1. Auto brands and purchases are not their areas of expertise, so I will have to describe my decision clearly.

2. Both groups are probably motivated by personal interests, such as profits, tax benefits, and personal likes and dislikes in autos.

3. Both groups are also motivated by professional concerns, such as prompt service, storage space, costs, and performance.

4. Both groups are well informed on retail and wholesale issues, so the car decision should also reflect their knowledge about and interest in retail and wholesale purchasing.

As Sarah investigates the concerns that her readers will have about the feasibility of company cars, she will have to keep all these assumptions in mind so that she can answer her readers' questions and meet their needs for information.

Learning More about Your Audience's Reading and Work Environments

When researching your readers and their needs for information, you should investigate their reading environment as well (a noisy office, the field, a manufacturing plant, or somewhere away from the workplace altogether) because that information will help you determine what form your document should take. For example, a reader in a noisy, busy office will probably be interrupted often; offer information in small doses with frequent summaries and highlights and provide overviews, rather than minute details, at least in preliminary documents.

If your readers are at a field site (literally at the site of their work), however, you will probably offer specific details about how to do something or what something should look like, rather than including background information, theories, or other kinds of information that doesn't apply directly to the setting. Because these readers may be exposed to all sorts of weather, you also need to consider how to protect the reading material from rain, wind, snow, and heat. Further, you should keep the document to a manageable size because the readers are unlikely to have a desk nearby.

You also need to consider the specifics of your readers' work environment and its culture, especially when you are writing to readers outside your organization. In particular, you will want to determine how the readers expect your writing to look and sound and how long or detailed they expect it to be, based on their experiences with writings from their own organization and from your competitors. Appearances can mean a lot in workplace documents; consider how professional the documents are that your readers are used to seeing and make sure your writing follows suit. (For more on appearances, format, and design, see Chapter 9.) Strategy Review 3.1 contains variables you should consider when assessing your audience.

LEARNING MORE ABOUT YOUR AUDIENCE

The following variables concerning your readers' backgrounds, work conditions, knowledge, use of information, and predisposition toward your topic can help you make crucial decisions about the amount and kind of research you should conduct:

1. *Background knowledge:* Someone who knows the technical details of a project might respond quite differently to your ideas compared to someone who has heard only secondhand accounts of your work. Further, your readers' educational, economic, social, and working backgrounds can provide several clues about their frame of reference for your writing.

2. *Use of information:* The immediate usefulness of a workplace document can determine how carefully it is read and how closely the recommendations are followed. Further, *how* information will be used (to clarify, make decisions, evaluate, etc.) can also affect how readers interpret information.

3. *Secondary audiences* (the readers beyond your primary readers): Keeping secondary readers, such as your immediate reader's boss or subordinates, in mind as you write can prevent embarrassing omissions, oversimplifications, or even tactlessness and can also affect how you organize and present information (see Chapter 4).

4. *Reading and comprehension skills:* Thorough readers expect careful descriptions and analyses that will answer their questions; they often mark the copy with detailed questions and additional considerations. Readers who just skim information appreciate highlighted details and frequent summaries to make sure they see the major points (see Chapter 9).

5. *General reaction to idea:* Some readers are notoriously prejudiced against certain kinds of ideas—for expanding their business, or downsizing its hierarchical structure, or adding a new product line, for example. Knowing their prejudices can prevent you from submitting in a straightforward manner an idea that is likely to irk your readers or arouse their immediate disapproval. A more indirect strategy that presents your reasons *before* making your pitch may win them over, however. (See Chapter 4 for more information on organizational strategies.)

6. *Preferences for various types of support and details:* Readers are often particularly impressed by statistics, graphics, or testimonials. Some readers believe everything that comes from certain business or technological philosophers (such as Peter Drucker, Tom Peters, or John Naisbitt), practitioners (such as Lee Iacocca or Bill Gates), or news sources (such as the *Wall Street Journal* or *U.S.*

(continued)

News and World Report). Investigate previous organizational documents that have won your readers' approval to see what kinds of evidence were used. Can you provide similar evidence for your ideas?

7. *Other demands:* Because such a tremendous amount of paperwork floods the workplace, readers often have to prioritize the documents they read. The more urgent problems or suggestions are likely to receive immediate attention. Explaining that a response to your idea can be postponed is a consideration that readers usually appreciate.

Learning More about Your Own Environment

Just as important as knowing about your readers' environment is knowing about your own work environment, including the organizational image and corporate culture. Even as a researcher, you reflect your organization's image and culture, and your investigations and findings should be appropriate to that image and culture (see Chapter 1).

Many of your decisions about the appropriateness of your research will depend on pure observation. Take time to see how reports are designed and their information arranged. Read several of your organization's research reports to get a feel for the amount of detail they include and the style and tone of your coworkers' and boss's writing. Evaluate several of your organization's proposals to see how they present the primary selling points of your products and services to your customers and clients. Study the kinds and sources of support that are offered as evidence of major and minor points in those documents. Investigating these simple details about your own workplace and its documents may take a little more time (at least initially), but it can prevent a lot of hard work on a doomed project.

Learning More about Your Subject

Once you have investigated your readers and their environment and reminded yourself of a few facets of your own environment, you are better prepared to understand the kinds of information you will need about your subject. Suppose that Sarah in our company car scenario has been asked to provide information that neither she nor anyone else in the company knows. In such cases, turning to her notes or searching her memory is silly; she simply does not have the information. So how is she going to get it? To determine the kinds of information she needs, Sarah opts to use a topical checklist, which is appropriate for almost any workplace message. (See Strategy Review 3.2.)

TOPICAL GUIDELINES FOR RESEARCH

One of the most difficult aspects of conducting research is determining what information is necessary. You can use the following topical guidelines to help you identify the parameters of information to investigate for your topic, purpose, and audience:

Major Points Regarding the Product, Service, or Issue

- Descriptions and definitions
- Use of the product/service/issue
- Benefits of the product/service/issue
- Users/beneficiaries of the product/service/issue

Supporting Details Regarding the Product, Service, or Issue

- History of the product/service/issue
- Future of the product/service/issue
- Users'/buyers' general attitude, likes, and dislikes about the product/service/issue
- Motivational strategy to encourage readers' support for the product/service/issue
- Amount of time and money provider must invest in the product/service/issue
- Amount of time and money user must invest in the product/service/issue
- Need to expand or narrow the product/service/issue
- Need to hire, fire, or reassign personnel to accommodate the product/service/issue
- Need to alter the quality of the product/service/issue
- Long-term profitability of the product/service/issue
- Competing product/service/issue
- Means of supplying the product/service/issue

Safety Factors

- Potential harm to users
- Potential harm to environment
- Routine maintenance
- Warranties and guarantees

(continued)

Legal Matters

- Support for claims
- Liability
- Contract for suppliers, distributors, and vendors

Graphic Support

- Photographs or illustrations of actual product
- Process graphics that demonstrate procedures
- Bar charts, flow charts, and the like that illuminate major/minor points identified above

---

Based on the results of her checklist, Sarah focuses on the particular kinds of additional information she might need:

- Purchasing information about general costs, fees, licenses, tags, and the like
- Leasing versus purchasing options
- Warranties (general and extended)
- Insurance information
- Service/maintenance information
- Sales team members' preferences for cars (colors, style, brands, etc.)
- Sales team members' specific needs (storage, mileage, passenger room, etc.)
- Trade-in/resale values
- Liability
- Tax savings or increases

Sarah values this list of topics because it shows her the kinds of questions she will have to answer for her readers, helps her see the kinds of information she needs, and even helps her start to figure out where to go for that information.

When you know your subject thoroughly, you are well prepared to answer questions, anticipate suspicions, and, thus, persuade an audience. Not knowing this information is dangerous, for you are likely to be asked numerous questions you cannot answer—questions that may make you look foolish, unprepared, or shallow.

Sources for Gathering Information

From the list of questions Sarah generated from her analysis of her audience and the topical guidelines about the company car scenario, as well as from the list of questions you will generate about the computer-purchasing scenario, you should

The Computer-Purchasing Scenario

Throughout this chapter, your opportunities to apply your knowledge center on the following scenario:

> Suppose your college or workplace is interested in learning about new computer systems or software programs that will help students or workers better conduct their work. Your current system (or programs) allows you to perform basic tasks but does not offer the broad range of possibilities that newer systems allow. Further, the current system is too slow or too limited to perform many current applications.

As you have read, some of the most important questions that will guide your research focus on your readers and their need for information.

1. Brainstorm a list of people who might be interested in reading your findings about new computer systems for your college or workplace. Consider their likely reactions to your suggestion that a new system is needed and to other aspects of your project. Then, list what you know about the reading environment and the work environment of each reader or group of readers. What specific strategies would you want to employ in your writing to accommodate these environments?

2. Using the topical guidelines in Strategy Review 3.2, identify topics that raise issues that are relevant to your project. Begin thinking about how you would find that information, especially as you read the next section on Sources for Gathering Information.

have a clearer sense of the role of research in two typical workplace situations. Now, where do researchers go to find useful information?

Sarah might consult the car dealers themselves, but for other information she will have to talk with insurance agents, the sales team, mechanics, lawyers, tax advisers, and perhaps some other people she hasn't even thought of yet. She might then consult consumer guides to purchasing automobiles, looking for the best values, the soundest engineering, and the highest resale values.

For your computer project, as well as for your own workplace projects, once you have learned more about your audience and their reading and workplace environments, your own environment, and your subject, you can use the list of questions you generated to begin a plan for research. The following discussion identifies three primary sources of information in the workplace: your own resources, your organization's resources, and external resources.

Your Own Resources

Before immersing yourself in research, you should consider the sorts of information you already hold about any given topic. Thus, in addition to asking what the audience already knows and needs to know about the topic, which is an integral planning strategy, as you learned in Chapter 2, you should ask yourself the same questions: What do I already know about this topic and what do I need to know?

Personal Experience and Observations

As the starting point for any research you conduct, you should begin by reviewing your own storehouse of knowledge, most often gained from personal experience and observations. Assessing upfront what you do—and do not—know about a topic will help you distinguish reliable information from information that demands greater scrutiny.

At the same time, you should consider the likelihood that what you think you know may not, in actuality, be the case. Be sure to apply your critical thinking skills to evaluate your observations and experience by asking questions, such as these:

- How certain am I of my facts?
- Could my experience be an isolated one that is based on my background, my position in the company, or the timing of the experience?
- Will my readers agree that my experience is valid as support for an idea or assertion, or will they be skeptical?

If you find that you are not sure of the universality of your experience and observations, you will need to conduct further research.

Your Project Notes

Depending on your position at work, your own work and notes may be the prime sources for your workplace writing. In fact, one of the greatest information-gathering skills you can possess is the ability to keep accurate records and notes of what you do on the job.

Work notes typically include the following kinds of information, which is kept in a daily log or checklist of accomplishments with dates, times, and other participants as appropriate:

- Projects addressed
- Details of specific tasks accomplished
- Lists of decisions made and why

■ Correspondence (phone calls, E-mail, memos, letters, etc.) with clients, vendors, distributors, internal divisions, management, and various departments such as the legal office, accounting office, receiving office, and delivery office

The system for keeping notes is largely up to you. Fortunately, several options are available, and you should choose the one that best suits you and your work: (1) a daily work log of appointments, subjects, and accomplishments; (2) a notecard system (preferably color coded) organized by project or some other scheme; or (3) a computer journal. Whatever system you adopt, you should try to make entries every few days, if not every day.

You will find that your notes will serve multiple purposes throughout your career. As a means of preserving information about a project you have worked on, they are quite useful; as a means of keeping track of your accomplishments, they are invaluable.

Your Organization's Resources

In addition to the information your notes and experiences provide, you should also consult relevant resources within your organization. These resources include the organization's stored documents and your coworkers.

Organizational Documents/Organizational Libraries

Most organizations keep careful records of their business transactions: reports, letters, memos, contracts, authorizations, disbursements, payment and fee schedules, shipping information, labor negotiations, and numerous other workplace documents. Because all these documents may help the organization define its position on any number of business issues, its filing and storage system is often viewed as the foundation for much of the work that goes on. In large organizations, a librarian is often in charge of organizing and storing the various documents that are generated every day—or at least the important documents. Even small companies keep records of their sales fluctuations, transactions, and promises and frequently refer to these records to make sure their work is on schedule or is sent to the proper address.

Of course, the increasing use of computers has radically changed the way information is stored, but because disks can crash and systems can go down (leaving an organization helpless for hours or even days), many organizations still keep their most important documents in hard copy as well as on computer disks. More progressive organizations often file their documents on CD-ROM disks, which are permanent (uncrashable) records that researchers can access, but cannot alter.

In the company car scenario, suppose the new company president told Sarah that the idea of company cars was considered several years ago, but dropped for some reason. Naturally, Sarah will want to know why the idea was deemed a poor one at that time. If the organization has a good system for filing its documents, she can probably retrieve the report rather easily. Additionally, Sarah can probably rely on the company's reimbursement and sales records to ascertain the sales force's patterns of travel, mileage, and additional expenses (for at least the past year) to get a clearer understanding of the current system's strengths and weaknesses.

Knowing what kinds of information your organization saves can be quite valuable to your research strategies. Be sure to find out where such documents are stored (or on which computer disks) and how to go about requesting them from the librarian—or the filing cabinet.

Your Coworkers

Your colleagues are another invaluable source of information on the job. They can help you remember events or ideas you may have forgotten, encourage a proper perspective on work and deadlines, and explain details that are more within their realm of expertise than yours.

Rarely does one person have all the information for any document that must be written because rarely does one person handle every aspect of a project. Typically, a project requires an entire team representing several departments within a company: marketing, designing, engineering, legal, sales, advertising, technical writing, and so on. Your project may also include the work of subcontractors, companies or people who do not work for your organization, but have been temporarily hired because of their specialization in some area.

To account for all the activities that go on during a project, you may have to interview several people from several different departments or organizations. (See pages 78–79 for information on conducting interviews.) That means, of course, that you'll have to accommodate their schedules, learn something about their role on the project, their language for describing that role, and their concerns and satisfactions with the project.

To research the feasibility of company cars, for instance, Sarah might find it useful to interview all of the following:

- The sales team: To learn their requirements for a company car and their personal preferences.
- The company president: To find out what constraints she sees in terms of budgets, liability, service, and the like.
- The legal department: To learn what kind of insurance and other legal responsibilities the company would assume for the cars.
- Insurance agents: To find out the kinds of coverage available and its limits.
- Car dealers: To find out what kinds of deals they would offer on purchases and leases.
- Other organizations' representatives who have company cars: To learn what their experience with company cars has been.

External Resources

Although your organization has numerous resources, you may find that you need information beyond your own organization's realm of expertise. Or you may want to know how similar organizations have dealt with situations similar to your own. In these cases, you should consider turning to external sources for the information you seek.

Traditional Libraries

In the workplace, you will rarely go to a traditional library and do the kinds of research you typically had to do in school. Most of these libraries do not have the kind of information you need and are, for the most part, practically irrelevant to the writing you will have to do. Occasionally, however, you may need to do a little background work, and that information may come from a standard library.

Your college library may have a computerized card catalog (such as Marquis) that allows you to learn the location and availability of books, journals, newspapers, and other publications by typing in the title, author, or a subject. Your library may also have access to a number of CD-ROM index systems, such as Info-Trac, ProQuest, and other databases, that carry copies of the abstracts or complete articles you want to read or download and print for your own hard copy. Many of these sources are free, although some charge for printing. Your reference librarian can help you conduct a search, typically using keyword descriptors (described more thoroughly below) to help you find information.

In the company car scenario, for example, Sarah would probably do well to examine consumer guides to see how they rate the safety, engineering, value, and other factors of various brands of vehicles. Such guides compare within categories, such as trucks, sport utility vehicles, luxury cars, sports cars, sedans, and minivans, so it is important that Sarah determine which category (or categories) best fits her organization's needs.

She might also research articles on the advantages and disadvantages of company cars, warnings about company car scams, tips for negotiating the purchase of a fleet of cars, and numerous other topics that might help her do the best possible job on this project. Learning from the experiences of others is one of the most important benefits of conducting thorough research through traditional sources of information.

Experts outside the Organization

In addition to the information you gather from your coworkers inside your organization, you might also obtain valuable information from those outside your organization. Such information may be organization-specific, meaning that it is only relevant for the respondent's organization, but it may also point out additional concerns that might have escaped your attention.

In the company car scenario, for instance, Sarah sees that her colleagues can provide valuable information about their travel patterns, expenses, and concerns about company cars. Still, none of these sales representatives has ever had a company car, so they can offer only suppositions about the potential problems and benefits of such a program.

Sarah decides, therefore, to investigate the feasibility of company cars by gathering information from other organizations that provide cars to their representatives. She knows of at least three such organizations and contacts them to ask about specific advantages and disadvantages, cautions, and any other information that might help her and her readers make a decision. She also asks these sources for supporting documentation concerning maintenance costs, trade-in values, and general satisfaction with the program so that she can provide more than just experiential information to her readers.

Taking research questions outside your organization can be a useful means of collecting a wider range of information than is available internally. At the same time, you must carefully ascertain the conditions surrounding that information to determine how closely the organization and the situations that generated the information correlate with your own organization and its situations.

Electronic Sources: The Internet and the World Wide Web

In traditional library settings, in high-tech offices, and in the comfort of their own homes, many researchers have discovered the value of electronic searches for information. Because of the initial expense, on-line (electronic) searches were originally conducted almost exclusively in libraries and large organizational settings. The remarkable decline of that expense, combined with the increased technological capabilities offered by personal computers, has led to the proliferation of electronic research in almost all workplace environments.

When on-line, you can access E-mail (electronic mail) from friends and correspondents around the world—typically at prices that are minuscule compared to traditional long-distance telephone charges. (Be careful! Some people have become addicted to the Internet and spend hours and hours every day "talking" on-line—an addiction that can prove quite costly.) You can also access various sources of information that might prove useful for your workplace research.

You can use the Internet's access to mail service and discussion groups (a number of people "linked" to each other for the purpose of discussing particular topics, such as tax law rulings, fine wines, and the likelihood of alien sightings) to talk to a number of people who share your work or recreational interests. You can browse Web sites to get updated information about your favorite sports team, the local news, and even tips for creating successful workplace communication (check out the Business Communications World Wide Web Resource Center at http:// www5.ios.com/-reach).

The name *World Wide Web* is a clue to both its extent and its construction. Accessible to anyone, anywhere, with the proper equipment and service, the World Wide Web is both an international resource and a host to a world of subjects. The "Web" part of the name refers to its construction: it has a hypertext format, which

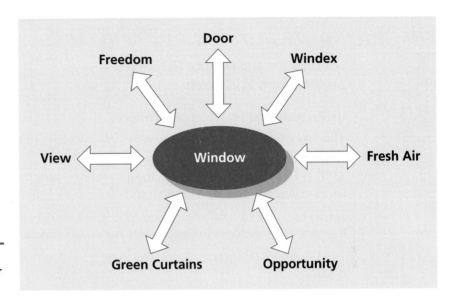

FIGURE 3.1

Associations That
Suggest Links to Other
Topics on the Web

means that subjects are linked to each other not by strict logic, but by association, much like a spider's web. Thus, rather than the linear thought processes (so often valued, especially in academic circles) in which A leads to B, which leads to C in regimented (logical) order, hypertext (and, thus, the Web) allows a user to exercise a stream of thought that may make sense only to that user. For example, consider the associations (or "links") made with the simple word *window* (see Figure 3.1). As this example shows, while one user thinks of window in metaphorical terms (the window of opportunity), another thinks of it in physical terms (like a door), and yet another thinks of processes (the windows need to be cleaned). In a Web search, all these links are possible, allowing users to track their own interests.

The Web is not merely a static bulletin board; increasingly, it is becoming an interactive site where you can find various kinds of information, ask questions, learn how to perform a variety of tasks, and so on. In fact, some of the most useful resources for some workplace writers are the grammar help sites, including the following (as of this publication date):

- http://www.columbia.edu/acis/bartleby/strunk
- http://owl.english.purdue.edu

Interesting groups and sites appear (and disappear!) all the time, so being familiar with the technology that links you to these sources is invaluable. While you are in college, be sure to take advantage of courses or extracurricular offerings that will put you in touch with such technology. (You may use this technology later when seeking employment—see Chapter 11.)

In the company car scenario, for instance, Sarah might decide that she wants to know about tax incentives for buying company cars, the best brands of cars,

THE WORLD OF WORKPLACE WRITING

Useful Sites and Helpful Resources on the World Wide Web

Useful Web Sites for Workplace Writers

The Copyright Website: http://www.benedict.com (discusses protected Web information)

EPIC (Electronic Privacy Information Center): http://www.epic.org (concerns issues relating to privacy and the Internet)

Jobweb: http://www.jobweb.com (lists jobs by profession and/or geography; includes helpful tips for job interviews and ranges for starting salaries)

The Library of Congress: http://www.loc.gov (lists the library's extensive holdings)

Medscape: http://www.medscape.com (provides on-line medical information about diseases and treatment)

NYNEX Interactive Yellow Pages: http://www.niyp.com/home_lycos.html (provides names, addresses, and phone numbers of more than 16.5 million businesses, like the yellow pages in the telephone directory)

World News on Line: http://worldnews.net (provides global news)

ZD Net: http://www.zdnet.com/home/filters/news.html (on-line magazine about computers and the Internet)

The White House: http://www.whitehouse.gov (provides history, tours, speeches, and current issues)

The U.S. Census Bureau: http://www.census.gov (excellent source for demographics)

Helpful Resources for Learning More about the Web and Conducting Searches

General Information

The Complete Web Guide: http://www.mit.edu:8001/people/cwward/webguide.html

Entering the World Wide Web: A Guide to Cyberspace: http://www.eit.com:80/web/www.guide

Guide to the Web: http://www.hcc.hawaii.edu/guide/www.guide.html

Netscape Tutorial: http://w3.ag.uiuc.edu/AIM/Discovery/Net/www/netscape

The World Wide Web for Dummies: http:www.mit.edu:8001/people/rei/www.intro.html

Web Search Guides

General Finding Tools: http://www.ucr.edu/pubs/navigato.html

Internet Search Tool Details: http://www.sunsite.berkeley.edu/Help/searchdetails.html

Locating Information: Directories and Indexes: http://www.info.anu.edu.au/courses/intro/wkbk/loc.html

Search the Internet: http://www.rs.internic.net/scout/toolkit/search.html

Search Tools: http://www.cs.rose-hulman.edu/%7dearinme/links.html

WebPlaces Internet Search Guide: http://www.webplaces.com

possible deals on a fleet of cars, and the organization's legal liability for company cars. Unfortunately, she does not have access to this information through the sources already described—her own knowledge and notes, her organization's records, and her colleagues' knowledge. She suspects the information is available, but she does not have time to go to the public library and look it up. How should she go about finding it?

Using her knowledge of the Internet and the Web, Sarah first asks for help from her on-line discussion group of professional transportation managers (who routinely discuss problems and solutions associated with their jobs). These managers put her in touch with people they know who have faced Sarah's dilemma. One suggests that she look at a couple of Web sites with which he is familiar. She also uses the on-line search engines (vehicles or avenues accessed through a particular Web site for finding additional—and typically more specialized—information) to locate more sources of information:

- *Consumer World* (http://www.consumerworld.org): Provides access to more than a thousand resources for consumers who want to investigate the quality, cost, problems, and benefits of a variety of products and services, ranging from health, home, and finances to tourism, bargains, and automobiles. Sarah follows this search to find information about trustworthy automobiles and their costs.

- *The Digital Daily* (http://www.irs.ustreas.gov/basic/cover.html): The IRS's on-line publication for individuals and businesses that have questions about the tax system, legitimate deductions, waivers, and so on. Sarah uses this site's What's Hot page to ask her questions about tax breaks for fleet vehicle purchases.

- *Internet Legal Resource Guide* (http://www.ilrg.com): A comprehensive resource for laypeople and legal professionals. This site offers information about all sorts of legal issues, including legal news, federal court decisions, and links to search engines. Sarah uses a search engine to research one of the on-line directory's resources concerning liability for organization-owned vehicles.

APPLICATION

Finding Sources of Information

Along with the audiences and topical guidelines you have identified for your computer project, you should have a list of questions that your readers will have about your topic. Consider the sources of information discussed so far:

1. Do you have any personal experience or observations that might be pertinent to the information your readers need? If so, what is it?

2. Do you have any project notes from working on a similar problem for another group or organization? What does that information contribute?

3. Do you have colleagues, or do you know people in the college/workplace system, who are knowledgeable about computer systems? What kinds of information might they contribute to your readers' understanding?

4. What kinds of information about computer systems might be available in your college's or workplace's documents? Who has access to that information? Is it available to you?

5. What sorts of information might be useful from general references in traditional libraries?

6. What sorts of experts outside your organization might have useful information for this project?

7. What sorts of information might you find over the Internet? (See the later discussion of how to access the Internet and the World Wide Web to check your assumptions.)

A number of other sites might also help Sarah, of course, but these three give you an idea of the information available directly through the Internet, as well as the process of using search engines to find more specific information.

A strict word of caution is necessary, however: Both the beauty and the beast of the Internet and the Web are their accessibility. Anyone can put any information on these formats, which is beautiful because people who heretofore have had no means of communicating with others (whether because of shyness or because they live in the remote outbacks) can now communicate, voice their concerns and opinions, and challenge all of us to be better human beings. That access is also beastly, however, because cranks and ill-informed (even though well-intentioned) users can also post information on the Internet. Inaccurate information is always dangerous, but it is especially treacherous in the hands of the naive who do not question the information they receive. Thus, when reviewing published information or on-line information, learn to ask yourself the following questions:

- What do I know about this person's or group's credibility? (Beware of anonymous contributors.)
- How reliable is the informants' work?
- How forthcoming are they about their means of gathering information?
- How likely is it that this information is flawed?
- Has the work been challenged by knowledgeable experts? If so, how did the contributors respond?
- What other interpretations of their data might be possible?

Remember, also, that all information from any outside source (and even some internal sources) must be documented in your work. Your experiences compiling a bibliography, list of references, or list of works cited for your college papers will be useful in the workplace as well, where it is just as important to credit others' ideas. (See Strategy Review 3.3 for a brief review and the Brief Usage Guidebook for a more detailed discussion with examples of documentation.)

STRATEGY REVIEW 3.3

DOCUMENTING SOURCES

You probably remember from other courses that you have to document the ideas of others when you use them in your writing. In general, follow these rules for documentation:

1. Document any idea that you borrow from other writers, listing the author's name, the title of the work, the date of publication or discovery over the Internet, and the location (volume number, issue number, page numbers for hard copy; the address of Internet or Web sites).
2. Document any idea that your reader might want to track down and read.
3. Document any idea that might make your reader skeptical of your information.

The Appendix at the end of the text provides more specific "how to's" for constructing a Works Cited list at the end of your document.

Strategies for Gathering Information

Now that you have determined the kind and sources of information you need, you are ready to develop some specific strategies for finding that information. The options described in this section—interviews, brainstorming sessions, surveys, the Internet, and other methods—are certainly not the only ways to find information, but they are the methods most frequently used in the workplace. Further, you will see that some categories overlap; that is, you may *interview* people via the *Internet,* making the Internet both a resource and a tool for gathering information.

Interviewing Internal and External Sources

Because people so often hold the information you need, developing good interviewing skills may be critical to your development as a writer and as a worker. The basic purpose of interviewing, of course, is to give you direct contact to the specific people who hold the information you need. Thus, you should interview people when you are certain of all of the following:

- They have access to the information you need.
- They have time to give you that information.
- You can contact them easily (via telephone, over the Internet, or in person).
- They are likely to be able to describe or articulate exactly what they know, as well as what they like, dislike, fear, or need.
- They have complete information within their areas of expertise.

Obviously you should not waste time trying to interview people who cannot provide the information, the access, or the descriptions you need. You should have alternative candidates for the interview—and sometimes even alternative methods for gathering information. (See Strategy Review 3.4.)

STRATEGY REVIEW 3.4

CONDUCTING FORMAL INTERVIEWS

A few standard guidelines for interviewing may help you set up and organize the interview to keep it as professional as possible. Remember, most people appreciate an interviewer who is prompt, organized, informed, and thorough:

1. Draft a list of the kinds of information you need—technical, financial, or whatever. Then decide whether you are more likely to get the information you need from closed-ended questions (questions that generate "yes" or "no" responses) or open-ended questions (questions that leave the interviewee free to respond in detail).

2. Decide who inside or outside your organization is the most appropriate person to interview for the information you need. Interviewees find it very frustrating to have to spend time with someone who is asking questions that are not within their realm of expertise.

3. Schedule a particular amount of time with that person so you won't be interrupted by other calls, meetings, or duties.

4. Ask permission to tape the interview, but be sure to take notes as well in case the recorder malfunctions.

5. Be particularly aware of definitions and explanations you will need for your writing. If you don't get complete information or if you don't understand the information, ask for explanations and clarifications.

6. For particularly difficult information, try paraphrasing what the interviewee said and ask if that's what was meant.

7. Ask the interviewee for any other information you might need to write your document.

8. Be respectful of the person's time and leave when you agreed to leave. When an interview runs over an hour, the information (as well as the interviewer–interviewee relationship) often becomes strained. Ask for a follow-up session if necessary.

9. Thank the interviewee.

In the company car scenario, Sarah decides to interview the current sales force at her company to get their general reactions to the idea of company cars. She decides that a list of open-ended (rather than yes–no) questions will help her learn valuable information about the sales team's likes, dislikes, fears, and concerns. Knowing that these representatives are busy and want to be on the road selling as much as possible, she draws up a short list of questions to obtain information she cannot find from other sources:

1. How do you feel about the company's purchasing company cars, rather than reimbursing you for wear and tear on your own vehicle?
2. What advantages do you see in such a plan?
3. What disadvantages do you see in such a plan?
4. If we go with company cars, what are your requirements for space, size, and storage?
5. What additional or special features would you like?
6. Can you recommend some brands we should consider within our price range?

From her interviews, Sarah learns that, on the whole, the representatives like the idea of a company car, but are most concerned about personal features, such as color, style, and comfort. As a result, she plans (at this stage in her thinking at least) to recommend that the representatives be allowed to choose from a selection of colors, that the car be a sport utility vehicle rather than a sedan, and that special comfort features (such as lumbar support seats, air conditioning, and CD players) be considered standard equipment.

Brainstorming with Colleagues

In lieu of formal interviews with colleagues whom you do not know very well (if at all), you may brainstorm with your coworkers, which is a far less rule-bound process than interviewing (see Chapter 5 for more information on brainstorming). The advantage of brainstorming with your coworkers is that their memories and notes are likely to hold different bits of information that might be useful to you—information you overlooked or did not regard as significant. Consider the following information that was generated during the sales team's brainstorming about company cars:

> **Kay:**   I think it's important that all members of the team be allowed to express their individuality, meaning that some choice in color or model is going to be paramount to our being happy with the company car selection.
>
> **Doug:**   I don't care so much about the color or brand of the cars, but I do know that I need plenty of room for hauling these heavy catalogs. And I think small cars tend to make you stoop and lift with your back—not good if you have a back like mine.
>
> **Bob:**   My big concern is service. Right now, my nephew can work on my car, and he drops everything when my car has to be repaired. He knows I cannot spend all morning waiting around an auto repair shop; I make my living on the road, and if I am not calling on customers, I am losing money.
>
> **Lorraine:**   That's true, but some other matters of cost also need to be considered. Right now, we get to write off our mileage and car expenses as tax deductions. Has anyone figured out how much that deduction means for us at tax time?

From these conversations, Sarah has gained information that she might have overlooked had she relied strictly on her own notes, memory, or organizational or local library. Getting help and information from others throughout the research phase of your work is a useful way to make sure you see your work from more than one angle.

Surveying Internal and External Sources

To conduct on-the-job research successfully, you must be able to identify the most efficient means of gathering information from the most knowledgeable sources. Occasionally, you will not have enough information about readers, clients or consumers, or your subject matter to fulfill your goal of communicating some much-needed information to a less-informed reader. In such cases, you may not even be able to turn to published information in libraries or on computer data files; to make matters worse, your colleagues and teammates may be just as lost as you or may not have the time to meet with you for an interview or brainstorming session. Furthermore, external sources may be far away or have tight schedules that leave no time for interviews.

In these cases—and to solicit a broader perspective on your topic—you may try to find a representative population of people who are (or are similar to) the clients, customers, or other specific group about whose needs you are writing. To get the information you need, you can survey these people to get their responses, experiences, and impressions about your subject. For example, you may survey some of your clients or consumers to find out how satisfied they are with your product/service, how they would like to change it (safer? more efficient? less expensive? a different color? a better fabric?), and what new products or services they would like. To conduct a survey, you must first decide on the kind of information you want, how you will get it, and then how you will use that information. (See Strategy Review 3.5.)

Next, just as you have to decide whom to interview or include in a brainstorming session, you will also have to decide whom to survey. Randomly distributed surveys are rarely useful because they do not necessarily target respondents who most closely resemble the real users of a product or service. It may seem obvious, therefore, that you would go directly to the source for information you want. Special considerations, however, may change your mind about the wisdom of *always* going to the primary source for information.

In the company car scenario, for instance, Sarah wants to know how other organizations' representatives feel about their company cars:

- Are they happy with the make and model of the car they drive?
- Are they happy with the maintenance and repair contracts?
- What is a suitable mileage allotment?
- Are the car's storage and hauling room adequate?
- Have the representatives' tax deductions changed significantly (by more than 10 percent)?
- What standard and optional features on the vehicle are desirable?

Sarah realizes, however, that the very difficulties she faces in interviewing her own company's sales force will be magnified if she tries to survey another organization's sales force. First, the sales team members are likely to be on the road, not waiting around to answer her survey. Second, they may not feel that their experiences are relevant to Sarah's situation. Third, they may not have thought about many of the questions she is asking. In short, it might be better to find someone else to answer these questions.

Sarah decides, therefore, that it might be better to ask the transportation managers of some other organizations (those who hold her job in other organizations) what concerns they have had about the company car fleet. An alternative would be to survey sales managers or maintenance and repair personnel about the car fleet, an approach that will likely yield quite different responses, based on their experiences and expertises.

CONSTRUCTING SURVEYS: A PRIMER

After you determine what information you need, who has that information, and how you will use it, you are ready to construct your survey. Whether you conduct a telephone survey, a mailed survey, or a face-to-face survey, the information generated can help you answer important questions in your workplace document.

Although it is beyond the scope of this text to give you strategies for writing a scientifically valid survey (entire textbooks are written on this topic), you may conduct a survey on the job to get a sense of how your audience, customers, or co-workers feel about the particular products, services, or projects on which you are working. Therefore, you do need to know a few basics:

1. Determine how long you can reasonably expect to hold your respondents' attention. Are they likely to feel great passion about this subject? Perhaps you can hold their attention for twenty minutes. Are they likely to have little interest in this subject? In that case, perhaps you can hold their attention for three or four minutes.

2. Keeping your time limit in mind, list the most important questions you feel you *must* ask during the survey. Then, list the secondary (or more minor) questions that will provide additional details and information.

3. Determine whether you should ask open-ended questions, which allow respondents to discuss or relay their experiences, or closed-ended questions, which require respondents to answer "yes" or "no," or to give predetermined responses (multiple choices or rankings). Remember that open-ended responses are likely to garner more information, but that information can be difficult to tally and difficult to organize for presentation to others. Closed-ended questions are easy to tally, but may not accurately reflect the respondents' true feelings.

4. Now arrange the questions on your list (see item 2) from the easiest, most general, and least personal to the most difficult, most specific, and most personal. Remember that your respondents are likely to be offended by questions that they feel are none of your business. In fact, many people look for reasons to refuse to answer a survey; part of your job will be assuring people that their participation is important and easy.

5. Ask questions your respondents should be able to answer. Do not ask them questions that are beyond their experience or understanding; they are likely to make up the answers and skew your data.

6. Ask unambiguous, straightforward questions. Do not skew the responses by giving the respondents hints of how they should answer ("Did you vote for the loser in the last election? Would you vote for him again?"). Also be sure to ask only one question at a time. This question is actually two questions: "Does your company provide cars, and will they consider buying a foreign

car?" The respondent is likely to be confused by having to answer "yes" or "no" to two separate questions and is probably further confused by what the questioner means by the word *consider*. The respondent could interpret *consider* to mean "to think about fleetingly and then dismiss altogether" or "to think about carefully—to the point of test-driving the car."

7. Use vocabulary and terminology that your respondents understand. If you overwhelm respondents with unfamiliar words, they are likely to either disregard your survey altogether or make up answers.

8. Always be considerate of the respondents' time, feelings, experiences, and responses. Be sure to thank them sincerely.

Once you have devised a survey, you may conduct it in person, over the telephone, or through a mailed questionnaire. As Table 3.1 shows, there are advantages and disadvantages to each method. Clearly, no method of conducting surveys is without problems, meaning that you will have to consider how rapidly you need the information, how much money you can spend gathering information, whether you have access to knowledgeable respondents, and how you intend to use the information your survey provides. On the positive side (evidenced by the innumerable surveys that are conducted daily in the United States), well-constructed surveys can provide information for on-the-job writers that is obtainable in no other way.

TABLE 3.1 Advantages and Disadvantages of Survey Methods

Method	*Advantages*	*Disadvantages*
in-person	■ establishes rapport ■ holds attention ■ surveyor can assess respondent's gender, class, race, age, and other details that may be pertinent to the topic	■ respondent may be busy or unwilling to respond ■ time-consuming for both respondent and surveyor, especially if surveyor must locate a number of respondents ■ respondent may feel the need to over- or underreport information to impress researcher or to avoid embarrassment
by telephone	■ saves time, energy, and gasoline ■ surveyor can increase number of respondents	■ respondents often resent interruptions during dinner, work, or family time ■ respondent may be easily distracted ■ too easy for respondent to simply hang up
by mail	■ allows respondent to set aside time for thoughtful responses	■ easily lost, misfiled, or forgotten ■ sometimes quite expensive ■ response rate can be low, making data unusable ■ readers can misinterpret questions

Using Interviews and Surveys to Gather Information

After considering the internal sources at your disposal and listing the particular workers or divisions that might hold information you need for your project, determine which external experts (or organizations) might hold some useful information for you and your work. List the names of several colleges or organizations similar to your own that might have some useful information about computer systems.

Next, consider whether an interview or a survey might yield more and better information for your project. You may find that one group can be interviewed, while another group should be surveyed.

Then, devise a list of questions appropriate for an interview and another list appropriate for a survey. How do your lists differ? Why do they differ? Write a brief paragraph describing your purpose for these two strategies and your expectations as to the kind(s) of information they will yield.

Accessing the Internet and World Wide Web

As described earlier, the Internet is a powerful resource for finding all kinds of information, making it both a source of information and a tool for research. Depending on the work you do and the environment where you do that work, you may find innumerable valuable sources on the Internet, and using the Internet wisely can drastically reduce the amount of time you spend conducting research. In particular, the Internet offers the researcher four primary advantages:

1. The Internet has vast resources, which are frequently inaccessible by other means (meaning they exist only on-line), as described earlier in the chapter.
2. Information on the Internet is readily accessible; on-line sources are always available—not checked out of the library, ripped out of books, or misfiled by inattentive librarians or patrons.
3. Sources can be downloaded (electronically copied) and saved onto your disk (or mainframe) for later study and note taking.
4. Access and copying are free, unless you are paying for a service provider.

As described earlier, the Internet provides access to E-mail, discussion groups, and Web sites. Generally, accessing the Internet requires you to have the following:

THE WORLD OF WORKPLACE WRITING

Internet Surveys

Increasingly, some researchers are conducting surveys via the Internet because it offers access to more respondents and is faster than mail surveys. A word of caution is in order, however. If the information you seek is held exclusively by computer users, using the Internet to obtain that information is valid. For instance, if you are asking questions about, say, how much rudeness is tolerated in on-line discussion groups, you would be right to conduct such a survey via the Internet. Indeed, it would not make sense to mail the survey because many of the people on your list might not even own computers.

If, however, you should also question noncomputer users because they have equally valid experiences, then using the Internet as the sole mechanism for obtaining information would skew the data you collect. For example, if you want to discover attitudes toward a new bill pending before Congress that would monitor and censor explicit or obscene Internet materials, the response would be skewed if you surveyed only via the Internet. People who are not hooked up to the Internet also have valid opinions about such legislation—and may express them with the votes they cast in the next election.

In short, if you conduct a survey through the Internet, make sure that the medium (the Internet) does not preclude any relevant group from responding.

- A computer system (hardware and software, such as Netscape Navigator, Microsoft Internet Explorer, or any of the innumerable E-mail software programs)
- An account (typically provided by your college to its students or available through a commercial service provider)
- A service provider (America On-line, Prodigy, CompuServ, or any of a number of local and national servers)
- An E-mail address
- A password that is your unique code for access
- Addresses for correspondents, discussion groups, and Web sites—often available from on-line listings by topical interests

E-mail (Electronic Mail)

Perhaps the most frequent use of the Internet is electronic mail (E-mail). E-mail allows you to send correspondence electronically (rather than through the postal service or your organization's internal mail service). In addition to its use in standard correspondence, E-mail can also be used in research. With the addresses of correspondents (frequently published in internal or professional directories), you can ask for resources, experiences, or referrals to other potential correspondents who hold some information about your topic.

Discussion Groups: Usenet (Newsgroups and Listservs)

Discussion groups fall into two broad categories: newsgroups and listservs (also called Usenet). A *newsgroup* is the equivalent of a bulletin board (including the graffiti that often appear on posted notes). In other words, participants post their ideas or wishes, and other participants may read, ignore, or comment on those ideas or post related or even unrelated ideas of their own. Newsgroup participants vary in their knowledge and commitment to accuracy, so be especially wary of information you find here. In addition, because of the bulletin board format, information that appears one day may easily disappear the next, making it difficult to check your facts or verify information.

A *listserv* is a more interactive communication to which participants must actively subscribe (as to a magazine). Typically an academic site, a listserv brings together people with similar interests—people who treat diseases of quarterhorses, investigate Cajun history, or monitor congressional legislation regarding veterans' affairs. Because such groups are typically well read and current on their information, you may find knowledgeable sources here, and you can contact them directly because their E-mail numbers are often displayed whenever they contribute to a discussion. (Remember, however, that a message you send to a participant must have the *participant's* address—not the listserv's address, which would post your question to everyone in the group.)

Web Searches

Web sites (collections of interlinked on-line documents representing a single person, an organization, or an entire industry) tend to offer more permanent information than is available from newsgroups and listservs, primarily because it often takes considerable time to design useful Web pages that constitute a site. Although individuals may create their own Web pages, for your research purposes you will generally find more useful information on the sites created and maintained by organizations. (See Strategy Review 3.6.)

To conduct a Web search, you need an Internet server and a *browser*, a specialized program that gives you access to the Web. Many colleges and organizations subscribe to Netscape Navigator or Microsoft Internet Explorer to give their users access to the Web. Some organizations, however, purchase text-only access, which provides access to the text, but not the graphics, on the Web.

To use the Web effectively as a research tool, you should be familiar with search engines—the electronic equivalents of the subject index in a card catalog or the standard index at the back of a book. A search engine, such as Alta Vista, Yahoo, or Lycos, allows you to conduct a keyword search, meaning that you can narrow your search by suggesting parameters for the topic you are researching in much the same way that you use keyword searches to find information in your school library's on-line catalog. In this strategy you describe your primary areas of interest by joining topics (*finances* and *senior citizens*), narrowing those areas (*mutual funds* and *senior citizens*), and then narrowing again if necessary (*mutual funds* and *senior citizens* and *fraud*). Other searches may require you to use "or" (for comparable terms or secondary interests) or "not" (for exclusionary topics): (*mutual funds* or *certificates of deposit* and *senior citizens* and *fraud*). A reference librarian will help you conduct a keyword search in the library, but you may need a helpful colleague to get the hang of a successful keyword search on your personal computer.

STRATEGY REVIEW 3.6

CONDUCTING A WEB SEARCH

In general, if you have the right hardware and software and can point a cursor and click a mouse, you can access the Web. These simple steps introduce you to the process:

1. Click on the icon for the server (Netscape Navigator, for instance).

2. Choose a search engine that accommodates your interest:
   - Yahoo (http://www.yahoo.com)
   - Lycos (http://www.lycos.com)
   - Alta Vista (http://www.altavista.digital.com)

   For our purposes, try Alta Vista.

3. For *experimentation* and to browse the subject areas, click on blue words, the words on which the cursor turns to a hand, or the images matching the sites in which you are interested.

   For a *keyword search*, list your keywords with phrases in quotation marks. Advanced keyword searches may be separated by *and, or,* or *but* to define the parameters of your search. The first sites shown will have the most "hits"—the most appropriate sources, given the parameters your keyword selection has generated.

4. Click on highlighted items to go to related items in other documents. (You are now browsing the Internet.)

5. Record useful information either by downloading documents or taking good notes. Be sure to save the URL addresses of sources you will use.

6. Be sure to copy all information about addresses, authorship, sponsoring organizations for the site, and the date you found the material; this information will be required when you list references in a Works Cited section at the end of the document you write.

Applying Other Strategies for Research

In addition to conducting traditional and corporate library research, interviews, brainstorming sessions, surveys, and on-line searches and relying on your personal experiences (often chronicled in your work log), you may have to conduct formal research on the job. Such formal research, however, is typically understood to be part of your job and is not incidental to it. Laboratory technicians know they will be working with blood tests, chemical tests, or other tests, for example, and they know they are expected to write the results of their tests in their work logs, their daily reports, and (for some researchers) in research journals and other scholarly publications. Workers in other jobs, such as architects, know they are expected to build models of their ideas and describe the most important features, building materials, and safety components.

Building models and conducting laboratory tests are examples of the scientific and other research that undergirds workplace writing. Because these forms of research are so discipline-specific, however, they are not covered here. But do be aware that the term *research* means a great many things in today's workplace. Finding out about products, services, consumers, buyers, suppliers, supervisors, and creditors is part of knowing about work. Uses, costs, benefits, side effects, additional uses, disadvantages, packaging, marketing, recycling, safety, and energy efficiency are just a few of the millions of workplace topics that you may have to know about. Being able to find that information—through books and documents, people, on-line resources, or tests and experiments—is one of your most valuable workplace assets.

The Ethics and Elements of High-Quality Research

Although quality research demands time, you should devote yourself whole-heartedly to doing quality work when asked to research a topic. Knowing that readers will rely on your information to perform their jobs, make decisions, or plan a future should remind you of your ethical responsibility to them.

In general, three hallmarks of quality research will mark your work as ethical and usable:

1. *Thoroughness:* In spite of time limitations, you should still be committed to providing complete information, which means that you should present both sides of the topic you are discussing, point out its advantages and disadvantages (or strengths and weaknesses), and look beneath the surface to find the deeper implications of the topic for your readers. The purpose of most congressional legislation, for instance, is to improve conditions in the United States, but without thorough research, laws intended to protect citizens may backfire and create worse problems than those the legislation was designed to correct—a result that sometimes occurs.

2. *Timeliness:* Major problems can result when researchers rely on obsolete data. Make sure the information you use is as up-to-date as possible. If it is dated and you cannot get more current information, be sure to warn your reader in prominent (and numerous) places that the information is useful merely for historical interests and trends and may not be reliable today.

3. *Accurate:* It should go without saying that research should be accurate, and most people (unless they are unethical) do not intend to present inaccurate data in their writing. More often, they simply misread or misinterpret facts and figures. Check and recheck your information to make sure your dates and numbers are accurate; look again for "no," "not," and other negators that can be overlooked in quick readings (and quick typing and proofreading) and ask for help, if necessary, in interpreting data.

Finally, your most useful research strategy is a critical mind. Learn to ask questions about what you read:

Who says so? Why should I believe them?

Could alternative explanations also be reasonable?

Does anything seem odd about this research or its findings?

Under what conditions and with what biases was this research conducted?

What are the experiences and background of this research author?

Who supports the research author's work?

How similar is the research author's situation to the one about which I am writing?

What if the research author's claims are inaccurate?

Acknowledging your dependence on other sources of information and then learning to evaluate those sources critically will drastically reduce the likelihood that you will naively accept everything that appears in print, on-line, or on television as truth.

Summary

In presenting an overview of the research process, this chapter has emphasized that although the process is described in stages, it has no particular linear order. You may, for instance, sit down and draft as much as you can about your topic or writing assignment based exclusively on the information you already know or have readily available in your notes. Then, you may form a research plan to provide the missing details in your draft. Or you may want to conduct your research first, so that you will have all your information at hand before you begin to work on a draft (see Chapter 5).

Two essential concerns should guide your research: first, you must consider your objectives, which will entail learning more about your readers and yourself; second, you must investigate your topic thoroughly and ethically. Although you may think you only have to research your topic, you would do well to find out more about your readers as well, concentrating on how much they already know about the topic, how reliable that information is, what additional information they need from you, and the forms in which they are most likely to understand your information. You should also try to learn more about the readers' backgrounds and their intended use for the information you provide. In addition, you need to investigate your readers' environments to find out how their work areas (office, manufacturing plant, sales floor, etc.) affect their reading and the amount of attention they can devote to your documents.

Learning more about your own environment will bring you back to several issues of organizational image and culture: What characteristics feature prominently in your workplace documents that distinguish your organization's work from that of other (perhaps competing) organizations? Should you adhere to those forms and characteristics to present a unified organizational "look" for your documents? On what basis should you deviate from those forms?

After finding out more about your readers, you should next investigate your subject matter thoroughly, relying on your own notes and memory, your coworkers, library materials (in both standard libraries and your organization's library), and people inside and outside your company who might respond to a survey or interview, giving you information to which you otherwise would not have access. Investigate resources available on the Internet for basic and additional information that you might need for a more universal perspective on your topic.

Regardless of your methods, you should keep the three hallmarks of good research in mind as you work:

- Be thorough.
- Be up-to-date.
- Be accurate.

These mantras will help ensure that you treat your subject ethically and provide the kind of information your readers will need to conduct their own work.

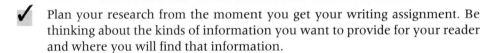

CHECKLIST

✓ Plan your research from the moment you get your writing assignment. Be thinking about the kinds of information you want to provide for your reader and where you will find that information.

✓ Keep notes of your work and your coworkers' contributions to each project you are assigned.

✓ Conduct interviews with subject matter experts to gain a more thorough understanding of your topic.

✓ Plan your interviews carefully. You want to make sure you get all the information you need, while limiting your conversation to a reasonable and productive amount of time—say, one hour.

✓ If your interviewees do not know the answer to a question, ask if they can refer you to someone who has the information you need.

✓ Find out who is in charge of your company's documents, and learn the proper procedure for requesting those documents. If you need special security clearances to gain access to some of the company's more sensitive records, find out how to get those clearances.

✓ Make friends with a reference librarian at your college or public library. The librarian can be an invaluable guide on finding information you may need for your workplace writing.

✓ Familiarize yourself with the standard resources and reference works, available in almost any college library, that will provide statistics and other background information for your work.

✓ Conduct surveys to get a broader range of responses from people with whom you do not have daily or easy contact. Be sure to construct surveys that will target people who can provide the accurate and thorough information you need.

✓ Take advantage of the innumerable resources available on-line through databases, personal correspondence (E-mail), discussion groups, and Web sites.

✓ Make friends with the computer experts in your college or organization, especially those with the information and the patience to teach you to become adept at on-line searches for information.

✓ Be sure to review the information in the Appendix at the end of this textbook to refresh your memory about crediting other people's ideas and information. Stealing ideas on the job can have serious repercussions, but none is more serious than the damage to your reputation.

✓ Be gracious with people who provide you with information. Remember that they are doing you a favor by making time for you; providing you complete, accurate, and up-to-date information; and making your writing assignment easier.

EXERCISES

Individual Exercises

1. Consider the following topics and audiences. For each topic, choose the most logical group of readers in the second column; be prepared to defend your choice (you should see lots of interesting options). Then, choosing one item from the topics column and one *or more* audiences from the readers column, form a research plan that answers these questions: What specific kinds of information do you think each audience wants? Under what circumstances would this information be useful to these readers? How would you go about getting that information? Be prepared to defend your choices.

Topics	*Audiences*
a. new cars	a. senior citizens
b. financial investments	b. teenagers
c. colleges in Hawaii	c. bankers
d. computer prices	d. hairdressers
e. parking on campus	e. nature lovers
f. energy savings on washing machines	f. do-it-yourselfers
	g. newlyweds
g. building a bluebird house	h. new professors
h. trimming hedges	i. travel agents
i. repairing a car's air conditioner	j. college graduates
j. managing subcontractors	k. war veterans
k. vacation spots in the tropics	l. entrepreneurs
l. sound tax investments	m. alumni at homecoming weekend
m. tips for traveling alone	

2. For one week, keep a daily log of your activities at school or on the job. Note especially the kinds of details you're responsible for and the relationships you have with your teachers, supervisors, colleagues, and subordinates. Also note the progress you make on various projects, obstacles that have hindered your progress, and creative means you have devised to overcome these obstacles. At the end of the week, organize your notes as though you were making a presentation to your boss or teacher that demonstrates how hard you have worked and how productive you have been. How would you structure your presentation (and what language would you use?) to convince your boss or reader that you have too many responsibilities? That you want more responsibilities? Turn in both your log and your presentation to your instructor.

3. Go to your college's library or the local public library and see what kinds of government publications are available. How might you use such publications in your work? How might workplace writers in other companies use some of this information? List and describe five publications that you think might be useful in your career. Be sure to explain why you believe those publications might be useful.

4. Find at least ten reference works in your local or college library. After briefly scanning the introductions to these works, describe the kinds of information they offer and under what circumstances you might find the information useful in your career. A summary paragraph for each work should be sufficient.

5. Ask your reference librarian about your library's collection of CD-ROMs. What forms of information are available in this format? List five references that you might find useful in your job; provide a scenario for each that shows the situations in which you might use the CD-ROM.

6. Choose a topic about which you know a great deal—a work-related topic, a hobby, or something you have learned in school. First, think of someone who might genuinely want or need to know more about your topic, and then list the kinds of information you think this reader would want to know. How much information would the reader need in order to understand the gist of your description? Then, without using any reference works, write a paragraph or a page—following your instructor's requirements—that describes this topic to your reader. Be prepared to explain your topic selection, your reader selection, your arrangement of the information, the amount and kinds of details you have provided, and your word choices.

7. Explain where you would go to find more information about the following:
   a. Career options for someone in your major
   b. Geographic regions where you might find plenty of job opportunities in your career specialization
   c. Some companies in your area of specialization that make more than $1 million a year
   d. A list of magazines and professional journals in your field
   e. A list of professional organizations in your field and the yearly dues for each organization
   f. Colleges or universities in your region (or in another region) that offer graduate programs in your field
   g. Types of organizations where graduates from your college in your major have gone to work

   For three of these topics, list Web sites that should include the information. If possible, print the information and be prepared to turn it in during class.

Collaborative Exercises

1. What do you know or what can you assume about the following readers or groups of readers? What do they read on the job? What kinds of information are they looking for when they read on the job? Do they have particular preferences for the presentation of that information? For the research behind that information? Are your feelings and impressions about these read-

ers based on stereotypes? On what grounds have you formed those stereotypes? In what ways are the stereotypes useful to you? In what ways are
they harmful?

loan officers	lawyers	police officers
teachers	physicians	college presidents
professors	animal trainers	construction workers
mechanics	weight trainers	computer programmers

2. Because you might need to provide background information on some project, product, or service you are working on, an appreciation for "history" is
   important, even though it is workplace history, rather than the formal history you have studied throughout school. From the following lists, choose
   three products or services that originated in Western culture and three that
   originated in a non-Western culture. Prepare a brief history (one or two
   paragraphs) of each product or service you have chosen. The histories
   should be directed to your classmates. For the products or services from non-
   Western cultures, be sure to include their history *within their own cultures,* as
   well as in Western culture.

   From Western Cultures
   a. Coca-Cola
   b. computers
   c. compact discs
   d. football
   e. airplanes
   f. eyeglasses
   g. hot air balloons

   From Non-Western Cultures
   a. fireworks
   b. paper
   c. thatching a roof
   d. saki
   e. jinriksha
   f. pyramid
   g. catamaran

 ONGOING ASSIGNMENT

■ Given the work you have done so far in identifying your primary organization's culture and planning a document that will help newcomers fit in,
  what sorts of additional research might you want to conduct? To ensure that
  your document includes more than your own observations and experiences,
  what precautions might you need to take?

■ Using the topical guidelines in Strategy Review 3.2, devise a research plan
  based on your audience, your purpose, and your readers' need for information. Where will you go for that information? How might you use some of
  the strategies described in this chapter to help you uncover valuable information?

CHAPTER 4

Constructing and Organizing Information for Your Reader

- **The Rationale for Organizing Workplace Documents**
- **Strategies for Organizing Workplace Documents**
  - *Organizing by Anticipated Reader Response*
  - *Organizing by Reader Needs*
- **Summary**
- **Checklist**
- **Exercises**

Have you ever had a day when you just couldn't get organized? Perhaps you went to the cleaners and found you had left your soiled clothes at home. Or you went to get gasoline and realized you'd passed the post office where you had intended to mail your rent check; then you had to backtrack across ten blocks of traffic. Even if you don't consider yourself particularly well organized, zigzagging around town to run a few simple errands is time-consuming and irritating.

Just as you try to organize your errands, you will want to organize your writing for several important reasons: organizing saves time, it outlines a clear path, and it makes sense. Furthermore, you can organize tasks and information in various ways—for example, by priorities, deadlines, steps in a process, budget issues, location, and, of course, alphabet. As you can see, all tasks should not be organized in the same way; for instance, it would be silly to arrange your grocery shopping list by alphabet. Similarly, it would be futile to list solutions to a workplace problem before identifying the problem. Understanding that information can be arranged in a variety of ways will make you a better writer, one who realizes that the *choices* you make when organizing information can affect your readers' comprehension and use of that information. The letters in Figure 4.1 on page 97 and Figure 4.2 on page 98 illustrate the advantages of providing an organizational scheme for your writing that readers can follow.

This chapter focuses on the various organizational strategies that serve the readers of workplace documents. After you understand more clearly the principles on which organization is based, you will learn some specific strategies for organizing your information: problem/solution, cause/effect, chronological, comparison/contrast, immediacy/remoteness, general to specific, and specific to general.

It is important to remember that organization is part of the writing process, which means that you do not have to make all the organizational decisions about your work at a specific time in the process. Nevertheless, getting a sense of the proper organization of your information during the planning, researching, and drafting stages (see Chapters 2, 3, and 5) will enable you to see more clearly what information will be important in your final document and will give you a better sense of where you are going with your document.

At whatever point in the writing process you make your final decisions about organization, you should return to this chapter to make sure your document has a logical structure. Once you have composed, say, a chronological report, you can use the elements in this chapter or in the final checklist to make sure you have constructed that chronology correctly.

The Rationale for Organizing Workplace Documents

Although some people joke that a well-organized desk is a sign of a disturbed mind, developing a reputation as a well-organized person will generally work to your advantage. People feel more confident about your capabilities when you can

THE STATE OF

A L A B A M A

STATE DISASTER AND RELIEF OFFICE
9001 Merlington Avenue
Montgomery, AL 38511

3 April 2000

Mr. Bernard Manze
843 Riverside Drive
Chesterton, AL 38589

Dear Mr. Manze:

1

Good news, **Bernard Manze!** You can pick up your money any time after Tuesday, November 2! And remember: the payments are exempt from local, state, and federal taxes.

2

We recommend you hire an accountant and an attorney who will oversee the appropriate distribution of your settlement to the proper government agencies. And, because this money is offered as federal relief money, you must verify your expenditures on housing, food, and clothing.   **3**

4

We hope you are recovering from the drastic devastation of the recent flooding, and we will be happy to answer any questions you have about your settlement.

4

Best wishes,

Janice C. Farrington

The Honorable Janice C. Farrington
Secretary for Disaster Relief

---

1. sounds like a lottery winner

2. why? no context

3. first mention of source of money and context

4. goodwill closing

FIGURE 4.1   A Letter with No Clear Arrangement or Context Confuses Readers

---

quickly find information in your files or on your computer disks, organize your workday to accommodate various project schedules, and write important information in a logical fashion.

To understand the various strategies for organizing information for an entire document, as well as for the individual paragraphs that make up that document, you will need to know the following:

- What your reader needs to know
- How your reader will use the information you provide

- In what order your reader needs and expects to find this information
- What additional evidence your reader will need to be persuaded by your arguments
- How your reader is likely to interpret or feel about your information

---

THE STATE OF

A L A B A M A

STATE DISASTER AND RELIEF OFFICE
9001 Merlington Avenue
Montgomery, AL 38511

3 April 2000

Mr. Bernard Manze
843 Riverside Drive
Chesterton, AL 38589

Dear Mr. Manze:

1   **1**

We are sorry to learn of your flooded home, caused by the recent hurricane and high waters of the Mahweh River. We have read your claim and have determined you are eligible for disaster relief funds of $50,000.

2

To collect your settlement, please follow these instructions:

1. Your check will be mailed as soon as you call Damian (1-800-555-1212) to verify your receipt of this letter and your current address. Many residents have had to move because of the floods, so we need a current address where we can contact you.

2. Your settlement will be paid in a single installment of $50,000.

3. You do not have to pay applicable local, state, and federal taxes. Nevertheless, we strongly encourage you to consult a financial adviser who can help you reserve your money to pay for repairs or replacement of damaged items.

Should you need additional information, or if you have additional damages, please do not hesitate to call our office.

3

Best wishes,

Janice C. Farrington

The Honorable Janice C. Farrington
Secretary for Disaster Relief

Column notes (left margin):

1. context and goodwill established

2. procedures/ additional information

3. goodwill closing

FIGURE 4.2   A Letter Organized to Provide Context and Useful Information for the Reader

In this chapter, we will use a scenario involving the organizational decisions that Ben Ames, director of Mahweh Water Control, and Maria Lopez, researcher and technical trainer, make when discussing numerous issues related to the water of the Mahweh River. Currently, excessive flooding and some control problems in the paper industry have allowed the river's water to be contaminated by toxic wastes from a local paper mill. Chapter 13 will build on the work you do in this chapter to describe a problem/solution report that Ben writes; for this chapter, however, letters and memos provide most of the examples of organizational strategies.

The following outline reveals Ben's general analysis of his first writing situation, which will become more specific once he focuses on his particular audiences and their needs:

His readers need to know that several factors have contaminated the Mahweh River, threatening the wildlife of the river and making it hazardous to use for drinking water.

His readers will use this information to decide what changes to make in their work endeavors and lifestyles.

His readers need the information in this order:
1. Proof that a problem exists
2. Factors that are currently causing the problem
   a. Chemical spills (biggest problem)
   b. Agricultural runoffs (second biggest problem)
   c. Excessive rainfall and flooding (third biggest problem)
   d. Lack of awareness and preventive strategies (fourth biggest problem)
3. What can be done
   a. Negotiate safety strategies with corporations
   b. Negotiate safety strategies with farmers
   c. Expand legislative directives on Water Purity Act
   d. Hold additional training sessions for all water quality personnel
   e. Hold information sessions for residents and general public

His readers expect to find the information in this order:
1. Clarification of problem in the introduction
2. Discussion of problem in the body
3. Solutions or recommendations in the conclusion

His readers need additional persuasion, such as the following:
1. Statistics on current levels of contamination
2. Review of factors creating toxic levels in the river
3. Map of the river, showing affected areas
4. Descriptions and pictures of river areas affected by contamination
5. Descriptions of safety strategies for corporations, farmers, and legislators
6. Sample training materials that will educate water quality employees; statistics on other rivers' improvements after employee training

His readers are likely to feel concerned about the problem Ben has identified, grateful for some of the suggestions, and, perhaps, nervous or even defensive about others.

Ben has already clarified a number of issues that will be important, regardless of who his readers actually are. Now, as he tailors the information for specific audiences, he will give additional consideration to organization, based on each audience's needs and likely reactions to the information. If the readers are corporate representatives from the local paper mill, for instance, they are probably most concerned about the amount of contamination that is contributed by their mill and may be looking for ways to help out—or to avoid responsibility. Legislators may be looking for ways to help their constituents (the area citizens who live along the Mahweh or the big businesses that have contributed significantly to their election campaign coffers). People who live along the river want to know how this contamination will affect their property values and when they can expect the cleanup to begin. Workers in the water quality facility may be eager to learn how their jobs will change in light of the new contamination levels.

As this scenario shows, organizing information requires you to see the big picture, as well as the specifics of the particular project on which you are working. In organizing information, therefore, you need to stand back and see how your project fits into the larger scheme of all the organization's projects, and you may have to consider how your project fits into the community as well. You will then be better prepared to decide whether your subject is a problem, a solution to one or several problems, an important bit of background information, or part of a simple or larger process that may determine the success of your organization. Once you can determine how your project and writing assignment fit into the scope of your work and goals, you can make some decisions about how your writing should be organized and how you can make that organization evident to your readers.

Strategies for Organizing Workplace Documents

Writers typically use one of two approaches for communicating information. One approach is organizing by anticipated reader response—information is arranged according to how you think your reader will react (positively, negatively, or neutrally) to the information. The other approach is organizing by reader needs and expectations—information is arranged according to the order in which the reader will use or want to know the information and according to where the reader expects to find the information. Both approaches require you to integrate concern for the reader with the appropriate presentation of information, which involves making sure that the reader concludes that your information is complete, accurate, and up-to-date and that you have presented the information with great care for relevance and ethical considerations. (See Strategy Review 4.1.)

In addition to showing that you understand the information and are concerned for your reader, well-organized documents also signal that you know how things are done. Violating the reader's expectations about the order of information, for instance, may suggest that you have not considered the reader's needs very carefully or that you simply do not know how to accommodate the reader's needs in memos, letters, reports, and proposals (forms that we will discuss in Part II of this textbook).

What does it mean to "violate a reader's expectations"? Quite simply, based on their experiences with reading and with life in general, readers expect certain kinds of information at certain times in their reading, and they expect that information to be discussed in certain, predictable ways. If, for instance, the author of a mystery novel announces "who done it" in the first chapter, you would certainly be justified in believing that the author does not understand the genre of mystery writing. Similarly, workplace documents have standard features and patterns of organization, too; understanding the genre in which you are writing—memos, letters, reports, proposals, and manuals—and then using the appropriate organizational strategy for the kind of information you are presenting and the audience's needs will help send the message that you are a competent workplace writer.

STRATEGY REVIEW 4.1

ORGANIZING FOR EMPHASIS

In the documents you create, you will often want to organize for emphasis, most often by putting the most important information in prominent places in your document. Thus, in addition to the overall organization of your workplace writing, you will also have to attend to the internal organization of each segment and paragraph. Just as you consider organizing by purpose (the direct and indirect approaches) and organizing by content (problem/solution, cause/effect, chronological, comparison/contrast, immediacy/remoteness, general to specific, and specific to general), you will have to determine which strategies work best for individual segments and individual paragraphs.

A common experience will clarify the reasoning behind organizing for emphasis. What happens when you walk into class and find out your teacher is about to give a pop quiz on the material you were supposed to have read last night? If you have a moment and have the textbook handy, you probably attempt some of these cramming strategies:

- Read the chapter summary and checklist.
- Read the marginal notes provided by the author or the previous owner of the text.
- Look at the major and minor headings.

(continued)

- Look at the graphics and read their captions.
- Read the first sentence of every paragraph.
- Read the last sentence of every paragraph.

The last two strategies—reading the first and last sentences of every paragraph—show that you count on the writer to provide an overview in the first sentence and conclusions or summaries in the last sentence. Thus you assume that by reading these sentences you will obtain details and insights that you might miss by concentrating on the other four strategies.

In the workplace, readers also count on writers to provide the most important information in certain places: in headings and subheadings, in marginal comments (often summaries of main ideas), in summaries and checklists, in graphics and captions, and in opening and closing sentences of paragraphs. Savvy writers use these places to feature important information that they want their readers to note.

The following discussions of strategies for organizing workplace documents use simple examples to demonstrate organizing techniques. More extensive examples appear in later chapters on informational and instructional reports, analytical reports, and proposals and are referenced throughout this chapter. Thus, the concept of organizational strategies, presented here in simplified form, will serve as the basis for your understanding the strategy in longer documents, such as reports and proposals.

Organizing by Anticipated Reader Response

As with any aspect of workplace writing, organizing by anticipated reader response requires you to consider your readers carefully, focusing on what you want them to do or think immediately after reading your document. Organizing by reader response may take either a direct approach or an indirect approach.

Using the Direct Approach

When writers anticipate a positive or neutral response to their communications, they use a *direct approach* and put the main idea first. This approach might seem preferable for all workplace communications, given that your readers are busy and won't want to wade through an entire document to find the main point. As you'll see when we discuss the indirect approach, however, the direct approach works only when the main idea is unlikely to cause your readers any consternation—unlikely, in other words, to hurt their feelings, disinterest them, depress them, anger them, or make them dislike you to the point of ignoring your suggestions and ideas. Thus, you should use the direct approach in the following circumstances:

- When presenting good news to the reader: A promotion, settlement of a complaint in the reader's favor, hiring, a bonus or raise, award of a contract or scholarship, acceptance into college, a goodwill message, or the arrival of a long-awaited product or service.

- When presenting routine information that the reader expects to read: Orders for products or services, announcements about upcoming events, confirmations of orders and reservations, descriptions of services or products, or appreciation for favors.

- When requesting information, products, or services that the reader expects to be asked for: Sales catalogs, basic product/service information (costs, materials, warranties, etc.), samples of products, or printed information (brochures, price lists, schedules, etc.).

- When alerting the reader to imminent danger to equipment or people or issuing other cautions that you cannot risk the reader overlooking.

The following examples of opening sentences in letters demonstrate the direct approach. Note that they clearly announce the subject of the letter and reveal the writer's intent.

- Please accept the following order for 200 pounds of Southard Coffee blends.

- Congratulations on your promotion to senior vice president at SE Bank & Trust.

- Would you please send me Meredith College's most recent course catalog?

- We are delighted that you will be staying at the Grove Park Inn from August 22 through 26.

- As a junior at the University of Central Florida, I am interested in learning more about your company's internship program. Would you please send me a brochure about Carolina Dental's internship opportunities and responsibilities?

Not only do these opening sentences immediately tell the reader what the writer wants, they also suggest what kinds of information might be in the remainder of the letter (which is typically rather short). For example, what would you expect the rest of the letter ordering coffee to do?

- Rave about the company's coffees?

- Specify how much of which flavors the writer wants?

- Describe a typical morning at the office when all the employees gather around the coffee urn?

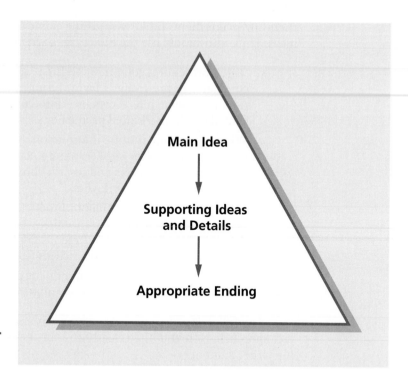

Main Idea

Supporting Ideas and Details

Appropriate Ending

FIGURE *1*

The Model for the Direct Approach

An advertising copywriter might rave about the company's coffees, and a creative writer might describe the social scene around the coffeepot; but a workplace writer will get to the point, telling the readers what they need to know. In this case, the writer will specify how much of which flavors he wants to order.

The direct approach allows you to tell the readers what you want from them or what you want them to know; then you can use the remainder of the document for necessary details, evidence, or explanations of your primary message. Figure 4.3 shows the organization of a direct message. If, for instance, Ben in the Mahweh Water Control scenario wants to congratulate a worker on quickly identifying the source of the toxic contamination in the Mahweh River, he should tell her that information in the first sentence of the first paragraph of the memo (see Figure 4.4).

Of course, not all documents using the direct approach convey good news; in fact, warnings of danger and problems can also merit the direct approach, especially if you are afraid your reader might overlook your communication or misinterpret your message. In such cases, putting the most important information first is crucial to your role as a communicator. Figure 4.5 on page 106 is a sample letter that delivers bad news in a direct approach; Chapter 12 offers an extended example of a report following the direct approach.

In the Mahweh River scenario, for example, it is essential that Ben deliver the messages on page 105 to their audiences in a direct manner.

Audience	Message
Area citizens	Do not drink the water. It is contaminated.
Legislators	Emergency bills need to be passed to provide drinking water for citizens, stop the primary sources of contamination (agriculture and industry), and start to clean the water.
Farmers	Stop using agricultural sprays and pesticides immediately.
Paper mill	Stop production immediately.
Media	The river is contaminated.
Fishers and restaurants	Do not eat the river's fish or sell them for eating; they are contaminated.

MAHWEH WATER CONTROL

memo

To: Maria Lopez
From: Ben Ames *BA*
Date: 24 September 1999
Subj: Raise for January 2000

good news announced in opening sentence

Congratulations, Maria, on your outstanding work—and your $1,750 raise for this year. You certainly deserve our thanks for a superb job. The test you developed to detect sulfur contamination will likely save our residents a great deal of worry about their drinking water.

details and support for good news

We were all impressed with your daily work, but your special efforts to get the sulfur-testing equipment ready for the rainy season made a tremendous difference in our ability to evaluate the damage caused by the recent flooding. I have no doubt that your work enabled us to detect—and correct—what could have been an overwhelming catastrophe for all of us who depend on the Mahweh River.

goodwill closing

Again, thanks for your hard work, and I look forward to another year of working together.

FIGURE 4.4   The Direct Approach for a Good News Message

bad news in
opening sentence

emphasis added

details of bad
news

solutions for bad
news

goodwill closing

MAHWEH WATER CONTROL

7000 WATERFORD DRIVE
SHAWNEE, ALABAMA 38591

5 September 1999

Dear Area Citizens:

By now, you have heard that the Mahweh River—and your drinking supply—is
unsafe. We recognize the inconvenience, but it is essential that you DO NOT
DRINK THE WATER UNTIL YOU ARE NOTIFIED THAT IT IS SAFE.

The water is contaminated by pollution from agricultural runoffs, industrial spills,
and flooding. Although the river can routinely handle some toxins, the combination
of problems has resulted in serious contamination of the drinking supply. The
recent effects of the hurricane season and the increased use of the water for
purification by several local industries have all contributed to the problem.

Currently, we are working with water cleanup crews from several states, and
the governor has promised to work diligently for disaster relief funds. In the
meantime, we continue our work to make your drinking water safe again.

We will be happy to answer any questions you have about the drinking water
supply if you call us at (123) 482-4820.

Sincerely,

Ben Ames

Ben Ames, Director

F I G U R E 4.5   The Direct Approach for a Bad News Message

To write a successful document using the direct approach, make sure that
you can anticipate a positive or neutral response to your communication or that
the message you have to communicate is too serious to risk its getting lost in an
indirect pattern (discussed in the next section). Then, state in a simple sentence
what you want your reader to understand after reading your communication.
You may find that the sentence you have constructed will be a good opening sentence for your communication.

Using the Indirect Approach

After working on becoming a more direct communicator, you may be tempted to believe that directness is the *only* way to communicate in the workplace. The direct approach, however, does not always work to the writer's advantage. In some cases, presenting the primary idea first may anger readers or turn them off to your explanations and development of the rest of your ideas.

What kinds of issues, topics, and purposes are likely to irritate readers or make them respond unfavorably to direct writing? Many, if not most, people resent the following:

- Bad news about their jobs (firings, layoffs, denied promotions)
- Bad news about their finances or credit (credit refusal, bank overdrafts, nonpayment of bills)
- Requests for donations
- Offers of services/products the reader has not requested
- Complaints
- Refusals to settle complaints
- Refusals to accept invitations, honor debts, or accept jobs/promotions

Consider how you would respond to the following opening sentences:

- You're fired.
- Your application for a Visa has been rejected.
- Your parole is denied.
- Please donate $5,000 to be a member of the Chancellor's Club.
- Your tuition is going up 29 percent next year.
- Your campus parking privileges have been revoked.
- You owe us $457 in fines for overdue library books.

You probably would feel a variety of emotions: anger, confusion, disappointment, embarrassment, outrage, and contempt. Surely, though, the writer did not intend for you to feel any of these emotions. Ironically, had the writer presented the information in a different way—through a different organizational structure—you probably would not have responded quite so negatively to these messages.

Although some readers claim to prefer to receive bad news upfront, at the very beginning of the document, most readers react negatively to writers' efforts to be absolutely blunt with them. International readers are also likely to be highly offended by the bluntness they perceive in Americans' direct approach correspondence. Thus, for bad news or for information that is likely to make the reader feel ambivalent, good writers most often use an *indirect approach*. A document organized using the indirect approach follows this pattern:

- *First paragraph/section:* A neutral introductory opening.
- *Second paragraph/section:* The reasons for the decision or current state.
- *End of second paragraph/sections:* The bad news in as few sentences as possible—preferably in only one sentence and sometimes only by implication—provided the reader clearly understands that the news is bad.
- *Third paragraph/sections:* If possible, an alternative solution and its advantages for the reader.
- *Final paragraph/sections:* A pleasant or neutral conclusion that avoids harping on the bad news.

Thus, the indirect approach follows the model in Figure 4.6.

Remember, however, that the purpose of the indirect approach is to protect your readers' feelings, not to mislead them. If your communication is in danger of violating your ethical responsibility to the truth, you should revise your language or the structure of your document to clarify that truth (see Figure 4.7 on page 109 and Figure 4.8 on page 110).

Although we will discuss bad news letters/memos and the indirect approach they typically follow in Chapter 10 on letters and memos, you can begin to understand the rhetorical nuances (the persuasive strategies of language, style, and organization) of such an approach from the documents shown here. Figure 4.9 on page 111 offers another sample of an indirect message that demonstrates this strategy.

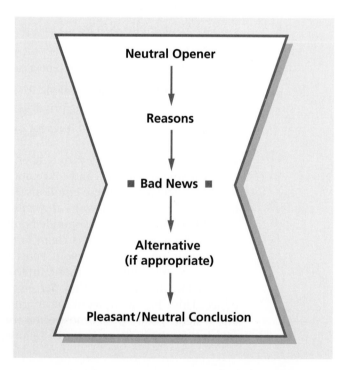

FIGURE 4.6

The Model for the Indirect Approach

MAHWEH WATER CONTROL
7000 WATERFORD DRIVE
SHAWNEE, ALABAMA 38591

17 September 1999

Mr. Preston Davis, CEO
Davis Paper Mill
Route 5, Box 395
Chesterton, AL 38589

Dear Mr. Davis:

pleasant opening

We appreciate the work you and your engineers have done in the wake of the Mahweh River flooding and contamination. Clearly, our efforts as partners to protect the river have paid off, and we are grateful for your quick work.

background

As you know, the Governor's Task Force has engaged federal investigators from the Environmental Protection Agency to ascertain the causes of the damage done to the Mahweh River and neighboring industries, residential areas, and wildlife preserves. In its assessment of the water's chemical makeup immediately

finding

following the first fish kill two weeks ago, the EPA has found the high level of nitrogen to be attributable to the agricultural runoff during end-of-the-season

*finding
(no cause/source)*

harvesting and regeneration. The high level of sulfur, however, has done the most damage to the river.

action requested

We hope to work with you on the environmental awareness aspects of the project and to give the Davis Paper Mill a large share of the credit for its concern for the river. We both make our livelihoods and our homes along this river, Mr. Davis, so I am pleased that we can be partners in making our river safe again.

pleasant closing

If you have any questions, please call me during work hours at (213) 492-5929 or at home at (213) 492-6839.

Sincerely,

Ben Ames

Ben Ames, Director

FIGURE 4.7   Bad News and Indirect Approach with Unclear Message

MAHWEH WATER CONTROL
7000 WATERFORD DRIVE
SHAWNEE, ALABAMA 38591

17 September 1999

Mr. Preston Davis, CEO
Davis Paper Mill
Route 5, Box 395
Chesterton, AL 38589

Dear Mr. Davis:

pleasant opening

We appreciate the work you and your engineers have done in the wake of the Mahweh River flooding and contamination. Clearly, our efforts as partners to protect the river have paid off, and we are grateful for your quick work.

background

As you know, the Governor's Task Force has engaged federal investigators from the Environmental Protection Agency to ascertain the causes of the damage done to the Mahweh River and neighboring industries, residential areas, and wildlife preserves. In its assessment of the water's chemical makeup immediately following

finding

the first fish kill two weeks ago, the EPA has found the high level of nitrogen to be attributable to the agricultural runoff during end-of-the-season harvesting and regeneration. The high level of sulfur, however, has done the most damage to

finding
bad news

the river and is directly attributable to the paper mill because neither farms nor hurricanes produce high levels of sulfur. The EPA will be in touch with you directly

solution

about the specific damage from sulfur and about the task force recommendations for economic restitution for the Mahweh River's cleanup.

offer to help

Although the Mahweh Water Control cannot help with the financial aspects of the river's recovery, we do hope to work with you on the environmental awareness as-

context for statement is now clear

pects of the project and to give the Davis Paper Mill a large share of the credit for its concern for the river. We both make our livelihoods and our homes along this river, Mr. Davis, so I am pleased that we can be partners in making our river safe again.

pleasant closing

If you have any questions about the EPA findings, or about the environmental impact education plan, please call me during work hours at (213) 492-5929 or at home at (213) 492-6839.

Sincerely,

Ben Ames

Ben Ames, Director

FIGURE 4.8   Bad News and Indirect Approach with Clear Message

davis paper mill

memorandum

To: Gloria Thurber
From: Jason Ridge   JR
Date: 4 December 1999
Subject: Raises and bonuses for the third quarter

subject line does
not give away
bad news

neutral opener

Gloria, we appreciate your thorough documentation of your team's work over the past six months on the Mahweh River fiasco. You have clearly done some outstanding work and have put a lot of time into the project.

reasons

In spite of your hard work, however, the cleanup of the river has tremendously set back our production plans, as well as our budget. Thus, the increases in corporate revenues that we hoped for have simply not materialized. Your request for a raise,

bad news

therefore, will be carried over to the next fiscal period when I will review each account manager's contributions and salary inequities, and I will remember the

alternative

hard work you have put in and your graciousness in acknowledging this turn of events.

pleasant/neutral
conclusion

We value your contributions, Gloria, and we look forward to a much more productive and profitable period next quarter for the entire company.

FIGURE 4.9   The Indirect Approach for a Bad News Memo

Again, such strategies for writing direct and indirect communications apply to all forms of workplace communication, including proposals, letters, and reports. Consider how your reader is likely to react to your information and then organize that information accordingly. With standard communications, however, when the reader is unlikely to react hostilely, the best strategy is to *put the most important information first*. Remember that readers are busy and typically resent having to thumb through your document (or worse, to read every section of it) to find the information they need. If they are likely to be angry or bitter about your message, however, your best bet is to try the indirect approach.

Organizing by Reader Needs

Although most workplace communications are organized in either a direct or an indirect fashion, writers must also make other decisions about organization. These decisions depend on the answers to two questions:

APPLICATION

Applying Organizational Schemes

In the Applications throughout this chapter, consider the following scenario:

> You are an engineer working for Advance Aeronautics, a company that makes small engines for private airplanes. The new engine (RJ7) you and your teammates have designed over the past two years is a remarkable piece of machinery that increases the power of small-engine airplanes while reducing tremors and vibrations. Unfortunately, the engine has also raised a significant environmental concern—noise pollution. The Environmental Protection Agency (EPA) will not approve the design as it now stands because of this concern. Therefore, you and your teammates must find some way to address and reduce the noise levels.

First, determine what approach you would use—the direct or the indirect—to tell your teammates that the engine has not met EPA regulations. Then, using the memos in this chapter as a model (and referring to Chapter 10, if necessary), organize the message you feel would be most appropriate.

- What does my reader need to know first? Second? Third?
- Where does my reader expect to find that information?

Workplace writers' responses to these questions often result in common organizational structures for their documents: problem/solution, cause/effect, chronological, comparison/contrast, immediacy/remoteness, general to specific, or specific to general. The writers' decisions about using these standard organizational strategies are guided by their concerns for the audience, the information, and the purpose of the document. Two cautions, therefore, are essential at this point:

1. Few writers start out to write a problem/solution or cause/effect document. More likely, after they have written a first draft that accommodates the information, audience, and purpose for a document, they realize that their writing follows one of those patterns (or some other pattern). Then, they revise to clarify those organizational structures in their document.

2. Even though these organizational structures dominate workplace writing, they do not always exist discretely; in other words, an overall problem/solution report may still have chronological elements or cause/effect explanations. As you examine and revise the organizational patterns in your workplace documents, be sensitive to the organizational structures *within* organizational structures. Then, review this chapter's guidelines for successfully organizing the information.

The following descriptions and examples of these organizational structures are the results of decisions writers make about their audiences, their information, and their purpose(s) for writing. These examples will help you understand some common patterns that writers find most effective in particular workplace circumstances. Later chapters provide more extensive writing samples that follow the organizational strategies described here.

Problem/Solution Organization

Problem/solution documents typically have one of two types of readers: (1) readers who, even before reading your work, know that a problem exists and want to know the solution(s), or (2) readers who do not know or have to be convinced that a problem exists before hearing the solutions. Thus, the order in which you present information in a problem/solution document will depend on how knowledgeable your reader is about the problem.

Of course, you would expect a problem/solution structure to reflect its name, with the opening sections of the document focusing on the problem(s) being addressed and the latter sections describing the solutions. Such an organization, in its extended form, works best only for readers who do not know or have to be convinced that a problem exists.

For readers who already know a problem exists, you don't have to be so careful about breaking the news and can use a direct approach. Thus, the document typically opens by reminding the reader of the problem and then quickly moves on to the solutions—"We need to follow these steps to solve our problem." The latter sections may clarify the problem or provide evidence of the problem's significance (How serious is the problem and what aspects of the company does it affect? How critical is it that the problem be solved? What could happen if we ignore the problem?). The problem section may also include some background information about the problem (perhaps even a cause/effect discussion or chronological history) and a description of additional or related problems that should also be addressed.

In the Mahweh Water Control scenario, for instance, the first communication with Davis Mill's CEO has to convince Mr. Davis that the Mahweh River is, indeed, polluted. Therefore, Ben uses this organizational scheme:

- *Discussion of the problem:* Contamination records and statistics.
- *Analysis of contamination:* Water samples and controlled experiments by independent and federal analysts.
- *Source of contamination:* Paper mill discharges due to high water from hurricane and poor internal treatment measures.
- *Possible solutions:* Cleanup methods and restructuring treatment measures.

To meet the goals of the organizational scheme, here are some questions Ben might answer in the report:

What is the mill's routine sulfur discharge?

What was the level during the spill?

What is the sulfur level now?

Who or what caused the sulfur spill?

Can the water and the spill be cleaned? How?

What are the effects of the spill?

How long will the effects last?

How can we prevent spills?

How can we know when spills have occurred?

If Mr. Davis already knows about the problem, however, then Ben's communications might focus on solutions, following this order:

I. Introduction and brief overview of the problem   [1 page]

II. Solutions to Mahweh River contamination   [15 pages]
    A. Shut down the mill permanently.
    B. Use alternative chemicals that contain less sulfur.
    C. Improve the system for removing sulfur by-products.
    D. Contract with waste services to transport by-products to a safer locale, especially when the river's water level exceeds eight feet.
    E. Conduct routine pump checks in each zone (once per day).

III. Sources of problems from Davis Mill for Mahweh River   [8 pages]
    A. Sulfur discharge from Mill 1
    B. Failed pump at zone 3
    C. Excessively high water levels from hurricane and rain
    D. Other contributing factors

IV. Significance of ignoring the problem   [6 pages]
    A. Danger to workers and area citizens
    B. Polluted water
    C. Poor morale and productivity—lower profits
    D. EPA fines or prison or both

V. Conclusions   [3 pages]

This organizational scheme is aimed at readers who already know a problem exists and are most interested in how to solve it. Next, they might want to know some background information, such as what caused the problem and even how important it is to solve the problem. Finally, readers might want to know what the writer's conclusions are about the problem and its solutions; thus, the conclusion may reflect recommendations for structuring the solutions, advice about proceeding, or ideas that need to be researched further.

The most frequent errors writers make in constructing problem/solution communications are to overstate or understate either the problem or its solutions. Some writers trivialize a problem, leading readers to believe that it is not serious. Other writers make too much of a problem, creating hysteria where calm should be the order. Similarly, some writers overstate the value of a particular solution, claiming that it is a cure-all when it is only a Band-Aid. Careful investigation, fact checking, and consultation with your colleagues and others knowledgeable about the problem and its potential solutions will help you avoid some of these pitfalls and maintain credibility with your readers. (See Strategy Review 4.2.)

STRATEGY REVIEW 4.2

ORGANIZING BY PROBLEM/SOLUTION

When organizing by problem/solution, be sure to determine how much your readers know about the problem, as well as their attitudes toward it. If they agree that the problem is as severe as you claim, you can follow the direct approach, providing a brief overview of the problem and then moving directly into a discussion of solutions. If the readers must be convinced that a problem exists, discuss the elements of the problem clearly and completely, perhaps even using the indirect approach that lets you present reasons and evidence before you conclude that a problem exists.

In either case, the following strategies will help you review your organizational decisions for problem/solution documents:

1. Identify the problem in terms the reader will understand; accountants understand budget issues, legal teams understand liability issues, and technicians understand technical or procedural issues. Keep your reader's background and expertise in mind as you organize your information.

2. Focus on solutions, if at all possible. Unless you are certain that your reader needs all the details of the problem at this stage, moving on to solutions can be a useful way of contributing to your organization's well-being.

3. Identify areas for further research of your solutions (costs, competing products, timing, scheduling, etc.).

Cause/Effect Organization

Cause/effect organization is closely related to problem/solution because it also typically grows out of a problem. In this organizational structure, however, your readers may already know about the problem and its solutions. Now, they want you to explain how the problem occurred ("How did we get into this mess?") and indicate what subsequent problems were created. For example, your readers might know that the problem is a sulfur spill into the Mahweh River, but until they find out what *caused* the spill, they may not feel very confident about your proposed solutions, their own safety, or the security of their livelihoods.

Most cause/effect documents follow the prescribed order: an explanation of causes leads to an explanation of effects. In a medical report, for instance, stress, poor diet, no exercise, and smoking may be presented as causes that lead to a particular effect: heart attacks. Remember, however, that the causes and effects in one situation may lead to additional causes and effects in other situations. In a different situation, for instance, the effect (heart attack) may be presented as a cause that leads to other effects: damage to cardiovascular tissue, shortness of breath, chest pain, and even death. On a more positive note, the heart attack could also lead to the patient's commitment to moderate exercise, a low-fat diet, and regular physical checkups.

Similarly, the damage to Mahweh River is both a cause and an effect that may lead to additional causes and effects:

Problem/Cause	*Effects*	*Extended Effects*
The pressure gauge on the pump in zone 3 did not register the high sulfur levels and the high flood waters of the Mahweh River	Sulfur spill Contaminated water Mill shutdown Poor morale among employees Poor relations with the community	New system for routine maintenance and checking of pressure gauges and pumps Better system for managing high flood waters Better system for managing sulfur discharges Better system for cleaning pipes Stronger sense of commitment to the community Decreased chances of later spills and damage

As in problem/solution documents, you may have to reverse the order in a cause/effect document, explaining the effects before you explain the causes. In that case, you will be organizing an *indirect* document that explains the results or effects of the situation before describing the source or cause of the problem. Such an organizational strategy is typically used when the writer does not want to accuse someone or something of causing problems until the reader is convinced of the significance or insignificance of those problems. (See Strategy Review 4.3.)

As the director of the Mahweh Water Control, Ben might be reluctant to accuse Davis Paper Mill, which employs nearly half of the area's workforce, of polluting the Mahweh River. After he has described the high levels of sulfur in the water, its effects on the water quality, and the results of his *thorough* investigation of water safety records and the mill's own records, however, this conclusion will be unassailable. By reserving the cause of the problem until the end of the document, he brings his readers along with his reasoning, leading them to the same inescapable conclusion he has reached: the mill is, indeed, at fault. Had he opened his report with such a conclusion, his readers might not have been persuaded; they might even have decided that Ben held a grudge against the mill and was using his report to undermine it. To present his findings most persuasively, Ben organizes his report following this strategy:

- *Problem:* Polluted water.
- *Effects:* Unsafe, undrinkable, and unusable water; massive wildlife and fish kills.
- *Cause:* Excessively high levels of sulfur.
- *Ultimate cause:* A pressure gauge in the Davis Paper Mill's pump in zone 3 failed to read the high levels of sulfur and the high flood levels of the river, allowing the pump to continue substantial discharges into the Mahweh River during its highest flood stages.

STRATEGY REVIEW 4.3

ORGANIZING BY CAUSE/EFFECT

Cause/effect, like other organizational strategies, requires great attention to relationships between ideas. It is easy to assume that because two events happened at the same time, one of those events necessarily caused the other. One of the keys to successful cause/effect organization, therefore, is being able to separate events and look at each one critically and in isolation before trying to link them together. Asking yourself whether cause and effect is the *only* possible explanation for the two events is a good way to question your logic.

Once you are certain that a cause/effect relationship exists, the following guidelines will help you organize your work:

1. Work exclusively with accurate, thorough, up-to-date information when trying to understand and present the cause of some effect; assigning the incorrect cause for certain effects or failing to see the full ramifications of a cause is a sign of incomplete thinking and research.

2. Recognize that cause/effect works for positive situations (the investment in Rancid Air Corporation increased our profits by 10% last year) as well as for negative situations (the investment in the Rancid Air Corporation devastated our public image).

3. Once you identify the cause, determine whether anyone or anything benefits from the praise or blame associated with it. If there is no benefit (the person who solved the problem has already been promoted or the pump that failed has already been replaced), don't dwell on the cause; focus instead on the effects. If your readers need you to identify the *source* of the problem or solution, however, you will need to emphasize the causal element.

4. Be especially careful with your language in writing cause/effect documents. A tremendous difference exists between absolute relationships and probable ones, and your language will clarify the certainty of your claims.

APPLICATION

Applying Organizational Patterns

In a full-length report to the management of Advance Aeronautics, you must describe the situation with the noisy RJ7 engine, including the EPA's concerns and recommendations. A number of organizational strategies could be useful to you:

- *Problem/solution:* The problem of noise and possible solutions.
- *Cause/effect:* The causes of the noise and its effects on the environment.
- *Chronological:* A work log, detailing your team's discovery of the noise problem and attempts to correct it (what you did first, second, third, etc.).
- *Comparison/contrast:* The similarities and differences in noise levels of the RJ7 engine and Advance Aeronautics's UW4 engine.
- *Immediacy/remoteness:* Some quick tune-ups that would reduce the noise plus some long-term design changes that will muffle it.
- *General-to-specific:* The major problems with the noise and the smaller contributing factors.
- *Specific-to-general:* The smaller factors that contribute to the overall noise level.

Now, consider how your message and organizational strategies would change if the report is to be written for the investigators from the EPA. What sort of problem/solution and cause/effect message would you construct for this audience?

Chronological Organization

One of my favorite examples of chronological procedures comes from the television show *M*A*S*H*. Two of the main characters (Hawkeye and Trapper John) have to dismantle a bomb that has landed in the MASH unit's compound. Their commander, Colonel Henry Blake, reads the instructions for performing this delicate procedure to them. Reading a phrase at a time so that Hawkeye and Trapper can perform one task before going on, Henry tells them to cut the green wire, which they do. Then, he reads, "But first, make sure the . . . ." You can imagine what happens: the bomb explodes. Fortunately, it is a propaganda bomb filled with fliers encouraging the enemy to surrender rather than an explosive bomb, but the point is clear: chronological information can be read and followed in ways the writer may not intend—unless the writer pays careful attention to details and can predict how readers will follow the information.

On the job, chronological organization is most frequently used when describing processes or when giving instructions. Descriptions of *processes* that the reader wants to know about, but does not intend to actually perform, are typically written in the third person (he, she, it, they). For example, readers may want to know how a product is manufactured, what steps a hospital takes to ensure quality, or how the accounting department will review some financial data. But the readers themselves will not have a hand in manufacturing the product, ensuring quality, or reviewing the data. Thus, when writing about a process, the writer describes the work that employees or others do—in the order in which they do those tasks. Sometimes, humans will not even be involved, as in descriptions of the process of photosynthesis, desalination, or cross-pollination. Drawing on our Mahweh River scenario, Figure 4.10 shows a chronological process description of the procedure for removing sulfur from water.

Like process descriptions, *instructions* present information in chronological order, but unlike process descriptions, instructions are written for people who will

heading helps orient the reader	**Application of Chemicals**
	The desulfurization process requires two chemical compounds: STG-47, which will
language addresses the process, not the reader or performer	neutralize the sulfur, and WWU-3, which will cause the breakdown of STG-47. The agents are released in incremental dosages that conform to the following three-day timetable:
overview of application measurements	Hour 1 32.5 gallons of STG-47
	Hour 20 42.2 gallons of STG-47
	Hour 25 17.8 gallons of WWU-3
	Hour 48 42.2 gallons of STG-47
	Hour 70 20.9 gallons of WWU-3
	This application method ensures that the exact proportions of all chemicals are
cautions	released at the critical intervals for absorption and desulfurization. Deviations in timing and/or measurements will not only negate the desulfurization process, but will also . . . .
heading helps orient the reader	**Action of Chemicals**
	The blend of chemicals addresses the sulfur content of the river, while equalizing
overview of process rationale	the effects of the added chemicals. This process relies on the acidity of the STG-47, which later breaks down with the addition of the WWU-3. At the first
details	application, STG-47's chemical nutrients are suspended in the water, moving with the current of the river. The second application of STG-47 increases the acidity
transitions help reader focus on the order of the process	of the river's compounds and directly attacks the remnant sulfuric content. Next, the water is ready to absorb the WWU-3; its time-release formula will lessen the severity of the STG-47's acidic effects. As the flood waters continue to recede . . . .

F I G U R E 4.10   Excerpt from a Process Description, Showing a Chronological Organizational Scheme

THE WORLD OF WORKPLACE WRITING

Your Role as an Instruction Writer

In the workplace, technical writers often see instruction writing as their job, especially in the computer industry where these writers compose software documentation, telling readers/users how to use a new software package. Other writers create training materials, telling readers how to perform some process that will be part of their jobs: how to install a circuit breaker, how to sell a new satellite dish system, how to hook up a dishwasher, or how to measure fertilizer for crops. In small companies that do not have a technical writing staff or in your own entrepreneurial ventures, however, you may have to write such instructions yourself, meaning that you must attend to all these details and reader needs.

Another possibility is that, in your role as technician, auditor, or health care specialist, you will be paired with a professional writer assigned to document the procedures you perform on the job. In this case, you will have to communicate clearly the steps and special conditions relevant to chronological procedures. Your knowledge of proper chronological explanations will help you work with this writer and will save valuable time in the revising process.

actually perform the procedure described. Thus, the relationship between the writer and the reader is much closer than the relationship established in process descriptions because the reader relies directly on the writer's clear descriptions and chronology. If you have ever been frustrated by complex instructions, you know the importance of good instructions.

In addition to their chronological arrangement, instructions have several special requirements. (See Strategy Review 4.4 on page 122.) For instance, a good instruction writer will do all of the following:

- Take special care to introduce the instructions so that the reader will have a context for performing the tasks.
- Address the "doer" of the instructions as "you," the reader, whom the writer assumes will be performing these tasks.
- Number the steps in the instructions so that readers will know which steps to perform in which order and can quickly find their place if they are distracted or have to put down the document to perform a task.
- Define any special terms so that the reader will know what's what when performing the procedure.
- Provide transitions that warn the reader that one step follows another ("next," "afterward," "then"), that one step goes on simultaneously with another ("meanwhile," "simultaneously," "at the same time"), or that one step causes other things to happen in the procedure ("consequently," "therefore," "thus").

■ Include graphics for most instructions, a strategy you will learn more about in Chapter 8.

In the Mahweh Water Control scenario, Maria writes special instructions for the water technicians to follow when measuring the sulfur content of the river. She assumes the readers have general knowledge of the equipment they are using, so she proceeds to describe the steps they will follow to get accurate readings on the sulfur content. Note her use of instruction features (an introductory orientation for the reader, a "you" address, and enumerated steps) that guide the reader through the process (see Figure 4.11).

---

overall warnings
come before steps

WARNING: To perform the desulfurization, technicians must wear protective gear: gloves, masks, and safety goggles.

WARNING: The steps in administering chemicals at river zone C must be followed *precisely;* deviations may harm the technician and the environment.

Instructions:

overview of chemi-
cals needed in
procedure

Roman numerals
break steps into
discrete stages

I. Inspect the chemical barrels at the site to ensure the following quantities:
    • 116.9 gallons of STG-47, separated as follows for application:
        • 32.5 gallons
        • 42.2 gallons
        • 42.2 gallons
    • 38.7 gallons of WWU-3, separated as follows for application:
        • 17.8 gallons
        • 20.9 gallons

writer uses under-
stood "you" to
address the reader/
doer

enumerated steps
take reader/doer
through the process

II. *With safety equipment on,* at hour 1, prepare to apply 32.5 gallons of STG-47:
    1. Remove drum lid carefully, being certain not to spill contents.
    2. Using the 3.5 distancing measure on the forklift, move container to the application site's funnel.
    3. Set the base of the drum into the funnel silo.
    4. Tilt the drum at 47° until no more of the compound spills.
    5. Tilt the drum at 90° until no more of the compound spills.
    6. Tilt the drum at 130° until no more of the compound spills.
    7. Return drum to its base.
    8. Return lid to the drum.
    9. Using the retractor on the forklift, set the empty drum in the blue zone, marked at the application site. . . .

FIGURE 4.11   Excerpt from Instructions, Showing a Chronological Organizational Scheme

STRATEGY REVIEW 4.4

ORGANIZING BY CHRONOLOGY

Writing a chronological description requires the writer to do the following:

- Determine whether the reader intends to perform the process (instructions) or learn more about the procedures (process descriptions).
- Determine exactly how much the reader already knows about the procedure.
- See *every* step in the procedure, attending especially to the little steps that might be overlooked.
- Predict which steps might cause the reader difficulty and provide pictures or detailed descriptions that should remove that difficulty.
- Determine which steps must be done in a particular order.
- Use transitions that explain relationships between steps.
- Use comparisons or analogies that describe the procedure according to some task or process the reader already knows.

Comparison/Contrast

Frequently, your work will require you to look at more than one incident, situation, or set of circumstances. In these cases, you will often have to compare (find similarities in) or contrast (find differences between) two or more sets of information. Your challenge is to make sure your reader doesn't see only similarities where differences exist or only differences where similarities exist. Thus, your job is to clarify the relationship between these sets of information.

Because *comparisons* are used to explain similarities, they frequently allow you to explain complex information in terms of a process or scenario that your reader already understands. The following comparisons, which are part of our everyday understanding, demonstrate the value of these structures:

- An X ray is a photograph of your internal bone structure.
- A synthesizer allows musicians to alter the sounds of their instruments, just as most word processing programs allow you to alter the type font of your text.
- A computer's keyboard is like a typewriter's keyboard.
- A dentist's suction instrument is a small vacuum cleaner for removing water and residue from the patient's mouth.

Of course, it is possible to oversimplify similarities, so you will have to be careful about the comparisons you construct. After all, you might frighten someone (especially a child) if you tell her that the dentist will put a vacuum cleaner in her mouth.

Along with comparisons, you may also have to offer some *contrasts*. Contrasts are especially important when readers are likely to misinterpret the seriousness or triviality of a situation because they think it is similar to other situations.

Comparisons and contrasts—along with the criteria on which they are based—often carry strong *rhetorical* implications, meaning that readers are likely to be persuaded on the basis of the writer's choice of comparisons or contrasts. In fact, readers sometimes muster strong opinions about problems or solutions, causes or effects, or any other kind of information based on the writer's selection of criteria. Automobile manufacturers, for instance, would be very concerned if a

---

THE WORLD OF WORKPLACE WRITING

The Role of Ethics in Comparison/Contrast

On the job, you will have numerous occasions to compare and contrast processes, equipment, situations, problems, and solutions. For example, you might compare the marketing features of a highly successful product with the features of a proposed product to prove that the latter will be a moneymaker and should be manufactured. Or you might contrast marketing features to prove that the proposed product should be abandoned. It is crucial, therefore, that you consider the *ethical* bases of your comparisons and contrasts. Although you might select any criteria to form your comparison or contrast, you are ethically bound to select *relevant* criteria.

As an example of the ethical and unethical selection of criteria to support a writer's position, suppose that you have been asked to write a report recommending the selection of a special pump to help neutralize chemical spills. In recommending a pump, you may consider the following criteria:

safety	cost	insurance
service	ease of use	performance
other options	reliability	maintenance

If you wanted to skew the data to give your best friend, who is an equipment dealer, your company's business, which criteria might you select and which might you omit? If you know that your friend's pump is very expensive but also highly reliable and easily maintained, you would probably downplay the issue of cost— perhaps an entirely ethical decision given the importance of the work the pump will do. But what if you also know that a less expensive pump is available that is even more reliable and performs better than the pump your friend sells? Clearly, you are now ethically bound to investigate, compare, and contrast the two pumps and then recommend the best pump for your organization's needs.

writer compared their new car to an Edsel, a car that was a disastrous failure in the 1950s, but note how many of them like to compare their cars (favorably, of course) to a Mercedes, Lexus, or some other luxury car. In a different example, political debaters frequently compare U.S. foreign policy involvements to the involvement in Vietnam—a sure way to make the American public wary of such entanglements. Some writers, in fact, choose comparisons and contrasts with the specific motive of inflaming audience members or calming them.

Thus, by *comparing* your topic to other topics with which readers have positive associations, you can create a positive impression, which should encourage your readers to like your idea, product, or service. By *contrasting* your topic to other topics that have positive associations, you can create a negative impression, which should encourage your readers to dislike the idea, product, or service you are presenting. Hence, the strategy is to create an impression through the positive or negative presentation of your own topic and comparable topics (see Table 4.1).

In the Mahweh Water Control scenario, for example, a team of technicians might think that the procedure for removing sulfur from water is the same as the procedure for removing phosphate or some other contaminates. As the lead researcher on sulfur contamination, Maria will have to clarify that misunderstanding by pointing out the differences, while noting that some similarities do exist. If, instead, her readers rebel against learning the sulfur removal process, thinking that it is too difficult or makes no sense, then Maria will have to point out the similarities of the two procedures, while providing special notes about their differences (see Figure 4.12). (See Strategy Review 4.5.)

sets up discussion of similarities	The process for desulfurizing the river is similar in many ways to the process of desalinating water. Both processes rely on chemical agents that remove or negate the undesirable compounds. Both processes also rely on timely applications of those chemicals. And both processes are highly effective in treating water problems.
similarities	
warns reader of differences	The similarities in the procedures' effects, however, do not extend to the application procedures themselves. For desulfurization, an entirely new procedure—with additional safety precautions—is imperative. First, desalination requires little
differences are enumerated to show more than one or two	more than standard protective gear; desulfurization requires extensive protection due to the acidity of the chemicals involved. Second, the chemical agents used in desalination can be applied in bulk dosages; desulfurization requires precise timing and incremental applications. Finally, the toxins in the desulfurization process mean
transitions separate and distinguish differences	that imprecise measurements or timing can not only negate the positive effects we seek, but can also cause extensive environmental damage in their own right. . . .

F I G U R E   4.12   Excerpt Showing a Comparison/Contrast Organizational Scheme

T A B L E 4.1	Strategies for Comparing Ideas, Products, or Services for Special Results				
Presentation of Your Topic		**Presentation of Comparable Topic**		**Results for Your Topic**	
positive	+	positive	=	positive	
positive	+	negative	=	positive	
negative	+	positive	=	negative	
negative	+	negative	=	negative	

STRATEGY REVIEW 4.5

ORGANIZING BY COMPARISON/CONTRAST

Constructing an ethical comparison or contrast requires that you investigate thoroughly and keep an open mind:

1. Acknowledge your own biases (for or against) an idea before you begin researching and writing. Then, try to control those biases as you work.

2. Be sure to investigate both similarities and differences. You must be careful not to be so carried away with similarities that you fail to notice differences or become so enthralled with differences that you fail to notice similarities. You must also point out these aspects to your reader.

3. Set up your comparisons of ideas, products, or services using specific criteria that you announce in your writing. Some sample criteria include the following:

costs	advantages	disadvantages	safety
resale values	maintenance	guarantees and warranties	service
profits	selection	additional benefits	image

4. Organize the discussion according to these criteria, not according to idea A versus idea B, which requires the reader to make the actual comparisons and contrasts.

5. Write a sound conclusion that reflects the criteria you have used for your discussion. Showing that one idea is better than another, according to the criteria used, and then recommending the opposite idea in your conclusion (despite the evidence offered by the criteria) suggests stubbornness, an undesireable characteristic in workplace writers.

Immediacy/Remoteness Organization

Because successful companies spend a great deal of time planning their strategies for ongoing success, many of their workplace documents attend to details that need to be taken care of immediately and other details that need to be kept in mind for future action. Following this plan, you may arrange some of your documents according to when their information will be used. In a problem/solution report, for instance, you may find that some solutions need to be put in place immediately, while others are long-range plans that may take months or years to implement. (See Strategy Review 4.6.)

Several factors may influence the timing of business's plans:

- Costs
- Other projects or commitments
- Personnel
- Materials
- Legal issues and requirements
- Insurance regulations
- Labor disputes
- Competition
- Morale
- Location
- Space
- Computer capabilities

APPLICATION

Applying Organizational Schemes

Having read more about chronological, comparison/contrast, and immediacy-to-remoteness organizational schemes, how could you use each scheme to provide useful information to the EPA readers? Remembering to address their key concern—noise pollution—determine the kinds of information that would appropriately be used with each of these organizational strategies.

What steps might you describe in a chronological report? What kinds of comparisons and contrasts might you make with the company's UW4 engine? What sorts of solutions or tactics might be best presented in an immediacy-to-remoteness organizational scheme?

When you know your reader is looking for information organized according to deadlines, costs, plans, implementation schedules, or other factors, be sure to arrange your information in the relevant order. Demonstrating that you know which actions should be taken immediately and which can wait will signal that you understand and appreciate the need for careful timing in the workplace.

In the Mahweh Water Control scenario, for instance, consider how important it might be for the Davis Paper Mill to come forward immediately with the news of the sulfur spill. If the mill's executives delay presenting information to the media and avoid taking responsibility for the spill, the citizens are likely to react strongly against the mill. A better strategy is to take immediate measures to investigate and clean up the spill. Doing so will garner a great deal of public support that could have gone against the company had it handled the crisis more underhandedly, complacently, or ineptly.

STRATEGY REVIEW 4.6

ORGANIZING BY IMMEDIACY/REMOTENESS

Immediacy/remoteness documents, which are used primarily for planning situations, show readers which details or work that needs immediate attention and which can wait. Because so many workplaces depend on schedules and plans, this organizational strategy will be especially valuable if you work in an area of the organization that juggles timing, budgets, and new products and services.

To construct a useful immediacy/remoteness document, be sure to follow these guidelines:

1. Based on your workplace's mission, determine the information or recommendations that readers should know and/or act on immediately; such information is likely to involve one or more of the following:

   ■ Any danger posed to or by your organization's products or services

   ■ Potential problems that can seriously damage the work that goes on in your workplace, employee morale, or the organization's image

   ■ Legal rulings that might jeopardize your organization's well-being

   ■ Competitors' moves that can challenge your organization's profits

   ■ Negative attention to your organization from the media, consumer activists, or political activists

2. Although a proactive stance is desirable in the workplace, determine which actions or recommendations readers can delay for a while. A wait-and-see attitude is quite valuable in many workplace situations, especially where additional time may well correct the problem without damaging any relationships or work your employees value.

General-to-Specific Organization

Workplace situations often require you to have a general understanding of concepts such as profits, personnel, legal matters, public relations, and product development. The *general* information you hold about these topics provides you with a context from which to discuss and learn more about these issues when they become more important to your job. In addition to this information, you will need *specific* knowledge about issues related to your job, your department, and your mission in the workplace.

In workplace writing, a general-to-specific organizational structure frequently makes the most sense when your readers do not know very much about your subject or its context. The general-to-specific structure allows you to compensate for their lack of knowledge by presenting some background information "to bring them up to speed," as businesspeople say, before bombarding them with details for which they have no context. A simple example demonstrates what can happen when you begin your document with specifics before providing the reader with a general context (see Figure 4.13). Imagine how managers who do not know the reasons (the general context) for the deductions are likely to respond to this announcement of specific steps the company's board of directors is planning to take.

Figure 4.14 presents a revised version, in which the general conditions are presented before the specifics. Although no workers want to take a cut in salary

---

davis paper mill

memorandum

To: Upper-level Managers
From: James Beam, CEO   *JB*
Date: 24 January 2000
Subj: Salary recoup for cleanup

vague reason with
no context

Because of the cleanup, starting with next week's paycheck, we will deduct

brash plan, likely to
anger readers

- 10% from managers' salaries over $75,000;
- 7.5% from managers' salaries over $50,000; and
- 5% from managers' salaries below $50,000.

closing assumes a
behavior and
attitude that are
highly unlikely in
the circumstance

Thanks for your understanding.

F I G U R E 4.13   Specifics without Context Cause Problems for Readers

davis paper mill

memorandum

To: Upper-level Managers
From: James Beam, CEO   *JB*
Date: 24 January 2000
Subj: Salary recoup for cleanup

context

general overview
of the situation

As you probably know, the environmental cleanup agreement we reached last week with the EPA did not go in our favor financially, although we have gotten line employees back to work—at least temporarily. We will return to the bargaining table the first week of next month, when we anticipate a much more equitable contribution from the state and federal agencies that are at least partially responsible for the flood stages that the Mahweh River reached prior to the sulfur spill. (The unprecedented and unannounced release of 50 million gallons of water from the upriver Falls Lake dam created the greatest basin flooding in the history of our region.)

general action

benefits

In the meantime, we ask your cooperation in a rather drastic move: a one-time *only* cut in your pay (for the end-of-July paycheck only) that will free some funds to pay for some of the beginning cleanup measures. In compensation, we will give each of you a corresponding percentage of company stock, which, despite our problems, continues to rise in market value because, we are told, the public has overwhelmingly approved of our upfront handling of this crisis.

Starting with next week's paycheck, we will deduct

specifics of plan

- 10% from managers' salaries over $75,000;
- 7.5% from managers' salaries over $50,000; and
- 5% from managers' salaries below $50,000.

goodwill
conclusion

This move is certainly not popular with the board of directors, but we do feel confident that it will allow us to get through this very difficult time for the Davis Paper Mill. We appreciate your professionalism and your dedication to the company; your sacrifices will be remembered and rewarded.

FIGURE 4.14   Context before Specifics (General-to-Specific) Aids Reader Understanding

for any purpose, they are much more likely to understand this temporary pay cut when the general situation is presented first, followed by the specifics of what the plan will mean to them. Thus, like the indirect approach, the general-to-specific organizational structure frequently is used to convey bad news by presenting the context and reasons before the specifics.

The general-to-specific organization also works for good news when the reader is likely to be confused by reading the specifics of the writer's message without a general context. By presenting the context before the specifics, the writer prepares the reader to understand the critical details offered in the remainder of the document. (See Strategy Review 4.7.)

STRATEGY REVIEW 4.7

ORGANIZING BY GENERAL TO SPECIFIC

A general-to-specific organizational scheme works best when readers need the larger context before they can understand the various components of your message. To use this scheme effectively:

1. Determine what the big picture is—the overall message or context for your document—and lead with that information.

2. Determine the smaller details or parts of the puzzle that comprise or contribute to that big message.

3. Talk to authorities in the areas from which the smaller details come to make sure you understand the details thoroughly.

4. Present those details as separate components of the overall message.

Specific-to-General Organization

In many of your classes, you have probably learned the dangers of generalizing information. That danger exists in the workplace as well. Nevertheless, carefully researched generalizations can play an important role in helping managers and analysts understand trends, causes of problems, and potentially profitable moves. By looking at a set of specific data, workers can predict consequences, results, strategies, roles, and needs. Thus, one value of specific-to-general organization is that it demonstrates larger conclusions—or allows readers to draw their own conclusions—based on a set of more specific facts.

In special cases, the amount and type of the readers' knowledge, rather than the topic, make the specific-to-general organizational structure preferable to other structures. In these cases, the readers are typically aware of the small picture—the details and day-to-day operations of their part of the company, laboratory, or manufacturing plant—but they lack the big picture. They do not see how their work fits into the larger goals of the company, how plans in one division will help employees in other divisions, or how seemingly simple problems can cause widespread or long-term problems for the company.

Specific-to-general patterns are common in several work arenas. In medicine, for example, physicians compile a list of specific symptoms before reaching a general conclusion (or diagnosis). Your writing instructor will look at several of your writing assignments before generalizing about your writing abilities. And your college adviser is likely to discuss specific details about what you like to do before suggesting a general major in which you might excel.

Returning to the Mahweh Water Control scenario, consider the following specifics that Maria and Ben reviewed to see what generalizations they might logically reach about the Mahweh River spill:

1. The Mahweh River has not flooded in a hundred years.
2. A number of events combined to flood the Mahweh River:
   a. The tremendous rainfall during the hurricane
   b. The release of several hundred thousand gallons of water from the dam upriver to prevent flooding upriver
   c. The wet season just prior to the hurricane
3. The Davis Paper Mill depends on the low flood plain of the Mahweh River for the minimal and environmentally sound practice of releasing overdrains into the river.
4. The high level of water after the hurricane should not have affected the levels of sulfur discharged into the river.
5. The mill did, indeed, discharge too much sulfur into the river.

What might Ben and Maria conclude about this situation? They might surmise that something happened between the routine discharges on prehurricane days and the posthurricane discharge, but they would probably hesitate to suggest that one of the engineers did not monitor the discharge or the pumps properly, or that one of the technicians neglected to measure the sulfur content of the discharge.

APPLICATION

Applying Organizational Schemes

Having read more about general-to-specific and specific-to-general organizational strategies, consider both the big picture and the small details that the EPA readers might need in your description of efforts to correct the noise levels of the RJ7 engine.

What information about your organization and its mission might fit into your discussion? What details about specific strategies your design team has employed might be useful?

Unsupportable charges, even if they are logical based on the facts of a situation, can tremendously damage morale in an organization. Thus, in moving from specifics to generalizations, you must consider the context of the issue within your organization's culture as well as the need for logical, thorough, and well-supported generalizations. (See Strategy Review 4.8.)

STRATEGY REVIEW 4.8

ORGANIZING BY SPECIFIC TO GENERAL

A specific-to-general organizational scheme typically works best for information that might be difficult for your reader to understand or agree with at first. In short, your reader does not see the big picture and consequently cannot understand the conclusions you intend to present in your document. To construct this organizational scheme, follow these guidelines:

1. Identify and describe the various smaller pieces of the puzzle—the details of your message. This segment most likely will include a brief overview of information your reader already knows to provide a context for your message.

2. Include additional details that your reader needs to obtain a sense of your overall message.

3. Lead your reader along with the details, linking them through problem/solution, cause/effect, chronologies, and other organizational strategies to flesh out your message.

4. Conclude with the generalization based on these details that forms the overall message of your document.

Summary

This chapter has described several organizational strategies that you will find useful as a workplace writer. You may not make all your decisions about organizational structure at this stage of the writing process, but you will certainly want to return to this chapter when you review the organization of any document you write.

One of your first decisions about organization will be whether to organize by anticipated reader response (direct or indirect) or by content (problem/solution, cause/effect, chronological, comparison/contrast, immediacy/remoteness, general-to-specific, or specific-to-general). Your readers and their needs will help you make this decision.

The direct organizational strategy works best for readers who are expecting the news or information you have to deliver. In the insurance business, for example, claims adjusters expect to receive letters (and phone calls) about insurance claims—damaged homes, wrecked cars, or stolen possessions. In that case, because the reader expects to be reading about your wrecked car or damaged home, you don't have to "break the news" to the reader. Instead, you can use the direct approach in your letter. But, if you are writing about the wrecked car in your weekly letter to your parents, you might want to break the news more gently by assuring them that you are fine before telling them that the car has been wrecked.

Thus, the indirect approach is appropriate for readers who are unlikely to be expecting the news or information you have to deliver. These readers need to be prepared for your news, and you can best accomplish that task (and retain their goodwill) by opening with a neutral buffer and then explaining the reasons or the facts behind your bad news before presenting the bad news itself. After presenting the bad news, you should try to offer alternatives or benefits of an alternative plan. Finally, your closing should avoid references to the bad news and should try to retain an element of goodwill.

Other organizational strategies—problem/solution, cause/effect, chronological, comparison/contrast, immediacy/remoteness, general to specific, or specific to general—require your understanding of the big picture, as well as the more minute details about which you may be writing. Seeing how a particular problem fits into the structure of your business's routine dealings or long-range plans will help you determine how useful any given organizational strategy might be. For example, it would be embarrassing to suggest that your reader (the company's CEO) immediately update all the computers in your division when the CEO has already planned to move the office to a new building equipped with state-of-the-art computers. Instead of using a problem/solution strategy, you might use the immediacy/remoteness organizational structure; this would enable you to acknowledge that new computers are on the way, while pointing out that certain upgrades are essential for the smooth running of your division in the meantime.

Above all, remember that you can alter your organizational scheme at any time in your writing and revising process. For your final document, however, you should have an arrangement of information that seems sensible to your readers and meets their needs. In other words, there is no universal rule about organizing except that you should think about your readers' needs for information; let that consideration guide all of your decisions about your organizational schemes.

✓ CHECKLIST

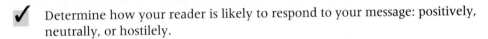 Determine how your reader is likely to respond to your message: positively, neutrally, or hostilely.

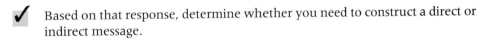 Based on that response, determine whether you need to construct a direct or indirect message.

If you construct a direct message, follow these guidelines:

- Begin with your main idea, completing the sentence, "The main thing I want my reader to know is . . . ." Then, revise for a more appropriate opening sentence.
- Provide all necessary details for the reader of the direct message.
- Conclude the direct document with an upbeat message of goodwill.

 If you construct an indirect message, follow these guidelines:

- Begin with a neutral buffer—a statement with which the reader will agree or at least find inoffensive.
- Provide reasons for the bad news before delivering the bad news punch.
- Try to keep the bad news to a minimum, and work to present a tactful resolution, if at all possible.
- Describe alternatives that might satisfy the reader.
- Conclude the document with an appropriate message of goodwill.

 In a problem/solution document, be sure to do the following:

- Identify the problem in terms the reader will understand.
- Focus on solutions, if at all possible.
- Identify areas for further research of your solutions (costs, competing products, etc.).

 In a cause/effect document, be sure to question your connections between cause and effect; just because one event follows another does not mean it is an effect of that event.

 In a chronological document, determine whether your information should be written as a process description or as instructions: Do your readers want to know how something happens (process description), or do they intend to perform the task themselves (instructions)? In either case, follow these guidelines:

- Strictly adhere to the correct chronology of events in your discussion.
- Test your information to double-check the order of your steps.
- Determine the usefulness of graphics for your discussion (see Chapter 8).
- Use cues to help readers know the relationship between steps ("next," "then," "simultaneously").
- Ask other readers to test your information for accuracy and order, whenever possible.

In a comparison/contrast document, determine whether readers need to focus on the similarity or dissimilarity of two products, services, or ideas. Then, follow these guidelines:

- Organize information according to criteria or ways in which the two subjects are alike or different; do not analyze subject 1, then subject 2.

- Be certain your reader understands the basis for your comparisons and contrasts. (It makes little sense to say that electric hedge clippers are similar to an electric carving knife if the reader has never seen an electric carving knife.)

- Be scrupulously careful in your discussion to point out both similarities and differences; be careful not to mislead the reader about the subject's capabilities, safety, or other qualifications.

 In an immediacy/remoteness document, follow these guidelines:

- Determine the information or recommendations that readers should know and/or act on immediately.

- Determine the information or recommendations that readers can delay for a while.

 In a general-to-specific document, which is used when readers need the larger context before they can understand the various components of the message, follow these guidelines:

- Determine what the big picture is—the overall message or context for your document—and lead with that segment of the document.

- Determine the smaller details or parts of the puzzle that comprise that big message; arrange those details as separate components of the overall message.

 In a specific-to-general document, which typically works best for information that might be difficult for your reader to understand or agree with at first, follow these guidelines:

- Identify and describe the various smaller pieces of the puzzle—the details of your message.

- Lead your reader along with the details, linking them to culminate in the overall message of your document.

 Whatever organizational strategy you choose, be sure to consider its appropriateness for your message and your readers (and their feelings) throughout your writing process.

EXERCISES

Individual Exercises

1. Determine who your audience would be if you were to write about the following situations. Then determine whether you would use the *direct* or the *indirect* organizational approach for each situation. Be prepared to defend your decisions.

   a. You are requesting that your professor change your grade from a C to a B.

   b. You are disgusted with your newspaper's delivery system.

   c. Your best friend was promoted to senior accountant.

   d. You were overlooked for a promotion you think you have earned.

   e. Your organization will be three weeks late shipping an order to an important customer.

   f. Your organization wants to order thirty-five new computers.

   g. The lawsuit against your organization was dropped; report that information to the stockholders.

   h. Your organization is sponsoring a new educational program.

2. Choose any three scenarios in exercise 1 for which you would use the direct approach. For each scenario, do the following:

   a. Write the opening paragraph.

   b. Determine what kinds of supporting details you would add, and write those sentences.

   c. Write a pleasant, appropriate closing.

3. Choose any three scenarios in exercise 1 for which you would use the indirect approach. For each scenario, do the following:

   a. Write a neutral opening statement.

   b. Write the reasons/bad news paragraph.

   c. Write the alternative paragraph.

   d. Write the concluding paragraph.

4. How is your reader likely to take the following bad news? List the reasons you might offer to explain the bad news. Then, list the alternatives you might offer.

   a. No pets are welcome at the bed and breakfast.

   b. Employees' contributions to the health care fund will increase by 4 percent.

   c. The new Pluto station wagon has been recalled.

    d. A hiring freeze means Amelia will not get the new administrative assistant she was promised.

    e. Vacations are canceled.

    f. The warehouse is overstocked.

    g. The electricity in the Branchwood subdivision will be turned off for three hours on Tuesday.

    h. The bookstore has sold out of the textbook for Physics 4300.

5. What might be the causes of the following problems? What solutions might you investigate? Where would you go for more information about the problems, causes, and solutions?

    a. Low morale among employees

    b. A decrease in orders placed by telephone

    c. An increase in complaints about your company's delivery workers

    d. Too many errors entered into the new computer system

    e. Declining sales in a retail clothing store

6. Write a chronological description of one of the following processes. How would the description differ if you were writing instructions? What assumptions are you going to make about your audience?

    a. Making your favorite dinner

    b. Changing the oil in your car

    c. Cleaning an aquarium

    d. Dropping or adding a class at your school

    e. Choosing classes for next semester

    f. Renting an apartment

    g. Brewing homemade beer

7. What similarities and differences do you see in the following pairs of items? Choose three of the pairs of items, and for each pair, write a brief paragraph that compares and contrasts the items. Begin the paragraph with a topic sentence.

    a. A computer and a typewriter

    b. A savings account and a checking account

    c. A life insurance plan and a retirement plan

    d. A hot air balloon and a gas balloon

    e. A fan and an air conditioner

8. Determine which of the following steps you have already completed and which steps you will face in the future. Then, determine which steps you should complete immediately and which steps can wait a while; your response, of course, will depend on where you are in your academic and professional career.

- Get a job
- Apply to graduate school
- Apply for a loan to move to another state
- Sign up for coursework in your major
- Change your major
- Quit your job
- Start your own business
- Open a savings account
- Investigate an internship or cooperative education experience
- Talk to a career counselor
- Talk to your adviser
- Buy your books and school supplies for the upcoming semester

Defend your priorities to various audiences, such as your parents, your business associates, your partner/spouse, your accountant, your boss, and your academic adviser. How did your strategies for arguing change? Did your priorities themselves change? If so, why?

9. Based on the following specifics, what generalizations might you make with some additional research? Where would you go to conduct that research? For what audience might you have to write a letter describing the situation?

   a. John's employees despise him. His department is poorly organized, and its sales are down again this quarter. His employees call in sick frequently.

   b. The engine makes a lot of noise, smokes, and is hard to start.

   c. The Umsteads' investment portfolio is stagnant. They are paying more in taxes this year than ever, and their financial analyst never returns their phone calls.

10. Review the following paragraphs and determine the proper order of the sentences. Be sure to start with the topic sentence or main idea and omit irrelevant or unethical statements.

    a. What kinds of people get promoted here? What is the appropriate rate of advancement? What criteria do managers use to evaluate and promote employees? It makes little sense to align yourself with the company troublemaker. If you want to get ahead, it's important to make friends with people who are knowledgeable about your company. Make sure your relationship is aboveboard. If people think you are sleeping with your mentor, they will lose respect for you. They should know a great deal about the company's products and services, of course, but they should also know something about the company's culture. Choose a mentor who is unselfish with his or her time, who will answer your questions, and who does not feel threatened by you. Most important, you should seek out the help of someone who carries a great deal of respect in your workplace.

b. You should make sure that you and your partner have the same business philosophies about reinvesting in the company, keeping supplies in stock, and hiring additional personnel. You will learn all sorts of things about your partner that you never imagined before you went into business together. Going into a business partnership is a lot like getting married. I'm not talking about putting the cap back on the toothpaste either. How will you settle disagreements? If one of you pouts and the other always gives in, a real relationship (business or personal) doesn't stand much of a chance. What if one of you wants to get out of the business? For example, Kim's partner started selling supplies to their competitor. Having a plan for resolving conflicts is crucial to a successful partnership.

c. The meeting starts promptly at 3:00, so if you want a seat, you'd better get there early. We'll have a big discussion about how to develop good study habits so that you can do well in college. Only an idiot would miss this session. Cookies and soft drinks will be provided. Mr. Jamison from Career Counseling will be on hand to answer questions about the importance of good grades when you start hunting for a job. We will be through by 5:00, so you can catch the 5:10 bus back to your apartment. See you there! If you are unsure about juggling a full college course load, and you don't know how to organize your time, you will want to come to our College Study Skills Session.

Collaborative Exercise

Choose a simple process that you learned as a child, such as how traffic lights regulate traffic, the safety procedures a school bus driver follows when picking up children, or how your allowance was calculated. In language appropriate for a child reader, write a description of that process. Next, choose a simple task that you learned to perform, such as sharpening a pencil in a rotary sharpener, planting seeds in a vegetable garden, or playing a childhood game. In language appropriate for a child reader, write instructions for that process.

Write a separate paragraph evaluating the process description and instructions you wrote for the child reader. Answer the following questions in your paragraph:

a. What kinds of special considerations did you make for your audience?

b. What kinds of pictures might you add to make your description and instructions clearer?

c. What do such writing tasks teach you about writing for *adult* audiences, especially the kinds of readers for whom you will be writing on the job?

d. What sorts of decisions will you have to make about chronological organization for your on-the-job writing?

 **ONGOING ASSIGNMENT**

■ Consider the planning and research you have done so far for your manual introducing newcomers to your campus or workplace. Which organizational strategies described in this chapter might be useful? Following the model in the Application on p. 118, how might you use each of the organizational strategies to present a different kind of information for a slightly different purpose in your manual? Which organizational schemes are going to be most relevant for your audience, purpose, and topic?

CHAPTER 5

Drafting Your Workplace Documents

Quite simply, and to many novice writers' chagrin, there's no magic formula for writing a draft. There is no right way to go about it, but on a positive note, there is also no wrong way to go about it. The only goal at this stage is to get something on paper or on your computer screen.

Unfortunately, some writers freeze when they come to this often deceptively simple task of getting started. Or they may begin again and again and again but are never quite satisfied with their writing; they keep starting over until, finally, they have to keep something because the document is due the next day. You, too, may have procrastinated with your own writing projects; perhaps you believed that if you waited long enough, you would be enlightened about the direction your writing should take. More than likely, though, all you ever felt was panic.

To help you avoid delays and the accompanying panic, this chapter will give you some strategies for getting something on paper—strategies that good writers use to create the first draft, based on their plans, research, and organizational decisions (see Chapters 2, 3, and 4). Then, you can practice some prewriting strategies to draft the introduction, discussion, conclusions, and, if necessary, appendixes. You will probably like some of the strategies but feel uncomfortable with others. That is all right because the key to writing well is finding strategies that are comfortable for *you*. The strategies that work well for you may not work for others. The strategies presented here are useful for all kinds of workplace documents— letters, memos, reports, proposals, manuals, or any other kind of communication (see Part II for these forms)—and may be employed at any stage in your writing

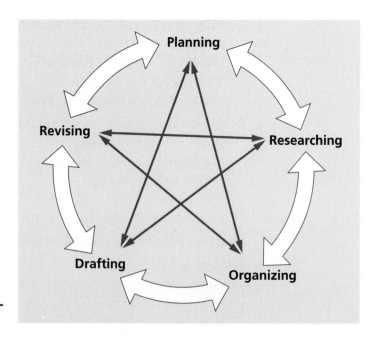

FIGURE 5.1

A Model of the Writing Process

process. Figure 5.1 should remind you of the way the stages of the writing interrelate. As a result, you will find that some of the strategies presented here have already been discussed in earlier chapters. (See Strategy Review 5.1.)

STRATEGY REVIEW 5.1

REVIEWING YOUR PLANS, YOUR RESEARCH, AND YOUR ORGANIZATIONAL DECISIONS

One of the most useful starting points for writing a draft has nothing to do with turning on your computer or arranging your pen and paper. Rather, you should reconsider your plans for writing (Chapter 2), your research (Chapter 3), and your organizational options (Chapter 4). By reviewing your *plans,* you refresh your memory about your actual writing assignment—its content/context, audience, purpose, scope and limitations, methods, definitions, and plan of development, as well as your role as a writer. When you transfer those plans into a draft, you may revise some elements, but the plans should help you establish at least the major ideas you want to communicate to your readers.

By reviewing your *research* within the context of your plans, you can begin to see which information will serve as main ideas and which will support those ideas. You may also discover that you need more evidence or that some research is a bit skimpy or overstated. Now is a good time to look for and fill gaps in your research.

Next, you should consider (or reconsider) the *organization* of your document. As discussed in Chapter 4, decisions about organization may come at the prewriting stage or may be part of your revision strategy, but most writers recommend considering organization at the drafting stage to clarify how your ideas fit together. Knowing, for instance, that you are following a problem/solution organizational scheme allows you to divide your work into a problem section and a solution section. Doing this allows you to see your writing as smaller tasks, rather than as one overwhelming chore. The simple strategy of dividing your work can alleviate much of the anxiety you may feel about a writing assignment.

Reviewing your plans, your research, and your organizational options should remind you that writing is a *recursive,* not a linear, process in which successful writers often go back and forth between the stages of work.

Experimenting with Prewriting Strategies

Once you have reconsidered your plans, reviewed your research, and reconsidered your organizational strategy, you are ready to start on the document itself. In this chapter, we will follow the drafting strategies that Collin Outland uses to draft a discussion of flexible hours for the Radiology Department of Cedars Hospital. Because the hospital has lost several of its top employees to Jamestown Memorial,

Collin's boss has asked him to investigate the feasibility of introducing flextime in their organization. Flextime is a work plan that allows some employees to set their own hours to accommodate their preferred work schedules (nights or days; mornings or afternoons) or other responsibilities, such as young children or elderly parents. As he works, Collin uncovers another problem in the Radiology Department that might contribute to the high turnover rate: a tyrannical manager, John Schmidt.

In the initial stages of his writing project, Collin drafted a plan of work, conducted some research, and adopted an organizational strategy (problem/solution) to support his writing project:

- *Audience:* The manager of the Radiology Department and top-level managers at Cedars Hospital. They *are concerned about* the high turnover in the Radiology Department *and wonder whether* flextime might work for the department and provide incentives for employees to remain.

- *Purpose:* Thus, the purpose of this document is to review the characteristics of a good flextime model; to review Cedar Hospital's structural needs for employees' work schedules; and to combine these two topics to see if a flextime plan will work for the Radiology Department.

- *Research sources:* (1) Management books and articles on structuring flextime; (2) on-line discussions with organizations that use flextime; (3) surveys of employees to see if they are interested in flextime; and (4) interviews with top managers to learn their concerns about flextime.

- *Organizational schemes:* Probably a problem/solution organization that emphasizes solutions because readers already know about the problem; this scheme would be combined with strict criteria to determine the feasibility of the idea for Cedars.

Looking over these plans, Collin realizes that although he has the information to start writing, he still does not feel comfortable about putting those first words on the screen.

If you, like Collin, feel that your current strategy does not really help you get into the writing task, or if the first phase of your writing is typically filled with panic and a sense of blankness, or if you waste a lot of time starting over and over again, you may want to consider some useful *prewriting strategies*. As we discuss them, it is important to realize that although these are common strategies, they are not the only ones. Furthermore, although we call them prewriting strategies, you can return to them throughout your writing, at any stage, to help you move along with your first or even subsequent drafts.

Talking Out

Increasingly valued in the workplace are opportunities for workers to talk over their problems and ideas—whether they involve personnel issues, quality control, sales leads, or advertising strategies. Writers frequently use this strategy, too; in fact, you have probably done so, unknowingly perhaps, when you met with a writing instructor to talk about an assigned paper. Simply put, *talking out* a written communication means telling a listener your plans for the communication or asking questions about it. Issues you may talk about include the following:

- Your perception of your topic
- Your audience and its needs
- What you want to tell the reader first, second, third, and so on
- Concerns about the ethics of some bit of information
- Alternative organizational strategies
- Sources of your information
- The proper tone of your document
- Whether to include certain statistics
- Formatting decisions you will have to make
- Concerns about the length of the document
- Attempts to understand the readers' likely reaction to your communication
- What you'd *really* like to say (but perhaps don't dare)

All these issues may not come up, of course, but they represent a sample of the concerns that writers often discuss with others—their bosses, their coworkers, their colleagues in other departments, other writers, researchers, and even their best friends, spouses, or partners outside the workplace. Sometimes the listeners may respond with questions or advice, but often they just listen.

The following brief dialogue is an excerpt from Collin's talking out session for the Cedars Hospital report:

Collin: I've got a report due Wednesday on the Radiology Department's high turnover rate. You know they lost two technicians last spring. We replaced them, but then lost three more. I'm not sure how to present some of this information to managers.

Boyce: What do you think is the problem?

Collin: It looks as though there's a problem with morale, but most of that problem seems to hinge on the director's inflexibility. We suggested looking into a different managerial system for the Radiology Department, but I think that created a lot of fear. I mean, for one thing, the director runs that department with an iron fist and makes a lot of people miserable. But they are reluctant to complain because they are afraid he'll retaliate against them.

Boyce: Is it likely that would happen?

Collin: Yes, and that's the rub. Currently, we need the employees in the department to speak out if we are going to make significant managerial changes. But they won't do it publicly because of their fear. The director has been known to give really bad schedules to people he sees as his enemies. And they are always afraid that their salaries and chances for promotion will suffer. Most of them are afraid they will get a poor letter of recommendation if they do try to leave. The truth of the matter is that without a change in the director's views on how to run an efficient department, the high turnover is going to continue. But I don't think I could say that in the report.

Boyce: Do you think you could just present the data in the report—you know, about the high turnover and the possibility of a morale problem, but offer more specific instructions to the director in his confidential annual evaluation?

Collin: That's possible. Do you think he would understand the seriousness of his moves? And, would the technicians believe that anything had changed if they don't hear about the specific instructions to the director? Also, would it be ethical to keep that conclusion out of the report itself?

Boyce: I think you could make him understand the seriousness. But you've got a point about the ethics angle. Perhaps you could . . . .

What good does this strategy do? For some people, talking out a problem or situation (whether in writing or some other context) helps them clarify their options, questions, and decisions—even when the listener doesn't offer any advice. When students go to their writing instructor's office, they often ask how to proceed with their writing projects. When the instructor asks what their instincts tell them, they often come up with very acceptable responses. In other words, they really don't need the instructor's guidance as much as they need a sounding board—someone to listen to them think or plan out loud.

The danger, of course, is that you may irritate people if you take up too much of their time or pester them too often about your assignments. Some people cannot construct even the simplest writing assignment without talking to every available (and sometimes not so available) listener. You will have to be respectful of your listeners and their obligations; your most considerate move, therefore, is to ask for an appointment when your listener can spend some time with you on your assignment. That way, you should have the listener's undivided attention as you discuss and clarify some of your choices in writing on the job.

Brainstorming

Similar to talking out your assignment is *brainstorming*, which involves unrestricted thinking about a topic. Unlike talking out, however, you typically brainstorm alone or with a group of writers who share your writing assignment. Using this strategy, you list—on paper or on your computer screen—every idea that crosses your mind about the topic, the readers, the major and minor points, and the results you want the document to accomplish. You may be as whimsical or as methodical as you want, but most writers who use this technique argue for the whimsical approach because it does not limit their thinking. This freedom allows you to come up with creative aspects you might not have considered in a more formal, restricted, critical thinking process.

Collin, for instance, brainstormed and came up with the following list of ideas for his report on the morale problem in the Radiology Department:

morale	director	inflexibility	complaints
lawsuits	turnover	job sharing	management
retraining	replacement	performance	temporary help
reassignment	jerk	fear	termination
subcontract	flextime	guidance	retaliation

Notice that there's no particular pattern to these words; some of the ideas seem repetitive, and the list includes various parts of speech (verbs, nouns, adjectives). Collin will incorporate some of these words or ideas directly into his report, but others (like "jerk") will never appear in the final draft.

At this point, Collin is ready to make some decisions about how to use his list of ideas. He may decide, for instance, to begin with the facts: the high turnover rate and the low morale in the department. Then, he may decide to focus on ways to make the department more flexible: hiring temporary workers and allowing job sharing and flextime. Next, he is ready to talk about the technicians' issues with John Schmidt, the department manager—especially his inflexibility and propensity for retaliation. Wanting to end the report with solutions instead of problems, Collin may conclude with suggestions for improving the department or, more specifically, for improving the manager's performance through retraining, reassignment, or management seminars.

From this example, you can see that brainstorming is a valuable technique, especially when you do not have listeners to participate in a talking out session. Be sure to get all your ideas on paper or on the computer, however, because you do not want to overlook any significant ideas.

Freewriting

When confronted by a blank page or screen, many good writers recommend going ahead and starting to write even if you do not have a clear idea of what you intend to accomplish—a prewriting strategy called *freewriting*. By writing about the information you hold, you may see a main point develop; that point then allows you to focus on that issue, sharpen your sense of what you want to accomplish, and see a clearer structure for presenting the information. In fact, some writers claim that starting with a firm idea of what their writing should accomplish can sabotage their writing. Once they abandon their fixed notions, a more useful slant on the topic may emerge—one that more adequately meets both the writer's true purpose and the reader's needs.

Unlike brainstorming, where you list ideas as words or phrases, in freewriting you put your ideas into sentences. You write for a specific amount of time, writing or typing any ideas that come to mind exactly as you think of them. The key is to continue writing, not stopping for any reason. If you are temporarily stymied, you can write "I have no idea what I'm talking about," "What in the world is this leading to?" or even "asdlfkajsdf; alkdjfa; slkfja; slfja; slkfjadsljfa; sdljkfa; ldjkf." What's important is that you keep writing or typing, working through your uncertainty until you're back on the topic and adding more ideas and information.

At the end of a freewriting period (which may be a limited amount of time—say, five minutes measured by an egg timer you keep nearby), you can develop the useful ideas and delete irrelevant ones. Or you may see an idea that you'll want to use later but not at this particular point in your writing.

Figure 5.2 shows a paragraph from Collin's freewriting about adding a flexible workforce to the Radiology Department. Of course, you immediately notice

One possibility for increasing the flexibility, and therefor the work satisfaction in teh radiology deparment is to institute a plan for hriing temporary workers when the case load is quite high or workers are out sick. These temporaries are usually ~~women or men who are~~ brtween jobs or women who have had babies and don't want ot be out of the home for too long, like a full-time job would probably make them be. But they are all certified of course. We might also look into the idea of job sharing. Some radiology technicains at largers hospitals don't work as many hours as our techs do they might want ot work here partime.

Solution? · define · conditions · people? · Stereotypes? · Sounds awkward · relevance? · new idea start new para · address in separate segment on certification

FIGURE 5.2 Collin's Freewriting for His Report on the Radiology Department's Workforce

some typographical errors, disorganization, redundancy, and awkward wording. All these weaknesses would be cleared up in a subsequent draft, but for now Collin at least has something concrete for his discussion of flexible workstaffs. And having something to work with is often the best result of freewriting.

Formal Outlining

Some writers are perfectly comfortable with the strategy of *formal outlining,* which they learned in their early years of writing instruction. Many writers like the aesthetic appeal and the visual logic of an outline.

Strategy Review 5.2 shows the standardized structure of a formal outline. Given the formal nature of outlining, you should adhere to a few rules, which will be especially important when you convert your outline to a table of contents for longer documents (see Chapter 15):

1. Your outline cannot have an A without a B or a 1 without a 2. The guiding principle of outlining is that you are *dividing* major issues into smaller or minor issues. As you know from math, you cannot divide something into fewer than two entities. If you divide a stack of coins, for instance, you must have at least one coin in a second pile or you haven't divided the pile at all.

STRATEGY REVIEW 5.2

THE HIERARCHY OF FORMAL OUTLINES

One characteristic of formal outlines is the structure of the lists, which does not vary from subject to subject. The unchanging hierarchy of formal outlines allows writers/readers to know that the relationship between ideas with Roman numerals versus ideas with Arabic numerals will always be the same; in other words, the system provides information even when the subject matter is unknown. The hierarchy of formal outlines is as follows:

    I. Roman numerals for major headings or ideas
       A. Capital (uppercase) letters for second-level headings or ideas
          1. Arabic numerals for third-level headings or ideas
             a. Small (lowercase) letters for fourth-level headings
             b. small letters for fourth-level headings
          2. Arabic numerals for third-level headings or ideas
       B. Capital letters for second-level headings or ideas
    II. Roman numerals for major headings or ideas

THE WORLD OF WORKPLACE WRITING

Scientific Notation

Few works extend much beyond four levels into fifth- or sixth-level headings. When they do, many writers prefer to use scientific notation because it is a simpler system than the Roman and Arabic numerals and alphabet letters of formal outlines.

In fact, many organizations, especially government and legal organizations, insist on scientific notation in formal documents. Some organizations even require each paragraph to have an individual number, which makes it easier to refer to the information in the paragraph. A scheme for scientific notation follows:

1.0 Major ideas are numbered sequentially, followed by a 0.
    1.1. Secondary (minor) points are numbered first by the major heading under which they fall (the first "1"), and second by which point under the major heading they are (the second "1").
    1.2. The second minor point under the first major idea.
        1.2.1 A third-level point that is the first point under the second minor point under the first major idea. This point can be considered the first minor, minor point.
        1.2.2 Another third-level idea; it is the second minor, minor point.
2.0 The second major idea.

---

2. Although you may divide your discussion into as many smaller segments as you deem necessary, at some point you may end up with so many little segments that your discussion appears to have no substance. Combine smaller elements of your discussion to prevent choppy or superficial treatment.

3. Your outline must be grammatically parallel. Although parallelism is discussed more thoroughly in the Brief Usage Guidebook at the end of this text, you should remember that equal ideas must share the same grammatical structure. If the first item in a list begins with a verb, all subsequent items must begin with verbs. If the first item begins with a word ending in "-ing," all subsequent items must begin with words ending in "-ing." This grammatical convention signals to readers that each grammatically parallel topic carries equal emphasis.

Figure 5.3 is a formal outline that lays out the topics and their relationships to each other for Collin's report for Cedars Hospital. The advantage of this formal outline is that it clearly constructs the order of ideas for Collin's report; further, it shows relationships between ideas. You'll note, for instance, that the idea on de-

title reflects subject
focus

major heading
provides context for
remaining discussion

three problems, to be
discussed in detail

major heading

four forms of alter-
nate workforce to be
considered

three characteristics
of leadership needed

plan of action

The Cedars Hospital Department of Radiology: Developing a Flexible Workstaff

I. Introduction and Overview of the Department of Radiology

II. Problems in the Department
   A. High turnover rate
   B. Low morale
   C. Fear of administration

III. Solutions for the Department
   A. Alternate Workforce
      1. Temporary workers
      2. Job sharers
      3. Flextime workers
      4. Part-time workers
   B. Leadership
      1. Flexibility
      2. Vision
      3. Commitment

IV. Conclusion: A Call for Leadership and Goodwill

FIGURE 5.3 Formal Outline for Collin's Report on the Radiology Department's Workforce

veloping an alternate workforce is just as important as the problem of high turnover. Thus, a formal outline allows you to establish the order and relationships of the topics you'll be discussing before you begin your draft.

Listing and Mapping

Many writers are uncomfortable with the rigidity of formal outlining and simply list their ideas. More formal than brainstorming, a conscientious *listing* strategy requires you to challenge, however briefly, the relevance of each item as you add it to your list. In other words, listing is censored brainstorming.

    Listing also helps you to see relationships even as you construct or revise your list. Knowing which points are likely to be major points and which are likely to be minor points helps you categorize your list of ideas as you construct it. Then, you can graphically map (with arrows, numbers, or other icons) the relationships between ideas on your list. If you do not know these relationships as you begin to list ideas for your document, you will have ample opportunities later to revise your list, combine related ideas, and delete concepts that do not belong in your document. (See Strategy Review 5.3.)

COMBINING LISTING AND MAPPING TECHNIQUES

You may recall from Chapter 2 the strategy that Nicholas used when he listed ideas for the progress report on the boat design project. After listing his ideas, Nicholas drew a "fence" around the ideas that were relevant to his project, leaving out the ideas he wanted to discuss but decided were irrelevant to this particular writing project.

Mapping strategies involve graphic maneuverings of listed ideas and allow you to visualize the relationships between ideas in your list. The following mapping strategy shows a different kind of graphic construction, which Collin uses for his project:

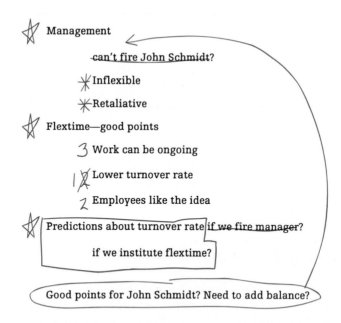

Notice that Collin has deleted the references to firing John Schmidt and has put stars beside the ideas he wants to include. The 1, 2, and 3 under flextime indicate the order in which Collin thinks he'll discuss these points. Collin also is considering adding some comments on Schmidt's good points to the management discussion.

Other techniques for getting started on a draft are certainly possible, and you may find that your own process involves two or three of these strategies. As long as you are comfortable with your method for beginning to write, it hardly matters what that process is. If you are uncomfortable with your current process, however, try some of the prewriting strategies in the following Application for getting something on paper.

APPLICATION

Applying Prewriting Strategies

For the Applications in this chapter, you can use the following scenario to practice some of the drafting strategies you learn:

> Using your workplace, your home, or your parents' home (assume your parents are elderly) as the site for your investigation, determine the usefulness of security systems and recommend a system that is financially feasible, reliable, and manageable for those who must turn it on and off.

The following outline of a writing plan will help you understand the parameters of your writing project:

- *Subject:* Security for your workplace, your home, or your parent's home.
- *Purpose:* How to protect the site from break-ins.
- *Audience:* The users of the system (if you choose your home as the site, then the audience may be your spouse, children, or roommates).
- *Scope and limitations:* (1) Recommendations cannot cost more than $x for the initial outlay or $x in yearly fees (the financial limitations of users at the selected site will determine these parameters); (2) the system must be reliable; (3) the system must be easily turned on and off.
- *Methods:* Review of security data; interviews with security agencies; review of literature on security systems; interviews with users about their needs.
- *Definitions:* Types of security systems will be defined.
- *Plan of development:* Description of problem, advantages and disadvantages of three popular security systems, recommendation of best system.

With a partner and a tape recorder, talk out the concerns you have about completing this project. Note any special concerns you have about your audience's needs for information. At the end of your talking out session, address the following questions:

(continued)

1. What kinds of information and concerns did you reveal in your session?
2. What kinds of help did you get from your partner (questions, prompts, additional concerns)?
3. How will your concerns translate into the draft you want to write?

On your own, try a few more prewriting strategies for your security system project. Try at least two of the following strategies, making sure that you try at least one *new* strategy that will challenge you to explore a technique that is different from those you currently use:

1. Brainstorm a list of concerns related to your topic, your audience, your purpose, or other elements of this project.
2. Setting a timer for five minutes, freewrite about the element of your writing project about which you know the most.
3. Construct a formal outline, following the guidelines in the text and Strategy Review 5.2.
4. Devise a list of topics, showing the relationship of the ideas to each other via mapping.

Putting Prewriting Strategies to Work

As an additional strategy for helping you get started writing, good writers often recommend that you start with the segment of your document (letter, memo, report, etc.) that you know best; in other words, write about your own contributions to the project before you write about your colleagues' contributions. Or you may want to write about the final stage of a project before you write about its initial stage. Your revising process will allow you to reorganize these segments of your document into the most logical order for your readers' needs (see Chapter 6).

Combining the technique of writing your "easiest" segment first with some other strategies can help you overcome the helpless feeling sometimes associated with writing:

1. Allow yourself plenty of time to write. If you wait until your deadline to write, you are almost certain to experience more anguish, blankness, panic, and unproductive periods.
2. Remember that this is just a rough draft—it isn't supposed to be perfect.
3. If you run out of ideas, return to the talking out, brainstorming, freewriting, outlining, and listing strategies.

4. Perform any necessary rituals you associate with writing—getting into your favorite bathrobe (if you're at home, of course!), turning on soft music, brewing a fresh pot of coffee, or sharpening pencils. (Just be sure these rituals do not extend into serious procrastination ploys.)

5. Talk to your readers as if they were standing right in front of you. What is the main point you want them to know? How do you know your point is accurate? What do you want them to know next?

6. Try tape-recording your ideas. Don't worry if you ramble as you talk, but try to get on tape all the ideas necessary for your document.

7. Start your first sentence with "What I really want to say is . . . " and fill in the blank.

8. Keep your sense of humor. Laughing at yourself prevents frustration and can help you stay focused on your writing assignment.

9. When all else fails, take a break—quit for a while, work on some other project, take a walk, or find some other diversion that will let you clear your mind.

Most important, you should allow yourself enough time to write so that you don't take your first draft too seriously. Although it will certainly be the basis for your final document, the draft must go through some changes if it is to be the best writing you can produce. If you take your first draft too seriously, you are likely to "fall in love" with your writing and be resentful or even obstinate about making changes in it. Recognize your draft for what it is: a draft that will require additional thought and work before it becomes the polished document you ultimately will pass on to a reader.

Drafting the Introduction for Workplace Documents

In workplace writing, introductions for almost all documents (except some letters and memos) provide the same kinds of information. The introduction should convey the following information (notice that the elements are identical to those in the plan you constructed for your writing in Chapter 2):

- *Content/context:* The overall subject of your communication and its importance to the organization or some specific part of the organization.
- *Audience:* The intended readers of your work.
- *Purpose:* The writer's reason for communicating and the reader's reason for reading.
- *Scope and limitations:* The parameters of your discussion—what you do and do not intend to discuss in the document.
- *Methods:* The sources of your information.

- *Definitions* (optional—depending on the readers' knowledge): Clarifications of any terms your readers may not know or terms that may be used in a special way in the context of your document.

- *Plan of development:* An overview of the major points that follow in your document—typically presented in only one or two sentences.

Rather than including separate sentences for each element of your plan in the introduction, however, you will compress and combine the information into a few readable sentences.

For Collin's report to the administrators and manager of the Radiology Department at Cedars Hospital, this strategy is put into action in Figure 5.4. You'll note that no definitions are provided in this introduction because Mr. Schmidt, the reader, is familiar with the work of his department. Were the same report being sent to readers who are not radiology specialists or administrators, however, several definitions would have to be provided.

As you become more comfortable with these elements of the workplace document's standard introduction, you'll see opportunities for combining information, especially the content/context, audience, and purpose. The following sen-

<table>
<tr><td></td><td>The Cedars Hospital Department of Radiology: Developing a Flexible Workstaff</td></tr>
<tr><td>subject</td><td rowspan="8">This report describes the current working conditions in the Department of Radiology at Cedars Hospital. This department is staffed by six full-time radiology technicians and two overseeing physicians; the department currently serves the hospital's traditional patients, but also serves the emergency room and four outpatient centers in the metropolitan Boise area. From this report, readers will be able to ascertain the problems of high turnover and low morale in the department and will be able to determine what sorts of steps might alleviate these two problems. The report focuses on developing alternative workstaffs via temporary hires, job sharers, flextime workers, and part-time workers; the report does not consider the budget ramifications at this time (a later report, if desirable, will address budgetary factors). The information for this report was gathered from the department manager, the radiology technicians, and the physicians assigned to the department. Current health care literature in periodicals and books and on the Internet has provided additional information on alternative workstaffs. Following this introduction, the report addresses the specific problems in the department, following by a discussion of solutions, which hinge on the viability of creating an alternative workstaff (and pool of workers) for the Radiology Department.</td></tr>
<tr><td>context/background</td></tr>
<tr><td>purpose for reader</td></tr>
<tr><td>scope and limitation</td></tr>
<tr><td>methods/sources of information</td></tr>
<tr><td>plan of development</td></tr>
</table>

FIGURE 5.4   Draft of the Introduction to Collin's Radiology Department Report

tence, for example, gives you an idea of how smoothly those elements can be combined:

> This report will help the department manager [audience] make a decision [purpose] about investing in new workforces [content] to increase our staff, which is currently suffering from high turnover rates and poor morale [context].

As you can see, introductions in workplace documents are somewhat, if not radically, different from the introductions you have written for papers in other classes. That's because, unlike readers of essays or fiction, readers of workplace documents are not reading for pleasure. They are reading for information so that they can learn or do something—usually something crucial to their jobs. They do not care to be entertained or amused; they want to be informed. A well-written introduction should tell your readers all of the following:

1. They are reading material that is appropriate for them—that is neither over their heads nor irrelevant to their needs (established through your statement of audience, purpose, and scope and limitations).
2. They will see the relevance of your work to the workplace as a whole (content/context).
3. They will know what they can and cannot expect to find in your work (scope and limitations).
4. They will be able to understand difficult terms because you have explained important terminology for them (definitions).
5. They can rely on your information because it was gathered through credible, current resources (methods).
6. They will find particular kinds of information in your document in a specified order (plan of development).

APPLICATION

Drafting the Introduction

Based on the parameters you established for the report on a security system for your home, your parents' home, or your workplace, outline the kind of information you need to provide in a document written for the appropriate readers. (Although you would never write such a document to your partner or parents because we do not communicate with our loved ones via reports, the same strategies you use to write in the workplace will serve nicely for our purposes.) Then, draft the introduction.

By providing these elements in the introduction, you preview for your readers the kinds of information they can expect in the rest of your document. You also signal that you know how workplace documents are introduced, further demonstrating your competence as a workplace writer.

Drafting the Discussion for Workplace Documents

Based on the information you have previewed in the introduction, the remainder of your document should deliver on your introductory promises. Thus, the discussion section of your document should describe more thoroughly the major points you want to make (*claims*); it should also include supporting details that prove the accuracy of your statements (*evidence*) and provide coherent links between the claims and the evidence (*logic*).

Constructing a Claim

As you learned in the previous section on writing the introduction and in the previous chapter on organization, most workplace documents begin with a major premise or *claim*—a statement asserted and then supported by evidence or proof. Claims typically grow out of situations that you identify as good or bad, right or wrong; thus, a claim is an assertion based on the goodness or badness of a situation and/or how it should be preserved or changed.

In the Cedars Hospital scenario, Collin makes the following claim:

Flextime will improve the working conditions in the Radiology Department.

This statement acknowledges that the current situation is less than ideal (because a change is being suggested). Then, using the direct approach (see Chapter 4), Collin can organize the remainder of his writing project to describe flextime and support the idea he has raised in his claim.

Dangers in constructing a claim lurk in the following constructions, however:

1. *"All-or-none" statements.* A key characteristic of poor writing (and weak thinkers) is an all-inclusive claim that *everything* or *nothing* can go wrong, that *everyone* or *no one* is doing the job right, that we *always* do things this way, or that we have *never* done things this way. The danger in these statements is that just one contrary example negates their accuracy and punctures your argument. Carefully describing the context in which events occur and people act is critical to establishing a valid claim.

2. *Broad generalizations.* Similar to "all-or-none" statements are broad generalizations such as "Technology is sweeping the world." In fact, a number of developing countries have extremely limited access to technology (from refrig-

erators to computers), and many Americans with plenty of money and access still refuse to use computers. Such generalizations can lead to simplistic and poorly thought-out arguments.

3. *Obvious statements.* Obvious statements are the crutches of insecure writers. Uncertain of how to present the heart of their arguments, they rely on statements that are indisputable, but that also provide no new information to the reader: "In today's society, you can no longer assume that you and your possessions are safe." One of the primary reasons this statement would be considered obvious is that no one is arguing otherwise; no one, for instance, is saying "In today's society, you can go wherever you want and assume that you and your possessions are safe."

Weak claims are a problem because they cannot be adequately supported, making your job as the writer far more difficult than it should be. And without support, these statements can make the writer seem foolish or naive.

This discussion of good and bad claims presupposes a direct approach to your topic. Occasionally, however, you may decide that the indirect organizational approach is preferable for your writing project. Then, you will reserve the major premise for the conclusion of your work, slowly building your evidence until you reach the ultimate claim. As Chapter 4 explains, such a strategy works best when readers are likely to be offended by or skeptical of your claim.

As one of the readers of Collin's report, John Schmidt, for example, would probably be offended if Collin opened the report with accusations and criticisms of Schmidt's management style. Collin decides, therefore, to focus on a different major claim: that flextime will improve the working conditions in the Radiology Department. He may reserve his suggestions for revamping Schmidt's management style for the conclusions and recommendations at the end of the report—or save them for an employee evaluation (see Chapter 13) that is entirely separate from the report.

Identifying Sources of Evidence

Readers often find information in workplace documents unconvincing. The writer hasn't provided enough information to support the claims, or the readers' own instincts and logic make them skeptical about the information. Consider the following claims and determine how believable you think they are:

1. Being poor can be fun.
2. ONPEP can make you look ten years younger in five days.
3. A college education is a waste of time.

If you feel skeptical about any of these statements (or all of them, perhaps), you will expect the writer to provide a good deal of persuasive information to be provided in the remainder of the paragraph or document. The following information might help persuade you that these statements have some validity:

1. Humorous testimonials from newlyweds who describe how they have pinched pennies and worked together to make a life for themselves as a couple

2. Scientific experiments with photos of "before and after" treatments; testimonials from satisfied customers; publications in highly respected medical journals

3. Evidence from skilled laborers that they do not need college training; testimonials from other workers who do not want to be promoted

Providing the larger context—and special situations—that establish the validity of suspicious statements may be part of your work in writing on the job. Make sure you provide enough information that readers know they can rely on your work.

Writers most frequently rely on the following kinds of evidence to support or clarify their statements:

- *Statistics:* Numerical data and percentages.
- *Examples:* A scene, event, story, or fact that provides at least one account of the phenomenon in question.
- *Testimonials:* Accounts from people who have experienced the phenomenon.
- *Eyewitness accounts:* Descriptions from people who saw the phenomenon but were not directly involved.
- *Experiments:* Attempts to recreate the phenomenon at will; *scientific* (valid and reliable) experiments demand closely guarded conditions that employ a set number of factors (or controls).
- *Specifics:* A breakdown of the components of a larger topic.
- *Credible sources:* Support of knowledgeable and recognizable experts on the topic.
- *Survey results:* Responses generated from questions posed to those with, presumably, firsthand experiences about a particular phenomenon; responses may be presented as statistics, discussions, graphics, and the like.
- *Anecdotes:* Stories or narratives that support the phenomenon.
- *Graphics:* Pictures, charts, and graphs that provide visual evidence of the phenomenon.

All forms of evidence are not appropriate for every topic, and some evidence will be inappropriate for the reader's needs. Other kinds of evidence will fall short because the reader simply does not value the source.

In the Radiology Department scenario, for instance, Collin would not provide evidence from experiments because flextime is not a scientific phenomenon that would be performed under laboratory or controlled conditions. He might, however, provide some statistics about the number of flextime workers, graphics showing the increasing number of American organizations that are trying flextime, and perhaps even testimonials from people who have worked in a flextime situation. Considering all forms of evidence and your readers' attitudes toward them will help you select the proper evidence to support your claims.

Challenging Your Evidence

Throughout this text, you have read cautions about the ethics of organizing and incorporating information into your communications. Using valid supporting evidence is crucial to proving your claims. It is essential to realize, however, that evidence can be flawed or manufactured. And some of it, though impressive, may not be relevant to your topic or may not prove your claims. The following discussion shows what can go wrong with each form of corroboration and encourages you to challenge all your information.

Statistics

Political watch groups are notorious for skewing data to "prove" that their way of thinking is correct. From a single set of statistics, they can deduce any number of interpretations. The trick, of course, is that, in themselves, statistics do not mean anything; they require analysis, interpretation, or cause and effect explanations. And as you learned from Chapter 4's discussion of cause and effect, any number of causes can lead to any number of effects. Attributing the right causes to the right effects requires serious work and clear thinking. When dealing with statistics on the job, be sure to ask a reliable statistician to clarify your interpretations if you are unsure of them. (Taking a business statistics course in college is a good idea, too.)

Examples

Like statistics, examples can be skewed when ideas are inaccurately linked. Most problematic is offering a single example as a model for a larger principle. In fact, that's how many inaccurate stereotypes arise.

Many southerners, for instance, would have a problem with the designation of either President Bill Clinton or Senator Jesse Helms as a "typical southern politician." In some cases, of course, a single example may prove your point: "Jake Neuss is a thief; for example, he was caught red-handed and later convicted of stealing $4,000 from the Widows' and Orphans' Society." You hardly need more examples of Jake's thievery to prove your claim. But be sure to offer more than one example for ideas or claims that are likely to be challenged.

Testimonials

Because of problems with understanding what happens to us, many people offer testimonials that are simply wrong. Their descriptions of certain events or experiences may be distorted for any number of reasons: the drink they had at dinner, their predisposition to believe in certain phenomena, or the payoff they received from the questioner. Some testimonials strain our common sense, while others play on our indulgence in wishful thinking.

For instance, numerous "miracle" products flood the market each year; their sponsors make millions off the gullibility of a public all too willing to believe testimonials about rapid weight loss, youth pills, or hair-growing tonics. For a testimonial to be credible, the speaker (testifier) must be of high character, the claim must be believable on some level, and the medium in which the testimony is offered should be respectable as well.

Eyewitness Accounts

Just as testimonials are sometimes unreliable because the testifier was disreputable or, more innocently, too close to the event to be objective, eyewitness accounts are often erroneous because of fear, haste, or loyalties. Court records, for instance, are filled with witnesses who have lied under oath because of their desire to help or hurt the defendant or because of their confusion about the particulars of the event. Even in the best of circumstances, when eyewitnesses intend to be accurate, their memories or vision can be clouded. In television courtroom dramas, for instance, the eyewitness often adamantly identifies the defendant, only to learn that the real culprit was someone who resembled the defendant or wore clothing similar to the defendant's.

On the job, eyewitness accounts are common when reporting problems or accidents; be sure to get the most complete information possible from as many sources as possible. But also be sure to state that your information is based on eyewitness accounts, which may lend either credibility or skepticism to your information. You will have to determine how much your reader should rely on the accuracy of those accounts.

Experiments

Experiments are frequently sponsored by organizations or groups with something to gain. Such experiments can sound very impressive when, in fact, readers should be skeptical about their results. Many people, for example, are suspicious of experiments on smoking that are funded by the tobacco industry. Impartial experimenters and scientific experiments demand closely guarded conditions that employ a number of factors (or controls) in any given experiment in a stringent attempt to rule out fraud or skewed data. Many companies, such as pharmaceutical companies, not only test new products in their own laboratories, but also hire independent laboratories to test the products.

When using information derived from experiments, be sure to check the source of the experimentation and any possible connections with the company or agency that will benefit from the experiments. Further investigation into the reputation of the laboratory or the scientists involved will also help you assess the reliability of the results.

Specifics

As you learned in Chapter 4's discussion of generalities and specifics, writers have to be cautious about attributing certain specifics to a large "umbrella" generalization; similarly, they must be careful about generalizing based on a limited set of specifics. Sometimes, a single detail, inaccurately attributed to a generalization, will endanger the credibility of the entire argument.

If you want to prove that your boss is incompetent, for instance, you will have to provide some specifics of his incompetence. But presenting a list of a hundred errors he has made will likely raise suspicions about your motives. In other words, overstating a case by providing too many specifics or by incorporating specifics that are trivial or do not really prove your boss's incompetence can damage your credibility.

You will have to decide how many specifics you will need to make certain generalizations; consulting with your colleagues is a useful check. Investigate your facts carefully, making sure that the specifics you offer truly contribute to your overall argument.

Credible Sources

The support of knowledgeable people is often enough to persuade us to believe any number of ideas. Experts on the economy, resources, labor, marketing strategies, legal issues, personnel policies, and numerous other business concerns are frequently cited in workplace documents.

One of the biggest problems with business research, however, is that credible sources sometimes contradict each other: one group of experts says the economy is getting stronger while another group claims the economy is in serious danger. In this case, credibility often depends on how often the group is correct, rather than on more common gauges of credibility such as the institutions or think tanks with which they are affiliated.

Survey Results

As Chapter 3 warned, a unique combination of problems can arise from using survey results as proof in a workplace document. First, because surveys typically rely on the respondents' personal experiences, you must be wary of their interpretations of those experiences. For example, in many early gender surveys, only a few women in very drastic cases claimed they had experienced any discrimination or harassment on the job. As women have become more educated about what constitutes discrimination and harassment, however, they have also become more aware of how many of their experiences result from inappropriate workplace behaviors. Second, surveys frequently offer results in statistical formats, introducing the problems of skewed data discussed earlier under Statistics. Third, although surveys are supposed to be conducted with rigid controls, many of them do not adhere to the scientific methods of experimentation required to produce valid and reliable results.

One of the easiest ways to create an invalid or unreliable survey or to obtain distorted data is to ask an inappropriate group of respondents to answer a survey. Asking men whether women have been sexually harassed in the workplace, or vice versa, would produce questionable results—although these surveys would produce interesting accounts of gender-crossed *perceptions* of harassment in the workplace. A well-formed survey means having access to people who actually know the information you seek.

Anecdotes

Anecdotes are similar to testimonials and eyewitness accounts. An anecdote is a story or narrative that is supposed to support the described phenomenon. Although they are typically quite entertaining or startling and are frequently attributed to well-known people, anecdotes can cause great problems because they are often fictitious. For instance, the story of George Washington's cutting down the cherry tree and then professing his honesty is a historical anecdote—it never happened, yet (ironically) the story has been used through the years to teach children the importance of telling the truth.

Using anecdotes to enliven a workplace communication may also cause problems because the stories can trivialize the point you are trying to make. When you tell a humorous or outlandish story, the reader may have difficulty retaining a proper perspective about the remaining message. When in doubt about the effect an anecdote will have, stick with the facts.

Graphics

Like statistics, graphics can be used to prove almost anything because disreputable people can distort the pictures that are supposed to provide evidence of the phenomenon. Although we will talk more about the ethical use of graphics in Chapter 8, you should know that when used to prove an idea, graphics must be carefully constructed to match readers' expectations about their use.

Irrelevant Data

Sometimes information is valid, but it simply doesn't belong in a particular document. Some writers, whether intentionally or not, introduce irrelevant data into their workplace writing—because they want to pad a document they feel is too short or because they are not thinking clearly enough to delete irrelevant information. Incorporating irrelevant data into a workplace document may not be unethical per se, but hiding the real information from readers is. And confusing readers by including information they do not need can certainly damage your reputation as a clear thinker.

Several kinds of irrelevant information can crop up in workplace communications, but most of it involves one or more of the following:

- Statistics that are impressive or even startling, but do not have much to do with the topic
- Graphics that are showy, but do not really help the reader understand
- The writer's inappropriate commentary on a situation or event, frequently presented as speculation, attempts at humor, or derision
- Repetition of earlier points
- Improper context for argument

Although issues of relevance will also be important in the revising process (see Chapter 6), if you already see irrelevant ideas that you might be tempted to incorporate in a final document, you should eliminate them at this early stage.

THE WORLD OF WORKPLACE WRITING

Avoiding Logical Fallacies

Because readers rely on the information you provide, workplace writing requires you to be particularly certain of your data. Investigating reasons for problems can take unusual turns in the workplace; you should be sure of your information before you point a finger at people or events that have created difficulties or before you praise people or plans that have resolved difficulties. For example, a common problem with cause/effect is assigning the effects to the wrong causes. Typically, the confusion is caused by proximity in time. The writer thinks—erroneously—that two events are linked because they happened at the same time. Or the writer decides that because one event occurred before another, the first event *caused* the second. Careful analysis will help prevent you from making such errors in logic and judgment.

Other problems arise when you jump to illogical conclusions. For example, the following specifics can lead to several possible conclusions:

Specific Details

1. Teachers have to be evaluated every semester by their students.
2. Students hate getting bad grades.
3. Students often evaluate a strict grader negatively.
4. The students' evaluations are considered when the teachers' boss determines the appropriate amount for the teachers' merit pay raises.
5. Negative evaluations, brought on by students' resentment of teachers with high standards, can hurt the teachers' chances of getting fair merit pay raises.

(continued)

General Conclusions

1. Students should not evaluate teachers.

2. Students' evaluations should not be considered at all in determining merit pay raises.

3. Students' evaluations should be considered as only one measure in determining appropriate merit pay raises.

4. Teachers should give everyone an A so they'll be sure to get good evaluations.

5. Because students evaluate easy teachers more positively, only teachers with negative evaluations should get merit pay raises.

Although some of these conclusions may seem absurd, the general results demonstrate the kind of interpretations to which the specifics can lead. In fact, only by extending the argument does the absurdity of these conclusions become clear.

Many readers and writers who are inexperienced with a particular topic fall victim to illogical conclusions because of their lack of knowledge. Thus, the careful workplace writer investigates and offers sound proof that conclusions are truly sensible and do not mask underlying inconsistencies or absurdities.

Linking Your Claim and Your Evidence through Logic

Many writers become so familiar with how their evidence supports their claim that they forget that the reader might not see the connection. Thus, the relationship between your situation (your claim) and the evidence you offer (often obtained from other sources) may not be clear to the reader, who is asking "What does this have to do with the topic?" To counter such confusion, you must carefully construct a bridge between your claim and your evidence. Several strategies will help:

1. Acknowledging differences in situations

2. Using transitions to describe relationships ("similarly," "consequently," "on the other hand")

3. Constructing "if . . . then" reasoning

Collin, for instance, uses his research as a basis for explaining how flextime might work for Cedars Hospital and constructs bridges between his claim and his evidence (see Figure 5.5). With his claim fully supported by the evidence, and those two elements linked by logic, Collin can proceed to draft the discussion.

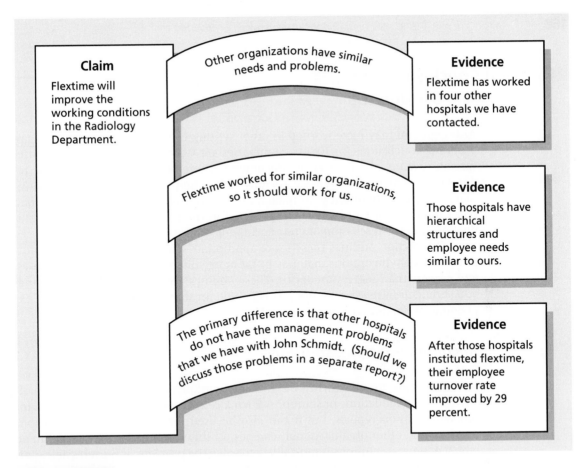

Claim

Flextime will improve the working conditions in the Radiology Department.

Other organizations have similar needs and problems.

Evidence

Flextime has worked in four other hospitals we have contacted.

Flextime worked for similar organizations, so it should work for us.

Evidence

Those hospitals have hierarchical structures and employee needs similar to ours.

The primary difference is that other hospitals do not have the management problems that we have with John Schmidt. (Should we discuss those problems in a separate report?)

Evidence

After those hospitals instituted flextime, their employee turnover rate improved by 29 percent.

FIGURE 5.5 Bridges between Collin's Claim and His Evidence

 APPLICATION

Drafting the Discussion

Draft the primary claim you want to make about a security system for your chosen site. What sorts of evidence will be most useful in persuading your readers? What kinds of evidence should you avoid—perhaps because it would be too technical for your reader or is not the kind of evidence they would value? Then, build bridges between your claims and your evidence that will establish the logic of your ideas for your situation. You may wish to follow the bridge model (Figure 5.5) Collin used to draft his discussion.

Then, depending on your instructor's requirements, draft the discussion sections of your document. For our purposes here, however, you may draft just one argument or segment of your discussion.

Drafting Conclusions for Workplace Documents

Although you may have learned in other writing classes that summaries are appropriate conclusions for papers, summaries are typically offered as front matter (prefatory material) in workplace documents. Therefore, a summary is a weak, redundant ending for a workplace document. You may, of course, offer a few summary statements to orient your reader, but effective conclusions do far more than recap information you have already offered in the prefatory material, the introduction, and the discussion of your document.

This section outlines these more appropriate endings for your communications, offering you options that may be far more suitable for your topics, purposes, and readers than mere summaries. These endings are all based on the idea that you should *draw conclusions,* not just conclude. In short, they depend on your explaining "What does this mean for us?"

Recommendations/Solutions

One of the most useful conclusions for many workplace documents is a section offering recommendations or solutions. Such a conclusion is most typically used for problem/solution reports, but it can also be used for cause/effect, comparison/contrast, and other organizational schemes. In this section, you may recommend which of several solutions is most likely to solve the problem, is most feasible, or is least disruptive. (See Strategy Review 5.4.)

Although instincts are important in the workplace, a reader will rarely be satisfied that they are the best grounds on which to base important decisions. Thus, you must explain the criteria on which your recommendations are based. Furthermore, your criteria must match the reader's expectations and needs. Imagine how embarrassing it would be to offer recommendations based on a sense of urgency and moving from immediate-to-remote implementation stages when your readers think your recommendations are based on costs. In other words, you might lose all your credibility if you have proposed an expensive plan because it offers the most immediate relief for the problem, but your readers expect you to offer the most cost-efficient plan.

Your recommendations may correspond to the following criteria:

- Costs or other budget matters
- The mission of the organization
- Space
- Personnel needs
- Deadlines (legal, business, environmental, or other forms of deadlines)
- Tax structures
- Immediate-to-remote implementation schedules

- Equipment or technological needs
- Materials availability
- Locations

STRATEGY REVIEW 5.4

LISTING RECOMMENDATIONS

In reports and other documents, recommendations are frequently presented as lists, a formatting issue discussed further in Chapters 9 and 15. For now, however, you should consider whether you want to list your recommendations or describe them in paragraphs. Lists are simpler to read and easier to recall than paragraphs, but they may oversimplify your recommendations when you want to make sure your readers understand all that your recommendations entail.

Collin's report on the operations and problems of the Radiology Department at Cedars Hospital concludes with the list of recommendations in Figure 5.6. The bases on which he makes these recommendations are highlighted for you.

overall
recommendations

. . . In conclusion, the results of the surveys, interviews, and additional research performed for this report suggest that the Department of Radiology should investigate the feasibility of hiring an alternative workforce for its staffing needs. Specifically, the manager should begin the following steps:

specific
recommendations

1. A specific recruiting strategy (outlined in Appendix A) for bringing in temporary workers
2. An advertising campaign for hiring part-time workers
3. An announcement on the Internet and on the hospital's web site of positions to be filled
4. An internal initiative to institute job sharing and flextime among current staff members

concluding
recommendations

To improve morale in the department, these steps for restructuring the workstaff should be followed up with special morale-building incentives: careful review of job performance records, pay increases, promotions, and disciplinary procedures.

FIGURE 5.6 Recommendations as a Conclusion for Collin's Report on the Radiology Department

Significance or Consequences

Instead of offering recommendations or solutions to problems, a conclusion may explain the significance or consequences of certain problems or workplace situations.

Collin's report on morale problems in the Radiology Department, for example, might conclude that if the problem remains unresolved, the consequences *to the readers* are lower profits, lower morale, even higher turnover, and poor patient care. Of course, significance and consequences may also be positive, based on good news presented throughout the document. When the department manager realizes that his inflexibility has caused serious problems for the department, his changed attitude may result in higher job satisfaction for the workers in the department, higher productivity, and better patient care—all resulting in improved morale as well (see Figure 5.7).

The most important point to remember is that you should present the significance or consequences in terms that affect the reader, presumably someone who is strongly concerned about the best interests of the organization. When the reader's personal best interests conflict with the organization's (as in our scenario where the restructuring of management will severely weaken the manager's powers), you will have to decide how best to offer such consequences. In this

conclusion consequences consequences of no change are lost employment and higher costs	Failing to recognize and address the problems in the Department of Radiology can have long-lasting, severe consequences for Cedars Hospital and its reputation for excellent patient care. It would be unreasonable to expect the remaining staff of the department to continue working in the current conditions. The costs of hiring an entirely new radiology staff could be as high as $59,000, based on conservative estimates of advertising/recruiting costs, initiation classes, and errors.
major consequences severity; consequences	Most severe, of course, is the damage done to patient care and, thus, to Cedars' outstanding reputation. Because so many of our patients do go through the Radiology Department, and because understaffing and poor morale are so easily sensed by patients, the problems in radiology could easily reverberate throughout the hospital, increasing dissatisfaction in numerous other departments whose workers feel that radiology is too slow and is creating a backlog of service to patients. . . .

FIGURE 5.7   Consequences and Significance as a Conclusion for Collin's Report

case, you may find that the reader could better handle other responsibilities; thus, the manager would lose some power in one area, but gain power in another. However you resolve the conflict, your ethical responsibility, of course, is to protect the *organization*'s best interests.

Trends and Predictions

Many conclusions suggest trends and offer predictions about how certain issues, covered in the discussion of your document, are likely to affect your company. *Trends* are patterns of activities, behaviors, or attitudes. Trends in business describe the dominance of certain business philosophies, consumer buying habits, or hiring practices. *Predictions* use trends as a basis for estimating or forecasting future activities, behaviors, or attitudes. Business experts, for instance, might predict an even heavier reliance on technology, more emphasis on employee leisure hours, and greater demands for equity in the workplace.

Many trends and predictions in workplace documents are based on precise research and marketing information. To compete, most organizations try to anticipate consumer needs for the future as well as for the present. Some companies realize their products are likely to be short-lived. For example, toy manufacturers know that their products are likely to be fads. Yo-yos, for instance, go in and out of fashion with children, as do hula hoops, trolls, marbles, and certain dress-up fashions. These companies try to anticipate fluctuations and are constantly looking for new toys that will catch children's eyes and become "must-haves" (especially at Christmas). Only by understanding trends and making accurate predictions can these companies stay in business beyond the life of the latest frenzy.

Other organizations have identified numerous factors that will determine their products' or services' long-term viability, and they consider each of these factors whenever they embark on a new plan or strategy or review their current and projected successes. These factors include the following:

technology	globalization
legal status	diversification of product lines
competition	social concerns
aging of the population	political climate
health issues	costs and interest rates

Organizational planners attempt to anticipate changes in consumer needs, buying power, and other concerns. They stake their careers on being able to predict how long consumers will want their organization's products or services and what consumers are likely to want next. If the needs of your organization's customers are changing, so that the organization's products or services must also change, you will probably learn to predict such patterns; in the meantime, you may be asked to participate in teams whose primary concerns are to watch for signs that consumer needs are changing and then create products and services that meet the new needs.

In the Radiology Department scenario, the workers have shown a preference for a flexible work arrangement. In doing so, they are part of a trend: many productive workers prefer hours that allow them to be at home with their children or let them work when they are at their peak. Knowing the value of trained workers, many organizations are accommodating such preferences. Organizational planners predict that the way American workers work will change even more drastically in a future filled with technology and conflicting demands.

Plan of Action

Some conclusions require combining solutions, consequences, trends, and predictions into an appropriate plan of action. In such cases, your document's discussion section alerts readers to changes or problems in the workplace; your conclusion sets out a particular strategy for acting on those changes or problems.

A plan of action addresses the cynical, but all too frequent, response to many workplace suggestions—"Nice idea, but how are we going to accomplish it?" Incorporating a plan of action in your conclusion demonstrates that you not only have a clear view of solutions, consequences, or predictions, but have also devised a tactic for what to do next.

Collin's conclusion in his report on the Radiology Department may offer suggestions for solving the department's problems, describe the consequences of ongoing high turnover and poor morale, or even predict that the problems are likely to persist if nothing changes in the department. Most readers, however, will also appreciate an outline of a specific plan for what to do next (see Figure 5.8).

Be sure to investigate the feasibility of your plan of action, as it will have to work within the context of your department or organization. You will have to talk with several of your colleagues and your supervisors to determine exactly how doable some of your ideas are, but arguing for a plan's feasibility or investigating its feasibility further is also part of the purpose of constructing a plan of action.

Questions for Further Research/Investigation

As the discussion of plan-of-action conclusions pointed out, you will sometimes have to conclude workplace documents with ideas for further research or investigation. Such conclusions may be frustrating for writers who want to provide all the answers in a single document. Nevertheless, the limitations of your assignment—along with the urgency of meeting your deadline—frequently mean that you cannot present an all-encompassing document.

In many workplace documents, conclusions about the need for further research and its direction are standard. Even when ideas are thoroughly investigated and presented as desirable, several investigations may be set up as part of

order of steps	In summary, we need to institute an immediate plan of action, following these steps:
awareness of issue	1. We need to help our employees understand that we know there is a problem, that we are aware of several causes of the problem, and that we
plan of action	are working on a strategy to correct the problem. A series of employee/ management meetings should be scheduled.
awareness of issues	2. We need to investigate and then initiate a plan for instituting alternative work schedules. Based on our current research, the best strategy appears to
	a. survey employees to see who wants to work what kind of schedule;
	b. determine how many employees need to remain as traditional, full-time
plan of action	employees and how many can work alternative schedules;
	c. produce a mock-up schedule, with blanks for unavailable workers that might later be filled with temporary or part-time hires;
	d. develop a policy statement for the work of alternative workstaff; and
	e. advertise open positions and flex hours that are available for radiology technicians.
awareness of issues	3. Because one of the primary problems with high turnover and poor morale also hinges on the management of the Radiology Department, we also
	need to investigate more thoroughly the work habits, temperament, and
plan of action	judgment of the current manager. Initial research suggests Mr. Schmidt might benefit from retraining, especially in areas of management sensitivity and accommodation of diversity. Ongoing strategies for working with Mr. Schmidt include . . . .

FIGURE 5.8   Plan of Action as a Conclusion for Collin's Report

the implementation schedule to alert organizational planners to problems they may not have anticipated.

In the Cedars Hospital scenario, even if the alternative workforce is presented as the most desirable solution for reducing high turnover in the Radiology Department, ongoing research/investigations will determine the best schedule for the workers, the hours that will require the most workers, and special benefits requirements. In short, planners want to know about potential problems before they arise. Thus, it is critical that ongoing investigations provide useful information about day-to-day operations (see Figure 5.9 on page 174).

Whatever content you deem most appropriate for the conclusion you write, your decision should be based on the type of information that will be most useful for your readers. Although a brief summary may be useful, it is hardly the most valuable information you can provide at the conclusion of a workplace document.

purpose of
additional research

To determine the correct path for the Radiology Department's growth and stability, we need to investigate a number of ideas about creating an alternative workstaff:

specific questions to
be answered

1. How many workers actually want to work an alternative shift?
2. How successful are alternative workstaffs in hospital environments?
3. Does patient care suffer with the frequent turnover of staff members?
4. Do worker benefits and insurance change because of the changed schedules?
5. Are there any hidden factors that might affect the efficiency of an alternative workforce?

results of research

additional or
alternative plan

Additional research and surveys should help us answer these questions and file a completed report within thirty days. In the meantime, we should also investigate the best means of restructuring the management situation in this department, perhaps by instituting mandatory retraining through our new management seminars. . . .

F I G U R E 5.9   Questions for Further Research as a Conclusion for Collin's Report

APPLICATION

Drafting the Conclusion

Given the introduction and discussion you have crafted, determine the kind of conclusion that is best for your readers and their needs. Does the information you have provided in the document support that type of conclusion? Why or why not? Draft the conclusion.

Drafting Appendixes for Workplace Documents

As you draft your introduction, discussion, and conclusion, you may find numerous pieces of information that might interest or be useful to your reader but fall outside the scope of your document. Including this information might enhance your image as a careful writer but might also irritate your readers if this material gets in the way of more relevant and useful information. In such cases, good writers construct an appendix, where the information will be accessible to readers without obstructing the primary purpose and information of the document.

Most good writers recommend drafting the appendix the same way you draft all the other segments of your documents. As you prepare the appendix, you are likely to see parts that need to be reworked in light of your audience, their needs, and your purpose. The following are some of the materials most commonly included in appendixes:

- Complex calculations that would overwhelm readers if placed in the body of the document
- Additional sources of information
- Lists and addresses of references
- Oversized graphics, maps, blueprints, and the like that cannot be reduced and incorporated into the body of the document
- Works cited (see the Brief Usage Guidebook)

There is no prescribed order for appendix materials, although the order should correspond to the order in which the materials are discussed in the document. Thus, if your document refers to calculations, then addresses, and then maps, your appendix should provide that information in the same order: calculations, addresses, and maps.

When preparing the report on the Radiology Department, Collin decided that several items were more suitable for the appendix than for the text of the document itself: a spreadsheet of schedules for radiology technicians, a list of management seminars that the manager should attend, tallied results of his survey, and preliminary budget calculations for the effects alternative schedules would have on the department's profits.

Remember, however, that an appendix is not a dumping ground for all of the additional information you find on your topic. Rather, it is a carefully constructed resource that, if tapped, will extend the reader's knowledge.

Summary

In this chapter, you have learned some strategies for drafting your workplace documents. A common strategy for getting started is to review your ideas from the planning, researching, and organizing phases, described in Chapters 2, 3, and 4. You might also remember that beginning with your easiest segment, whether it's the introduction, part of the discussion, or the conclusion, can help alleviate some of your stress about looking at a blank page or computer screen.

Other strategies that many successful writers use to get started include various prewriting techniques. *Talking out* is the process of discussing your ideas and your concerns for your draft with a partner or colleague. From your discussion, you should gain some insights about ways to present your information to your audience in order to achieve the purpose you have established for your document.

Brainstorming, which generates an unrestricted list of ideas about your topic, can be especially useful when you aren't sure what the parameters of your discussion should be. By reviewing the topics you have listed, you should be able to detect which topics go together and which should be deleted from consideration. Then, you may be able to make some decisions about the arrangement or organization of your ideas.

Freewriting draws on the brainstorming strategy, but requires you to write your ideas in sentences, moving along without censoring your ideas or stopping. At the end of a freewriting session (typically timed in five-minute increments), you should look at your writing and determine which ideas are valuable and deserve inclusion or further development in your draft. Again, you may be able to make some decisions about the order of the information for your final draft.

For those who are especially keen on organizing their ideas at the drafting stage, *formal outlining* offers both a strategy and a structure for ordering information. Many writers find the aesthetic appeal of a formal outline reassuring because it reminds them that they know where they are going with their topic. Thus, they avoid the feeling of floundering that sometimes stymies writers.

Those who do not like the rigidity of a formal outline may find simple *listings* useful at the drafting stage. In this strategy, the writer makes a limited list of ideas (unlike brainstorming where no limits are imposed) and draw arrows, circles, dots, or whatever to associate similar items (an additional technique called *mapping*). Lists also allow writers to include examples and specific types of support they intend to use to develop a topic—elements that technically are "not allowed" to appear in a formal outline.

Next, the chapter addresses the kinds of content you should provide in a workplace introduction, discussion, conclusion, and appendix—all in the context of what your reader needs and expects to find in your document. The standard introduction for workplace documents includes content/context, audience, purpose, scope and limitations, methods, definitions, and plan of organization. Following this scheme, you can provide the information your reader needs to understand what follows in the remainder of your document.

The discussion section of a workplace document requires you to provide the details and proof (*evidence*) of your primary assertions (*claims*), which are most often made in the introduction. Writers rely on a number of strategies for presenting details and proof in their works: statistics, examples, testimonials, eyewitness accounts, experiments, specifics, credible sources, survey results, anecdotes, and graphics. All these forms of evidence, unfortunately, can also be used in unethical ways, so you must take special care as a writer (and as a reader) to use information properly to enlighten your reader and protect your own reputation. You must also build bridges between your claims and your evidence, showing the relationship of those ideas to your own situation.

Conclusions in workplace documents are rarely summaries because most introductions summarize the document's findings. The final segment of a document should draw conclusions—not summarize. In concluding a document, you may need to offer recommendations or solutions to the problem your document addresses, describe the significance or consequences of your subject, offer predictions or describe trends based on the information you have uncovered, offer a plan of action, or raise questions for further research. Such content at the end of the document leaves your readers with a clearer sense of how to interpret your message and what to do with it.

Finally, you should determine whether any of your ideas belong in appendixes instead of in the document proper. Appendixes are excellent places to put oversized documents (such as blueprints, maps, and spreadsheets); they also should include any technical or scientific information that might overwhelm the reader if placed in the text of the report. Works cited throughout your report also belong in a list in the appendix.

Although all writers (even bad ones) have their own strategies for generating drafts, the key is to make sure you are comfortable with your process. If you feel you waste too much time or panic when trying to draft a document, try some of the strategies and insights offered here. You may modify these approaches in any way you want, and you may return to them at any stage in your writing process.

CHECKLIST

✔ Review your plans, your research, and your organization for your document, according to the information in Chapters 2, 3, and 4. You may need to alter your plans or find additional information. If so, make a list of questions and find the answers or leave blanks in your draft where that information will go.

✔ Try some of the prewriting techniques discussed in the chapter—talking out, brainstorming, freewriting, outlining, and listing and mapping—especially if you have trouble putting your ideas on paper or on screen.

✔ Construct an introduction for workplace documents that includes the following:

- Subject
- Purpose
- Audience
- Scope and limitations
- Methods
- Definitions (optional)
- Plan of development

Draft the discussion for your documents to provide *evidence* that supports the main idea (or *claims*) of the document through the following:

- Statistics
- Examples
- Testimonials
- Eyewitness accounts
- Experiments
- Specifics
- Credible sources
- Anecdotes
- Graphics

 Check your facts and carefully consider their accuracy, currency, and relevance to your work.

 Link your claims and your evidence by building logical bridges.

 Draft a conclusion for your documents that draws conclusions and does not simply summarize the document. The conclusion should offer the following:

- Recommendations or solutions
- Significance or consequences
- Trends or predictions
- Plan of action
- Questions for further research/investigation

✔ Place additional ideas, information, and even some forms of support (especially complex calculations and formulas) in the appendix of a workplace document so that you will not overwhelm the reader with too much complex information at one time.

 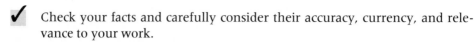

EXERCISES

Individual Exercises

1. Write a brief description of your process for beginning to write. You may want to include such information as the following:

   a. How close to your deadline you begin your first draft

   b. Any special rituals you go through to prepare for writing

   c. What you do when you first turn on your computer or set out your paper and pens

   d. How often you usually start over

   e. Whether you use any prewriting strategies

   f. How you know something's not going right in your draft

   g. How long you usually take to write one page of the draft

   h. How frequently you stop to read what you've written

   i. Whether you make changes in your draft each time you pause

2. Arrange the following words and phrases into either a formal outline or a list that clearly demonstrates the organization of ideas and their relationship to each other. Be sure to establish an appropriate audience before you begin your arrangement. Add or delete any items that may not serve your reader's needs. The topic is running a home cleaning service.

if the owners are at home	vacuuming	dusting
mopping	windows	rugs and carpets
pets	keys and locked areas	hardwood floors
linoleum	insurance	crews
transportation	supplies	directions to houses
tips	advertising strategies	uniforms
hardwood paneling	antiques, china, and	theft
sexual harassment	other breakables	paychecks
state and federal taxes	references	laundry
billing	guarantees	

3. After establishing an appropriate group of readers and their needs, what kinds of evidence would you expect to have to provide for the following statements?

   a. The Milwaukee plant should be closed.

   b. The clerical division should be restructured.

   c. We should expand our market into Australia.

   d. Our company's health benefits are inadequate.

   e. We need to update the look of our stores/offices.

4. Using a topic that you devise or your instructor assigns, try some prewriting strategies: talking out, brainstorming, freewriting, outlining, and listing and mapping.

5. For each of the following claims, compose a list of evidence (specific details or reasons) that might prove or support that claim. Be as creative as you wish, and include as many forms of support as you can. Then, compose a separate list of specific details or reasons to refute each claim. Again, include as many forms of support as you can. Based on the evidence for and against the claim, choose a position and construct a reasonable bridge between the claim and the evidence that would apply to you and your own life situation.

a. A dog is a person's best friend.

b. Our school needs to have more computers available to students.

c. The summer school session is too short.

d. Teachers at this school really care about their students' learning.

e. All students should take Introduction to Psychology.

f. All employees should know CPR.

g. Students should not be required to buy textbooks.

6. Using the claims in exercise 5 and the evidence you generated there, devise as many concluding scenarios as possible. Then, after establishing a particular audience's needs and expectations, determine the most appropriate conclusion and write a paragraph expressing it. An example is provided for you:

Claim: All employees should know CPR.

Recommendations: Initiate CPR training sessions.

Significance/consequences: (1) We can save the lives of fellow workers. (2) Our insurance rates will go down. (3) Employees will feel safer in the workplace.

Trends/predictions: As our worker population ages, more workers are subject to heart attacks while on the job. Knowing CPR can help employees save lives. Our employees will be interested in this program if they are trained while on the job, receive their regular salary, and receive a bonus when they have completed the training and are certified.

Plan of action: (1) Contact the local chapter of the American Red Cross to schedule training sessions. (2) Advertise the sessions to employees, emphasizing that the training will go on during their work schedules and that they will be paid for the time they spend in the sessions. (3) Have employees register for the sessions in the worker lounge on Monday and Tuesday. (4) Send notices to supervisors, listing the employees who are excused from work during the training sessions. (5) Take attendance at every session. (6) Provide bonuses for those who complete the CPR training and get their certification.

Questions for further research/investigation: (1) How many employees are interested in this program? (2) How much will the training cost, especially in downtime? (3) What are the supervisors' attitudes toward the training and downtime? (4) How successful is the training likely to be in helping prevent deaths on the job? (5) In addition to heart attacks, what other medical problems are met with CPR procedures? (6) Are there additional medical programs that we should investigate for their usefulness? (7) What effects will this training have on our insurance rates?

Audience: Executives concerned about the company's high insurance rates

Conclusion: Although the idea of instituting a CPR program is a good one, we need more information before we begin the training sessions. Specifically, we should consider these questions: (1) How many employees are interested in this program? (2) How much will the training cost, especially in downtime? (3) What are the supervisors' attitudes toward the training and downtime? (4) How successful is the training likely to be in helping prevent deaths on the job? (5) In addition to heart attacks, what other medical problems are met with CPR procedures? (6) Are there additional medical programs that we should investigate for their usefulness? (7) What effects will this training have on our insurance rates?

When these questions are answered satisfactorily, we may begin on a CPR instruction course for our employees.

Collaborative Exercises

1. Work on a writing project following the pattern in a–e below. Use the following topics:

- A report on ways to improve your campus's appearance
- A letter to a scholarship committee on why you should be awarded a $10,000 scholarship
- An investigation of how student fees are spent at your school
- A recommendation to give students more access to their teachers
- Suggestions for rearranging certain features of your school's library
- Suggestions for restructuring the requirements in your major (obviously, you and your partner must have the same major)
- A description of the various kinds of counseling services offered at your school
- A description of the grade appeals process at your school

a. For each of the topics, brainstorm (solo) a list of ideas. Then, choose a partner and brainstorm together on one of the topics. Be sure to note ideas that your partner offered but you had not thought of.

b. Next, your teacher will time you in a five-minute freewriting exercise on the topic you and your partner have selected.

c. Based on the list you brainstormed (and possibly your freewriting), create a formal outline or list of ideas you'd want to include in a document written to an appropriate reader.

d. Teaming with another pair of writers with a different topic, talk out your plans and problems for this writing assignment.

e. Prepare a one-page paper describing the topic you have selected and the primary points you would want to make in a document. You may use an outline or a list of topics to show your instructor how you want to group ideas and the kinds of support you would offer.

2. Divide the following topics with a partner. Then take turns talking out your ideas for writing a report on your topics for an appropriate audience.

    a. An investigation of access to buildings on your campus for people with disabilities

    b. An investigation of strategies for recruiting minorities at your school

    c. An investigation of security at your school

    d. An investigation of graduation rates in your major

    e. An investigation of graduate schools in your major

    Next, describe the contributions you gathered from your partner. Did your partner offer advice? Encourage your own exploration of the topic? Redirect your thinking? In what ways? Write a paragraph assessing the session for your instructor.

 ONGOING ASSIGNMENT

Draft the document for the new student/new employee orientation manual you have worked on throughout the course. Keep these parameters in mind as you prepare your draft:

- The manual can be no longer than ten pages.
- The manual should address a specific audience.
- The manual must be approved by your boss or the dean of students.

CHAPTER 6

Revising Your Workplace Documents

From your earliest instruction in grade school until your current efforts in this class, you probably remember your writing instructors telling you to revise your work. Unfortunately, many writers do not know what *revising* a piece of writing actually means. This chapter will clarify the *process* of revising and will provide specific tactics you can use when reviewing your draft to make sure that it will work for your readers.

The importance of revising cannot be overemphasized. Your readers count on you to provide information efficiently; they rarely have time to puzzle over parts that don't make sense to them or wade through extraneous details to find your message. Thus, to avoid their disdain, you should revise your documents to meet your readers' needs.

Unfortunately—but understandably, perhaps—after producing a draft of a workplace document, some writers find it difficult to alter the writing they have worked so hard to create. That's why Chapter 5 cautioned you not to "fall in love" with your first draft; it's hard to change a draft if you feel it's perfect the way it is. By taking a second, third, and fourth look at that draft and applying the principles and guidelines offered here, you will see numerous changes that can be made to meet your readers' needs for information and to achieve the other goals you have set for your document.

On the job, of course, only your most important documents and your most remote readers merit the time and concentration this chapter's revision techniques require; for more familiar readers and more routine documents, you can pare down your revision schemes. As you practice the strategies described in this chapter, many of them will become second nature to you. You will develop a feel for particular weaknesses and correct them without giving much thought (or effort) to the process.

At this stage, however, revising needs to be a conscious process, and as described here, you will find that it requires numerous readings of your original draft. As you practice, though, you will learn that you can combine some of these strategies, perhaps performing the steps for writing concisely with those for creating tactful communication. Because you will have other tasks to do on the job, you also need to develop some specific strategies to help you move smoothly through the revising process—seeing and correcting the major problems with your draft, adjusting the minor problems, and, unfortunately but realistically, letting a few minor weaknesses go. At some point, after all, you have to turn in your writing assignment, whether on the job or in a class such as this one.

Prioritizing Your Revisions

The following lists are examples of problems you may find in your writing. The first and second lists give you an idea of the major and minor problems you *must* attend to in order to protect your document's usefulness and your own credibility.

The third list provides examples of minor weaknesses that you should certainly correct if you have time—attending to small details boosts your credibility—but that you may have to abandon due to time constraints.

Major Problems in Drafts That Writers Must Attend to and Correct

- Improper audience considerations—work written for the wrong audience, the audience's feelings not considered, or the audience's needs not met.

- Inappropriate organization for readers' needs and goodwill—work does not address what readers need to know first, second, and third and fails to anticipate their reactions (positive, negative, neutral) to the ideas and information presented.

- Unclear purpose—writer and reader miscommunicate about what the writer's intentions are in the document; the reader concludes that the writer does not have a real purpose for writing.

- Inaccurate, unsupported, or out-of-date information—reader bases decisions on wrong information, with the result that the reader looks foolish and the writer's credibility is ruined.

- Inappropriate methods—writer constructs invalid surveys, interviews inappropriate respondents, or otherwise generates erroneous information from unreliable sources (this weakness typically demands a startover, but some inappropriate methodology and the information it generates can occasionally be salvaged).

- Indefensible conclusions—writer draws conclusions that are not substantiated by the information provided.

- Inflated or deflated style—writer uses inappropriate level of formality for the audience, uses vocabulary that is too colloquial or too pompous for the audience, or creates unclear, wordy, or tactless communications.

- Problems with graphics—clarity is compromised; writer fails to provide appropriate graphics for the reader's needs or level of understanding or fails to explain how the reader should interpret the graphics.

- Problems with spelling, grammar, or punctuation—reader misreads communication and is frustrated by the writer's carelessness or lack of knowledge of standard grammar.

Minor Problems in Drafts That Writers Should Make Every Effort to Correct

- Occasional wordiness
- Occasional structural weaknesses (topic sentence buried, for example)
- Occasional (brief and minor) deviations from the main point
- Graphics that are not quite as professional looking as they should be
- Matters of formatting (improper use of headings, subheadings, type sizes and fonts, and the like—see Chapter 9)

Minor Weaknesses in Drafts That Writers Should Correct, But May Have to Abandon

- Occasional misspellings (usually, although not always, corrected through spell checkers)

- Occasional punctuation problems that do not affect the reader's interpretation or understanding

- Up-to-date information simply not available (writer must address delays in getting current information)

- Less-than-desirable type size or font

All of these problems should be corrected, of course, but it is crucial that you be able to recognize and correct those in the first two lists.

The remainder of this chapter provides some strategies for recognizing these problems in your own drafts. At first, take the strategies one at a time, ponder them, practice them, challenge them, and apply them again. At this stage, they are likely to seem clumsy and tedious, and you may be eager to dismiss them as too time-consuming. If you practice them, however, you will become quite adept at incorporating these considerations into your revising process, and the speed of your revising will increase dramatically.

Accommodating Initial Revisions: The Big Picture

As a first step in revision, you need to step back from your work and look at its overall strengths and weaknesses. The centerpiece for all the questions you ask during revisions should be audience accommodation, as demonstrated in Figure 6.1. The following questions can help you address the primary issues of revising drafts. Be sure to take each set of questions separately, and work through your entire draft with only that set in mind.

- *Centerpiece—audience accommodation:* What evidence in my document demonstrates my consideration for a particular, identifiable reader or group of readers? (Consider the amount of explanation and detail you have offered; definitions for terms with which the readers may be unfamiliar; graphics for additional clarity and simplification; comparisons to ideas or products with which they are familiar; the arrangement and movement of ideas from general to specific, problem to solution, and so on—see Chapter 4.)

- *Topic and purpose:* Does my document have a clear topic and a clear purpose? Do these topics and purposes match my assignment? Have I strayed from the topic or undermined my purpose at any place in the document? Or do I work so hard to prove my point that I resort to unethical claims, descriptions, or omissions?

- *Information and findings:* Is the information I present relevant and appropriate for this audience and its needs? Do my findings (or conclusions) make

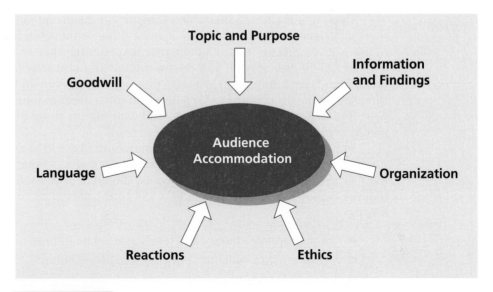

FIGURE 6.1   Model of Initial Revision Concerns

sense based on the case I have described? Are my conclusions appropriate for this group of readers? Have I made clear connections between my claims, my evidence, and the situation I am describing?

- *Organization:* Is the document's organizational scheme clear to my readers? Is it appropriate for their needs? Do I provide a clear sense of what comes first, second, third? Are those steps or details logical for my readers' needs? Do I follow through on the organizational scheme—clearly presenting well-ordered causes and effects or clearly listing the chronological steps we should take to resolve the problem I am discussing?

- *Ethics:* Have I stated the constraints of my information and findings so that they will not mislead readers? Have I incorporated only relevant, ethical details, clearly targeted for my readers' needs? Have I omitted snide comments, attempts at humor, unnecessary details, or unethical claims?

- *Reactions:* Have I carefully constructed my document to accommodate my readers' likely reactions to my topic? Do I avoid harping on bad news or other details and information that are likely to irritate my readers? Have I allayed their fears or misconceptions, reinforced their confidence and self-respect, and otherwise accommodated their reactions?

- *Language:* Are the language and structure of my sentences clear? Are they too formal? Too informal? Too wordy? Too blunt?

- *Goodwill:* Do I maintain the goodwill and respect of my readers? Do my competence and credibility come through in each sentence of this document?

Thus, revising for audience accommodation means attending to details of need, understanding, ethics, and company culture. Although it may be tempting to use your workplace writing to tell your readers what they want to hear, your own credibility may suffer if you do not present accurate information and interpretations of that information in a form that your readers can understand. And although you may be tempted to keep only your own needs in mind (the need to be perceived as knowledgeable, credible, and competent), those needs will best be met by accommodating your readers' needs first.

Although these considerations are paramount in the final draft (the finished product), you will want to include them at various stages of your drafting process, too. Each subsequent draft, in other words, should help you refine the elements that are considered most desirable in a workplace document, including the following:

- The appropriate amount and levels of accurate information
- A clear sense of audience, purpose, and organization
- A style that is clear, concise, and tactful
- A final document that has been carefully proofread and is free of spelling and grammatical errors

Revising for Appropriate Information

Earlier chapters on planning your workplace document, conducting research, and drafting a rough document focused on determining what kinds of information would be most important for your readers, how to get that information, and then how to write it in a workplace document. At this stage of the revising process, you need to question those early decisions. An *informational revision* requires you to challenge your claims, your evidence, and the logical bridges you constructed to connect your claims and evidence to your particular workplace situation (see Chapter 5). Because you may need to add or delete information or even redefine your goals for your revised draft, you should attend to an informational revision before you revise for audience, purpose, organization, and style. After all, it makes little sense to struggle over the details of the style of a paragraph that you may delete once you realize it offers no useful information to the reader.

Revising for appropriate information is frequently combined with revising for audience and purpose, but the two processes can be separated by the following considerations:

- Revising for appropriate research
- Revising for useful conclusions
- Revising for accuracy
- Revising for completeness
- Revising for currency
- Revising for relevance

Revising for Appropriate Research

At this stage in your revising, you should review your research, making sure you have provided details that match your readers' needs. You should also reconsider whether the research itself is likely to prove what you intend it to prove. And you should ensure that the research has been generated from sources that are likely to convince your reader.

As we discussed in Chapter 3, many readers assign special importance to research conducted by certain groups. Frequently, the organization's culture determines which research is preferred. If your organization is conservative, you would probably be wise to rely on conservative estimates and research. In an organization that emphasizes inventiveness, creativity, or risk taking, you may succeed with bolder research. In other words, if your organization operates on the belief that the economy or society is disintegrating, your readers are unlikely to be receptive to research based on an optimistic view of the economy or society. If your organization operates on the belief that the economy or society is in an upswing, however, your readers will probably not be persuaded by research (and recommendations generated from that research) based on conservative estimates that discourage risk taking and inventiveness.

Revising for Useful Conclusions

Next, you should consider the conclusion of your document to make sure that you have provided the kinds of information your readers expect and on which they can act. No reader wants to read an entire document only to find out in the conclusion that nothing can be done. At the same time, you should be careful not to overstate the options available to your organization. A careful balance of realistic options, consequences, trends, and plans will make your document most useful to your reader, while protecting your credibility as a writer. When revising conclusions, therefore, you should consider these questions:

- Do I present appropriate solutions to the problem? Are the solutions sensible, affordable, and in line with my company's or my client's way of doing things?

- Do I present consequences of actions, policies, or philosophies that are clearly supportable, based on the document's discussion of various situations and issues?

- Do I present trends and predictions that are clearly supportable, based on experience and on new factors in the industry, economy, and society?

- Do I present a clear plan of action that is doable in terms of my company's or my client's finances, resources, personnel, and deadlines?

- Do I clearly indicate which ideas need to be researched or investigated further, ensuring that my reader will understand that I am not presenting all the solutions at this time?

Revising for Accuracy

Revising for accuracy means looking carefully at the information you have provided to make sure you have presented it in the manner it was intended to be used. Because statistics, for example, are such an important part of many workplace documents (and of the decisions that will be based on those documents), you should check not only the numbers you present in the document (a matter of proofreading) but the interpretation of those numbers as well.

APPLICATION

Revising for Accuracy

To see how revising for accuracy can affect the information presented, consider the following responses to the question "How important is salary in your consideration of a job offer?" How would you interpret these statistics?

Males
- Very important—30 percent
- Important—42 percent
- Somewhat important—20 percent
- Not important—8 percent

Females
- Very important—28 percent
- Important—40 percent
- Somewhat important—18 percent
- Not important—14 percent

A quick reading of these statistics might suggest that men care more about their salaries than women do. But suppose that a more careful investigation finds the following details:

- Number of men surveyed: 2,443
- Number of women surveyed: 1,911
- Number of men responding to this question: 1,978
- Number of women responding to this question: 814

Understanding the context of questions and answers in statistical surveys is crucial to presenting accurate data (which should further prompt you to take a good business statistics course while you are in college).

Now that you know more about the context of the data, does your interpretation change? Write a paragraph describing what the numbers might mean.

Constructing accurate information involves far more than just statistical interpretations, however. It also means that you are sensitive to other kinds of problems that may arise with information and support, problems addressed in Chapter 5's discussion of drafting a workplace document.

Revising for Completeness

As Chapter 5's discussion of drafting pointed out, you must also be concerned with ethical presentations of information, which means presenting *complete* information. The television news media, for instance, are frequently lambasted for offering "sound bites," statements removed from their larger context, which, if provided, might change the meaning of those statements and viewers' understanding of them.

Incomplete or inaccurate attributions may also occur when writers do not understand or clearly present the relationship between ideas and their contexts. Several medical specialists, for instance, have proposed legalizing marijuana for terminally ill patients. Unfortunately, their statements have often been repeated without the context of "terminally ill patients." As you can imagine, speakers or writers find it very frustrating to be quoted out of context, and you must take special care not to make that kind of error in your workplace writing. Another potential error is to propose ideas for implementation in the workplace without noting that they are appropriate for only a specified environment. Ideas that work on the West Coast may not succeed in the Midwest, and ideas that work for clothing retailers may not be appropriate for computer retailers. Providing complete information means you present not only the information you want your readers to know, but also the context in which it was generated.

Revising for Currency

Other problems with accuracy arise when outdated information is presented as current. Your readers have every right to expect your information to be up-to-date, and they will generally presume that all information is, indeed, current. The researcher who cites ten-year-old job satisfaction figures, for instance, may not accurately represent job satisfaction among current workers, which may have suffered because of downsizing, new managers, or mergers. You must make every attempt to get the most current information for your communications. If you're not using the most recent figures on a particular issue, you must explain clearly and prominently in your document that current figures were not available.

Revising for Relevance

Finally, you must revise your information for relevance. Many writers are tempted to include startling details and impressive statistics and graphics throughout their documents in the belief (erroneous) that doing so will make the reading more enjoyable. They fail to remember that readers are reading to be enlightened, not to be entertained. Therefore, any details, statistics, and graphics that do not support the main point and purpose of the document should be edited from the final version.

Some writers recognize that some of their materials are irrelevant, but are determined to include them anyway in much the same way that an inept after-dinner speaker insists on telling a joke although it has nothing to do with the message. Even though the writer strives to make the irrelevant material relevant, the reader's reaction is still likely to be "Interesting, but what does it have to do with the issue?" Because you do not want readers to have that reaction to your writing, you will have to rigorously edit irrelevancies from your documents.

In revising for appropriate information in a document, therefore, you should consider each of your statements in light of the following questions:

1. Are the numbers accurate (copied correctly)? Are they interpreted correctly?

2. Is the context of the information clear? Have I explained the circumstances in which these ideas were offered and in which they will work?

3. Is the information the most current available? Is that good enough? What are the results of using information that is not up-to-the-minute? What cautions do I need to offer the reader about relying on dated information?

4. Do every sentence and every minor point contribute to the major idea I am trying to present? Have I edited statements that may get in the way of the reader's understanding?

By attending to matters of appropriateness in content, you are well on your way to producing a good final document.

Revising for a Clear Sense of Audience, Purpose, and Organization

In your review of the information you have provided in your document, once again consider your audience, your purpose(s) for writing and your readers' purpose(s) for reading, and the organization of your document. All of these issues, of course, involve the relationship between you and the reader and have been important factors in every stage of the writing process we have examined. Most important here is a word of caution: be careful not to overplay to your readers. Some writers are so conscious of what readers *want* to hear that they ignore their corresponding obligation to provide what readers *need* to hear. Maintaining the delicate balance between what readers want to hear and what they need to hear is one of the ways that the workplace writer facilitates success in today's organizations.

Revising for Audience Needs

Although you have already considered some audience needs in your planning, researching, and drafting stages, you will want to attend to them much more conscientiously at this stage. Primarily, you will want to consider the following:

- What your readers already know about your subject and what they need to learn
- Any special terms that should be defined or clarified for your readers
- The kinds of research they expect and trust
- The kinds of conclusions that will be most useful for their own work

Readers' Knowledge and Needs

Finding out what your readers already know about your subject is part of the ongoing writing process, but you should have a fairly clear idea at the earliest stages when you are planning and researching information for your document. If your readers know little or nothing about your topic, you may have to spend a great deal of time educating them by explaining the history of the situation, its context, and why it is important to the company and to them.

Most dangerous is assuming that your readers know about a situation that is actually totally new to them. In such cases, readers are likely to dismiss your communication because they don't understand what you're writing about or why you're writing to them. As a competent workplace writer, you will have to find out—primarily from talking with your prospective readers or with colleagues who interact with them—what they do and do not know about your topic.

After you determine what your readers already know about your subject, you will have to revise your writing to make sure you have provided the information they *need* to know (see Figure 6.2). This concern dovetails with your primary purpose for writing—to provide the information your readers need to know.

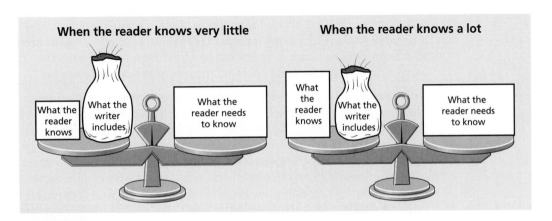

FIGURE 6.2 The Balance of Information

Occasionally, your readers may not want to know the information you are offering; they may be hurt when you explain that their "great idea" is a miserable failure, that their work is unsatisfactory, or that they will not be promoted. In these cases, you will want to carefully consider the organization of this bad news (see Chapter 4) and the style and language you use (see Revising for Tactfulness, Tone, Attitude, and Sexism below). In other cases, readers may not want to know the information you are offering because they think it is boring, too difficult to understand, or irrelevant to their work; in these cases, it is your job to make sure they understand the importance and relevance of the document to them. If you argue successfully that your report, for example, explains the *only* way their vacation time will be approved, you are more likely to win your readers' attention.

Special Terminology

As part of your consideration of what your readers already know and what they need to know, you should consider whether you have used any special terms that should be defined or clarified for your readers. In workplace situations, and the documents that arise from those situations, you may find that specialized terminology does not translate from one division of the company to another.

How will you know whether you need to define terms? Three questions should guide you:

1. Do my readers' backgrounds (education, position in the company, experience with this situation) suggest they would know this term from other readings or routine work situations? If readers have worked in a particular division of the company for years, they should know the terminology used in that division. You will have to be more careful, however, when you are writing for someone outside your division. As a general rule, the more technical and division-specific a term, the more likely you will need to define it.

2. Does this term have an alternative meaning that my readers would more commonly use? For instance, when I tell my students that their lists are not *parallel,* they typically think I am talking about a matter of formatting—the alignment of their lists along a particular margin. I have to explain carefully that I am talking about a grammatical structure—not a formatting structure—and then define what "parallel" means in this specialized use.

3. Do I have access to my actual readers or to people who would represent this group of readers? Can I ask them directly whether they understand these terms? Of course, access is less likely when you are writing to someone outside your company. To ensure that their written materials will be understood by readers outside the organization, many organizations spend a great deal of money researching vocabularies and associations with certain terms. Marketing research companies, for instance, have learned that consumers have negative connotations about the term "used cars"; hence, the change to "previously owned cars" and now "program cars." Writers use the results of these "vocabulary tests" whenever they communicate with a particular group of

readers, taking care to define and explain terms and contexts that will affect the readers' understanding and associations of terms used throughout the document.

In fact, some organizations have to define terms so often that they have devised a glossary of terms that can be customized for any workplace document. After writing, say, a manual for a particular group of readers, the writer can highlight terms that should be listed in the glossary; the computer provides that glossary with terms already defined (a process called "boilerplating"). The writer may have to make minor adjustments to the definitions, but the work is essentially standardized.

Revising for the Writer's Purposes and the Readers' Purposes

As you continue to check for appropriate information throughout all your revising stages, you are now ready to face one of the most challenging aspects of writing in the workplace: the requirement to balance the writer's purpose for writing with the readers' purpose for reading (see Chapter 2's description of planning for the writer's and readers' purposes).

Determining the best ways to match your purposes with the readers' purposes requires careful attention to *rhetorical* strategies—persuasive options that writers use to convince readers. The first requirement for using an appropriate rhetorical strategy is to determine what motivates readers to act or believe as they do. Common motivators are

money	prestige	power	appearances	goodwill
credibility	popularity	safety	efficiency	praise
leisure	ethics	health	independence	education
fairness	productivity	fear	security	quality

When designing rhetorical strategies, you must be careful to use only ethical or legitimate motivations; for instance, it would be unethical to play on a reader's concern for quality when the solutions you propose have nothing to do with quality. Similarly, you must not play to a reader's fears when there is nothing to fear. Determining the appropriate content, style, and visuals that will match these appeals is the writer's true mission in assessing the reader's purposes for reading.

Realizing that readers frequently have more than one purpose for reading is also important. Although their primary motivation may be to protect the organization or its employees, for instance, their secondary motivation may be to support a strategy that will make them look good. Or they may be concerned with how to balance profits with ethics and safety. Once you discover what motivates your readers, you should try to account for all these motivations—again, being careful not to overstate your case.

THE WORLD OF WORKPLACE WRITING

Anticipating Readers' Reactions

Although we say that readers read for information, they typically read that information in light of their motivations, and those motivations are going to create reactions to your work. Most readers' reactions stem from positive, negative, or neutral answers to these questions about your work:

- Will this idea generate or cost us (or me) money?
- Will this idea give me more power or take it from me?
- Does this idea harm anyone or the environment?
- Is this the ethical thing to do?
- Will my job (or my employees' jobs) be more secure if we follow this strategy?
- Is this strategy fair to all employees?

Thus, accommodating readers' needs for information and the motivations that will affect them must also be balanced with the readers' likely reaction to your ideas. Generating goodwill and appropriate responses is a primary concern for workplace writers.

At the same time, you should also be aware of your own primary and secondary motives for writing. Your primary motivation is, most likely, to inform, persuade, clarify, simplify, or summarize information. But your secondary motivations may range from trying to impress your readers with your insights to trying to make life a little easier for yourself and your team.

Problems arise when your readers' motivations for reading and your motivations for writing conflict. If your readers are concerned about employee safety and you are writing to convince them to adopt a highly profitable, but slightly dangerous, procedure, your ethical responsibility is to meet the readers' needs—not your own. In other words, you must explain the dangers, but you may also explain why you believe the higher profits may be worth the risk. Then, your readers can make the decision, based on the full presentation of the facts.

Revising for Organizational Clarity

A clear revision based on your readers' needs should include any necessary changes in organization. The organization, of course, should be a natural consequence of the audience and purpose you have identified in the introduction of your document. Just as certain groups will need special kinds of information (background, consequences, cause and effect, and so on), they will also need to find that information in a particular order.

In revising the organization of your document, therefore, you should not only be able to identify *what* you have placed first, second, and third, but you should also be able to defend *why* you have placed the ideas in that order. Why, for example, did you place the solutions before the problem? The cause before the effects? The current situation before its history? Each of these organizational choices can be useful in particular circumstances and can also be adjusted for particular audiences and purposes. (See Strategy Review 6.1.)

STRATEGY REVIEW 6.1

REVISING FOR ORGANIZATION

In revising your work, you should consider the following challenges to its organization, presented here with bracketed responses for a report on absenteeism at XYZ Corporation:

The first major point I offer is __[an overview of the problem of absenteeism]__.

It is the first point because __[my readers need this context to understand how widespread the problem is and why the solutions appear so drastic]__.

If I saved this point until later, __[my readers would be confused and might be irritated with my recommendation to spend $1,450 to solve the problem]__.

My second point is __[an explanation of the significance of the problem of absenteeism]__.

It is not the first point because __[my readers need the context and proof that the problem exists first]__.

It is not the third point because __[my readers might be tempted to dismiss the whole problem if they do not understand immediately how serious it is]__.

In addition to considering the order of your information, you should also consider your readers' likely responses to that information. Again, if you know your readers are likely to interpret your information in a positive or neutral light, you should use a direct approach; if they are likely to be frightened or irritated by your information, you should use an indirect approach (see Chapter 4).

Finally, you should revise your organization at every level of your document, meaning that you should reconsider the arrangement not only of the total document, but of each section, paragraph, and sentence as well. In Chapter 4, we discussed the importance of constructing topic sentences and placing one at the beginning of each paragraph (see Strategy Review 4.1). As you revise, go through your document, reading each paragraph's opening sentence and determining whether it does, indeed, provide the most important information in that paragraph. Try highlighting each opening sentence; then, carefully review each subsequent sentence in the paragraph, asking these questions:

- Does this sentence belong in a discussion of my topic sentence? Or does it belong in some other paragraph?
- Does this sentence contribute additional information, clarification, examples, or details to that topic sentence? Or does it merely restate the topic sentence?
- Does this sentence logically follow the preceding sentence and logically lead to the next sentence? Do I need to add transitions, additional sentences, or other elements that will clarify the relationship between these ideas?

Being able to defend your organizational decisions requires great insights about your audience, your purpose for writing and the readers' purpose for reading, and the context and culture of your particular company. Such insights also require you to be a clear, ethical thinker. Be sure that the organization of your work does not bury important information, but also be sure that it does not overstate or understate the seriousness of your ideas.

Revising for Appropriate Language and Style

From the previous sections, you should have a clearer sense of how to revise the content of your document, your motivations for writing it, and the order of the information you present in light of a particular audience and set of purposes. In short, you have revised *what* you have to say. Now it is time for you to revise *how* you say it. Revising for style requires careful attention to readers' needs because poorly written workplace documents can confuse, frustrate, or irritate readers; poor writing can also make them doubt your knowledge, competence, and ability to think clearly.

Many writers puff up rather simple concepts to try to appear really smart or use specialized jargon so that only specialists in the field can understand the arguments. On the job, you will have many opportunities to include or exclude readers by the language you use. To perform ethically and competently, however, you should present information in the clearest, most concise, and most understandable language possible. If technical terminology must be used in a document for people outside your field, definitions should be provided as explained earlier.

Revising for Clarity

Several structures can cause problems with clarity; many of them are considered more thoroughly in the Brief Usage Guidebook at the end of this text. A brief discussion here, however, will point out some of the structures you should watch for as you revise your workplace documents.

Modifiers

A primary problem arises from the inaccurate placement of modifiers—words and phrases (usually taught as adjectives and adverbs) that describe other words and phrases. When modifiers or modifying phrases and clauses are misplaced in sentences, readers may be confused about what is actually being described (see the Brief Usage Guidebook, section I2). Look what happens to the meaning when "only" is moved in the following sentences:

> Only the man in the warehouse can apply for worker's compensation. [No person outside the warehouse can apply; no women can apply.]

> The only man in the warehouse can apply for worker's compensation. [No women can apply; there is only one man in the warehouse.]

> The man in the only warehouse can apply for worker's compensation. [There is only one warehouse.]

> The man in the warehouse can apply only for worker's compensation. [He cannot apply for any other benefits.]

> The man in the warehouse can apply for only worker's compensation. [He cannot apply for any other form of compensation.]

To convey the sense that the writer intends, words must be arranged in a particular order. Be sure to stand back from your writing and evaluate the order of information in your sentences carefully to make sure that modifiers are attached to the appropriate words and phrases.

As you revise, *bracket* all nouns and their modifiers; then, determine whether each modifier really contributes any additional meaning to the idea—the idea may already be clear just by its definition. Stretch your vocabulary to find the perfect word that can stand alone and communicate your ideas precisely.

Punctuation

Few nonprofessional writers know all the rules of punctuation, but fortunately, you need to learn only a few rules to prevent most serious misreadings in a workplace document. Those few rules are important, however, because problems with punctuation can create dangerous misinterpretations of on-the-job writing. Consider, for instance, how readers might misinterpret the following sentence:

Original: After hanging the man straightened the pictures.

At first reading, you may have thought the writer was talking about "hanging the man," rendering the rest of the sentence confusing, to say the least. Adding an object—what is being hung—and a comma clarifies the meaning:

Revision: After hanging the pictures, the man straightened them.

Other punctuation issues are taken up in sections L–R of the Brief Usage Guidebook at the end of this book. Be especially careful to use punctuation as a means of ensuring clarity in your workplace writing.

Ambiguity

Ambiguity—sentences or phrases that can be read in more than one way—is one of the most difficult flaws to spot in your own work. Because you know exactly what you mean, you may not see that a reader could misinterpret your information. Reading more slowly and more critically will help, but you should also enlist the assistance of other writers or editors to help you find ambiguous statements in your writing.

Problems with ambiguity occur when the reader could just as easily adopt one interpretation of a sentence as another. In the following sentence, for instance, how would you decide which vial should be shaken?

Original: Before mixing the nitroglycerin with the sodium, shake the vial for four seconds.

Asking "which vial?" may not occur to you unless you know that shaking some chemicals can cause an explosion. As the sentence reads, the reader has a 50–50 chance of shaking the right vial—or the wrong one! A revision clarifies the meaning:

Revision: Shake the sodium vial for four seconds before mixing in the nitroglycerin.

Most problems with ambiguity can be resolved by asking and answering the following questions:

- Which one?
- What kind?
- In what way?
- To whom?
- How much?

Asking this series of questions at the end of each of your sentences is a painstaking process, but it helps to ensure that your sentences are clear and unambiguous.

With practice, you will soon be able to work more quickly and will see ambiguities without having to spend so much time on the process. For now, however, taking it slowly will help you detect these problems and will generate specific answers to correct them.

Pronoun References

Pronoun references help you add coherence to your writing and prevent singsong patterns. But problems with pronoun references can also confuse your readers. (See the Brief Usage Guidebook, section H.) The following sentence and its revisions illustrate the vagueness that can be introduced by improper pronoun usage and offer strategies for clarifying pronoun references:

> **Original:** Richard told Jermaine that he had wrecked his car.
>
> **Revision:** Richard told Jermaine, "I have wrecked your car."
>
> **Revision:** Richard told Jermaine, "I have wrecked my car."
>
> **Revision:** Richard told Jermaine, "You wrecked your car."
>
> **Revision:** Richard told Jermaine, "You wrecked my car."

Imagine how much more confusion would be introduced with the addition of another male in the sentence: "Stanley listened while Richard told Jermaine that he had wrecked his car." Now whose car has been wrecked and who did the wrecking? Stanley? Richard? Jermaine? Clear pronoun references will ensure that your readers understand your meaning. (See Strategy Review 6.2.)

STRATEGY REVIEW 6.2

CLARIFYING PRONOUN REFERENCES

In addition to "this," which novice writers often use to refer to any element previously covered in a paper, other pronouns are frequently asked to do more than they can do to clarify and extend meanings. In your own writing, *circle* the following pronouns, making sure they have clear references—and only one reference—when you use them:

this	that	these	those	us/we/our
it	they	she	he	

If you cannot find the corresponding reference for the pronoun, revise your use of the pronoun or the sentence. Remember, too, that you are always safe to include a noun after many of these pronouns (this book, that idea, these children, those henhouses).

Revising for Conciseness

As you revise for clarity, you may have to add words, phrases, or even sentences to ensure that your reader will understand your meaning. If the additions clarify your meaning, by all means include them. Some writers, however, create long-winded documents or overexplain their ideas, going over and over a point that can, if well written, stand alone. Problems with conciseness usually occur for these reasons:

- The writer does not have a clear sense of the readers and their understanding of particular ideas.
- The writer believes that longer documents and longer words are more impressive than shorter documents and shorter words.
- The writer is trying to sound important.
- The writer is trying to imitate other documents in the field.

Redundancies

A primary problem with conciseness arises from *redundancy*—the repetition or modification of ideas that can stand alone. The following list of tautologies, paired words whose modifiers are unnecessary because of the definition of the noun, provides examples of redundancy:

Unexpected surprise (if it is a surprise, it is unexpected)

Major crisis (if it is a crisis, it is major)

True fact (if it is a fact, it is true)

Sudden explosion (as opposed to a slow explosion?)

Sum total (if it is the sum, it is also the total)

Free gift (if it is a gift, it is free)

Babbling incoherently (as opposed to babbling coherently?)

Unnecessary redundancies (are some redundancies necessary?)

Unexplained/unsolved mystery (if it were explained, it wouldn't be a mystery)

Workable solution (if it isn't workable, it isn't a solution)

Viable alternative (if it isn't viable, it isn't an alternative)

Unsubstantiated rumor (if it is a rumor, it is unsubstantiated)

End result (if it is a result, it must come at the end)

Mutual agreement (if it is an agreement, it must be mutual)

Other redundancies are created when writers include *genres (or sets) as part of the description* of the subset:

Red in color

Warm in temperature

Precipitation in the form of rain

Scaly in appearance

Sarcastic in nature

Mahogany in hue

Silky in texture

Equally irritating is adding the "-wise" ending to these sets: temperature-wise, color-wise, appearance-wise, and the like. Clarifications may be added, however, when the reader might misinterpret your meaning. Consider the difference between describing chili as hot in temperature versus hot in spiciness. Good writers, of course, have other words at their disposal; they might substitute "scalding" for hot in temperature and write simply "spicy" for hot in spiciness.

Hedges

Still other impediments to conciseness are created when writers introduce *unnecessary hedges* or fumble for ideas, using common words and phrases such as the following:

kind of	generally	really	sort of
particularly	likely	perhaps	possibly
probably	I would guess	very	may/might

Nevertheless, in some contexts, hedges can play an important role:

- They may prevent blanket statements that make a possibility a certainty: Perhaps we should fire the CEO. (To assert that we should fire the CEO denies the possibility that the CEO should not be fired.)
- They may prevent equating two ideas that have important differences: A dentist's suction instrument is almost like/kind of like a vacuum cleaner. (To assert that a dentist's suction instrument is exactly like a vacuum cleaner would create false impressions and misunderstandings.)
- They may allow the writer to emphasize certain ideas: We will be particularly vulnerable to a higher tax liability if the merger goes through. (To say only "vulnerable" may not alert readers to the problem as effectively as emphasizing that higher tax liabilities are likely.)
- They may prevent the writer from sounding like a know-it-all: If we continue to manufacture large, gas-guzzling cars, we are likely to lose the Japanese market. (To assert that the production of large, gas-guzzling cars will definitely cost us the Japanese market may ignore the increasing number of Japanese millionaires who want larger cars.)

Circle all hedges in your writing, and make sure they provide the kind of focus on possibilities, differences, emphases, and tones that you want to create. If any hedges dilute statements that should be strong assertions, you should edit them from your document.

Introductory Missteps

Wordy introductory statements or setups also hinder conciseness. Writers typically use such statements to try to distance themselves from the message they are sending:

It might be said that	It is clear that
You should understand that	It is with this principle in mind that
There is little reason to believe that	It is crucial to note that
It is generally thought that	There are many people who

Note that most of these constructions open with "it is" or "there are"—particularly weak openers for most workplace documents. Consider the following weak openers and their more straightforward revisions:

Original: There are those who say that the Japanese market is growing rapidly, while the European market is declining.

Revision: Many say that the Japanese market is growing rapidly, while the European market is declining.

Original: It is with this principle in mind that we should consider reversing our international strategies.

Revision: Therefore, we should consider reversing our international strategies.

Bracket every "It is" or "There are" opener in your document; then, look for the real subject and get on with your discussion.

Extenders

A common weakness in workplace writing is stretching a perfectly good verb into a noun form, typically by adding "-tion" to the end of the verb, as in *exclamation, realization, alteration,* and *communication;* whenever possible, these words should be recast as strong verbs (exclaim, realize, alter, communicate). For example, consider the following sentence's extenders and their revision:

Original: We asked him to provide a confirmation of the details in the laboratory's report.

Revision: We asked him to confirm the details in the laboratory's report. (weak noun revised as strong verb)

The following list presents some common wordy combinations, which consist of a verb such as "make," "offer," or extend" plus a word ending in "-ation"

THE WORLD OF WORKPLACE WRITING

Looking for Good Writing Models?

Many students try to imitate the writing they read on the job, but every workplace includes many poor writers whose work should not be used as models. Many business writers, for instance, fill their correspondence with oddities, such as "per your request," and "herewithal." To make sure you edit this kind of nonsense from your writing, ask yourself a simple question: "Do I talk this way?" If you do not *talk* to real people this way, why *write* to them this way? Be careful about the role models you select for writing in the workplace; look for clarity and a human voice instead of obfuscation (often intended to mislead) and pomposity.

plus "of" or some other preposition—constructions that undermine strong verbs that can usually stand alone:

make a presentation about = present	make a decision = decide
offer a recommendation for = recommend	put one's trust in = trust
hold an election = elect	make a proposition = propose
reach a conclusion = conclude	will be beneficial to = will benefit
extend congratulations = congratulate	express appreciation for = appreciate
offer a suggestion = suggest	make an accusation = accuse

Circle every "of" in your document because this preposition frequently sets up weak nouns that should be revised as strong verbs. Then, see if you can revise the phrase to omit the "of" construction. Remember, however, that "of" is a perfectly good preposition and may be necessary to introduce a prepositional phrase that cannot be revised.

If you can remove redundancies, hedges, wordy introductions, and extenders from your sentences without damaging the meaning, you should do so. If, however, the changes you make are likely to create harsh statements that may hurt or irritate your reader, you should consider the advice presented in the section on tactfulness.

Revising for Naturalness

Writers sometimes try to lengthen their work and make it sound more impressive by using complex or unusual words when simpler words are preferable. As earlier chapters pointed out, replacing ordinary words with "thesaurus" words can mislead readers and make the writer seem foolish. The first rule for generating good prose is to use appropriate words that carry the exact meaning the writer intends. Often the most precise word is also the least pretentious.

Pompous Language

Think about how you talk with your friends versus how you talk with your parents, your boss, and your teachers. When you are with your friends, you do not think about what you say, so you use a different vocabulary, tone, and language structure than you use when you are with your parents, teachers, and bosses and are more consciously monitoring your language.

Although engaging workplace writing emphasizes the value of speaking and writing naturally, traditional rules of good grammar and etiquette remain in place. But you don't have to resort to the stuffiness that we associate with English butlers in the movies—the kind of language that seems out of touch with our everyday lives.

Using more natural sounding language helps us connect with readers. Consider the following *pompous or overblown words* and their more natural replacements, which are closer to the way human beings actually talk:

Pompous or Overblown	*Replacement*
accommodations	rooms
facilitate	help
prioritize	rank, list
transpired	happened
cognizant	aware, know
termination	end, firing
interface	talk with
utilize	use
mechanize	automate
facilities	rooms (meeting rooms, convention halls, bathrooms?)

Clichés

You will also want to avoid *clichés* in your writing. Clichés are descriptive phrases that have lost their originality and spark because of overuse:

that's the way the cookie crumbles	crowing like a rooster
let's get the ball rolling	take a number
raining cats and dogs	jumping on the bandwagon
take the ball and run with it	playing someone for a fool
make an end run around	set up shop

The Voices on Television

Listen to ordinary people being interviewed on local television news programs. Many of them use bloated language in an attempt to sound important or intelligent. You may notice how silly and pompous they actually sound. You'll also probably notice that the news broadcasters themselves (except for sportscasters) typically use ordinary words; listen to how natural they sound.

Take notes on the interviews you see on local television stations; if the speaker's language sounds unnatural to you, determine why and explain what the speaker should have said to be more natural. Be prepared to discuss your findings and ideas in class.

In addition to these routine clichés, business has generated its own overused phrases. These business clichés typically appear in letters but may also occur in other workplace documents:

The undersigned (I, we)

Per your request (as you asked)

Please find enclosed (here is . . .)

Kindly instruct the committee (please tell the committee . . .)

As per our telephone conversation (as we agreed on the phone)

The aforementioned item (the item)

To convince yourself that these phrases are, indeed, unnatural, consider how often in a day (or even a week, month, or year) you say "undersigned," "per," "aforementioned," or "please find enclosed." If you think a butler is much more likely to utter such a phrase than you are, you should probably drop it from your writing repertoire.

Passive Voice

Some writers try to lengthen their communications or make their writing more impressive by using *passive voice* and by *switching a sentence's real subject and object:*

Original: It is a misunderstanding to think that the antiestablishment movement of the 1960s will be perpetuated by the reopening of the Hendrix investigation.

Revision: Reopening the Hendrix investigation will not perpetuate the 1960s' antiestablishment movement.

Not to be confused with past tense, which places the action of the sentence in a previous time, passive voice removes the doer of the action from the place of honor: the subject slot. The Brief Usage Guidebook at the end of this text summarizes the difference between passive and active voice (see section E); for now, the following example should help your understanding:

> **Original:** The jury was shocked by Ms. Passini's exclamation that her innocence would be proved. (Passive voice: The jury [in the subject slot] is sitting passively while Ms. Passini is doing the action [exclaiming].)

> **Revision:** Ms. Passini shocked the jury by exclaiming that her innocence would be proved. (Active voice: Ms. Passini [in the subject slot] is doing the action.)

In spite of some old advice about avoiding passive voice in workplace documents, the passive voice actually has some value:

- When you do not know who did the action: The safe was robbed last night.
- When the doer is clear: The groceries were stocked in the wrong place.
- When you do not want to place blame: "The car got dented last night, Dad."
- When the doer is unimportant: The garden was festooned with brightly colored lanterns, putting everyone in a festive mood.

If your information does not fit into one of these special cases, however, you should consider revising your sentences into the active voice.

When you revise your final document, *underline* all verbs and determine whether they are active or passive voice (see the Brief Usage Guidebook). If you can recast passive voice as active voice without damaging the sense of the sentence, do so.

Revising for Tactfulness, Tone, Attitude, and Sexism

A frequent casualty of revising for conciseness and naturalness in workplace writing is tactfulness—the proof of the writer's concern for the readers' feelings. Some writers mistakenly believe that their message is so important that tact is unnecessary, or they may believe that their readers do not deserve a tactful communication, or they may think that a tactful version of a command sounds unnatural.

Tactfulness, diplomacy, and general etiquette, however, are crucial in maintaining goodwill among coworkers, between companies and their clients, and between any other groups that interact. Your attention to tactfulness, diplomacy,

THE WORLD OF WORKPLACE WRITING

Why Be Concerned with Good Manners?

Numerous arguments may be raised against tactfulness (it's time-consuming, nobody else does it, it's unnecessary in standard business relationships), but probably none is as pernicious as the idea that tactfulness "just isn't part of my nature." Such an argument is no more acceptable than saying "I was raised by wolves who placed no value on kindness or respect."

An equally offensive objection is that being tactful means deferring to others, which may be appropriate when dealing with one's boss, but not when dealing with one's coworkers or subordinates. In reality, being nice only to the people who have power over you is a form of brownnosing—not politeness. Put yourself in others' positions: Don't you appreciate being asked politely to stay overtime and help out on the team project? Isn't that preferable to being ordered to stay late?

Tactfulness, diplomacy, and other forms of etiquette indicate that you are an educated person. Although all educated people are not tactful, all tactful people are educated in a very important sense: they know how to make people feel valued—one of the most important forms of knowledge in any environment.

Fortunately, like any other required behavior, thoughtfulness, tactfulness, and proper business etiquette can be learned. At least one business etiquette handbook (such as Letitia Baldridge's *Complete Guide to Executive Manners*) is a must for anyone who hopes to be promoted to a position that will require business meetings, lunches, dinners, fund-raisers, and other social-business encounters. Although such books do not necessarily explain how to be tactful in written communications, they do typically cover proper dress, invitations, greetings, and the social obligations that are part of business functions.

and general business etiquette will help your organization run more smoothly and will portray you as a careful, conscientious, sensitive human being.

Etiquette and tactfulness are systems of behavior recognized by reasonable people (and you *do* want to be reasonable, don't you?) as the proper way of handling difficult people and difficult situations. In conversations, we regard a calm, even voice as a sign of self-control. "Please," "thank you," and "you're welcome" are markers of graciousness and appreciation. Refraining from embarrassing other people, admitting and apologizing for mistakes, and taking steps to protect other people's sensibilities undergird successful communications that can enhance the goodwill in a business relationship.

To communicate tactfully, you must first recognize the need for a balance between clarity/conciseness/naturalness and tactfulness. Although the clearest,

---

MEMORANDUM

To: Brittany Cooper
From: Jeremy Daniels
Date: September 14, 1999
Subj: Restructuring production lines

context and
thanks

When the huge order for B-plate markers came in, we were swamped, and we are grateful for your efforts to help us keep up with production.

current situation

Now that those orders have been met and delivered, we see that to stay in business, we have to find a way to prevent another slump. Therefore, we are restructuring our production line to enable fewer workers to handle greater responsibilities. Unfortunately, that means we will have to let some of our workers go, and as of October 31, we will no longer have a position for you. But you will receive a check for two weeks' severance pay, which will be mailed to your home address at the end of October.

bad news

good news/
alternative

pleasant closing

We will keep your employment records on file so we can give an accurate reference for you when other employers call. If demands for our product increase, which we certainly hope, we will call you and the other workers laid off to see if you want your position back.

FIGURE 6.3 A Sample Letter Exhibiting Tact

---

most concise, and perhaps even most natural statement to an incompetent employee may be "You're fired," a more tactful approach takes a little longer to draft. The letter of termination in Figure 6.3 demonstrates that approach. As you can see from this example, you have already learned one way of incorporating tact into your business communications: writing an indirectly organized letter that explains reasons before delivering the bad news. Such an organizational structure demonstrates your concern for the reader's feelings.

Other strategies for incorporating tact depend on the following:

- Your incorporation of simple markers of tact
- Your knowledge and selection of proper words and their connotations

- Your understanding of sentence structure's effect on tone
- Your reliance on positives, rather than negatives
- Your avoidance of absolute statements
- Your avoidance of sexist language and assumptions

Markers of Tact

First, your communications should routinely include *simple markers of tact*, such as "please," "thank you," and "you're welcome." Acknowledgments of appreciation and kindness demonstrate your thoughtfulness and attest to your expectations of sociable behavior in the workplace. From your own experiences, you know that you like to do business with organizations whose employees act as if they sincerely appreciate you. Doing business with people who act as if they are doing you a favor by waiting on you or by taking your money isn't as pleasant.

Proper Word Choice

Although including simple markers of tact in business communications is valuable, tactfulness involves a great deal more than saying "please" and "thank you." It also requires that you *know proper words and their connotations.* Calling a woman a "siren" when you mean that she is attractive, saying a product is "cheap" when you mean it is inexpensive, or referring to someone as "infamous" or "notorious" when you mean he is well known can hurt people's feelings or misrepresent your ideas. (See Strategy Review 6.3.)

How do you spot such errors in word usage? For one thing, make sure you know what words mean when you use them. Just because you hear someone use a new word that *sounds* as if it means what you want to say doesn't mean that you understand all of the word's potential undertones. Because a thesaurus rarely explains subtle differences in usage, a dictionary is your best tool to investigate word meanings. Most useful are dictionaries that include synonyms and usage notes that point out the subtle shades of meaning between words and explain common misuses. The following sample usage note is from the *American Heritage Dictionary* (3d ed. 1993. Boston: Houghton Mifflin):

> **Native American . . . :** *Usage Note:* The term *Indian* has always been a misnomer for the earliest inhabitants of the Americas. Certainly wherever confusion between the peoples indigenous to the Americas and the inhabitants of India might exist, *Native American* is an obvious choice. It is also preferred by many contemporary writers when emphasizing ethnic pride. However, it should not be assumed that *Indian* is necessarily offensive or out of date. . . . (908)

MAKING THE BEST USE OF YOUR THESAURUS AND DICTIONARY

Using a thesaurus indiscriminately is a major source of miscommunication. Even common words that typically cause few problems can be dangerous in the hands of a thesaurus abuser. For example, a dictionary's description of a thesaurus's synonyms for "slide" clarifies the subtle differences in meaning and helps the writer select the word that most closely fits the meaning required:

> **slide . . . :** *Syns: slide, slip, glide, coast, skid, slither*. These verbs mean to move smoothly and continuously over or as if over a slippery surface. *Slide* usually implies rapid, easy movement without loss of contact with the surface; *coal sliding down a shute. Slip* is often applied to accidental sliding resulting in loss of balance or foothold: *slipped on a patch of ice. Glide* refers to smooth, free-flowing, seemingly effortless movement: *"four snakes gliding up and down a hollow"* (Ralph Waldo Emerson). *Coast* applies especially to downward movement resulting from the effects of gravity or momentum: *The driver let the truck coast down the incline. Skid* implies an uncontrolled, often sideways sliding caused by a lack of traction: *The bus skidded on wet pavement. Slither* can mean to slip and slide, as on an uneven surface, often with friction and noise: *"The detached crystals slithered down the rock face"* (H. G. Wells). The word can also suggest the sinuous, gliding motion of a reptile: *An iguana slithered across the path.* (*American Heritage Dictionary* 1281)

These differences in usage become even clearer when we misuse a term. Consider the simple sentence "He *glided* over the ice with his hands *sliding* down his partner's arms." Replacing the italic words indiscriminately with other terms results in awkwardness (or hilarity):

> He *slithered* over the ice with his hands *slipping* down his partner's arms.
>
> He *coasted* over the ice with his hands *slithering* down his partner's arms.
>
> He *slid* over the ice with his hands *skidding* down his partner's arms.
>
> He *slipped* on the ice with his hands *gliding* down his partner's arms.

Sentence Structures

In addition to word choice, your choice of *sentence structures* can also have a profound effect on the tone of your communication. You probably remember one of your parents telling you when you were a child "not to take that tone with me." The problem was not so much what you said as how you said it.

Being short, sarcastic, or condescending with people—in speaking or in writing—can quickly mark you as someone with a bad attitude. Just as you don't like being around people who snap or treat you as if you are stupid, others will not want to be around you if you sound that way. Sometimes, however, we may not realize that we sound snappish or patronizing; here are some examples with notes about what makes them sound as they do:

"I told you I wanted that report by Tuesday." (Emphasis on "told" suggests only an idiot would have to be told again.)

"Okay, let's go over this one more time. Take the little yellow tag and wrap it around the big black tire." (Emphasis on "one more time" sounds exasperated, as if this is your last chance. Use of "little" and "big" mimics the way adults talk to children, not to other adults.)

"If I had wanted the sale to start Wednesday, I would have started the sale on Wednesday." (Emphasis implies that the speaker/writer never makes a mistake; you were wrong to think she or he might have erred on the day.)

All these sample sentences let you hear the writer's irritation and anger, creating a tone that may occasionally be useful in workplace writing—but only rarely. More

APPLICATION

Revising for Tone and Reactions

Evaluate the following sentences to see why you react as you do to their tone and messages:

1. Had I known the work was going to be late, I would have rescheduled the rest of the shipment.

2. The bridge is out. I did not know the bridge was out. Nobody told me the bridge was out. So here I am, waiting behind three hours of traffic, because the bridge is out.

3. Nobody told me the work had to go through a committee. I did not even know about a committee. Had the proper person told me about the committee requirement, I would have followed the procedure. How can I be expected to follow the procedures when nobody told me what the procedures were?

4. Get the contract signed. Get it to the post office before 5:00. Get a receipt for it. Get it in the mail.

work gets done in the workplace when people cooperate and share goals than when they are at odds with each other, order each other around, or correct each other.

Positives versus Negatives

Another way to check the tone of your work is to rely, as much as possible, on *positives rather than negatives.* Rather than talking about what you cannot do, emphasize what you can do. Rather than seeing the bad side of a situation, look for the good side. And rather than focusing on what's not right, see if you can find things that are right. In other words, look for solutions instead of just finding problems. The following negatives are revised to emphasize the positives:

> **Original:** We cannot ship that order before December 12.
>
> **Revision:** We can ship the order on December 12, ensuring that you will receive the mattresses by December 15.
>
> **Original:** I can give you only a $200 raise this year.
>
> **Revision:** I can give you a $200 raise this year, and I can increase your employee discount to 25 percent.

As you can see, putting a positive spin on information can have a different effect on the reader. Although you must be careful not to bury or misrepresent important information, thereby risking your credibility with your readers, you can still present most information in a positive, rather than a negative, light. The reader is much more likely to be satisfied with your plan, your response, or your information if you present it positively.

Tactless Absolutes

A final way you can increase the tactfulness of your communications is to carefully *avoid making absolute—"always" and "never"—statements,* a danger you learned about in Chapter 5's discussion of constructing claims. In certain contexts, such as when evaluating employees' performances, such statements are defeating, if not downright humiliating; in other cases, they may make the listeners/readers defensive. Consider the following example:

> You *always* whine about how much work you have, but you *never* do anything.

Such a statement may certainly seem to be true of some people, but telling them in this manner is likely either to make them feel worthless or to increase their combativeness. Certainly, you don't want the employee to respond by sniveling and saying "I can't do anything right." This response requires you to counter your own argument, providing evidence that the employee does, indeed, do many things right. But you also don't want the employee saying "Oh yeah? What about the Jamal account? Who stayed here seven nights in a row to finish it?" This response requires you to provide more information about times the employee was not helpful; you quickly get into a contest over who has the best memory—rather than a true evaluation of the employee's work.

Clearly, you do not want either response from the employee in such a situation. But the tactlessness of the absolute statements almost guarantees that you will get one of the two responses. Temper your writing with a little kindness, and absolute statements are likely to disappear from your communications.

Sexist Language

Revising your work to *avoid sexist language* can also demonstrate your consideration for people's sensitivities in the workplace. Many good definitions of sexist language exist, but in general it refers to language that reflects the assumption that specific workplace roles are gender-bound; such traditional assumptions are skewed, out-of-date, and inconsiderate, however. The following are examples of traditional male and female roles:

Traditional Male Roles	*Traditional Female Roles*
judge	court clerk
CEO	secretary
policeman	meter maid
preacher	choir member
truck driver	waitress
lawyer	paralegal
physician	nurse
professor	teacher
soldier	day-care owner
scientist	receptionist
auto mechanic	homemaker
coach	librarian

Such sexist assumptions about the "proper" roles for men and women are quickly disappearing in American society, primarily because of the increasingly diverse roles that people adopt according to their individual strengths.

Most well-educated people understand the importance of equal opportunities for a variety of roles in our society; unfortunately, our language sometimes continues to reflect stereotypical thinking about gender roles. Be sure to revise your work for stereotypes such as referring to the police officer as *he* and the nurse as *she*. Writers have found several ways to handle sexist pronoun usage in their writings:

> **Original:** Each scientist should record the results of his experiments.
>
> **Revision:** Each scientist should record the results of his or her experiments. (The added pronoun acknowledges that the scientist may be male or female. Many writers [and readers] find this construction awkward unless they are trying to make a specific point about individual behaviors or attitudes. Therefore, many opt for the second revised version.)
>
> **Revision:** Scientists should record the results of their experiments. (Change referent and its pronoun to plurals.)

In addition to watching for sexist pronoun usage (see the Brief Usage Guidebook, section H5), you should also be careful to assign roles and expectations to people on the basis of their capabilities, not their gender (What man will be the new manager? Which of the women—or worse, "girls"—will be promoted to ad-

APPLICATION

Revising for Sexist Language and Implications

The following statements reveal some rather pernicious stereotypes and their extension to other aspects of our language (and our culture). How would you revise these statements to eliminate the sexist implications?

> John's promotion is going to be interesting. He's going to have to work with all those girls at the cashiers' stations. Can you imagine him having to listen to them gossiping and chitchatting? They're going to whine about wanting Saturday nights off to be with their boyfriends. Then, at Christmas, they're going to want time off to go shopping. He's going to have to schedule their work so they can come in late and get off early whenever they don't feel well. It'll never work out.

> Janet's promotion is going to be interesting. She's going to have to work with all those foul-mouthed guys in the delivery area. They're going to be cussing and scratching and talking about what they did with their girlfriends the night before—all that locker room talk. And you can bet they're going to give her a hard time because she's a woman. She's going to be scared to death of them or else she's going to be so hard-nosed and rough that they're going to hate her guts. It'll never work out.

ministrative assistant?). Look for sexist terms that, with a little thought, can be easily revised to be gender-neutral:

policeman = police officer	mailman = mail carrier/deliverer
lady truck driver = truck driver	male nurse = nurse
fireman = fire fighter	spokesman = speaker
salesman = sales clerk/representative	craftsman = artist, worker, artisan

Eliminating sexist language and stereotypes demonstrates your knowledge of the real world, where women and men no longer have to function in limiting, gender-specific roles. Make sure your language reflects your awareness of these truths.

Proofreading the Final Document

After revising for the appropriateness of information in your document, along with the proper sense of audience, purpose, organization, and style, you have almost completed your mission in generating text as a workplace writer. (Visual design and graphics elements, commonly called nontextual elements, are described in Chapters 8 and 9.) The final step is to proofread your work, making sure you have caught all errors in spelling, grammar, and mechanics (punctuation).

Many workplace writers have a tough time proofreading their own work—primarily because they are so familiar with the information, its organization, and other communication elements that they have lost the critical edge required to proofread a document carefully. Therefore, many writers arrange with other writers to switch final documents and proofread each other's work. Such an arrangement is extremely valuable—provided both writers are also good proofreaders.

If you have such an arrangement with coworkers or classmates, be sure to give them enough time to proofread the document thoroughly. If you do not have such an arrangement, make sure you allow enough time to proofread your own work thoroughly. Most writers recommend at least a twenty-four-hour "cooling off" period between writing the final draft of your document and proofreading it. When you return to your document after this period, you will have forgotten some of the elements and will see them with a fresh perspective that will enable you to find errors you missed earlier.

Although many word processing programs include spell checkers, these programs cannot catch some kinds of errors:

- Grammar mistakes
- Misspelled words that are also real words ("war" for "was" or "being" for "begin")
- Omitted words
- Repeated words

- Errors in numbers (28496 for 24896)
- Errors in sequences (1, 2, 4, 5)
- Punctuation mistakes (semicolons for commas)

Do use your computer's spell checker, but do not forget that you are the ultimate proofreader, and your final document will put *your* credibility on the line—not your computer's. (See Strategy Review 6.4.)

STRATEGY REVIEW 6.4

PROOFREADING TIPS

The following tips for proofreading should come in handy; be sure to read through your final draft looking for each type of error. Trying to catch every error in a single read-through rarely works.

1. Look for words you frequently misspell. (I often type "univeristy" when I'm trying to type "university"; now I've learned to look for "university/univeristy" in all my writing—especially when I am typing on a typewriter instead of a word processor.)

2. Read your work out loud. Doing so will often help you find words you have omitted or repeated.

3. Read your work from the back to the front. This strategy keeps information "out of order" and prevents you from glossing over errors.

4. Be particularly sensitive to the tense of verbs in each paragraph. If you begin with a past tense verb, make sure all subsequent verbs are also in the past tense. Look for the frequent "-ed" or "-en" markers at the end of past tense verbs.

5. Review the grammatical structure of items in horizontal or vertical lists to make sure they are parallel—all items should start with the same grammatical form (verbs, participles, etc.).

6. Be sure to check the spelling of all names, towns, and products.

7. Be sure to check all numerical data—addresses, phone numbers, statistics, order numbers, and the like.

8. Look for words with double consonants or vowels. (A third consonant or vowel might creeep in!)

9. Review grammar and punctuation rules (see the Brief Usage Guidebook) for structures or problems that your English teachers have frequently noted in your writing.

The message that you have good ideas, reasonable arguments, and a nice style rarely gets through when your writing is full of proofreading errors. Such errors tend to jar the reader, just as potholes jar riders in a car. Careful proofreading can help ensure a smooth ride.

Summary

Although some professional writers can create a pretty good draft in a single attempt, they rarely try to do so. Instead, they write a draft with the understanding that they will return to it again and again to revise for accuracy, audience considerations, purpose, organization, and style.

Honing the content of a workplace document requires a clear sense of what the information actually means. Writers are responsible for explaining the context as well as the content of all information they provide in their documents. Writers also review and revise the document in light of the readers' needs for definitions of special terminology, appropriate research, and useful conclusions. Then, writers revise to make sure that the readers' purposes for reading and their own purposes for writing share some common ground because writing from only the writer's perspective and only for the writer's purpose typically results in unethical and uninformative workplace writing. Writers also revise for organizational clarity, demonstrating their understanding of the order in which readers need and expect to find information.

After revising the content of a workplace document—the "what" that writers want to communicate—good writers also review the style—the "how" of communication. In revising for style, these writers consider the clarity of their statements, looking for ways to ensure that the reader does not become confused. They also consider the conciseness of their statements, remembering that readers are likely to get frustrated with redundancies, hedges, useless introductions to sentence content, and extenders that mask strong verbs as weak nouns or hide them in wordy phrases. Next, they review the tone of the work to make sure it is both natural and tactful. Good writers realize that excluding pomposity, clichés, and passive voice and including markers of politeness, appropriate word choices, and properly constructed sentences can help to generate goodwill and a cooperative work environment. To this end, these communicators also seek to construct positives instead of negatives, to avoid absolute statements, and to correct sexist language and attitudes in their work.

As a final step, once the writers are certain that all their information is correct and stated appropriately, they begin the process of proofreading. If possible, they exchange documents, knowing that a reader with a fresh perspective will catch more errors than they would find in their own writing. When another reader is not available, writers must rely on their own proofreading skills, developed through the tips offered at the end of the chapter, to ensure the accuracy of spelling, grammar, and mechanics in the document.

✔ Begin the revising process by considering the content carefully. It makes no sense to revise and proofread a paragraph or section that you may delete.

✔ Reconsider your audience—what readers already know about your subject (Have you repeated information they already know?) and what they need to know (Have you omitted vital information?).

✔ Reconsider your own purpose for writing and your readers' purposes for reading; find a way to mesh the two.

✔ Revise for appropriate information:

- Make sure all information is accurate (Are numbers correct, details straight, and sources quoted correctly?).

- Make sure all information is complete (Is the full context provided? Is my work telling the whole story?).

- Make sure all information is current (Is this information as recent as possible?).

- Make sure all information is relevant (Does this information further my point?).

✔ Revise for stylistic concerns, such as clarity, conciseness, naturalness, and tactfulness.

✔ To revise for clarity, be sure that modifiers and punctuation lead readers to the correct conclusion. Also be sure that the content includes no ambiguity (through either lack of logic or vagueness).

✔ To revise for conciseness, eliminate redundancies, unnecessary hedges, introductory missteps, and extenders.

✔ To revise for naturalness, eliminate pomposity, clichés, and unnecessary passive voice.

✔ To revise for tactfulness, incorporate simple markers of politeness ("please" and "thank you," especially); review your word choices and sentence structures; present information as positively as possible; avoid absolute statements; and eliminate sexist language and attitudes from your writing.

✔ Proofread carefully. Agree to co-proofread with a partner. Take extra time to work on a piece of writing, set it aside, then return and proofread it again.

EXERCISES

Individual Exercises

1. Read paragraphs A, B, and C. For each paragraph, determine the following:

　a. Who the intended readers are and what their purpose for reading is.

　b. What the writer hopes to accomplish.

　c. How appropriate the research is for the readers and their purpose.

　d. What kinds of conclusions might be reached from the paragraph.

　e. Whether each sentence in the paragraph contributes to the topic sentence, which is underlined for you. If a sentence does not contribute to the readers' understanding, explain whether the sentence should be omitted or should go in a different paragraph with a different topic sentence.

Once you have eliminated unnecessary or irrelevant information, revise the paragraphs for clarity, conciseness, and tactfulness.

A. <u>Our company's no-smoking policy was instituted for two reasons.</u> First, substantial evidence supports the idea that secondhand smoke is dangerous to non-smokers. With the increased number of colds and allergy attacks being reported, we felt it would be better to require smokers to go outdoors to smoke. But they cannot just get up from their desks any time and go outside. They have to wait until breaks. Second, our insurance representative said we could lower our group insurance rates if fewer people smoke. We are hoping that the inconvenience of having to go outdoors to smoke may encourage more people to quit smoking altogether. Of course, we cannot govern what our people do after hours, but perhaps this strategy will help.

B. <u>The new shipping zones have caused several problems for our delivery people.</u> Nobody knows where some zones are. Some of the zones that used to include both small and larger clients are no longer in the same zone, meaning that our trucks are overloaded for certain zones and underloaded for others. In the past, our trucks could balance orders for large companies with orders for small companies—all going to the same zone. Now, we have to send two big trucks to one zone, costing the company more money. Then, we have to send little shipments to almost every zone because there's no room on the big trucks for those deliveries. And some of the workers are complaining that they get only large shipments that require more back-breaking labor, while other workers get to carry the light stuff.

C. <u>Stadium seating has been reorganized to give our biggest supporters the best seats.</u> In the past, some of the regular Bears fans had better seats than members of the Bears Den. Students, on the other hand, were separated by the band. The new arrangement keeps all students together, which can be a problem for security except that they know where all the students are sitting now and can keep an eye on them for drinking and unruly behavior. The alumni section and members of the Bears Den have equally good seats. And since many of the alumni are Bears Den members, that's no problem anymore. The biggest problem is what to do with the faculty. Some people think they should have seats away from the students, but that would mean they would have to sit at the top of the stadium. But somebody has to sit at the top of the stadium; why not the faculty?

2. List ten terms that are specific for the field in which you intend to major. What considerations should you make about the following readers' knowledge of those words and their context? How would you define the terms for these readers?

   a. Your parents

   b. A sixteen-year-old

   c. A coworker in another division of your company

   d. A business professor

   e. An English professor

   f. A customer

   g. An engineer

   h. A television newscaster

   i. Your congressional representative

3. Revise the following sentences to eliminate problems with clarity, conciseness, and tactfulness:

   a. The parts of the reservation process help the individual hotel so they don't have unnecessary business to deal with.

   b. For the cost of hiring one more person for both night and day shifts and installing an 800 number you could hire a computer reservations service. It's not impersonal either, hiring a service is just like hiring a 24-hour employee at your inn.

   c. A small business will profit from a consulting firm because they keep the personal touch without devastating their resources.

   d. There are many people who want to invest in stocks without knowledge of how they operate.

   e. Women are generally unaware of the extent of gender biases. This is a result of women's learning to expect different treatment and conforming to different rules from men. An example of this is behavior of men that typically is discounted will be considered objectionable in a woman.

   f. As per your request, we investigated the dubious nature of the Hills's business holdings and have found them wanting.

   g. A review of operations reveals that freight bills for Do-Good Trucking have steadily increased from $478,011 in 1995 to over $1,309,492 in 1998. This is an increase of almost 100 percent in three years.

h. It is typical for expenses to increase as a company grows. One explanation is the increase in the size of the administrative staff.

i. Creating a no-hassle, enjoyable experience for customers with faulty tailpipes was only part of the success behind the car company's handling of the recall situation.

j. I don't think it would kill the salesmen to take a day off their routes to come in and help with inventory. After all, if it weren't for us keeping up with the stocks and supplies, they wouldn't have anything to sell.

4. Drawing on the strategies presented in the chapter, revise and proofread the following paragraphs:

a. Companies must communicate effectively with many audiences to be successful in today's competitive sales market and work place. Whether the audience is a company's employees, members of the board of directors, shareholders, long-time clients, prospective customers, or the media, corporate communication must transmit messages effectively to the different target audiences and produce the desired results. A consistently high-quality message that is meaningful to the audience can build trust, win respect, garner favor, create understanding, reap profit, and more. communication has long been recognized as an external necessity in the areas of corporate public relations and marketing of goods or services. However at a time when many companies are facing economic uncertainly and downsizing, published literature notes that the corporate communicator's role is coming to be viewed as even more critical.

b. When crises or questions of credibility occur in corporations, communicators are the ones often on the firing line with the media. As the company's main link to the media, the corporate communicator usually serves as the spokesman for the company. quick responses and sensitive statements are necessary to provide information, calm fears, dispel rumors, and dissipate any negative effects possibly caused by the crisis. Moreover, complete disclosure during day-to-day business operations and during crisis situations can help a company regain the trust of the various publics that might be really hungry to bring the company down. The main point is you have to really be on your toes when you're in charge of a company's communications—especially during crisis situations—because the wolves are always at your door.

Collaborative Exercise

1. For each of the following topics, list three separate audiences who might be interested in some aspect of the topic. What kinds of information would be most useful for each group of readers? What kinds of conclusions should the report offer them?

a. A report on oil production at the local refinery

    b. A policy statement on sexual harassment

    c. A revision of a particular company's hierarchy

    d. An explanation of the company's retirement benefits

    e. A description of how to make candles

    f. The procedure for appealing a grade

    g. How parking fees are collected at your school

    h. The administration and role of the local Humane Society

    i. The advantages and disadvantages of college ROTC programs

    j. How professors at your school are granted tenure

An example is provided for you:

Topic: The advantages and disadvantages of college ROTC programs.

Readers and their motives: Students interested in the program; parents concerned about students' decisions; academic counselors reviewing the program; potential employers investigating the kinds of experiences ROTC students have had.

Conclusions:

- *Student:* I should/should not enroll in ROTC; I should learn more about ROTC.
- *Parent:* I should/should not encourage my child to enroll in ROTC.
- *Academic counselor:* ROTC is a good deal for certain students.
- *Potential employers:* ROTC is/is not good preparation for the work we expect from employees.

 ONGOING ASSIGNMENT

- Using the draft you created for Chapter 5's Ongoing Assignment, revise the manual you have created for newcomers to your school or workplace. Be sure to complete the informational revision before moving on to the stylistic revision. What kinds of changes have you made in your draft? What kinds of weaknesses do you want to keep in mind for special attention in your future workplace documents?

CHAPTER 7

Collaborating on Workplace Writing

225

Contrary to the popular image of writers working alone in cubicles cut off from the rest of the world, most workplace writers find that isolation is a rare phenomenon. As you have learned, the well-being of any organization depends on communication among its employees and with clients, vendors, and other groups; and communication means interaction, not isolation.

One of the most important ways that workers interact is through a collaborative project, assigned in the workplace because various viewpoints and expertises are needed to ensure that the project will be accurate, comprehensive, and coherent. This chapter focuses on the advantages and dangers of collaboration and offers some strategies you can use to make collaborations work more smoothly. After comparing the collaborative and competitive workplace models, the chapter describes two dominant work patterns and the most common roles that collaborators assume. Finally, the chapter addresses a general fear about collaborative efforts: conflict. Realizing that conflict most likely results from one of four sources—process issues, document issues, relationship issues, and personality issues—will help you develop strategies for recognizing and managing conflict before it overwhelms you and your workgroup.

Collaborative tasks most often operate within and reflect the specific constraints of an organization's culture (or the cultures of any number of organizations that may be involved in the project). Therefore, you should review Chapter 1's discussion of organizational culture to refresh your memory of how an organization's culture establishes expectations and behaviors, which can lead to miscommunication and sabotage in collaborative efforts.

The Competitive versus the Collaborative Workplace Model

Although education emphasizes both individual performance and social integration, the dominant image of the American workplace has historically been one of intense competition. Increasingly, however, many organizations are recognizing that when competition dominates their organizational cultures, their employees compete against each other—rather than working together to compete against the *real* competition. In these organizations, sales representatives do not pass on leads to other representatives, even when they cannot get the sale themselves. Messages get lost; phone calls are not returned; and workers criticize each other to anyone who will listen.

As an antidote to this competitive and destructive workplace model, organizations are encouraging collaboration among workers to achieve their goals. Unlike the secretive and often brutal nature of competition, collaboration often allows workers to set their own goals or establish their own process for meeting a goal. Information is shared rather than hoarded, and ideas become group property where they can be explored and put to work in ways that the original "owner" of the idea may never have considered. In collaborative team efforts, you can expect a number of work-related and socially based changes from the competitive model:

- Experts from various departments in your organization serve as resources for your project.

- Work assignments are flexible, allowing workers to work on processes and products that differ from their routine job assignments.

- Multilevel cooperation encourages information exchange and access to knowledgeable coworkers.

- Individual workers have more control over the message, medium, and other elements of the written document.

- A higher level of participation, motivation, and sense of ownership toward the final product exists, typically resulting in increased morale and loyalty.

In this chapter, we will follow the scenario of Alexa and Natalie, a writer and a computer scientist, respectively, who are collaborating on a project with Michael, a graphics illustrator, and Sherry, their editor, to develop a users' guide for the Internet. All four team members work for Buffalo Internet, a provider of Internet services. Alexa's expertise in writing will help the team determine the kinds of information needed and the best means for presenting that information for novice Internet users. Natalie's expertise with how the system operates and the kinds of access it can provide will form the basis of the subject matter for the project, while Michael's expertise in illustrating computer screens and processes will help users visualize their tasks and options. Sherry's knowledge of writing, computers, and graphics will enable her to oversee the group's work and help in decision making at a number of levels and stages in their project.

At their first meeting, the group members recognize that they depend on each other to produce a successful manual. They are enthusiastic about the project because they realize it is important to their organization's well-being and to their clients' satisfaction with the service Buffalo Internet offers. They also understand that to create a useful document, they must engage in a collaborative effort that will bring together their various expertises, viewpoints, and experiences.

Advantages of the Collaborative Workplace Model

At its best, collaboration encourages sharing, discussing, negotiating, and other key activities in building relationships and exchanging ideas. All these activities converge to form the basis of strong collaborative skills, which are important in both the classroom and the workplace where collaboration offers several advantages:

- The additional information and perspective a partner or team members can offer a project (by raising questions, playing devil's advocate, pursuing alternative strategies, etc.).

- Fewer chances of errors, fraud, and oversights.

- A realistic means of dividing labor and, thus, meeting schedules and deadlines; or a more integrated approach to work that encourages idea development at every stage of the collaborative project;

- A forum for communicating about special workplace issues, such as employee benefits, representation in the workforce, quality assurance, and even future directions for the organization. In the classroom, collaboration can result in students becoming more involved in the educational process, as they have a voice in their reading materials, testing procedures, projects, and even the topics for some of their lessons. Collaborative assignments require students to develop negotiating and problem-solving skills.

- More reliable data and interpretations of data.

- Greater incentives to study and learn (for most people, learning in groups is more fun and more successful than learning alone).

- Less dependence on high-level executives/teachers to make all the decisions.

- Improved morale among workers/students who feel their ideas are valued.

The new emphasis on collaboration has attracted the attention of various academic disciplines because it reflects the way many American businesses now conduct their work. Even prominent MBA programs, historically known for the intense competition their coursework engendered among students, are emphasizing collaborative skills. Similarly, medical students are encouraged to collaborate with each other (within and outside their specializations) to understand the whole effects of their patients' symptoms and possible treatments. In short, collaboration has taken on a special significance in a variety of work relationships, and many business forecasters predict it will continue to proliferate and become the dominant model for work in industrialized nations.

Variations on the Collaborative Model

Although so far we have talked about collaboration as if it were a singular concept, in reality collaboration may take a number of forms in the workplace—most notably, as a division of labor or as an integrated task (see Figure 7.1). You may find that you will use both of these strategies at various stages in your collaboration.

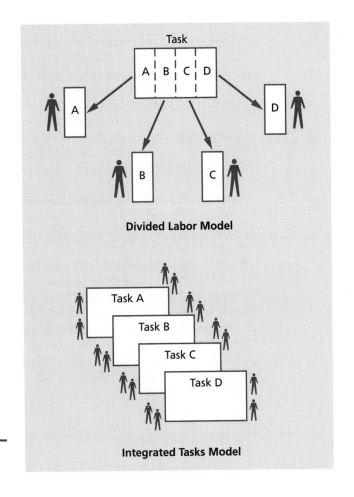

Divided Labor versus Integrated Tasks
Collaborative Models

Divided Labor

The most common means of collaborating is probably the divided labor strategy. Its purpose is to divide the tasks equitably (according to expertise, time, other projects, etc.) among team members.

In the Buffalo Internet scenario, for instance, Natalie conducts all the research for the project, drawing heavily on her own knowledge of the Internet's resources. Then, she offers her notes and findings to Alexa, who drafts the manual. Alexa turns her draft over to Michael, who determines where and what kinds of graphics are needed and then draws those graphics. Sherry reviews the draft, making corrections, asking for more information, and suggesting alternative wording and graphics to improve the manual. She then returns the draft to Natalie, Alexa, and Michael to make the corrections, additions, and deletions.

This divided labor model appeals to many collaborators because it allows them to use their strengths and to work at their own pace, provided they accomplish the work by the group's deadline. Because collaborators can be physically separated, divided labor is often the most sensible approach when workers are in different segments or branches of an organization.

The key to successful division of labor is *equitable* division—the shared sense that the tasks have been divided so that no one spends more or less time on the project than others (or at least not without a significant reward for the additional work or a clear sense of why the work was distributed unevenly). When teams collaborate frequently, however, the sense of equitable distribution may change, with one team member taking on more work for one project while others take on more work for other projects.

The advantage of the divided labor model is that it requires less time than many other kinds of work assignments, including the integrated tasks strategy (discussed next). By dividing the labor, many workers feel they can complete a task in a fraction of the time required for the integrated approach. The disadvantage of the divided labor model, however, is that it is highly susceptible to miscommunication; writers who go off to write on their own without a clear sense of their mission and without intermediary feedback may produce completely unacceptable drafts as their contribution to the final product. Further, divided labor often leads to fragmented documents; no matter how hard the editor works to commingle the drafts into a whole, the individual voices and styles of the various writers may prevail. Finally, because these workers work alone, many invariably feel that they have worked more than others in the group, that their work was of significantly higher quality than the others' work, or that the others failed to appreciate their efforts.

Integrated Tasks

The alternative to divided labor as the collaborative strategy is integrated tasks, a complex and sophisticated model that, nevertheless, frequently results in much higher quality work than the divided labor model. In the integrated tasks model, workers collaborate on every segment of the work process—never going off to their own offices or workstations to work alone.

In the Buffalo Internet scenario, Natalie may initiate a discussion among the group members to try to understand the novice Internet user's needs and fears. As they talk, Michael realizes that a graphic of the overall Internet structure would provide a foundation for much of the information that Natalie wants to offer. Alexa gains some insight on how to set up the text discussion that will support and clarify the illustration Michael envisions, while Sherry suggests adding a central character to "act out" the user's questions and frustrations. Now Alexa may have to revise her initial ideas to make a place for this character/user in the context of the manual.

The advantages of the integrated tasks model include a greater feeling of having explored all ideas and a greater sense of ownership of the final document. Workers also tend to feel they have contributed equally because they are all par-

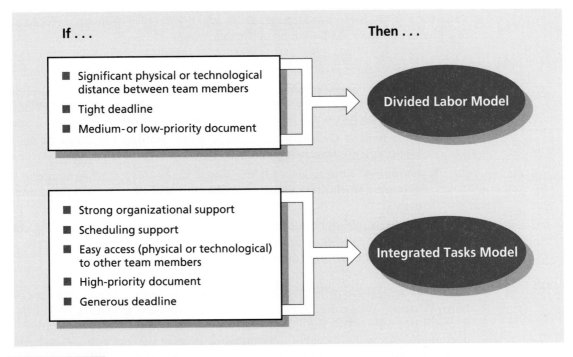

FIGURE 7.2 Factors Affecting the Choice of a Collaborative Model

ticipating in every aspect of the work. In addition, the final document tends to sound more unified because it is a group effort, rather than a combination of multiple voices speaking in different segments of the document.

The primary disadvantage of the integrated tasks approach is that it often requires considerable time. Scheduling can become a nightmare if the organization does not support the approach. Unfortunately, many shortsighted organizations do not see that the integrated approach's quality more than compensates for the additional time required.

Thus, the choice of the divided labor approach versus the integrated tasks approach may turn on resources and organizational philosophy, rather than on which model is more familiar to the group members. Figure 7.2 summarizes the factors that can affect the choice of a model.

Featured Roles in Collaborative Groups

Team projects are common assignments in both small and large organizations because many projects require expertise in marketing, engineering, writing, safety factors, legal issues, design, budgets, and numerous other areas that are far too diverse for a single person to manage. Thus, when you collaborate on a workplace document, you may work with all of the following:

- *Subject matter experts* or *content specialists:* Colleagues (such as engineers, accountants, technicians, researchers, and others) from the technical divisions of your organization who have specific knowledge of the subjects about which you will frequently be required to write.
- *Other writers:* Colleagues with experience drafting the kinds of documents you are now being asked to create.
- *Illustrators:* Colleagues with the visual know-how (and equipment) to enhance the clarity, quality, and visual appeal of your workplace documents.
- *Editors:* Colleagues whose knowledge and experience with writing conventions, as well as subject details, allows them to correct, improve, or approve the writing you produce.

Your work with these colleagues may vary widely in tone, content, and expectations. Whatever the project, however, your ability to learn, get along, and be flexible will not only affect the quality and comprehensiveness of your workplace documents, but will also signal how much of a "team player" you are—whether your coworkers look forward to an assignment with you or consider it some kind of punishment.

Experienced collaborators use a number of strategies to help them to succeed in a group, but perhaps none is as important as having a positive attitude. Recognizing that every collaborative experience gives you additional insights into your organization, its mission, and its workers can help you understand how important your work is and how it fits in with the other tasks going on in your environment. Thus, whether you work with a partner or with a team, and regardless of your collaborators' personalities and the role you play in the group, you will want to use these guidelines as the foundation of your approach to collaboration:

- Prepare thoroughly.
- Share ideas willingly.
- Keep remarks brief and relevant.
- Maintain an open mind.
- Listen carefully.
- Give and receive constructive criticism willingly.
- Help reconcile differences of opinion.
- Focus on the group's objective instead of on [your] own. (Hulbert 53)

You are now ready to apply these guidelines to working with your collaborative team members.

Working with Subject Matter Experts

Depending on your role in your organization, you may be the subject matter expert (frequently known as a SME) with whom professional writers are paired, or you may have to work with SMEs. These content specialists are characterized by their special knowledge of the topic about which you (or other writers) are asked to write. They may serve any technical, clerical, or specialized role in the organization; but for our purposes, they are not the primary writers on a project.

In the Buffalo Internet scenario, Natalie's expertise is invaluable to the group, but having her write the document could easily be disastrous—simply because she knows so much about the Internet. In short, the team realizes that Natalie's knowledge is invaluable but far too sophisticated for novice users. Thus, the team uses Natalie as a resource without confusing her needs and level of background knowledge with the audience's limited knowledge and extensive needs. Through question-and-answer repartee, the group can hone Natalie's extensive knowledge into manageable bits of information that their audience can use. For-

THE WORLD OF WORKPLACE WRITING

Difficulties in Working with Subject Matter Experts

Although working with subject matter experts is generally a pleasant experience, getting information from them can also be a great deal more difficult than just asking for the information—for a variety of reasons:

- The SMEs may not understand what you want.
- They may be stressed by their own deadlines and find your requests for information bothersome.
- They may be irritated that you don't know the information already.
- They may feel that it is not their job to explain complex, serious issues to "the little people."
- Their schedules may not allow them to meet with you for an adequate amount of time.
- Their technical jargon may not be clear to you.
- They may not know how to explain the subject to nontechnical personnel.

Although you should not be overly sensitive in any of your work relationships, you should realize that a request for information can be viewed as an intrusion. Understanding that you are asking for a favor, however, must be balanced with the realization that both you and the content expert are doing the organization's work—and that you must cooperate to accomplish that work.

tunately, Natalie understands her role and offers to provide details and additional information where necessary; she is aware that the manual's readers know as little about the Internet as she did a few years ago, when she, too, was a beginning Internet user.

Working with content experts can be a pleasure, especially when they recognize that your job is difficult and that you do not have the technical expertise they have. In many cases, you will find that they are more than willing to take the time to accommodate your questions and explain their work. The guidelines in Strategy Review 7.1 will help you establish a good relationship with SMEs from the outset.

STRATEGY REVIEW 7.1

WORKING WITH SUBJECT MATTER EXPERTS

The following guidelines for working with subject matter experts will help you develop useful strategies for getting the cooperation you need to write your document:

1. If you need to meet with the SME on a one-on-one basis, arrange a special appointment, clearly explaining how much time your session will require.

2. Whether you are working in a partnership or a group, clearly explain the kinds of information you will need to make sure the expert has all the necessary files and data when you meet.

3. Do your homework. Before going to the expert, read as much as possible so that you will be somewhat knowledgeable about (or at least familiar with) the topic.

4. Ask specific questions. Don't ask the expert to "tell me all about this product."

5. Don't pretend to know more than you do. When you don't understand a description, term, or some other bit of information, ask. Don't wait until the expert has used the term for half an hour before admitting you don't know what it means.

6. Ask the expert for advice on describing the product or process to the group of readers you have identified as the audience for your document.

7. If the expert provides written material to be incorporated into your work, use it, if possible. If you need to make some changes, be prepared to explain them in terms of clarity, simplicity, and readers' needs—not just "because it sounds better."

8. If you need to schedule additional sessions, do so at the end of your meeting. Many topics require hours of collaboration, but your expert may become

restless or irritable if you plan a three-day session. If you have any control over your schedule, you may want to set up daily appointments from, say, 8:00 to 10:00, which will give you time to meet your own deadline without monopolizing the expert for three entire days.

9. Thank the expert (and all other group members). Everyone likes to be appreciated, and the content expert has made your job possible, not just easier.

Remember, too, that you may be the SME on some projects. If so, you will want to revise some of the guidelines in Strategy Review 7.1 to fit your new role. Most important, however, is realizing that you and the writer(s) are working toward a common goal: the success of your organization. Talk with the writer(s) about your expectations for the collaboration, the kinds of information you can provide, and the way you prefer to work. Then, be flexible as the writer(s) responds with other ideas about your collaboration. One of the special requirements of collaboration is negotiation—you will never have everything your own way, regardless of the role you play.

APPLICATION

Collaborating with Subject Matter Experts

For the Applications in this chapter, your teacher will serve as the subject matter expert about a favorite hobby, and the rest of the class will be divided into collaborative teams. Each team will assign an appropriate role (researcher, writer, editor, illustrator) to each member of the group.

After announcing the topic of the hobby, the teacher will allow you time to conduct some research on your own about the hobby. Your group may delegate this task to one or two members or approach it as an integrated task.

Next, if your group is using the integrated tasks approach, the teacher will meet with the entire team to provide information about the hobby. If your team is using the divided labor approach, the teacher will meet with *only* the researchers and/or writers.

After this meeting, write three or four pages describing some aspect of your teacher's hobby for readers who are totally inexperienced with that hobby. Again, your team may either delegate this task to one member or use an integrated approach. Remember, however, that at this stage your task is to gather information and draft a description—not produce a final product.

On a separate page or two, describe the process of gathering information and preparing to meet with your content expert; include the details of the decisions you made about your collaborative process.

Working with Other Writers

Collaboration in the workplace frequently pairs writers with other writers, and many people assume that such pairings are relatively stress-free. After all, both collaborators come from similar educational backgrounds, share common goals, and value the written word. Actually, working with other writers can be an excruciating experience. When one writer comes from an academic background (perhaps, has an MS or an MA in technical writing) and the other comes with technical experience (became a writer after years as an engineer, for instance), the differences in perspectives, habits, and rules about writing can be monumental. Other problems arise when writers have different styles of writing, different pet peeves about language usage, different processes for writing, or different rules about grammar, mechanics, and usage. You may even feel some of these tensions when you collaborate on writing projects for this course.

Getting along with other writers requires an appreciation for their writing habits and writing styles. Collaborators who appreciate each other will not take a narrow-minded approach to writing and the writing process. They will not insist, for example, that every writer start with the introduction, that "which" and "that" are interchangeable in standard English, or that the company's piped-in music should be turned off. Of course, you may find some habits intolerable—the overuse of certain words or descriptions, the inflated tone of the work, or even a

---

THE WORLD OF WORKPLACE WRITING

Negotiating the Draft

On the job, you are likely to find that you will frequently have to negotiate about written documents—primarily because we all have ideas and idiosyncrasies about how to communicate those ideas. Because ideas can be expressed in innumerable ways, conflicts over the message itself, the purpose of the document, or even who the real audience is can creep into good working relationships and cause friction.

Even after you have resolved conflicts, you may still disagree about the particular wording of an idea. Establishing a strategy for resolving "wording differences" at the beginning of the collaboration can help you eliminate some unnecessary conflict. Workplace writers frequently use the following strategies to prevent difficulties:

1. Defer to the group leader or editor.
2. Test the separate versions on coworkers outside your group.
3. Test the separate versions on representative readers.
4. Negotiate a compromise in which you give in on this point in exchange for writing another segment of the document the way you wish.

writer's constant failure to complete tasks on time. Some successful collaborators begin with a list of pet peeves that lets their partner(s) know what habits really bother them. (See Strategy Review 7.2.)

STRATEGY REVIEW 7.2

WORKING WITH OTHER WRITERS

Following these guidelines for working with other writers can help prevent many of the conflicts that might otherwise arise:

1. Select—at the outset—the grammar handbook, style manual, dictionary, and other reference works that you will rely on to resolve differences over grammar, documentation styles, spelling, graphics, and other elements of your document.

2. List your favorite and least favorite roles in writing: planning, researching, drafting, organizing, revising, designing, formatting the document. With luck, your partner(s) will prefer other roles, and you can divide the work accordingly.

3. If you decide to divide the labor, clarify the roles each of you will take and the segments each of you will write. Miscommunications about roles and segments waste time and put you and your collaborator(s) in the position of having to make choices at a stage in the process when such issues should have been long resolved.

4. If you adopt an integrated approach to your writing, be particularly sensitive about dominating the process. Give all contributors a chance to finish an idea or offer their own views for moving ahead.

5. Negotiate the outline of the work and milestones for completing particular aspects of the work.

Following these guidelines can help prevent some rather inconsequential differences from controlling the work relationship you establish with your partner or team of writers. Further, the guidelines acknowledge that we all have different styles and work habits, which affect our writing just as they do every other part of our lives.

From your own collaborative experiences in this classroom, you have probably realized the importance of following the suggestions in each of the previous chapters, especially the advice for planning your document. Collaborators who work without a plan often have no clear sense of their audience, purpose, and message. Yet, as you know, neglecting these elements in any kind of writing can be fatal. As you work with other writers, you will find that employing those early strategies can alleviate a great deal of anguish at later points in your draft.

Working with Illustrators

Because most workplace writers are not graphics experts, they eagerly rely on those who are. But that does not mean that writers should have no input into decisions about graphics in a document. On the contrary, most illustrators want the writers' ideas. When the writers have no ideas to offer, the illustrator must read the document (a waste of time that should be spent perfecting the graphics the document needs).

Working with illustrators means making sure they have the information they need to do their jobs. In particular, illustrators need to know who your readers are, what their needs are, what the document's purpose is, and what the goal of the entire project is.

When you are collaborating on a workplace document with a graphics expert, perhaps the most important thing to remember is that a different form of communication is involved. Although your collaborations with subject matter experts, other writers, and editors require negotiation of content and style, you are still working with the written word. Now, you must negotiate the visual aspects of your work, a negotiation that requires a basic understanding of graphics and illustrative concepts (see Chapter 8). In addition, you need to be able to (1) trust the illustrator, (2) tell the illustrator what you do and do not like, and (3) employ your diplomatic skills. (See Strategy Review 7.3.)

S T R A T E G Y   R E V I E W   7 . 3

WORKING WITH GRAPHICS ILLUSTRATORS

Working with a graphics illustrator gives you a chance to work with a different kind of subject matter expert. Unlike the content expert, the illustrator holds expertise in an area that complements your ideas but does not necessarily shape them, although good graphics can certainly augment content. Successful collaborators respect the illustrator's expertise and follow these guidelines:

1. Have some idea of the kinds of graphics you want to use—and why. You should not assume that the illustrator will choose the appropriate ideas to present graphically.

2. Provide a rough (thumbnail) sketch of the graphic you want the illustrator to create, or take graphics from other documents that you like to show the illustrator what you have in mind.

3. Listen to your illustrator's suggestions; you might be surprised at how your ideas can be represented graphically.

4. Ask questions if you don't understand what the illustrator is suggesting. Like other experts, graphics illustrators have their own technical jargon, which may confuse you. But also learn some of that jargon, especially if your work will require frequent associations and collaborations with illustrators.

5. Be sensitive and up front about deadlines and budgets (your own and the illustrator's). The illustrator may show you a number of "gee whiz!" possibilities—possibilities that can cost thousands of dollars in some printed documents. If your budget does not allow for such graphics, ask for a scaled-down version that is more economically feasible.

Once you have described what you want, the illustrator will construct a rough draft, which you should approve before the illustration is incorporated into your final document. Consider these questions as you preview the graphics:

Content

- Is the subject right?
- Is it the subject you asked for from the illustrator?
- Is the meaning clear?

Appearance

- When the illustration is placed on the page, will I notice it? (Squint your eyes and look at the page.)
- Is the illustration well executed? Does it look sloppy and should not? Does it look neat and should not?
- If the illustration is in color, are the colors correct? Do the colors give me the right feeling?

Style

- Will the illustration have the intended effect on readers?
- Do I like the illustration? Will others like it?
- Does the type of illustration seem appropriate for the document?
- Does the illustration overpower the text?
- Is the illustration too busy or too colorful?
- Is the tone right?
- Does the illustration have the feeling I want? Is it out-of-date, faddish, or conservative?
- Will different members of my audience react differently to it? How? Does that matter? (Tanner and Larson 153)

What happens if you hate the illustration the graphics expert offers you? Again, be diplomatic; talk about the illustration, not the artist. Instead of saying "You didn't do what I asked you to do," try "This illustration doesn't look the way I imagined it would." Then, put the blame on yourself: "I did a lousy job explaining what I want. Let me try again." Then, offer specifics; most often, you will want to focus on the following kinds of revisions:

- The perspective
- The color
- The size
- The amount of detail
- The visibility of the parts
- The lightness or darkness
- The connections or relationships between parts
- Implied textures

Rather than telling the illustrator, "Something's just not right about this illustration," be as specific as possible. Again, communication is paramount. Remember, too, that diplomacy, clarity, and accuracy are just as crucial in working with illustrators as they are in any other collaborative relationship.

In the Buffalo Internet scenario, Michael produced graphics showing the overall process of using the Internet and its connections, but Alexa realized the illustrations were drawn exclusively from Natalie's perspective as a sophisticated Internet user. As a result, the graphics were far too detailed for the novice user, identified as the audience of the manual. Working with Natalie and Michael, Alexa helped the group reshape its idea and the visual representation of the Internet model; the result was a more manageable and understandable tool for the novice reader.

Working with Editors

The primary role of editors is to suggest changes or make corrections in documents that could otherwise confuse, irritate, or even harm readers. In short, the editor is one of the primary connections between the company's work (about which you are writing) and the consumer. The writer's relationship with the editor, therefore, is an important one, but it may also be strained because many of us feel defensive about anything we write.

Chapter 5's discussion of drafting reminded you not to fall in love with your drafts because they will invariably change in your revising process (see Chapter 6). Similarly, even after you have concluded your revisions and produced what you feel is a final document, your editor may make additional changes—making it doubly unwise for you to fall in love with the document you submit to your editor.

It should help you to know what editors will do with your work, once you have completed the draft. Many editors divide the editing process into two functions: substantive editing (editing for content) and copy editing (editing for grammar, punctuation, proofreading, spacing errors, and so on). Although relatively few writers have problems with editors during the copy editing stages, problems during the substantive editing process are likely to be more harrowing—for both the writer and the editor. The following list outlines the questions editors will be asking about your document:

- What is the purpose of this document?
- Who will read it and why?
- What should readers do or know as a result of reading it?
- What do they already know about the subject?
- In what circumstances will they read it? (In good light or poor? Inside or outside? While doing a task?)
- Will they read it straight through or selectively?
- Should they memorize the contents or just use the document for reference?
- What will they do with the document once they have read it? (Throw it away? File it? Post it?)
- What are their attitudes toward the subject of the document? (Will they be inherently cooperative? Unsure? Hostile?) (Rude 206–07)

Thus, the editor brings a fresh perspective to your work. You may find that the answers you thought you had provided may not be so clear to the editor and may, therefore, require some revision. In short, the editor serves as a representative for the audience and may offer suggestions that will make the difference between a mediocre document and a truly excellent one. Consider the editor's points carefully and incorporate helpful suggestions whenever possible.

To promote a good relationship with your editor, you should first understand that it is the editor's job to make you look good. As hard as it is to accept criticism sometimes, the editor's comments may prevent your work from being criticized by readers or by the upper-level administration in your organization. It is far better to discuss differences with the editor—all in the name of producing the best document possible—than to let your ego keep you from making changes that could substantially affect the quality of the final document. (See Strategy Review 7.4 on page 242.)

APPLICATION

Negotiating Collaborative Roles

Continuing the teacher's hobby scenario, reconsider the roles you and your group assigned in the first Application; pay particular attention to matters of expertise and temperament. After reassigning roles, describe briefly who will be doing what and how you reached those decisions about role assignments.

S T R A T E G Y   R E V I E W   7 . 4

WORKING WITH EDITORS

To promote a good working relationship with your editor, you should consider these pointers:

1. Make sure you and your editor share the same vision (purpose, readers, use, and longevity) and goals (sales background information, legal protection) for the document you are writing. Differences in views and goals can be a source of numerous problems with a draft and its revisions.

2. Understand the editor's suggestions or criticisms thoroughly before trying to make changes. You can make substantially more work for yourself if you fail to get this clarification.

3. Understand whether the editor is offering a suggestion or a request for changes. Your draft may require simple clarifications, rather than a drastic rewrite.

4. Do not get caught up in trivial matters, such as formatting or optional punctuation marks, as the fodder for disagreements with your editor.

5. Separate your ego from your document.

6. Forgive the editor who isn't as tactful or diplomatic as you might like. Although all relationships work better when tactfulness is the foundation, social courtesies may suffer under duress, especially with tight schedules and cramped budgets.

Document Issues

Once you understand the roles of the people with whom you are likely to collaborate, you are ready to discuss some particular document issues that will have to be negotiated with your partner(s). The editor's functions about which you just read, in fact, help clarify some of the document issues you and your team members will face. Although some of these issues are likely to be known from the outset of your assignment (perhaps even specified in the assignment), you may have to brainstorm with your group to make sure you all agree on other aspects.

Some of the most common points of negotiation about the document itself stem from differences and options you have studied in previous chapters:

- *Audience:* Who is reading the work and why? What do the readers know already? What do they need to know? (See Chapter 2 on planning.)
- *Purpose:* What are we trying to accomplish with this document? (See Chapter 2 on planning.)

- *Message:* What is the primary information we want to convey to our audience? What secondary information is also important? (See Chapter 3 on researching and gathering information.)

- *Organization:* How can our ideas best be arranged to accommodate the readers' needs and our own purposes? (See Chapter 4 on organizational options.)

- *Length:* How much detail do we need to incorporate to provide the whole picture? How long can we realistically expect to hold our readers' attention?

- *Tone:* Should the document sound friendly and inviting or threatening and stern? How formal or informal should it be? What means do we use to achieve that tone? (See Chapter 6 on revising.)

- *Graphics:* At what points will readers need graphics to simplify, clarify, emphasize, or synthesize information? Where will the readers need visual breaks? (See Chapter 8 on graphics.)

- *Design:* What elements of appearance can we control to make the document more readable and appealing to readers? What should the cover and the pages look like? Should we use color? What special features would present an innovative or conservative image? (See Chapter 9 on document design.)

- *Format:* How should information be arranged on the page to be most readable? Wide margins? Large type font? Plenty of white space? (See Chapter 9 on document design.)

Miscommunications or misunderstandings about any of these elements are likely to cause long-term problems in the collaboration. You can imagine what would happen if a group that has been asked to describe the company's new software program reconvenes to find that one group member has assumed the readers are novice users, while another group member has assumed they are advanced or expert users. The group may have to start over and rewrite the entire document.

Similar consequences may result from misunderstandings about the purpose of the document, its organization, or its length. You should also be sensitive to secondary factors as well, such as secondary audiences, purposes, or designs. Be sure to settle these document issues as early as possible in your collaboration.

Process Issues

The process issues in a collaboration are the administrative details that support the work, although they do not contribute to the production per se. In other words, these details allow the work to proceed smoothly. Process issues may be established or resolved by the group members, by the leader, or by some external agent, such as a documentation manager or even the CEO. In many companies, such issues are not negotiable, but you should make sure that you and your team members know all these issues as you begin your work.

One of the basic process issues has already been described: whether to use the divided labor or the integrated approach to collaboration. Your group's decisions about how to work are at the heart of all process issues, which include the following tasks and decisions:

■ *Data and draft exchanges:* With the innumerable technologies and workstyles now available in the workplace, group members will have to decide how they will exchange information. It is no longer inconceivable, after all, for a group to be comprised of members from Texas, New York, Idaho, Japan, and Germany. Even collaborators in a single building can sometimes find it difficult to exchange information.

Although group members used to communicate by traditional (slow) methods (mail, telephone), they are now much more likely to work via technology (E-mail, faxes, disk exchanges, conference calls, telecommunications hookups, and so on). Networked software that allows multiple users to contribute to any segment of a document during any phase of its development has been a tremendous boon to collaboration. As a result, group members will have to make sure they agree on the means of data exchange, that they have compatible hookups and software, and that they are all technologically sophisticated enough to manipulate the technology they are using.

■ *Scheduling:* How will the work proceed? At what times will the group meet? What other workers should be included at various stages of the process (illustrators, editors, subject matter experts, printers, etc.), and how do you schedule their time? Scheduling requires someone who is capable of seeing the big picture and knowing all the little steps that go into completing a successful document. Nothing is more frustrating than to be facing a deadline and then finish your part, take the work to the printer, and find that the printer wasn't expecting your document and has just accepted a week-long rush job. Waiting your turn is not only exasperating, it can be deadly in terms of corporate scheduling.

■ *Milestones:* Milestones are the various markers set at intervals in a project that allow the group to measure how far it has come and how far it needs to go. Milestones are frequently presented as lists or graphics:

  1. The first rough draft of the entire document and visual markers
   2. Graphics discussed with illustrator (on hold for editor's approval)
    3. The revised draft with rough graphics completed—send to editor
     4. Work returned from editor; revisions begin
      5. Graphics sent to illustrator
       6. Draft completed; final graphics inserted
        7. Final document sent to printer

Group members try to set realistic milestones that will both motivate them and encourage their progress. Unrealistic milestones can undermine the group's morale, creating tension between members and encouraging sloppy writing. When milestones are too generous, however, group members may think they have all the time in the world and become distracted by other projects—a perfect way for deadlines to sneak up on a group.

■ *Evaluations of the work:* Because many workers are sensitive to criticism of their work, it's important to understand at the beginning how the work is going to be evaluated and who will be doing the evaluating. Having your work evaluated by other group members is quite different, for instance, than having it evaluated by the editor, a representative sample of readers, or the CEO. Similarly, being evaluated on the basis of your team spirit, morale, and hard work is not the same as being evaluated on the basis of your knowledge of grammar, punctuation, and usage.

   If nobody spells out how the work will be evaluated and by whom, you should ask. Although you should do your best work regardless of the answers, it may help to know whether the evaluation process is formal or informal and whether you or your team members can recommend modifications in that process.

■ *Revision:* Handling revisions on a project can be sensitive, especially if you must revise your partner's work. Establishing from the outset that work will be exchanged can prevent people from feeling (later in the process) that someone is taking over their work and changing everything. As you revise others' work, or as they revise yours, be sure to keep your ego in check. Evaluate revisions and suggestions with an open mind—will this change improve the document? (See Chapter 6.)

■ *Fact checking:* Are we absolutely certain that our explanations are accurate, that our figures were copied correctly, and that our analysis is logical? As an ongoing part of your work—and especially, perhaps, your revising process—your group must decide on strategies for fact checking, returning to original sources of information and ensuring that the information in your document is accurate. (See Chapter 3.)

■ *Deadlines:* On what dates will various segments be completed? How rigid are those deadlines (not to be missed? can fudge a day or two?)? What happens if deadlines are missed? Are there any rewards for beating the deadline? Making sure that everyone understands how deadlines are to be interpreted is crucial, both to the project itself and to the morale of the group members. People are easily frustrated when their coworkers are late with promised materials. Missed deadlines can set back the entire project, cause scheduling conflicts, and even sink a project altogether.

In short, process issues help you and your partner(s) make some decisions about how your work will evolve and how you will monitor its progress. Handling these details at the beginning of your collaboration is likely to prevent hurt feelings, misunderstandings, and poor morale at the end of the process.

Resolving Document and Process Issues

In as much detail as you deem necessary for your instructor, describe the document and process issues you and your teammates resolved before (and perhaps even during) the writing of your document. Be sure to pay special attention to the rationale for your decisions.

Relationship Issues

No less important than the process and document issues that successful collaborators negotiate are the relationship issues. As in any relationship, many elements are left to chance, and that spontaneity is one of the pleasures—or perils—of the relationship. In some collaborations, you may immediately bond with your teammates and predict that you will be friends and respected coworkers long after your assignment is completed. In other cases, you may take an immediate, intense dislike to your collaborators, perhaps finding their voices, attitudes, or mannerisms grating.

Regardless of your immediate impressions, you are going to have to work with this person or group, and your social skills as well as your business, technical, and communication skills are going to be crucial to the collaboration's success. In this section, we will examine four special issues that can make or break a collaborative relationship.

Choosing a Leader

Because collaboration emphasizes shared responsibilities, many collaborative teams do not choose leaders; instead they simply reach a consensus about the work that needs to be done and the quality of the work that is produced. Other groups do choose a leader so that the group members can concentrate on the work (researching, drafting, revising) rather than on the "administrative tasks" that producing workplace documents may require: scheduling, budgeting, working with editors, getting approvals from upper-level administrators, and so on.

Interestingly, even in groups that do not specifically choose a leader, a leader often emerges. This person may be someone who storms in and takes control or someone who subtly nudges, encourages, guides, or placates group members. Most groups find the first type of leaders, the takeover leaders, to be a real problem because they tend to stifle discussions about alternatives and are likely to offend group members who want to share in the collaborative process. Such leaders often hurt feelings, alienate group members, and, ultimately, produce a document in which the group members take no pride. If you and your group choose a leader, be careful not to let takeover types push you into voting for them. If you do not take a stand against them at the very beginning of the process, you really cannot make a stand later in the collaboration (at least not without a mutiny, which invariably saps the energy of the entire group).

Many collaborators say they seek the following qualities in leaders:

- *Flexible:* Don't have to have their own way; see alternative means for achieving goals.
- *Knowledgeable:* Know the subject, the sources of information, and the documentation process.
- *Probing:* Encourage a number of responses and alternatives for each idea posed.
- *Open-minded:* Carefully consider each idea presented.
- *Organized:* Value schedules and deadlines as paths for succeeding.
- *Experienced:* Have worked on similar projects, perhaps even as the leader.
- *Tactful:* Don't shoot down other people and their ideas; look for something useful in each statement or suggestion or at least find a gracious way of moving beyond the suggestion.

Although you may find that certain leadership characteristics are especially valuable for particular forms of collaboration, these qualities will usually help you identify a person in your group who will make a good leader.

Encouraging Ownership

Most successful groups find ways of dividing work and coming together that will make each member of the team feel important. A variety of strategies and work relationships may lead to this sense of importance, which typically results in all group members feeling "ownership"—taking pride in the final product and feeling that they have made important contributions to it. In other words, ownership is the feeling that the project has solidified into something to which each group member is proud to have contributed.

In some collaborations, however, ownership never quite develops. Perhaps you have worked on a project where you felt that none of your ideas mattered, that your insights were discounted, or that your suggestions were ignored. When the final document was produced, did you feel that you had had little to do with it—that the group would have produced exactly the same document without your help or without having you on the team? Perhaps you have written a paper for an instructor who kept saying "Do it this way," "Say it this way," or "No, don't

THE WORLD OF WORKPLACE WRITING

Encouraging Ownership and Keeping Up Morale

Some of the nation's greatest athletes provide excellent examples of the collaborative spirit in their on-camera interviews, when they give credit to their teammates for assistance, outstanding plays, and leadership. These athletes recognize that they could not succeed without the help of their teammates; in fact, when athletes take too much credit for their success, their teammates often "teach them a little lesson" in the next game by refusing to block for them, refusing to pass the ball to them, or carrying out other maneuvers that deflate the athlete's performance—and ego.

In the workplace, no one wants to work with those who boast of their own accomplishments and claim all the credit for group efforts. As a worker, you should be known for giving credit to others for their work and letting them contribute what they are capable of contributing. Developing the habit of crediting others increases morale and the sense of ownership in workplace projects, makes others more willing to work with you, and increases your own sense of team spirit.

say that." At the end, you may have felt that the paper was more your instructor's work than your own.

Encouraging ownership means encouraging contributions and then valuing those contributions from your group members. Corrections and improvements can be made without taking the pleasure out of work. Although no members will have everything their own way, the final product should contain various notable contributions from each member.

Keeping Up Morale

One of the more difficult challenges facing groups involved in long-term projects is maintaining morale. Any number of setbacks related to the writing, budget, graphics, length, or numerous other factors can deflate the group—especially if members thought the project was almost completed, only to learn that they will have to put in another month's work.

Many groups try various strategies to keep up their morale. Some initiate nonwork activities (going out to lunch together, playing volleyball, or going on retreats) to help the group bond and provide a break from work. Others set aside a little time at the beginning of their sessions for chitchat and social discussions. Most of these strategies aim to take the members' minds off the work for a while. Then, some redirection can help the group return to the project invigorated and ready to work.

Personality Roles in a Collaborative Group

Describing the makeup of a collaborative group by its members' activities is a useful way to discuss the roles that members play, but it overlooks a crucial factor in all collaborative endeavors: personality. If you have ever had to work for or with someone you dislike, you know that personality can play a significant role in how you feel about and, thus, how you work with others. Of course, the people you consider "pushy" may have called themselves "motivated." And your "high standards" may have been "pickiness" to your coworker. Regardless of the specific interpretations of personality traits, however, personality plays a significant role in how well we work as individuals and as partners or team members.

You will probably recognize from your previous collaborative experiences some of the most common functional roles that are largely determined by personality types:

Functional Roles

- *Coordinator:* Ties ideas together and shows relationships among ideas.
- *Encourager:* Encourages other group members to participate.
- *Evaluator:* Offers judgments about the ideas presented to the group.
- *Gatekeeper:* Guides the flow of information among group members.
- *Harmonizer:* Tries to maintain a cooperative, productive climate; tries to resolve conflicts.
- *Information giver:* Provides facts and opinions in areas of expertise.
- *Information seeker:* Asks for facts and opinions from other group members.
- *Initiator:* Gets the collaborative process started.
- *Liaison:* Volunteers to obtain information from others outside the group.
- *Standard setter:* Works to maintain the group's focus on reaching a sound decision.
- *Summarizer:* Ties loose ends together; brings closure to the discussion at various points.

Dysfunctional Roles

- *Blocker:* Prevents the group from reaching a decision; interrupts; criticizes.
- *Competitor:* Expresses different views primarily for the sake of arguing; believes his or her ideas are always correct; attacks others.
- *Recognition seeker:* Monopolizes the discussion; focuses attention on self rather than on the group's objective; brags; clowns.
- *Repeater:* Continually repeats one or two ideas; repeats ideas presented by others.
- *Withdrawer:* Does not contribute to the group effort; acts bored or indifferent. (Hulbert 53–54)

As useful as these descriptions are, they do not account for the different work styles and personalities that you may encounter in coworkers from non-American (or non-Western) cultures. Table 7.1 explains how cultural differences often influence collaborative behaviors. Note, however, that these explanations are not limited to cultural differences, but also apply to personality differences within a single culture.

Understanding the various roles that group members may play on a team assignment—and the cultural factors that may motivate those behaviors—can help you see ways of encouraging positive behaviors and discouraging negative behaviors. You should not, however, be so concerned for harmony that you stifle substantive conflict, which can lead to useful alternative perspectives—one of the primary advantages of collaborative groups (see, for example, Burnett). In fact, too much harmony can actually cause group members to lose interest in a project, because they feel that it will proceed just fine without them. Even with natural dif-

T A B L E 7.1   Possible Behaviors and Explanations in Collaborative Relationships

Behavior	*Rationale*	*Implication*
may not respond with a definite "no"	to prevent both parties from losing face	may take on more work than others in the group
may be reluctant to admit a lack of understanding or to ask for clarification of information	to do so might place speaker in a position of revealing ignorance	may pretend to understand
may avoid criticizing others	to avoid embarrassing self or others	may not respond critically to other members of group or on evaluation forms; may avoid confrontation
may avoid initiating new tasks or performing creatively	to avoid making a mistake and appearing foolish	may accept assigned tasks, but may not volunteer
may avoid asking for promotions or deserved benefits	to protect supervisor from possibly refusing and to protect self from humiliation	may not emphasize own part in group on evaluation form
may feel discomfort with compliments	to avoid the imbalance between parties such compliments create	may not seek verbal approval from teacher or other group members
may avoid complaining about product or service	to prevent other party from feeling a sense of failure	may not indicate problems with group members on evaluation form

Source: Deborah S. Bosley. "Cross-Cultural Collaboration: Whose Culture Is It Anyway?" *Technical Communication Quarterly* 2.1 (1993): 57.

ferences about work styles and writing options, however, diplomacy and respect for others' opinions will be paramount in the group's search for ideal content, tone, organization, graphics, and design.

Conflict in Collaborative Relationships

Although conflict might seem to be a relationship issue—and, indeed, it is—it may also be a process issue or a document issue. That's because the *source* of conflict, which is the most important realization to make about all conflict, may lie in differing views about how the document should look or sound when completed (document issues), how the work should proceed (process issues), or how workers' personalities affect group interactions (relationship issues).

Foremost, it is unrealistic to expect every group situation (or partnership) to run smoothly all of the time. Recognizing the source of any conflict will help you determine how to handle that conflict. Process issues and document issues may require reflection and postponed decisions. Personality issues may require division of labor, negotiation, patience, or even reassignment.

It is also important to remember that conflict can have positive results, especially when it involves process or document issues. Indeed, the fear of conflict can stifle a group's potential for exploring alternatives and perhaps finding a better solution than the original suggestion.

Sometimes, however, conflicts with your partner or your group members will have negative effects. In that case, you should be prepared to try a number of strategies for resolving the conflicts:

- *Self-monitoring:* Examine your own behaviors, attitudes, and motivations. Try to understand—honestly—why your collaboration is not working. In what ways have you contributed to the problem? In what ways has the collaborator contributed? Remember, very few poor relationships are the fault of just one person. If you sense that your collaborators are exasperated by your chitchat at the beginning of sessions, your late arrivals, or your rehashing of details of the last session, change your behavior.

- *Other-monitoring:* Examine your partner's or the rest of the group's behaviors, attitudes, and motivations. Try to determine whether the conflicts are personality differences or substantive differences. If they are personality differences, try to get the person or the group to focus on the work. If they are substantive differences, try to encourage negotiation and trade-offs.

- *Negotiated discussion:* Try to talk diplomatically with your collaborators about their expectations from you and the group's sessions. If the other members have some valid complaints or ideas for redesigning the sessions, go along with them. But, if your partners are merely irritated about having these sessions, see what you can do to lessen the irritation. Ask about rescheduling them. Try a different environment for the sessions (perhaps the company's coffee shop or outside the building altogether).

■ *Confrontation:* Occasionally, you may have to confront your coworkers, spelling out the problems you see and explaining why they have been difficult to work with. Some people do not seem to know that their attitudes or behaviors are problematic. Again, you will have to be as diplomatic as possible (rudeness rarely resolves conflicts), but you should clearly note your own expectations about your working relationship. You should be prepared to receive some criticism of your (and perhaps the rest of the group's) work habits, too. Then, see what resolutions you can reach.

■ *Managerial pressure:* If the preceding four steps have not produced any improvements, your manager will probably step in and either try to resolve the conflict or take a stronger role in your collaboration.

■ *Reassignment:* When all else fails, you, your partner, or some of your group members may be reassigned. As a last resort, that may be exactly what you all want. But remember that your ability to get along with others (even difficult others) sends a powerful message about your work ethic, your character, and your potential for promotion. Being reassigned may get you out of a painful situation, but it may also hurt your image in the long run.

Finally, remember that if your group determines early how it will resolve conflicts, you can often prevent them from getting blown out of proportion and defeating the team effort.

APPLICATION

Negotiating Relationship and Personality Issues

On your own, describe the relationship and personality issues that affected (either positively or negatively) the success of your group's work and its final document. This description should be a personal reflection in which you honestly evaluate your coworkers; it will be submitted separately and confidentially. Your report should include descriptions of all of the following:

1. The leader of your group and that person's strategies and successes in leading

2. Your feelings of ownership over the final document

3. Any attempts to encourage morale throughout the project

4. Any personality issues that created functional or dysfunctional roles

5. Any conflict that arose in your work and how (or if) it was resolved

Summary

This chapter's focus on collaboration has emphasized the cooperative spirit that characterizes many workplace relationships. Many American corporations see the advantages of having their employees (from line workers to managers to the CEO) work together to create solutions for company problems, new ways of doing business, and visions for the future.

As exciting as such cooperation is, it also defies many assumptions about the workplace, especially the belief that work depends on competition, killer instincts, and an overriding concern for the bottom line. Certainly, competition is still a major part of the American workplace, and no one would promote and adopt collaborative strategies if those strategies were not profitable. But that's the point: collaboration is profitable. Higher productivity, improved morale, and greater company loyalty are just a few of the signs that collaboration is working.

This chapter outlines some of the fundamental elements of collaboration. It focuses on the advantages of collaboration over competition and then explains that collaboration may involve either a division of labor or an integrated approach. Dividing the labor requires an equitable distribution of assignments and tasks; workers typically write in at least some semblance of solitude and then reconvene to share drafts via hard copy or disks. In the integrated tasks approach, all group members participate in every phase and aspect of the work, including outlines, organization, research sources, the wording of draft versions, revision strategies, and formatting choices.

Collaborative writers are likely to be paired with someone (or several people) whose expertise is quite different from their own, usually subject matter experts (SMEs), other writers, illustrators, or editors. The collaboration requires that all participants combine their knowledge, strengths, and insights to produce a successful document.

Collaboration requires that team members agree on certain *document issues*: audience, purpose, organization, length, tone, graphics, design, and format. A number of *process issues* also need to be clarified at the beginning of the project. Specifically, teammates must agree on the means for data and draft exchanges, schedules, milestones, revisions, fact checking, deadlines, and evaluations of the work. They should also be sensitive to *relationship issues*: choosing a leader, encouraging ownership, and boosting morale. *Personality issues* also play a significant part in collaborative successes; checking your own personality and resulting behaviors can help you determine whether your attitudes are serving a functional or dysfunctional role.

Finally, learning to recognize the source of conflict and having some strategies at hand for resolving conflict are important tools for the successful collaborator. Because conflict can be productive, you do not necessarily want to stifle it, but you should recognize when discussions about process issues and document issues cross the line into attacks on personalities and relationships.

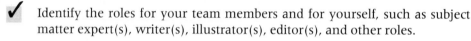
CHECKLIST

✓ Determine whether your group's and project's characteristics make the divided labor strategy or the integrated tasks strategy more workable.

■ Use the *divided labor strategy* when

there is a great deal of physical distance between participants,

the group is pressed for time, and

the document is a medium to low priority for your organization.

■ Use the *integrated tasks model* when

your work has strong organizational support,

your schedule is open to a number of workers,

you have easy access (physical or technological) to other members of the team,

the document is a high priority for your organization, and

you have a generous deadline.

✓ Identify the roles for your team members and for yourself, such as subject matter expert(s), writer(s), illustrator(s), editor(s), and other roles.

✓ Resolve document issues:

■ Audience and purpose of the document

■ Message of the document

■ Organization of the document

■ Length of the document

■ Tone of the document

■ Graphics for the document

■ Layout and design features of the document

✓ Resolve process issues:

■ Data and draft exchanges

■ Scheduling

■ Milestones

■ Evaluations of the work

■ Revisions

■ Fact checking

■ Deadlines

✓ Resolve relationship issues by following these guidelines:

■ Choose a leader who is flexible, knowledgeable, probing, open-minded, organized, experienced, and tactful.

- Encourage ownership of the work.
- Keep up morale.

✔ Identify functional and dysfunctional roles and work to resolve those personality issues.

✔ Identify sources of conflict in collaborations, realizing that conflict over document and process issues is likely to have positive results, whereas conflict over relationship and personality issues is likely to be negative.

✔ To resolve relationship and personality conflicts, you may engage in a number of increasingly confrontational strategies:
- Self-monitoring
- Other-monitoring
- Negotiated discussions
- Confrontation
- Managerial pressure
- Reassignment

EXERCISES

Individual Exercise

1. Describe a collaborative project (successful or unsuccessful) in which you participated. Consider the final document, the process, and/or your relationships with your teammates. What aspects of your experience might be explained by the new knowledge about collaboration you acquired from reading the chapter?

Write one or two pages describing the collaboration. If it was successful, evaluate the strategies you used to make it a successful experience. If it was unsuccessful, describe alternative strategies that might have improved the final work and your feelings about the project.

Collaborative Exercises

1. In a group of four or five classmates, brainstorm on your idea of the perfect teacher. What qualities would such a teacher have? What policies would the teacher use to run the classroom? What kinds of tests, projects, or other assignments would the teacher assign? How would the teacher motivate you to learn?

2. Submit the document you completed for the Applications in this chapter.

3. Following the same instructions as in the Applications, select a member of your team whose hobby or work you and your group members want to know more about. With that person acting as the subject matter expert, conduct your research, write a draft, select material that should be illustrated, and edit and revise your document, which should inform a reader unfamiliar with the hobby or work about the basics of your topic. Submit the final document to your instructor.

4. Brainstorm with your group members about the physical layout (attractiveness, safety, and accessibility) of your campus, identifying areas that need improvement. Be prepared to discuss your ideas and questions with a representative from your college's groundskeeping or security division.

   When the representative meets with your class, pose your questions tactfully, but be sure to get all the information you need to write a problem/solution discussion. Identify portions of the text that need graphics; then, edit the work and submit it to your instructor.

 ## ONGOING ASSIGNMENT

- For your manual on your primary organization's culture, describe any help you have received from subject matter experts—coworkers, other students, executives, teachers—that has helped you refine your ideas for the project. Describe as thoroughly as possible your preparation and strategies for getting the right information from these resources.

- Next, identify material that should be illustrated to help the newcomer understand your message about your organization's culture (perhaps offering an illustration or photograph of the proper attire or a flow chart of the chain of command).

WORKS CITED

Bosley, Deborah S. "Cross-Cultural Collaboration: Whose Culture Is It Anyway?" *Technical Communication Quarterly* 2.1 (1993): 57.

Burnett, Rebecca. "Substantive Conflict in a Cooperative Context: A Way to Improve the Collaborative Planning of Workplace Documents." *Technical Communication* 38 (1991): 532–39.

Hulbert, Jack. "Developing Collaborative Insights and Skills." *Bulletin of the ABC* 57.2 (1994): 53–56.

Killingsworth, M. Jimmie, and Betsy G. Jones. "Division of Labor or Integrated Teams: A Crux in the Management of Technical Communication?" *Technical Communication* 36 (1989): 210–21.

Rude, Carolyn. *The Process of Editing.* Belmont, CA: Wadsworth, 1991.

Tanner, Beth, and Pete Larson. "'Worth a Thousand Words': Choosing and Using Illustrations for Technical Communication." *Technical Communication* 41.1 (1994): 150–53.

CHAPTER 8

Using Graphic Elements in Workplace Documents

Have you ever thought about how difficult it would be to explain to someone who has never seen the process how to tie a shoelace, inflate a balloon, or change a lightbulb without showing the person how to do it? We learn many of life's most basic lessons from watching others or looking at diagrams or photographs or illustrations.

In the workplace, much vital information is also communicated through visual images, charts, and graphs. Most often, workplace writers incorporate graphics to do one or more of the following:

- Present quantitative data and relationships
- Compare single datum or sets of data
- Show structural patterns in time or space
- Simplify schematic or analytic information

As an example of the usefulness of graphics, consider the following information:

> In 1997, XYZ Corporation hosted its annual stockholders' meeting and attracted 454 people. As a result of the meeting, 123 people immediately signed up for additional shares of stock, with 201 signing up for additional shares within three months, and 12 people dropping their stock. In 1998, when we used a video of our organization's accomplishments and plans for developing the laser instrument, 503 people showed up for the meeting, and 396 signed up immediately for additional stock; 115 people bought additional shares within three months, and 4 dropped the stock.

What does this tell you about the relative success of XYZ Corporation's 1997 and 1998 stockholders' meetings? What can you conclude about the effectiveness of the video? You had to look back over the paragraph before you could answer those questions, right? Now look at Figure 8.1, which presents the same information in a graphic format. Isn't it easier to compare the data?

Although the benefits of presenting complex information graphically are rather obvious from this example, graphics serve a number of other purposes in workplace documents, including the following:

- Highlight selected information
- Emphasize important details or trends
- Simplify complex information
- Clarify information that could be misinterpreted
- Provide a mental image or orientation of the process or product being described

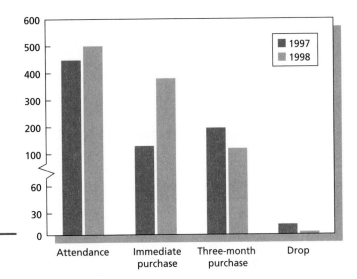

FIGURE 8.1

Stockholders' Meetings and Stock Purchases

- Show relationships between ideas, trends, or statistics
- Justify claims
- Attract the reader's attention
- Give the reader a break from the text

Graphics should serve at least one of these functions; don't put them in to impress your reader or to cover up the fact that you have little to say. And don't expect your reader to gain the full meaning of your ideas from the pictures alone. Suppose you had seen only Figure 8.1. Would you have understood the information? Would you have known what was being purchased immediately or what "drop" meant? When you explain graphics to your readers, you make sure they do not mistake your meaning.

Depending on your major and your career plans, your college work may require you to take special courses in graphics, design, and computer-aided design. If you choose a career as a city planner, you may use the information from those graphics courses to draw the layout of the city's new development project. If you choose a career as a tool machinist, you may use the information from your graphics courses to help you design new tools to meet the technological challenges of an automated society. In addition, you will also have to use graphic elements when you write reports or proposals to prospective clients or to your supervisor.

In this chapter, you will not learn to become an expert illustrator, but you will learn about some graphics you can use to present information visually—and persuasively—in your workplace documents. First, you will learn how graphics can accommodate your audience's needs, as well as how to incorporate graphics into your text, talk about them meaningfully, and document your sources for the graphics. Then you will learn how to incorporate tables or figures based on the kind of information you are presenting. As you will see, both forms of visuals require your attention to fundamental do's and don'ts. Finally, you will learn more about the rhetorical or persuasive signals that graphics send to your readers.

Accommodating Audience Needs

As you draft your document, note where and what kinds of graphics you want to use to clarify, simplify, or emphasize the information you are discussing. If you are unsure whether to use a graphic for a particular idea you are trying to communicate, ask yourself the following questions:

- Will a graphic help the reader understand, or could it get in the reader's way?
- What kind of graphic(s) will this audience understand best?
- What can I do to make my graphics clear, informative, and appealing?

One of the most important choices you will have to make when designing your graphics is how sophisticated they should be. Graphics software programs are particularly useful for this purpose because they can show a range of representations, from the simplest concept to the most complex rendering. Your graphics program can only show you the possibilities, however. You will have to determine the appropriate complexity based on your audience's ability to understand and the kind of message you want to send.

Consider the representations of a flower in Figure 8.2. Which representation would be better for a kindergarten class? Which would be appropriate for a group

FIGURE 8.2

The Complexity of the Drawing Suits the Audience's Level of Sophistication

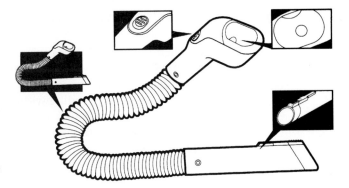

FIGURE 8.3

An Illustration Showing an Entire Object and Highlighting Parts for Emphasis

Graphic provided courtesy of Black & Decker® Household Products Group, SnakeLight™ Flexible Flashlight © 1995.

of professional florists? Why would either graphic be inappropriate for the opposite group? Clearly, the choice depends on the audience's familiarity and comfort with the concept being illustrated. Don't overwhelm readers with complex illustrations when simple illustrations are more appropriate to their level of knowledge. Similarly, don't insult readers with amateurish illustrations when more complex illustrations are required.

The simpler the drawing and the concept, the easier the illustration is to understand. Although complex equipment, such as the workings of a computer, cannot readily be simplified, you can take small segments of the overall concept and illustrate them, as in Figure 8.3. Moving from part to part of the equipment will help you focus on one segment at a time—a strategy that is much more useful than trying to explain the entire object at once.

In this chapter, our scenario will follow the work of Action Advertising, a newly formed advertising agency that is trying to attract new clients from small businesses in the Seattle market. The members of the collaborative team—the owner of the company (Adriena Dunlow), the head of the graphics department (Warren Montel), illustrators Maya Sanchez and David Stowe, and writers Belinda Mason and Taylor Ronkowski—recognize that their first job is to sell the agency to these small businesses. They plan to produce a brochure that can be mailed to organizations that earn less than $500,000 a year and currently are not represented by an advertising agency.

The group recognizes that the primary reason these organizations do not have agency representation is the misconception that the services offered are too expensive for small businesses to afford. Thus, they know that a highly sophisticated brochure and graphics will lose the audience. At the same time, they realize that an unsophisticated product will not work either because the small business owners might decide they can do just as acceptable a job as the agency. Throughout this chapter, we will follow the decisions that the group makes about the graphics represented by the agency. Next, however, a few points about handling graphics will help you understand the complexities of incorporating graphics and acknowledging their sources in your documents.

Incorporating Graphics into Your Text

Some excellent newsmagazines run outstanding graphics along with their stories, but the writers do not refer to the graphics and do not give readers an opportunity to stop reading to look at the graphics. If readers get caught up in the text, they turn the page to continue reading without looking at the graphics. Thus, to look at a graphic, readers have to stop (sometimes in midparagraph) before turning a page, a practice that irritates many readers or causes them to ignore the graphics altogether.

Many writers try another tactic with equally bad results. They put all their graphics at the end of their documents, which forces readers to flip back and forth through the document as they read. Once again, many readers become irritated and lose interest in the graphics or forgo them altogether.

Much more convenient for your readers (and attention grabbing) is to place graphics in the text with a clear explanation of what they contain. Your discussion of the graphic need only be minimal, but it should indicate what you want readers to note—or, in other words, why you incorporated the graphic in the first place.

Referring to a graphic is quite simple; you have seen many such references in your textbooks. Consider the following examples:

- . . . the relationship between years with the organization and salary is highly suspicious. (See Figure 1, below.)
- As Figure 1 shows, the relationship between economic trade sanctions and our . . . .
- Figure 3 illustrates how the piston moves from . . . .

If your graphic is too large for the space available on the page, or if it will require an entire page, put it at the top of the next page, after the reference, and then tell the reader where the graphic is: "As Figure 4 on page 15 shows, ..." Helping your readers find information in your work improves their understanding and also enhances your credibility as a workplace communicator.

Acknowledging the Source of Your Graphics

Unless you are using your own organization's records and graphics for the information you present visually in your workplace documents, the source of the information for your graphics should be acknowledged directly below the graphic. Even when you are using material from your company's information stock, you should still be prepared to tell readers—especially those who may be skeptical about your graphic—where your information comes from.

Just as you don't want readers to wonder where you found the information in the text of your document, you do not want them to wonder where you got the information for your graphics. Therefore, you should document the sources of your graphics, although you will not use endnotes, footnotes, or parenthetical notations, as you would to credit text sources. Instead, you should follow these requirements for documenting sources:

- *Situation 1:* A graphic that you copied from another source:

  [graphic of a pie chart]

  Figure 1: Pie Chart Showing Types of Cases Handled by Hilton Law Partners

  Source: *Hilton Law Partners: 1994 Annual Report.* Greenville, NC: 1995.

- *Situation 2:* A graphic that you created using information from a source:

  [graphic of a pie chart]

  Figure 1: Pie Chart Showing Types of Cases Handled by Hilton Law Partners

  Information gathered from: *Hilton Law Partners: 1994 Annual Report.* Greenville, NC: 1995.

- *Situation 3:* A graphic that you created using information that you generated:

  [graphic of a pie chart]

  Figure 1: Pie Chart Showing Types of Cases Handled by Hilton Law Partners

  When both the information and the graphic are your own, you do not acknowledge or mention a source.

In attributing credit for information and graphics you use in the text of your work, you not only demonstrate your ethical considerations for fairness and integrity, but you also send the message that you welcome readers to check your facts. By telling them where they can find the information you have found and used in your work, you lend credibility to your facts and figures.

Illustrating Comparisons and Relationships for Quantitative Data

When you realize that quantitative (or numerical) information in your text is either too complex or too dense for your readers to understand or to maintain their interest, you should add a graphic. Most frequently, quantitative data are visually represented in tables, charts, and graphs. Tables present information in tabular columns; charts present information in visually significant designs; and graphs present information along x and y axes that intersect (or do not intersect) in significantly meaningful ways. Strategy Review 8.1 on page 264 gives a general discussion of graphics software.

T H E   W O R L D   O F   W O R K P L A C E   W R I T I N G

The Ethics of Graphics Use

Just as you must be concerned about the ethics of your text, you must also concentrate on the ethics of your graphics. Misleading readers (whether intentionally or not) damages your credibility. Be sure to check your numbers and your facts before you incorporate them into your graphics. And be certain that the visual representation of those numbers and facts is not skewed by inappropriate graphics choices or by inaccurate drawings that over- or understate the message.

How would you interpret the figure below? Although the illustrator's point is that there are more cows in one state than in the other, you might reasonably conclude that cows grow larger in one state than in the other. Think of the difference that would make if you were raising cows. You would want to know what kind of food or environmental conditions lead to larger cows.

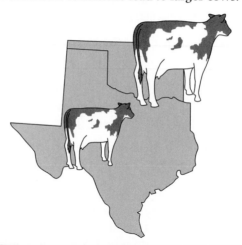

GRAPHICS SOFTWARE

Innumerable software packages have tremendously affected the type and sophistication of graphics that workplace writers can produce themselves—or have graphics illustrators produce for them. Several factors determine how useful and attractive those graphics will be when they are reproduced in your document.

A graphics program may produce either *bitmapped* (raster-based) or *object-oriented* (vector-based) graphics. The bitmapped graphics programs allow you to create soft images, which are popular for creating special rhetorical effects, such as sensitivity, warmth, or affection. Because bitmapped programs use a series of dots (called pixels) to form patterns and pictures, their capabilities are limited. You cannot add layers to the graphic, nor can you save large graphics because of the amount of drive space they require.

The object-oriented graphics programs produce sharper images and are useful for layering images, creating or enhancing special effects (by changing color, size, shape, etc.), and moving images within the graphic. As a result, some illustrators caution users about the potential for using such programs in unethical ways. Ethical illustrators, however, use the options to create a number of valuable effects, such as focusing on the target object or image and enhancing clarity.

A high-quality printer essentially "guarantees" the high quality of the image produced by an object-oriented program. In contrast, scanned images are recorded in bitmapped form and can only become object images if illustrators trace specific images around the forms with a mouse or stylus.

Be sure to check with your illustrator or print specialist before determining which kind of program to use for your workplace document's graphics. Costly misunderstandings can quickly deflate the value of graphics and, thus, the effectiveness of your document.

Tables

Does the text include a lot of *numbers, percentages, sums, statistics,* or *measurements*? If so, readers are likely to get confused. A *table* of the numerical data can help clarify the information. Tables are especially useful when you want readers to have exact numbers or percentages—not just representative drawings of those numbers (which are best presented in graphs).

Table I, which shows how a table can clarify numerical information, also illustrates the key features of an effective table.

Table I: Sales and Profits for Action Advertising: 1996–1999

Year	Sales Percentages	Sales Contracts	Gross Margins	Net Profits
1996	4.9%	214	10.8%	$824,434
1997	5.2%	243	12.2%	$924,933
1998	5.5%	322	12.5%	$1,243,434
1999	6.3%	399	14.2%	$1,534,909

Source: Sales Reports, 1987–1990. Slack & Camden, Inc. Washington, DC 2000.

When constructing a table, follow these guidelines:

- Align columns properly; be particularly careful about decimal points.
- Make sure headings for rows and columns are clear and readable.
- Make sure information in rows and columns is easily readable—not crowded or confusingly abbreviated.
- Round off large numbers and indicate the scale (e.g., Numbers are rounded off to thousands).

- Make sure lines between entries (called "rules"), if used in a dense table, do not overwhelm or darken the table.
- Number the table consecutively with other tables and give it an informative title.
- Clearly indicate the source of your information.

In addition to numerical comparisons, tables may also be used to provide textual and conceptual comparisons, as Table II shows.

Table II: Table Presenting Textual Information

Salesperson	Code	Sales Territory
Chang	Q1	Hong Kong, Japan, and China
Wright	R5	Belgium, France, and Holland
Perez	Q2	Peru, Brazil, and Chile
Littlefair	P3	Great Britain and Northern Ireland
Page	P2	Northwestern United States and Canada
Monte	T1	Mexico and El Salvador
Aydini	Y9	Kuwait and Saudi Arabia

Tables can also be constructed with a column that makes the comparisons for the readers; consider how useful Table III is because it provides all the information the readers want, rather than forcing them to draw their own conclusions about when to use which machine class.

Table III: Table Making Explicit Comparisons

Fittings	Machine Class					
	1	2	3	4	5	6
0.41	GOOD					
0.79						
0.96						
1.04						
1.6						
2.8		SATISFACTORY				
3.6						
4.9		IMPROVEMENT				
5.3			DESIRABLE			
6.1						
8.2						
8.4		UNACCEPTABLE				
9.3						

Unless the information you are presenting in a table is extraordinarily complex, you should consider tables as a generic graphic form that is relatively easy for the majority of readers to understand. By presenting information in parallel columns, tables enable readers to compare numerical data, concepts, and conclusions, as shown in the previous examples.

Action Advertising's collaborators considered using a table to show readers the financial benefits of advertising for one of the agency's first clients, Linda's Catering. To add extra emphasis to the table, the illustrators changed the font of the headings and used boldface type (see Table IV). They also used a screen (a computer/desktop publishing option) to shade important information. (Although most screens are gray, you may opt for a light color, such as a pastel blue, to shade information, provided the information is still easily readable.) The illustrators presented their table to the team, asking for suggestions or approval for its incorporation into the brochure.

Table IV: Advantages of Advertising for Linda's Catering

	Sales Percentages	**Sales Contracts**	**Net Profit Percentages**
(1998) No advertising	4.9%	28	—
(1999) Advertising	5.5%	58	+ 39%

Source: Sales Reports, 1998–1999. Linda's Catering, Inc., Seattle, WA 1999.

The team members liked the idea of using a real client for the brochure and table, but realized they would have to get permission from Linda's Catering to include this information. Perhaps a discount on her next advertising campaign would persuade Linda to allow Action Advertising to use the information in its brochure; if not, the team would have to use a different organization or combine information from various clients for the table.

STRATEGY REVIEW 8.2

PLANNING AND INTEGRATING GRAPHICS

When planning the text of your document (see Chapter 2), you should already begin to see some opportunities or even necessities for incorporating graphics to help your reader comprehend your message. Incorporating graphics considerations into your planning process will help you determine whether the graphics will be a supplemental element of your document or a focal element. A supplemental element is incorporated to clarify or simplify the text, whereas a focal element serves as a central point around which text will flow. For instance, a writer

(continued)

may use a graphic to represent every stage of a process, using each graphic to supplement the textual description. Another writer may use an elaborate graphic of an entire process as the focal point for the remaining discussion. Such decisions depend on your audience's ability to digest small versus large amounts of information at a time. Clearly, your decisions about your audience will affect your use of graphics in workplace documents.

Flow Charts

Does the text describe the *complex relationships between workers or departments or between stages of a process,* resolving questions about who answers to whom or about the sequence of segments of a process? A *flow chart* can outline the relationship you want to describe (see Figure 8.4).

When constructing a flow chart, follow these guidelines:

- Relationships between segments of the chart should be clear; for example, solid lines between elements typically represent permanent links, while dotted lines indicate tentative or optional links.
- All offices, segments of the process, or possible responses should be accounted for.
- Labels should be readable. If labels are too small to read, enlarge the entire flow chart; if it will not fit on the page, turn it horizontally (with the text or image facing outward, not into the binding of the document).
- Geometrical figures should be consistent within levels of the hierarchy.
- If the information is not from your own organization's files, sources should be clearly noted.

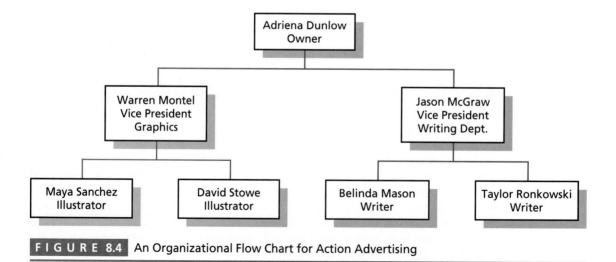

FIGURE 8.4 An Organizational Flow Chart for Action Advertising

As long as flow charts have a clear top and bottom, even general readers should be able to understand the information you present. To highlight specific portions of a flow chart, use a thicker rule (or design line) around the emphasized portion, or shade that information. Again, make sure that the shading or rules do not obscure the information.

Pie Charts and 100% Column Charts

Does the text explain the *parts that make up a whole*? Does it help you account for the entirety of some subject? A *pie chart* or a *100% column chart* can show this information (see Figures 8.5 and 8.6). Almost all readers are familiar with pie charts and 100% column charts. In fact, most readers find such graphics quite pleasing because they appear to account for all the information.

When constructing a pie chart, follow these guidelines:

- The divisions should begin at 12:00 (the top of the circle).
- The parts should proceed from the largest to the smallest segment.
- The number of segments should not crowd the chart. You may combine the smallest percentages as "other," as long as you explain in the text what constitutes that category.
- All segments should be labeled.
- The segments must add up to 100 percent.

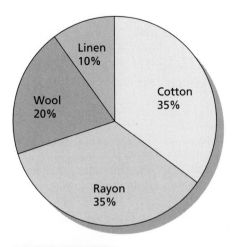

FIGURE 8.5

A Pie Chart Showing Production Rates of XYZ Fabrics, Inc.

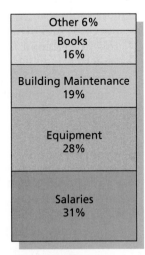

FIGURE 8.6

A 100% Column Chart Showing Where Tuition Money Goes

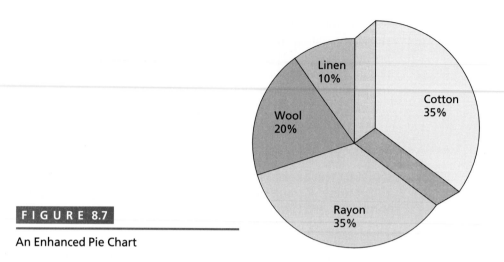

FIGURE 8.7

An Enhanced Pie Chart

- Labels for all segments should be readable (don't make readers turn the page upside down to read labels).
- Any color used should enhance rather than detract from the chart.
- Sources of information should be clearly noted.

A 100% column chart follows some of the same rules as a pie chart: the segments must add up to 100 percent, be labeled and readable, and be clearly attributed to sources. In a 100% column chart, however, the largest segment is at the bottom, and the divisions move up to the smallest segment at the top.

As desktop publishing and other computer graphics programs have become more sophisticated, plain pie charts and 100% column charts have practically disappeared; these charts are usually enhanced with pictorial representations that provide additional commentary on the topic. You can add color to enhance the segments on which you want your readers to focus, for example, or you can pull out a slice of the pie or enlarge a segment of the column chart as long as the enhancements do not distort the meaning (see Figure 8.7).

Line Charts and Graphs

Does the text describe *more than one set of numerical information,* combining, for instance, profit percentages with specific years or salary dollars with educational levels? A *line chart or graph* can help you display those concurrent trends, as Figure 8.8 shows.

When constructing a line chart, follow these guidelines:

- The *x* (horizontal) and *y* (vertical) axes should be clearly labeled.
- The numbers on the axes should be in consecutive intervals; if not, use two squiggly lines to indicate where the break occurs.
- Sources of information should be clearly noted.

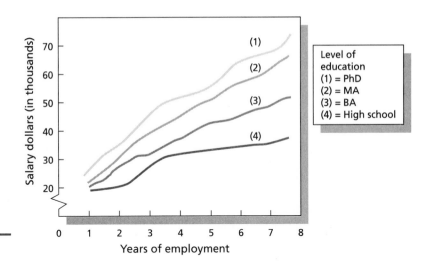

FIGURE 8.8

A Line Chart

Most readers have little trouble with line charts and graphs, but you must make sure that the kind of information you present is familiar enough to readers to be understandable (for example, the academic degrees in Figure 8.8). Very complex, geometric line charts can easily overwhelm novice readers.

STRATEGY REVIEW 8.3

DIFFICULTIES WITH THREE-DIMENSIONAL GRAPHICS

Be especially careful when using three-dimensional figures on line graphs, bar graphs, and other visual representations. Three-dimensional figures are appealing, but distortions are easily introduced (see Figure 1). In addition, many three-

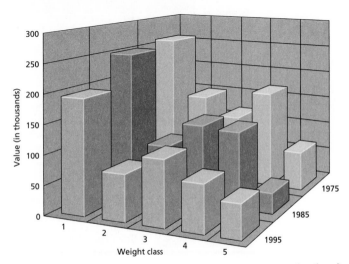

FIGURE 1 A Three-Dimensional Bar Chart That Distorts Information

(continued)

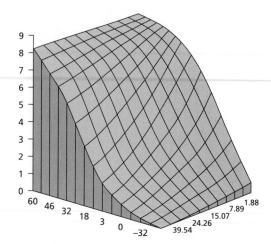

FIGURE 2   A Graphic That Is Hard to Read Because of Three-Dimensional Distortions

dimensional figures are hard to read (see Figure 2). To test the ease of understanding a graphic, pick any point in the graphic and see if you can easily find a corresponding meaning; if not, revise or delete the graphic.

Bar Charts and Graphs

Do you need to present *numbers in relation to ideas*? A *bar chart* is a useful means of presenting more than one form of information at a time. When well drawn and explained in the text, bar charts are also relatively easy for readers to understand. In Figure 8.9, for instance, students' test results on state tests are compared to

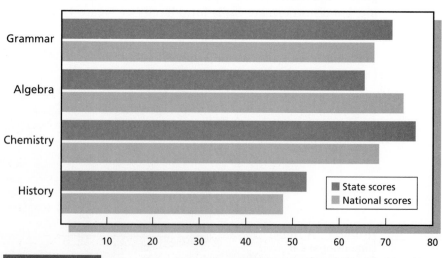

FIGURE 8.9   A Bar Chart Comparing State Test Scores to National Test Scores

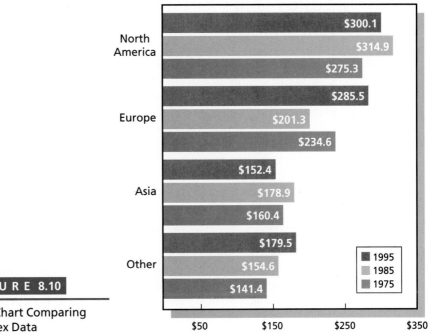

Airplane Ticket Sales

North America: $300.1, $314.9, $275.3

Europe: $285.5, $201.3, $234.6

Asia: $152.4, $178.9, $160.4

Other: $179.5, $154.6, $141.4

1995
1985
1975

$50 $150 $250 $350

FIGURE 8.10

A Bar Chart Comparing
Complex Data

their results on national tests; the figure shows that in all subjects except algebra, students score higher on their own state's tests than they do on national tests.

One of the advantages of using bar charts is that you can compare more than one set of data in a single graphic. For instance, you can compare *the number of airplane tickets* sold to *various destinations* over a *twenty-year period*. Figure 8.10 simplifies the information for you.

When constructing a bar chart, follow these guidelines:

- Be sure all measurements are exact.
- Be sure all columns are easily distinguished from each other; columns can be plain, shaded, vertically striped, horizontally striped, or dotted, for example. Color can be a useful distinction unless your reader might photocopy your graphic, in which case all the colored areas are likely to end up white or gray.
- Do not crowd the individual sets of bars; about five is all anyone can stand to look at in one graphic.

For Action Advertising, the opportunities for using graphics to demonstrate quantitative data are numerous, but the team members focus on the audience's needs and the rhetorical implications of their options. Knowing that pie charts are almost universally understood and may be a little too simplistic for their audience and message, the team members exclude pie charts. Confident that they can pre-

THE WORLD OF WORKPLACE WRITING

Costs of Graphics

Improvements in in-house, desktop publishing capabilities have caused the cost of graphics to decline dramatically. Nevertheless, graphics remain one of the most expensive elements of workplace documents because of the additional costs of preparing and printing them.

For many of your workplace documents, you will have to abide by a budget, and you should determine early in the project how much of that budget can go toward reproducing graphics. When in doubt, consult a professional printer—or your computer graphics guru—to help you make informed decisions about graphics costs. These experts may also point out some less expensive alternatives that can help you stay within your budget.

sent any information in the remaining formats given the proper focus, the team members look at their information carefully to determine whether graphics will enhance the details they want to provide. Finally, they decide to offer a graphic to support their claim that their clients' profits have increased since they began advertising (see Figure 8.11).

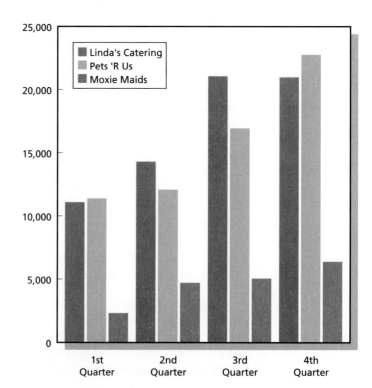

FIGURE 8.11

A Bar Chart Showing Clients'
Increased Profits since Advertising

Illustrating Quantitative Data

For the Applications in this chapter, assume the following role and situation:

> Your team has been asked to evaluate the environmental impact of a new airport and industrial park on your region. Knowing that the area contains thousands of acres of wetlands, which are easily susceptible to environmental changes, you are concerned that business leaders, economists, and legislators may trivialize your group's findings, ignore the effects on the wetlands, and go ahead with the proposed development.
>
> Your study shows that the 4,200-acre industrial park will affect 75,000 acres of surrounding wetlands. Further, the fisheries industry will suffer an estimated 37 percent total reduction in accessible estuaries, with almost 10 percent of that area being unrecoverable (and unusable for other purposes). Of that 10 percent, 15 percent will be lost in the first year of construction and 12 percent in the second year; the best guess is that a loss of approximately 8 percent of that 10 percent will be felt in the third year. Most disconcerting is that these numbers do not even begin to reflect the physical damage the area will suffer—fish dying along the banks of the river, algae kills, and an unrelenting stench from the effects of the new industrial park.

Determine what sorts of quantitative details you want to introduce in a report to the developers, legislators, or business leaders who will read your report. Recognize also that many of these readers are not accustomed to reading sophisticated or complicated graphics; you might also consider that copies of your report may go to members of the public at large. What do you want them to understand about your concerns and findings?

Next, construct appropriate graphics to present your findings. Write a brief explanation of the graphics that tells readers what you want them to understand from viewing the graphics.

Illustrating Physical Features

So far, our discussion of graphics has focused on opportunities to represent numerical data, a common task for graphics in workplace documents. Depending on your particular organization and its mission, you may also have to present the physical features of an item or site or relationships between segments or parts. The most common techniques for presenting these kinds of physical features are photographs, maps, illustrations of parts of the whole, illustrations of processes, exploded diagrams, cutaway drawings, blueprints, and projection drawings.

Photographs

Does the text describe a *physical object* that readers need to see in order to understand it? A *photograph* can express the reality of that object. Photographs are also useful ways to incorporate people into your presentation; doing so can add interest and help humanize an otherwise dull topic. You can also use photographs to convey a sense of relationships in the topic's coverage; for example, you could use a drawing to show how to put on a seat belt on an airplane, but more effective is a photograph of a human being fastening the seat belt.

When using a photograph in a document, be sure to attend to these matters:

Print Quality

- Evaluate, critically, the quality of your photograph. A photograph that is hazy, dark, or light will look twice as bad when reproduced in a document.
- Avoid using paper clips, staples, or other attachers that can deface the photograph. Do not write on the front or back of your photograph; the writing may come through on the photograph when you reproduce it.
- Consider whether you will scan the photograph into your document or have it professionally printed. Although scanning is increasingly sophisticated, it can restrict the number of copies you can produce in a desktop-published document, and it may not give you the expandable image you want. Professionally printed photographs in documents can be quite expensive, however. Ask your illustrator and printer how the printing technique will affect the quality of your photograph.

Focus and Scale of the Image

- Crop the photograph to eliminate any surrounding details or images that may obscure the message you are trying to send.
- Check the lighting of the photograph to make sure distortions and shadows do not interfere with the primary view.
- Use real people whenever appropriate to humanize your topic and to emphasize the diversity of your organization; include men and women and members of various ages and races in your photographs.
- Use an item for comparison, such as a ruler, thimble, human being, or some other reasonable measure, beside the object you are photographing when you want to emphasize the size of an object.

The issues of focus and scale are particularly important when using photographs in your workplace documents. In the photograph in Figure 8.12 much of the detail of the featured subject matter is lost due to poor cropping and focus. Note the improvement in the message's clarity when the photograph is cropped to emphasize the content (see Figure 8.13).

The Action Advertising team decides to use a photograph showing the results of the agency's work. The team members believe that a photograph of cus-

FIGURE 8.12

A Photograph before Cropping
Photo courtesy of NASA

FIGURE 8.13

The Same Photograph after Cropping
Photo courtesy of NASA

tomers lined up at the Fresh Market Bazaar (one of the agency's accounts) will catch readers' attention and reinforce their message that "advertising pays." Now they must decide how to reproduce the image. Because they use high-quality graphics computers in their work, the team members decide to scan in the image of the photograph, which will allow them to remove shadows, enhance colors, and remove distracting details from the photograph.

Maps

When discussing *geographic regions or features,* you can use *maps* to show the particular areas or features (such as rivers or mountains) you are describing. You may find maps useful, for instance, when describing sales territories, target markets, or special features of a region. You might also use them to illustrate a discussion of an area's water supply or hazardous winter road conditions. Maps may also be used to show demographic data, as in Figure 8.14 on page 278.

When you use a map in your document, attend to the following issues:

Physical Features

■ Use an up-to-date map. New roads, for instance, can make a graphic of an organization's sales routes obsolete. Global maps are particularly sensitive to change as countries adopt new names or alter their borders.

■ Label small areas only if they are relevant to your discussion. For example, in a map of the United States, you should label the states in New England only if they are emphasized in your discussion. If your focus is on the Northwest or the South, however, you don't need to label the New England states.

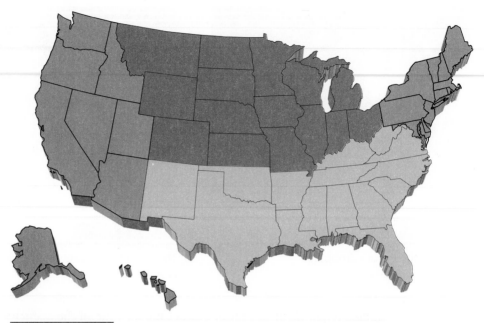

FIGURE 8.14   Map of the United States Showing the Four Segments of the Country Designated by a Market Research Group

■ Indicate major roads, rivers, mountains, or other features that are relevant to your discussion. For example, when weather forecasters predict that a hurricane may affect all areas east of I-95, their maps highlight that major interstate.

Scale and Proportion

■ Indicate which direction is north. Map readers expect that north will be at the top, so you should orient your map that way.

■ Keep areas in the correct proportion. Distorting the size of an area for emphasis is unethical and confusing because it suggests that the area is larger than it actually is. Instead, pull out the segment you want to emphasize.

■ Include a legend with the scale to which your map is drawn (for example, 1 inch equals 10 miles) only if the purpose of your map is to indicate distances, not physical features.

Most readers have little trouble understanding a clearly drawn map. Remember, however, that the more information in the map (terrain features, highways, rivers, cities, counties, airports, etc.), the more difficult it is to comprehend.

To make maps more interesting, consider adding color for emphasis and appeal. You can also add graphic representations to communicate additional messages, such as putting dollar ($) signs over the areas that are the organization's most profitable territories.

Illustrations of the Parts of the Whole

Does the text describe *a physical object or the various parts* of a piece of equipment? With an *illustration of the parts of the whole,* you can show the reader how the equipment looks and label the various parts without encountering many of the potential distortions of photographs. Figure 8.15 is an example.

When constructing an illustration, follow these guidelines:

- The perspective on the illustration should be clear and/or labeled (straight on, slanted, from the back, etc.).
- The parts you want to emphasize should be clearly labeled.
- Large parts that will help orient your reader should be clearly labeled.
- Labels should be readable.
- Lines drawn to parts should not cross unnecessarily, creating a chaotic effect.

Computer-generated illustrations, such as the one in Figure 8.15, are often more effective than hand-drawn illustrations because they provide more options for emphasizing relevant or important parts. Further, if the design of the equipment you are depicting changes, a computer-generated illustration can be more easily modified than a hand-drawn illustration. The Action Advertising team, for example, decides to add a computer-generated illustration of a stack of dollar bills to convince readers that advertising will help them get more for their money. In Figure 8.16 the stack of dollar bills symbolizes the *whole* concept of profitability.

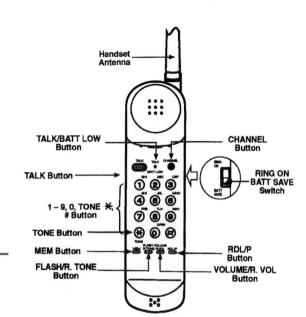

FIGURE 8.15

An Illustration Showing the Parts of the Whole

Reprinted by permission. © 1993 Uniden America Corporation.

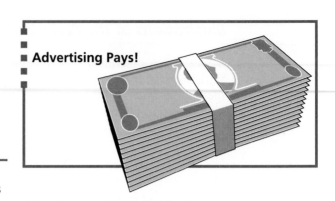

FIGURE 8.16

Computer Clip Art Conveys
Special Meaning to Readers

Illustrations of Processes, Steps, or Procedures

Illustrations are also useful for explaining *processes, steps, or procedures,* especially when that information is so complex or abstract that it cannot be represented with photographs or other visuals. In fact, you are probably familiar with such illustrations from your science texts, where they show the processes of photosynthesis, passive solar heat transfer in a greenhouse, or precipitation. Figure 8.17 shows the process of installing a battery in a cordless vacuum cleaner. Notice how the use of human hands adds context to the illustration.

When using illustrations to describe a process, steps, or procedures, follow these guidelines:

- Clarify the order in which the process, steps, or procedures take place; number the steps or draw arrows in your illustration if appropriate.
- Indicate repetitious actions by drawing circles or arcs to emphasize the repetitions.
- Include warnings at dangerous stages of the process (see Figure 8.18).

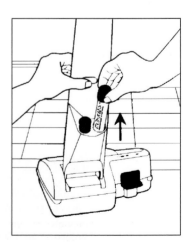

FIGURE 8.17

Hands Help Provide Context for Illustrating the
Process of Installing a Battery

Graphic provided courtesy of Black & Decker® Household
Products Group, Floorbuster™ Cordless Room Vac. Model
SV3000 © 1996.

FIGURE 8.18

A Warning of Danger in a Process

Exploded Diagrams

Does the text describe *how the various parts of equipment fit together*? An *exploded diagram* showing how the parts should be assembled is quite useful (see Figure 8.19). When designing an exploded diagram, follow these guidelines:

- Use dotted or colored lines to show the connections between parts.
- Make sure each nut, bolt, or fastener is clearly visible to the reader.
- Draw the parts to a specified scale, keeping their proportions to each other accurate.
- Pull out intricate parts from the rest of the illustration for focus.
- Make sure all parts are clearly labeled, perhaps using numbers or letters that correspond to a legend that lists the individual parts.

Cutaway Drawings

Does the text describe the *inner workings of some piece* of equipment? A *cutaway drawing* reveals what photographs and standard illustrations cannot show. Unlike an exploded diagram, which shows how an object is assembled, a cutaway drawing shows readers the internal dimensions and features of the object or how it should be positioned to operate correctly (see Figure 8.20 on page 282).

1. Unit base

2. Jar base

3. Blade assembly

4. Gasket

5. Jar

6. Lid

7. Cap

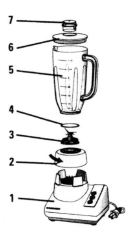

FIGURE 8.19

An Exploded Diagram Showing How to Assemble a Blender

Graphic provided courtesy of Black & Decker® Household Products Group, PowerPro™ Blender © 1996.

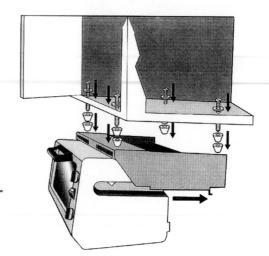

F I G U R E 8.20

A Cutaway Drawing
Graphic provided courtesy of Black & Decker®
Household Products Group, Toast-R-Oven™
Broiler with Mounting Hood.

When designing a cutaway drawing, follow these guidelines:

- Clearly label the part of the object that you are illustrating.
- Clearly label the components of that part.
- Indicate the larger components to help orient the reader.
- Indicate the smaller parts on which you want the reader to focus.

Depending on the audience's need for information, a cutaway drawing is a relatively simple concept for most readers to comprehend. Make sure, however, that distracting details are omitted and that only the relevant internal features are shown.

Blueprints

Does the text describe the *design or layout of an area*? If so, a standard *architectural blueprint* will clarify the proportions and special features of the design. Of course, drawing architectural blueprints is a highly specialized skill; nevertheless, understanding the basics of such drawings can be useful in whatever organization you work. Unless you are in the architectural design business, you may rely on simplified drawings that show the design or layout of the area you are describing (see Figure 8.21).

When constructing a blueprint, follow these guidelines:

- Indicate walls, doorways, halls, and windows.
- Indicate special features for computers, storage, electrical outlets, phone jacks, and the like.
- Include dimensions for length, width, and height.
- Include any special notes about construction.

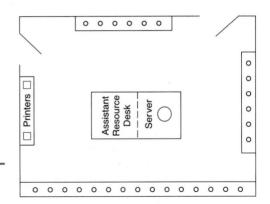

FIGURE 8.21

A Simplified Blueprint of a
Computer Workstation

Projection Drawings

Does the text describe a *single object from a variety of views?* If so, special *projection drawings* can clarify the angle and the appearance of that object (see Figure 8.22).

When illustrating your ideas with projection drawings, follow these guidelines:

- Clearly label the angle from which you are showing the object or plan.
- Show each angle that will help the reader understand.
- Keep the proportions of each view consistent.

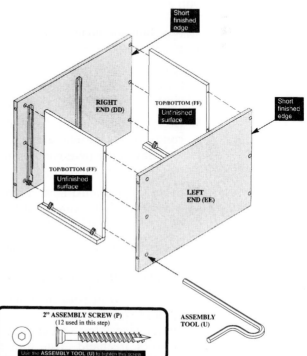

FIGURE 8.22

A Projection Drawing—A View from the
Top, Left-end Side

Reprinted by permission from Sauder®
Woodworking © 1996.

Illustrating Physical Features

Based on the scenario introduced in the first Application in this chapter, consider what sorts of physical descriptions and graphics might be useful for your information and audience. Consider as many options as possible for an extensive report on the environmental impact of the industrial park. Next, select two of these options and sketch the graphics for them. Construct the introductory and explanatory text to accompany these graphics.

Using Graphics Professionally: Additional Do's and Don'ts

Understanding the numerous forms of graphics and the special rhetorical services they perform for your readers can help you make clear decisions about when and how to use graphics. Although graphics illustrators may be available to you, knowing some general do's and don'ts of all graphic construction will prove useful as you work with these illustrators or as you draft and design your own graphics:

1. A graphic should send one clear message; putting too much information in a graphic can overwhelm readers and confuse your message.

2. Because one of the purposes of graphics is to give your readers a visual break, be sure to allow enough space between the text and the graphic to rest your readers' eyes. Crowding the graphic negates much of its value.

3. Every graphic in your document must be numbered. Tables are numbered consecutively with other tables using Roman numerals (I, II, III, . . .). Figures have their own consecutive sequence that ignores the table numbers. Figures are numbered with Arabic numerals (1, 2, 3, . . .).

4. Every graphic must have a title that identifies the type of graphic it is (pie chart, line graph, cutaway diagram, etc.) and the type of information it provides; for example:

   Pie Chart Showing the Uses of Cotton in the United States

   Cutaway Diagram of an Automatic Drip Coffeemaker

5. Like the rest of your document, graphics should look professional. Computer programs can help you construct professional-looking graphics. If you do not have access to a graphics software package, however, you may have to work freehand. You should still use precise measuring instruments (rulers, T squares, protractors, etc.) to construct your graphics.

6. The printing process and reproduction method for including graphics in documents affect numerous decisions about the number and kind of graphics you can use. Be sure to consult with a graphics specialist about your opportunities and limitations.

7. Graphics should be in ink, never pencil, even when you are sketching a rough diagram for an art specialist.

8. Color can enhance graphics and help the reader to see more quickly the point(s) you want to emphasize. Make sure, however, that you don't overuse color and overwhelm or confuse your reader. And be certain that the color is suited to the printing process.

Controlling the Rhetorical Message of Graphics

Throughout this text, you have learned to consider the rhetorical undercurrents of your writing—both the explicit and the implicit messages that are communicated by the actual text of your workplace documents. You should also learn to evaluate the appropriateness of the rhetorical messages you send in your graphics. Consider, for example, Figure 8.23 on page 286 whose purpose is to help readers focus on physical characteristics so they can provide accurate descriptions of suspects for the police. Although the information in this graphic is useful and the graphic itself is clearly reproduced, what additional, and certainly unintended, message do you see here? If you answer that the graphic suggests that all criminal suspects are men, you are well on your way to understanding the rhetorical value of graphics—and figuring out what to do to improve that rhetorical message. In this case, the authors of the publication should have added a graphic of a female to show the kinds of physical characteristics readers should focus on to describe a female suspect.

APPLICATION

Considering the Rhetorical Significance of Graphics

Sometimes the best way to be sure you understand all the nuances of your graphics is to consider how they can be misused. Return to the graphics options you considered for the two previous Applications in this chapter (both the options you accepted and those you discarded). Which options had the potential for rhetorical overtones that would further your message that the proposed industrial park is hazardous to the environment? Which had the potential for unethical or distorted overtones? Which had neutral overtones that, consequently, contributed neither information nor meaning? How have these determinations affected your choice of graphics? What are the ethical repercussions of your choices?

FIGURE 8.23 The Rhetorical Significance of the Choice of Graphics

East Carolina University *Emergeny Procedures Manual*. Reprinted by permission of the Justice Academy.

Be sure that the graphics you select for your workplace documents convey the appropriate message both at the most obvious level and at the more subliminal level. Using a photograph showing all men, all women, all elderly persons, all Hispanics, or some other exclusionary group to depict your organization's workers suggests a lack of diversity in your organization, which may be correct, of course, or may mislead your readers about the culture of your organization. Similarly, a photograph showing men wearing business suits and women in less professional attire suggests that only men have management positions in your organization. Including numerous people in a variety of roles typically sends a better message about your organization.

Summary

Graphics can enhance the information you are trying to convey in your workplace documents by simplifying, clarifying, or emphasizing it. Used appropriately and ethically, graphics can make the difference between a boring or confusing document and an interesting, clear one.

Just as you consider your readers when making decisions about the text of your workplace documents, you should also consider the audience when making decisions about graphics. Knowing the kinds of graphics that readers can understand will prevent you from including useless (and often expensive) graphics. Similarly, recognizing that too many or crowded graphics can overwhelm your readers will help you place your graphics appropriately in your text.

Graphics are especially useful for comparing numbers, percentages, and other data. Tables, charts, and graphs are the graphic forms most often used for presenting numbers and, occasionally, text. Graphics are also useful for showing pictorially (through illustrations, photographs, and maps) information that might be bland in textual descriptions. Be sure to use graphics whenever the text of your discussion is complex or highly detailed.

Reproducing graphics can be a highly sophisticated procedure that can cost a great deal of money, and if the method is not chosen wisely, it can result in blurred, foggy, or pointless visuals. Be sure to work closely with a professional artist and printer who will help you get the best graphics for your money.

After determining the appropriate graphic for conveying the information you need to discuss, be sure to introduce your graphic with a clear explanation of what the reader should see. Then, stop the text to insert the graphic, giving the reader the opportunity to visualize your information. Clearly indicate the sources for your graphics if the sources are outside your organization; even if your organization has produced the graphic or the information on which it is based, you may need to cite specific sources for skeptical readers.

Finally, be certain to evaluate your graphics for ethical and rhetorical concerns. Over- or understating your point with graphics is just as unethical as such misstatements in the text. Similarly, the rhetorical significance of graphics should not elude you. Make sure that your graphics include representative populations and that a proper sense of fair play is at work when you select graphics.

Working with graphics can be an exciting part of planning and creating workplace documents. Knowing more about your options and how to work with professional graphic artists allows you to have more input on that aspect of your work.

CHECKLIST

✔ Add graphics to your document to serve the following purposes:
- Highlight selected information.
- Emphasize important details or trends.
- Simplify complex information.
- Clarify information that could be misinterpreted.
- Provide a mental image or orientation of the process or product you are describing.

- Show relationships between ideas or trends or statistics.
- Justify your claims.
- Attract the readers' attention.
- Give the readers a break from the text.

✓ Choose the right graphic to communicate your message to your audience.

✓ Consider whether your graphic is suitable for your readers' abilities to understand.

✓ Consider whether you are presenting quantitative (numerical) data or the physical features of some object or process before deciding which graphic to choose. Then, review the kinds of information that are best presented by the individual graphic forms:

Quantitative Data
- Tables
- Flow charts
- Pie charts or 100% column charts
- Line graphs or charts
- Bar graphs or charts

Physical Features
- Photographs
- Maps
- Illustrations of parts or the whole
- Illustrations of processes, steps, or procedures
- Exploded diagrams
- Cutaway drawings
- Blueprints
- Projection drawings

✓ Consider how sophisticated or simple your drawing should be for your audience and your message.

✓ Draft your graphics, just as you draft your text. Then, revise them for accuracy and interest.

✓ Check with professional illustrators to determine the printing method to be used for your document and the resulting limitations or opportunities for your graphics.

✓ Make sure all parts of the graphic are readable.

✓ Use color (if possible), text type, and labels to clarify and enhance the appeal of your graphics.

✓ If you don't have a computer program to design your graphics, you should still produce a professional-looking graphic. Use precise measurements for graphics: use a ruler, protractor, T square, and other appropriate tools.

✓ Tell your reader what to look for in the graphic.

✓ Explain the graphic to your reader.

✓ Insert the graphic into your text as close as possible to your discussion of it. If the graphic must be placed on another page, tell the reader where to find the graphic.

✓ Label all graphics with a table or figure number and an informative title.

✓ Acknowledge the source(s) of your graphics.

✓ Consider the rhetorical message of your graphic in addition to its explicit message.

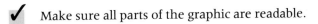

EXERCISES

Individual Exercises

1. Determine the characteristics of an audience that would care about the differences between two breeds of dogs (e.g., parents looking for a dog for their child, a single person living in a small urban apartment, an elderly couple living on a farm). Then, explain which graphic form you would use to compare a rat terrier and a springer spaniel in terms of each of the following:

   a. Physical appearance
   b. Longevity
   c. Weight and height
   d. Primary features

2. If you were to design the "female" version of the male suspect graphic in Figure 8.23, what specific features would you want readers to note if they were trying to describe a female suspect? What options for each feature would be appropriate for identification?

Collaborative Exercises

1. With your partner or team members, go through a number of news-magazines, such as *Time* and *Newsweek,* and choose five particularly appealing graphics. What aspects of the graphics are especially pleasing?

Next, evaluate the usefulness of the graphics. Do they provide relevant information? Why were they included with this article?

Then, look for references to the graphics in the text. If you find references, write them down and be prepared to share them with classmates. Evaluate the usefulness of the references in terms of the following:

a. Encouraging you to stop reading and look at the graphic

b. Telling you what you should see in the graphic

c. Complementing the information in the text

If you do not find any textual references to the graphics, determine where in the article you would include a discussion of each graphic; then write that textual discussion.

2. Given the following information, prepare a graphic appropriate for general readers:

Investing $2,000 a year for 30 years at 4 percent yields $112,170. At 7 percent, that $2,000-per-year investment yields $188,922. And at 11 percent, a $2,000-per-year investment results in $398,036.

Next, write a sentence or two to introduce the graphic to general readers and to explain to them what they should understand from the graphic.

 ONGOING ASSIGNMENT

Based on the work you have done in planning, drafting, and revising the text of a manual for newcomers to your organization, what kinds of graphics might be appropriate?

■ Begin by brainstorming a full list of possibilities.

■ Determine what kinds of information most need a visual aid.

■ Determine which graphics are feasible if you are using software available to you on your college campus or through your workplace.

■ Determine the printing method that is most likely to be necessary for the kind of graphic(s) you want to include.

Designing and Formatting Your Workplace Document

Each year, market researchers, publishers, public relations and advertising personnel, car and clothes designers, and countless others spend a great deal of time and money perfecting the visual appeal of their products. Visual appeal is comprised of a product's packaging, design, color choices, display, the type style of the descriptive text or logo, and numerous other factors that shape our initial impressions of a product or service. An attractive package may appeal to consumers who would not even notice the same product in plain wrappings.

Company logos in particular are designed and displayed to attract attention. The designers and displayers of Mercedes-Benz's emblem, McDonald's arches, Nike's swoosh, Colombian coffee's Juan Valdez, and Apple's Macintosh all count on your having positive associations with the companies and their products, and they hope you look for the logos when making relevant purchases. Other companies are known by the distinctive color packaging of their products: the all-green packaging of many gardening products, the red of Coca-Cola, and the blue of IBM (known in the computer industry as "Big Blue"). Many nonprofit organizations, such as the American Red Cross, the Shriners' Hospital, and the Smithsonian Institution, also have immediately recognizable visual symbols: the large red cross, the poster children at the Shriners' Hospital, and the photographs of the Smithsonian buildings (especially the castle) all bring instant recognition to the organizations. Thus, for many companies, their visual representations are part of their culture.

Just as organizations strive to ensure that their products and symbols express the appropriate visual images, members of those organizations must work to make sure their documents convey the proper image and appeal as well. In this chapter, you will learn to consider the visual appeal of your workplace documents, and you will learn some strategies for making them both more attractive and more readable for your audience.

You have already learned from Chapter 8 that appropriate graphics add clarity and emphasis to points you want to make, thereby increasing reader interest in and comprehension of your workplace documents. Although you will make several decisions about the visual appeal of your document as you plan and draft it, other decisions will have to wait until you are ready to produce the final document. At that time, you should consider all your options for improving the visual appeal of your document; specifically, you will have to consider the design and format:

- *Design:* The overall appearance of the document, determined by its size, the cover, the color of the paper, the type size and style, and other features.

- *Format:* Matters of textual shaping, such as margins, columns, lists, headings and subheadings, boxes, shading, and other features.

These visual elements need not be addressed in a specific order, but some of your choices may affect earlier decisions—for instance, a shift to a larger type size often affects the placement of text on a page, and a different type font can throw off the margins of your lists.

Although you may rely on personnel in your organization's graphics department to help you fine-tune the visual elements of your documents, you will have to know some terminology to understand what the illustrator has in mind or to describe what you want (see Chapter 8 on graphics). In many smaller organizations, you will have to make all of these decisions yourself. Thus, understanding your options and some general principles of design and format will help you to ensure the visual integrity of your workplace documents.

Of course, with the increased availability and sophistication of desktop publishing systems (software and printers), the features described in this chapter are only some of the options you have for designing and formatting workplace documents. Regardless of the proliferation of options, however, the keys to their successful use remain the same: (1) be consistent in your use of design and format features, and (2) err on the side of simplicity rather than chaos.

Design for Informative and Persuasive Documents

Just as you have made a number of content decisions based on what you want to accomplish and what your reader needs to know, you will also make design and format decisions based on these two elements. In short, the options for your document's design will be influenced by its purpose and audience.

Informative documents—those whose primary purpose is to relay information and only to a lesser degree to persuade—often require structured formats that leave you with little choice. Information briefs and press releases, for instance, typically appear in a traditional format of paragraphs with, perhaps, headings and subheadings and a few graphics. The readers of such documents want information in a simple, readable format that allows for little creativity.

In contrast, persuasive documents often allow for a great deal of creativity. These documents generally need to make information friendly and relevant to a clearly focused purpose. Additionally, readers need to believe that the information presented is useful and important to their lives. Because most workplace documents contain at least a modicum of persuasive intent, your knowledge of layout and design features will serve you well when creating persuasive reports and proposals, brochures, and even Web pages—specific types of documents whose design and format options are addressed at the end of this chapter.

Throughout this chapter, we will follow a scenario involving Bunting College, a small liberal arts college that is embarking on a major campaign to recruit new students. Bunting has a solid history as a fine school, but over the years its adherence to a classical curriculum with no attention to technology, combined with its aging faculty, has sent the message that the school is a bit out of touch with the twentieth, much less the twenty-first, century.

A new college president is beginning to breathe life into Bunting and has recruited top students to work with the faculty on a campaign to show off the new Bunting College curriculum and philosophy in a series of brochures, letters, a Web page, videos, and newsletter articles. At this stage, the committee must present a short report on its progress to the board of trustees and ask the board to continue funding the recruiting campaign. The committee recognizes that while the report's purpose is both informative and persuasive, it is mostly persuasive. Throughout this chapter, we will follow the committee members' decisions about the design and format options for this report. The chapter's Applications will give you the chance to make decisions for formatting a similar document for your own college.

Audience Factors in Design and Format

In workplace writing, you want to make sure that your product—your finished document—will attract and hold the attention of your readers. Consider your own preferences for reading materials:

- What about the covers of books (or brochures) attracts your attention?
- How do you react to books that have tiny print and long chapters?
- How do you react to books that have no pictures?
- How do you react to brochures that are all text?
- How do you react to works that have page-long paragraphs?

If the appearance of reading material does not match your preferences, you may have a difficult time making yourself read important documents or assignments, and you may forgo reading them altogether if given the opportunity.

To compensate for readers' reluctance or anxiety, writers of successful workplace documents employ visual elements that make the document more appealing to readers, establish the proper rhetorical theme, aid the readers' memory or recall of key issues, and make the ideas more comprehensible. These visual elements begin with the design and color of the cover and include lists, various type fonts and sizes, headings and subheadings, boxes and shaded text, and margins and white space within the document itself. The goals are quite simple: to make the documents more inviting and more comprehensible for the readers.

In the Bunting College scenario, the audience (the board of trustees) recognizes the need to modify the Bunting curriculum and image, but the trustees are uncomfortable with a rapid shift to an entirely new image. The recruiting committee, therefore, wants to be certain that the board members, many of whom graduated from Bunting and feel nostalgic about their alma mater, understand that Bunting's traditions are not being sacrificed for technological additions to the curriculum. Instead, the committee wants to present these technological updates as a means of moving the curriculum—still a liberal arts curriculum—into the next century. That understanding of the audience will guide the decisions the committee makes about the document's message and appearance in the remainder of this chapter.

Design Elements

The *design* of a workplace document determines its overall appearance. Design elements include the size and shape of the document; the texture and appearance of the cover; the color of the pages, sections, graphics, and cover; and the style and size of the type used for the text and headings. This section presents some options along with some guidelines for making decisions about these elements. You should explore these options in terms of your organization's culture. In other words, how conservative or creative your organization is will determine how open its leaders and clients are to unusual visual elements in your workplace documents.

Paper Size

Most traditional or conservative organizations (and most are at least somewhat traditional) rely on standard-sized workplace documents, meaning that their reports, letters, and proposals are all produced on standard 8½-by-11-inch paper. Other organizations use slightly larger or smaller paper for their routine communications. Using smaller sheets of paper for memos and form letters is popular because it avoids wasting paper when the message merits only a sentence or paragraph.

Variations in paper size send the message that this organization is a little different, and many executives or graphics managers believe that odd-sized paper generates interest in their organization. Readers may, indeed, notice the difference, but many of them may respond negatively, thinking the organization doesn't know the proper paper for standard business communications. When deciding about page size, therefore, the company will have to balance its desire to appear different with concern about how the readers will react to such variations.

As with all your design decisions, paper size can send interesting rhetorical messages about your content. Consider the value of using an oversized brochure or document to indicate company growth or the larger size of your product. In contrast, smaller documents or brochures can signal individual servings or smaller portions of your product. In short, alternative paper sizes can be quite effective when trying to persuade an audience to take a certain view of your topic. When trying merely to inform an audience, however, standard paper sizes may be best.

Because readers frequently have strong expectations about paper sizes, you must determine whether it is a good idea to accommodate or violate those expectations. Your primary considerations about page size, therefore, should address these questions:

- What is the standard page size for the type of document I am producing?
- What are the advantages of adhering to that standard? Will my readers be more comfortable with the standard size or with some alternative size? Will the page size indicate what they should expect in the content of my work? Can I present as much or more information in this size?

- What are the disadvantages of adhering to the standard size? Will my readers overlook this document, thinking it is just like every other document? Will using the standard size make the document seem boring?

- What are the advantages of using a larger or smaller size? Will the larger paper be more dramatic? Is such drama appropriate for this document? Will the smaller paper indicate simplicity? Will the smaller paper be appropriate for, say, pocket instructions?

- What are the disadvantages of using a larger or smaller size? Will the larger paper seem overwhelming and bulky? Will it get in my reader's way? Will the smaller paper make the print difficult to read? Will it indicate small thinking? Does it send a rhetorical message I do not intend?

The committee members in the Bunting College scenario carefully considered their options for the paper size of their report. A smaller report, they feared, might suggest the scaling down of the curriculum, while a larger report might overwhelm the readers. Finally, they opted for a standard-sized report out of respect for the traditional members of the board.

Covers

Many workplace documents, such as reports, manuals, and proposals, have hard-stock covers that protect the document and give the work a finished, booklike appearance. When choosing a cover for your communications, you should consider the rhetorical message you wish to send and then design elements that will help you communicate that message.

Which cover in Figure 9.1, for instance, do you think most readers would find more visually appealing? Why? You probably chose B, the cover with the graphic. Regardless of your understanding of sales charts, you have probably seen enough of them to associate the left-to-right upward climb with progress, a message the creator of this cover certainly hopes to communicate. Thus, even this simplistic design sends the rhetorical message that the contents of the report will provide strategies for XYZ's growth. (See Chapter 8 for more on graphic design and rhetorical interpretations.)

In selecting a cover for your document, you will also consider other elements of visual design such as an appropriate color, the style and size of the font for the title and other text, and the use of graphics (see Chapter 8 for graphics). Coordinating these matters, while keeping the cover relatively simple, will challenge you to put your knowledge of design, graphics, and format to good use.

The Bunting College committee, for instance, decided to look for a way to blend the college's tradition with the modifications to the curriculum and philosophy. The committee members brainstormed about how to represent the traditional elements: the college seal, the stone arch at the entrance to the college, and the stately administration building. Then, they brainstormed about the best way to represent the new curriculum and philosophy: a computer, a computer-generated symbol of the twenty-first century, or some other high-tech image.

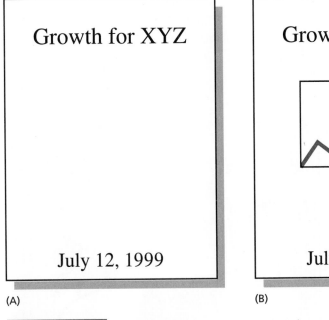

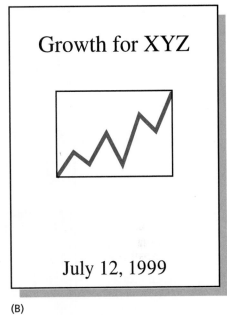

(A) (B)

F I G U R E 9.1 A Plain (A) versus a Graphically Enhanced (B) Cover for a Workplace Document

In the end, the group decided to use the cover in Figure 9.2 on page 298 for their report. How do you think the board members responded to this cover? What sorts of expectations do you think the cover aroused about the content of the report? Do you think the cover is appropriate for the committee's message?

Color

Color in a workplace document can have dramatic effects and can take on significant rhetorical meanings for your reader. Whether used in the text to highlight important information, in headings or subheadings to help organize your document, or in graphics to direct your readers' attention to special segments, color is perhaps one of the most effective tools workplace writers have for enhancing the visual appeal of their documents. Unfortunately, color is often misused or overused; when it is, it contributes to the chaos that many readers feel when reading overdesigned documents.

Just as you probably use highlighters to mark important ideas in your textbooks, you can use color in your workplace documents to highlight information and show readers where they need to pay special attention. Of course, overusing color for highlights confuses readers because it suggests that everything is important.

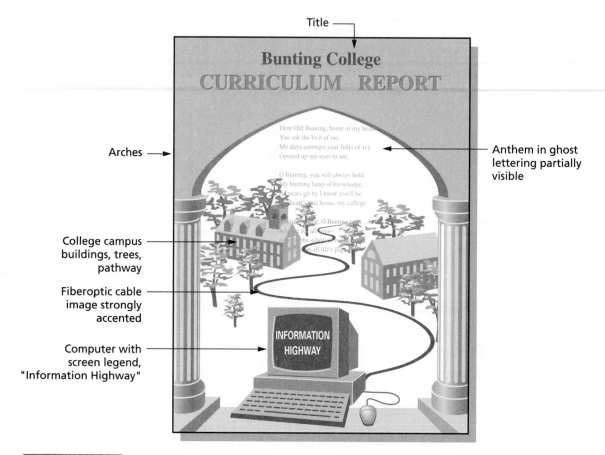

FIGURE 9.2 A Cover Idea for a Report to the Board of Trustees of a College

Colored headings, as in this book's design, are useful for emphasizing new segments or for organizing segments according to the readers' needs. For example, a report may have green headings for sections engineers should read, brown headings for managers, and gray headings for marketing personnel. Colors may also denote special topics: green for financial segments, red for safety segments, and so on.

Colors may also be used for special pages in a document. Especially in lengthy documents, colored pages may serve as dividers for sections of the document. In organizations where documents are written on a variety of reading levels for different groups of readers, different colored pages may be used for entire segments, say, white for highly technical readers, ivory for business executives, and gray for lay readers. Thus, color coding pages within a document is a popular way to send different messages to different readers.

If you use color in your document, you should consider the following questions:

THE WORLD OF WORKPLACE WRITING

Color and Meaning

As a reader, you are familiar with many business metaphors, such as "red ink" to refer to debt or losses and "black ink" to refer to a profit. For American readers, other colors also take on special symbolism:

- Yellow suggests caution or cowardice.
- Green suggests "go" or envy.
- Purple suggests dreamy, fanciful, or ornate as in "purple prose."
- Blue suggests tranquillity.
- Red suggests danger, caution, warning, or stop.
- White suggests good, clean, pure, or chaste.
- Gray suggests dull, boring, depressing, or conservative.
- Gold suggests high quality, top grade, or flashy.

Although this symbolism does not always translate into workplace documents, it can be useful in designing your work. At the same time, you should note that context can influence interpretations of color. Red, for instance, when used for notes in a manual, typically warns readers to be cautious, but as a color for clothing, it often suggests power. Green means "go" on a traffic light and suggests "growth" in gardening paraphernalia, but it suggests "envy" in emotional terms— substantially different interpretations for the same color.

Additionally—and significantly—colors often take on very different meanings in other cultures. White, for instance, is the color for mourning in East Asia, while red is the color for brides. Black may be our color for mourning, but it is the color for power in East Asia. Consider whether your audience is an American or an international one before you rely on colors to enhance the message of your document.

- Does my reader share my cultural understanding of the messages attached to certain colors? In other words, although American readers may associate red with danger, readers from other countries may not. What color would be more appropriate to catch their attention?
- Does the color enhance or impede the legibility of the text? As useful as color can be, it can also reduce the visibility of text. Be sure not to use yellow ink on white paper, for instance, or black ink on dark purple paper.
- Have I limited the use of color so that it makes a statement when and where I want? The overuse of color, like the overuse of any other element in your workplace documents, can confuse readers or even lead them to disregard colored segments.

Generating Information for Future Exercises

With your instructor's help, investigate the changing curriculum at your college, focusing on a new or revamped program that may not have attracted much attention on campus. Your instructor may set up an information session with the coordinator of the program, or you may have to do all the investigating on your own. In either case, ask a number of questions aimed at generating information to produce text for potential students of this program; for example:

- What is the purpose of the program?
- What kinds of students will be interested in this program?
- What career advantages would students who major or minor in this program have?
- Who are the primary faculty teaching in this program, and what are their interests?
- What are the curriculum requirements of the program?
- What are the admission requirements of the program?

Your instructor will help you determine whether your text will eventually be formatted as a brochure, a newsletter article, or a Web page. If you produce a hard-copy document, determine what options for paper size, cover, and color you want to consider at this early stage and why.

- Have I determined the financial implications of using color? Because color costs more to reproduce than standard black-and-white text, you may need the approval of your boss before planning to include color in your document. Be sure to check on the budget before relying too heavily on color to make your points in your communications.

Type Style

Because of the proliferation of word processing and desktop publishing packages that offer a variety of type styles and sizes, workplace writers have a number of options for designing the text of their documents. These options can get you into trouble, however, if you don't know what you are doing. One of the biggest dangers is using too many type styles in a single document. The result is chaos. And you certainly do not want your documents to be considered chaotic—especially after you have spent so much time drafting and revising to create a competent, coherent, professional communication.

Two groups of type styles are available: serif and sans serif styles. *Serif* type styles (such as Times Roman, Century, Palatino, Courier, Bookman) have strokes (or serifs) at the edges of each letter:

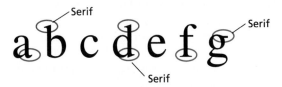

Serif type styles are considered traditional, for they originated before the printing press at the time when books and letters were copied by hand by scribes. Hence many companies use serif type to send the rhetorical message that the company is traditional. In addition, research frequently finds that serif styles are more readable than sans serif styles.

As you have probably figured out, *sans serif* type styles have no strokes or serifs along the edges:

a b c d e f g

Sans serif styles (such as Helvetica, Futura, Gill Sans, Avant Garde) sometimes help readers follow the horizontal line of text. Rhetorically, they are frequently used when the writer wants to send the message that this document is about something new or improved. Some organizations prefer their work to be set in sans serif type because of such undertones: "We don't want to look traditional and stodgy; we want to look fresh, innovative, and creative."

Both the serif and the sans serif style offer a number of alternative fonts. Consider, for instance, the following variations:

Serif	*Sans Serif*
Courier	Helvetica
Bookman	Futura
Century	Avant Garde
Palatino	Gill Sans
Times	

Further, to test the rhetorical differences such type styles imply, consider what entertainment, dress, food, and music you would expect to find at the following parties:

You are invited to attend a party on October 30, 2000.

You are invited to attend a party on October 30, 2000.

You are invited to attend a party on October 30, 2000.

You are invited to attend a party on October 30, 2000.

Do you notice that you read each line a little differently; do your expectations about the party also change?

In the workplace, of course, your decisions about type styles should coincide with your organization's guidelines and its culture. Most organizations, for example, do not use scripted fonts for their workplace writing—elegant scripts are usually reserved for invitations and other special occasions. Nor do most organizations use extremely casual fonts that look like handwritten communications; again, such fonts would send the wrong message about an organization that is trying to appear professional and attentive.

Thus, you should choose a typeface from within the confines of "acceptable" type styles—the professional and clean-edged serif and sans serif styles available on most word processing programs. Your decisions about type style should also coincide with your rhetorical intentions. Because you may not be able to anticipate how others will interpret your choices, be sure to ask colleagues what message your selection sends.

Type Size

Small print is standard in a variety of contracts and offers involving everything from employment to cars to credit cards. Such print sends an important rhetorical message: "You really don't have to worry about these details." Experience, however, has taught us to be wary: "In your own best interest, you'd better be aware of these details."

Small type has other disadvantages as well, especially for those who are visually impaired. Sensitive companies are willing to pay a little more for the added length of a document printed in a more legible type size. Most readers consider any type size smaller than 9 points to be difficult to read. Further, many readers assume that works printed in smaller type are boring, technical, or otherwise difficult; perhaps you react that way when you are required to read books with tiny print.

In contrast, larger print offers several advantages for readers, most importantly, that it is more legible—up to a point. Type that is too large looks juvenile (remember the big print of your first-grade reader?) and slows the reader. In the workplace, "juvenile" type not only insults the reader, but it also suggests that the writer has little to say and has increased the size of the type to expand the number of pages.

When determining the optimal type size for your documents, you should consider the following:

- The message you want to communicate to your readers: Minor details? Important information? Regular text?
- Your readers' visual capacity: Any visual impairments?
- Your rhetorical message: This can be skimmed quickly; this should be read carefully.

THE WORLD OF WORKPLACE WRITING

Reader Preferences versus Reader Successes

Research has played a key role in helping writers and designers move beyond their own preferences to figuring out what readers as a group like and dislike about the appearance of a document. Research can produce conflicting answers, however, depending on how the questions are phrased. In some cases, the answers differ depending on whether readers are asked which text features they like or which ones they read best. For example, research commonly shows that readers dislike small type, especially the 6- and 8-point type shown here:

This sentence is in 6-point type.

This sentence is in 8-point type.

Ironically, however, research also shows that readers read 6- and 8-point type much faster than larger type sizes. Further, readers can adapt to small text in small doses—say, in a table—when they may not in a complete document.

Would you give more weight to reader preferences or reader successes if you were choosing the type style for a workplace document? Most researchers conclude that readers' preferences should take precedence over other criteria because readers may have such strong negative reactions to, say, small type that they may not try to read a document that does not consider their preferences.

Similarly, you should realize that your own preferences will not always match those of "most" readers. Although you may still want to experiment, you should also be aware that some guidelines are more rigid than others because they involve crucial factors such as legibility and legality.

Although some workplace documents are printed in 12-point type, most are printed in 10-point type. Remember, too, that different type styles appear to be different in size; you may have to adjust type styles and sizes for the optimum effect and readability:

This is 12-point type in Helvetica.
This is 12-point type in Century.

This is 10-point type in Helvetica.
This is 10-point type in Century.

This is 9-point type in Helvetica.
This is 9-point type in Century.

Thus, your general text will usually be in 9- to 12-point type, with 10-point type being optimal for word-processed documents. Major headings may be a little larger than the standard text size, but few are larger than 14 points:

This is 14-point type in Helvetica.
This is 14-point type in Century.

The key to creating effective headings and subheadings is consistency. Headings that are the same size and style and are placed in the same way communicate that the information is the same level of importance (see Chapter 4 on the use of headings as an organizational tool). If you use a 12-point, centered heading in boldface type for your first major point, you should use the same style of headings for your second, third, and fourth major points. If you use a 10-point flush left, underlined subheading for your first subpoint, the subheadings for your second, third, and fourth subpoints, as well as for the subpoints under all your other major points, should follow the same style. Notice the consistency of the headings and subheadings in this textbook, for example.

Design factors—page size, covers, colors, type style, and type size—set the tone for the document's content or message; carefully consider all your options, along with the rhetorical messages they communicate, when you design your document. Because of the proliferation of desktop publishing packages, color printers and copiers, and other technological advances, you can incorporate many of these options into your routine workplace communications, rather than saving them for expensive, professionally reproduced documents.

APPLICATION

Making Design Decisions

Having gathered information about the new or revamped program you are describing to potential students and having chosen a document form for the information, you are ready to make some design decisions about your document. Describe the decisions you have made about the following:

- Paper size
- Cover
- Color
- Type size
- Type style

Be prepared to defend your choices.

Format Elements

As you have seen, many design elements, such as color and text style and size, affect the readability of workplace documents. Format issues also affect readability because they address matters of textual shaping, such as margins, columns, headings and subheadings, lists, highlighting, boxes, and shading, which can make documents easy or difficult to read and remember. Thus, format elements, like design elements, will require you to make some complex decisions.

Margins

The key to decisions about margins is to allow enough space between the edges of the paper and the text so that the text is framed, but not crowded (see Figure 9.3). In workplace documents, text pages typically have a 1-inch border at the top, right, and bottom and a 1½-inch margin on the left if the document is to be bound. Because of the use of running headers and footers on many desktop published documents, however, you may have to adjust the top and bottom margins accordingly.

In some special cases, you may extend the margins to give the page a cleaner, less cluttered look. Pages full of white space (areas with no text, graphic, or other

Operation Plan

The goal of IHOC Health Care is to provide affordable, at-home care for postoperative open heart surgery patients. In order to give the best care possible, IHOC will provide the following:

- Qualified nurses to assess patients' progress. IHOC will use only registered nurses who are experienced with the care of cardiac patients.
- Trained nutritionists to educate patients on how diet can affect their health.
- Trained exercise therapists to educate patients on the benefits of various exercises and to encourage them to use the exercise equipment IHOC provides.

FIGURE 9.3 Text Framed by Appropriate Margins

sort of design) are expensive, however, and are often reserved for coffee table books or, in the workplace, for annual reports. Sometimes, though, documents with complex information may have wide margins to allow readers to make notes in the margins.

The other critical issue with margins is whether you want them to be justified or unjustified, terms that denote the appearance of the right-hand margin of text. Justified margins (like those in this book) are even; unjustified margins are ragged. Research shows that readers read ragged or unjustified margins more easily than justified margins, which, in informal documents, may have excessive hyphenation or unusual spacing between words. Readers also lose their place more easily when reading successive lines of justified text. Professional printers, however, can correct these problems with justified text, so justified margins are acceptable for professionally produced documents.

Columns

Desktop publishing systems and more advanced word processing packages also allow routine communications to be formatted in multiple-column layouts—options once reserved for professional printers or manual cut-and-paste systems. Traditional workplace documents, such as letters and internal reports, are still produced using a single column of text, but many important documents, such as annual reports or proposals, now use two- or three-column layouts. The primary advantage of such layouts, with which you are no doubt familiar, is the added professional (printed) look of the page.

If you want your document to send the rhetorical message that it has been specially produced for a special reader and a special occasion, you might want to consider using a two- or three-column layout; keep these points in mind, however:

- Too many columns clutter the page and lead to narrow columns that are difficult to read.

- Columns can lead to a number of problems such as rivers of white space and overhyphenation. These problems are more acute when margins are justified.

- Graphics must not interfere with the reading of the text.

- Space between columns must be ample enough to give the reader a clear sense of the columns.

- The size and style of the typeface also affect the readability and visual appeal of columns.

Numerous other rules also apply to columns, but these few suggest the range of issues you must accommodate if you select this format.

Headings and Subheadings

Throughout this text, you have seen the advantages of using headings and sub-headings to separate ideas, indicate the document's organization to readers, and provide visual breaks. When you use headings and subheadings, take care not to abandon them at the bottom of the page with no text underneath them. (It hardly makes sense to have a *heading* sitting alone at the *bottom* of the page, right?) Also, be sure not to stack headings (have a heading and subheading together with no text between them). You need at least an introductory sentence to clarify the re-lationship between the heading and subheading (see Figures 9.4 and 9.5). Finally,

stacked
headings
disorient
reader

SWOT Analysis

Strengths
IHOC has several strengths that will enable it to control the competitive forces in the home health care market. The power of buyers will be controlled by imposing high switching costs on the patients after they begin IHOC's rehabilitation program. After doctors prescribe IHOC's services as treatment for patients, it will be more expensive for both the patients and the hospitals for patients to return to the hospital for rehabilitation. The level of service . . . .

FIGURE 9.4 Stacked Headings Provide No Means of Interpretation for the Reader

introductory
statement

SWOT Analysis
The following sections describe the Systemic Workers Operational Treatment's analysis of the benefits of our operational plan. Following the strengths, we have analyzed potential problems that the plan incurs and offered some solutions.

Strengths
IHOC has several strengths that will enable it to control the competitive forces in the home health care market. The power of buyers will be controlled by imposing high switching costs on the patients after they begin IHOC's rehabilitation program. After doctors prescribe IHOC's services as treatment for patients, it will be more expensive for both the patients and the hospitals for patients to return to the hospital for rehabilitation. The level of service . . . .

FIGURE 9.5 An Introductory Statement between Headings Orients the Reader

check the parallelism of your headings and subheadings (see the Brief Usage Guidebook). Just as they should be consistently formatted, they should also be grammatically consistent.

Lists

Information that consists of several items can be presented more clearly in lists than in standard text paragraphs. Lists are especially useful if readers need to be able to recall the information. Figures 9.6 and 9.7 show how much more useful information is when listed. Strategy Review 9.1 gives examples of icons that may be used in your list design.

> When planning your trip to the beach, be sure to pack items that cannot be rented, such as personal items (toothpaste, toilet paper, hair dryers, soap), linens (towels and sheets—although we do provide pillows and blankets), reading materials, and food. A lot of people forget to pack paper towels, pillow cases, and soap.

FIGURE 9.6   Lists in Paragraph Form within Text Are Difficult to Organize and Comprehend

> When planning your trip to the beach, remember the items that we provide for you and those you must bring for yourself. We provide these items:
>
> - Pillows
> - Blankets
> - A few toys and games for children
> - Kitchen paraphernalia:
>   - Pots and pans
>   - Coffeemaker
>   - Eating and cooking utensils
>   - Kitchen towels
> - TV and VCR and modest stereo system
> - Deck chairs

FIGURE 9.7   Listed Items Are Much Easier to Comprehend

What kinds of information can best be listed? Whenever you present instructions, you should consider using a list so that readers can readily return to their place in the text after performing each step. You should also consider listing information that contains many details and descriptions. In such cases, you can use boldface or italic type for the main idea or underline it; then, you can add the other details as subtext for the item. Finally, you can list information that you want readers to be able to recall as important features of a main idea. The following list, for example, presents the most important information in this paragraph to show how writers and document designers pull out relevant or important information, especially when it shares the same subject ("lists" in this example):

■ *When you present instructions,* you should consider using lists so that readers can readily return to their place in the text after performing each step.

■ *When information contains highly complex details and descriptions,* you can use boldface or italic type for the main idea or underline it; then, you can add the other details as subtext for the item.

■ *When you want readers to be able to recall specific items as important features of a main idea,* you should consider listing those items.

STRATEGY REVIEW 9.1

DESIGNING LISTS

When designing a list, you will have to select an icon to go before each item in the list. The following are examples of commonly used icons:

● A bullet, made by typing an "o" and coloring it in if you do not have a bullet key on your software program

* An asterisk

Δ A triangle

❏ A box, which is particularly useful if your list requires the reader/user to check off items or completed steps

✓ A checkmark

✍ A writer's hand, which can be useful when you want to signal that the reader must sign in a particular place or write a response

→ An arrow, which is useful when you must indicate directional information

Once again, you should consider the rhetorical message of your selection; be careful not to choose an icon that is startling, juvenile, or otherwise inappropriate for your audience or your document's seriousness of purpose.

In the Bunting College scenario, the committee members felt it was important to provide the audience with lists of strategies they were employing to recruit new students. They wanted to make clear that they were using a variety of strategies to find new students and were not relying on a single approach. The list reinforced the comprehensive nature of the committee's work and won the approval of the board members who voted to continue funding the recruiting committee's work.

Highlighting: Outlining, Shadowing, Italicizing, Boldfacing, and Underlining

Throughout your text, you will probably have numerous points that you want to emphasize. Most standard word processing packages give you numerous options for outlining, shadowing, *italizing*, **boldfacing**, and underlining. Used sparingly—and consistently—such features can provide the emphasis you want. When overused, however, like any other format or design technique, all of these features are annoying and difficult to read. This paragraph, for example, would most likely annoy a reader:

> Throughout your text, you will probably have numerous points that you want to emphasize. Practically any standard word processing package gives you numerous options for outlining, shadowing, *italizing*, **boldfacing**, and underlining. Used sparingly—and consistently—such features can provide the emphasis you want. When overused, however, like any other format or design technique, all of these features are annoying and difficult to read.

Boxes and Shadings

Many desktop publishing programs allow you to set off text in boxes or shaded segments (like the Strategy Review boxes and World of Workplace Writing boxes in this text). As with all other options, the key to using these features is consistency and moderation.

Boxes are particularly useful for presenting ideas that can be set off from the primary text:

- Summaries of the text
- Additional addresses, references, and the like
- Related points that should not be part of the actual text, such as the information in the boxes throughout this text

Boxes can also be useful for presenting ideas that are integral to the text:

- Warnings
- Legal clauses
- Conclusions
- Other essential information

In these cases, the boxes should be set within the text itself as highlighted information (see Figure 9.8).

Too many boxes, however, can make readers wonder which information is actually essential—the boxed or the unboxed information. Further, too much boxed information may suggest to readers that too many additional issues are cluttering your primary message.

Be particularly careful when shading text because some printers make it too dark (so the text is unreadable) or too light (so the text looks unshaded). Finally, many copiers do not reprint shaded text very well, either blackening it or reproducing it as regular text.

. . . Upon your arrival at the realty company, you should be prepared to provide the following:

- ✓ A check or money order for the balance owed
- ✓ A security deposit, written as a separate check
- ✓ An information card (enclosed) with emergency listings
- ✓ A signed copy of the rental agreement (enclosed)

At that point, we will give you the key to your cottage, and you are on your way to enjoying a fun-filled week at the Crystal Coast.

FIGURE 9.8 Boxed Information Inserted into the Text for Emphasis

Making Formatting Decisions

Having made the appropriate design decisions for your college document, you are now ready to consider the shape of the text of your document. Remembering that you want an easy-to-read and rhetorically sensitive format, explain the decisions you have made about the following elements:

- Margins
- Columns
- Headings and subheadings
- Lists
- Highlighting
- Boxes and shadings

Be prepared to defend your choices.

Applications and Document Factors

You may find yourself working in organizations that produce pamphlets, brochures, newsletters, or Web pages, all of which depend heavily on good visual design. Therefore, the basic principles of design and format are even more important for these documents than for letters, reports, and other technical documents. If your job description calls for you to produce these types of documents, you should consult a specialized book such as K. C. McAdams and J. J. Elliot, *Reaching Audiences: A Guide to Media Writing* (Boston: Allyn & Bacon, 1996).

Pamphlets and Brochures

Government agencies, businesses, and nonprofit organizations of all types distribute pamphlets for multiple purposes: to convey information, create a special image, publicize a mission, and even argue an opinion. For a briefer presentation, they may use a brochure to provide quick descriptions of goods and services they offer.

A *pamphlet* is a short, paperbound booklet or folder, sometimes stapled along a center fold. Page size may vary from relatively small (5½ by 8¾ inches) to large

(8½ by 11 inches). Like a book, a typical pamphlet presents its message on two facing pages inside the folder, as well as on the front and back covers. A careful look at any pamphlet you receive in the mail will show how it illustrates the design concepts already discussed in this chapter, including a systematic format for headings and typography, white space, lists, boxes, and other special features.

Three important design principles guide the writer's and artist's use of design tools when constructing a pamphlet:

- *Unity:* The components of a page comprise a single visual unit; thus, photographs must match the subject, and headings and text must deliver a single, consistent message.

- *Balance:* Either the visual "weight" on the right and left sides of the page should be equal, or the two sides should complement each other. Designers use text, white space, and art to achieve balance.

- *Proportion:* The visual "weight" at the top and bottom of the page, including both text and graphics, should create a sense of proportion. Many professional designers weight the top and bottom of a page unequally to avoid a boring visual design.

A *brochure* is a single sheet of paper (usually thick card stock), often folded into three panels, with text and graphics on each panel. The designer of a brochure keeps in mind the principles of unity, balance, and proportion noted above but with this difference: these principles now apply to the brochure's three or more panels, taken individually and as a whole. The brochure creator carefully arranges the information on one panel so that it leads visually, without confusion, to the neighboring panels. (See Strategy Review 9.2.)

STRATEGY REVIEW 9.2

PAPER SIZE AND DISPLAY CONSIDERATIONS FOR BROCHURES

Choosing a paper size for special documents you (or your team) may be asked to create on the job may be more difficult than for reports. Brochures, for instance, come in a variety of sizes and shapes, many of them clearly intended to arouse the reader's interest.

Although traditional brochures have a three-panel design and open into the standard 8½-by-11-inch page, some alternative designs can be eye-catching. Smaller or larger sizes can help your brochure stand out from others—especially when several brochures from competing companies or institutions are likely to be displayed at the same time. Consider, for example, the way travel brochures are

(continued)

displayed at travel agencies; the larger brochures can certainly attract attention. Just folding an 8½-by-11-inch page once instead of twice can give your brochure an interesting look.

The title may or may not be the most prominent feature on the brochure's cover. If the brochure is to be displayed in a rack (most often with competing brochures), though, you should make sure that the most eye-catching feature extends above the rack. Otherwise, readers may never lift your brochure from the rack to consider it.

If you analyze the brochures you receive in the mail, you may find that many of them exhibit one of two common styles of brochure design: a symmetrical, evenly balanced layout (see Figure 9.9), or an asymmetrical, somewhat diagonally balanced layout (see Figure 9.10).

Newsletters

Many organizations produce newsletters for the public or for employees. Among other things, these publications may provide technical information for product users, news about personnel or company policies, statistics on sales or marketing, or information on promotions. Newsletters often appear in an 8½-by-11-inch format, using most of the design techniques discussed in this chapter. One distinctive feature is the use of newspaper-like column widths for text; photographs, type styles and sizes, headings, distinctive boxes and panels for special features, white space, ruled lines of varying thickness, and clip-art images are used to achieve unity, balance, and proportion. An attractively designed cover page encourages readers to turn the page and keep reading.

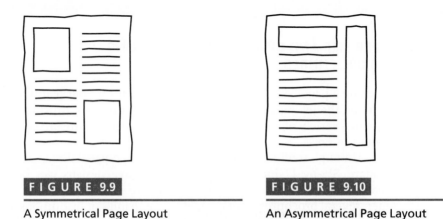

FIGURE 9.9

A Symmetrical Page Layout

FIGURE 9.10

An Asymmetrical Page Layout

Web Pages

Now that the Internet and the World Wide Web have become part of almost every organization's promotional and publicity mix, Web pages have become an important way to present information to the public. Businesses use Web pages for advertisements and sales. Governments at all levels publish announcements, reports, research results, and much-used forms on Web pages. Educational and health institutions use Web pages to relay course work, report data needed by various departments, and provide access to research facilities. With the expanding uses of the Web, you are likely to be involved in designing Web pages as part of your job assignment.

Readers of Web pages depend on one of several commercial software "browsers" to deliver material on screen in semistandardized formats and commonly use search engines with Web browsers to find material. (See Chapter 3's discussion of Internet search techniques.) Not only can Web pages display useful and interesting graphic images, but they have radically changed the rules of document design through *hyperlinking*—attaching "hot buttons" to images and words and inviting readers to "jump" to a new section of the document or to entirely different documents that interest them or seem relevant to their topic. Audiences for Web pages expect to be given options and choices about what to read and what to pursue.

To create a complete Web page, you will have to write coded computer instructions that are, in effect, bracketed around individual text and graphic elements (often a software package can help). The resulting text and graphic material are coded in a form that can be set up for the Web system server—a large traffic-control computer run by an institution or commercial service. If you are planning to create a Web page, consider some of these factors:

- A number of standardized browser formats are in wide use, but because different browsers may decode markup elements differently, your message may appear somewhat differently on your audience's screens than on your own.

- Simple graphic images will translate easily on most Web browser software, but some software will not be able to decode complex graphics, audio, or video. Even with the right software, these complex files can be bulky and time-consuming to deliver, as well as to create.

- A review of other pages will help you determine what kinds of elements are simplest and most effective.

If you are creating a Web page yourself, you will probably need instruction in a suitable software package or Web-page manual. Some basic information about the process can be gleaned from general books, such as P. W. Agner et al., *Multimedia in the Classroom* (Boston: Allyn & Bacon, 1996).

Summary

The previous chapter on graphics demonstrated the value and variety of visual images in workplace documents. Used with concern for the reader, all visual elements can help readers read and understand your message. Similarly, the design and format issues discussed in this chapter can also help readers find their way through your text, understand complex messages, and focus on key issues.

With desktop publishing systems so widely available, almost any workplace writer can use design and format features to enhance the visual impact of a routine document. Of course, visual impact can be a tricky business, for you certainly do not want your document to overuse or misuse visual elements. The dramatic effects made possible by many word processing programs and desktop publishing systems are dramatic only if used with discretion. Too many design and format features can complicate a text and overwhelm readers. In designing and formatting a workplace document—whether a report, a newsletter, or a Web page—simplicity and understatement must always win out over clutter and chaos.

Design features, such as paper size, covers, color, and type style and size, can enhance the visual appeal of a workplace document; such features can draw the reader into the document, lessen the reader's anxiety about reading it, or actually encourage the reader to read. The rhetorical message of design features must also be carefully considered: type that is too large creates a juvenile-looking text, type that is too small is hard to read, and script type styles look more appropriate for a wedding invitation than for a workplace document. Misused options sabotage the message you are trying to send.

Formatting features—margins, columns, lists, headings and subheadings, highlighting, boxes, and shadings—can help readers find their way through complex text. Again, consistency and moderation are the keys.

When designing or formatting documents, you should consider the following questions:

1. Does this feature enhance the text and overall message of my document, or am I just showing off?

2. Is this feature used consistently throughout my document, or does it sometimes suggest one message and later mean another?

3. Does this feature require any additional space or costs? Does my publication budget allow for such extras?

Finally, some highly specialized workplace documents—most notably, pamphlets and brochures, newsletters, and Web pages—have special requirements for format and design because of their highly specialized purposes and audiences. Be sure to consult special texts, in addition to the introductory information offered here, for more specific guidelines on creating these documents.

Used inappropriately, design and formatting features can make your work resemble a poorly designed traffic circle. But used appropriately—in moderation, with a specific purpose, and with consistency—these features can help readers navigate through complex information, find important and relevant details, and understand the organization of your document.

✔ CHECKLIST

✔ Make all decisions regarding design and format in light of the following:
- Your audience's receptivity to such features
- Your audience's need and ability to navigate through your text
- Your organization's culture
- Your publication's budget
- Your document's importance
- Your document's primary and rhetorical messages

✔ Use a standard paper size (such as 8½ by 11 inches) for traditional messages from a conservative organization to its conservative clients.

✔ Use unusual paper sizes to make your organization or your message stand out in a highly competitive and innovative market.

✔ Use traditional paper sizes for routine communications when budgets are tight.

✔ Use graphics on the covers of workplace documents for added visual appeal.

✔ Choose a color that sends the appropriate rhetorical message for the cover of your document.

✔ Use color to enhance graphics, highlight important information, direct readers' attention, and signal levels of reader accommodation in a text.

✔ Choose a serif type font (Times, Roman, Monaco, etc.) for routine messages in a conservative organization.

✔ Choose a sans serif type font (Avant Garde, Helvetica, Geneva, etc.) for innovative messages in a more creative organization.

✔ Choose type sizes ranging from 9 to 12 points for the text; remember that different type styles can affect the optimum size of the type.

✔ Reserve larger type sizes for visually impaired readers and for headings in the text.

✔ Use standard 1-inch margins to frame a document's text; allow a 1½-inch left-hand margin for works that will be bound.

✔ Vary the margins when you need to allow extra room for notes or other marginal features.

✔ Use unjustified right margins for easier reading.

✔ Use columns when you want to professionalize a document's appearance, but do not use columns for routine correspondence and reports.

✔ Use headings and subheadings throughout the text of your documents to help readers find their way to the information that most concerns them and to demonstrate the organization of your document.

✔ Be consistent when you create headings and subheadings, assigning one size, placement, and style to headings throughout your document and a different size, placement, and style to subheadings.

✔ Use lists to pull out complex, detailed, or itemized information from the text.

✔ Emphasize critical information with outlined, shadowed, *italicized*, **bold-faced**, or <u>underlined</u> text.

✔ Put related information or summaries in boxes or shaded segments set off from the primary text.

✔ Include integral information in boxes set within the primary text.

✔ Use all design and formatting features with a clear sense of purpose, consistency, and moderation. If you cannot explain why you have selected a design or format option, you should probably delete it and rely on standard text to communicate your message.

EXERCISES

Individual Exercises

1. Collect several examples of professionally published or desktop-published materials, such as the following:

brochures	college catalogs	magazines
manuals	textbooks	annual reports

    a. Examine the materials you have selected, and compare their use of the design and format features discussed in this chapter:

paper size	margins
covers	columns
color	lists
type style	headings and subheadings
type size	boxes or shadings

    b. For what kind of audience were the materials prepared? How do you know?

    c. What is the primary message of each document? What is the rhetorical message? How do the visual elements of each document convey or enhance its rhetorical message?

    d. How well designed and formatted are these documents?

    e. What does each document say about the organization that produced it?

    f. Would you have changed anything in each document? Why? For what effect?

2. Choose one of the following groups of magazines, and obtain one issue of each magazine in the group. Paying special attention to design and format features that are particularly well chosen, given the content and audience, write a comparison of the design and format of the issues you obtained.

    a. *Newsweek, Time,* and *U.S. News and World Report* (all newsmagazines)

    b. *People, TV Guide,* and *Reader's Digest* (all written for the same level of audience)

    c. *New Yorker, Southern Living,* and *Mirabella* (all written for the same level of audience)

    d. *Seventeen, Ladies' Home Journal,* and *Cosmopolitan* (all women's magazines, but for different ages and interests)

    e. *Sports Illustrated, GQ,* and *Esquire* (all men's magazines, but for different ages and interests)

Collaborative Exercises

1. With a partner or team, write a three-page comparison of three World Wide Web pages you have printed out. What special features distinguish these pages from other pages? Might any of the features be especially useful, given the Internet medium on which the pages are displayed? What are the pages' purposes? What kind(s) of audience might they attract? Do these pages meet their audience's needs?

2. With a partner or a team, design a Web page for this class. What kind of audience do you anticipate? What are its needs? What kind of content should the Web page incorporate? What special design features should you consider? After answering these questions, design the page.

 ## ONGOING ASSIGNMENT

- Based on the information you have learned and experimented with on design and format for this chapter, what kinds of decisions are you prepared to make about your organizational culture manual? Be sure to consider any budget constraints you face, as well as time and software/printing limitations. Further, consider carefully the rhetorical implications of all your choices and their appropriateness for your audience, your purpose, and your message.

CHAPTER 10

Letters and Memos

Many novice writers believe the myth that workers have administrative assistants who handle their writing responsibilities. Most workers find, however, that they have to compose their own correspondence and reports. Even workers (usually higher-level managers and executives) who have assistants to write routine correspondence for them or draft form letters and memos for common situations and events find that complex situations call for their own writing solutions—not those of a clerk or assistant.

In other words, serious communication issues in the workplace rarely fit neatly into boilerplate forms. Such issues require special considerations for audience, context, message, and rhetorical uses of the language that allow writers to communicate clearly, ethically, and persuasively—considerations for which *you* will be responsible. And whether you communicate via hard copy (paper) or on-line (using E-mail or other networked systems), you need to know the information this chapter presents regarding letters and memos:

- The most common messages in letters and memos
- Strategies for organizing these communications
- Various formats for letters and memos
- Additional touches, such as humor, personal messages, and response generators

Addressing both hard-copy and electronic communications (E-mail messages sent over linked computer networks), the chapter focuses on the following:

- The receivers of such messages
- The receivers' dependence on and preference for certain organizing strategies
- The formats that are most likely to communicate your message along with a professional image for your company and for you
- Matters of tone that can help your communication succeed

Again, you must consider the information in this chapter in terms of your organization's culture, for many organizations have their own style and design for letters and memos. Noting such conventions will signal your observational abilities and show that you know "how things are done." Most important, of course, is that attending to style, message, and format in writing correspondence clarifies your meaning and improves your readers' understanding.

The Technology of Letters and Memos

The proliferation of computers is the major reason that workplace writers have taken responsibility for their own correspondence. Writers at all levels of an organization find it easier to write their own communications than to dictate to an assistant. In fact, although we tend to think of computers in terms of their more glamorous uses, such as for graphics and desktop publishing, they may be used most frequently to correspond with coworkers, clients, suppliers, lawyers, professional organizations, and government agencies. Dashing off a quick memo about a schedule change and crafting a lengthy letter outlining a legal stance are typical applications of computers in today's workplace.

Moreover, although memos and letters continue to dominate workplace communication, with the increased use of E-mail, that correspondence is being conducted in a much more abbreviated (and often more informal) style. If your computer is hooked up to the Internet or to an E-mail network, you have probably already experienced some of the fascination and frustration that such a system offers. Most valuable to organizations, of course, are the paperless communications that can be sent in seconds, whereas letters sent by mail may take days to reach their readers. Because interoffice memos can be misrouted or delayed in delivery, E-mail is frequently used internally as well.

As appealing as the new technology is, it still has not replaced traditional letters and memos—and probably never will entirely. For several reasons, paper versions (hard copy) of communications are preferable:

1. Paper provides concrete documentation of ideas, policies, and agreements.

2. It offers a professional touch that many feel is lacking in electronic communications.

3. It presents an organizational image that is hard to produce electronically.

As the last two points suggest, elements of organizational culture can be lost or misconstrued in electronic communications. For all of these reasons (and others, which we will discuss throughout this chapter), therefore, you need to learn how to write a proper, hard-copy letter and memo. At the same time, you will probably have increasing access to more and more technology, so the chapter also discusses how on-line communication differs from hard-copy communication and offers cautions and strategies for coping with these differences.

Messages of Letters and Memos

Letters and memos tend to be used for different kinds of messages, and as a result, they differ in other ways as well. *Letters* usually are formal communications that are sent to readers outside the organization. They generally are printed on letterhead stationery and adhere to a corporate letter format that includes standard forms for the date, inside address, paragraph indentions, and complimentary closing (see Standard Features of and Formats for Letters and Memos later in the chapter).

Because letters typically are written to readers outside the organization, they deal with a variety of issues: a supplier's inability to meet a schedule, a customer's

TABLE 10.1 Comparison of Rhetorical Situations for Letters and Memos	
Letters	**Memos**
■ addressed to outsiders	■ addressed to insiders
■ audience may be varied	■ audience more defined
■ tone likely to be formal	■ tone may be formal or informal
■ informative or persuasive	■ more likely to be informative
■ often introduce a new strategy, settlement, product, etc.	■ often introduce a problem, solution, policy, or routine matter such as meeting schedules, etc.
■ may be organized directly or indirectly	■ may be organized directly or indirectly
■ rarely longer than two pages	■ range in length from one paragraph to as much as twenty pages (a short report)

complaint about the organization's product, and a contractor's use of a particular vendor, to name only a few. In short, any kind of communication between the organization and the outside world—whether clients, customers, suppliers, service agents, legal representatives, or government agencies—may be communicated through letters.

At the same time, organizations also engage in a great deal of internal correspondence, and much of it is transmitted as memos. Whether transmitted as hard copy or on-line, memos deal with matters that are particular to the *internal* workings of the organization. Many are short and address routine events in an organization—reminders about meetings, policies, or upcoming events, for example. Others are longer and even take on a report format (see Chapters 12 and 13); these memos allow writers/employees to exchange ideas about improving services, products, or policies. Still other memos may alert readers to potential problems, offer solutions, or inquire about procedures.

Thus, letters and memos are distinguished primarily by whether the *reader* is inside or outside the organization and by what that reader needs to know. Table 10.1 summarizes their differences and also shows that letters and memos share a number of features: for instance, their audiences frequently overlap, as do their purposes and organizational schemes. Thus, whether you write a letter or a memo is a decision you will make based on the situation, readers, and purpose you and your communication face.

Hard Copy or On-Line: How to Choose the Medium

Have you ever heard the adage "The medium is the message"? It means that the *way* a message is communicated (the medium—telephone, computer, paper, poem, singing telegram, or whatever) is a rhetorical part of the message itself. For example, when you send someone a poem to tell how you feel about that person,

THE WORLD OF WORKPLACE WRITING

Hard-Copy versus On-Line Communications: Security Checks

Because memos document the internal workings of an organization, many organizations are very guarded with their memos—often shredding them at the end of each business day. And because few computer safeguards have proved 100 percent effective against hackers and industrial saboteurs, organizations are more than a little leery of communicating vital internal workplace information via E-mail. Knowing whether to communicate by hard copy or on-line can be one of the more pressing decisions you will have to make as a workplace writer—every bit as pressing as your decisions about audience, purpose, and content.

you are saying something significant by virtue of sending *poetry*, which we associate with love and romance. As another example, to be told over the telephone that your current love interest no longer wants to see you is more devastating than to be told in person—the telephone is part of the message "I don't want to see you so I am telling you by telephone."

In professional communications, sending a message on-line versus by hard copy may also reveal something about the content. An on-line message may mean "I acknowledge that you are up-to-date with current technology; you are not afraid of computers and new ideas; you enjoy a fast-paced exchange of ideas." A hard-copy message may mean "This is important; I want you to hold this information in your hands, take special note of it, and then file it." Be sure, therefore, to pay special attention to the rhetorical significance of your choice of hard-copy versus on-line media for communicating your messages.

Imagine what would happen if you needed to communicate with someone by 2:00 this afternoon and forgot to put your message in the mail. You could phone, but what if the person is in an important meeting and cannot be disturbed? Can you leave a message? Can you count on the person to return your call before 2:00?

If you opt to send a fax, can you be sure your fax will reach the person—especially if it is not expected? The person may go through a series of daily meetings without checking for fax messages or without rummaging through a pile of faxes to find your very important message. Additionally, a fax is hardly secure and may go through the hands of numerous coworkers before reaching your intended reader. If your message is in any way confidential or private, faxing is clearly not your best option.

In contrast, electronic mail is one of the great advantages of computer systems because it frees us to communicate pretty much whenever we please (except, of course, when the system is down!), rather than waiting for postal or tele-

TABLE 10.2 When to Use Hard Copy, Faxes, and E-Mail for Your Communications		
Send Hard Copy When . . .	*Send a Fax When . . .*	*Send E-Mail When . . .*
■ the reader needs formal correspondence—hard copy on letterhead stationery—for legal or contractual records ■ the information is sensitive, and you have reason to fear that your on-line system may be accessed by outsiders ■ the document is longer than three or four screens of text ■ time is not critical ■ you have great confidence in your message delivery system (postal service, internal delivery, or specialized service) ■ your audience is not comfortable with current technology or does not have access to it	■ you want to send "hard copy" quickly ■ time is critical ■ security is not an issue (anyone who handles the fax may decide to read it) ■ the message is not longer than fifteen or twenty pages ■ the reader is expecting the fax (call ahead and tell the reader you are faxing critical information)	■ time—in terms of getting information *to* and/or *from* a correspondent—is critical ■ the reader does not have to keep your correspondence on file or can save and print it from the computer ■ the message is not longer than two or three screens ■ the reader understands the informality and "looseness" of E-mail correspondence ■ the reader does not need a formal document (although E-mailed messages may be legally binding) ■ the reliability, speed, or security of traditional delivery systems is suspect

phone services that may be slow, busy, or antiquated. That freedom is especially appealing when you consider that time zones are the prime obstacle to global communication—while our audience sleeps, we are at work, often trying to communicate with them.

Nevertheless, not every message can be communicated by E-mail. For one thing, access to E-mail networks is not universal, and some people aren't comfortable with such technology even if they do have access. Other factors also affect the usability of E-mail, such as the length of the message; it simply isn't practical to submit a ten-page report over E-mail, much less a hundred-page report (although you can often attach a file of a lengthier document to your cover message). Table 10.2 provides a summary of when different media are appropriate.

Organization of Correspondence

Besides understanding your audience and the purpose of your correspondence, another important aspect of effective communication is presenting the information in the proper order. And because the organization affects the reader's reaction to the message, a good way to predict the best organizational strategy for a letter, memo, or on-line message is to determine how the reader is likely to read and react to the message.

Determining the Medium for the Message

Continue with the Application scenario of Chapter 9, in which you designed a document for students who might be interested in a new or revamped curricular program in your college. At this point, you should be ready to determine what sort of cover letter, memo, or E-mail message you are going to create to introduce and present that document to various audiences. Your audiences include all of the following:

- The director or chair of the program itself
- The students already in the program
- Your school's board of trustees
- Your school's highest academic officer
- Potential students

What decisions about the appropriate medium have you made? Will you use the same medium for each of the different audiences? If so, why? If not, why not?

Hard-Copy Letters and Memos

After determining which format (letter or memo) to use for your hard-copy message, you will have to determine the order in which to present your message; again, the reader's situation should help determine your options. This section focuses on the organization of hard-copy letters or memos, which depends on the situational and rhetorical implications of your message; strategies for organizing on-line communications are in the next section.

Good writers organize their hard-copy letter or memo depending on how readers will likely react (positively, negatively, or neutrally) to the content. (See Strategy Review 10.1.) If a positive or neutral response is expected, information is arranged in the order the reader will use or want to know the information and according to where the reader expects to find it (see Figure 10.1 on page 329 and Figure 10.2 on page 330). If writers anticipate a negative reaction, they try to soften the blow by omitting blunt or hurtful statements, especially in the introduction (see Figure 10.3 on page 330 and Figure 10.4 on page 331). You should review Chapter 4's discussion of organizing messages according to anticipated reader response.

ORGANIZING BY ANTICIPATED READER RESPONSE: GOOD NEWS/BAD NEWS

As you recall from Chapter 4's discussion of organizing strategies, most readers like to receive good or neutral news up front, but prefer not to be lambasted by bad news in the opening sentences. Thus, Figure 1 shows the organizational structure for *good or neutral news,* and Figure 2 shows the organizational structure for *bad news.* See Figures 10.1 through 10.4 for examples and annotated strategies.

FIGURE 1   Organization for Good or Neutral News

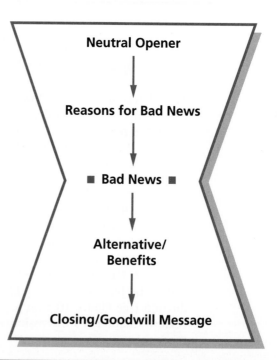

FIGURE 2   Organization for Bad News

The Upper Cut Salon

28-A Bensonhurst Drive
Magnolia, NC 48294
Ph: 743-382-5829

8 April 1999

Mr. Howard Long
Jernigan Hair Products
392 Maple Lane
Bonion, NJ 58203

Dear Mr. Long:

good news

With the Christmas rush, we were remarkably busy, and—as always—Jernigan products were one of the featured product sales that kept our shop so busy.

information

With spring, however, we are seeing even more traffic, and we need to increase our standing order. Please adjust our order accordingly:

details

Product	On Order	Revised to
Humidity GONE!	10 bottles	17 bottles
Moisture Balance	5 bottles	14 bottles
Frizz No More	6 bottles	10 bottles

goodwill/pleasant closing

Thanks so much for understanding our situation. We appreciate your working with us.

Sincerely,

Kelly Maness

Kelly Maness
Owner

encl: copy of initial order form

F I G U R E 10.1 Using the Direct Approach in a Routine or Neutral Letter

Americans Fight Against Hunger

To: Maria del Gratis
From: Kristen Black 𝒦ℬ
Date: 22 October 1999
Subject: Raise for 2000

good news first

details/reasons

Congratulations, Maria, on your raise for 2000. We looked at the quality and quantity of your work and realized that you certainly deserve our thanks for an outstanding job—along with a $1,000 per year salary increase.

goodwill closing

We hope you realize how valuable you are to our organization; we take such pride in your work and in your dedication to our goals. We look forward to another year's progress in the fight against hunger.

1003 Deion Drive
Minneapolis, MN 26342-1003

(823) 389-3332
Fax: (823) 389-2322

FIGURE 10.2   Using the Direct Approach in a Memo

---

m
e
m
o

Stacy & Associates

To: Edna Thurber
From: Jason Ridge   𝒥ℛ

Date: 4 December 1999
Subject: Raises & bonuses

goodwill

neutral/pleasant opener

Edna, we appreciate your thorough documentation of your team's work on the Andreas account over the past six months. You have clearly done some outstanding work and have put a lot of time into the project.

reasons

bad news

alternate plan

In spite of your hard work, however, we did not win the Andreas account; thus, the increases in corporate revenues that we hoped for have not materialized. And because we cannot hand out bonuses from funds that do not exist, your request for a raise cannot be granted. Your request will, however, be carried over to the next fiscal period when I will review each account manager's contributions and salary inequities.

goodwill closing

We value your contributions, Edna, and we look forward to a much more productive and profitable period next quarter for the entire company.

FIGURE 10.3   Using the Indirect Approach in a Memo

The bank that puts you first

SE BANK AND TRUST

110 Hunt Hill Place
Kingston, SC 28391
(223) 832-5839
FAX: (223) 832-7219

20 April 1999

Mr. David Maroules
402 Johnson St.
Pine Bluff, SC 28392

Dear David,

goodwill/personal
opener

When we received your credit application yesterday, I was amazed to see that you have almost finished your English degree. It's hard to believe that the kid I used to baby-sit is ready to go out on his first job.

reasons

bad news and
alternative

We are pleased that you have landed a job with Douglas and Associates, and we are confident that you will be able to establish a good credit rating after you pay off some of your college debts. Because our loan policies require at least eight months' employment or substantial collateral, we are sorry to have to turn down your loan application. Won't you reapply in January after you have been at Douglas Associates for eight months?

additional
alternatives

We know how difficult it is for young college graduates to pay off their debts and establish credit. Because we have faith in your future and want to help you out when you need it most, we offer the New College Graduates' Prime Account. The NCGPA is a special account that handles your repayment of college loans (at the amount you set) and establishes a savings account for your monthly deposits (again, at the amount you set). At the end of a six-month trial period, we will review your NCGPA records and, if all is in good shape, will initiate your loan application for $10,000.

goodwill closing

We appreciate your considering SE Bank and Trust for your banking needs, and we are eager to establish an NCGPA for you. We wish you much luck in your new position with Douglas and Associates.

Sincerely,

Linda Bascom

Linda Bascom
Associate Vice President

FIGURE 10.4 Using the Indirect Approach in a Letter

T H E   W O R L D   O F   W O R K P L A C E   W R I T I N G

Sales Letters: Good News or Bad News?

How do you feel when you receive a sales letter asking you to buy a new car, invest in real estate, or join a new CD club? Many people are thrilled to get such exciting offers, but others are irritated at receiving "junk mail." Sales letters present a unique dilemma for writers who may not know how readers are likely to respond to their correspondence.

Although larger organizations hire marketing specialists to create sales letters, smaller organizations (or your own entrepreneurial venture) may require you to write sales letters. If so, you should consider how the reader is likely to respond to the product or service you are selling, as well as to the presentation of your message. If readers are likely to be excited about your product, you may present your ideas in a direct fashion, beginning with the main point of your letter:

> FINALLY! We have dozens of direct TV systems in stock. We know you have been waiting for months for a direct TV system, but you don't have to wait another day. We can install your new system within 24 hours of your purchase.

At other times, you will have to convince your readers of the value of your product or service. In these cases, writers often rely on the indirect approach to arouse their readers' interest in the product or service before making a sales pitch. The following paragraphs are the opening of a sales letter addressed to homeowners with families:

> No one likes to think about crime in their neighborhood, but if no one on your block has been vandalized or burglarized in the past 12 months, you're part of a very small percentage of crime-free neighborhoods in our city. Unfortunately, there's no guarantee that your neighborhood will remain crime free. You could be vandalized or burglarized tonight, while you and your family sleep just inches away from a thief.

> Fortunately, there is something you can do. The Microtonics Security System is a 21st-century alarm system, designed by police officers, security researchers, and—yes—former thieves who know the most common tactics for breaking into homes and for shutting down many ordinary home security systems.

When writing sales messages, consider whether your readers are likely to be delighted to hear the news that your product or service is available or annoyed with another piece of junk mail. Then, organize and plan your message accordingly.

On-Line Correspondence

An essential consideration when organizing your on-line message is how thoroughly your reader reads such messages. Many readers "check their mail" by looking at their list of messages:

enniwm@ame.siv.edu	NO SUBJECT	1-18-99
wkelsiw@ske.wkr.com	OFFICE PARTY	1-18-99
tiwqrl@ ske.wig.com	RESERVATIONS	1-18-99
slean@ske.wig.com	SNOW SKIS 4 SL	1-19-99
ssouth@ske.wig.com	CRISIS-MERGER	1-19-99

Does anything in this list suggest that one message is more important than the others? If you are like most readers, you would quickly open the last message—CRISIS-MERGER. The subject notice tells you there's something important here. Or if you recognize the sender "wkelskiw@ske.wkr.com" as your boss, you will probably open that message before turning to messages from writers whose addresses you do not recognize. But, then, how motivated are you to open the other three messages?

Many readers scroll through their messages looking for crises, recognizable writers (such as their bosses), or really interesting messages. After reading those messages, they may return to the other messages later or even delete them without reading them (a dangerous, but frequently practiced, strategy).

So how do you get readers to pay attention to your message? First, if your message is truly urgent or critical, indicate that it is important. You should never mislead readers with the subject line of your messages, however. (You may recall the old story of the shepherd boy who cried wolf—when you really need to get someone's attention, you won't be able to if you have a reputation for making all your messages sound urgent when they really aren't.) The subject line of the E-mail memo is your first opportunity to clarify the topic and importance of your message.

Second, because E-mailed messages reveal only about the first twelve lines of text, you must make sure that your message's main point is communicated in those twelve lines or at least that readers know something important is coming on the next screen. The attempt to crowd important ideas onto the first screen has been blamed for the "rushed" sense of E-mail correspondence, however. An alternative is to create your E-mail message on standard software that can be dumped into an E-mail program. This way, you can take your time composing your message, making sure you convey the proper tone and sense of audience, while avoiding the costs of time spent on-line.

Organizing a good news E-mail message is simple because you can follow the same structure as for a hard-copy good news message: main idea, supporting details, closing. With this approach, the main idea falls naturally into the opening twelve lines of displayed text. But organizing a bad news E-mail message can be troublesome because you have to put enough information into those twelve lines to keep the reader reading without being rude or hurting the reader's feelings. Consider the messages in Figures 10.5 and 10.6. With Figure 10.5, the readers may believe that the message is unimportant, when, in fact, it is critical. In Figure 10.6, the message is revised so that it is not impeded by the format of the computer screen.

unclear subject—
"sorry" for what?

general
knowledge

all information
about party?

[screen break]

bad news

problem

change of plans
must go to work
consolation
sentence

To: asuzslack@uva.edu
From: enwelles@cis.vm1.ecu.edu
Date: 9 September 2000
Subj: Sorry

routine information

Johanna is hosting this year's office party at her home at 622 Wyndham Avenue in the Brookshire section. If you need directions for how to get there, don't hesitate to ask her for a map she's drawn for us.

I know we are all looking forward to this party. What a relief it will be to get away from some of the pressure we have all been under in the last few weeks with inventory and the reorganization of the downtown store. I can't tell you how much I appreciate all your help and selflessness.

Mr. Dawson is quite pleased with the speed with which we completed both the reorganization and the inventory. I tried to tell him that this is by far one

crucial new information

of the best working groups with whom I have ever been associated. So you can imagine how disappointed I am to have to tell you that we will have to delay the party for a couple of hours so we can meet with Mr. Dawson to convince him that the inventory has been counted accurately. I'm pretty sure that the problem is with the professional counters he hired to go in after us and check our counts. Some of the smaller items that we know about are not immediately visible to them. Also, we know where some of the overstock is stored that they know nothing about.

Nevertheless, I cannot convince Mr. Dawson that all of these discrepancies are actually not discrepancies. So, I appreciate your coming into the store at 6:30 (or staying late if you are scheduled to work). We'll still be at Johanna's by 8:30.

FIGURE 10.5   Display Can Make the Reader Miss Bad News

better summary of
the *real* message

To: asuzslack@uva.edu
From: enwelles@cis.vm1.ecu.edu
Date: 9 September 2000
Subj: Party Delay—Two-hour Call-in for Inventory Discrepancies

current situation

We are all eager to attend Johanna's office party because we have all been
working incredibly hard over the past two weeks with inventory and the downtown store's reorganization.

reasons

Professional inventory counters were hired to check our figures, but they did not
know where all the small items and overstocks are kept, so our figures appear to

bad news
modest consolation

contradict their work. A modest inventory crew—Susan, Stan, Jimmy, and Sean—
can clear up the problems in a couple of hours. Thanks for coming in at 6:30; I am
almost certain we'll be out by 8:30 and on our way to Johanna's party.

To compensate for this interruption of your leisure time, this extra time

[screen break]

better compensation

counts as overtime and will be paid time and a half plus a free half day's vacation
later in the year.

F I G U R E   10.6   Revised Organization Overcomes the Effect of the Display

Additional Persuasive Touches: Humor, Personal Messages, and Response Generators

Although letters, memos, and E-mail may have different audiences and messages,
they frequently share an aim or purpose: to persuade. Constructing a persuasive
message typically depends on finding the right tone, details, and organizational
strategy that will appeal to the reader. As the sales letter in Figure 10.7 on page
336 shows, knowing what motivates people to act or believe as they do is an integral part of constructing a successful document. Similarly, knowing the strategies
that help create such motivations are useful additions to your storehouse of correspondence techniques.

In Chapter 6's discussion of revising for tactfulness, you learned techniques
for making your communications more diplomatic, an important element of

CitiScapes Security Systems

2904-B Langston Avenue
Boulder, CO 49193
823-523-6843

17 July 2000

Ms. Madison McCall
401 East Street
Boulder, CO 49192

Dear Ms. Madison:

gentle opener

The things that go bump in the night—your cat? Your teenager coming in late? Your house settling? Or is it a burglar? The simple explanations are not so simple anymore.

motivation to solve problem

More than anything else, you want to keep your family and your home safe. We can help. CitiScapes Security Systems has 20 years' experience in home security systems, and we offer a range of options to protect you, your family, and your property. Three of our most popular models are

solutions/(sales)

- Basic security option: Access codes, lights, and links to law enforcement.
- Deluxe security option: Access codes, lights, sirens, and links to law enforcement.
- Failsafe security option: Access codes, bars, lights, cameras, sprinklers, sirens, routine patrols, and links to law enforcement.

motivation

From the very first night of installation, you can sleep easier and go out of your home knowing it is protected from break-ins.

motivation

If you will call us for an appointment, we will make a thorough inspection of your home, probably finding accesses that you didn't know a criminal could take advantage of. And we can install your new security system within 48 hours. After you read our enclosed brochures, we will gladly answer any questions you have when you call for an appointment with one of our security representatives.

motivation

call for action

call for action

Please take the time to make this important call now.

Sincerely,

Angela Ledfoot

Angela Ledfoot

encl: brochures

F I G U R E 10.7   A Sample Sales Letter Addressing the Reader's Motivation to Buy

Organizing Your Message

Reviewing Chapter 4's discussion of organization if necessary, consider how you might organize the cover letter, memo, or E-mail message that describes the content of your brochure, its purpose, and any additional details you want to include. The following details about your audiences may help you make some decisions about their likely reactions to the brochure or document you have created:

- Director or chair of the program: Extremely knowledgeable about the topic
- Students in program: Basically knowledgeable about the topic
- Board of trustees and academic officer: Know very little about the topic
- Potential students: May know general subject matter but not details about the topic

Determine the order in which you want to present information to each audience, creating four different outlines or plans, if necessary.

---

every communication. Occasionally, you may also want to add a persuasive humorous or personal touch to your letters and memos. Though readers typically prefer to think you are serious about your message, humor, personal touches, and response generators may convey a lighter tone and help you get the response you want from your readers. Although such touches should never be used to manipulate readers, they can humanize some correspondence.

Most writers recommend self-effacing humor and warn against poking fun at others. Although a few groups (politicians, the government, and bureaucrats) seem to be safe targets for humor, the joke can backfire if, say, your reader is sympathetic to that group or has a spouse who works for them. Poking fun at yourself is much safer.

In hard-copy communications, you can also add personal messages. Adding a handwritten PS at the bottom of a letter is a popular technique. If you're on a first-name basis with the reader, you might also want to draw a line through the formal salutation of the letter, replacing the reader's title and last name with her first name (see Figure 10.8 on page 338).

Finally, some writers, especially writers of sales letters, add a personal message to encourage readers to respond. Figure 10.8 demonstrates all three touches: humor, personal message, and response generator.

WORLDWIDE TRAVELS
231 Peace Lane
Mobile, AL 29592

2 February 1999

Ms. Laura Larconia
920 Deyton Drive
Princeton, AL 28391

Dear ~~Ms. Larconia~~ *Laura*:

situation

humor

resolution

I cannot believe I left for my two-week vacation without finalizing the plans for your trip to Jamaica. (I guess that shows how much I needed that vacation!) Fortunately, Jeanelle realized my oversight and made the arrangements for you.

goodwill

To assure you that you really are a top priority client, I'm enclosing a coupon for a 10% discount on your next trip.

Bon voyage!

Ben

Benjamin Dial

P.S. We have special rates on Mediterranean cruises! Great tour packages! Call me—

FIGURE 10.8 A Sample Letter Incorporating Humor, a Personal Message, and a Response Generator

THE WORLD OF WORKPLACE WRITING

Appropriate Humor in E-Mail Messages

One of the first lessons many on-line message writers learn is how to make "pictures" for their readers using standard type; two simple examples are shown here:

> :) (a smiling face on its side)
>
> : ((a frowning face on its side)

As you are probably aware, such images are not really professional—just as smiley faces are also considered juvenile in hard-copy professional correspondence. *Remember:* When technology offers you the chance to draw pictures, you should carefully evaluate the wisdom of doing so, especially in professional documents (see Chapter 8).

Of course, many of these same strategies can be used to personalize an on-line communication: calling the reader by first name, adding humor, and incorporating personal messages and response generators. The E-mail printout in Figure 10.9 illustrates these strategies.

To: enisaia@cis.vml.edu
From: rbbenne@cis.vml.edu.sdsu
Subject: proposed delay on copier acquisitions
Date: 2 February 1999

first name

punctuation
inserts emotion

understatement/
humor

personal plea

ISAIAH—What in the world are we going to do without the new copiers!!?? Do I sound frantic? Yes!!! I am. We have a huge deadline with the Massachusetts legislature on a proposal for expanding our programs to find parents who have refused to pay child support. That proposal must go to the General Assembly this week, and next week the legislators will vote on the issue. If we miss this deadline, we cannot offer the proposal until next year at the earliest. Yes, we can go to the local copy shop, but it isn't exactly equipped to run off the 200-page reports we need for all the representatives. HELP—Please advise—We need our copiers!!!

FIGURE 10.9 A Personalized E-Mail Message

Standard Features of and Formats for Letters and Memos

With a better sense of the content of letters and memos (their general messages, organizational structures, and humor and personal touches), you are ready to format them into a standard documentation form—one that most readers will immediately recognize as a letter or memo format. Because all on-line messages are formatted the same (as memos), you have very few options for differentiating the format of your E-mail message. For hard-copy documents, however, you can add innovative elements to the standard format to produce an appropriate "look."

You are undoubtedly already familiar with the basic elements of both memos and letters. The "To," "From," "Date," and "Subject" headings are key indicators that a document is a memo. Similarly, the letterhead, inside address, date, salutation, and complimentary closing signal that a document is a letter.

In the standard memo format, all elements are in a single column, but this format is sometimes modified. Consider the following format, which is seen more and more often in business because the double-column arrangement takes up less space than a single column:

To: Date:
From: Subject:

Some organizations have added other elements that make it easier for readers to respond to the memo or to understand what it requires of them:

To: Branch managers   **Reply to:** James Aquino, Public Relations Office
From: Betsy Impanse   **Action required:** Submit proposals by 3/4/99
Date: 1/3/99
Subject: Travel allotments for second quarter 1999

The headings in boldfaced type on the right let readers know immediately to whom they should address questions or send responses; further, they also know that the memo requires them to do something—in this case, submit proposals by a particular deadline. These elements are variations of the traditional memo and acknowledge the special needs and standard questions that readers have when reading memos:

1. I have a question—do I call Betsy Impanse?
2. Do I have to do anything because of this memo?
3. Is there a deadline for my response?

The format also ensures that readers do not have to hunt through the memo to find crucial information and reminds writers to include all the pertinent information when writing the memo.

Like memos, letters also have a standard format, although you are likely to find more variations in letters than in memos. Figure 10.10 shows the standard

standard letterhead
information

PEACHTREE PLAZA

1000 Runion Avenue   (586) 485-2847
Tungsten, AZ 48275   (586) 485-7586

date

2 November 1999
          2–6 lines

inside address

Mr. George Alexander
Fit To Be Tied
Peachtree Plaza
          1 line

formal salutation

Dear Mr. Alexander:
          1 line

text is single-spaced
with a double
space between
paragraphs

For the past seven years, we have appreciated your tenancy in the Peachtree Plaza.
Most important is that you demonstrate the same care for your customers as we
try to take of our tenants.

Over the past seven years, of course, a great deal has changed at Peachtree:

- A major renovation of the west wing that updates the appearance of all stores
- New escalators designed to enhance the safety of our customers
- A new advertising strategy that encourages customers to shop here
- A cooperative advertising plan that benefits all merchants

And, of course, such innovations cost money. But with good negotiations and great
concern for our tenants' welfare, we have limited the increase in our costs to only
8.2%, much of which we have absorbed through restructurings. As a result, we
will need to raise your rent, but by only a modest 6%. Thus, your new monthly rent
will be $6,500.00, beginning on January 1, 2000. Please sign the enclosed contract,
renewing your option on the store's space and agreeing to the new rental rate.

As a bonus for your contract renewal, Mr. Alexander, we are running a free advertising insert in the DAILY PLANET, and we will contact you soon about featuring Fit
To Be Tied as one of our more popular stores. You might want to be thinking about
the after-Christmas sales and Valentine's Day specials you might want to feature.

As always, we are eager to do all we can to ensure your comfort as a tenant at
Peachtree Plaza.
          1 line

complimentary
closing

Sincerely,
                    3 lines

signature

Belton McNair

writer
writer's title

Belton McNair
Management Coordinator
          1 line

enclosure

encl: new contract

FIGURE 10.10 The Format Features of a Standard Letter

format and identifies the elements of a formal letter. These elements are standard in American professional communications although different organizations may modify them slightly. Three common modifications for letters, for instance, are the *block* format, in which all typed text is aligned along the left margin (see Figure 10.11); the *semiblock* format, in which the first line of each paragraph is indented (see Figure 10.12 on page 344); and the *modified block* format, in which the date, complimentary closing, and signature are aligned along the center line (see Figure 10.13 on page 345). Most contemporary writers prefer the simplicity of the block format. Other creative modifications may be made depending on the image the organizations wants to convey (e.g., traditional, innovative, high tech, high class). For example, the *letterhead* may be aligned along the left margin, centered at the top, or split between the top and the bottom.

Regardless of these numerous variations, however, a few elements of letter format are considered inviolate and unchangeable by those who know how standard letters are to be correctly formatted:

1. Choose an appropriate, professional-looking font and type size. Most readers do not consider script or cursive type fonts to be professional and find type that is too small difficult to read. They also tend to associate type that is too large (i.e., 12 point and larger) with juvenile messages. If you know that your reader is visually impaired, however, you should use a larger type font (see Chapter 9 on document design).

2. Include your name *only* in the complimentary closing—never in the return address or as part of the introductory paragraph.

3. Use standard postal abbreviations (ME, NC, IA, NY, WI) for U.S. states—all capital letters with no periods and no spaces.

4. Include the full inside address—name, position, company, address, city, state, zip code.

5. Unless you and the reader are on a first-name basis, punctuate the salutation with a colon. If you are friends and refer to each other by your first names, punctuate the salutation with a comma. If you are friends, but still refer to each other by your surnames (Mr., Mrs., Ms.), you may punctuate the salutation with a comma.

6. Determine the preferred title of the person to whom you are writing—Mr., Dr., Professor, Mrs., Ms., or Miss. A woman who prefers her married title may be offended if addressed as Ms., for instance. A quick phone call or a well-placed inquiry can prevent your offending a reader. When in doubt or when such inquiries are not reasonable, use Ms. Further, make sure that the person is, indeed, the gender that you assume: both men and women are named Pat, Chris, Stacy, Sam, Sidney, Kay, Kelly, Ashley, and dozens of other names.

   If the person is a government official (judge, governor, senator, diplomat, etc.), look up the proper title of address in an etiquette or business etiquette handbook (see, for example, Letitia Baldridge's *Complete Guide to Executive Manners* [New York: Rawson Associates, 1985]).

WORLDWIDE TRAVELS

231 Peace Lane
Mobile, AL 29592

2 February 1999

Ms. Laura Larconia
902 Deyton Drive
Princeton, AL 28391

Dear Ms. Larconia:

I cannot believe I left for my two-week vacation without finalizing the plans for your trip to Jamaica. (I guess that shows how much I needed that vacation!) Fortunately, Jeanelle realized my oversight and made the arrangements for you.

To assure you that you really are a top priority client, I'm enclosing a coupon for a 10% discount on your next trip.

Bon voyage!

Ben Dial

Benjamin Dial

FIGURE 10.11 In the Block Format, All Text Is Aligned Flush Left

7. When writing to an unknown reader or group of readers, address them by their roles as readers of your communication; for example:

> Dear Friend of the Cleveland Orchestra:

> Dear Personnel Committee Members:

> Dear Homeowner:

> Dear Macintosh User:

Do *not* address such readers as "To Whom It May Concern," "Dear Ladies and Gentlemen," or "Dear Sir(s)."

WORLDWIDE TRAVELS

231 Peace Lane
Mobile, AL 29592

2 February 1999

Ms. Laura Larconia
902 Deyton Drive
Princeton, AL 28391

Dear Ms. Larconia:

indent first line
of paragraph

    I cannot believe I left for my two-week vacation without finalizing the plans for your trip to Jamaica. (I guess that shows how much I needed that vacation!) Fortunately, Jeanelle realized my oversight and made the arrangements for you.

indent first line
of paragraph

    To assure you that you really are a top priority client, I'm enclosing a coupon for a 10% discount on your next trip.

Bon voyage!

Ben Dial

Benjamin Dial

F I G U R E   10.12   In the Semiblock Format, the First Line of Each Paragraph Is Indented for a Less Formal Effect

8. Use standard margins that are neither too wide nor too narrow. Most readers prefer a 1-inch margin on all sides of the text (see Chapter 9). You may have to adjust these standards or adjust the vertical spacing of your letter to give it the proper look.

9. Single-space all letters (and memos), but double-space between paragraphs.

10. Try to center your letter vertically on the page, realizing that the optical center of a page is approximately one-third down the page, not at the mathematical one-half point. If you cannot center a short letter exactly, be sure that the greater part of the letter appears slightly higher than the mathemat-

WORLDWIDE TRAVELS
231 Peace Lane
Mobile, AL 29592

date starts on
center line

2 February 1999

Ms. Laura Larconia
902 Deyton Drive
Princeton, AL 28391

Dear Ms. Larconia:

I cannot believe I left for my two-week vacation without finalizing the plans for
your trip to Jamaica. (I guess that shows how much I needed that vacation!)
Fortunately, Jeanelle realized my oversight and made the arrangements for you.

To assure you that you really are a top priority client, I'm enclosing a coupon for a
10% discount on your next trip.

complimentary
closing starts
on center line

Bon voyage!

Ben Dial

Benjamin Dial

FIGURE 10.13   In the Modified Block Format, the Date and Complimentary Closing Are
Aligned on the Center Line

ical center of the page. Do not resort to double-spacing to vertically position
your letter. Figure 10.14 on page 346 and Figure 10.15 on page 347 demonstrate how additional spacing can help improve the attractiveness or visual
appeal of a short letter.

11. Make sure the complimentary closing of your letter sounds professional.
Most readers consider the following closings appropriate:

    Sincerely,
    Sincerely yours,
    Cordially yours,
    Cordially,

ACTION AGENCY, INC.ⅢⅢ➡

TEMPORARY SERVICES

2200 PLANKTON BLVD.
MIAMI, FL 14384

(322) 435-2945
FAX: (322) 435-4922

17 January 1999

Mr. Edward Petralski
723 Alexandria Lane
Coopersville, TN 58139

Dear Mr. Petralski:

We received your letter of application and résumé last week and are pleased that you will soon be relocating in the Greater Miami area. We think you will find our gentle climate much more pleasant than the cold weather we know you have in Tennessee this time of year.

Because of our gentle climate, however, we rarely have calls for heater repairmen. And even if we did, we probably would not have many calls for temporary workers. May we suggest you contact some individual air conditioning and heating specialists in the area? We have enclosed some photocopies from the Greater Miami yellow pages of companies in our area that might have temporary employment for you.

Good luck,

Midge Madrix

Midge Madrix
Technical Supervisor

encl: photocopied yellow pages

(margin notes:)
letter is
top-heavy

optical center

mathematical
center

FIGURE 10.14   A Brief Letter, Improperly Balanced

ACTION AGENCY, INC. ⅢⅢ➡
TEMPORARY SERVICES

2200 PLANKTON BLVD.
MIAMI, FL 14384

(322) 435-2945
FAX: (322) 435-4922

17 January 1999

Mr. Edward Petralski
723 Alexandria Lane
Coopersville, TN 58139

Dear Mr. Petralski:

We received your letter of application and résumé last week and are pleased that you will soon be relocating in the Greater Miami area. We think you will find our gentle climate much more pleasant than the cold weather we know you have in Tennessee this time of year.

Because of our gentle climate, however, we rarely have calls for heater repairmen. And even if we did, we probably would not have many calls for temporary workers. May we suggest you contact some individual air conditioning and heating specialists in the area? We have enclosed some photocopies from the Greater Miami yellow pages of companies in our area that might have temporary employment for you.

Good luck,

Midge Madrix

Midge Madrix
Technical Supervisor

encl: photocopied yellow pages

additional vertical spacing and narrower margins help letter accommodate optical center

optical center

mathematical center

FIGURE 10.15 A Brief Letter, Properly Balanced

More formal closings sound archaic to some readers, but are nevertheless appropriate in some situations and for some readers:

> Yours very truly,

> Very truly yours,

For more personal closings, you may opt for these:

> Best wishes,

> Warm regards,

> Fondly,

Never appropriate for organizational communications are these closings:

> Love,

> Honestly,

> See ya,

Note that in all closings the first word is capitalized, the second word (if used) is lowercase, and the closing itself is followed by a comma.

12. Leave three lines of space between the complimentary closing and your typed name; your typed title goes immediately underneath your name. Your signature goes in the space between the closing and your typed name:

> Sincerely,

> *Jo Allen*

> Jo Allen
> Codirector of Technical and Professional Programs

13. Include "encl:" (for enclosure) two lines below your title if you are sending attachments with the letter. You should also specify what you have included:

> encl: résumé and writing samples

APPLICATION

Formatting Your Message

Depending on your decisions in the first two Applications in this chapter, design and format your message as a letter, memo, or E-mail message. Your instructor may ask you to draft and design as many messages as your audiences and their situations require or may have you draft and design a message to only one of your audiences. Be prepared to submit your final copy as the basis for classroom discussion or for credit.

14. If your letter's information is too long for one page, be sure to put basic information (usually, the reader's name, date, and page number) at the top of the second page (and any additional pages) in case it is separated from the first page:

> Taylor, p. 2
> 23 January 1999

Remember, too, that all pages after the first page are printed on plain stationery (not letterhead) that matches the quality and color of the letterhead stationery itself.

Summary

Even if your organization relies on E-mail for the majority of its routine in-house correspondence (and, increasingly, for its correspondence to outside agencies), you will still have to write letters to clients or customers, suppliers, and other readers outside your organization. Letters and memos (both hard copy and on-line) conduct much of an organization's business—with all kinds of audiences and for all kinds of purposes. To write such correspondence, you need a clear sense of the information you are conveying, its details, and the goodwill you want associated with your writing and your organization's work.

When you write hard-copy messages, anticipating whether readers will respond positively, neutrally, or negatively to your correspondence can help you decide how to organize your information. For good news or routine messages, you should present the most important information first. For bad news, you should open with a neutral statement, explain your reasons for refusing a claim or for any other bad news you have to present, and then state the bad news in one place only and conclude with a goodwill gesture or statement.

The content and organization of sales letters depend on how you anticipate readers will respond to your product or service. As a representative of your organization, you may find it difficult to believe that some people will not be as enthused about your product or service as you are; nevertheless, realizing whether readers will be eager to buy your wares or resentful of your intrusion on their privacy will help you determine whether to organize your sales letter as a direct or indirect communication.

On-line communications modify these direct and indirect organizational strategies because the screen typically displays only about twelve lines of text. Consequently, writers must communicate their primary message in those twelve lines (in case the reader doesn't scroll to the next screen to finish reading the message) or indicate that the message is so important that the reader will scroll to the next screen.

After drafting the correspondence, you should follow your organization's formatting standards to design your letters and memos. As Chapter 9 demonstrated, the appearance of all your workplace documents says something about your (and your organization's) professionalism and image, while enhancing your reader's ability to find or recall important information in your work.

CHECKLIST

For Hard-Copy Messages

✔ Use the memo format when sending messages to readers inside your organization.

✔ Use the letter format when sending messages to readers outside your organization.

✔ Organize information in letters or memos according to how you think the reader will interpret the message—as either routine information, good news, or bad news.

✔ For routine or good news correspondence, put the most important information first.

✔ For bad news correspondence, open with a neutral or pleasant introduction. Next, explain the reasons for the bad news; then, present the bad news in one sentence only or, even better, merely by clear implication. If possible, offer a conciliatory alternative that might lessen your readers' disappointment or hurt. Finally, conclude the communication with a pleasant ending that is designed to maintain the goodwill of your readers.

✔ Special touches, such as humor, personal messages, and response generators, can help make you and your organization more human to your reader. Do not, however, use such touches to manipulate your readers; they typically sense the deception and resent your attempts to manipulate them.

✔ Follow the standard layout features of letters and memos unless your organization uses a different design. The proper appearance of letters and memos sends a message that you are professional, while helping readers find certain kinds of information.

✔ Set a professional tone in your work by using proper titles of address and professional complimentary closings that show your respect for readers.

For On-Line Messages

✔ Communicate your primary message in the opening twelve lines of text, or convey to readers the importance of their scrolling to the next screen(s). Although the subject line of an on-line message is also a useful way to forecast the message, do not expect all readers to pay attention to the subject line.

✔ Retain your sense of professionalism in spite of the informality that on-line correspondence encourages. Remember to be diplomatic and precise in your communications.

Respond promptly to on-line communications, just as you do to hard-copy communications.

 Incorporate strategies for personalizing on-line communications, such as mentioning your reader's name or adding humor or other personal touches.

EXERCISES

Individual Exercises

1. Determine who your audience would be in each of the following situations. Then determine whether you would use the *direct* or the *indirect* organizational approach for each situation; next, determine whether you would write a letter, memo, or on-line message. Be prepared to defend your decisions.

   a. You are requesting that your professor change your grade from a "C" to a "B."

   b. You are disgusted with your newspaper delivery system.

   c. Your best friend was promoted to senior accountant.

   d. You were overlooked for a promotion you think you have earned.

   e. Your company will be three weeks late shipping an order to an important customer.

   f. Your company wants to order thirty-five new computers.

   g. The lawsuit against your company was dropped; report that information to the stockholders.

   h. Your company is sponsoring a new educational program.

   i. Your company is now offering dental insurance.

   j. Your company's dental insurance does not cover braces or other orthodontic work.

   k. Your company is instituting a firm "No Smoking" policy.

   l. Your department was named "Department of the Year."

   m. You will be hiring Jenny Masterson as your new technician.

   n. The wheelbase of the new car design is not wide enough to offer the necessary stability.

   o. Your company agrees to resolve Juana Ruble's complaint about her new television in her favor.

2. Choose any three of the scenarios in exercise 1 for which you would use the direct approach. Do the following for each scenario:

   a. Write the opening paragraph of the communication you selected in exercise 1.

b. Determine what kinds of supporting details you would like to add; write those sentences.

c. Write a pleasant, appropriate closing.

3. Choose any three of the scenarios in exercise 1 for which you would use the indirect approach. Do the following for each scenario:

a. Write the neutral opening statement of the communication you selected in exercise 1.

b. Write the bad news paragraph.

c. Write the alternative paragraph.

d. Write the concluding paragraph.

4. Write an appropriate letter to each of the following:

a. Your scholarship benefactor: Express your gratitude for the donation to your education.

b. One of your former high school teachers: Explain your current direction in college.

5. Write an appropriate memo to each of the following:

a. Your professor: Explain how you plan to use writing in your career.

b. Your boss: Ask for one hour off each day to pursue your college studies and writing projects.

Collaborative Exercises

1. With a partner or group, identify a reader or group of readers who are likely to take the following messages as bad news. If you had to present the bad news to these readers, what explanations might you offer for the news? What consolations or alternatives might you offer?

a. No pets are welcome at the bed and breakfast.

b. Employees' contributions to the health care fund will increase by 4 percent.

c. The new Pluto station wagon has been recalled.

d. A hiring freeze means Amelia will not get the new administrative assistant she was promised.

e. Vacations are canceled.

f. The warehouse is overstocked.

g. The electricity in the Branchwood subdivision will be turned off for three hours on Tuesday.

h. The bookstore is out of the textbook for Physics 4300.

i. Rezoning laws prohibit the building of chicken houses in MacGregor Downs.

j. The Board of Health has ruled against constructing a restaurant on this site.

2. Choose three situations from collaborative exercise 1 and write a bad news, hard-copy letter for each situation. How might your letters change if you were sending the news on-line?

3. For each of the following groups of readers, list three topics that they might consider to be good news:
   a. Naval commanders
   b. Instructors/professors at your college
   c. Grocery store clerks
   d. Highway patrol officers
   e. Interior designers
   f. Students at your college
   g. Parents of kindergartners in your community
   h. Neighbors in your residential area
   i. Fans of the Rolling Stones
   j. Subscribers to your local newspaper
   k. Advertisers on a local radio station

4. For each of the groups of readers in collaborative exercise 3, list three topics that they might consider to be bad news:

5. Select three of the good news topics you identified in collaborative exercise 3:
   a. Write the introductory paragraph for a hard-copy letter on each topic.
   b. Write the introductory paragraph for an on-line letter on each topic.

6. Select three of the bad news topics you identified in collaborative exercise 4:
   a. Write the introductory paragraph for a hard-copy letter on each topic.
   b. Write the introductory paragraph for an on-line letter on each topic.

7. Suppose you have been asked to devise strategies for a sales letter for each of the following products or services:
   - A book on gardening
   - A new rod and reel
   - An automatic pet feeder
   - A diet program
   - Membership in a local book club
   - New cable television offerings
   - A hunting club
   - An indestructible mailbox
   - A bird feeder
   - A college degree program
   - A computer graphics program
   - An infallible radar detector
   - A residential cleaning service
   - A pool cleaning service

a. List the types of readers who would be likely to purchase each product or service with very little convincing from you.

b. List reasons why reluctant readers might change their minds and purchase the product or service.

An example is provided for you; the product in question is a gold credit card:

Readers Likely to Purchase
- Travelers
- Shoppers
- Those who entertain clients at dinner
- Those who have needed emergency cash at some time
- Those who like the prestige of gold cards

Reasons Reluctant Readers Might Change
- Really low interest rate
- No annual fee
- Bonus points or reward percentages on purchases
- Special services for card members at various shops and resorts
- Fear of emergencies involving themselves or family members

8. Select any product or service in collaborative exercise 7, and write a sales letter for it to readers in group (a) and another sales letter to readers in group (b). Then write an E-mail message on the product or service to readers in group (a) and another E-mail message to readers in group (b).

ONGOING ASSIGNMENT

- Using the information from this chapter about the technology, organization, and format of standard correspondence, determine the appropriate form of correspondence to let your organization's management know that you have completed the corporate culture document, including all of the following steps:

  a. Gathered all the information for the document

  b. Drafted an outline for the document

  c. Drafted the graphics for the document

  d. Made the appropriate design decisions for the document

  As an alternative, determine the appropriate form of correspondence to let management know that you have completed the document without discussing the individual steps.

- After determining what you know about your audience and the purpose of your correspondence with them, draft and format the message using the insights offered in this chapter.

CHAPTER 11

Employment Communications

The Résumé and Letter of Application

Although your college major may prepare you for a number of career paths, at some time you will have to decide which paths are most appropriate and desirable for you, based on your interests and abilities. If you are majoring in business, for example, you may be qualified to work as an entry-level accountant, retail manager, or human resources counselor. You will find it difficult, however, to write a single résumé and a generic letter of application that best present your abilities for all these jobs. Far better is tailoring your qualifications for one of these career paths.

Another key to finding the perfect job is to allow plenty of time to work on your employment correspondence and plan to produce numerous drafts before getting your résumé and letter of application right. More than likely, your first draft will look like a first draft—incomplete, poorly organized, sloppy, or overblown. Remember, your résumé and letter of application represent you, and you will want them to be top quality.

Some students and professionals hire professional résumé services or use computerized résumé programs to write their résumés. Certainly, that's the easiest way to do a résumé, but unfortunately, these services and programs typically take a formulaic approach that makes almost all résumés (and job candidates) look and sound alike. Only you know you, and you should be your own best source of information about your experience and qualifications.

Writing your own résumé gives you an additional edge: it helps you to prepare for an interview. After you draft the responses to the résumé worksheet, you may find several aspects of your background that may not be appropriate for the résumé or letter of application, but should be brought out in an interview. In short, writing your own résumé and letter of application is a great way to review what you are, what you can do, what you would like to do, and what you can offer a prospective employer.

This chapter provides, first, a clearer understanding of your audience to help you make some critical decisions about your employment communication package—the letter of application and résumé. As you will learn, even though these documents are essentially about you, the most successful ones demonstrate a keen awareness of readers as well. This chapter will also present strategies for drafting and revising your résumé and letter of application, describe three format options for presenting your qualifications (the option you choose will depend on your readers and your qualifications), and offer some specific do's and don'ts of creating a professional résumé and letter of application. Although there are some good computerized résumé writing programs, you still need to consider the various *options* for presenting your qualifications that computer programs rarely offer. This chapter will help you understand how to write a professional résumé and letter of application so that you will not be limited by the constructs of a computer program. Where to look for jobs is discussed in Strategy Review 11.1.

APPLICATION

Find Your Ideal Job

Before you begin your job search, spend some time thinking about what you truly enjoy doing. Then, make a list of all of those activities or challenges.

Many people overlook the possibility of an "ideal" job because they are set on thinking too broadly: "I want to be an accountant." That's a fine goal, but remember that you can be an accountant in a number of fields. Can you think of any hobby or interest you have that might allow you to find the most appealing accounting job, rather than just any accounting job? Perhaps you could combine your experience in accounting with your love for sailing to land an ideal job as an accountant with a yachting firm.

What kinds of job possibilities can you think of that the following job seekers might not have considered?

Academic major: Engineering

Hobbies: Car repairs, car racing

Job possibilities: _____

Academic major: Fashion design

Hobbies: History, museum tours

Job possibilities: _____

Academic major: Technical communication

Hobbies: Hot air ballooning, fixed-wing flying

Job possibilities: _____

Academic major: Business and French

Hobbies: Traveling, investment analyses

Job possibilities: _____

Now try to combine your own interests and experiences:

Academic major: _____

Hobbies: _____

Career possibilities: _____

S T R A T E G Y   R E V I E W   1 1 . 1

WHERE TO HUNT FOR JOBS

Although many people have found their first important jobs through obscure avenues, almost everyone agrees that having a plan for your job search is a much more sensible strategy. Be prepared to investigate each of the following resources, for many jobs listed in one source are not found in others:

1. The classified ads in the newspaper.
2. The Internet's numerous job listings and search engines, such as Yahoo.
3. Your college or university's career counseling center.
4. Cooperative education and internship opportunities.
5. Your professional organizations. Network with other members, and be sure to read the organization's professional publications, which often list job openings.
6. Information interviews with professionals in your field. Find out how to prepare to join the profession and the kinds of discipline-specific information you should include in your employment communications.
7. Career fairs, often hosted by your college or university.
8. Information-exchange fairs, which allow various organizations to provide information about themselves, such as their mission, their future projects, and the skills they seek in potential employees.
9. Various social and civic organizations, which provide excellent networking opportunities.
10. Management recruiters, although these professionals are likely to be of more use to you later in your career.

Audience and the Employment Communication Package

Unless they are sending the employment package to a specific person they know in an organization, most job seekers have only a vague idea of who might be reading their documents and may assume the reader has plenty of time to ponder each applicant's qualifications and suitability for a position in that organization. In most cases, nothing could be further from the truth. Readers of résumés and letters of application are likely to have a stack of such documents to wade through, typically before getting on to their *other* job responsibilities. That lack of time means that you have to communicate effectively and quickly. Getting to the point with both your résumé and your letter of application means focusing on the key factor that is likely to catch the reader's attention: evidence that you have the skills and qualifications needed for a particular position.

Sending hundreds of letters and résumés to organizations you've selected at random will rarely result in a successful search. More beneficial will be careful research and consideration of your audience—both the individual reader and the organization where that reader works. For the most part, you may assume that readers of résumés and letters of application have these qualities:

1. They are busy people. On average, most readers of résumés spend only forty-five seconds reviewing an application package. If your information is under- or overdeveloped, you are unlikely to use that forty-five seconds wisely.

2. They are frequently *not* in the résumé business. In other words, many readers of letters and résumés are engineers, laboratory supervisors, and sales managers—not personnel or human resources employees.

3. They are frequently not in your area of specialization, so you should not assume they will understand acronyms and the significance of some of your qualifications. You should explain that information carefully and concisely.

4. They are as likely to be looking for a reason to disqualify you from consideration as to include you, especially when they have a number of applicants for a job. Most people in hiring positions want to find the "just right" person for the job, just as you want to find the "just right" organization for which to work.

As you revise your résumé and letter of application, keep these ideas about your readers in mind; their foibles, preferences, and biases will play a key role in determining whether you get an interview.

Drafting the Résumé: A Worksheet Approach

To help yourself draft your résumé, complete the ten tasks listed on pages 359–365. List as much information as possible (brainstorm!), including even information that seems irrelevant, unimpressive, or repetitive. You will decide what to include and exclude as you revise and format your résumé.

1. List your name, your current and permanent addresses, your telephone number(s), and your E-mail number (especially if you are going into a high-tech industry):

Susan Juarez

School Address:
1704-A Ascot Way
Peterson, WI 72833
(377) 473-9689
sjuarez@samen.gskm.wisconsin.edu

Permanent Address:
107 Square Drive
La Jolla, CA 28382
(224) 434-2221

2. *Optional:* Construct one phrase that tells the reader the kind of position you want and the special skills you have that you'd like to put to work:

> Job Objective: An entry-level technical communication position where I can use my computer skills and collaborative experience.

> Job Objective: A management trainee position in human resources that involves hiring, training, and reassigning employees.

> Job Objective: A career counseling position that focuses on developing and coordinating cooperative education opportunities for students.

The danger in constructing a Job Objective—and the reason many instructors and textbook authors argue against it—is that the objective is often too vague, too limiting, too naive, or too predictable. Avoid statements such as these:

> . . . opportunity to work with people (too commonplace)

> . . . opportunity to help others (too vague)

> . . . opportunity to manage others (too vague—perhaps presumptuous?)

> . . . opportunity to be my own boss (don't work well with others?)

> . . . opportunity to travel (jet-setter? unsettled?)

> . . . opportunity to move up (too ambitious? power hungry?)

3. List your *after-high school* educational background. Include your degree and major(s), institution, its location, and date of (expected) graduation, beginning with your most recent, most impressive, or most relevant degree for the position you seek. You may also include your overall grade point average (and/or your grade point average in your major) if you believe it will impress your prospective employer. Because different fields regard different grade point averages as "impressive," check with advisers in your major to determine whether you should list yours. Be sure to include any special workshops, management or technical seminars, discipline-related licenses or certifications, or other educational experiences in addition to your standard college course work.

> Education:

> M.B.A. The Fuqua School of Business. Duke University, Durham, NC: 2000.

> B.S. in Biology, minors in Business and Industrial Technology. University of Maryland—College Park: 1997. (overall 3.7 GPA on a 4.0 scale; in major, 3.9)

> A.A.S. in Environmental Engineering. Lakeland College, Mentor, OH: 1995. (3.5 in major)

> Management and Technical Seminars:
> Communicating with Men and Women in Management (1999)
> Basic PWR Systems Training (1997)
> Total Cost Management (1996)

4. List the names of all organizations where you have worked (as either a paid or a volunteer employee), followed by their locations (using postal abbreviations for the states), your job title(s), and dates of your employment. Repeat as often as necessary. For example:

    The Rusty Pelican, San Diego, CA: Host, 1999.

    Top O' the Cove, La Jolla, CA: Busboy, 1997–99.

    The Marine Room, La Jolla, CA: Waiter, 1996–97.

    Algiers' Landing, New Orleans, LA: Busboy, 1996.

    U.S. Army, Ft. Bragg, Fayetteville, NC: Paratrooper with the 82nd Airborne, 1992–96

5. For each job, list your accomplishments and responsibilities using *action verbs* (not "responsible for" or "duties included"), which will make your work appear more dynamic. Be careful not to overstate your experience, though. The following action verbs work well on résumés:

managed	reviewed	calculated	analyzed
designed	completed	negotiated	performed
wrote	supervised	organized	applied
produced	handled	ran	scheduled
contributed	sponsored	represented	worked
oversaw	coordinated	distributed	monitored
presented	trained	installed	contracted
planned	developed	collected	appraised
collaborated	supported	hosted	sold
studied	learned	helped	arranged
advised	budgeted	controlled	adjusted
revised	specialized	customized	researched
documented	standardized	evaluated	hosted
directed	reported	represented	

In describing your work experience, be specific; add details about numbers, money, and the like. *Note:* If you are reluctant to specify dollar amounts (which may compromise the confidentiality of a previous employer's financial status), try to present monetary amounts in percentages, such as "increased sales by 12% over 3 years."

Top O' the Cove, La Jolla, CA: Busboy, 1997–99.

*   Managed 6 other busboys
*   Bused 75–100 tables per night
*   Handled $200–$400 in tips for servers
*   Arranged formal place settings
*   Helped close the restaurant at night and prepared for next evening's seatings
*   Coordinated service and seating with host and waiters

U.S. Army, Ft. Bragg, Fayetteville, NC: Paratrooper with
the 82nd Airborne, 1992–96.
- Trained on B-29s with 40 other paratroopers
- Named squad leader within 3 months
- Made over 100 successful jumps
- Flew classified missions
- Promoted to sergeant
- Honorably discharged, 1996

Although many students have work experience that translates into the career they seek, a few students still graduate with no paid work experience. In that case, focus on the experience you do have—academic credentials and projects, volunteer work, and internships. The key is in recognizing and presenting transferable skills.

6. As you complete this work experience segment, determine the specific skills or qualities *you* would want an applicant to have if you were reviewing résumés from potential candidates. What should this "ideal" person be able to do? Some possibilities include, but are certainly not limited to, the following:

- Delegate duties
- Work on or lead committees assigned specific tasks
- Evaluate the work of others
- Solve problems
- Analyze data
- Write different forms of communication in acceptable formats (reports, proposals, etc.)
- Negotiate with difficult people
- Handle complaints
- Use particular computer programs
- Use specialized tools or pieces of equipment
- Accommodate federal, state, and local regulations concerning the organization's work
- Juggle a number of responsibilities
- Organize work schedule (for self and/or others)
- Speak a foreign language
- Collaborate successfully with others
- Work well alone with little direction or motivation from others
- Manage a budget
- Meet deadlines

Check the items that characterize what will be expected of you on your job. Be sure to add additional qualities that will help you prove you are a hard worker. Then, underneath each item that applies to you and is relevant to the position you want, list the specifics of your experience that prove your capabilities. For example:

> *Work on or lead committees assigned specific tasks*:
> - Member, committee to reorganize work schedules (Rusty Pelican)
> - Leader, committee to redesign the host station (Top O' the Cove)
> - Member, committee to select new team leaders (Top O' the Cove)
>
> *Manage a budget*:
> - Managed a $32,000 household budget
> - Managed a $6,500 budget as treasurer for The Royal Preservationists

7. Describe your personality as honestly as possible. Use the following list of possible descriptors, adding any others that describe you better:

ambitious	motivated	analytical	problem solver
peacemaker	negotiator	diplomatic	well rounded
intelligent	good speaker	good listener	flexible
meticulous	loyal	conscientious	creative
determined	enthusiastic	socially adept	poised
team player	self-motivated	logical	careful
clearheaded			

Given what you know about the jobs and organizations to which you are applying, which of your attributes might be worth mentioning and proving, or developing further, in a résumé or perhaps later in the letter of application or even in the interview?

Next, list particular instances in which you can demonstrate or prove that you have each quality you have marked. For example:

> *Diplomatic:*
> - Convinced the members of our senior project team to be more tolerant of one member's ideas; in the end, one of her ideas was quite useful in setting our project apart from the other teams' projects.
> - Coordinated work of volunteer staff at the local nursing home, settling a debate among volunteers about weekend work hours and encouraging a more unified spirit for helping the residents.

8. Answer "yes" or "no" to the following questions:
   - Are you willing to travel? Anywhere in the United States? Anywhere in the world?
   - Are you willing to relocate? Anywhere in the United States? Anywhere in the world?
   - Are you willing to be promoted? To any level? To do any task?
   - Are you willing to work alone? To work in a team setting?
   - Are you willing to return to school for more education/training?

In light of what you know about the positions and organizations to which you are applying, list your responses that are likely to serve you well.

9. List your work or volunteer experiences and any accomplishments that you are especially proud of. Consider, but do not limit yourself to, these suggestions:

   ■ Grade point average (a 3.2 on a 4.0 scale)

   ■ Positions you have held (manager at Hardee's; worker on family farm)

   ■ Awards (Most Improved Student)

   ■ Community service (volunteer for the American Red Cross)

   ■ Professional service (newsletter editor for your student organization)

   ■ Scholarships (the Clinton Keeler Fellowship)

   ■ Honors (member of Phi Beta Kappa)

   ■ Leadership roles (student government representative; president of the Campus Club)

   ■ Combined experiences (maintained a 3.2 grade point average while working twenty hours a week on the family farm)

   ■ Computer skills (comfortable with Windows and DOS packages)

   ■ Military service (learned the value of discipline and loyalty; worked on technical deploys in the Persian Gulf)

   ■ Athletic participation (participated in varsity hockey for two years)

   ■ Membership in professional or civic organization (member of Students in Administrative Management Careers)

   ■ Other extracurricular activities (band, choral groups, cheerleading)

   ■ Hobbies, especially if they are in some way relevant to the job you want (e.g., applying for a feature writer's position—"enjoy photography"); if they indicate something about your personality, social standing, or maturity (e.g., applying for country club manager's position—"participate in dressage, fox hunting, and polo"); or if they are likely to interest the interviewer (e.g., applying for a travel agent's position—"traveled extensively throughout Africa and the Mediterranean")

   ■ Foreign language proficiencies—specify reading or conversational knowledge and level of fluency (advanced reading knowledge of French; fluent in Spanish; modest reading knowledge of German)

   ■ A special project in school or at work (completed a business plan for an entrepreneurial venture between students in industrial tooling course and the local hardware manufacturing company, resulting in $2,500 profit in three months)

   ■ Domestic responsibilities (provide a home for three children—serve as cook, nurse, counselor, chauffeur, teacher, and banker)

10. List people you have worked with and believe would attest to your credentials, potential, character, and work ethic. You may choose professors, former/current employers, and coworkers. You may choose your minister if you have worked at your church or if the minister has special knowledge of

your character and work abilities. When selecting references, ask yourself these questions:

■ Has this person had a chance to see the best work I can do?

■ Does this person have any personal or professional grudges against me?

■ Does this person have any reason not to recommend me for a position?

■ Will this person write a professional letter or act professionally in a telephone interview with prospective employers?

Based on your answers, narrow your list to three or four people who would offer the most convincing evidence of your suitability for a position. Arrange an appointment with (or call or write) these people and ask if they feel comfortable recommending you for a position. *Never list references without asking their permission first.* Then, you may want to keep their letters of recommendation on file at your institution's career counseling and placement service.

After completing these ten tasks, you probably have a lot more information than you thought you'd have. You're now able to select the most important, most outstanding, and most impressive aspects of your abilities. (See Strategy Review 11.2.)

STRATEGY REVIEW 11.2

OMITTING IRRELEVANCIES FROM YOUR RÉSUMÉ

You have probably seen résumés that have included all sorts of information. Generally speaking, however, most of this additional information should be excluded because it is either illegal for the employer to consider, likely to obscure your true qualifications, or likely to take up space that can be better used. In general, avoid references to all of the following:

■ Your age, race, gender, or religious affiliations. Such information is illegal for employers to consider in the hiring process because it is irrelevant to how well you can perform your job.

■ Your health status—everyone claims to be in "excellent" or at least "good" health.

■ Your physical appearance, unless the position for which you are applying has a height/weight requirement. Do not include a photograph because it would indicate your age, race, gender, and physical appearance—issues that are irrelevant to your qualifications for a job.

■ Your church's specific denomination (Baptist, Catholic, Lutheran) when discussing your *volunteer* work—unless you are applying for a job with a church. In any application, however, you may include your work as "Director of the Church Youth Choir" (not "Director of the Stoney Branch Methodist

(continued)

Church Youth Choir"). If you have worked as a paid employee of a church, you should, of course, list the church's full name.

■ Your political affiliation (Democrat, Republican, Independent) unless you are applying for a job with that political party. You may, however, include your work with a political party without specifying the party: "Advance Team Coordinator for 1992 Presidential Election Nominees visiting George-town University."

■ Casual aquaintances you know at the organization where you are applying for a job. You would be embarrassed if that person were asked about you and didn't remember who you were or if that person carried little respect within the organization.

■ Your high school unless you are young (under twenty) or have some *unique* high school experience: Valedictorian, Morehead Scholar, and the like. It looks pretty silly for a thirty-five-year-old person to recount high school glo-ries on a résumé.

■ Courses taken in your major. A reader expects you to have completed cer-tain courses by virtue of your major. You may, however, list relevant courses that will distinguish you from others who graduate in your field. For instance, courses in business/technical communication, speech communica-tion, industrial psychology, Russian, and Japanese are good additions to the résumé of a business student who wants a job in international business.

■ Hobbies that sound impressive, but do not really interest you. You would be embarrassed if the interviewer wanted to discuss your impressive hobbies, wouldn't you?

Now, highlight the items you think are most important to include. Next, highlight secondary items that you may include if there's room on your résumé. Don't throw out anything yet—some of the information you have generated may be more appropriate for your letter of application, discussed later in this chapter, or for helping you prepare for the interview.

Choosing a Format for Your Résumé

After completing the résumé worksheet, highlighting your primary and sec-ondary accomplishments, and adding and deleting information to strengthen the content, you are ready to make some decisions about the format of your résumé. This section presents three formats, which will give you some ideas about how you can craft the appearance, wording, and organization of your résumé to in-crease the reader's interest in you as a job applicant. After focusing on what you know about the organizational culture to which you are applying, you will have to consider your own qualifications and credentials, and you will have to determine the order and means of emphasis that will best sell your strengths to the reader. At this stage, be flexible. You may be surprised at the format and style that best present you to a prospective employer. (See Strategy Review 11.3.)

STRATEGY REVIEW 11.3

SPECIAL DESIGN FEATURES OF RÉSUMÉS

Regardless of the other decisions you make about your résumé, some general suggestions about design can help you create a polished, professional résumé that emphasizes the information you want to emphasize.

1. Make the heading of your résumé your name, address, and phone number—not the word "Résumé." Because of their specialized format, résumés are obviously résumés. Your name is the most important information on your résumé; make it your heading.

2. Vary the type size (but not the type style) or presentation of important information, such as headings and special qualifications. **Boldface** type, *italic* type, and underlining are particularly useful for drawing the reader's attention to your special qualifications. Be careful about shading information, however. When copies are made, the shading may turn black, obscuring the information you've tried to highlight.

   Standard 9-, 10-, and sometimes 12-point types are best, depending on the style or font you have selected. Type that is too small looks cramped and is hard to read; type that is too large looks juvenile—as if you are trying too hard to fill the page.

   Some companies use Optical Computer Readers (OCRs) that scan all résumés into a similar format and search for words and phrases (such as "sell," "sold," "manage," or "oversee") that indicate you have particular kinds of experience. Such scanners can distort or omit letters printed in unusual fonts, turning your carefully crafted résumé into gobbledygook. Your best bet, therefore, is to select rather traditional type styles instead of script, all capital letters, or all boldface type.

3. Do not use script or other unusual type styles that may distract or irritate readers or send the message that you are unaware of the standard conventions for résumés (and, possibly, other communications as well). In addition to the scanning problems, unusual type may also suggest that you are too unconventional to fit into the organization. Of course, if you are entering a highly creative or artistic field (graphic arts, retail display, design, etc.), you may take more liberties to show off your creativity. Ask your professors and career advisers how unconventional you should be.

4. Use other textual features, such as indentations, bulleted lists, and spacing to create an easily readable format that will help readers see the most important information.

(continued)

5. Aim for a one- or two-page résumé. Unless you are an older student with a lot of work experience, you probably can explain all your qualifications in a single page. A longer résumé may make you seem long-winded and even suggest that you have padded your résumé. Of course, if you need two pages to present your qualifications completely, by all means, use them.

6. Leave ample white space throughout your résumé to improve its readability. No one wants to read cramped information. At the same time, do not overuse white space so that it looks as though you are spreading out information to fill the page.

The Chronological Résumé

The chronological résumé, which lists information in reverse order beginning with the most recent experiences and accomplishments, has historically been the most used résumé format in the workplace. Unfortunately, it rarely sells a traditional (eighteen- to twenty-two-year-old) *student's* qualifications, making it one of the least desirable methods of presenting your abilities if you fall into that category. It also does not present well those with little or no paid work experience and those who have taken numerous (and varied) part-time jobs to work their way through school. Instead, the chronological résumé works best when you fit into one or more of these categories:

- You have paid work experience (not just academic or volunteer experience) in your field.
- Your experiences have become increasingly impressive, complex, demanding, or visible within an organization.
- You are remaining in the same field, although you are changing companies or applying for a promotion within the same organization.
- Your experience correlates exactly with the position for which you are applying.
- You need to be able to account for all your time (for example, if your job requires that you be bonded for security reasons) to demonstrate that you have not been, say, in prison.
- You are writing to a highly conservative organization that expects all résumés to be chronological.

The key to a chronological résumé, of course, is chronology. If items appear out of order, they may confuse readers or make them think you are trying to hide something. In short, you must be meticulous about dates and duties. The chronological résumé in Figure 11.1 emphasizes time because the placement of dates as the first bit of information in each entry allows readers to glance down the left column to see if any gaps appear in your employment record.

name and address
take most impor-
tant place

Jamison Turnage
223 Melrose Drive
Reno, NV 47382
(341) 573-2843

specific job objec-
tive, but open to
possibilities

Job Objective: An entry-level position in a design firm where I can advise
clients about fabric options

education dates
first, then additional
information

Education: 1999–2001: A.A. in Interior Design. Watauga College: Raeford, NV.
Grade point average in major: 3.9 on a 4.0 scale

Special Seminars

1999: Alternative Fabrics (Seminar, sponsored by DuPont
Synthetics, Inc.)

1999: Ethnic Influences on Design (Seminar, sponsored by the
Boston Museum)

date first, then
job information

Experience: 2000. Summer. Management Intern with Fabulous Interiors,
Raeford, NV.

work details

- Managed three summer interns
- Oversaw $75,000 budget for clients
- Consulted with 10 clients about interiors options (fabrics,
wall coverings, paint, flooring, upholstery, accents)
- Accompanied store owner on buying trip to New York
- Offered full-time position, but returned to complete college
education

date first, then
job information

1999. Summer. Sales Intern with Fabulous Interiors, Raeford, NV.

work details

- Consulted with 7 clients about fabrics, wall coverings,
paint, and flooring
- Sold $35,000 in materials and services
- Named Outstanding New Employee for July

date first, then
job information

1996–98. Part-time Assistant at Margie's House O' Wow Designs,
Reno, NV.

work details

- Took orders over the phone (average $350 per day)
- Maintained four room displays
- Arranged catalogs from over 75 companies
- Ran errands and made deliveries

dates first

Honors and   2001: Outstanding Senior in Interior Design. Watauga College.
Awards: 2000: The Margie Hunter Scholarship for Designing Women.
1999: The Eye for Detail Award.

References: Furnished on request.

FIGURE 11.1   A Chronological Résumé

The Skills and Accomplishments Résumé

When your qualifications are best presented by some criteria other than dates, you should consider using a skills and accomplishments (SA) résumé. The SA résumé works best when you fall into one or more of these categories:

- You are applying for your first major job within a field.
- You are changing careers.
- You want to combine experiences from two or more fields.
- Your paid work experience to date is limited.
- Your volunteer experience and academic work are your strongest selling features.
- Your experience is transferable to the position you want.

For most students, the SA résumé should begin with a list of your educational experience, starting with the degree on which you are currently working (assuming you intend to use this degree in the job you are seeking). Then, the SA résumé allows you to discuss your special projects (both academic and volunteer). As the SA résumé in Figure 11.2 shows, experiences are organized according to two, three, or four of your outstanding qualities. You'll have to decide which of your qualities are most characteristic of your skills and abilities and will sell you best to a prospective employer.

The Titles Résumé

Many human resources advisers say that not only are you likely to change jobs nine or ten times during your worklife, but you may also change careers three or four times. The titles résumé emphasizes the positions you have held, arranged in order from the most impressive job title to the least impressive (regardless of the chronology of those positions). The point is to show that you have had experience in several management levels in one or more organizations. The second point the résumé makes is that your skills are transferable—that the work you did (and management experience you gained) for one organization translates to the next organization's needs. Thus, the titles résumé works best when you fit into these categories:

- Your management skills are more important than the technical products or services with which you have had experience.
- You have held at least two impressive job titles.
- You are trying to get a position that also carries an impressive job title.
- Your skills are transferable.

The titles résumé, because it is often written for a specific position, may include details that are far more concrete than those you would include in a

Melvin B. Lane
2939-B Pensacola Lane
Orlando, FL 29485-3858
(329) 385-3858

Job Objective: An entry-level journalist's position with a small newspaper, with an opportunity to write special features

Education: B.A. in Journalism, minor in English/Writing. Central Florida University. Orlando, FL (1999). GPA 3.3 in major, 3.2 in minor on a 4.0 scale.

Special Coursework:
Media Influences on Small Town America
Interpersonal Communication
American Ethnography

Skills and Abilities:

Writing

- Wrote feature story on ethnic influences in central Florida—
  - Picked up by UPI and AP news services
  - Won award for Best Feature Story, *The Floridian* (1997)
- Wrote local news briefs, abbreviated from UPI and AP stories
- Wrote "Police News," based on police logs
- Edited the work of two other part-time journalists

Interpersonal Relations

- Convinced reluctant merchants to discuss economic difficulties of preseason merchandising for feature story
- Interviewed leading personalities among Seminole Indians for Christmas feature
- Presented part-time journalists' grievances to management
- Maintained good rapport with police officers
- Led senior reporting project, "Central Florida University—Evidence of Diversity in Academic and Campus Life"
- Traveled successfully throughout South America during summer of 1999

Researching

- Researched ethnic influences on Christmas celebrations in central Florida
- Investigated the magic of Disney World for adults
- Researched the influence of local elections on local citizens
- Interviewed local politicians on campaign issues for 1998 campaign
- Worked with Professor Jan Camarillo on her research on Seminole Indians in Florida

Positions: Part-time journalist, *The Floridian*, 1997–1999.
Staff reporter, *The Central Florida Gazette*, 1994–1997.

References: Furnished on request from Career Counseling and Placement Services, Central Florida University, CFU 213, Orlando, FL 29486.

Margin annotations:
- most important information first
- relevant course work for this particular job
- special skills highlighted
- evidence of skill
- evidence of skill
- evidence of skill
- particular jobs and dates of employment

FIGURE 11.2 A Skills and Accomplishments Résumé

standard résumé. In Figure 11.3 on pages 373–374, for instance, the job objective is more specific, and details about education are relegated to a lower status (and placement) on the résumé. The figure also shows how you can use this format to emphasize management experience.

A final note about formatting your résumé: you may be tempted to try various gimmicks with your résumé, but your best bet is to follow the standard guidelines presented throughout this chapter. Even though gimmicks may make your résumé stand out, they are also likely to turn off your reader (creating a negative impression). For experienced résumé readers, a professional-looking résumé that presents your qualifications effectively is the most impressive presentation you could want.

Refining Your Résumé's Content

After you review the information in your worksheet and draft your résumé according to the format that best presents your qualifications, you should also review the revising strategies you learned in Chapter 6; then, you should become familiar with some basic do's and don'ts specific to refining a résumé:

1. Never lie on a résumé or "pad" your experiences. Word about your deception can spread quickly throughout an industry, making it difficult or even impossible for you to get further work in your profession. Hardly worth the price of a little exaggeration, right?

2. Do not use full sentences in a résumé; instead, list information. Readers should be able to glance quickly over your qualifications, achievements, and special skills. (If readers spend only 3–7 seconds glancing at a résumé and only 45 seconds actually reading one, they must be able to see your most impressive qualifications at a glance.)

3. Present your most valuable and impressive qualifications and experiences first or at the earliest and most appropriate opportunities.

4. Talk about your experiences in terms that make sense to your reader. If you do not know whether your reader will be a technical expert or a more generic human relations officer, use generic terminology throughout your communications, possibly with technical terms in parentheses.

5. Include details and specifics that clarify your responsibilities and capabilities. Mention the specific number of people you managed, a range of the amounts of money for which you were responsible, the specific number of courses you took in your academic specializations, and so on.

6. Include traditional categories of information, such as education, work experience, and computer skills, that prospective employers expect to find in your résumé. Excluding these categories suggests you have no education, work experience, or computer skills.

most important
information first

Elizabeth Sessoms Johnson
211 Pine View Drive
Houston, TX 93823
(422) 832-4839
sessjohnc@iitvax.bitnet

very specific
position sought

Job Objective: To use my experience in computer retail, merchandising, and management to lead Johnson Components through its merger with Winston Parts, Inc.

Leadership Experience:

most impressive
title first
then details of
employment

<u>President.</u> The Sauer Computer Group. Houston, TX: 1999–2004

- Led company to its *Fortune 500* status, maintained since 2000
- Negotiated $3 million merger between the Sauer Components Company and the Smithson Design Group
- Improved sales 24% over 7 years
- Prevented company's insolvency in 1999

accomplishments

- Oversaw all operations, from the Sales Division to the Design Division to the Marketing Division
- Restructured the Design Division to bring in a team of 7 computer specialists
- Initiated the design, development, support, and marketing of XY200, a $1 million computer program designed to support home computer accounting packages

second most
impressive job
title

<u>Vice President, Marketing.</u> The Lawson Company. Dallas, TX: 1995–1999.

- Coordinated public relations campaign to reposition The Lawson Company as a leader in home computer packages

accomplishments

- Implemented results of usability tests to redesign support packages for computer programs—decreased calls to Helpline by 43%
- Developed advertising campaign for television, radio, and print media
- Led team that redesigned the packaging and display of Z2000 computer package—sales increased 23%

third most
impressive job
title

<u>Vice President, Sales.</u> The Lawson Company. Dallas, TX: 1990–1995.

- Initiated Sales Drive '82, a $150,000 sales event
- Coordinated the work of a 95-member sales force

accomplishments

- Developed training packages for sales teams, emphasizing gender relations, technical expertise, and service contracts

FIGURE 11.3 A Titles Résumé, page 1

Johnson, p. 2

- Instigated sales retreats, resulting in better communications between sales associates and sales managers
- Promoted sales agenda in management meetings

Awards and Recognitions:	- *The Texan*'s Woman of the Year, 2003 - Who's Who Among American Businesswomen, 1999 - The Jackson Management Leader, The Lawson Company, 1998 - Speaker of the Year, The Texas Business Communication Council, 1998 - Valedictorian, The Babcock School of Business, Wake Forest University, 1987 - Valedictorian, Meredith College, 1983

(margin note: outstanding awards listed in reverse chronological order)

Education:	MBA, The Babcock School of Business. Wake Forest University. Winston-Salem, NC, 1987. (Valedictorian) BA, English. Meredith College. Raleigh, NC, 1983. (Valedictorian) Special Technical and Management Seminars: - 12 management seminars - 7 computer design seminars - 4 computer documentation seminars - 3 communication seminars

(margin note: education is last because, at this level of employment, it is either assumed or irrelevant)

References are confidential and will be furnished on request.

FIGURE 11.3   A Titles Résumé, page 2

7. Demonstrate your knowledge of the field in which you want to work by stating your familiarity with various types of equipment, computers, and other tools routinely used in your field.

8. Determine whether you want to list the names and addresses of your references on your résumé—*after you ask for permission to use them as references, of course.*

9. Proofread your résumé—again and again and again. Use your spellchecker, but do not rely on it because it cannot catch errors in dates, unusually spelled names, and grammar. Very few problems with a résumé can be as damaging as a simple typographic error because such errors suggest you are sloppy—hardly a quality you want to display to prospective employers.

These guidelines should help you to understand the "standards" of résumé writing—the guidelines and assumptions that practically all experienced résumé readers share. Because they constitute the norms of résumé writing, violating these guidelines may imperil your job search.

Drafting the Letter of Application: A Worksheet Approach

How do employers decide which college graduate with a degree in business (or landscaping, engineering, or history) to hire over other college graduates with identical degrees? Typically, the employers try to find the candidate whose experiences most closely match the needs of their organizations. If you write a letter of application that makes those connections *for* the readers, you demonstrate your suitability for the job, while distinguishing yourself—and what you have to offer—from all those other applicants.

In this section, you will learn some valuable strategies for drafting and refining your letter of application. Because a successful letter of application depends so heavily on your knowledge of the organization to which you are writing, your research on the organization (see The World of Workplace Writing on page 376) is crucial here; you'll want to review your notes about promising organizations before you begin your draft. The sample letter in this section (Figures 11.4 and 11.5) coordinates with the résumé in Figure 11.1, so be sure to review that résumé as well.

Completing the three tasks listed on pages 375 and 377 will help you draft your letter of application. Again, plan to spend some time on these tasks; doing so will help you present yourself in the most professional light.

1. Select a two-column format on your computer screen, or draw a vertical line down the center of a sheet of paper. On the left side of the screen or paper, list what you know about the organization to which you are applying, based on your research. You may include, but should not limit your list to, the following kinds of information:

   - Geographic location(s)
   - Products or services offered
   - Recent mergers, diversifications, or acquisitions
   - Kinds of equipment, computers, and processes used
   - Management philosophy
   - Future plans
   - Competitors
   - Status among competitors—role in the industry
   - Divisions in the organization for which you might be suited

THE WORLD OF WORKPLACE WRITING

Researching an Organization for Employment Communications

What kinds of information should you know about an organization to which you are applying? The most important information to know is the organization's primary product or service. Because of diversification, buyouts, and mergers, however, many companies make more than one product and may oversee the management, production, and distribution of thousands of products.

You may also want to investigate other kinds of information:

■ The organization's general financial picture and any reports of possible reorganizing or downsizing

■ Any suggestions of expanding, diversifying, buying another company, or merging with another company

■ The organization's history and management philosophy

■ The organization's hierarchical structure and levels of management

■ The organization's record of hiring and promoting women and minorities

■ The organization's environmental record

So how do you find out about an organization? First, turn to your career counseling center. The volumes of literature the counselors keep about companies can make your research a great deal easier.

You can also try these research techniques:

■ Request a copy of the organization's annual report, which typically reviews the organization's accomplishments over the past year and describes its strategies for remaining competitive.

■ Study published analyses of the organization in *Standard & Poor's Corporate Records, Standard and Poor's Register of Corporations, U.S. Industrial Outlook,* Dun and Bradstreet's *Million Dollar Directory,* and other resources (see Chapter 3).

■ Interview current workers in the organization; also talk with professors, advisers, and career counselors.

■ Read about the organization in trade periodicals and in your local or state newspaper.

■ Check out the organization's Web page on the Internet.

- Financial status
- Qualifications of employees typically hired
- Job expectations and pressures

2. On the right side of the screen or paper, list your own qualifications, preferences, experiences, and abilities that match, as closely as possible, each of the points you listed in the left-hand column for step 1.

3. Review your résumé for strengths that may offer additional benefits to the organization, given what you know about that organization.

THE WORLD OF WORKPLACE WRITING

Frequently Asked Questions about Writing Employment Correspondence

1. *Do I have to send a letter of application with the résumé?* Absolutely! The letter of application presents you to the reader; by itself, a résumé seems a stark, if not confusing, introduction. Most important, the letter of application helps the reader understand the résumé in light of your interests, career ambitions, and experience.

2. *Must I reveal a salary history or give a desired salary range?* From your research with career counselors, information interviews with professionals, and discussions with your professors, you should be able to identify a salary *range* that you can expect in your first (or subsequent) job. An inflated or deflated salary request can damage your possibilities of a job offer, so be sure to keep your request within a reasonable range.

   Most career counselors suggest you play it straight when negotiating your salary, although you may err (slightly!) on the side of generosity. In other words, if you know that most people in a job such as the one you seek make $20,000 to $22,000, you would probably be wise to ask for $21,000 to $23,000. The prospective employer is likely to go for the lower end of the scale you present, so be sure you can live with the lower figure.

3. *What if my grades aren't that great?* Although most recruiters realize that all college students are not dedicated solely to their studies, you can hardly blame them for wanting evidence that you are serious, knowledgeable, and will work out well for them. As you draft your résumé, emphasize what you have learned. And if family responsibilities or part-time or even full-time work responsibilities have distracted you from your studies, be sure to emphasize that experience in its most positive light—for what it has given you in terms of work ethics, tuition, maturity, and responsibility.

With her job application package, Jamison Turnage (see her résumé in Figure 11.1 on page 369) is seeking a job with Interiors Galore, an internationally known, award-winning design house. Although Interiors Galore has not advertised for a specific position, Jamison knows the management routinely hires a couple of college graduates each year. Thus, she plans to submit a blind solicitation for a position. Based on her knowledge and research of Interiors Galore, Jamison made the following list:

Interiors Galore	*Me*
1. sells to upscale clientele	1. worked with team on redecorating historic district
2. sells $1 million/year	2. sold $75,000 per year
3. handles 200+ clients/year	3. worked with 10 clients at a time
4. has formal showroom	4. did display work; attended buying shows in New York in formal showrooms
5. won award for ethnically diverse fabric use and designs	5. helped design African American display for new Nevada Museum of History display; attended Boston Museum's seminar on ethnic influences in design
6. mentioned in *Fabrics Today* for innovative fabric use	6. won three college awards for innovative design
7. teamwork required	7. worked on two team projects— led one team

Working from the information she developed in the letter of application worksheet, Jamison used the following pointers to help her draft the letter of application:

In the First Paragraph

- Aim for a confident, but not arrogant, tone.
- Do not open with a rhetorical question or with a gimmicky or shocking statement. You certainly don't want to turn off readers at the beginning.
- Specify the position for which you are applying. If you do not know about a specific position, specify the division for which your experience would be most suitable: for example, sales, advertising, engineering, or writing.
- Explain how you know about the position (newspaper advertisement? advertisement in trade journals? word of mouth? electronic bulletin board? professor? career counseling center? friend?). If your letter and résumé are a blind solicitation, you may explain how you know about the organization itself.

- Offer a brief (one or two sentence) overview of your primary qualifications (education, work experience, or both) and personal qualities (attention to details, ability to work in collaborative settings, professionalism, etc.) that will interest the reader.

- Limit the first paragraph to no more than four or five sentences—a long opening paragraph overwhelms readers.

In the Middle Paragraph(s)

- Select two or three highlights of your experience or of your professional qualities that correlate to *significant points you know* about the organization to which you are writing. For instance, if you speak Japanese fluently and know the organization is expanding into the Japanese market, that connection should help you get the reader's attention. If you know the company uses a particular kind of computer equipment and software, your familiarity and innovations with that system might impress the reader.

- Provide additional evidence that you know something about the organization's plans, history, products/services, or market and that your own interests and experiences would be useful.

In the Final Paragraph

- Refer to your enclosed résumé, but don't just state "I have enclosed a résumé for your review." Phrase your reference so that it provides information as well. For example, "The enclosed résumé shows that . . . " or "As the enclosed résumé shows, . . . " or "The highlights of my work experience, presented on the enclosed résumé, prove that . . . " are good ways to refer to your résumé.

- Ask for an interview.

- Tell the reader *where* and *when* you can be reached: "at (919) 555-2837 after 5:30 on weekdays," for example. Even though you have listed your phone number on the résumé, you should make the information available in the letter's conclusion as well. Again, the point is to make it easy for your reader to contact you. (*Note:* If you have taped a silly or humorous message on your answering machine, you might want to replace it with a more serious message because potential employers may be calling you for interviews.)

Based on her worksheet, Jamison drafted a letter of application to Interiors Galore (see Figure 11.4 on pages 380–381). See if you agree with Jamison's notes about the letter's strengths and weaknesses. Because the letter of application introduces your résumé, it is your first opportunity to sell yourself to a prospective employer. Jamison recognized some problems, such as length and tone, immediately, but other matters escaped her until she read the letter aloud and critically. Then she realized that some of the information was overwhelming in the letter but would stand on its own in the résumé.

223 Melrose Drive
Reno, NV 47382
22 March 2001

Mrs. Ernestine L'Amour
Interiors Galore
1001 Park Avenue
New York, NY 10012

Dear Mrs. L'Amour:

As a student of the interior design industry, I have combined my college experience with three years' work in interior design. After I graduate in May, I hope to work in the interiors industry, and I believe my experience and design awards are evidence of my creativity, my professionalism, and my potential as a fabric adviser. I would like to be considered for an entry-level fabrics adviser's position at Interiors Galore. I am particularly interested in your work with historic homes and ethnic influences, as I want to get right into that area of work.

I have long followed the industry's trade journals, and I know that Interiors Galore won an award as a front-runner in fabric innovation. I, too, see great potential in the use of ethnic fabrics and influences in creating unique effects for clients. In 1999, as part of our junior class project, I helped select the fabrics for a new display on African Influences for the Nevada Museum of History. The *Reno Observer* called the display "a rich, respectfully elegant use of fabric to recreate the timeless influence of Africa on our state's history." My team was awarded the Eye for Detail Award by Watauga College's Interiors Alumni Association for our work on the museum display.

For my senior project, my team helped plan the redecoration of several homes in the historic Reno district; our choice of fabrics (heavy brocades in rich eggplant and celestial golds) was approved by almost all the influential women in the region. My college work has also been recognized by my winning two other awards: the Outstanding Senior in Interior Design and the Margie Hunter Scholarship for Designing Women.

But my experience goes far beyond being a good student. I have enclosed a résumé, which shows I also have retail experience that has allowed me to put my ideas on

Margin annotations:

not sure she's a Mrs. or likes this title

too drawn out

request is buried

too pushy?

doesn't seem relevant

good evidence ⎤
             ⎬ keep
good evidence ⎦

too long?
too much information—save until interview

doesn't fit here

combine into more meaningful sentence

FIGURE 11.4   Jamison Turnage's Draft of Her Letter of Application, page 1

L'Amour, p. 2
22 March 2001

the line for clients' approval. During summers, I have worked with as many as 10 clients at a time, helping them select fabrics for new and renovated homes. Most of these homes were in the most influential districts of Reno, NV, with many of them appraised at over $1 million. I know that Interiors Galore works with an exclusive clientele, and I believe that my creativity, along with my diplomacy, will suit such clients quite well.

I plan a trip to New York in April, accompanying Anne Tyson, owner of Anne's Fabulous Interiors in Faeford, on a buying trip. Of course our trip includes Interiors Galore's show on Saturday, April 8. I realize that the middle of a show is a poor time for an interview, so could we schedule a time to meet on Monday, April 10? I look forward to hearing from you soon.

Sincerely,

Jamison Turnage

encl: résumé

Margin annotations:
good point

spelling!

add phone number and times when available

weak, abrupt ending

add 1 line space

sign it!

too much space

FIGURE 11.4 Jamison Turnage's Draft of Her Letter of Application, page 2

Like all correspondence, a letter of application should look professional and be error-free. Several other problems commonly occur in letters of application:

- Gimmicky, overconfident, or shocking openers
- Mere restatement of the résumé
- Emphasis on who you know, rather than what you can do
- Emphasis on education as classes, not work preparation
- Presumptuous or pleading tone
- Long-winded, overblown prose or short, choppy sentences
- Apologetic for minimal experience and qualifications
- "I" at the beginning of every sentence
- Emphasis on the writer, rather than on "the organization plus the writer"

APPLICATION

First Impressions and the Letter of Application

Evaluate the following letter of application, identifying its strengths and weaknesses; then, determine what the letter's total presentation says about the writer:

> 12 January 1996
>
> 209 Seats Ave.
> Phoenix, AZ 28473
>
> Human Resources Director
> The Hardware Store
> 1111 Pine St.
> Chicago, IL 90037
>
> Dear Sir:
>
> Are you ready for an innovative new manager at The Hardware Store? I am interested in a management position with The Hardwre Store. I have 7 years' experience working in Chamber's Hardware here in Phoenix. I have worked summers and Christmas vacations since I was 16.
>
> I have enclosed my résumé. With my college degree, I am now ready to move into management. I think my qualifications are exactly what your store needs. Let me show you what I can do for you.
>
> Please let me know when we can meet for an interview.
>
> Sincerely,
>
> *Jeff Simple*
> Jeff Simple
> College Graduate
>
> encl: résumé

If you received this letter, would you be interested in interviewing Jeff? Probably not. Unfortunately, Jeff has made the same kinds of mistakes that many college graduates make when writing the letter of application:

- He has assumed that a man will be reading his letter and résumé.
- He has relied on a rhetorical question as an opener—a poor strategy because the reader may quickly respond "no."
- He has misspelled a word—particularly bad in this case because it's the store's name.
- He talks exclusively about himself—not about The Hardware Store and what he knows about it.

- He has written the letter in short, choppy sentences.
- He assumes that his work experience qualifies him for a management position.
- He assumes that a college degree qualifies him for a management position.
- He assumes he can "fix" The Hardware Store.
- He offers no evidence that he already has *specific* experience that will be valuable to The Hardware Store; instead, he wants to prove himself *after* he gets the job.
- He doesn't provide a phone number and explain when he's available for a conversation.
- He has written a letter that's too short and does not take advantage of the full page he has to sell himself.
- He thinks his college graduate status is worth a final mention.

Refining the Letter of Application

When you have drafted your résumé and letter of application, be sure to consider what you know about the organization to which you are applying. How precisely do your qualifications match the organization's needs? Have you demonstrated that match in the content of your résumé and letter?

In addition to the standard revision strategies presented in Chapter 6, consider the following special pointers for revising your letter of application:

1. Check all names and addresses and telephone, fax, and E-mail numbers.
2. *Read the letter out loud.* Listen for sentences that may not be worded fluently. You may also hear sentences that sound out of place or flat.
3. Revise the organization of your résumé and letter to provide the clearest evidence of how your qualifications fit the organization's needs.
4. Revise each paragraph into a clear entity that sells one or a related set of skills you have.
5. Aim for a readable, one-page letter.
6. Polish your documents' layout and design so that important information is readily recognizable and all information is easily readable.
7. Proofread again and again. Use your spellchecker and ask your friends and advisers who are good proofreaders to review your work.

Based on her own analysis of her letter and the suggestions for revising, Jamison revised her letter (see Figure 11.5 on pages 384–385). What do you think of this version? How to reproduce your communications is discussed in Strategy Review 11.4 on page 385.

changed term of
address to Ms.

shorter opener,
but kept strongest
selling features

direct request for
position

relevance added
match made

kept good evidence

omitted paragraph
on historic
renovations

refers to résumé
in embedded
sentence

work details

match made

ongoing
professional
development

223 Melrose Drive
Reno, NV 23844
22 March 2001

Ms. Ernestine L'Amour
Interiors Galore
1001 Park Avenue
New York, NY 10012

Dear Ms. L'Amour:

Having combined my college studies with three years' work in interior design, I
believe my experience and design awards are evidence of my creativity, my
professionalism, and my potential as a fabric adviser for Interiors Galore. Would
you please consider me for an entry-level designer's position with your firm?

I would particularly like to work for Interiors Galore because of its award-winning
status, noted in last month's *Interiors Today,* for fabric innovation. I, too, see
great potential in the use of ethnic fabrics and influences in creating unique
effects for clients. In 1999, as part of our junior class project, I helped select the
fabrics for a new display on African Influences in Nevada for the Museum of
History. The *Reno Observer* called the display "a rich, respectfully elegant use of
fabric to recreate the timeless influence of Africa on our state's history." My team
was awarded the Eye for Detail Award by Watauga College's Interiors Alumni
Association for our work on the museum display.

As the enclosed résumé shows, I also have retail experience that has allowed me to
put my ideas on the line for clients' approval. During summers, I have worked with
as many as 10 clients at a time, helping them select fabrics for new and renovated
homes. Most of these homes were in the most influential historic districts of Reno
and Raeford, NV, with many of the homes appraised at over $1 million. I know
that Interiors Galore works with an exclusive clientele, and I believe that my
creativity, along with my diplomacy, will suit such clients quite well.

I plan a trip to New York in April, accompanying Anne Tyson, owner of Anne's
Fabulous Interiors in Raeford, on a buying trip. Although our trip includes
Interiors Galore's show on Saturday, April 8, I realize how busy you will be prior
to the show. Could we schedule a time to meet on Monday, April 10? You may

FIGURE 11.5   Jamison Turnage's Revised Letter of Application, page 1

request for interview
and phone numbers
and times available
added

better closing

L'Amour, p. 2
22 March 2001

reach me at (919) 726-3747 on weekdays after 5:30, and I will bring my portfolio
of work for my clients to the interview.

I look forward to hearing from you soon.

Sincerely,

Jamison Turnage

Jamison Turnage

encl: résumé

FIGURE 11.5   Jamison Turnage's Revised Letter of Application, page 2

STRATEGY REVIEW 11.4

REPRODUCING YOUR EMPLOYMENT COMMUNICATIONS

Regardless of the content or the layout of your résumé and letter of application,
the following matters of presentation are standard; violating these conventions
may make it difficult for readers to find pertinent information and may even send
negative messages about your professionalism:

1. Use high-quality paper (20-weight bond) available at most print shops or
   quick-copy centers.

2. Buy additional stationery and envelopes in the same color and texture as
   your résumé to create a unified "look" for your employment documents.

3. Use a conventional paper color and size for your résumé and application letter unless you are in a highly creative field, such as graphics or display (then
   talk with your professors and advisers about your options). Most acceptable
   is white, ivory, or light gray paper that measures 8½ by 11 inches.

4. Use laser printers for printing your résumé and letter of application. Never
   use a dot matrix printer (even one that is *almost* letter quality).

5. When you reproduce your résumé, be sure to get a flawlessly clean copy.
   Then, go to a reputable copy shop and specify the paper you have selected
   for your work. Be firm about the quality of the reproductions you expect; do
   not accept copies that are too light, too dark, or misaligned on the page.

Summary

In this chapter, you have learned some strategic do's and don'ts for writing employment communications; you have also seen models of various résumés and letters of application, designed to show you various options you have in writing these employment communications. Central to each of these strategies and formats is one question: "What best presents *you* to a reader?"

As you plan your employment communications, begin by talking with professors, career advisers, and members of the profession you want to join to learn more about the experience and knowledge your employers will expect of you. Research is one of the most crucial preparatory strategies at your disposal for helping you create a professional résumé and letter of application.

The résumé and letter of application worksheets in this chapter will help you identify the information you want to include in your final documents. The information you generate from these worksheets will help you decide what your most valuable experiences and qualifications are for any particular job.

The formats provided here for chronological, skills and accomplishments, and titles résumés also provide some options for you. They allow you to personalize your résumé while presenting your qualifications in the best possible light. Your best bet may be to experiment with several formats before deciding on the one that is best for you—you might be surprised at the results.

Experience may be the strongest selling feature of your employment communications package, so be certain to include the numerous experiences you have had beyond (or perhaps instead of) full-time, permanent employment. Consider your academic projects, volunteer work, and other experiences that have required you to use particular kinds of knowledge and/or skills or have helped you develop professional characteristics and work habits. (Those experiences are especially useful if you are applying for your first position and have relatively little paid work experience that is directly relevant to your chosen profession.)

Finally, be sure to look at the numerous tips and strategies provided throughout the chapter. These suggestions are based on research gathered from employers who specified their expectations and preferences for the content, organization, and appearance of professional letters of application and résumés.

CHECKLIST

Writing the Résumé

 Never pad your résumé.

 Allow plenty of time to work on drafts of your résumé. You may want to experiment with a variety of formats before deciding which one best presents your qualifications.

✔ Make sure the most important details of your experience and education are presented properly.

✔ Make sure you include relevant details that translate into the work you will be doing in the new position.

✔ List your qualifications using action verbs, not "responsible for" or "duties included."

✔ Provide specifics of your experience to clarify the amount of responsibility you have held.

✔ Select a readable type font and size and incorporate enough white space to make the résumé readable—neither cramped nor sprawling.

✔ Use high-quality paper, a laser printer, and a reputable copy shop for printing and reproducing your résumé.

✔ Enlist the help of a trusted friend or professional to help you review your résumé draft.

✔ Proofread again and again and again.

Writing the Letter of Application

✔ Be sure to complete your research of an organization before beginning to write your letter of application.

✔ Follow the worksheet's strategies for identifying significant facts about the organization to which you want to apply, and then match those facts with details from your own experience.

✔ Rank the items on the worksheet from most impressive, most useful, or most relevant to those that will carry less weight in your letter of application.

✔ In your letter of application, follow these guidelines:
- Aim for a confident, but not arrogant, tone.
- Begin by specifying the job or area in which you want to work.
- Organize the letter's introduction to present your strongest selling points first.

✔ In the body of the letter of application, offer proof that you have the experiences and qualities the organization seeks in its employees.

✔ In the conclusion of the letter, restate your interest in the job, and offer your phone number and times when you can be reached.

EXERCISES

Individual Exercises

1. For each of the following jobs, what personal and professional qualities (besides a college degree) do you think employers seek? If you were reviewing résumés, letters of application, and interview notes, what would you want to find evidence of? How might the successful applicant meet your expectations? An example is provided for you.

   a. Proofreader

   b. Nurse

   c. Landscaper

   d. Minister

   e. Teacher

   f. Insurance sales representative

   Accountant: Able to meet deadlines and handle pressure; knowledgeable about general accounting practices.

   Evidence: Completed college degree in four years; worked two part-time jobs while in college; completed parts 1 and 2 of accounting board examinations.

2. Revise the following groups of items for parallelism. (For help, see the Brief Usage Guidebook at the end of this text.)

   a. Worked on a cruise ship

   b. Guest relations

   c. Answering questions and giving directions

   d. "Most Cheerful Cruiser"

   e. Help cruise director arrange tournaments

   f. Consulting with clients about flower preferences

   g. Planted shrubs

   h. Mulched

   i. Borders

   j. Fertilizer

   k. Pruning

   l. Landscape design

   m. Environmental/ecological concerns

   n. Guided tours through museum

   o. Answering questions

   p. Tour groups of five to fifteen guests

   q. Promoted to head tour guide

   r. Researched eighth-century home furnishing

   s. Knowledgeable about the history of significant artifacts

3. Revise the following list so that the credentials are presented with fresh, active verbs:

   a. Responsible for arranging flowers, taking orders, delivering flowers, charging accounts

   b. Handled customer complaints, additional charges, returns, and credits

   c. Was in charge of customer service, women's clothes, and children's clothes

4. Revise the following list so that it provides more specific information. You may have to invent some details to clarify the applicant's responsibilities and achievements.

   a. Painted houses

   b. Waited tables

   c. Worked in clothing store

   d. Delivered pizzas

   e. Served as fraternity president

   f. Participated on varsity golf team

   g. Worked part-time as nursing attendant at local nursing home

5. Evaluate each of the following job objectives. Do you think each one is strong? Or is each likely to send the reader the wrong message? Be prepared to defend your answers. If you do not like any of the job objectives, present an alternative version.

   a. I want to work in a company that will challenge me.

   b. I want to use my computer skills to develop software that will entertain children.

   c. I want to explore my potential as a manager in a small, private engineering firm.

   d. I want to capitalize on my aggressive ambitions to succeed as a corporate manager.

   e. I want to write feature stories for a culturally aware publication.

6. What do you think each of the following hobbies says about the writer? For what kind(s) of jobs should the writer list each hobby?

   a. Volunteering at hospital

   b. Surfing

   c. Surfing the Internet

   d. Playing golf

   e. Photography

   f. Hiking

   g. Gourmet cooking

   h. Bungee jumping

   i. Reading

Collaborative Exercises

1. How would you organize the following pieces of information about an organization and about a prospective job candidate in order to make that information work for the job applicant? Using the information, write a résumé and letter of application for a position as a rafting guide.

About the Organization

- Recognized as outstanding tour group in the Natahala River
- Has ten fully equipped rafting fleets
- Requires AAA rafting and tour guide certifications
- Has a 100 percent safety record
- Requires completion of safety course prior to hiring
- Large, multinational clientele
- Hosts overnight trips
- Hosts trips lasting three to five days

About the Applicant

- Eight years' experience rafting through Devil's Chasm outside Thunder Bay, Canada
- Experienced with kayaks, rafts, inner tubes, and canoes
- Worked as a guide through the National Park Services, Natahala River Refuge
- Completed AAA rafting certification, but not tour guide certification
- Speaks Spanish fluently
- Has taken several overnight trips, but never hosted them

2. You and your partner(s) are human resources personnel; that is, you daily review résumés and letters of application for positions in your firm. Evaluate the following excerpts from introductions to letters of application and determine whether you would want to keep reading. Why or why not?

Whether it's feeding turkeys or shoveling manure, I have vast amounts of experience working on turkey farms. In fact, after seven years of working here every summer, weekend, and holiday, I feel ready to cluck myself. But seriously, if your new turkey operations need someone with a keen knowledge of feeding, breeding, and house maintenance, I'm your girl.

The stage is set. The lights dim. The curtain goes up. And, suddenly, loud clanging, scrapes, and muffled cries are heard from behind stage. If such an uproar is as mortifying for you as it is for me, let me direct the stage management for your next production. My strength lies in organization—and in letting others know where things belong—so that such mishaps do not detract from the real production that audiences have paid to see.

With a B.S. in psychology and three years' experience working in a research clinician's lab, I am prepared and eager to work for Cutter Laboratories. My areas of specialization focus on laboratory rat experiments with topical anesthetics, an area I know your own technicians have been studying since the late 1980s. My work with Dr. Carter Sawyer has revealed some of the verifiable psychological impacts on rats of such anesthetics, and we published our findings in *Experimental Psychology* (1992—vol. 3).

Extended Collaborative Exercise

3. Prepare a draft of your résumé and letter of application for a particular job of your choice. Then, exchange drafts with a partner (or partners) and answer the following questions about each other's drafts:

Reviewing the Content

About the Résumé:

a. What information on the résumé is most outstanding? Is that the information that *should* be emphasized?

b. Are the writer's name, address(es), and phone number(s) presented as the headings for the résumé? If more than one address or phone number is listed, is it clear when the reader can reach the writer?

c. Has the writer included a job objective? Is it clear and useful or is it naive, arrogant, or vague?

d. Has the writer written a chronological, skills and accomplishments, or titles résumé? Is that selection appropriate for the writer's qualifications and experiences? Why or why not?

e. Is the educational information clear, accurate, and impressive?

f. Do additional courses/seminars listed strengthen the résumé, or are they predictable inclusions in light of the writer's major?

g. If the writer created a chronological résumé, is every item in chronological order?

h. If the writer created a skills and accomplishments résumé, are the outstanding qualities or qualifications readily clear? Are they appropriate for the position?

i. If the writer created a titles résumé, are the job titles and responsibilities clear? Do they make a good argument that this person should be considered for the position?

j. If the writer listed honors and awards, is it clear on what basis each was given?

k. If the writer listed references, is it clear how to reach each one? Is the relationship between the writer and the reference clear or at least presumable?

About the Letter of Application:

a. Does the letter open with a direct request to be considered for a particular job in the organization?

b. Do the supporting details indicate that the writer knows something about the organization to which he is applying and show that the writer sees a place where he will fit into this organization?

c. Does the writer clearly show how her own credentials and experiences would serve the organization?

d. Is the letter formatted professionally? Is it addressed to a specific reader? Is it signed? Does the letter reflect an overall sense of dignity and professionalism?

Reviewing the Form and Design

a. Are all items and topic sentences in the résumé and letter of application relevant?

b. Did the writer use the appropriate paper (color, size, weight)?

c. Are the copies good ones—clear, clean, error-free?

d. Is there plenty of white space so readers don't feel the information is cramped?

e. Is the white space contained so readers don't feel the information sprawls?

f. Did the writer use the amount of pages necessary to present the relevant information?

g. Overall, is the presentation professional? Neat? Attractive? Readable?

Forming an Opinion

a. Based on your partner's résumé and letter of application, how would you describe that person?

b. Do you have any suggestions for how the résumé and/or letter of application might be improved?

c. How successful was your partner in presenting the desired information and image in these employment communications?

➡ ONGOING ASSIGNMENT

■ Based on the work you have done so far to create a newcomer's manual for your primary organization, include a segment for *potential* newcomers. Describe for job applicants the skills, education, and responsibilities expected of employees in your organization (or students at your college).

CHAPTER 12

Informational Reports and Instructions

- **The Audience for Informational Reports**
- **The Purposes of Informational Reports**
- **Topics for Informational Reports**
- **Definitions of Terminology in Informational Reports**
- **Types of Informational Reports**
  Background Reports
  Mechanism Descriptions
  Laboratory Reports
  Process Descriptions
- **Instructional Writing**
  The Instructional Audience
  Writing Instructions
- **Summary**
- **Checklist**
- **Exercises**

Letters and memos conduct most of the day-to-day operations of organizations, but special situations call for special communications, usually in the form of reports. Although some letters and memos are, themselves, reports, we most often think of *reports* as lengthy workplace documents (even ranging to thousands of pages in multivolume works) that communicate about a specific situation, problem, need, or status either within or affecting an organization. Although the uses, frequency, and appearances of reports vary from organization to organization, most reports are more thorough, more sensitive, or more specialized than traditional letters and memos.

With the exception of proposals (a specialized report form discussed in Chapter 14), reports can be classified as either *informational* or *analytical*. An informational report is based on a request to investigate a situation and report specific facts about it; thus, the informational report requires a summary, overview, or explanation. An analytical report is based on a request to investigate a situation and then draw conclusions about its causes, effects, solutions, or any other findings; thus, the analytical report requires you to draw meaning from the information you have, typically to predict consequences or recommend solutions. Table 12.1, which compares a series of reports written about company cars for the XYZ Company, summarizes the differences.

In this chapter, you will learn more about the readers of informational reports and their needs; then, you will learn some of the most frequent topics and purposes of informational reports. Next, the chapter describes the primary types of informational reports, addressing the purpose, content, and reader needs that guide the writing of each type. Strategy Review boxes provide questions that guide your revisions of the various report forms. Although these reports are dis-

TABLE 12.1 A Comparison of Informational and Analytical Reports

Informational	Analytical
1. a description of how company cars are handled in most organizations	1. an investigation of the efficiency of company cars for XYZ
2. a presentation of XYZ's transportation costs over the past three years	2. a discussion of why costs are soaring and likely to continue to rise
3. a description of criteria to be used in analyzing company car possibilities	3. a comparison of car makes and models that concludes with a recommendation of which is best for XYZ
4. a discussion of insurance, maintenance, and other costs associated with company cars	4. a plan to maximize the advantages of company cars while minimizing extra costs

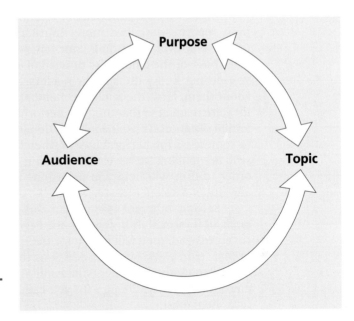

FIGURE 12.1

A Model of the Interrelationship of
Purpose, Audience, and Topic

cussed as freestanding, which they may certainly be, the chapter also points out
that informational reports may also serve as the basis for analytical reports and
may be incorporated into them (see Chapter 13).

Whether a report grows out of a specialized topic and its corresponding elements, the writer's organizational purposes and intended consequences, the audience's need for the report's information, or some combination of these three elements (see Figure 12.1), you will quickly see the value of incorporating audience,
purpose, and topic in all your decisions about the content, structure, tone, and
other elements of an informational report. Ultimately, however, informational reports update or clarify information that allows the audience to draw its own conclusions, make its own decisions, and/or proceed at its own pace.

The Audience for Informational Reports

Although reports are written on various topics and for various purposes, like all
other workplace documents, reports share one essential element: they must be
valuable to somebody. Reports written for the sake of reports contribute to the
paper glut that saps the efficiency and energy of productive workers, and, ironically perhaps, no form of report runs a greater risk of being unnecessary than the
informational report. In the right situation, however, an informational report is
invaluable to its readers. As a workplace writer, therefore, you must carefully
consider how you can make your information relevant to the work and interests
of your readers.

Because of the workplace environment, as well as the topics and purposes of most reports—described more thoroughly below—you are likely to know the people who will be reading your reports: your supervisor or manager, that person's boss, or the employees or head of a department or organization. But even if you do not know the specific readers, you can make some useful assumptions about them. First, the audience members are rarely reading for pleasure; instead, they are reading so that they can perform their jobs or understand a current or potential situation. Thus, the informational reports that you write are usually critical to someone's job performance. Remembering that your readers are busy people who are looking for usable information (not information they have to rework in order to use) will help you determine the organization of your report and the amount of detail to include.

Second, different readers of a particular report may be looking for different kinds of information in that report. Few readers will read a report from cover to cover. Instead, they will search for the information or sections that directly relate to their own work or to the decisions they have to make. Using a variety of formatting options (headings, subheadings, tables of contents, tabs, and other elements discussed in Chapter 9), you can help readers find the segments that concern them most.

Finally, although readers always count on you for accuracy and thoroughness, they may or may not have some experience with the topic of your report. When you are presenting information to readers who have no previous experience or familiarity with the topic, you must first create a context for the information. The context is an initial layer of background information to which the audience must be exposed before taking on the new information (see Figure 12.2).

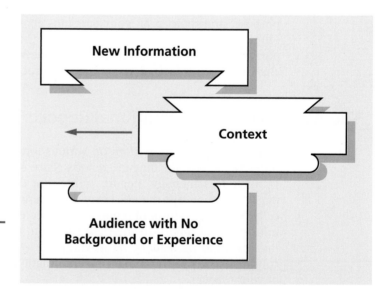

FIGURE 12.2

An Audience without Appropriate Background and Experience Requires an Additional Layer of Information

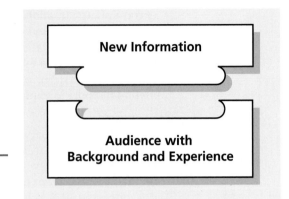

FIGURE 12.3

Accommodation of an Audience
That Has Some Familiarity with
the Topic

When readers have some experience with the topic, they already have a context in which to acquire and process the new information (see Figure 12.3).

Thus, when your readers have no experience with your topic, be sure to provide background and details that will establish a context for your writing. When your readers do have some experience with your topic, however, be careful not to insult them by providing basic details and background information that will be common knowledge to them. Instead, briefly review your shared knowledge (the information that you and the reader both hold about your topic), but focus the majority of your report on information that is new to the readers.

Throughout this chapter, we will continue with the company car scenario set up in Chapter 3 on researching and gathering information. Sarah Snow, you will recall, is responsible for investigating the feasibility of having her company provide cars for its sales representatives. Even though she will ultimately be writing a feasibility study, at this point, she must write an informational report to describe the concept of company-owned vehicles to her managers and to her sales team. She realizes that both groups of readers have several questions about how company cars would affect their business and their work styles. We will follow Sarah's decisions and her resulting documents throughout this chapter.

The Purposes of Informational Reports

The primary purpose of all informational reports is to provide detailed information to a specialized audience. More specifically, reports often fulfill one or a combination of the following purposes:

- *To inform or introduce:* One of the greatest challenges in contemporary organizations is keeping up with the mounds of information available about technology, market trends, tax laws, transportation and distribution developments, personnel issues, trade regulations, and all the other topics that affect any given organization. Informational reports help inform audiences of current affairs. In addition, informational reports directly support analytical reports—policy changes, sales analyses, market analyses, and so on—by establishing the foundation (or givens) for them. A common purpose of all reports, therefore, is to make sure key people receive timely information about relevant matters. For our company car scenario, Sarah might use an informational report to explain to readers the concept of company-owned cars.

■ *To persuade:* Typically, persuasion is associated with analytical reports in which the writer analyzes data, reaches some conclusion, and then tries to convince readers that it is accurate, realistic, or probable. Few reports, however, are actually devoid of persuasive elements; even in information-only reports, you still want to convince your readers that you have a firm grasp of the concepts and details you are describing (that you see both the big picture and the minor, but significant, details) and that you are reporting those details ethically (documenting sources properly, relaying facts and figures accurately, interpreting figures correctly, and portraying the positives and negatives responsibly).

■ *To consolidate:* Because information comes from so many sources—journals, books, news releases, the Internet, colleagues, and numerous other sources—many organizations frequently ask for informational reports that review and consolidate information about a particular topic. For instance, a multinational corporation might want a synthesis of information about legislation affecting its international markets; a health organization might want a synthesis of information about recent cancer research; and the coaching staff of a college basketball team might want a synthesis of information about new NCAA recruiting policies and violations. When you write such a synthesis without interpreting what the information might mean to your reader, you have written an informational report. In our scenario, Sarah might produce a report that describes the advantages and disadvantages of company-owned cars.

■ *To clarify or simplify:* Given the overwhelming amount of information in the workplace, readers frequently rely on informational reports to clarify a new policy, a legal ruling, or other complex information. On their own, for instance, readers might not understand how the tax system encourages companies to own their sales representatives' cars. As the report writer, Sarah must summarize and simplify that tax information in light of the readers' need to understand.

■ *To standardize:* The erratic application of rules and policies is a source of frustration in many organizations. Reports that set out standard procedures for handling such matters can tremendously improve an organization's efficiency and morale. Thus, Sarah might have to prepare informational reports on the standard procedure for selecting company cars or deciding who gets to drive them.

■ *To update:* Perhaps the greatest danger facing most organizations is outdated information. Whether it concerns market trends, investment opportunities,

THE WORLD OF WORKPLACE WRITING

Ethics and Informational Reports

Although matters of accuracy and ethics are most frequently associated with persuasive reports (because writers have the power to choose particular words, phrases, analogies, and bits of information that may affect the readers' understanding and sense of an issue), accuracy and ethics are integral parts of all reports—and, indeed, of all workplace documents.

As an ethical communicator of information, you are responsible for choosing elements that honestly portray the situation, process, solution, or technology in the reports you write. Even simple word choices can have ethical dimensions. For instance, calling a particular automobile model "cheap" rather than "inexpensive" is likely to affect how your readers interpret the suitability of that automobile. Distorting the criteria used to evaluate cars is also unethical, just as it is unethical to rely on only one car manufacturer's literature and then focus on the advantages of those cars. Further, burying information in small print or appendixes is also unethical because it places vital information in places where it is likely to be overlooked.

In the end, remember that your own reputation is at stake. If readers find that you have misled them by careless word choices—or, worse, by intentional exaggerations or omissions of crucial information—you may have a difficult time reestablishing your credibility.

technological capabilities, or personnel availability, outdated information can be even more damaging than no information at all. For example, if executives have no information about safety issues related to a particular auto model, they might decide, based on costs alone, that the Backyard Minivan is the best option for company cars. Additional research, however, might show that the Backyard Minivan has been named in hundreds of lawsuits and is currently facing additional testing to ensure its safety. The executives would look foolish if they placed an order for a hundred minivans without having this updated information.

- *To instruct:* Many reports' primary goal is to educate their readers, and this education can be accomplished in a number of ways—many of them already discussed under the preceding purposes. Thus, updating, standardizing, and persuading are all means of educating readers. Writers also educate readers through instructions, which frequently take on highly specialized forms in the workplace. For readers who need to know how to operate a piece of equipment or fill out application forms, instructions perform a critical role in the workplace. Instructions, along with their special requirements, are described at the end of this chapter as the last form of informational report.

Information for its own sake is rarely as useful to an organization as information that has been interpreted or analyzed to provide some special meaning for that organization. Therefore, most informational reports eventually become the bases for analytical reports. You will learn more about turning your informational reports into analytical reports in Chapter 13.

Topics for Informational Reports

In your first English classes, your instructor may have asked you to provide a plot summary of some short story you had read. Most likely, your instructor was measuring your ability to comprehend a piece of writing: Did you understand the sequence of events and their relationship to each other in the story? Did you understand the characters' motivations, actions, and intent? Did you understand, in fact, what happened in the story? The ability to understand the big picture, as well as the minor details, is good preparation for the informational reports you will be asked to provide in the workplace.

In the workplace, however, readers need informational reports not to determine whether *you* understand what is going on, but to help *them* understand what is going on. Just as you may have explained to your best friend (who didn't have time to read the day's assignment) what happened in the assigned reading, you may now have to explain to readers through summaries and other details the information they have never had the time or opportunity to assimilate.

The need for informational reports arises from various events in the workplace—from routine operations to pressing problems. Some reports are prepared daily (for example, accountings of the preceding day's profits or updates on a design team's progress), whereas others are prepared weekly, monthly, quarterly, or even yearly (annual reports, for example). Sometimes a specific type of report will be prepared only once in an organization's lifetime, as when a final report on a merger with another organization is written.

As Chapter 2's discussion of planning pointed out, your supervisor or manager will frequently assign reports to you, although on occasion you may take the initiative to address a situation on your own. For example, you may realize that your new CEO needs a history of the organization (or your department) in order to understand its operations or needs an explanation of the form of total quality management that your organization has adopted. Only very rarely, however, do workplace writers sit at their desks or in their laboratories or workshops and try to think of something to write a report about. Instead, they respond to a specific request to address a particular audience need.

The remainder of this chapter describes some of the most common informational reports in the workplace. As you read, make sure that you understand the role such reports play both as freestanding documents and as potential sources for analytical reports and that you also understand the basic strategies for writing them.

Developing an Informational Document

Either individually, with a partner, or as part of a team, you should work toward developing a guide to restaurants (or theaters or laundry services) in your area. Because this document will be an informational report, you will describe and present options, but you will not analyze the quality of the restaurants (or other businesses).

At this stage, decide who your readers will be and why they will read your guide. Then, clarify your guide's purpose accordingly. Finally, determine whether you want to limit your topic in some way, such as including only one district of your city or covering only one type of restaurant such as fast-food restaurants, fine dining establishments, or quirky cafés.

Definitions of Terminology in Informational Reports

Occasionally, you may find yourself working in such a cutting-edge environment that you will be compelled to create and define new terminology for your readers. In other cases, your readers may not be familiar with your field's or your organization's specialized terminology, so you will have to provide definitions for them.

Generally, definitions make up *part* of a workplace document—not the entire document—and concern abstract notions and distinctions between unknown, commonly misunderstood, or confusing terms. Depending on your readers and their understandings, your definitions may be *brief* or *extended*. A brief definition is typically a one- or two-sentence explanation of a term that follows a standard format:

Term = group/class + distinguishing features.

In other words, the term's meaning is comprised of the category of objects or processes to which it belongs (class), along with the elements that distinguish it from other objects or processes in that group (distinguishing features). For example:

Odometer = a measurer of distance that is standard equipment on an automobile.

The biggest problem in writing a brief definition is that the features that distinguish the item must be exclusive to it. Do you see any problems with the following brief definition?

Dog = an animal that barks and wags its tail.

After a moment's thought, you probably realized that some dogs do not bark and that some dogs do not have tails to wag. Further, seals bark, and they tend to wag their rear ends when they are moving or excited. Is a seal a dog, too? Creating unique distinctions that will help readers clearly understand your term can be a challenge, but it can also be an interesting exercise in critical thinking and problem solving. Again, working with your colleagues who can help point out weaknesses in your definitions is invaluable.

Typically, the more complex the term and the more essential it is to the readers' understanding, the more likely you are to need an extended definition. To create an extended definition, start with the brief definition formula, and then extend it by answering any (or all) of the following questions:

- What is the history of this object, process, or phenomenon?
- What is it made of?
- How does it work?
- What does it do?
- Who uses it?
- What is it similar to?
- How is it different?
- What does it look like (shape, color, weight, height, length, thickness, or other characteristics)?
- What rules govern its operation?
- What are some examples of this term?

On numerous occasions, your writing tasks will extend beyond informing readers of problems, situations, and other common workplace topics. In these situations, you must provide the very beginning understanding of a topic or term, and your ability to write clear definitions to meet those needs will help you communicate with the reader.

Types of Informational Reports

The following descriptions of common informational report forms will clarify not only the purpose for each type of report, but also its audience and the common topics it addresses. Remembering that informational reports serve an incredibly important function for those who are not yet knowledgeable about situations, equipment, procedures, and other workplace issues will help you stay focused on your readers and their needs.

In these descriptions of four informational report forms, we build on the company car scenario to demonstrate the audience/purpose/topic relationship in each type of report. Notice how the audience accommodation and writer/reader purposes change from report form to report form.

Background Reports

From your experience with television news, you are probably familiar with background briefings at the White House between the president's staff and members of the media. These briefings are designed to bring the reporters "up to speed"—to make sure they know the foundation on which the new information, to be released during the press conference, will be based. This background information does not require interpretation or analysis: it is presented as facts on which all subsequent information will rest.

In the workplace, numerous reports are also written "for information only," meaning that the report writer merely wants the reader to be familiar with the background or events surrounding a particular situation. Most likely, the writer does not want the reader to act on the information in the report, perhaps because the situation has already been handled or because the topic is highly sensitive, the sources of information a bit suspect, or the general atmosphere of the workplace poorly suited for action. Because background reports merely summarize the current or background situation, they often read more like a term paper than a workplace report. The background report may even merge with the other forms of informational reports, described later. Nevertheless, background reports are incredibly important to appropriate readers because they fill in details that are otherwise missing from the readers' store of knowledge, and they often prevent embarrassing questions or assumptions that might damage morale or the progress on a project.

Although the topics for background reports vary, most of them provide either generic information about trends in the market or specific information about the history of some event. A request for generic information might begin like this: "The CEO says we need to look into putting our sales catalog on-line. I don't even know what being 'on-line' means. What's it all about?" Questions such as "How did we plan our expansion into Saudi Arabia?" or "What were the legal steps we went through to resolve that EPA investigation last year?" might lead to reports providing specific information about an event. For example, in our company car scenario, a report on how sales representatives' travel expenses currently are handled might be useful for the new CEO who is proposing that the company investigate the advantages of owning company cars. This historical perspective will help the CEO determine how effective the current system has been and whether it should be altered.

Because background reports contain little information on which to act, writers should carefully consider how their report *can* be used:

- As the basis for an analytical report?
- As a historically and/or legally accurate record?
- As evidence of actions?
- As evidence of the thinking behind certain actions?
- As speculation?
- As gossip?

Although you cannot necessarily control how readers will use the information you provide in a background report, you should specify how you intend the information to be used. (See Strategy Review 12.1.) A simple statement of purpose in the introduction of your report (as you learned to compose in Chapters 2 on planning and 5 on drafting) can clarify your intent:

> This background report should help readers understand how car reimbursements for automobile expenses have historically been handled at XYZ Corporation. This information can then be used to analyze the feasibility of investing in company-owned cars for our sales representatives and, perhaps, for our upper-level management.

Such a statement of purpose not only provides a guideline to help you determine which information is and is not relevant for your report, but also shows your reader the kind of information you have provided (and excluded) from your work.

STRATEGY REVIEW 12.1

THE BACKGROUND REPORT

Writing a background report requires astute attention to details, tone, and sources of information. When you are asked to write a background report, be sure to consider the answers to these questions:

1. Have you determined the purpose behind the request for a background report? Is it an ethical purpose? Does the requester want you to document some event or check into someone's past? For what purpose?

2. Have you researched the situation carefully, drawing from as many sources as possible? Your own observations and recollections may be valuable in many situations, but they probably should not be the sole source for this document. Ask sources if they are willing to be quoted for your report. If they are not, do you want to use their information for your report?

3. Have you determined the best organization for your report? Historical accounts should, of course, be arranged chronologically, but other topics (such as why night employees prefer a particular policy) might be better served by alternative organizational patterns (see Chapter 4).

4. Have you drafted the report, being certain to incorporate the crucial elements of a standard introduction—subject, purpose, audience, scope and limitations, methods, definitions (optional), and plan of organization? These elements will help you control the content and uses of your background report (see Chapter 5).

5. Have you incorporated graphics, as needed, into the text—especially where they show relationships between ideas (see Chapter 8)?

6. Have you inserted headings, subheadings, and other layout features that will clarify the information and organization for your readers (see Chapter 9)?

7. Have you revised carefully, keeping the needs of the readers in mind (see Chapter 6)?

Figure 12.4 shows an excerpt from a background report that reviews XYZ Corporation's handling of transportation for its employees. Special features in the report, noted in the margin, address particular reader concerns or needs for information.

Mechanism Descriptions

Mechanism descriptions are used most frequently in technical and engineering settings. These reports explain to readers how a particular mechanism, tool, or piece of equipment is put together and how it works. You may be called on, for instance, to describe how an engine works, how a safety lever operates, or how one piece of equipment can be converted to work in additional ways, such as how a drill can be converted to a screwdriver.

The underlying rhetorical purpose of mechanism descriptions—a purpose that is likely to be revealed in later analytical reports—may be to explain why a mechanism has failed to work or to persuade readers that it will, indeed, work. Again, your first consideration must be your audience: How much do readers already know about this mechanism? Why do they want to know more? How will they use this information? In planning to write a mechanism description, consider what you want readers to know about the mechanism and present an ethical description that acknowledges both the strengths and the weaknesses of that mechanism. In addition, you may also need to include sections on one or more of the following:

- The history of the mechanism—early versions of the device, other attempts to construct such a mechanism, and, perhaps, why those attempts failed.
- The uses of the mechanism—whether it can be used for only one purpose or to perform multiple tasks.
- A description of the mechanism—its color, shape, size, weight, height, and materials.
- The moving parts of the mechanism—gears, hands, pistons, blades, or flywheels.
- The stationary parts of the mechanism—bases, cover, pedestal, or cylinders.
- How those moving and stationary parts fit together—by cables, nuts and bolts, or belts.

**Summary of XYZ's Handling of Transportation
for Sales Representatives**

This report describes the current method of handling transportation for sales representatives at XYZ Corporation. The report should help the new CEO, Branch McGraw, gain a historical perspective on this method as well as begin to make some assessments about the possibility of changing the system. The report describes the earliest moves to a systematic handling of transportation and reimbursements but does not address the various accounting procedures that have been used over the years. Following this introduction, the report addresses the early years when the corporation established its sales transportation methods and then addresses the philosophy and move to a systematic transportation policy.

The Early Years: Establishing a Sales Team

In 1966, XYZ Corporation opened its doors as a building supplier for contractors and do-it-yourselfers. Sales teams, as such, were merely clerks who received orders from customers at the front desk and then went to find the requested items in catalogs and in the warehouse.

By 1970, the owners of XYZ had decided to develop the company's own line of specialized products, with emphasis on higher-end lines of windows, doors, and exterior finishings. With this decision came the move toward an external sales team that would call on contractors and, later, on home builders/owners themselves.

In the early years, these sales representatives owned their own cars, as they do now, and were paid $.12 per mile for their gasoline, oil, tires, and wear-and-tear on their vehicles. Representatives were encouraged to trade cars regularly for increased safety and reliability, but limits on the age of cars were not incorporated into the organization's policy until some years later.

As the sales teams grew, a more systematic approach to handling transportation was desirable so that budget estimates could anticipate expenses.

The Beginnings of a Transportation Philosophy

The first move away from the established reimbursement system actually had little to do with reimbursements. In fact, it was more of a determined philosophical initiative, based on the assumption that quality products demand a quality image. Some of the sales representatives were driving old vehicles while representing XYZ, and the owners of the corporation decided that these vehicles conveyed a poor image of the company.

Marginal annotations:

topic, purpose, and audience

scope and limitations

plan of organization

earliest background establishes chronological organization

shift to second phase of chronology

FIGURE 12.4   An Excerpt from a Background Report, page 1

Summary of XYZ's Handling of Information
p. 2

In response, the owners imposed several limitations on the kinds of vehicles representatives could drive:

- The vehicle could be no more than three years old.
- The vehicle had to be either white, black, or red.
- The vehicle had to be maintained properly (both internally and externally).

Although the sales representatives understood the philosophy (and even seemed to approve of it), they heartily disliked rules imposed on their car purchases. The company's take-it-or-leave-it attitude also irked them. . . .

The Current State of Sales Representatives' Transportation

Currently, our sales representatives drive sport utility vehicles, pre-approved by the company, because of their maneuverability and appropriateness both on and off the road. The construction sites to which our teams must drive make regular cars less suitable, and sport utility vehicles are also useful for hauling small deliveries, which occasionally our teams must make.

According to a recent survey, the sales representatives like these vehicles, considering them sporty, utilitarian, and fun to drive. The contractors who comment about the vehicles note their attractiveness, but occasionally make caustic remarks about the cost of the vehicles (and, consequently, our price margins).

Currently, our representatives are reimbursed on a modulated scale that acknowledges that older cars require more maintenance:

$.30 per mile for a 1-year-old car
$.31 per mile for a 2-year-old car
$.32 per mile for a 3-year-old car

The greatest perceived problem with this scale is that it seems to encourage representatives to hold on to older cars because they receive more reimbursement. . . .

Conclusion

Currently, our sales staff is comprised of seven representatives who travel for the company. Three additional inside sales members are not affected by the transportation guidelines set forth in the company policy manual.

A final survey of sales representatives found that four like the current system of reimbursement and three do not like the system. A company-owned car policy might rectify the concerns and dislikes of those who are unhappy with the current system.

moving to
current
situation

continued, but
omitted from
excerpt shown

to-the-minute
review and
opinions of the
system—with
no analysis
from writer

FIGURE 12.4 An Excerpt from a Background Report, page 2

- Similarities to and differences from other mechanisms—a computer's similarity to and difference from a typewriter, for instance.

- Who (and in what capacity) might find the mechanism useful—specialists, novices, scientists, technicians, or do-it-yourselfers.

- Any special requirements for using the mechanism—voltages, a dust-free environment, safety gear, oxygen tanks, safety goggles, gloves, or special clothing.

- Any warnings or safety precautions—shut-off procedures and fire precautions.

Graphics such as a photograph or line drawing of the mechanism may also enhance your description (see Chapter 8). (See Strategy Review 12.2.)

Figure 12.5 presents a description of an odometer, a device used to measure mileage for leased company cars. This description is aimed at the reader who wants to know, "How will the mileage be reliably calculated on our company cars when we are ready to trade them in?" In this case, the reader wants both an overview of how the mechanism works and *specifics* on how the odometer's reliability is gauged.

S T R A T E G Y   R E V I E W   1 2 . 2

THE MECHANISM DESCRIPTION

When writing a mechanism description, ask yourself the following questions:

1. Have you determined how readers will use your mechanism description? How will your description aid them in performing their jobs, making decisions, or recognizing appropriate uses of the mechanism? Will they have to write analytical documents based on your informational report? Have you presented the best criteria for discussing the mechanism in light of that possibility?

2. Have you considered all possible means for developing your mechanism description? In light of the mechanism itself, which ones will be useful for your description as well as for your readers and their reasons for reading your description?

3. Have you determined the best way to organize your description? Most mechanism descriptions are arranged from a particular view of the mechanism—front to back, top to bottom, side to side, and the like. How will the reader approach or first see the mechanism? Is that the best way to begin your description?

4. Have you drafted your introduction, clarifying the subject, purpose, audience, scope and limitations, methods, definitions (optional), and plan of organization? These elements will help you keep your readers' needs in mind as you write and revise your description.

(continued on page 410)

Reliability Assurances for the
New Fleet's Odometer Readings

context, audience,
and purpose

The purchase of a fleet of company cars is almost complete, but a few matters of quality control have yet to be addressed. Specifically, the owers have asked for a thorough investigation of the reliability of odometer readings for the cars. Although test research can be performed that would precisely measure the odometers' reliability, we have neither the time nor the instruments to perform such tests. Our research, therefore, is a compilation of data gathered from other researchers who have conducted highly specialized calibrations on Milers, the odometer brand installed in our new company cars.

scope and
limitations

methods

plan of
organization

This report describes those odometers in terms of their historical performance and reliability, the parts that measure reliability and gauge working conditions, and the particular reliability ratings the odometers have generated over the past five years.

first major topic

The Historical Assessment of Milers Odometers

history/rationale

Milers odometers were first manufactured in 1952 in direct response to the frequent failure of other odometers. Through the years the Milers odometer has been tested and found to surpass all other odometers in reliability and low maintenance. . . .

initial tests

comparison

The Milers odometer has performed significantly better than its closest competitor, the Gauge Plus odometer, over the past twenty years. As Figure 1 shows, tests verify that Milers odometers have had fewer failures and less variance in calibration than Gauge Plus odometers:

graphic
comparison

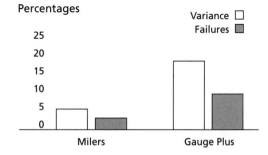

Figure 1: Bar Chart Comparing the Milers and Gauge Plus Odometers

Reliability Assurances for Odometer Readings
p. 2

Parts of the Milers Odometer

parts description

One of the soundest features of the Milers odometer is the pin drop that holds the gears in place. If something happens to the pin drop, the entire mechanism quits operating. This means that the speedometer also quits working, immediately alerting the driver to the failure.

introduces graphic and tells reader what to look for

Figure 2 shows the pin drop and the gear shaft of the Milers odometer. Note that the . . . .

graphic enhances description

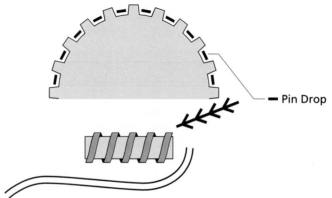

Figure 2: Illustration of the Pin Drop in the Milers Odometer

As this illustration shows, the pin drop cannot release from the . . . .

FIGURE 12.5 An Excerpt from a Mechanism Description, page 2

---

5. Have you looked for opportunities to use graphics in your description? Cut-away drawings, illustrations, and photographs may be particularly useful to your readers (see Chapter 8).

6. Have you revised your document, remembering to focus on the kinds of information the readers will need and the ways they will expect to see that information?

Laboratory Reports

As you might guess, a laboratory report typically describes the testing, research, and other work that goes on inside a laboratory. Unlike a research report, which interprets or analyzes the data (see Chapter 13), laboratory reports rarely include much interpretation of the data they list. Instead, they usually chronicle work in progress—the daily or weekly readings or measurements on whatever phenomenon, mechanism, or organism is under study. A research report, for example, might discuss the extreme temperatures to which an engine may be subjected and recommend suitable temperature ranges for operation, whereas the laboratory report will document the particular tests and the routine findings of those tests.

Depending on the size and funding of any given project, laboratory reports may be written by technicians or by the principal investigator or researcher. As a record of observations and measurements, laboratory reports can verify the rigor with which a study was conducted, the accuracy of data and figures, and the particular treatments, times, or variations noted regarding the subject or specimen. The researchers can then use this information to write the methods section of their research reports, to justify their request for additional funding, or to support their diagnoses or other interpretations of their data. Figure 12.6 shows an example of data from a laboratory report. As presented, this information may mean little to you or any other reader, but after it is interpreted by the principal researcher in an analytical research report, readers will understand that engine 3 shows tremendous variance between Condition 1 and Condition 2, resulting in its overheating at 91°C.

Laboratory reports are frequently form oriented; that is, they adhere to a chart or fill-in-the-blank format that demands particular pieces of information at every interval of the investigation. As such, they may not require very much writing per se—unless, of course, the principal investigator or researcher asks that unusual patterns or variations be noted. (You can probably see how such observa-

	Condition 1	*Condition 2*	*Results*
Engine 1	87°	92°	engine a bit jerky; some discoloration of coolant
Engine 2	84°	88°	engine stable; no discoloration of coolant
Engine 3	74°	91°	engine overheated; coolant discolored

FIGURE 12.6 Data from a Laboratory Test on Company Car Engines

tions can easily turn into the fodder for an analytical report, described in Chapter 13, which will require you to interpret such readings or speculate on their causes.) Then, the ability to describe such information and observations becomes critical to the overall research project, making your job and your writing as a laboratory technician even more crucial.

If you are writing a complete laboratory report, you must be conscientious about the criteria you set up for observation and categorization, and you must be certain to apply your criteria as consistently as possible. Again, objectivity plays a large role in this form of informational report, and as we have seen, objectivity is pretty much a matter of perspective (just as other elements of your writing situation are). Nevertheless, any perceptions that you have been unfaithful to the data or have not accurately reported what you saw or found in your experiments may have severe repercussions on your work, your credibility, and, ultimately, your job. (See Strategy Review 12.3.)

STRATEGY REVIEW 12.3

THE LABORATORY REPORT

If you have to write a laboratory report, the following strategies will help guide your decisions; further, if your laboratory report will be the basis for a research report (described in Chapter 13), the information you present may be even more critical:

1. If you are using a prepared form for your report, have you reviewed the form carefully and determined exactly what kind of information each question is soliciting?

2. If you are not using a form, have you considered making one of your own that will let you look for consistent kinds of information during each of your observations? Generous margins can be used to note additional observations and descriptions, whenever necessary.

3. Have you used appropriate measurements, spellings, and descriptors in your observations?

4. Have you specified even the slightest differences you have noted about the performance, appearance, sound, smell, or feel of the item in your routine observances?

5. Have you used graphics for any aspects of your experiment that are difficult to describe in language? You may find the proper words at a later time and incorporate them with the graphic into a clearer, more useful research report.

6. Have you revised the report to provide the appropriate information for your readers' needs, based on how the readers will use the information you provide?

Process Descriptions

In many organizations, standardized procedures allow the smooth and timely operation of daily routines. Such procedures may involve posting revenues and accounts receivable, taking inventory, acknowledging contributions, or helping people apply for retirement benefits. In addition, many people like knowing how things are done—even if they are not directly responsible for performing that task. As a consumer, for instance, you might like to know how your meat is inspected, even though you do not intend to inspect meat yourself. You might want to know how microwave ovens work, how a thermometer measures temperature, or how computers process data and analyze statistics. To find out such information, you would read *process descriptions*, which describe how something works or how something is made. (See Strategy Review 12.4.)

On other occasions, you may need to know how to perform certain tasks or functions yourself: how to load a software program onto your computer, how to use a food processor, or how to change the oil in your car. In these cases, you would read *instructions*, which provide step-by-step guides to performing a particular task. On the job, instructions help your reader perform routine or specialized tasks according to the organization's way of doing things.

Thus, the primary difference between process descriptions and instructions lies in who (or what) is performing the task: if readers merely want to know how something works, happens, or is made, they will read process descriptions. If they want to perform the task themselves, they will read instructions. As a writer, you must determine your readers' intentions and purpose for reading.

STRATEGY REVIEW 12.4

THE PROCESS DESCRIPTION

The discussion of organizing information in Chapter 4 presents sound advice for developing the information you need for writing process descriptions (and instructions). When writing process descriptions, be sure to reconsider these issues:

1. Has your introduction provided the reader with an overall sense of the process you are describing—or at least what the final product will be?

2. Does your introduction include the standard information—subject, purpose, audience, scope and limitations, methods, definitions (optional), and plan of organization?

3. Have you drafted the information, beginning with the segment of the process with which you are most familiar?

4. Have you revised the draft to put information in the correct order and to explain clearly the relationship between various steps of the description?

5. Have you reviewed the document again to be sure that you have not omitted steps and that your reader will understand your descriptions?

(continued)

6. Have you incorporated graphics that show the progress of the description, the cycle of the process, or the stage at which the reader is currently reading?

7. Have you highlighted special features or requirements that the reader might need to know?

8. Have you incorporated headings and subheadings that tell readers at which stage of the activity they are?

9. Have you read your description as if you were a first-time observer of the process and then revised it as needed? Have you asked someone who is familiar with the process to read your description to make sure you have not omitted steps? Have you asked someone who is unfamiliar with the process to read your description to make sure it is clear?

Figure 12.7 presents an excerpt from a process description, describing how an automobile dealership sets up procedures for selling and buying back company cars. Be sure to note the difference in tone between this description and what you would expect from instructions, which more often address "you" the reader because the writer assumes that you are reading instructions to *do*, not merely to learn or understand.

Instructional Writing

"When in doubt, read the instructions." That bit of humor (and wisdom) underscores the state in which many of us find ourselves when trying to assemble a complicated piece of machinery or work through a complicated procedure. Our brains may tell us we can figure it out for ourselves, but the complexities of fitting tab A into slot B tell us otherwise.

Considering the daily barrage of instructions that we face (how to open the milk container, how to take medicine properly, and how to use an ATM), it is little wonder that we have become somewhat oblivious to instructions and to the strategies that good instruction writers use to communicate their message. Further, the new wave of on-line instructions for operating computer software (which are too complex to treat in this text) means that we have instructions embedded within processes, creating special problems for instruction writers and readers. In fact, you may be somewhat surprised to discover that the relationship between writer and reader is not always as straightforward as it may seem, as this section describes.

The Instructional Audience

Audiences for instructions are assumed to be potential performers of the tasks described. The word *potential* is included in recognition that a number of readers read instructions to determine whether they are capable of performing them (or

George Foss Auto Warehouse:
Procedures for Providing Company Fleets

This report reviews the process by which George Foss Auto Warehouse (GFAW) buys and sells company fleets. For companies with more than three employees driving company cars, this report assesses the procedure that we follow when contracting with a company to provide its fleet. (For individual company purchases, these guidelines do not apply—see the sales manager.) Our procedures have been developed with the highest industry standards in mind, as well as the most generous system for buying and selling company cars. The remainder of this process report describes the role we play as procurers of fleets, as well as the roles the individual corporations will play.

Step One: Assessing Corporate Needs

The most critical step in providing company cars is one that many dealerships overlook: determining corporate needs. Although most dealerships simply determine the number of cars your company needs and let you pick out the car that the purchasing agent likes best, we at GFAW spend time talking with the drivers of these cars, determining their needs for the following crucial elements:

- Storage and space requirements
- Prestige
- Hauling
- Safety
- Mileage

Then, we talk with the budget officers of the corporation to determine the price range for initial purchases. Although some flexibility in pricing may be standard practice in buying automobiles, we set our initial prices at the lowest possible price because of the volume business your company is offering us. Thus, the prices you will receive on the cars you select are below wholesale price and could not be offered on a single purchase.

Step Two: Selecting the Car Model(s)

After assessing driver needs and the budget for the fleet, we meet with the managers/owners of the company and the members (or a representative) of the sales team to select the car model that best meets the drivers' needs and the company's image. We believe that if either group is dissatisfied with the selection, the fleet is destined to be a failure.

Marginal annotations (left column):

- title indicates topic and report form
- purpose/topic
- audience
- scope and limitations
- methods
- plan of organization
- first major phase as heading
- note parallel structure of headings
- note effective use of bulleted list
- second major phase as heading
- description and details

FIGURE 12.7 An Excerpt from a Process Description, page 1

George Foss Auto Warehouse
p. 2

In addition to models, we determine whether there are any restrictions on color. (Note: Although some dealerships insist that all cars be the same color, we have arrangements with the manufacturers that allow individual drivers to select whatever color they wish, although some popular colors mean a delay in shipping.)

third major phase as heading

Step Three: Selecting Special Options

After determining which car models will be ordered, we consider the addition of special options within the company's budget. We try to offer these options as packages because special requests can lead to delays in shipping, but we do fill special options at the company's request. Sunroofs, electric windows, and CD players are some of the options we encourage companies to consider—not because they increase the cost of these cars, but because their salespeople are going to be spending a great deal of time in these cars: their satisfaction (and these special features tend to increase satisfaction) is paramount.

fourth major phase as heading

Step Four: Purchasing and Ordering the Cars

Once the special features are selected, we are ready to place the order for your company fleet. We work directly with the manufacturer and distributors, so we can tell you the day your fleet will arrive, barring any unforeseen disasters.

details of costs

Your costs are determined by the model and special options you have requested. At the time of the order, we require a 50% payment on the 25% down payment. In other words, if your order will cost $100,000, we ask for $12,500. When the cars are shipped, we ask for the second installment of $12,500. After that installment, the remaining 75% is put on your corporate account and paid just as you would make payments on a personal car you own.

fifth major phase as heading

Step Five: Accepting Delivery

. . . (process continues)

Because mistakes do happen, and because we at GFAW want your complete satisfaction, we encourage you to inspect each of your purchased automobiles completely before accepting delivery. . . .

F I G U R E 12.7 An Excerpt from a Process Description, page 2

have the time, energy, materials, equipment, or inclination to perform them). You have probably thumbed through a recipe book, looking at ingredients of various dishes until you find a combination that sounds appetizing; then, you read the instructions to see whether you have the culinary skills, ingredients, and equipment to actually create this dish. As likely as not, you flip through a number of recipes before settling on one that sounds both appetizing and manageable. In short, readers of instructions may be reading to do, but they may also be reading to determine whether they can (or want to) do. Thus, the purpose of instructions is not just to explain how to do something, but also to reassure readers that they can, indeed, do that task.

Written instructions commonly incorporate the stylistic and formatting strategies we all associate with properly written instructions: stylistically, instructions address "you," the doer, in numbered steps. That attention to "you," the reader, will help you, the writer, remember that readers approach a set of instructions with varying skill levels. Thus, you must decide at the outset how sophisticated or naive your readers are about the task they are trying to perform. The numerical listing of tasks helps readers keep their place in the outline of steps and assures them you have accounted for each activity required. Your own meticulous attention to details will help you make sure you do not omit or misorder steps.

Reader Alerts for Instructions

Because readers of instructions are most often reading to perform a task (or to determine whether they can or want to perform a task), most instructions incorporate various forms of assurances that help readers as they proceed. Consider the advantages of reading special warnings and descriptions that acknowledge where readers typically go wrong in following instructions. The following phrases can alert a reader to danger:

> *not to be confused with* (the yellow–green liquid in the taller vial)
>
> *do not* (mix the two ingredients until a blue vapor appears)
>
> *just as you performed the step previously* (in the salinization process)
>
> *if you get a smoky odor* (discontinue the process and start over)

Most common, of course, are the warnings and cautions that accompany many dangerous procedures. The difference between a warning and a caution is an industry standard:

> WARNING signals potential danger to people.
>
> CAUTION signals potential danger to equipment.

Additionally, many industries use color (typically bright red, neon orange, or lime green) in their instruction manuals or in the workplace where danger lurks.

Finally, and perhaps most usefully, many instructions include graphics that show readers how the object is supposed to look at this stage, how pieces fit together, or how the computer screen looks in the current stage. By comparing their object with the graphic, readers can determine whether they are on the right track.

Writing Instructions

When writing instructions, remember the importance of strict chronological order (see Chapter 4) as a means for organizing information. Then, use the following guidelines in making your revisions:

- Make sure you have clarified the level of information the reader needs to perform the task. Decide how much you can assume the reader knows and how much specialized information you will have to provide for the uninitiated reader.

- Early in the instructions, describe all the needed equipment, materials, ingredients, and program and/or hardware/software requirements necessary to complete the task.

- Carefully review the order of information in your draft, making sure each step follows in a strict sequence, is adequately linked to previous steps, and is numbered accordingly.

- Address the reader as "you" throughout; clarify the doer of each step if more than one performer is involved.

- Include transitions within and between steps as needed to clarify actions that follow one another, precede one another, go on simultaneously, or have some other specialized relationship to another step.

- Carefully review your description of all the steps to make sure your reader can understand what is required at each stage.

- Include "signposts" that reassure readers that they are doing the right thing. Add warnings or cautions that anticipate whether they are about to do something wrong.

- Incorporate graphics that show the relationship of one step (or phase of steps) to another or show how the object (or computer screen) should look at this point.

- Review your draft to make sure your instructions are accurate, clear, and concise. Have you asked others who are familiar with the process to review your instructions? Have you asked someone who is unfamiliar with the process to try and perform your instructions?

In the company car scenario, the company's purchasing officer needs instructions for ordering and paying for an entire fleet of automobiles. Not only is the process unfamiliar, but the repercussions of ordering the wrong cars or the wrong options, or agreeing to the wrong purchase price, could be disastrous. Figure 12.8 shows an excerpt from these instructions. Note the common elements of

**Procedures for Receiving Delivery
of a Company Car Fleet**

These instructions describe the procedures purchasing agents should follow when receiving a company car fleet. The instructions should be followed scrupulously because miscommunications about ordering and delivery cannot be corrected.

These instructions describe the language and methods for filling out the attached receiving form (see Appendix A). The variations in responses for each category of information are limited. If you have questions about possible responses, please ask someone in our Purchasing and Ordering Division (POD) before submitting this form.

I. Physical Accounting and Receiving

1. Obtain your original copy of the purchasing agreement.

2. Check off each car as it is presented to you. Because many cars look the same, be certain to check for all of the following:

   ☐ Exterior color

   ☐ Interior color

   ☐ Interior fabric

   ☐ Roof color

   ☐ Options

     • Radio/CD/Cassette

     • Wheel covers

     • Arm rests

     • Steering wheel bands

3. Accept the keys *only after you have matched the car to your purchase order.*

II. The Paper Trail: Accounting and Receiving

1. Attach a copy of the original purchasing agreement to the receiving form (see Appendix A).

2. Find a copy of each invoice and compare it to the original purchasing agreement to match an invoice to each car received.

Margin annotations (left column):

audience
context/purpose
special concerns

attachment with
additional
information

source of help

first segment of
instructions

note consistent
use of understood
"you" as subject
of each step

boxes make
check-off easier

italic type
emphasizes
information

second segment
of instructions

reference to
attachment

FIGURE 12.8 An Excerpt from a Set of Instructions, page 1

Procedures for Receiving Delivery
p. 2

3. Verify the purchase order numbers and receiving numbers.

4. Verify the purchase price on the invoice and on the receiving form.

5.   Total the purchase prices from all invoices.

6. Add the tax, license, destination, and port fees for each vehicle.

7. Subtract the down payment, made before ordering the fleet.

specific references to other sites of information

8. Have the company owner sign the contract agreement for receiving (see Appendix B).

9. Initial the owner's signature, verifying your witnessing of it, and sign line 27 of the agreement.

10. Submit the original paperwork to our office, with the second copy going to your firm's legal representative. Submit the third form to your bank.

third segment of instructions

III. Removing the Vehicles from Our Lot

Because our liability ends when you sign the papers, any damages incurred on our lot or driving out of our lot are the purchasing company's responsibility. For a fee, however, our fleet drivers will deliver your vehicles to your primary site. To arrange for delivery, follow these instructions:

additional information forms

1. Fill out a copy of the Delivery Agreement (see Appendix C), which authorizes our drivers to move the vehicles from our lot to the destination of your choice.

2. Have your owner or a representative sign the legal release form (see Appendix D) and attach it to this contract.

3. Leave the keys with the POD.

4. Agree, with the POD and the Delivery Team Manager, on the date and time of delivery.

explanation of rationale

. . . (instructions continue)

5. Be prepared to sign a new acceptance form (see Appendix E) when the vehicles are delivered to you. This form acknowledges that all vehicles arrived in prime condition, barring routine roadwear such as mud splatters, rain streaks, etc. . . .

F I G U R E   12.8   An Excerpt from a Set of Instructions, page 2

Drafting Your Guide

Based on the parameters you have set (audience, purpose, topic limitations) for your restaurant guide, prepare a draft of the guide. Provide all the descriptions that would suit the readers' needs, but do not analyze the quality of the restaurants. Then, consider how other forms of informational and instructional reports could also be useful to your audience. Incorporate those forms, where appropriate, into your guide.

instructions: an introduction that provides a context for the reader, followed by numbered steps that take the reader through the procedure. Warnings, cautions, and reassurances are not particularly necessary in this example, although a few do appear.

As you review the instructions in Figure 12.8, consider whether *you* would feel comfortable undertaking this task. What additional information and description would have made the instructions more inclusive—that is, more likely to reassure you (or someone else with no fleet purchasing experience) that you could perform this task? Where would this information have been incorporated?

Summary

This chapter has introduced you to the purpose, audience, and content of informational reports. Realizing the importance of accurate information in the workplace, you should take special care to make sure that your reports meet the expectations of your readers by being concise, coherent, and well organized. Keeping in mind how the readers will use the information you include in your report should help you determine what content to include (and omit). Remember the readers are not looking for your opinions or your interpretation of the information you provide. (Those matters are taken up in Chapter 13 on writing analytical reports.)

Most informational reports help readers by introducing a topic, issue, goal, method, task, or some other matter that the reader has not previously understood, considered, or (perhaps) even heard of. Some reports provide background information, either historical or general information, on which readers may base future requests for additional information or questions of applicability to the organization. Other informational reports consolidate large amounts of information into a readable form; some simplify complex information by using simpler language or by adding examples or graphics; and some standardize policies and procedures throughout an organization. Finally, a number of reports update information, making the most current data readily available to the reader.

Readers of informational reports do not expect to find that information analyzed or interpreted for them. They either want to do the analysis themselves, or they want only an overview of ideas and relationships. Or they may be new to a topic or to an organization, or they may need a reminder of how certain events took place. Your ability to see the big picture will be invaluable to you as a writer of informational reports for a variety of readers.

In the workplace, you may have to write background reports, mechanism descriptions, laboratory reports, process descriptions, and instructions. Crucial to all of these reports, of course, is determining what the reader wants and needs from the report. If the readers want to understand what a new computer program can do, you need not provide instructions on how to install the program. If the readers want to understand how a particular piece of equipment operates, you need not compare all the brands of that equipment and conclude with the best brand. And if readers want to know how to perform a process, you need not overwhelm them with descriptions of other processes that are only remotely similar. In fact, as with most writing assignments, failing to provide the readers with what they need or providing more than they asked for can cause serious setbacks for your organization's (and even your own) growth and ability to meet users' needs.

The next chapter builds on your understanding of informational reports by emphasizing a highly specialized form of report: the analytical report. You can use the information you learned in this chapter about audiences and their needs, combined with their reasons for reading and the writer's purpose for writing instructions, to begin to clarify the crucial role that audience, purpose, and language play in analytical writing.

✓ CHECKLIST

 When assigned an informational report, be sure to clarify the following:
- Who the readers will be
- Why they will read the information
- What they will do with the information

 Based on your audience and its needs, determine the information you are assigned to present.

 Based on your assessment of the audience and its needs, determine in what order readers will want the information you have to present.

✓ Based on your audience, its needs, and the information you are assigned to present, determine what form your report should take:
- Background report
- Mechanism description
- Laboratory report

- Process description
- Instructions

 Review the strategies in this chapter for drafting and revising the critical elements of each of these report forms.

 Review Chapter 3's information on research to identify the best sources of information for your reports.

 Determine what kinds of graphics will most likely help you summarize, emphasize, or clarify information in your reports.

 Revise your work, trying to understand reader needs from the audience's perspective.

 Proofread.

EXERCISES

Individual Exercises

1. Devise an appropriate audience and purpose statement for an informational report or instructions for each of the following general topics:
   a. Sales of used cars in your area for the past year
   b. Advertising trends in your field
   c. The design of a new seat for passenger trains
   d. A plan for selecting ten museums in the United States that are worth seeing
   e. The use of computers in the writing courses at your college
   f. Means for evaluating teachers at your college
   g. The policy for keeping pets in an apartment complex
   h. The availability of scholarship funds at your college
   i. On-line research tools in your college's library

2. For each of the following general topics, prepare a purpose statement for a specific organization-based report. Choose any type of organization that you like, and add details to the topic as necessary to make the work appropriate for a particular audience with specific needs. Describe how you would approach each topic for an informational report and what your focus would be. What kinds of research would you conduct to find the information for each report (review Chapter 3 if necessary)? If your instructor encourages you, consider how the topic would shift for an analytical report.

a. Security for employees

b. A savings plan for employees

c. The use of employee discounts

d. Celebrating July 4 in America

e. The value of knowing a foreign language

f. Music in the workplace

g. Antismoking legislation

h. Collaboration in the workplace

3. Write a brief (three to five pages) history of your school or your place of employment. Determine carefully for whom you would write such a report and why. What particular kinds of information would that reader find useful? Useless? Why?

Individual or Collaborative Exercises

1. Select one of the following subjects and determine an appropriate audience for an informational report on the subject. Write a description of how the subject works. Then, write instructions for someone who would need hands-on directions for using the item.

a. Cellular phone

b. Remote control

c. VCR

d. CD player

e. Fax machine

f. Motion detector

g. Metal detector

h. Guide dog

2. Select any mechanism or process that is commonly used in your field. Write either a description for readers who want to know more about that mechanism or process or instructions for someone who wants to perform the process. Include a description of graphics you would include.

3. Write an extended definition (two to three pages) for one of the following terms:

a. Philosophy

b. Religion

c. Engineering

d. Tollbooth

e. Electric can opener

f. Microwave oven

g. Jacuzzi

h. Manufacturing

i. The brain

j. Shoes

k. Longleaf pines

l. Cordless phone

4. Write a laboratory report about one of the following topics, based on a series of criteria you select and observations you make:

   ■ The selection of food in your campus cafeteria

   ■ The makes and models of student vehicles in a particular campus parking lot

   ■ The makes and models of faculty vehicles in a particular campus parking lot

5. Describe the differences you would expect to find in the text and audience for a process description and instructions for each of the following subjects:

Process Descriptions	*Instructions*
a. Why a massage eases tensions	a. How to give a massage
b. How computers operate	b. How to install your word processing package
c. How glass is made	c. How to stain and preserve glass
d. Why lightning occurs	d. How to avoid getting struck by lightning
e. How X rays work	e. How to read an X ray
f. How the Internet works	f. How to use a Web browser

   Write a brief description (two to three pages) of one of the topics in the left column and a set of instructions for the corresponding topic in the right column. You should determine an appropriate audience and its purpose for reading before you begin to write either document.

Collaborative Exercises

1. With your partner or team members, select a campus issue you'd like to describe in an informational report of any kind (e.g., a description of how something works, a process, instructions). Possible topics include, but are hardly limited to, the following:

   ■ How to register for classes

   ■ An analysis of enrollments in your required courses over the past four years

   ■ The current process for evaluating instructors

   ■ Security on campus

   ■ The layout of the library's reference room

   After selecting a topic, do each of the following:

   a. Determine the purpose of your report.

   b. Determine the appropriate readers of your report.

   c. Determine the appropriate sources of information for your report.

    d. Determine the likely graphics for your report.

    e. Write an introduction for a five-page report on your topic.

    f. Write the complete report or instructions.

2. You and your partner/group members have formed a private foundation that provides scholarships for students in a particular field of study. After deciding on the field of study, list the criteria your group would use to evaluate scholarship applicants. Determine the number and amount of scholarships you would fund. For what purposes could the scholarship moneys be used? (Do you see that when the student selection committee evaluates students according to your criteria, the committee is analyzing, although your work at this point consists only of providing information?)

➡ *ONGOING ASSIGNMENT*

■ Continuing your ongoing assignment of developing a newcomers' manual for your primary organization (work or school), draft the manual according to the information-only strategies you have learned in this chapter. Your manual's length will depend on your instructor's assignment and specifications or may depend on your own sense of how much information your audience needs.

CHAPTER 13

Analytical Reports

As the previous chapter explained, informational reports present information in its raw form—clearly, accurately, and concisely, of course, but with no analyses, interpretations, or conclusions that would make the document so specialized that only a particular organization or division could use the information. For example, an informational report on new fast-food restaurants in Wynona Falls might chronicle the service and menu items these restaurants offer or describe their franchise arrangements, but it would not explore the effects of these restaurants on, say, TrendSetter's Restaurant's business. It would not analyze the preferences of local residents, describe ways TrendSetter's might change its menu, or predict that TrendSetter's will go out of business unless it makes substantial changes in its menu and service.

With analytical reports, however, writers do more than just present information. As you might expect, they interpret, evaluate, and configure information (especially data such as facts and figures about a given situation or organization) to make it useful to a *select* group of readers. Indeed, the purpose of massaging the information is to make it useful to that highly select group of readers.

Thus, readers of an analytical report will not only learn that TrendSetter's is being seriously challenged by these fast-food restaurants, but may also learn the sources and effects of that challenge, along with the best means, costs, and benefits of combating it. Most important for readers of the analytical report, however, is that it explains what the information means. For example, what does it mean that the number of Wynona Falls residents who eat in fast-food restaurants has increased 45 percent over the past eight months? What does it mean that patrons rate the service "fair" at TrendSetter's? And how can TrendSetter's change to become more appealing to diners?

To construct an analytical report, the report writer interprets information about TrendSetter's so as to make it useful *only* to a *specific* audience—those who oversee or are affected by TrendSetter's business. Such information would be useless to, say, the managers of a restaurant in your own area because the competitive challenges of the restaurant business and the means of dealing with them might not be the same. Thus, the advantage of analytical reports is that they provide highly detailed information that addresses a specific situation within a particular organization and its constraints.

This chapter gives you some experience writing the kinds of analyses that are common in the workplace. Once you have a clearer understanding of the audience for such reports, you will learn more about their purposes and topics. The remainder of the chapter then identifies and describes six common types of analytical reports: problem/solution reports, trip or field reports, research reports, feasibility studies, progress reports, and evaluation reports (for organizations, projects, and employees). Some analytical reports, especially those that evaluate the success of an organization, such as annual reports, are too complex for in-depth discussion in this text. Nevertheless, you may be asked to provide information for such reports, so your knowledge of their goals and structures can help you in your own career writing assignments.

Audiences for Analytical Reports

Readers of analytical reports expect information they can use immediately. Often these readers are too busy to conduct the analyses themselves—as CEOs typically are, for example. Or they may simply be out-of-field from the topic of the report; they do not have the background, experience, or training to understand the raw data without an explanation. For example, the restaurant employee (or hired consultant) who analyzes the traffic in TrendSetter's kitchen might record the following data:

1	1	21
3	4	28
2	2	15

What are these data likely to mean to the restaurant's decision makers? Even when you know what each column represents, can you figure out the meaning?

Column 1: Number of people in party.

Column 2: Menu selection by group (1 = soup/salad; 2 = sandwiches; 3 = entrées; 4 = daily special).

Column 3: Minutes between order taken and food presented.

From the information given, can you tell whether the overall picture is good or bad? Probably not—because no indication of "goodness" or "badness" accompanies these data. Once the data are interpreted, however, the analyst may convince the owner that the service is entirely too slow and that the primary problem is that the wait staff and cooks are in each other's way in the kitchen. Indeed, morale has decreased to the point that the groups intentionally antagonize each other: the cooks postpone cooking some waitpersons' orders, and the waitpersons take their time picking up the prepared dishes from the kitchen. The conclusion of the report—and solution to the problem—may be that the kitchen needs to be remodeled to provide a better flow of traffic, which will improve service and reduce the irritation. (See Strategy Review 13.1.)

One of the keys to writing a useful analytical report, therefore, is to determine not only the kind of information the audience needs, but also the exact level of explanation or interpretation required. Thus, one of your tasks will be to assess your readers' level of understanding and the best ways to explain your information to them. Do they understand comparisons? Analogies? Metaphors? Graphics? Your best strategy is always to have representative members of that audience read your document so you can revise it with a better idea of what is and is not clear. That strategy is often expensive and time-consuming, however, so you may have to rely on other methods of audience analysis that you have studied throughout this course and applied in all your writing assignments. Before you begin your report, determine all of the following about your readers:

■ Reason for reading
■ Intended use of the information
■ Primary area of expertise
■ Secondary area(s) of expertise
■ Experience with this topic
■ Experience with similar topics
■ Likely reaction to this information (positive, neutral, hostile)
■ Ability to understand the following:
  —Comparisons
  —Graphics
  —Examples
  —Other methods of explanation

STRATEGY REVIEW 13.1

ANALYZING GRAPHICS TO MAKE THEM USEFUL

Like any generic information, a figure or a table without any explanation rarely accomplishes the writer's mission (see Chapter 8). Instead, readers are likely to be irritated or confused by the graphic. Consider the following chart:

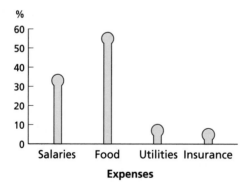

What does this chart mean? Salaries are 33 percent, food 55 percent, utilities 7 percent, and insurance 5 percent. But what are these percentages *of*? The monthly income of the restaurant? The daily income? The amount recently borrowed from the bank? And are these percentages good or bad? Better or worse than last month or last year? Clearly, the writer should interpret this graphic within the text of the report so that its information will hold some meaning for the reader.

Purposes and Topics of Analytical Reports

Most analytical report writers work from series of data that are either gathered specifically for the analytical report or are already available in informational reports on file with the organization. The writers review these data in terms of the topic and purpose of the report they have been assigned to write. Most reports meet one or more of the following purposes:

- *To interpret:* In contrast to an informational report, which describes or presents data, an analytical report interprets data. Thus, writers of analytical reports may have to explain what a particular set of numbers means for an organization. A good example of data that have to be interpreted—especially for an inexperienced audience—is tabular information that lacks complete labeling or explanation (see Figure 13.1). For example, if you have no experience with the stock market or with reading financial columns, you probably cannot interpret a newspaper listing of New York Stock Exchange transactions: What does $+3/8$ mean? Is that good or bad? Should you invest in this stock or not? Financial analysts and stockbrokers make their livings from understanding such information and interpreting it so they can use it in their work, which typically involves convincing their clients that a particular stock is a good investment.

- *To make relevant:* Analytical reports also take standard information (again, frequently from informational reports) and explain why it is important to the readers. For instance, if you own a plant that makes trailers, it might be interesting to know that boat sales are increasing. But it will be critical for you to see that *because* boat sales are increasing, *so, in all likelihood, is the demand for trailers.*

	SW-1	Low	Medium	Uprange
ee-8	−1.3	−2.3	5.3	3.45
ess 4.3°	.44	−2.3	−4.2	.4
aas.φ	−.33	−4.4	1.1	6.5
slas.e	.55	−2.3	6.4	9.6
wle.'Σ	.34	−5.5	2.4	89.3
qqq.zs	.22	.5	7.4	.6

FIGURE 13.1

Tabular Information without
Interpretation Will Be Unclear

■ *To predict:* Because most organizations rely on understanding what the future holds for them, reports that predict the future, based on current trends or anticipated changes, are invaluable. When travel agents learn, for instance, that the political situation in a particular country is becoming increasingly volatile, they typically recommend that their clients avoid the region until things calm down. When a popular hero is installed as the country's new president, the travel agents may decide that this area is, again, a safe place to send tourists. Reasonable predictions, which by definition cannot be certainties, should not be taken for granted in any organization or situation.

Finally, one of the most valuable uses of analytical reports is that they help decision makers make decisions or select the best option for a particular situation or need. Informational reports may describe a number of computer systems, but the operations manager of a large corporation will look for the follow-up analysis that recommends which computer system should be purchased for the clerical staff.

Overall, therefore, analytical reports help readers understand complex information. They explain what is especially useful, relevant, problematic, or prophetic about some generic information that might otherwise be useless to that organization.

Types of Analytical Reports

In the remainder of this chapter, you will learn about various kinds of analytical reports: problem/solution reports; trip or field reports; research reports; feasibility studies; progress reports; and organizational, project, and employee evaluations. As you read, you will notice that much of the information for each report could stand alone as an information-only report. You will also see, however, the value of the document's analytical segment, provided that the analysis is accurate, thorough, timely, and, of course, well written.

Problem/Solution Investigations

Being able to understand and describe problems is a key quality you should develop as a college student and as a worker–writer because recognizing problems (or potential problems) is half the solution. Problem investigations require critical thinking skills—being able to understand complexities that lie beneath the more obvious surface matters. For instance, almost anyone in an organization will understand that profits are sagging, that employees are discontented, or that a particular design or procedure is not working as it is supposed to work. A real problem investigator, however, looks far beyond these obvious manifestations of problems to find the real issues.

THE WORLD OF WORKPLACE WRITING

Analytical Reports and the Myth of Objectivity

Throughout your education, you have probably been taught the value of objectivity—of being able to listen to complete arguments or stories before deciding who is right, what is best, or what should happen next. Quests for objectivity are interesting and even noble in certain situations—such as jury trials—but generally, objectivity itself is unattainable. As thinking human beings with experiences, ideas, and emotions, we are shaped by who we are, where we have been, and how we have lived—all factors that preclude our objectivity on most subjects. Many philosophers, therefore, argue that we would do far better to acknowledge our biases and try to compensate for them if they are not productive biases, rather than trying to recreate ourselves and pretend we have no biases.

Because many workplace issues are mistakenly presented as matters requiring objectivity, workplace writers often have to face their own biases when asked to write analytical reports. If they know they favor a particular outcome at the beginning of the analysis, they should take special care to be fair to the alternative outcome. Otherwise, when pressed to be objective, they may conclude with recommendations that are uncomfortable and even unethical. For example, one "objective" writer, if asked to identify the least costly way for a manufacturing plant to dispose of its waste products, may well conclude that dumping the waste in the river is the least costly method. Another objective writer may argue that this solution is no solution at all—that it is unethical, illegal, and downright irrational. Writers who address controversial issues do so at the risk of "losing their objectivity."

Clearly, objectivity can be valuable in helping writers and decision makers understand their options and make the right choices. At the same time, objectivity can also sabotage more complex issues, especially matters of ethics, fairness, and high standards—three qualities that help build and sustain worthwhile organizations.

In the TrendSetter's Restaurant example, although many executives and employees may remark on the slow service at the restaurant, as a problem investigator you will have to determine the underlying problems that create the larger, more obvious problem. You may find, for instance, that a combination of factors is to blame: the small area for picking up orders, a large refrigerator door that opens into the food aisle, tense relations between cooks and wait staff who have no clear guidelines for their jobs, problems in scheduling lunch and dinner staff, or numerous other factors. Your research, conducted through a series of interviews or surveys perhaps, will help you identify these factors.

As useful as problem investigations are, they are typically only half the content in a workplace report. Most readers want more information than just the problem description; they want to know how to solve the problem. Thus, while a preliminary report might chronicle problems with prompt service at lunch, a follow-up report will focus on solutions, such as remodeling the kitchen, adding cooks or bartenders, seating large parties in a separate section of the restaurant, or having the wait staff prepare the salads. Often a single report covers both the problem and the solution, with the primary emphasis placed on the solutions.

Solving problems in the workplace may be simple or may require multilevel solutions. For instance, if the problem at TrendSetter's is that the salads are rarely fresh, the restaurant's managers may contract with a new produce wholesaler. But if the problem is low morale, the solutions are likely to be a great deal more complicated than a simple fix-it scheme. Raising employees' salaries or providing additional benefits may not be possible immediately, hosting a picnic to encourage organizational unity may come across as simplistic and offensive, and sudden displays of enthusiasm and praise might strike workers as insincere. Clearly, more complex, long-range plans are necessary for solving morale problems.

Figure 13.2 shows an excerpt from a problem/solution report dealing with TrendSetter's Restaurant. The excerpt focuses on the layout of the kitchen as a major source of irritation among employees and as a hindrance to faster service.

As a workplace writer, you will probably be asked to identify, investigate, and recommend solutions to problems at every level of your career. Many workers, including professional writers, describe their daily routines as problem solving—with the essential problem being a need for information that they resolve with their writings. Fortunately, you already have experience with problem solving, as you juggle your limited time to attend classes, study and complete projects and assignments, work, visit with friends and family, and pursue hobbies. Problem solving requires the same kind of balancing.

For most problem/solution reports, writers adopt a standard organizational pattern for the content:

1. Identify the overall problem.
2. Identify the smaller contributing factors to that problem.
3. Review the effects or consequences of the problem, explaining why the problem needs to be solved.
4. Identify a relevant range of potential solutions.
5. Target the solutions from step 4 that are most feasible, based on cost, expediency, space, personnel, user need, and other deciding factors.
6. Recommend a plan of action to resolve the problem.

If readers are familiar with the problem and, perhaps, even its intricacies, you may elect to summarize the first three steps briefly, devoting the majority of your report to the solution phases. Again, reader consideration is a key factor in your organizational decisions; you do not want to insult or bore readers who already know the problem by recounting its details. In that case, moving quickly to present solutions is your best tactic. (See Strategy Review 13.2 on pages 436–437.)

You're In My Way!
An Investigation of Problems at
TrendSetter's, Wynona Falls

context
purpose/audience

scope and
limitations

methods

plan of
organization

Following numerous complaints from the kitchen staff about the wait staff and
vice versa, we have investigated the problems so that the owners of TrendSetter's
can make some decisions about revising the way we do business at our restaurant.
The report specifically addresses the layers of personnel and morale problems
that have led to a decline in efficiency and, thus, in service to our clientele. The
report does not evaluate food selection, quality, or preparation per se, but instead
focuses on the processes that are contributing to poor service at the restaurant.
Based on interviews with the kitchen and wait staffs, along with a series of time
and motion studies, the report first describes the layers of problems and then
focuses on the specific problem that seems to underlie all the other problems:
the cramped kitchen.

first major point

Layers of Problems

dispel myths first

Listening to the complaints of the kitchen personnel and the wait staff at
TrendSetter's Restaurant in Wynona Falls, one might think that the problems are
strictly matters of personality conflicts and professionalism. The cooks complain
that the wait staff is constantly in the way; the wait staff complains that the cooks
are slow and result in irritated clients who leave poor tips. The result is hard
feelings between the groups, frustration, and, most recently, high turnover among
both staffs. . . .

real problem to
be set up here

second major point

The Real Problem: Cramped Kitchen Quarters

now describe *real*
problem

From the numerous interviews and studies conducted, we have concluded that the
real culprit at TrendSetter's is a matter of logistics. The poor arrangement of the
kitchen—dating from its days as a breakfast-only, short-order diner—leads to
chaos and ill feelings.

Specifically, the wait staff has no suitable place to prepare salads and pick up
orders; as a result, the waitpersons are constantly in the way of the cooks.
Meanwhile, the cooks have trouble maneuvering not only around the wait staff,
but also around each other and the awkwardly placed appliances in the galley.
Finally, slow-running disposals tie up the sinks, leaving the food preparers . . . .

FIGURE 13.2 An Excerpt from a Problem/Solution Report, page 1

third major point

offer solution(s)

conclusion

You're In My Way!
p. 2

Solutions

The best solution for this problem is to remodel the kitchen, creating more space
for the wait staff and upgrading the appliances to better serve the cooking staff.
Following the remodeling, both the kitchen staff and the wait staff will have to be
retrained in new food preparation, ordering, and pickup procedures. . . .

Conclusion

We recommend that a team survey a number of area restaurants, investigating
their kitchen layouts and the upgraded appliances we have recommended.
Following that trip, the team should conduct a feasibility study to determine
how applicable the solutions at other sites are to our plans for remodeling. . . .

FIGURE 13.2   An Excerpt from a Problem/Solution Report, page 2

STRATEGY REVIEW 13.2

THE PROBLEM/SOLUTION REPORT

When you have drafted a problem/solution report, consider these questions as a
means of checking your logic and your writing:

1. Have you determined the audience for your report and its purpose for reading? Because readers are most likely to use your report to make a decision,
   check your facts and figures again and again before finalizing your report.

2. Does your audience need extensive background information about the problem or only a simple summary? You may need to review the process of writing a good background report, covered in Chapter 12.

3. Did you determine how much explanation your audience needs about the
   seriousness (causes, effects, future consequences, etc.) of the problem? Have
   you provided evidence that supports your claims?

4. Does your language indicate how concerned the reader should be about this
   problem? Or does the language trivialize or inflate the problem?

5. Have you clearly and logically explained the criteria on which you have based the potential solutions—feasibility, cost, expediency, space, personnel, user need, or other factors? Are the reasons for your criteria selection clear to the reader? Are they ethical?

6. Did you determine in what order to present potential solutions—from best solution to worst or vice versa?

7. Have you added graphics to help readers visualize and to support your assertions of the problem's seriousness and the solution's desirability?

Trip or Field Reports

Although much business can be conducted by telephones and teleconferences, written documents and faxes, and computer networks, today's organizations still require many of their workers to travel. For example, your boss might ask you to travel for any of the following purposes:

- Arrange a complex business agreement in person
- Investigate a site for a building
- Collaborate with other researchers, engineers, or executives on a project
- Test a product or idea in the environment where that product or idea will actually be used

APPLICATION

Converting to an Analytical Report

Using the restaurant, theater, or laundry services informational report you constructed for Chapter 12, analyze the quality of those organizations according to criteria you establish that are meaningful for your audience. Consider such criteria as costs, service, selection, efficiency, and any other matters that affect your evaluation of the organization.

Prepare a special segment for your report on the quality of service provided by each establishment. For example, you might list issues you think the owners should cover with the staff or comment on how you would evaluate the employees with whom you had contact during your investigation.

- Evaluate the performance and efficiency of a branch office
- Interview employees and managers about the organization's current operations or its future

Although television tends to glamorize business trips, being on the road away from families and colleagues with people you do not know is hard—even grueling—work. Business travelers typically must also do a great deal of writing—usually in the form of reports about their findings.

Because situations that demand traveling are usually critical to an organization's well-being, collaborative teams are often sent to investigate and provide the information that the organization wants. For example, before an organization (whether large or small) decides to expand into another market area, it is likely to send a team to the area to investigate all of the following:

- The population's attitude toward the organization's product or services
- The population's need for the organization's product or services
- The likelihood the population will purchase the organization's product or services
- The competition
- Relevant environmental and governmental legislation and regulations
- The availability of trained workers and managers to staff the new facilities
- The accessibility of the area by air and land transportation

The organization might also ask the team to look into the quality of schools, the availability of day-care centers for employees' children, the potential for employees' spouses to find work, the general safety of the area, the climate, the availability of recreational outlets, and numerous other "quality-of-life" factors—information that could be obtained only from an on-site visit.

Based on the instructions from superiors who commissioned the report, the members of the trip team most likely will write an analytical report that will tell readers how suitable the area is for this particular organization's expansion, how likely the organization is to fit into the area, or even how well suited the region's transportation system is for the organization's needs. In short, teams are not sent to an area merely to look around and report what they see; they are expected to interpret their observations to provide some sort of meaning for the organization. (See Strategy Review 13.3 on page 440.)

This example has illustrated one use of trip or field reports in the workplace, but many other examples of the usefulness of going—in person—to conduct an investigation or conduct business could be cited. In short, a variety of information that travelers accumulate while representing their organizations (about site locations, mergers with other organizations, supply or labor relations, and so on) can be analyzed, interpreted, or explained to provide specialized information to readers. For our TrendSetter's Restaurant scenario, Figure 13.3 shows an excerpt from a trip report on other restaurants' kitchen layouts investigated by the team.

Trip Report: Results of Investigations into
Three Restaurants' Kitchen Arrangements

context/content

purpose

methods

This report presents our findings after visiting three restaurants in the region that do similar kinds and volumes of business as TrendSetter's in Wynona Falls. Specifically, we investigated the layout of the kitchens, looking for solutions to the traffic flow problems in our own restaurant. We talked with the managers of the restaurants, along with the cooks and wait staff, trying to find strategies we could incorporate into our own kitchen remodeling plan. The remainder of this report describes the layout features we found most useful and most applicable to our own situation.

plan of
organization

Arrangement of Floor Plan

first major topic

finding

details

The best kitchen layout was probably at the Silver Springs Restaurant in Topsail. Its floor plan reveals a concerted effort to open large aisles so cooks can pass each other in the kitchen, while designating a separate area for the wait staff to prepare salads and pick up food orders. The blueprint for this kitchen (see Appendix A) reveals special wiring that also allows appliances to be set up along the east wall, where the wait staff need never approach. . . .

second major topic

finding

details

Traffic Flow Patterns

The Georgian Room's kitchen was specially designed to prevent run-ins between the cooks and the wait staff. A long alley for the wait staff separates the food preparers from the cooks and allows . . . .

third major topic

finding

details

Appliance Setup

The appliance setup in Merle's Diner shows a careful consideration for the various functions of the kitchen staff. Because one refrigerator is kept for storage while another is stocked with the evening's most popular items, the cooks themselves can order the food preparers to . . . .

conclusion

Conclusion

results of trip/field
investigation

In conclusion, we found several useful ideas at all three restaurants we visited. The blueprints do not adequately explain how well the traffic flow works to keep kitchen staff and wait staff out of each other's way. The floor plan from the Silver Springs restaurant, the traffic flow configuration for the Georgian Room, and the appliance setup at Merle's Diner all suggest strategies we can incorporate into our plans for remodeling the kitchen at TrendSetter's.

We recommend that a feasibility study be conducted to determine whether some combination of those arrangements can be implemented in the space allotted for the new kitchen at TrendSetter's. . . .

FIGURE 13.3 An Excerpt from a Trip or Field Report

THE TRIP OR FIELD REPORT

When writing a trip report, reconsider the following ideas:

1. Have you identified the readers and their expectations for this report?

2. Do you have a clear sense of your mission and the criteria you are exploring?

3. Has your introduction established your readers, purpose, scope and limitations, methods, definitions, and plan of organization?

4. Have you arranged your report to set off (via headings and subheadings) the primary criteria and topics explored?

5. Have you used graphics to show relationships of ideas, maps of areas, and photographs of sites?

6. Have you clarified the sources of your information throughout the report?

7. Do you ethically describe both strengths and weaknesses of any topic?

8. Have you proofread?

Research Reports

In many fields, research and development are special or even primary components of an organization's work. In the pharmaceutical industry, for instance, more money may be spent on research and development than on manufacturing pills and medicines. In any research-based field, such as medicine, psychology, economics, and engineering, researchers seek answers to particular problems or puzzles, and the work that the researchers do is designed to provide at least pieces of those puzzles for other researchers and information users.

A researcher's primary job, therefore, is not only to generate information or data (through tests, experiments, surveys, and so on), but also to make some meaning of the results of those tests, experiments, and surveys. Thus, it may do the reader little good to know the kinds of data produced in laboratory reports (see Chapter 12). Only analyses of that data can truly make the information useful.

In order for the pieces of a research puzzle to be useful, of course, researchers must communicate their findings. Critical findings with immediate applications may require speedy, technical transmissions of data. In less dire cases, research results are commonly communicated through professional publications (research articles in journals), through follow-up reports to funding agencies, through presentations at professional conferences, or, if the information is an organizational or trade "secret," through reports and presentations that remain within the organization. Whatever the medium, research reports should convey the findings and verify that appropriate methods were used in conducting the studies, that figures were interpreted accurately, and that the conclusions are justifiable.

As a result of the rigorous methodology of quality research, research reports follow a rigorous, standardized pattern of organization:

1. Introduction
2. Methods
3. Results
4. Discussion

Failure to follow this organizational pattern has special meaning in research-based arenas: either the writer does not know the traditional pattern, or the researcher has something to hide by not following this pattern. Clearly, it is in the writer's best interest to conform to the readers' expectations concerning the organization and content of a research report.

In addition to the laboratory-based research described so far, innumerable other forms of research are conducted on-site. For instance, engineers are constantly experimenting and testing variations in mathematical formulas and the effect of those variations on the resulting product (an engine, a refrigerator, or even a bridge). In the TrendSetter's Restaurant scenario, for example, a production planner from the restaurant's headquarters conducted a time and motion study to see what caused the delays in service.

Because research reports are so highly specialized, their form receives no additional treatment here. They tend either to be produced by research and development corporations and thus are guarded as confidential data or are so beneficial to the profession that they are published in research journals. Nevertheless, knowing how to read a research report is likely to be important to you even if you never write such a report. And if you are going to write such reports, your instructors in those highly specialized areas will provide further instruction on the writing task and format.

Feasibility Studies

Before embarking on a new venture—a new product, market area, or service, for instance—most organizations conduct feasibility studies that are designed to answer the question, "After thorough investigation, does this [idea, product, plan] make sense for us to pursue?" As you can see from this question, determining whether the change "makes sense" requires the writer to analyze, evaluate, and make some critical decisions about the topic. Further, the emphasis on "thorough investigation" is also critical, for few successful organizations take on big projects or make big plans without plenty of research.

Before embarking on a major kitchen remodeling, for instance, the owners and investors in TrendSetter's Restaurant may spend months investigating (1) whether the remodeled kitchen would actually make a difference and (2) what kinds of remodeling should be done. In short, just because orders, food, and people tend to back up in the kitchen during hectic hours does not necessarily mean that the kitchen should be remodeled. Perhaps some other strategy could be devised to cut down on the delays, such as retraining the wait staff or hiring additional servers to move the food from the kitchen to the wait staff.

Feasibility studies require looking beyond the surface of a situation to determine all the hidden factors that may affect the success of an idea, service, or product. (See Strategy Review 13.4.) In the workplace, such factors may include, but are hardly limited to, the following:

- *Consumers' needs and attitudes toward the idea, service, or product:* Is there any evidence that consumers want this idea, service, or product? How widespread is that market? How affluent is that market?

- *Costs:* Can we afford to make this product, market it, and package it?

- *Distribution:* Can we afford to get this product or service to the people who need it and can afford it?

- *Salaries and wages:* Can we afford to pay the people who will have to develop the product and manufacture, package, inspect, and distribute it?

- *Taxes:* Can we afford the taxes we will have to pay on this product/service?

- *Laws/government regulations:* Can we work within the regulations imposed to protect the safety of our workers and customers, the success of our organization, and the reputation of our organization?

- *Space:* Do we have the space to store the raw materials needed to make this product? Do we have the space to manufacture the product? Do we have the space to store the product? Will buyers have space in their homes, offices, cars, or yards for this product?

- *Technological capabilities:* Do we have the right tools and technology to make and market this product or to perform this service?

- *Competition:* What other organizations are trying to make this product or perform this service? Are they better able to succeed than we are? What would it take to make us competitive with those other organizations?

- *Service/maintenance:* Can we service the machinery needed to make this product? Can we afford to pay mechanics or contract out the maintenance work?

■ *Language barriers:* Will we be working with, buying from, or selling to members of other cultures? Are we prepared to handle the language difficulties of global commerce?

■ *Workforce:* How stable is the workforce we need to be able to offer this service or make this product? Are workers readily available, trainable, loyal, and creative?

■ *Management personnel:* Do we have the managers who can oversee the production of this service or product? Are they adequately trained to understand, evaluate, and improve that production? What is their attitude toward the service or product (positive, negative, neutral)?

■ *Longevity of the idea, service, or product:* How long can we expect this idea, service, or product to be needed and profitable? Is that time frame worth our investment and efforts?

■ *Amount of time before return on investment:* How long before the product or service meets the needs of our consumers? Helps us make a profit? Earns us a quality reputation?

STRATEGY REVIEW 13.4

THE FEASIBILITY STUDY

When you write a feasibility report, consider these questions:

1. Did you begin by clarifying the audience for whom you are writing? How much do your readers know about the topic? How much background information will you have to provide for them?

2. When you drafted the introduction for your report, did you specify the subject, purpose, audience, scope and limitations, methods, definitions (if necessary), and plan of organization?

3. As part of the introduction's scope and limitations or methods section—or in a special section following the introduction—did you clarify the criteria you have adopted for this study? Is it necessary—for this topic and audience—to explain why each criterion is appropriate and how it will be measured or otherwise analyzed?

4. Have you organized your report by the criteria, addressing each one in a separate segment of the report?

5. Did you use headings to distinguish the criteria you are discussing and subheadings to show criteria that are interrelated?

(continued)

6. Did you use charts and other graphics to provide an overview or the particulars of the feasibility study?

7. Did you conclude the report with a specific assessment of the idea's feasibility—yes or no—or explain precisely why you cannot offer such a conclusion (perhaps describing the additional research you need to conduct in order to be able to determine feasibility)?

8. If appropriate for your topic, audience, and assignment, did you offer additional observations and recommendations that are also useful?

9. Did you revise, based on your audience's perspective and need to know? Remember, the readers are looking for thoroughness, accuracy, appropriate detail, and clarity throughout your report.

10. Did you design your work to make it visually pleasing and to direct readers to the most essential elements?

Figure 13.4 shows an excerpt from a report investigating the feasibility of TrendSetter's remodeling its kitchen according to a particular plan. Note the establishment of specific criteria that must be met in order for the venture to be considered feasible.

In short, feasibility studies require writers to look at an idea or project from every conceivable angle before the venture is undertaken. The writers may conclude that the idea is a good one, that it needs to be modified, or, perhaps, that it should be abandoned (at least temporarily). Feasibility studies show the thoroughness of your investigation and the soundness of your conclusions.

Progress Reports

Whether you work in a hospital, a corporation, or a laboratory, you will probably have to report your progress on your current project at consistent intervals (daily, weekly, or monthly). Progress reports are designed to let readers know how your work is advancing—or not advancing. Just as critical as knowing when a project will be completed is knowing what obstacles might prevent or delay its completion.

The complexity of the project usually determines the progress report's length, which can range from a single-page memo to a multipage work that highlights the developments and obstacles in a multifaceted project. A progress report on, say, the development of a seminar on retirement options might run three to four pages, while a report on the building of a new hotel/casino in Las Vegas might run hundreds of pages. Nevertheless, the kinds of information and the organization of progress reports remain essentially the same, regardless of length and complexity (see bottom of page 446).

Remodeling the Kitchen at
TrendSetter's Restaurant, Wynona Falls:
A Feasibility Study

Following the trip report from the team investigating kitchen layouts at area restaurants, we have conducted a feasibility study to determine how well the team's suggestions will fit into our own restaurant remodeling plans. Beyond the discussion of the suitability of the arrangement, we have also based this feasibility study's conclusions on costs and time to completion. We have consulted the architects who will draw up the actual remodeling plans and have asked representatives of the kitchen and wait staffs for their input on the ideas. Consultations with our accountants at headquarters have provided information about how long we can afford to close the Wynona Falls restaurant for remodeling. The following report describes those criteria and how well the preferred plan meets our objectives.

Suitability of Suggested Remodeling

The suggestions for remodeling the Wynona Falls TrendSetter's would alleviate a number of the difficulties observed and expressed by our personnel. Specifically, the new plan is extremely feasible as a means of solving the traffic flow problems, the outdated appliance problems, and the other problems resulting from these two primary headaches. Both the kitchen and the wait staff agree that . . . .

Costs

An initial concern for this project is the inherent costs of remodeling, along with the costs of upgrading the appliances. We may have to wait to upgrade the outside storage freezer, but the current costs of $42,000 for upgrading the inside appliances are certainly within reason.

Based on estimates, we have budgeted $94,350 for this remodeling project—a sum that is within the realm of acceptable expenditures for this kind of work. Further, given the profits of the restaurant over the years, we are convinced that the modifications recommended will help bring the restaurant back into the good graces of its clientele. . . .

Margin annotations: context; purpose; criteria; methods; plan of organization; first major point; second major point

FIGURE 13.4 An Excerpt from a Feasibility Study, page 1

<table>
<tr><td>third major point</td><td>

Remodeling the Kitchen at TrendSetter's Restaurant,
p. 2

Time to Completion

The biggest concern is the amount of time the restaurant will have to be closed for remodeling. Corporate headquarters allows no more than two months for shutdowns for any conversions. This project will take six weeks—provided it stays on schedule. Impending strikes in the transportation industry could affect the delivery of the appliances, but rumors indicate those strikes will be resolved within days. . . .

</td></tr>
</table>

third major point

conclusion

Conclusion

Based on our analyses of the blueprints for remodeling, the costs, and the downtime, we conclude that the remodeling project at TrendSetter's in Wynona Falls is completely feasible, with the possible exception of replacing the outside storage freezer at this time.

recommendation

Recommendation: **Begin construction immediately.**

F I G U R E   13.4   An Excerpt from a Feasibility Study, page 2

---

1. *An overview of the project:* Provide a context for your reader.

2. *A description of work completed:* Describe where you are in your work.

3. *A description of work to be done:* Explain what has not been done (no excuses or whining!).

4. *A description of obstacles that might delay the project, along with ideas or requests for helping eliminate those problems:* Present cause/effect or problem/solution information to advance the work.

5. *A timetable for completion of the major elements of the project:* Schedule the steps you will be taking to meet your deadline or to convince the reader that extending the deadline is necessary or advantageous to the project.

6. *Assurances that the project will meet the deadline or a request for a deadline extension:* Tell readers when they can expect your final product.

THE PROGRESS REPORT

After drafting the content for the progress report, you are ready to revise it; check to make sure that you have carefully considered your answers to these questions:

1. Have you determined who your audience is—your boss inside the organization or a client outside the organization?

2. Based on your audience, have you determined whether you need to use a letter, memo, or report format?

3. Based on your audience, have you determined how exacting you have to be about the information you present? Must you detail every delay or can you reassure the readers that the project will be completed on time?

4. Based on your readers and their concerns about the project, have you determined what factors demand special attention?

5. Did you begin the progress report with the standard introductory information—subject, purpose, audience, scope and limitations, methods, definitions (if needed), and plan of organization?

6. Did you organize the work according to the standard organization of a progress report as set out in the six steps in the text?

7. Have you used headings and subheadings throughout your progress report to help guide readers and to clarify your organization?

8. Did you include graphics of the remaining processes and time schedules for completing each phase?

9. Have you revised with the readers' needs clearly in mind? Remember, they should have no questions about where you are in the project.

Figure 13.5 on pages 448–449 shows a progress report that was submitted on TrendSetter's kitchen remodeling project. Notice that the report contains the six major elements described at the bottom of page 446.

Like other forms of workplace writing, progress reports help keep readers informed about current situations, problems, and achievements. As a workplace writer, you must present such information accurately and honestly. If your project is running into problems, it is far better to let readers know that delays are likely than to have them believe the project is proceeding on schedule. Again, goodwill and the work of your organization, as well as your own credibility, are at stake. (See Strategy Review 13.5.)

context

overview

purpose/audience

To: Graham Underwood
From: Tyrone Benson *TB*
Date: 22 May 2001
Subject: Progress on kitchen remodeling at Wynona Falls restaurant

Since detecting a problem with the service and kitchen layout at the Wynona Falls TrendSetter's Restaurant, we have been working to remodel the kitchen—the major source of the complications and slow service. The remodeling changes the flow of traffic into and out of the kitchen, reorganizes the counter space and appliances, and creates a more open environment for the cook staff. This report updates you on the progress of that remodeling.

first major topic

details

Work Completed

To date, the remodeling has moved well. The carpenters and electricians are through with the bulk of their work. The bricklayers have completed the outside renovation and have installed a new drive-thru window. In addition, the . . . .

second major topic

details

Work Remaining

The largest segment of work remaining is receiving and installing the new appliances. The large-capacity refrigerators and freezers are on back order, but should be installed by Friday, June 7, at the latest. The plumbing is all but finished—with some disposal work scheduled for later this week. . . .

third major topic

details

Obstacles

The greatest obstacle we are facing is the delayed shipment of glass bricks. The order from New Mexico has been stalled by poor weather and by the transportation workers' strike, which is predicted to be settled within a couple of days, making alternative shipment strategies unnecessary. We can use the extra time to consider our food orders and make additional arrangements for hiring and training new staff. . . .

fourth major topic

Timetable

Nevertheless, the work is almost on schedule. The slight delay in receiving the glass bricks might delay the reopening by a day or so, but that should not cause too many problems. The following time line shows the remaining work to be done before reopening:

F I G U R E   13.5   An Excerpt from a Progress Report, page 1

graphic illustration
of time line

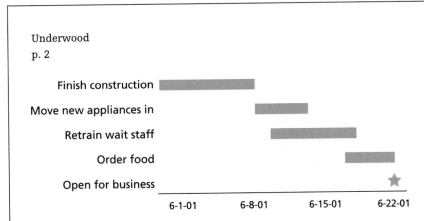

Underwood
p. 2

Figure 1: Time Line to Completion of Remodeling Project

assurances of
completion

In short, we have little reason to believe that our projected deadline is not reachable, although a one- or two-day delay may be inevitable. As stated above, that delay can be well used for retraining, hiring, and making other important decisions about our service, staff, and selection.

If you have any questions about this report or our progress, please let me know.

FIGURE 13.5 An Excerpt from a Progress Report, page 2

Evaluation Reports: Organizational, Project, and Employee

As organizations evolve over the years, their leaders are most concerned about the question, "How are we doing as an organization?" They seek answers to that question on three distinct, yet interrelated, levels:

1. In terms of meeting the organization's goals (profits, sales margins, growth, innovative projects, service assessment, number of customers/clients, product development and expansion, etc.)

2. In terms of completing individual and interrelated projects that forward the goals of the organization

3. In terms of the organization's employees (general abilities, safety records, ability to follow instructions, loyalty, promotability, general welfare, innovative ideas, etc.)

To find these answers, executives commission (or even write their own) evaluation reports that address the status of the organization, its projects, and its employees' work.

Organizational Evaluations

An evaluation report for an organization focuses on strengths and weaknesses and typically recommends new strategies for (1) remaining competitive, (2) keeping customers and employees happy, and/or (3) enhancing the organization's image within the profession or community. Because CEOs and other managers rely on internal evaluation reports to get a clear picture of the organization's status, such reports must be scrupulously honest in describing the organization's strengths and weaknesses. In a large organization, however, only rarely does one person write such an evaluation. Usually, the evaluation is divided among the various departments whose work is then analyzed and compiled into a larger, organization-wide report. Thus, although you may never have to write an entire organizational report, you may have to write your own department's report. If you are part of a small organization, though, you may, indeed, have to write the entire evaluation.

Internal evaluation reports are frequently the grist for the organization's annual report, a highly specialized external document that reports the organization's achievements (while usually minimizing its weaknesses) to stockholders, stockbrokers, and potential investors. Because annual reports are complex and must comply with many rules established by the Securities and Exchange Commission, these reports are not treated in this text. Nevertheless, knowing their importance and roles in publicly held corporations can help guide your considerations of analyses in organizational evaluations.

An organization's internal evaluation reports typically focus on its success in meeting goals and on its strengths and weaknesses. In addition, the reports typically emphasize profits, investments, expansions, divestitures, new projects, new services, new products, and changing management philosophies. Figure 13.6 shows the kitchen manager's organizational evaluation of TrendSetter's kitchen. Note that the manager, Mimi Devereaux, analyzes standard information about the restaurant's daily operations, plus information gathered from interviews with the wait staff and the cooks, to conclude that the restaurant needs to remodel its kitchen.

In essence, readers of an organizational evaluation are most concerned about the organization's (or a division's) current status, along with its potential strengths and weaknesses. (See Strategy Review 13.6 on page 453.) As you can see, such analyses draw directly from informational reports of sales, profits and losses, and other sets of data that are routinely recorded in organizations. They also rely heavily on the information offered in project evaluations (described on pages 453–455). The resulting information is then used to adjust strategies, personnel, and other factors that affect the operating practices of the organization.

<table>
<tr><td>

context

purpose and
audience

first finding

second finding

potential methods

scope and
limitations

plan of
organization

first major topic

overview of
discussion of
management

first subtopic

</td><td>

Where We Stand:
An Organizational Analysis of
TrendSetter's, Wynona Falls

This report presents an overview of the current organizational status for the owners and the manager of TrendSetter's in Wynona Falls. Its emphasis on the organization's strengths and weaknesses suggests some areas of growth and potential, but also identifies some obstacles that must be overcome in order for that growth to take place. Primarily, some changes in management decisions regarding scheduling and training of the staff are going to be crucial to the long-range viability of this restaurant. Some specific food management suggestions are also critical to the restaurant's appeal and, thus, its ability to survive.

Because the owners and manager have expressed concerns about the influx of fast-food restaurants into Wynona Falls (specifically, McTug's, Larry's, and the Burger Palace), we could also conduct a comparative analysis of the business at these three restaurants and that at TrendSetter's. But because that information would be beyond the scope of this analysis of TrendSetter's, we will wait for further instructions before embarking on that research.

Following this introduction, the report describes the general management strengths and weaknesses (regarding hiring, training, scheduling, and promoting the cooks and wait staff) and the food management strengths and weaknesses (regarding selection of food wholesalers, preparation of foods, menu selection, and presentation). Finally, we address matters of costs and service quality. The overview concludes with a general list of recommendations for improving the quality, productivity, and reputation of TrendSetter's in Wynona Falls.

Management Review

With the hiring of Jason McFree as its manager in 1998, TrendSetter's became far more competitive in the upscale dining market in Wynona Falls. McFree made a number of changes in the atmosphere of TrendSetter's by hiring more qualified wait staff and retraining the existing employees to cater to a more upscale clientele. Although those strengths certainly remain some of the hallmarks of TrendSetter's, a few specifics can be addressed that may pinpoint a few weaknesses.

Scheduling

Although scheduling wait staff is a large problem at every restaurant, we sense that it is particularly pernicious at TrendSetter's. In our observations, we noted that certain members of the wait staff were offered severely limited hours, while

</td></tr>
</table>

FIGURE 13.6 An Excerpt from an Organizational Evaluation, page 1

Where We Stand

p. 2

others seemed overworked. Although some of these workers are part-time and, thus, unable to work a full 40-hour work week, we noted a great deal of discontent among the staff. Some said that certain workers are punished for minor infractions, while others who had requested reduced hours were given additional work as punishment for infractions. A variation on this policy seems to be to assign certain members of the staff to nonpeak hours, thus reducing the likelihood of their making decent tips.

Scheduling must follow a consistent policy to ensure quality work. We recommend a schedule board that would allow the wait staff to schedule themselves, with certain limitations, and a review process (see Appendix A). Most important is that scheduling never be seen as punishment. Unless workers are to perceive all their work hours as punishment—in which case, they will quit—TrendSetter's must be careful that infractions are handled as a matter of training, not as a matter of scheduling. . . .

second subtopic

Training

Although the wait staff was extremely well trained in the presentation and removal of dishes, the workers were less well trained in the finer nuances of service. For example, one waiter had extreme difficulty opening a bottle of champagne, which sends a mixed message about exactly how upscale TrendSetter's is. On the whole, in fact, the staff seemed excellently trained about food, but poorly trained about wine selection and service. . . .

second major topic

Food Management

Our survey found little argument that TrendSetter's is serving the finest food in Wynona Falls. For atmosphere and quality selections, the restaurant consistently receives rave reviews. The only real problems we see in the management of foods are the availability and quality of fresh produce, the selection of chicken dishes, and the presentation of steaks.

subtopic

Produce

TrendSetter's long-standing policy of refusing to serve poorer quality food is one of the best decisions the managers here have made. This policy is known throughout the community and garners widespread support from patrons. . . .

FIGURE 13.6   An Excerpt from an Organizational Evaluation, page 2

STRATEGY REVIEW 13.6

THE ORGANIZATIONAL EVALUATION

The following questions will help you determine how effective your draft of the organizational evaluation (or your department's segment of it) is likely to be for your readers:

1. Have you determined whether your report is for internal use (for the CEO and other managers) or for external use as an annual report (for the public and stockholders)?

2. Have you identified your primary audience and determined its purpose for reading?

3. Have you considered the data you hold and your own ethical responsibilities to determine the kind of information you should offer the reader?

4. Do you understand how to read and interpret the financial documents that supply the data for your report? Consult accountants and financial coworkers for help, if necessary. Although you do not specifically have to *explain* the financial statements (balance sheets, expense accounts, and the like), you do have to *interpret* them to describe the organization's overall financial picture.

5. Have you drafted an introduction that provides a reading plan for your audience by focusing on the subject, purpose, audience, scope and limitations, methods, definitions (optional), and plan of organization?

6. Did you organize the report according to your assessment of the readers' needs for information?

7. Have you determined how to present bad news, if necessary, in the most appropriate—and ethical—manner? Make sure that you do not bury it or use so many hedges that the reader cannot understand your message.

8. Have you selected the internal design features, such as headings, subheadings, and graphics, that will help readers find the information they need in the report?

9. Have you revised the document with your readers' needs—and your ethical sensitivities—clearly in mind?

Project Evaluations

Unlike progress reports (discussed earlier in this chapter), project evaluations come at the end of a project. Their primary purpose is to assess how well the completed project met its goals. In most cases, the goal is to solve a problem or meet a need; thus, the project evaluation assesses how well the work of the project actually met the goal or need.

Because we all like to believe that our work accomplishes its goals, it is often difficult to admit that a project has failed. When a project succeeds, however, it is easy to boast about it and even overestimate its success. Establishing specific, measurable criteria is a useful strategy that can help you keep the right balance when assessing the success or failure of a given project. Most organizations try to avoid poorly defined goals, such as "increase profits during the next quarter" or "increase membership in the organization." Such objectives are difficult to measure in many cases—especially when, for instance, your organization may increase its profits and spending at the same time. Instead, setting specific, measurable criteria allows you to determine exactly how well your organization has met its goals:

- Increase sales by 20 percent and profits by 10 percent, while reducing spending by 2.5 percent.
- Increase membership by 200, while maintaining current membership status.

These goals are measurable, allowing analysts to determine whether the projects met their targets. (See Strategy Review 13.7.)

Project evaluations also allow writers to

- assess the value of individual contributors' work on the project,
- explain delays, cost overruns, or weaknesses in the project, and
- recommend improved strategies for future projects.

Thus, these reports serve an extremely useful role in most organizations.

STRATEGY REVIEW 13.7

THE PROJECT EVALUATION

In most successful organizations, at the same time a project is assigned to a worker or group of workers, a means of assessing its success or failure is also put into place. At the end of the project, the work is typically measured against the standards for success that were articulated as goals at the beginning of the project. The following questions will help you determine how well you have written your project evaluation:

1. Have you clearly articulated the purpose of the project?

2. Have you described the goals that were established as standards for your project?

3. Have you clearly described how well your project has met those goals?

4. Have you carefully described the strengths and weaknesses of the project's design and implementation?

5. Have you explained both predicted and unforeseen factors that contributed to the project's success or failure?

6. Have you described the roles of each participant in the project and evaluated the contributions each made?

7. Have you concluded with recommendations about whether similar projects should be carried out in the future?

In the TrendSetter's scenario, Mimi must set a realistic goal for reducing the delays in the kitchen; then, after the remodeling, she can assess the effect that the better organized kitchen has on the efficiency of the food preparation and service. Her project evaluation appears in Figure 13.7 on page 456.

Employee Evaluations

Although evaluations of the organization—especially of the organization as a whole—are usually written by divisional managers or vice presidents, evaluations of employees are written at all supervisory levels of the organization. Again, organizations use various criteria for evaluating employees, but most consider the following:

- *Competence in general workmanship:* Can this employee accurately and safely do the job for which he or she was hired?

- *Potential for promotion:* Do this employee's work and attitude suggest fitness for a higher position?

- *Collaborative strength:* Does this employee share ideas, accept criticism, and negotiate solutions in a team setting?

- *Work ethic:* Does this employee demonstrate a commitment to work, to doing things right the first time, and to taking pride in a job well done?

- *General attitude:* Does this employee contribute to or detract from the work and morale of others?

Some organizations require evaluations on a yearly basis and use the results to determine bonuses, merit pay raises, and even promotions. Other organizations evaluate employees more frequently—even at three-month intervals—as a way to stay abreast of employees' abilities and general satisfaction with their work.

As a supervisor who may have to write employee evaluations, you should know that checklists and general pronouncements are rarely useful; much more useful are descriptions of particular incidents or activities that support your evaluation of the employee. Further, given the litigious nature of our society, poor evaluations (or poor letters of recommendation) can lead to lawsuits from disgruntled employees. The best safeguard against such recrimination is clear, thorough documentation of the worker's abilities, disposition, and contributions to the workplace. (See Strategy Review 13.8 on page 457.)

**The Remodeled Kitchen at TrendSetter's, Wynona Falls:
A Project Evaluation**

context
audience
primary finding
methods

plan of
organization

The following report describes the results of the kitchen remodeling project at TrendSetter's in Wynona Falls. Corporate officers will find that the project met its goals while staying within the budget and the deadlines. Based on postproject interviews and additional time and motion studies, we conclude that the project has been successful in helping us alleviate problems with morale and service at this site. The remainder of this report describes more specifically the impact of the new arrangement, the costs, and the downtime.

first major topic

Impact of the Newly Remodeled Kitchen

primary finding

To say that morale and service at the TrendSetter's in Wynona Falls have improved would be a drastic understatement. The cooks and wait staff have new appreciation for each other because they are no longer in each other's way. Further, the turnover rate has subsided to a negligible level, while new applications for staff are coming in at an average of seven per week.

specific details

second major topic

The redirected traffic flow is one of the keys to this success. Time and motion studies show that the wait staff is rarely in the kitchen, and that wait persons have their food prepared and picked up in less than 12 minutes, a decrease of 4.8 minutes from the previous arrangement. . . .

Costs

Staying within the budget was a true test for this project. Compromises on appliances, however, and the delay on ordering the outside storage freezer kept the project within its budget. . . .

third major topic

Time to Completion

The downtime on this project did exceed our hopes by one day, but we used that extra day to retrain the wait staff, encourage positive thinking, and generate a festive air for the reopening of the restaurant. The delay may have cost us approximately $1,200 in business, but . . . .

conclusion

Conclusion

We conclude that the remodeled kitchen at TrendSetter's has been entirely successful. The plans for the kitchen were expertly carried out by the construction crews, and the retraining and development of new policies for the wait staff—mostly completed by the wait staff itself—have boosted morale even more. . . .

FIGURE 13.7   An Excerpt from a Project Evaluation

STRATEGY REVIEW 13.8

THE EMPLOYEE EVALUATION

Reconsider the following questions when you write an employee evaluation:

1. Have you determined the audience and its expectations for your evaluation?

2. Have you developed specific criteria—or followed your organization's standard criteria—for evaluating the employee?

3. If your reader is your employee, have you considered how the evaluation is likely to affect that person—positively, negatively, or neutrally?

4. Should you revise the wording, tone, or evaluation to lessen or heighten the reader's response?

5. Have you exercised good judgment, fairness, and clarity in the evaluation?

6. Have you provided examples of occasions on which your employee behaved or worked in the manner you describe?

7. Will the evaluation bring about the result you seek, such as improved or stabilized performance, increased safety consciousness, or improved disposition?

8. Have you revised for tone, clarity, completeness, and accuracy of data?

The employee evaluation in Figure 13.8 on page 458 shows the criteria used to judge TrendSetter's wait staff. The report assesses each individual's strengths and weaknesses and provides supporting evidence to document those judgments.

APPLICATION

Preparing a Problem/Solution Report

Based on your analysis in the first Application in this chapter, identify problems you observed at one of the establishments you investigated and suggest possible solutions. You may talk with the employees themselves or base your discussion on your own observations.

Assume that you are writing for the owners of the establishment. How persuasive will you have to be to convince them that a problem exists? What are the effects of the problem? How realistic are your solutions?

rating scale

rating

explanation
and examples

EMPLOYEE EVALUATION

NAME ___JAMIE FITZPATRICK___

DATE ___12-5-99___

Skills	Poor	Satisfactory	Good	Excellent
1. Ability to perform basic job functions				X
2. Ability to perform related job functions	X			
3. Ability to perform new job functions		X		

Comments: ___Jamie is exceptionally good at basic job functions: attending to customers, describing menu options, and cleaning her areas. She still has not learned many of the cashiering functions that are crucial to the credit card customer, however. These problems may not seem major, but she consistently has to ask other staff members to help her process payments, and the interruptions in their work are affecting their service. Consequently, Jamie must learn to manage the credit card functions.___

Training

	Poor	Satisfactory	Good	Excellent
1. Learns new techniques quickly		X		
2. Is able to help train new workers				X
3. Keeps up-to-date on her own			X	

Comments: ___Again, Jamie has problems learning new sales/credit card procedures. Nevertheless, she is exceptionally good at training new wait staff. Her knowledge of proper form and timing is a real plus for the new wait staff she trains. Jamie is pretty good at keeping up-to-date on her own, but occasionally has to be reminded of menu variations.___

Attitude

	Poor	Satisfactory	Good	Excellent
1. Attitude toward work				X
2. Attitude toward TrendSetter's				X
3. Attitude toward supervisor			X	
4. Attitude toward colleagues			X	

Comments: ___Jamie's attitude toward work is exceptional, and I am certain she would rather work at TrendSetter's than at any other restaurant in town. Her loyalty is impressive and filters down to the other workers and staff members. Her attitude toward her supervisor is also good, but there seems to be some occasional resentment about her schedule. Her attitude toward her colleagues is also good, although she occasionally loses patience with some of the new trainees.___

verification

Signature of Employee _____ Date _____

Signature of Evaluator _____ Date _____

FIGURE 13.8 An Excerpt from an Employee Evaluation

Summary

In this chapter, you have learned more about writing analytical reports. These reports require writers to do more than just present information; now, they must interpret, analyze, or enlist some other critical-thinking skill to make the information useful to their readers.

Because most readers of analytical reports are too busy to conduct the analyses themselves or lack the experience and knowledge to analyze the data, analytical reports serve an important function in the workplace. Indeed, one might argue that analytical reports are the most important type of documents that emanate from work because without them, workers would have facts and figures that had no meaning. What use is it to know that your organization served 92 customers last year, unless you also learn that that number is down 88 percent from last year? Or that the organization must serve at least 127 customers to break even? Or that management is committed to firing four workers if customers do not increase to at least 135?

This chapter has also described some of the most common purposes for writing analytical reports: to interpret information; to make information relevant to a particular reader, organization, or situation; to predict trends or consequences; and/or to help decision makers see all their options and select the best one(s). To meet these objectives, analytical report writers must be scrupulous in selecting the criteria that form the bases of their work.

Most analytical reports fall into one of the following categories, although the categories sometimes overlap:

- *Problem/solution studies:* These studies are conducted when organizations recognize a problem and seek ways for solving it; the study frequently analyzes and ranks solutions.

- *Trip or field reports:* These reports provide evaluations or interpretations of the conditions and/or events at a particular site.

- *Research reports:* These reports analyze the data produced during controlled experiments, surveys, or other methodologies.

- *Feasibility studies:* Organizations use feasibility studies to determine if a plan, product, service, or idea makes sense and will serve them well.

- *Progress reports:* Progress reports require writers to assess where they are with a particular project or assignment and report to the reader the accomplishments, obstacles, and remaining tasks for that work assignment.

- *Evaluation reports:* Evaluations of the organization focus on strengths, weaknesses, and goal attainment and may be reported in internal evaluation reports or in external annual reports; evaluations of projects focus on the completed work and its success or failure in meeting its goals; evaluations of employees focus on the strengths, weaknesses, and promotability of each worker and often serve as the basis for pay raises and promotions.

When constructing these documents, writers must carefully consider their audience's needs, as well as their own ethical responsibilities. Because others rely on the writer's interpretation of situations and events, the analytical report is one of the greatest responsibilities the workplace writer must shoulder.

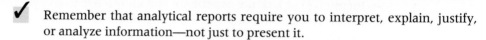

✓ CHECKLIST

✓ Remember that analytical reports require you to interpret, explain, justify, or analyze information—not just to present it.

✓ Check your information (or data) carefully before you begin to work with it. Make sure figures are correct and facts are documented, if necessary.

✓ Determine the audience's needs. What kind(s) of information should you provide?
- Interpretations of confusing or unfamiliar data?
- Explanations of the information's relevance to the reader's job or to the organization?
- Predictions of successes, failures, or consequences of certain plans, activities, products, or services?
- Selection of best options for solving a problem or meeting a need?
- Some combination of these possibilities?

✓ Determine how much background information your readers have or need. If the readers are capable of conducting this analysis but are simply too busy to do so, you may not have to explain many details about the methods of your analysis. If the readers are unfamiliar with such analytical procedures, you may have to explain a great many details about your methods and findings.

✓ Control your biases, especially if they are likely to shade your judgment or compromise your integrity.

✓ Let your readers' needs guide you in selecting criteria, determining the organizational structure, and making decisions about other matters throughout the report. These issues will help you decide what kind of report to write:
- Problem/solution report
- Trip or field report
- Research report
- Feasibility study
- Progress report
- Organizational evaluation report
- Project evaluation report
- Employee evaluation report

✔ For a problem/solution report, determine the following:
- How much information the reader needs about the problem
- How to define an "acceptable" solution
- How to compare potential solutions
- How to recommend the best solution

✔ For a trip or field report, concentrate on these issues:
- The specific mission of your trip
- The criteria for analysis
- Means for controlling your biases, unless they are relevant to your overall impression
- Recommendations of what the organization should do about the subject of your mission

✔ For a feasibility study, concentrate on these issues:
- Establish criteria for determining the sense or doability of this topic
- Organize your report based on the readers' need for information
- Craft a report that concludes with "yes" or "no" to the feasibility question or offers specific reasons why you cannot reach such a conclusion (at least not at this time)

✔ For a research report, provide the following:
- Introduction to topic of research
- Methods of research used
- Results of study
- Discussion of findings and implications

✔ For a progress report, provide the following:
- A review of your project
- A summary of work accomplished
- A summary of work to be done
- A summary of obstacles
- A timetable for completing the project

✔ For an organizational evaluation report, focus on these elements:
- The criteria for analysis
- The readers' need for absolutely accurate information
- The best organizational and design structures to emphasize crucial information

For a project evaluation report, determine the following:

- The goals of the project
- The accomplishment of those goals
- Failures in meeting the goals
- Contributions of others
- Suggestions for redirecting, continuing, or aborting the project

 For an employee evaluation report, determine the following:

- The appropriate criteria for analysis
- A means for controlling your biases
- A means for clarifying strengths and weaknesses you see in the employee's work
- Specific examples of the employee's strengths and weaknesses
- A method for wording your evaluation diplomatically

 Be resolutely fair and ethical in your analysis. Do not allow your biases to overshadow your selection of criteria and your assessment of data.

 Revise, keeping the readers' needs and expectations clearly in mind, and proofread.

EXERCISES

Individual Exercises

1. Devise an audience and purpose statement for an analytical report on each of the following topics:
   a. XYZ Corporation's sales for 1999
   b. Advertising trends in your field
   c. The design of a new seat for passenger trains
   d. A plan for selecting ten museums in the United States you'd like to see
   e. The use of computers in the writing courses at your college
   f. Means for evaluating teachers at your college
   g. The policy for keeping pets in an apartment complex
   h. The availability of scholarship funds at your college
   i. On-line research tools in your college's library

2. What criteria would you use to evaluate the quality of your academic program at your college? Be prepared to defend your criteria.

3. Choose one of the following as your audience, and prepare a progress report on your work toward a degree at your college. Then, describe how your tone would change if the progress report were to be directed to each of the other audiences.

- Your parents who are paying for your tuition
- Your parents who are not paying for your tuition
- Your partner, who is working two jobs while you are going to school
- Your academic adviser
- Your boss whose company is paying for your tuition
- Your know-it-all cousin who says you will never get a degree

4. Choose some work or volunteer organization (or division) with which you are familiar, and describe its culture and/or image (see Chapter 1). List the criteria you would use to construct a balanced, unbiased organizational evaluation, the criteria you would use to present a totally positive picture of this organization, and the criteria you would use to present a totally negative picture of this organization. What would be the audience, purpose, and ethics of each report? Write one of these three organizational evaluations (balanced, positive, or negative).

5. Describe a situation in which your work has been evaluated—as a student or as a worker. Discuss your reaction to the evaluation. Was it fair? Was it flattering or offensive? Try to reconstruct what, in particular, about that evaluation made it a favorable or unfavorable review of your work.

6. Select five places you would like to visit in your state. Then, giving yourself a modest budget, a limited amount of vacation time, and a list of desirable activities, rank the sites in order of feasibility. Next, suppose your budget or vacation time has been reduced, so you must omit one site. Which site would you omit and why? Explain in a memo/report to your traveling partner(s) (anyone you choose—partner, parents, siblings, children, friends) why you had to omit a site and how you selected that site.

7. Determine the feasibility of the following ideas for *you*. On what criteria did you decide an idea was good or bad? Could the unacceptable ideas be modified to make them more feasible for you?

   a. Get up two hours earlier every morning.

   b. Eat a more balanced diet.

   c. Learn to play a musical instrument.

   d. Invest $100 in the stock market.

   e. Volunteer at a local charity or retirement home.

8. Identify a problem in your work or school environment. How does your boss (or person who could change the situation) feel about that problem? What potential solutions do you see for that problem? What criteria would you use to determine their feasibility? Where would you go to find more information about the problem? List your information, but be prepared to write a report on the topic you have identified.

Extended Individual Exercises

9. Based on your current or previous employment or your experiences with volunteer or student organizations, address a problem you have noticed in the "workforce." Write a problem/solution report, carefully addressing a specific audience that has the power to make the changes you recommend.

10. Based on your current or previous employment, your community's needs, or other situations with which you are familiar, write a feasibility report proposing some special purchase or addition to that environment. You might recommend new equipment for your town's firefighters, a new traffic light at an intersection in your neighborhood, or a new computer system for your local school or workplace.

11. Make a grocery list with at least five items from several major categories, such as meat, frozen vegetables, fresh produce, and staples. Select three supermarkets and compare prices, quality, convenience, and any other criteria that will help you determine which supermarket is best. Write a trip report that explains your criteria and concludes with your findings.

12. Write a report based on your preliminary thinking for exercise 1, 2, or 8 above.

Collaborative Exercises

1. As a student you have probably been asked to evaluate your professors (and the courses they teach). What criteria do you think are most useful in evaluating the quality and level of instruction you have received?

Working with your partner(s), develop an evaluation form for professors and courses, based on your list of criteria. Be able to justify each item on your evaluation form.

2. With your partner(s), figure out how to read the stock market section of your newspaper. Select three corporations listed on the New York Stock Exchange and follow them for one week, pretending that you have invested $1,000 in each company.

Write a report in which you describe the status of one corporation's stock at the beginning of the week, in the middle of the week, and then at the end of the week. What (limited!) conclusions can you draw about the company after one week? What might explain any increases or decreases in the stock's value? What recommendations would you make to a friend who wants to invest in this company?

3. With your partner(s), determine whether your community should establish a new sports or recreational league (perhaps a soccer, football, tennis, bowling, or chess league) that would attract a particular population (teenagers, young adults, children, retirees). Determine the criteria you would have to use to measure the feasibility of your idea. Be very specific about the scope and limitations of your study—especially in terms of publicity, volunteer help, equipment and other costs, coaches, and the like. Answer the following questions, and then draft the feasibility report, paying special attention to the issues raised in the questions:

   a. Who would be your audience for this feasibility study?

   b. What kinds of information would the audience want to know?

   c. What kind(s) of research would you have to conduct on this topic? Where would you find that information?

   d. How long would your feasibility report be?

4. With your partner(s), gather data about computer programs that host E-mail: Pathway, Eudora Light, and others. Determine how you would analyze these programs in order to select one for installation in a computer laboratory on your campus. Then write the analytical report, comparing the programs you identified, explaining why you selected them over the numerous other programs, and recommending (to the manager of the laboratory) which program to purchase.

5. Brainstorm with your partner(s) to establish the criteria you believe characterize an excellent sports section in a newspaper. (How much attention is given to each in-season sport? How much attention is given to high school, college, and professional sports? How much attention is given to individual athletes?)

   Then collect newspapers for one week and analyze the sports sections. What conclusions can you draw about the coverage in that newspaper? Would you offer any suggestions or recommendations to the sports editor?

6. Brainstorm with your partner(s) to develop a brief survey that asks college students about their favorite newspaper cartoons. Try to elicit not only which cartoons they like, but why. Sample a random population of about fifty students, interviewing people in the cafeteria, in other classes (with the instructor's permission, of course), or in the dormitory. Or try to survey a number of men versus women students, freshmen versus seniors, and the like (such a survey is best conducted in dormitories and classes).

   Analyze the results of your survey. Did you find preferences among particular groups of cartoon readers (say, men versus women or freshmen versus seniors)?

   Write an analytical report for the editor of your local newspaper to use in determining which cartoons to keep publishing and which to delete.

ONGOING ASSIGNMENT

■ Based on the information you included in the newcomers' guide to your organization's culture, what assessment might you make about your organization? Do you consider it rigid or flexible? Is that rigidity or flexibility valuable or a hindrance to the organization's progress?

■ Write a report (two to three pages) to the organization's management explaining your assessment of its culture and offering recommendations to improve areas that might be detrimental to the organization and its ability to attract and retain high-quality employees.

Proposals

Have you and your friends ever speculated or joked about how you might make your first million dollars? Perhaps you have an idea for a new gadget that everyone will want or a service that people perform for themselves but would gladly pay someone else to do because they find the task difficult, boring, or disgusting. If you have ever said, "Somebody is going to make a million dollars from that idea" or "I wish somebody would develop a way to . . . ," then you have entertained some of the thought processes necessary to good proposal writing.

You can think about proposals in terms of the problem/solution reports you studied in the last chapter. Those reports often become the fodder for proposals—highly persuasive, specialized documents that offer products or services to an organization that needs and will benefit from those products or services. An organization may generate proposals internally to solve its problems, but just as often managers realize that the organization needs a product or service that is beyond the scope of its internal solutions. In that case, the organization looks for help from outside sources.

One of the primary means for finding that help is to issue a *Request for Proposals (RFP),* which asks interested parties (typically, other organizations) to describe how their product, service, system, or plan will meet the organization's needs and solve its problem. For example, the owners of TrendSetter's Restaurant (used as the basis for Chapter 13's scenarios) might agree that, based on a problem/solution report, they need a new produce vendor. They might issue an RFP that asks interested vendors to submit proposals covering a number of crucial issues: cost, selection, quality, availability, deliverability, complaint adjustments, and so on. Based on the proposals submitted, the owners would then select a vendor to be TrendSetter's new produce supplier.

Whereas for-profit organizations use proposals to attract clients or customers to purchase their services or products, nonprofit organizations use proposals to obtain funding for their work. Researchers in every field, for instance, often request funds from private and federal sources to pay research expenses such as salaries, equipment, travel, laboratory facilities, computers and software, and overhead (such as electricity, rent, and office supplies). You may already have had some experience with research proposals if your professors have asked you to submit a plan for a research paper or project (see the World of Workplace Writing box).

Social and welfare programs, special educational programs, and exhibitions and performing arts series are often funded by the government or by private foundations on the basis of merit, that is, by how persuasively a proposal writer argues that the program will benefit either a large number of people or a smaller group whose needs or interests are often overlooked. Even educational institutions, such as your college or university, request funds from donors and/or legislators for student scholarships (both academic and athletic), special programs, research priorities, teacher workshops, and new buildings or expansion. Your student organization may have requested funds to support a series of on-campus speakers, a

THE WORLD OF WORKPLACE WRITING

Proposals for Research

Although foundations that support research have highly specialized forms and applications for proposals, you have probably already been required (or soon will be) to write a brief proposal for research in some class. In requesting such a proposal, your instructor is trying to make sure *that your research topic is viable* (a subject that has answerable questions) and *that you know what conducting that research will entail* (time, budget, methods, equipment). Most classroom research proposals that are not approved pose questions that are unanswerable (at least in the classroom context), such as "When did time begin?" or are too big or too complex to be answered within the available time, budget, and other parameters, such as "What cures cancer?"

Successful proposals involve a narrow topic within a larger subject. The researcher either poses a question to be answered or states a hypothesis—a statement of belief that the research will either support or refute. The following are examples of questions that might be asked:

- Which mall attracts more customers during the December 20–25 shopping period?
- How much do elementary students know about babies?
- What U.S. city has the highest rate of unsolved crimes?

Those questions can be restated as hypotheses:

Hypothesis 1: The Bensonhirst Mall attracts more customers during the December 20–25 shopping period than the Montague Mall.

Hypothesis 2: Students in elementary grades know more about sex than they do about babies.

Hypothesis 3: Madison has a higher unsolved crime rate than any other city in the United States.

In writing a research proposal, you can use the following outline as a guide for constructing the answers to your instructor's questions:

OVERALL SUBJECT _____

NARROW TOPIC _____

    Question to be answered _____ OR

    Hypothesis offered _____

METHODS FOR ANSWERING THE QUESTION OR TESTING THE HYPOTHESIS:

    Literature review

    Survey/interview

    Advanced research methods (soil samples, tests, analyses, etc.)

field trip to another state, or a new software program for a computer laboratory. In short, every conceivable organization uses proposals to obtain things it needs.

In this chapter, you will learn more about the contexts and features of proposal writing. After a brief narrative that provides an overview of the proposal process, this chapter clarifies your role as a writer and what you need to know about your readers—information that will help you succeed as a proposal writer. Next, you will learn more about the types of proposals used in the workplace and will progress through the proposal writing process. The final section of the chapter shows the primary features of a proposal that readers consider when deciding whether or not to accept the proposal. Knowing these features will help you clarify and strengthen your own proposals.

An Overview of the Proposal Process

In the workplace, a *proposal* is a specialized report from an individual or a group, asking to perform a service or deliver a product to meet a particular need that the reader has. A *bid* is the cost estimate alone without the proposal's text that attempts to persuade readers of the applicant's suitability for the project. In the TrendSetter's Restaurant scenario, a bid based strictly on costs would not satisfy the owners because freshness, selection, and delivery arrangements are likely to be as important (if not more so) as costs. Further, the produce vendors themselves probably obtain the produce from warehousers, who purchase it from the farmers who actually grow the produce; thus, the proposal process might proceed as shown in Figure 14.1. As this example illustrates, the proposal process can be vast and may include dozens of organizations—all trying to convince others that their work or ideas are superior to those of their competitors.

Of course, TrendSetter's owners do not simply announce that they want a new produce vendor and then sit back and wait for vendors to submit proposals. Instead, the owners develop an outline of the information that they want each vendor to include in the proposal so that they can get a sense of the quality, costs, and benefits of the different vendors' services and products. The following questions offer a modest look at the restaurant owners' concerns at this stage:

1. What kind and amount of produce do we need, based on these criteria?
   - Menu selection and recipes
   - Number of customers
   - Storage facilities for produce
   - Clientele's expectations
   - Special catering/parties scheduled

2. What are the primary criteria for selecting the vendor?
   - Freshness
   - Quality

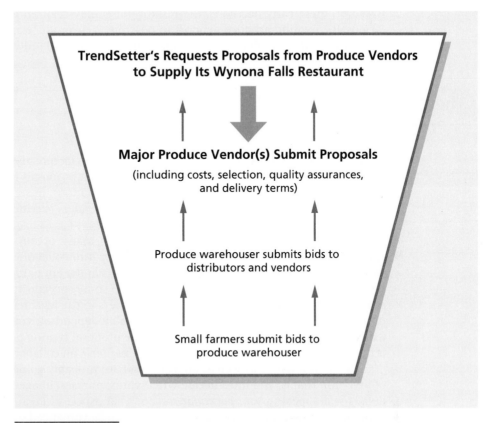

TrendSetter's Requests Proposals from Produce Vendors to Supply Its Wynona Falls Restaurant

Major Produce Vendor(s) Submit Proposals
(including costs, selection, quality assurances, and delivery terms)

Produce warehouser submits bids to distributors and vendors

Small farmers submit bids to produce warehouser

FIGURE 14.1 An Example of the Proposal/Bidding Process

- Variety
- Cost
- Reliability
- Required size of orders
- Ability to handle special orders
- Delivery standards
- Organic versus nonorganic produce

3. In addition to meeting our supply specifications, what other criteria should we use to select a produce vendor?
    - Amount of experience
    - Warehousers and farmers with whom the vendor contracts
    - Procedures for handling adjustments and complaints

Based on these early decisions, the restaurateurs may draft an RFP (Request for Proposals), inviting produce vendors to describe their produce and service (RFPs are discussed in more detail later). Thus begins the proposal process.

The Writer's Role in the Proposal Process

Perhaps more than any other form of report, proposals directly connect writers and readers via the "request-and-answer" format that proposals use. And because proposal writers are asking readers for business, donations, or some other form of support, the relationship between the writer and readers is critical to the success of the proposal.

Because of the importance of proposals to many organizations, proposal writers often work in teams, and your own entry into collaborative writing may well be through proposal writing. Various experts and team participants will construct particular segments of the proposal, with some specializing in product descriptions, others in cost estimates, and still others in the legal terminology of the proposal's promises. Your own role will probably depend on your area of expertise. The first role you are likely to play in the proposal writing process, however, is that of subject matter expert (SME). (See Chapter 7 on collaboration.)

Next, as a writer as well as an SME, you are probably going to play the role of inventor; that is, you must decide what words, phrases, images, and supporting details will appeal to *your particular readers*. That aspect of creativity is crucial to good proposal writing, for readers are unlikely to be convinced of your claims and the merits of your product or service if you do not craft a "just right" approach to winning their approval. To do so, you work with the content, tone, and "feeling" of your proposal—elements that require intense attention to the details that will motivate readers to trust you and your ideas.

Trustworthiness, therefore, is one of the final (but most important) qualities you must incorporate into your proposal writing. If the readers have the slightest sense that you are not being straightforward with your descriptions and your promises, they certainly will have no motivation to accept your proposal. As a highly specialized form of selling, proposals require the writer to acknowledge that the offered product or service is not a cure-all while assuring the readers that it will meet their needs.

Readers of Proposals

Proposal readers, like most report readers, are reading for special purposes. They do not care to be entertained (although they should not be bored either); instead, they are reading for information. Many proposal readers approach each proposal in one of three ways:

THE WORLD OF WORKPLACE WRITING

Ethics and Proposal Writing

Perhaps more than any other form of workplace writing, proposals may tempt writers to make false claims—slant the truth, misrepresent accomplishments and abilities, or skew some evidence of success. One writer, for example, had a great deal of trouble describing the level of expertise of his coworkers on a particular project. Another had difficulty saying that her organization was successful at meeting deadlines, given that its last three projects were late, although the delays were due to the sponsoring agency, not her own organization. A third proposal writer knew his product would best meet the sponsoring organization's need, but at a considerably higher price than his competitors' products. What claims could he make that would justify the higher price?

These examples illustrate just a few of the ethical dilemmas that proposal writers may face. Proposal readers and sponsoring (or granting) agencies are used to having to "read between the lines" for overstatements, misrepresentations, or facts that don't add up. As with other forms of communication, however, distorting information in proposals can have severe consequences for your organization, your career, and your self-respect. Most writers who have been caught in such misrepresentations will tell you that regardless of the value of the contract, losing your dignity and reputation is not worth the price.

1. How does your proposal *benefit* my organization?
2. What evidence do you offer that proves *you* are the best person/group/ organization for this job/funding?
3. On what basis can I *disqualify* you?

In short, some readers look for ways to include your proposal, while others read to disqualify it and select the "winner" by the process of elimination. Because you probably do not know which approach your readers will take, you should consider the following questions when revising and clarifying your proposal:

1. Have I shown how useful/appropriate our product or service is for the reader?
2. Have I provided all the evidence that we are the group/organization that can best meet the reader's needs?
3. Have I completely covered my topic and eliminated every obstacle that might prevent my organization from being awarded the contract or funds?

Other aspects of revising your document are addressed later under Revising the Proposal.

Types of Proposals

Regardless of their subject matter, context, or purpose, proposals typically fall into two classes: solicited and unsolicited. The main distinction between these forms is whether the reader expects to receive the proposal. *Solicited proposals* are requested by the reader or sponsoring organization; *unsolicited proposals* are initiated by the proposal writer. Some funding agencies, such as the National Science Foundation and the National Endowment for the Arts, expect and welcome proposals. In fact, these agencies stay in business because of proposals (and, of course, because of government funding). Other organizations, such as for-profit corporations, may solicit proposals only when they have a particular job they need done.

With an unsolicited proposal, the writers and their organization believe that once the readers and the receiving organization read the proposal and learn more about the offering organization's product or service, they will find that they need or want that product or service. In other words, the receiving organization may not even know that it wants a particular product or service until it reads an unsolicited proposal from an offering organization.

Regardless of whether the proposal is solicited or unsolicited, however, both forms require special persuasive strategies; thus, the rhetorical (or persuasive) aspect of writing becomes especially important. When writing a solicited proposal, you are likely to learn what appeals will motivate the reader by checking the RFP, which probably will specify that the proposal should include certain information such as qualifications or cost analyses.

When writing an unsolicited proposal, however, you will have to determine what is most likely to appeal to your reader. References to safety, quality, prestige, honor, security, health, profits, ethics, and—yes—sex appeal are often used to try to persuade readers. The following discussions of solicited and unsolicited proposals will help clarify the role of these appeals in proposals.

Solicited Proposals

As we have seen, a *solicited proposal* is a response to an RFP, a written or E-mailed invitation to submit proposals that is sent out by the funding (or sponsoring or granting) agency. Most RFPs come from organizations that have one of three purposes to be served:

1. The organization wants to hire another agency or organization to do a special job (which may be a one-time only job) for pay; for example, to deliver the official Christmas tree to the White House, to build a new wing for the local hospital, to arrange transportation for the city's newly founded ballet, or to design a new logo to be used on all the corporation's products.

2. The organization wants to fund certain kinds of programs (typically in the arts, economic development, social welfare, education, or related areas) that further charitable goals.

3. The organization wants to fund research projects that will contribute to a body of knowledge in a given field (e.g., sciences, humanities, education).

With its various agencies, the U.S. government is probably the best example of an organization that sends out RFPs for all three of these purposes. For example, the Smithsonian Institution (a government agency) may develop an RFP asking security firms to propose a new state-of-the-art security system; the National Endowment for the Arts (another agency) may develop an RFP offering to fund programs in the arts; and the National Science Foundation (a third agency) may develop yet another RFP offering to fund AIDS research.

When the writers in an organization draft an RFP, they specify for proposers the kinds of programs or ideas that organization seeks to fund and the particulars it wants to see in a proposal. As a proposal writer, you should follow the RFP's directions to the letter because variations, omissions, or unrequested additions may disqualify your proposal from consideration. Note that the RFP for the TrendSetter's scenario is very specific about the categories of information it wants (see Figure 14.2 on page 476). Writers drafting a proposal would be wise to use these categories.

Further, you should realize that, as strange as it may sound at first, *the lowest bid on a project does not necessarily win the project.* In addition to costs, other factors, which are often known only to the requesters, can significantly affect the awarding of a project:

- The requesting agency's experience with the proposing organization
- The reputation of the proposer
- The provisions for safety inspections and quality assurances
- The quality of materials
- The quality of the labor force
- The time to completion of the project
- The proposer's history of meeting deadlines

Of course, the writing of the proposal plays a direct part in the awarding of a contract:

- How persuasive is the proposal?
- How thorough is the proposal?
- Does the proposal address each item on the RFP?
- How understandable is the proposal? Does the proposal writer seem to be trying to hide something? Does the writer hedge on details, deadlines, or the organization's experience in this area?

A later segment in this chapter describes more thoroughly the evaluation procedures that most proposals face; for now, you should consider these questions as a means of supplying readers' needs in solicited proposals.

context and
purpose

first set of
requirements

second set of
requirements

document design
limitations

deadline

Request for Proposals

TRENDSETTER's, the nation's leading restaurant chain, seeks proposals for produce vendors to supply its restaurant in Wynona Falls. Licensed commercial vendors should submit, *in order:*

- Detailed lists of produce
- Detailed lists of costs
- Descriptions of delivery service
- Verification of organic subcontractors/farmers' growing practices
- Specifications for negotiating quality and complaints
- Descriptions of payment plans

Further, the proposal must include the following:

- A detailed history of the firm
- A list of other restaurants supplied by the vendor including three restaurants that may be contacted for references (include addresses and phone numbers)

The document must also meet the following design/content specifications:

- 3–4 pages
- Title page, including
  - Name of organization
  - Owners of organization
  - Years in business
- 10-point serif type only
- Double-spaced

Submit proposals (or further inquiries) by 20 December 1999 to Melinda Martine, TrendSetter's Restaurant, 1123 Gateway Plaza, Wynona Falls, SD 59344 or call (792) TRNDSTR.

FIGURE 14.2 TrendSetter's Request for Proposals

Unsolicited Proposals

In contrast to solicited proposals, which originate with the funding organization, *unsolicited proposals* originate with the product or service providers. Much like the writer of a sales letter, the writer of an unsolicited proposal has to persuade the readers that they need whatever it is the writer is "selling"—whether it is a research project investigating consumer habits, a series of seminars on improving workplace communications, or a maintenance contract to service the company's cars.

Because unsolicited proposals do not respond to RFPs, writers have to use their critical-thinking skills to determine which organizations or agencies might benefit from their wares. They may devise a list of prospects from reading the morning newspaper. Or they may know that certain industries stay in business by funding new projects, as publishing companies do by funding new books. Or they may even learn from social conversations that a particular organization might want to know more about the product or service they offer.

Figure 14.3 on pages 478–479 is an unsolicited proposal, written by a team of proposal writers at Strategic Advertising, that tries to persuade the owners of TrendSetter's to expand the restaurant's advertising. Note the kinds of content and motivational appeals the writers have included to support their proposition. Also note the letter format, which is often used for brief proposals; longer proposals will most likely require a report format, such as that shown in Figures 14.5 and 14.6 later in this chapter.

The Proposal Writing Process

Like all writing tasks, proposal writing should follow a carefully crafted, but recursive (back and forth) process that includes planning, researching, organizing, drafting, and revising; writers must also determine the special graphic and layout features the proposal needs to be clear and appealing. The following discussions address the process of writing a successful proposal. As you learned in Chapters 3–9 about the writing process, the order of these steps is not rigid, and you may return to any step at any time in the process.

APPLICATION

Developing a Proposal

Based on the information provided in Strategic Advertising's unsolicited proposal (Figure 14.3), do you think the writers stand a chance of having this proposal accepted? If you owned the restaurant, would you be interested in at least discussing these ideas with the Strategic Advertising team? Even without reading any further in this chapter, you should have a reaction to this proposal—positive, neutral, or negative. Describe your response, as well as the reasons for it, in a paragraph or two.

STRATEGIC ADVERTISING

2701 CANYON TERRACE
WYNONA FALLS, SD 59344   (792) 322-ADVT

18 November 1999

Ms. Melinda Martine
TrendSetter's Restaurant
1123 Gateway Plaza
Wynona Falls, SD 59344

Dear Ms. Martine:

knowledge of
TrendSetter's

Because TrendSetter's opened two years ago, many residents assume they know all you have to offer. But your expanded menu, extended dining hours, and catering services—as well as your larger dining area (which reduces the time spent waiting for a table)—mean that you have something new to offer the residents of Wynona Falls. A bold advertising campaign will attract the number and quality of clients you hope to reach.

offer

request

Would you please review the following ideas for forging that bold campaign and let us know if you would like to discuss these ideas—or others that you may have—with us?

Our Marketing Vision

theme of
campaign

A crucial part of our plan is maintaining the reputation for elegance and dignity that TrendSetter's has established over the past two years. We consider that image one of the essential elements in an advertising strategy that should incorporate all forms of media: television, radio, and newsprint.

methods

specific
suggestions

After first highlighting the menu selections, we would like to move on to the special facilities and services you offer: banquet facilities, catering, and lunches. We believe you can reach a much wider audience by sponsoring print and television/radio advertising. We would like to meet with you to show you some of our storyboards and layouts for the proposed campaign.

Benefits of Strategic Advertising

acknowledged fear

benefits overcome
fear

We realize that you are likely to be skeptical about handing over your business image to an agency since you have always handled your own advertising. One of the primary benefits of working with us is that it would free you to run your business, while we handle the production and arrangements for your advertising. Further, because you have final approval on all aspects of our plans, you remain in control of the advertising and image we design for TrendSetter's Restaurant.

FIGURE 14.3   An Unsolicited Proposal Letter from Strategic Advertising, page 1

Martine
p. 2

Some of the additional benefits we offer might entice you even further:

detailed benefits

- Guaranteed satisfaction
- Input on all phases of the planning and marketing
- Guaranteed lowest rates on all media contracts
- Free demographic information, based on latest research
- Two free meetings with account and marketing representatives
- Reasonable payment plan

Qualifications of Strategic Advertising

credentials and justification for awarding advertising contract to Strategic Advertising

Strategic Advertising has been in business for more than ten years in Wynona Falls. We know the area's residents and the businesses that support those residents. This knowledge gives us an edge over the larger agencies that are located in the capital. Our team is constantly conducting marketing research on the Wynona Falls area that will provide you with the most current information on area demographics—information to which you are entitled as one of our clients.

awards

team approach

That team approach to handling accounts is one of our strengths, evidenced by our winning the highly prestigious Sellers' Prize for South Dakota for the past four years. Rather than assign one agent to your account, which is standard practice in our industry, we assign a team comprised of researchers, text writers, graphic illustrators, account representatives, and company liaisons. This team is yours and works at your direction.

You are no doubt familiar with many of our clients and their businesses:

clients/testimonials

- Jade Market, Inc.
- Monroe Furniture Makers
- Purdue Ranches
- Jenny's Jewelers
- McCamerson's Fine Fashions

You are welcome to call any of these clients and inquire about our reputation for service and quality.

call to action

We are eager to go to work for TrendSetter's and would like to meet with you and discuss our services—and our ideas—further. Won't you call us and let us schedule an appointment to expand TrendSetter's high-quality profile? We look forward to hearing from you soon.

Sincerely,

J. Matheson

J. Matheson
President

FIGURE 14.3 An Unsolicited Proposal Letter from Strategic Advertising, page 2

Planning the Proposal

As with all forms of workplace writing, successful proposals most often begin with a well-thought-out plan. The worksheet in Figure 14.4 will help you identify the kinds of information your proposals should include. Based on your research and understanding of your readers' needs, you can outline the ways your idea, product, or service will meet those needs.

Researching the Proposal

Because all good writing depends on the strength of the information itself, proposal writers spend a great deal of time researching. Not only must they research the special needs of the requester, which typically are outlined in the RFP, but they may also research the requesting organization's environment to determine how specialized their product or service needs to be. They may also research their competition so that they can adjust their proposal to meet or surpass the benefits their competitors might offer.

Proposal writers also research their own product or service to determine how well it can meet the reader's needs. And they consider any additional benefits they can offer that might win the contract. Armed with this additional information about the reader, the competition, and the special features that are most likely to appeal to the reader, the writer can select the best information to include in the proposal.

Organizing the Proposal

The proposal should be designed to meet the special needs of the requesters or clients. Therefore, the order of the information should reassure the readers that the proposers are thoroughly familiar with those needs. As Chapter 4 on organization explained, you should organize your proposal according to the readers' needs for information. Often the RFP will specify the organization (and, thus, the major sections) of the proposal. When the order is not specified, you should consider the following pattern standard for proposals:

1. Overview of the organization's problem, showing that you understand the specific need, as well as the context for the proposal
2. Description of your product or service
3. Benefits of your product or service, as they pertain to the readers' needs
4. Additional benefits of your product or service that extend beyond the readers' specific requests
5. Your qualifications to perform this service or provide this product and your (or your organization's) experience with similar situations and needs

PROPOSAL PLANNING WORKSHEET

1. My readers are _____[names, titles, etc.]_____ .

2. The readers are
   - expecting my proposal (solicited proposal) or
   - not expecting my proposal (unsolicited proposal).

3. The readers are most likely to award this contract based on
   - the product or service itself,
   - my organization's experience and reputation,
   - the cost of my product or service,
   - rapid, dependable, qualified maintenance and service when problems arise,
   - our ability to meet a deadline, or
   - some other criteria _____ .

4. In addition, I should appeal to the readers' interest in
   profits   technology
   health   rapid service
   security   ethics
   safety   public image
   prestige   quality
   other appeals and interests _____ .

5. The strongest selling point of my proposal is
   - the product or service itself,
   - my organization's experience and reputation,
   - the cost of my product or service,
   - our ability to meet a deadline, or
   - some other criteria _____ .

6. My (or my organization's) abilities correspond to my readers' needs, as outlined in the following table:

The Sponsoring Organization Needs . . .	*My Organization Can Provide . . .*
1.	1.
2.	2.
3.	3.
4.	4.

7. The funding agency requested these additional features for the proposal:
   - Number of pages limited to _____
   - Cover page must include
     _____ name of organization
     _____ name of writer(s)
     _____ previous contracts awarded
     _____ date
     _____ other information
   - Number of copies to be submitted _____
   - Any special type style/size/features _____
   - Other features needed _____

F I G U R E 14.4 Proposal Planning Worksheet

6. Testimonials, statistics, or other proof of success

7. Concluding call for proposal acceptance

Although specialized proposals may require a different scheme, the organization of the majority of proposals follows this pattern.

Drafting the Proposal

The most complicated part of every writing task, of course, is the actual drafting of the document. Once you understand its organizational scheme, however, that chore is much simpler. By using some of the drafting strategies described in Chapter 5, you should be able to produce a working draft of a proposal that begins to address the readers' needs.

Figure 14.5 is a draft of a proposal written by Sue Banks, the owner and operator of Organically Yours, a produce vendor. The draft, which was written in response to TrendSetter's RFP, illustrates the planning, researching, and organizing that a proposal writer must do; also noted in the margins are the weaknesses in this draft that Sue wants to correct or strengthen in the final version of the proposal (see the next sections, Revising the Proposal and Criteria for Evaluating Proposals).

Revising the Proposal

Most of the strategies for revising the proposal closely follow the strategies for revising any workplace document (see Chapter 6). Writers must deliver clear prose, sensible organization, and complete and accurate information. Further, they must consider the graphics that will support or clarify the proposal's information, while appealing to the readers. Finally, they must attend to layout features that will help guide the readers through the document. The remaining keys to revision are echoed in the criteria that the readers use for evaluating the proposal, discussed next.

Criteria for Evaluating Proposals

When proposals are submitted, readers often form an immediate impression of the ideas, products, or services offered: good or bad—yes or no. Particularly with unsolicited proposals, readers may recognize that the proposal is not within the boundaries of ideas they consider or fund, that it does not meet any of their organization's needs, or that all funds are already designated for other projects. In that case, the proposal will be rejected on these grounds.

Other proposals, however, may strike the readers as interesting or even as ideal for their organization's needs or mission. When readers read a proposal care-

<table>
<tr>
<td>

title isn't very relevant—needs to connect OY to TrendSetter's

but they aren't <u>investing</u> in OY

cliché

name dropping? (move to later segment?)

subject and verb disagree

add imports

sounds smug and overly familiar

comma not needed

needs to be clearer

clarify

</td>
<td>

ORGANICALLY YOURS:
PRODUCE SUPPLIER FOR THE TWENTY-FIRST CENTURY

As a 27-year-old corporate produce vendor, Organically Yours (OY) is a smart investment for any upscale restaurant. We know your patrons are health-conscious, and our organically grown produce will suit them to a tee.

We currently service some of the best restaurants in the southern South Dakota region, including Stacey's, Margaux's, and MamaMia's Cuisine. Each of these restaurateurs will tell you that our quality is unsurpassed and our prices reasonable. We deliver on time and take great care that your order is correct and fresh.

We specialize in greens, such as turnips, lettuce, cabbage, and parsley. All forms of herbs are available through Organically Yours. All sorts of produce, in fact, bears the OY label: squash, potatoes, turnips, sweet potatoes, asparagus, mushrooms, cucumbers, tomatoes, celery, onions, carrots, peas, beans, peppers, and even hot peppers.

Our delivery service is as good as our produce: on time and correct. We pride our-selves on taking the time to make sure we have your order just right. It doesn't help for us to ship you cabbage when you need parsley, right? And our delivery trucks roll night and day, just to make sure you have the freshest produce possible.

We contract with some of the finest growers in our region (including McCrory's Farms, and Maple Hill Produce), and we import produce from outside the region for year-round availability (Tull Mill Farms, Nature's Way, and Arcadian Produce). Our verifications of growing practices assure you that all produce is, indeed, organically grown (see attached Certificate of Quality Produce).

We negotiate quality and complaints with each produce receiver at each restaurant, verifying that the selection and quality are what you want. If you have any problems with any of our deliveries, we will make immediate cost adjustments and will have the correct order to you within 12 hours. On special occasions, however, when produce is not up to our quality standards, we may have to refuse delivery to our clients. In such cases, we will contact you immediately to see if a substitution would be preferable.

</td>
</tr>
</table>

FIGURE 14.5 Sue Banks's Draft of a Solicited Proposal from Organically Yours, page 1

sounds too
flexible???

add current prices?

not relevant

not relevant

doesn't fit here

provide phone
numbers

too casual?

Organically Yours
p. 2

Our payment plans depend on the amount ordered and the length of the contract:

	$2,000–$4,999	$5,000+
1 year	15% interest	12% interest
2 years	12% interest	10% interest
5 years	10% interest	9% interest

Of course, market conditions determine the costs of the produce itself, so we cannot quote you prices.

Organically Yours has been in business for 27 years. I opened the warehouse in 1972 when I moved out from California because of my husband's poor health. Although the growing conditions in South Dakota are quite different from those in California, I have found that greenhouses, controlled properly, can replicate California's ideal conditions for growing produce. Our financial outlook, by all accounts, is good, and we anticipate building another warehouse in the spring.

We supply 33 restaurants in the southern South Dakota region, including the following, which you may contact for references:

Minah Byrd's
The Cooked Goose
Rebecca's
Mesquite Grille
Mashed Potato Mama's
El Greco's

We look forward to serving the needs of TrendSetter's and its patrons. Please give us a call and let's talk over a contract today.

FIGURE 14.5   Sue Banks's Draft of a Solicited Proposal from Organically Yours, page 2

fully, they are typically looking for a few critical matters—matters that can help the writer revise the drafted proposal:

1. The proposer is or represents a reputable organization that is willing to provide references.

2. The proposer has the qualifications, credentials, and licenses (if necessary) to complete the contract.
3. The proposer has experience handling this kind of project.
4. The proposer recognizes the importance of staying within a budget.
5. The proposer recognizes the importance of meeting a deadline.
6. The proposer stands behind all work.
7. The proposer is willing to allow spot inspections.
8. The proposer is willing to allow the funding agency some input on the project.
9. The proposer has accounted for hidden costs, such as overhead, in the proposal.
10. Related materials (such as paper for a seminar or laboratory equipment for a research project) are either covered in the cost analysis or assumed by the proposer.
11. The quality of the materials used is acceptable, if not exceptionally high.

Beyond relying on the standard elements of revision (see Chapter 6), successful proposal writers use their knowledge of evaluation criteria to revise their proposals. When you know, for instance, that readers are particularly interested in evidence that your previous clients or customers were satisfied with your product or service, you will be more careful to emphasize that information in your proposal.

For TrendSetter's, a proposal that meets the specifications of the RFP (refer back to Figure 14.2) will pass the initial test and attract the reader's attention. Once all the proposals that meet the specific requirements outlined in the RFP have been determined, TrendSetter's reader might use the following criteria to identify outstanding proposals and further narrow down the group of possible vendors:

1. Does the writer demonstrate a clear sense of our need?
2. Does the writer offer a clear means of meeting our need?
3. Does the writer have experience supplying similar restaurants?
4. Does the writer have a clear sense of the menu and clientele of our restaurant?
5. Does the writer have a clear sense of the financial parameters of our restaurant?
6. Does the writer offer clear evidence that this organization is the best to meet our needs?
7. Does the writer offer any additional benefits that we should consider?

At this point, you should review TrendSetter's RFP in Figure 14.2 and draft of a proposal from Organically Yours, a produce vendor, in Figure 14.5. The notes in the margins of the draft show the kinds of problems writers want to eliminate in their revisions. Now look at Figure 14.6 on pages 486–489, which shows Sue's final version of the proposal. How successful do you think she was in revising it?

better title emphasizes <u>both</u> businesses

experience and longevity as key selling factors

knowledge of TrendSetter's

partnership with OY

selection

offers current prices as a gauge for comparing competitors' prices

TrendSetter's and ORGANICALLY YOURS: Partners in Quality

Sue Banks, Owner

As a 27-year-old corporate produce vendor, Organically Yours (OY) is an excellent produce vendor for any upscale restaurant. We know your patrons are health-conscious, and our organically grown produce will ensure tasty, healthy meals that will enhance the TrendSetter's reputation for outstanding cuisine.

Produce Selection

We specialize in greens, such as arugula, turnips, lettuce, cabbage, and parsley. All forms of herbs are available through Organically Yours. All sorts of produce, in fact, bear the OY label: squash, potatoes, turnips, sweet potatoes, asparagus, mushrooms, cucumbers, tomatoes, celery, onions, carrots, peas, beans, peppers, artichokes, and even imported hot peppers.

Costs

Although market conditions determine the costs of the produce month by month, we can quote you a sample of the prices from this month's stock, per pound:

Lettuce and other greens	.64
Tomatoes, cucumbers, squash	.67
Peas, beans, potatoes	.54
Asparagus, artichokes	.99
Mushrooms	.93

FIGURE 14.6 A Revised Proposal from Organically Yours, page 1

TrendSetter's and Organically Yours

p. 2

OY's prices compare favorably to that of inorganic produce

We believe our prices compare favorably with the prices of even inorganically grown produce, making cost a nonissue in the produce growing business.

Delivery Service

dependability

Our delivery service is as good as our produce: on time and correct. We pride ourselves on taking the time to make sure we have your order just right. And our delivery trucks (refrigerated, of course) roll night and day

quality

to make sure you have the freshest produce possible.

Verification of Organic Subcontractors/Farms

quality suppliers

We contract with some of the finest growers in our region (including McCrory's Farms and Maple Hill Produce), and we import produce from outside the region for year-round availability (Tull Mill Farms, Nature's Way, and Arcadian Produce). Our verifications of growing practices

proof/certification

assure you that all produce is, indeed, organically grown (see attached Certificate of Quality Produce that certifies that planting, fertilizing, growing patterns, harvesting, and packaging have been monitored).

Negotiations for Quality and Complaints

"you"-oriented policies

We negotiate quality and complaints with each produce receiver at each restaurant, verifying that the selection and quality are what you want. If you have any problems with any of our deliveries, we will make immediate cost adjustments and will have the correct order to you

FIGURE 14.6 A Revised Proposal from Organically Yours, page 2

TrendSetter's and Organically Yours

p. 3

within 12 hours. On special occasions, however, when produce is not up to our quality standards, we may have to refuse to accept shipments from our suppliers, making the produce unavailable to our clients as well. In such cases, we will contact you immediately to see if a substitution would be preferable, and we will gladly confer with your chefs about substitutions for menu and recipe items.

helpful alternatives

Payment Plans

Our payment plans depend on the amount ordered and the length of the contract:

standard pricing contract, set up as a table for easier reading

Years under Contract with Organically Yours	Amount Ordered Annually	
	$2,000–$4,999	$5,000+
1 year	15% interest	12% interest
2 years	12% interest	10% interest
5 years+	10% interest	9% interest

History of Organically Yours

background/ history and longevity

Organically Yours has been in business for 27 years. The Eugene Banks family bought its first warehouse in 1972. Although the climate is quite different here in South Dakota, we have found that greenhouses, controlled properly, can replicate California's ideal conditions for growing produce. We purchased two additional warehouses in the first

F I G U R E 14.6   A Revised Proposal from Organically Yours, page 3

TrendSetter's and Organically Yours

p. 4

three years of operation to meet the demand from conscientious restaurateurs who wanted to have organically grown produce in their recipes and on their menus. Our business has grown so tremendously that we anticipate building another warehouse in the spring, but at the core we remain a small business with an ongoing commitment to freshness, quality, selection, and good health.

Other Restaurants Supplied by Organically Yours

We currently service some of the best restaurants in the southern South Dakota region, including four-star restaurants Stacey's, Margaux's, and MamaMia's Cuisine. In fact, we supply 33 restaurants in the region, including all of the following, which you may contact for references:

Minah Byrd's	Rebecca's	Mesquite Grille
(792) 322-4939	(792) 322-5748	(792) 321-3852
The Cooked Goose	Potato Mama's	El Greco's
(792) 466-3863	(792) 322-6878	(792) 466-2947

Each of these restaurateurs will tell you that our quality is unsurpassed and our prices reasonable. We deliver on time and take great care that your order is correct and fresh.

We look forward to serving the needs of TrendSetter's and its patrons. If you have any additional questions about our produce, service, or other matters, please do not hesitate to call Sue Banks at (792) 931-4323.

Margin annotations:

progress + growth = longevity

evidence and testimonials

phone numbers supplied for easy reference

call to action

FIGURE 14.6 A Revised Proposal from Organically Yours, page 4

Estimating Costs in Proposals

One of the most sophisticated points of a well-written proposal is the budget or costs estimate. In many industries, labor and materials are standard elements of the budget, but a company will quickly go bankrupt if the proposal writer does not include the costs of overhead (electricity, administrative assistants' salaries, and telephone expenses), equipment (initial cost, maintenance, and depreciation), and other often overlooked expenses.

If you are preparing your first proposal, be sure to look for all sorts of hidden costs, such as office equipment, building or rental costs, travel and telephone expenses, meals, overnight stays, special licensing fees, salaries for support staff, and labor expenses, that can skew the budget of your proposal. Gross underestimates can make you look naive or cause tremendous embarrassment if you have to ask the granting agency to renegotiate the budget. If the budget cannot be renegotiated, underestimates can cost your organization a great deal of money. Of course, overestimates can cause your organization to lose the contract altogether.

Summary

This chapter has described some of the most common purposes for proposal writing in the workplace. Writers often find themselves working in collaborative teams when writing proposals in order to take advantage of the expertise of the entire organization they represent. You may find it useful, therefore, to review the information in Chapter 7 on collaboration.

Proposals typically fall into one of two categories: solicited and unsolicited. Specifically, writers construct *solicited proposals* when they respond to an RFP (Request for Proposals). Organizations send out RFPs when they have a special need, want a particular job done, or want to fund certain kinds of programs or projects. Because the RFP often tells writers the exact kinds of information the funding organization seeks, writers would be wise to research and provide answers to those specific requests. Many proposals, in fact, are disqualified from consideration because they omit important information, do not format the proposal as requested, provide too much information, or violate some other explicit instruction set forth in the RFP.

Although many proposals are responses to RFPs in the workplace, numerous other proposals are *unsolicited*, meaning that the organization's writers take it upon themselves to offer a product, service, program, or other idea to another organization that they believe might benefit from that offering. For example, a security firm's writers might send out hundreds of unsolicited proposals to area businesses in the belief that at least a few of those businesses are likely to be interested in talking with them about their systems. Similarly, a coffee vending service might submit unsolicited proposals to every department in your college, asking for a contract to provide coffee equipment, supplies, and maintenance for faculty and students in each department.

As you can see from these examples, some proposals are nothing more than extended sales letters; more complicated services and products, however, demand extensive explanation, description, graphics, and even contractual sections. These documents serve specific purposes in selling expensive or complicated products or services, and their writers spend a great deal of time planning, researching, organizing, drafting, and revising these proposals. In many organizations, in fact, special teams of proposal writers are formed to create proposals as their sole job responsibility.

In smaller companies and in entrepreneurial ventures, however, every employee may be responsible for writing proposals—at least modest ones. If you are considering going into business for yourself, for example, you may have to write a proposal describing your venture for potential investors and for the bank from which you want to borrow money.

The proposal writing process, therefore, begins with a firm grasp of what readers look for when they read proposals and what might motivate them to accept your proposal. The answers to those questions should help you through the proposal writing process and result in a final proposal that encourages the reader's approval.

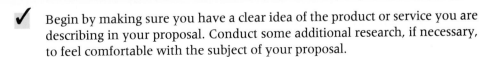

CHECKLIST

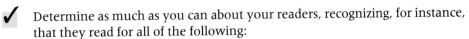

✓ Begin by making sure you have a clear idea of the product or service you are describing in your proposal. Conduct some additional research, if necessary, to feel comfortable with the subject of your proposal.

✓ Determine as much as you can about your readers, recognizing, for instance, that they read for all of the following:

- Clarity
- Accuracy
- Conciseness
- Attention to detail
- Elements of conviction or support
- Experience

✓ Recognize that your readers may also be reading for these reasons:

- To determine why you/your organization should be awarded the contract
- To disqualify your proposal from consideration

✔ If your proposal is solicited, turn to the RFP for specific instructions about these elements:

- ■ Content (needs)
- ■ Organization
- ■ Document details:
   Number of pages
   Type style and size
   Supporting documents and the like

✔ If your proposal is unsolicited, use your critical-thinking skills to determine the appeals (safety, profits, prestige, quality, and so on) that are most likely to motivate your readers to accept your idea, product, or service.

✔ As with any other sales tool, determine how your product/service/idea matches your readers' needs.

✔ Format the document according to any special requests the readers have made. Once you have met their requirements, look for ways to improve the overall image and visual appeal of your document, referring to the graphic and design features described in Chapters 8 and 9.

✔ Proofread carefully. Sloppy proofreading undermines your credibility—a primary feature of successful proposals.

EXERCISES

Individual Exercises

1. Suppose you are representing the following organizations and their products/services. What sorts of readers would be interested in proposals from each of these organizations? What might motivate the readers to respond—with additional questions or even contracts—to the proposals?
   - ■ A shoe manufacturer that specializes in athletic shoes
   - ■ A baby-sitting service
   - ■ A bakery
   - ■ A used-book store

2. Using the information and planning sheet from the first World of Workplace Writing box, identify a weakness or problem in your part-time or full-time job, or on your campus, that you are qualified to research and address. Submit the proposal to the appropriate instructor to gain approval for your research.

3. Using your imagination, select some product or service that you would like to have supplied at your current place of work or on your campus (perhaps a coffee service, a set of vending machines, or a postal service office). What elements and criteria would you want to see in proposals from various organizations that might want to supply that need? Construct an RFP that includes all the information you would seek.

Collaborative Exercises

1. With a partner or team, identify a special need in your community—perhaps a new sports league, an alternative campus newspaper, or a pet-sitting service. Next, identify an audience or even a group of audiences for whom proposals might be written. Write a brief, unsolicited proposal, being sure to start with a list of criteria and elements you think would motivate the readers to take you seriously.

2. As a good citizen, identify a problem in your community—a need not met—and attempt to solve it by garnering support and action via a proposal (two or three pages). You may, for instance, address the problems of any of the following:

   ■ A homeless shelter (not enough blankets, cots, or food)

   ■ Firefighters or police officers who work on Thanksgiving and have no holiday meal

   ■ A family that has lost its home and all its possessions in a fire

   ■ Elderly people who have no means of transportation to medical exams or supermarkets

   ■ A poverty-stricken family that has no money for heating bills

   First, identify the particular need you want to address. Then follow these steps to draft the proposal:

   a. Identify a group (church, civic, professional, student, etc.) that you want to target with your proposal.

   b. Thoroughly describe the need and the solutions.

   c. Thoroughly describe what you want the group to do.

   d. Investigate schedules, costs, and the like that will be necessary for the logistics of your solution.

   e. Draft the proposal, and then revise it according to the principles you have studied in this chapter and in Chapter 6.

3. Given the following RFP at the top of page 494, and using your imagination, write a brief (four or five pages) solicited proposal. Remember to keep your readers' needs firmly in mind as you plan, research, organize, draft, and revise.

**RFP
for a Service Organization to Wrap Christmas Presents
at the Uptown Mall**

The stores of the Uptown Mall request proposals from service organizations that want to make extra money at Christmas by wrapping gifts in the center aisles of the mall, December 1–24. Interested applicants should provide the following information by 1 November to Ursula Wheeler at Uptown Mall Offices, 232 Overlon Avenue, Fairbanks, AL 58392.

Content Details
- A description of the organization and its mission
- Number of workers committed to work
- Schedule of work by hours: 10:00 A.M. until 9:00 P.M.
- Previous experience with service projects
- References from benefactors of previous service projects
- Statement of commitment to project

Proposal Details
- Proposal should be typed, double-spaced.
- Proposal should be 2–3 pages.
- Proposal should include the organization's name, address, and phone number on the title page.

Please include any additional benefits your organization could offer that would make your proposal more attractive.

➡ *ONGOING ASSIGNMENT*

■ Based on the newcomers' handbook you created, determine the kinds of information that might be suitable for half- or full-day training (or orientation) sessions with the new employees/students. Write a proposal (three to four pages) to management (or to the dean of students in your college) outlining the kinds of information sessions you think are necessary and why. Be sure to describe all the benefits you see in offering these sessions.

CHAPTER 15

Elements and Options for Short/Informal and Long/Formal Reports

- **The Length Issue: Short and Long Reports**
- **Short/Informal Report Format Options**
- **Long/Formal Report Format Requirements**
    Prefatory or Front Matter
    The Introduction of the Formal Report
    Pagination of Formal Reports
    The Body of the Formal Report
    The Conclusions of the Formal Report
    The Recommendations of the Formal Report
    Optional Back Matter: References, Appendixes, and Indexes of the Formal Report
- **Summary**
- **Checklist**
- **Exercises**

In the three previous chapters, you learned some of the most common reasons for generating reports and proposals in the workplace. As a workplace writer, you must provide clear, persuasive, ethically balanced information in those documents because whether they address problems, descriptions, instructions, or routine work, your own credibility will be enhanced or eroded by the writing you produce. Your contributions to the welfare of the organization and its other employees will be noted whether your reports encourage progress (in terms of profit, technology, or conscientiousness), alert readers to dangers, or advise readers to consider alternatives to plans they have made.

When assigned a report on the job, you are likely to feel a little anxious at first, wondering what the reader needs or expects, how your writing and formatting options can help meet those needs, and how to make sure you do not overlook any important concerns. Consider, for example, the assignment facing April Tyndall, who works for a business that investigates the possibilities of purchasing other organizations. Her job is to investigate the feasibility of Coastal Corporate Investments (CCI) purchasing Dodge Boating, Inc., and then report her findings to CCI's owner. At the very beginning of her writing, she has a number of questions:

- Besides the owner of CCI, who might be reading this report and why?
- What questions do these readers have that I must answer?
- What kinds of details and support should I provide?
- What would be overkill? What would be inadequate?
- How long should this report be?
- How formal should this report be?
- What kinds of graphics should I use?
- How should I format the document?

Building on information you have learned in previous chapters about crafting the text and graphics of documents, this chapter demonstrates that length and format play crucial roles in your workplace documents. You will learn that short/informal reports and long/formal reports have special sections and formatting features that are designed to help readers find important information throughout the document. Thus, the chapter first describes the kinds of details, contexts, and reader needs and expectations that help writers determine the appropriate length of their workplace documents. Then, the main part of the chapter explains the special features that make a short report "informal" and a long report "formal," with the primary distinction between an informal and a formal report being the additional front and back matter included in formal reports but not in short/informal reports. Samples of short and long reports and their various elements will illustrate the most common expectations about the content and forms of these workplace documents. As always, all your decisions about report formats will depend on your organization's culture and its standards for formatting these documents, but some general guidelines can help you shape your workplace documents within those standards.

The Length Issue: Short and Long Reports

In college, you probably have reacted to all writing assignments with a question: How long does this paper have to be? Your professors have probably responded with a recommended or even a required length for the paper. On the job, your supervisors, like your instructor in this course, will sometimes give you an idea of how long your workplace document should be (a one-page memo, a five-page report, and so on). With that information, you are better able to judge the amount of detail you can reasonably include in the document—the longer the document, the more development and detail you can give the topic.

Often, though, you will be given a topic and no instructions about length—just get the job done. Pestering your supervisor with questions about the document's length seems adolescent. So how do you determine the appropriate length of a document?

For one thing, you should consider the *topic* itself very carefully. How complex is the issue, problem, service, or product about which you are writing? You may believe that the more complex the issue, the more you need to write, but that isn't always the case. For example, if you were asked to describe NASA's new rocket boosters for the space shuttle so that sixth graders could understand the description, would you write a hundred-page document? Of course not. The topic is complex, but a hundred pages on rocket boosters would overwhelm most sixth graders.

Thus, the second crucial element in the length decision is *audience*. How much does the audience *already know* about the topic? How much does the audience *need to know* about the topic? How much does the audience *want to know* about the topic? Considerations for audience, in other words, depend on your understanding of the following:

1. The readers' general familiarity with the topic (ranging from "thoroughly knowledgeable" to "no knowledge")
2. The amount of details the readers need to interpret, believe, or act on your report's information (ranging from "as many details as are available" to "no details—just an overview of the big picture")
3. The readers' interest in the topic (again, ranging from "great interest" to "no interest at all")

As a third element of the length decision, you must consider the *purpose* of your document. Is your purpose to make the reader(s) thoroughly familiar with your topic? Or is it to present an overview? Will it be difficult to convince readers of the value and sense of your idea? You may have to write a longer document if you anticipate objections. If your readers are not likely to be interested in your topic, but have to know something about it for their own job responsibilities, they will probably prefer a shorter document that gets to the point or summarizes the issues.

Finally, you should weigh your assignment's topic, audience, and purpose carefully so you can answer these questions:

1. Can I reasonably achieve my *purpose* regarding this *topic* for my particular *audience* in a one- or two-page memo?

    Yes, I can *inform* my *boss* in a one- or two-page memo of the *procedures for requesting that Burpsie Sodas be sold in our vending machine.*

2. Can I reasonably achieve my *purpose* regarding this *topic* for my particular *audience* in a three- to eight-page informal report?

    Yes, I can *convince* my *boss* in a three- to eight-page report that *absenteeism will be drastically reduced if we require a written physician's excuse from "sick" workers.*

3. Can I reasonably achieve my *purpose* regarding this *topic* for my particular *audience* in a ten-page or longer report?

    Yes, I need at least ten pages to *convince* my *boss* that *employees who are required to produce written excuses for missing work—along with other forms of adolescent treatment—are likely to rebel against the organization, be demoralized by the policies, and quit their positions to find work elsewhere.*

Short/Informal Report Format Options

Short/informal reports are most often formatted as memos, letters, or standard reports. The distinction between these forms has more to do with the introductory appearance of the document than anything else. As you would expect, the *memo format* (which, like all other memos, addresses readers *inside* the organization) opens with the standard memo headings: To, From, Date, and Subject. Additional organization-specific headings (such as Reply to and/or Action Required—see Chapter 10) may also be used. The opening sentence or paragraph of the memo report's text typically offers some background or a context for the topic that will be discussed in the remainder of the report.

For a *letter format*, which addresses readers *outside* the organization, the opening includes an inside address, salutation, and other traditional letter format features (see Chapter 10). Like the memo format, the letter format often opens with a sentence or even a paragraph that provides a context for the reader.

THE WORLD OF WORKPLACE WRITING

Informal and Formal Writing Style in Reports

In addition to length, reports are also frequently characterized by the degree of formality in the style of writing. How formal a report is depends on who the readers are and how much formality they expect or desire in a workplace document. The topic of the report may also affect the level of formality; legal and financial reports often take a more formal tone than, say, routine evaluations of employees.

Informal writing (and formal writing, too, for that matter) does not mean that grammar, mechanics, courtesy, and thoroughness can be abandoned. It does mean, however, that contractions are more acceptable than in formal writing, the style for documenting sources may be less rigid (perhaps parenthetical citations for references in the text, rather than a formal references page), the tone is a bit more familiar, colleagues are frequently referred to by first names only, and descriptions and explanations may be a bit briefer (although they should still be thorough enough for your reader to understand). Because many in-house reports are now produced electronically and "mailed" through the organization's computer network, even more informality has crept into these organizational documents.

Formal writing is often characterized by longer sentences, occasional inverted word orders (violating the traditional subject-verb order of most sentences), and a distant tone. Although writers of formal reports must carefully consider their readers at every turn, the work rarely addresses the reader directly and maintains a formal tone when referring to people—using a title (the Director of Communications) or a formal name (Ms. Schwartz). Similarly, writers rarely, if ever, refer to themselves as "I" or "me" in the text; instead, they use their position titles. Formal writing tends to cast sentences in passive voice more often than informal writing does (although active voice remains the preference of most readers). It may also be characterized by a loftier vocabulary (provided readers know what all terms mean), and it does not include contractions or slang.

In a memo or letter report, the context statement or paragraph often includes the following information:

- A reminder of the report's subject, who requested it, and for what purpose (if known and if appropriate to put in writing)
- A brief overview of the findings of the report
- A brief note of appreciation to any helpful personnel (supervisors, subject matter experts, research assistants, accountants, administrative assistants, etc.)
- An offer to clarify any information or follow up on the report (see Figure 15.1 on page 500)

context
major finding
purpose/topic

methods

offer to clarify/
follow up

> As we briefly discussed at Pamlico Tar River Foundation's oyster roast in early November, Dodge Boating, Inc., is a quite profitable enterprise. Following up on your interest in the company, our researchers and analysts have put together the figures you requested on the company's status and potential based on evaluations of the financial statements and examinations of the firm's tangible and intangible assets. We also held a brief meeting with Ms. Pamela Hawke, the current owner and CEO of Dodge Boating, who graciously answered all our questions about the history and current status of the company. We will be happy to clarify or follow up on any of the information in this report.

F I G U R E   15.1   An Opening Context Paragraph for a Memo or Letter Report

The *standard report format* dispenses with the memo's introductory headings and the letter's addresses and greetings and begins instead with a title. It then omits the context sentence or paragraph and goes directly to the introductory elements that are included in all reports and in all formats: the subject, purpose, audience, scope and limitations, methods, definitions (if necessary), and plan of development. If these elements of the introduction sound familiar, you will recall that they are exactly the same elements recommended for planning and drafting your professional communication documents (see Chapters 2 and 5).

Figures 15.2, 15.3, and 15.4 (see pages 501–504) show an opening page of an informal report in the three formats. As you can see, there are only two essential differences in the formats:

1. The material at the top of each example is different for each format.
2. The context segment is included only in the memo and letter reports—not in the standard report format.

In the standard report format, the context material that serves as the first paragraph of a memo or letter report (see Figure 15.1) becomes the *letter or memo of transmittal*—a separate communication that is attached to the cover of the report (described below and shown in Figure 15.6 later in the chapter).

In addition to the letter/memo of transmittal, reports may also carry a letter of authorization, a written request from the person who requested the report (described below and shown in Figure 15.7). Short/informal reports following the standard report format may, like the formal report you will study next, be bound (either spiral or saddle-stitched) and have a hard cover and a title page (see the next section's discussion of these features). The remaining features of the short report—headings, subheadings, lists, and graphics—are the same in all three

**Business Opportunities
& Investigations, Inc.**

111 Gawain Street
Benson, AK 58392
(433) 542-9485

MEMORANDUM

memo format

To: Charles Richmond, President
From: April Tyndall
Date: 6 December 2001
Subject: Investment in Dodge Boating, Inc.

finding

context

As we briefly discussed at our November board meeting, Dodge Boating, Inc., is a quite profitable enterprise. Following up on your interest in the company, our researchers and analysts have put together the figures you requested on the company's status and potential based on evaluations of the financial statements and examinations of the firm's tangible and intangible assets.

purpose

methods

scope and
limitations

plan of
organization

This report investigates the feasibility of purchasing a small boat design company: Dodge Boating, Inc., based in New Haven, AL. This report will outline the positives and negatives of the company, helping our investors determine whether purchasing Dodge Boating, Inc., would be a sound investment for them. Our researchers have relied on financial statements and their own evaluations of tangible and intangible assets, as well as a brief interview with Pamela Hawke, the current owner and CEO of Dodge Boating, Inc., to determine the potential profitability of this company. The report must rely on the boating firm's own records, rather than independent investigations of financial records, because we are not yet ready to invest earnest money in the purchase of the firm. After a brief overview of the current situation at Dodge Boating, Inc., the report offers a review of operations, then describes the assets and their valuations. The report concludes with an assessment of the positives and negatives of purchasing the company.

Overview of Dodge Boating, Inc.

report proper

Our researchers discovered a small boat design company based in New Haven, AL—Dodge Boating, Inc.—that is rumored to be profitable. The company is, in fact, extremely profitable, and its owner is considering retiring and selling the business. The company employs a dozen designers, twenty-seven machinists and technicians, and five full-time administrative personnel (including the owner). The company has operated for more than three years and has shown outstanding profits.

Review of Operations

A review of the operations reveals that the pretax profit for Dodge Boating steadily increased from $175,000 in 1997 to $225,000 in 1999 but dropped in 2000 to about $200,000 (see Figure 1). This increase . . . .

FIGURE 15.2 Memo Format for a Short Report

letterhead
stationary

Business Opportunities
& Investigations, Inc.

111 Gawain Street
Benson, AK 58392
(433) 542-9485

letter format

6 December 2001

Mr. Charles Richmond, President
Coastal Corporate Investments, Inc.
2332 Sudan Road
New Berne, AL 43627

Dear Mr. Richmond:

context
finding
methods

As we briefly discussed at Pamlico Tar River Foundation's oyster roast in early
November, Dodge Boating, Inc., is a quite profitable enterprise. Following up on
your interest in the company, our researchers and analysts have put together the
figures you requested on the company's status and potential based on evaluations
of the financial statements and examinations of the firm's tangible and intangible
assets.

purpose

scope and
limitations

plan of
organization

This report investigates the feasibility of purchasing a small boat design
company: Dodge Boating, Inc., based in New Haven, AL. This report will outline
the positives and negatives of the company, helping your investors determine
whether purchasing Dodge Boating, Inc., is a sound investment for them. Our
researchers have relied on financial statements and evaluations of tangible and
intangible assets, as well as a brief interview with Pamela Hawke, the current
owner and CEO of Dodge Boating, Inc., to determine the potential profitability
of this company. The report must rely on the boating firm's own records, rather
than independent investigations of financial records, because we are not yet
ready to invest earnest money in the purchase of the firm. After a brief overview
of the current situation at Dodge Boating, Inc., the report offers a review of
operations, then describes the assets and their valuations. The report
concludes with an assessment of the positives and negatives of purchasing
the company.

FIGURE 15.3   A Letter Format for a Short Report, page 1

Richmond
p. 2

Overview of Dodge Boating, Inc.

Our researchers discovered a small boat design firm based in New Haven, AL—
Dodge Boating, Inc.—that is rumored to be profitable. . . .

[Remainder of the Report]

After your review, I would be delighted to answer any questions you have about
the report, about Dodge Boating, or about any other possible investments. At that
point, our team will have completed a more detailed evaluation of Dodge Boating,
Inc., including a Level I Environmental Assessment. I look forward to hearing from
you.

Sincerely,

April Tyndall

April Tyndall
Account Representative

FIGURE 15.3   A Letter Format for a Short Report, page 2

formats: letter, memo, and standard report (see Strategy Review 15.1). Figure
15.5a on page 505 shows a letter of transmittal that sets up the short, informal report in Figure 15.5b on page 506. The annotations exemplify the standard elements of the short/informal report.

STRATEGY   REVIEW   15.1

VISUAL APPEAL AND ORGANIZATIONAL MARKERS: HEADINGS, SUBHEADINGS, LISTS, AND GRAPHICS

Whether you are constructing a long or a short report, you should remember the
value of visual appeal and the organizational markers you learned about in Chapters 8 and 9. These elements can break the monotony of a text-only report, clarify
or summarize information for readers, and help them find the most critical information in your report.

(continued on page 511)

Dodge Boating, Inc.:
A Business Evaluation and Purchasing
Feasibility Study

introductory
elements

subject and
purpose

audience

methods

scope and
limitations

plan of
organization

This report investigates the feasibility of purchasing a small boat design company:
Dodge Boating, Inc., based in New Haven, AL. This report will outline the positives
and negatives of the company, helping our investors determine whether
purchasing Dodge Boating, Inc., is a sound investment for them. Our researchers
have relied on financial statements and their own evaluations of tangible and
intangible assets, as well as a brief interview with Pamela Hawke, the current
owner and CEO of Dodge Boating, Inc., to determine the potential profitability of
this company. The report must rely on the boating firm's own records, rather than
independent investigations of financial records, because we are not yet ready to
invest earnest money in the purchase of the firm. After a brief overview of the
current situation at Dodge Boating, Inc., the report offers a review of operations,
then describes the assets and their valuations. The report concludes with an
assessment of the positives and negatives of purchasing the company.

Overview of Dodge Boating, Inc.

body

In our investigations into the Alabama-based boating industry, our researchers
discovered a small boat design company based in New Haven, AL: Dodge Boating,
Inc. Rumored to be profitable, the company is, in fact, extremely profitable, and
its owner is considering retiring and selling the business. The company employs
a dozen designers, twenty-seven machinists and technicians, and five full-time
administrative personnel (including the owner). The company has operated for
more than three years and has shown remarkable profits.

Review of Operations

A review of the operations reveals that the pretax profit for Dodge Boating
steadily increased from $175,000 in 1997 to $225,000 in 1999 but dropped in 2000
to about $200,000 (see Figure 1). . . .

[Remainder of the Report]

FIGURE 15.4   A Standard Report Format

Business Opportunities & Investigations, Inc.

111 Gawain Street
Benson, AK 58392
(433) 542-9485

6 December 2001

Mr. Charles Richmond, President
Coastal Corporate Investments, Inc.
2332 Sudan Road
New Berne, AL 43627

Dear Mr. Richmond:

context and
major finding

work accomplished

methods

As we briefly discussed at Pamlico Tar River Foundation's oyster roast in early November, Dodge Boating, Inc., is a quite profitable enterprise. Following up on your interest in the company, our researchers and analysts have put together the figures you requested on the company's status and potential based on evaluations of the financial statements and examinations of the firm's tangible and intangible assets. We also held a brief meeting with Ms. Pamela Hawke, the current owner and CEO of Dodge Boating.

appreciation for
staff support

finding reiterated

We appreciate the help your office staff, especially James Overton and Maria Sanchez, gave us in providing the criteria you use for determining whether to recommend investments for your clients. Based on your formula, our initial research shows that Dodge Boating, Inc., is a sound business opportunity for your investors, and we encourage you to continue with investigations.

offer to answer
questions
work remaining

After your review, I would be delighted to answer any questions you have about the report, about Dodge Boating, or about any other possible investments. At that point, our team will have completed a more detailed evaluation of Dodge Boating, Inc., including a Level I Environmental Assessment. I look forward to hearing from you.

Sincerely,

April Tyndall

April Tyndall
Account Representative

encl: report

FIGURE 15.5a A Letter of Transmittal Attached to the Cover of a Formal Report

title orients reader

purpose

audience

methods

scope and
limitations

plan of
organization

first major topic

background
orients reader

major heading sets
organization and
context/content

details

Dodge Boating, Inc.:
A Business Evaluation and Purchasing
Feasibility Study

This report investigates the feasibility of purchasing a small boat design
company: Dodge Boating, Inc., based in New Haven, AL. This report will outline
the positives and negatives of the company, helping our investors determine
whether purchasing Dodge Boating, Inc., is a sound investment for them. Our
researchers have relied on financial statements and their own evaluations of
tangible and intangible assets, as well as a brief interview with Pamela Hawke,
the current owner and CEO of Dodge Boating, Inc., to determine the potential
profitability of this company. The report must rely on the boating firm's own
records, rather than independent investigations of financial records, because we
are not yet ready to invest earnest money in the purchase of the firm. After a brief
overview of the current situation at Dodge Boating, Inc., the report offers a review
of operations, then describes the assets and their valuations. The report concludes
with an assessment of the positives and negatives of purchasing the company.

Overview of Dodge Boating, Inc.

In our investigations into the Alabama-based boating industry, our researchers
discovered a boat design company based in New Haven, AL: Dodge Boating, Inc.
Rumored to be profitable, the company is, in fact, extremely profitable, and its
owner is considering retiring and selling the business. The company employs a
dozen designers, twenty-seven machinists and technicians, and five full-time
administrative personnel (including the owner). The company has operated for
more than three years and has shown remarkable profits.

Review of Operations

A review of the operations reveals that the pretax profit for Dodge Boating steadily
increased from $175,000 in 1997 to $225,000 in 1999 but dropped in 2000 to about
$200,000 (see Figure 1). This increase of over 400% in three years shows the firm's
growth potential. As would be expected in the boating industry, designers' salaries
and materials costs (the major company expenditures) have steadily increased.
Fortunately for the company, however, the cost of shipping materials and
delivering finished goods decreased by nearly 50% in 1999. Conversely, the
contribution margin increased to an incredible 40% in 1999. Overall, all revenue-
generating factors have improved substantially over the three years.

The administrative expenses, although typically low, rose significantly in
1998. Although expenses do tend to increase as a company grows, expenses at
Dodge Boating grew dramatically, in part because of the increased size of the

FIGURE 15.5b A Sample Short Report, page 1

Dodge Boating, Inc.
p. 2

administrative staff. The administrative staff grew from a single individual in
1997, who was responsible for bookkeeping, typing, and receptionist duties, to
three individuals performing those tasks separately. Naturally, costs went up.
Further questioning revealed that the owner paid herself an exceptionally large
salary/bonus in 1999 (almost $200,000). Her compensation rose from $36,000
in 1997 to $52,000 in 1998 to an exorbitant $259,000 in 1999. Consequently,
administrative costs skyrocketed.

Also, as would be expected, operating income dropped dramatically in 1999.
During that year, the operating income dipped significantly, but explicably,
below the previous year's figures (Figure 1).

graph of information clarifies message in text

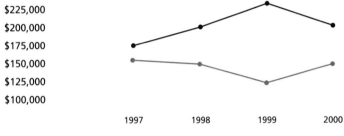

● Pretax profit

● Operating income

Figure 1: Comparison of Operating Income and Pretax Profits, 1997–2000

Inside Drawing Cards

In the boat design industry, the success or failure of the business most often
depends on the designers themselves. An owner must not only hire the best
designers, but must also keep them employed with the firm for many years.
Because salaries for boat designers are fairly consistent throughout the industry,
other incentives must be provided to encourage good designers to remain with
the firm. . . .

major heading

Assets

details

Business assets are divided into two categories: tangible and intangible. Tangible
assets are easily quantified and include cash, accounts receivable, inventories,
equipment, and real estate. Intangible assets are less easily measured and include

FIGURE 15.5b   A Sample Short Report, page 2

Dodge Boating, Inc.
p. 3

such items as trademarks, patents, contract rights, territorial rights, customer bases, reputation, name recognition, and market presence. Dodge Boating's assets include the following:

tabular form makes reading easier

Tangible	Intangible
• cash accounts	• boating contracts
• accounts receivable	• established clientele
• supplies	• geographic coverage
• repair parts	• reputation
• testing equipment	• name recognition
• design equipment	• design concentration system
• trucks	• location
• trailers	• warehouse leases
• boats	
• forklifts	
• office equipment, including computers	
• furnishings	

subheading

Valuations of Tangible Assets

The tangible assets of Dodge Boating, Inc., excluding cash in the bank, are valued at $3,205,558 (see Table I). These assets include equipment and parts, accounts receivable, office furnishings, and supplies.

Table I: Value of Tangible Assets

tabular costs

• cash accounts	$14,295
• accounts receivable	153,204
• supplies	23,499
• repair parts	19,945
• testing equipment	328,294
• design equipment	435,609
• trucks	722,011
• trailers	213,295
• boats	920,322
• forklifts	126,392
• office equipment and computers	154,387
• furnishings	94,305
Total value of tangible assets	$ 3,205,558

FIGURE 15.5b A Sample Short Report, page 3

Dodge Boating, Inc.
p. 4

subhead

Valuations of Intangible Assets

Valuation of intangible assets is quite subjective. Obviously, the true market value of intangibles and even of a business is always the amount that a legitimate buyer is willing to pay and a serious seller is willing to accept. However, one common approach uses a multiplying factor and the revenue generated by the business. Using the results of the summary of operations, which reveal the recent growth and success of the business, we have obtained the contribution margin, which eliminates any anomalies in the data such as the large bonus paid to the owner in 1999. Since the company is only three years old, the three-year contribution is appropriate to use, making $1,274,000 a realistic, and perhaps conservative, figure to use for the value of the intangible assets.

subhead

Valuation of the Business

Summing the tangible and intangible values results in an overall estimated value of $4,479,558. Of course, many factors could raise or lower this value, many of which are discussed below as positives and negatives of the business.

conclusions

Conclusions

Based on the analyses presented and the figures generated, we may assess the positives and negatives of your clients' investing in Dodge Boating, Inc.

Positives

bulleted list makes reading and recall simpler

- The business has operated at a profit during its more than three years' existence and recently has generated sufficient contribution margins to result in healthy profits. This trend should continue.

- The location of New Haven, Alabama, appears to be superior to any other city in eastern Alabama. Access to major roads, including US 83 and US 395, is a large contributing factor. Relocating within the Princeton Industrial Park would eliminate the warehouse rental expenses and would allow construction of a new warehouse that could be depreciated over time, thus providing tax relief.

- Distribution of revenues base is good. None of the three major design competitors controls enough of the business to cause concern.

FIGURE 15.5b　A Sample Short Report, page 4

Dodge Boating, Inc.
p. 5

Negatives

- The business currently operates effectively in a limited geographic area and market niche. Any growth outside this niche may be questionable until expansions and increased capital investments are made. Thus, although profit potential has not been reached, growth or size of the business appears limited until such investments are made.

- The business currently depends heavily on the owner/CEO. Because of her expertise in boat design, Ms. Hawke's name recognition, heavily associated with Dodge Boating, Inc., certainly contributes to the . . . .

- Lack of guaranteed or long-term contracts may be a cause for concern. Currently, the business tends to operate on a contract-by-contract basis, building special boats for highly specialized clients. If such special requirements could find a larger market, the concern over contract bases might be alleviated.

- The presence of an old EPA Superfund site on the property devalues the business. Although the suit is settled, future lawsuits are not out of the question. Relocating the company to the Princeton Industrial Park would resolve this negative.

Recommendations

Although the estimated value of Dodge Boating is $4,479,558, the positive and negative issues raised could substantially alter the value to any prospective buyer. Nevertheless, Dodge Boating still appears to be an extraordinary business opportunity. If a price close to the estimated value could be negotiated with the owner, it would be a wise investment for your clients.

Although offering an enhanced benefits package to designers would be a must, a more pressing concern may be maintaining the high morale that all the employees at Dodge Boating currently enjoy.

Finally, a multiple-year payment plan, including a continued involvement clause for the current owner for up to two years, might be essential for continued profitability of the company and should be negotiated.

Again, these are preliminary findings; more detailed studies should clarify this information and will be submitted to you within ninety days.

F I G U R E 15.5b A Sample Short Report, page 5

The sample reports included in this chapter—short/informal (Figure 15.5a and b) and long/formal (Figure 15.19)—give you a chance to see how headings, subheadings, lists, and graphics are used throughout the texts. Notice that headings and subheadings give readers a break from the text, indicate how the work is organized, and help them find the sections of your report that are most crucial for them to read. You should also note that the graphics are integrated into the text where they can summarize or emphasize the information presented in the text. Notice also that including bulleted or numbered lists of information, as opposed to traditional paragraphs, makes that information easier for readers to process and recall.

Long/Formal Report Format Requirements

The previous section showed you a few options for formatting short/informal reports—again depending on the standards used in your organization. Long reports follow a more traditional format, although certain elements may be altered as needed. Excerpts from a sample formal report appear throughout the chapter to show you various options and indicate how they might meet your readers' needs. These individual report elements are taken from a larger formal report that is presented in its entirety in Figure 15.19 at the end of the chapter.

Prefatory or Front Matter

Although long/formal reports use many of the elements found in short/informal reports (content features, headings, subheadings, lists, and graphics) to organize and present ideas, formal reports also require additional prefatory information (or front matter) that helps readers navigate through the lengthy document. In this section, you will learn about the purposes, content, and format of the most commonly included front matter—the letter of transmittal, letter of authorization, cover page, title page, abstract or executive summary, table of contents, and list of illustrations; samples of each will clarify their roles in the formal report. Accurate front matter will help your readers progress quickly through your report, allowing them to read sections that most concern them and skip sections that are not related to their interests or job responsibilities.

The Letter/Memo of Transmittal

The letter or memo of transmittal, which follows the appropriate letter or memo format depending on whether the report is sent outside the organization or remains inside, typically communicates the same kind of context information that you would have included in the introduction of a memo or letter report (see the earlier discussion and Figure 15.1):

- The opening reminder of the report's assignment and purpose
- A brief summary of the report's findings
- Appreciation for any outstanding assistance
- An offer to clarify any information or follow up on the report

Unlike the letter of authorization, discussed below, which is bound into the report proper, the letter of transmittal is typically attached to the front cover of the report with a paper clip so the reader can detach it and attach another letter of transmittal to secondary, additional, or future readers. (Because the letter of transmittal is the same for informal and formal reports, see Figure 15.5a to review the letter of transmittal.)

Cover Page

Formal reports are first recognized by their bound format and cover page. The cover page, which uses a hard stock of paper (much like thick construction paper and available from any copy shop), identifies the report and protects the more fragile pages inside the report. Although many organizations have standard covers or colors for all their reports, you can help set the tone of your work by using a particular color for the cover, if you have options. (For additional discussions of the uses of color in workplace documents, see Chapters 8 and 9.) Other aspects of the cover page, also discussed in Chapter 9, such as the quality or texture of the paper, its size, and its dimensions, may also signal how conventional or innovative your organization is.

The cover page presents standard information:

1. *A title for your work that sets the tone for the document:* The more creative the title, the more creative the work; the more serious the title, the more serious the work. A clever title that includes a play on words or suggests a frivolous approach is clearly inappropriate for a serious topic.

   The title also indicates how likely your work is to be confused with other reports. A short title, such as "Employee Morale in 1999," means that the reader should have no question about the content of your report. A longer title, such as "Employee Morale in the Arlington, VA Sales Office after the 1999 Merger Announcement," indicates that other reports on employee morale in other branch offices at other stages in the organization's history are also on file.

2. *The name(s) of the person, committee, or group for whom you are writing the report:* Such information is also useful to later readers of the report. When they see, for example, that your report was written for the executive officers of the organization, they may realize that it is unlikely to include the technical information they need. Instead, they may seek a different report written for, say, the technicians of the organization.

3. *Your (and your collaborative team members') name(s):* Reports in organizations are frequently known by the writer of the work—"Roger's report" instead of "the report on training new sales associates." Ironically, your name may also be dropped from a report—especially if your manager or supervisor intends to send it to other readers in the organization. Nevertheless, as the originator of the information in the document, your name (and your collaborators' names) should appear on the cover page.

4. *The date of the work:* Because some information becomes outdated very quickly, it is imperative that you date your work. A June sales report that is mistaken for a December sales report can wreak havoc in an organization that depends on current information.

5. *A descriptive abstract (optional):* Many organizations request that the cover include a brief (one to three sentences) overview of the content of the work. This descriptive abstract should provide more information than the title of the work, thus helping readers determine if this particular report is the one they need to read.

Figure 15.6 on page 514 shows a cover page that illustrates these features, as well as the spacing that makes each element stand out.

The Letter/Memo of Authorization

The letter or memo of authorization is a written request from your client, boss, or manager that asks (or authorizes) you to investigate a particular topic in your organization. Depending on the sensitivity of your topic, you may have to show such authorization to gain access to files or information you need for your report. You may also have to show the authorization to those you need to interview for more information. Because some organizations have multiple levels of security clearances, such a document may be your ticket into high-security files or may grant you access to others who have high-security knowledge.

With less sensitive topics, the letter/memo of authorization merely reminds readers of the context of the report and that they requested the report. Unlike the letter/memo of transmittal, described earlier, the letter/memo of authorization is typically bound into the report as its first page.

When writing a letter of authorization that other writers will use for gaining access to information, be sure to follow these guidelines:

1. Specify the exact topic you want covered.
2. Set some parameters for the research/discussion.
3. Recommend resources or helpful and knowledgeable people.
4. Set a deadline.

Figure 15.7 on page 515 shows how these elements work in a letter of authorization.

title offers context

DODGE BOATING, INC.:
AN EXTENDED FEASIBILITY STUDY

primary recipient/
audience

Submitted to
Charles Richmond, President
Coastal Corporate Investments, Inc.

Prepared by

writers

Business Opportunities & Investigations, Inc.

April Tyndall
Timothy Atkins
Pentros Abeynne

date

16 March 2002

abstract/summary

This report describes the results of a follow-up evaluation of Dodge Boating, Inc.
The original report (6 December 2001) suggested that investing in Dodge Boating
would be a generally sound move, and additional studies make an even stronger
case for the purchase. Based on extensive analyses, environmental statements,
and tentative purchase agreements, this report concludes that the purchase of
Dodge Boating should be an immediate priority for Coastal Investments, Inc.

FIGURE 15.6   A Cover/Title Page for a Formal Report

The Title Page

The title page in most formal documents is merely a copy of the cover page,
printed on traditional stock paper. If no letter of authorization is bound into the
report, then the title page is the first inside page of the formal report. (Because the
title page duplicates the cover page, this chapter's formal report example does not
include a title page.)

Coastal Corporate Investments, Inc.

2332 Sudan Road
New Berne, AL 43627
(312) 447-3923
FAX: (312) 447-3838

10 November 2001

Ms. April Tyndall
Business Opportunities & Investigations, Inc.
111 Gawain Street
Benson, AK 58392

Dear Ms. Tyndall:

content

authorization

As we discussed at the oyster roast last weekend, we want to purchase additional businesses in Alabama, particularly small (but, of course, profitable) businesses that have yet to realize their potential. Would you please pursue the research on Dodge Boating, Inc., letting us know whether the company would be a good investment for our clients?

specific request
limitation

In particular, we are interested in learning more about the assets and liabilities of Dodge Boating. We are not yet interested, however, in tendering an offer or even earnest money. Therefore, we realize you will have only limited access to the company's accounting books. Nevertheless, we hope you can make some initial judgments about whether to pursue this purchase.

offer to help

Our staff will be glad to provide you with a copy of the criteria we use in making such decisions about small businesses. James Overton and Maria Sanchez, our top account executives, will be happy to provide any other information you might find useful. You may reach them at extensions 773 and 355, respectively.

deadline

We look forward to your report, which we hope we can count on by the middle of December.

Sincerely,

Charles Richmond

Charles Richmond,
President

FIGURE 15.7 A Letter of Authorization Bound into a Formal Report

Abstract and/or Executive Summary

As opposed to the descriptive abstract (discussed above), an informative abstract is a more substantial overview of the contents and findings of the report. Almost all formal reports include an abstract after the title page. You must be careful not to offer so many details in this overview that it defeats the purpose of a "summary." To help you decide what to include in the abstract (see Strategy Review 15.2), remember that most readers will be looking for the answers to a few standard questions about the report:

1. What is this report about?
2. For what purpose(s) and audience(s) was it written?
3. Does the report have any special features or inclusions?
4. What are the writer's findings, as presented in the report?

S T R A T E G Y   R E V I E W   1 5 . 2

WRITING AND REVISING THE ABSTRACT

In the workplace, abstracts for reports commonly present overviews or summaries of the information that is presented in more detail in the report itself. When you write your abstract, draft and revise for the following concerns:

1. Have I captured the gist of the report, including all major findings and conclusions?
2. Have I allowed my reader to see quickly what the report is about?
3. Have I accounted for my reader's special concerns about this topic?
4. Have I written the abstract in coherent, carefully crafted prose?
5. Will my reader miss any substantial information by reading only the abstract?

When reading a report, executives typically seek information that will help them make decisions—information that is most often highlighted in the recommendations segment of the report. For these readers, report writers usually construct a special form of abstract: the *executive summary*.

The primary distinction between a traditional abstract and an executive summary is that the abstract is an overview for any audience and imitates the report's tone, emphases, and organization of information. In contrast, the executive summary is written for decision makers. Thus, it includes the results of the report's investigation and other information the reader/executive needs to make decisions. It reports that information in the order the reader needs it—not necessarily the order in which it appears in the main work. For example, an *abstract* for a formal report on new training techniques for sales associates would focus on the overall content of the report, while an *executive summary* would cast that information in terms of the decisions executive readers must make—perhaps emphasizing suggestions for funding new training sessions, scheduling time off for employees to attend the sessions, or compensating employees for voluntarily attending. Figure 15.8 illustrates this distinction between a traditional abstract and an executive summary.

Abstract general overview

This report describes the initial investigations into the feasibility of purchasing Dodge Boating, Inc., a small boat design firm based in Alabama.

The firm has enjoyed more than three years of stable, even rising, profits. Its strength lies in the morale of its employees, with designers, technicians, and machinists enjoying the mutual benefits of collaborating and sharing ideas.

The investigation shows that assets (both tangibles and intangibles) are a strength for Dodge Boating, Inc., but that some changes in locale and owner/profit sharing should be strongly considered before purchasing.

After investing some earnest money to see the firm's audited records (this report works only with unaudited statements), future reports should target the long-range viability of this company, especially its ability to open its designs for multiple users, rather than one-time contractors.

Executive Summary more budget/management issues covered

Initial investigations into the feasibility of buying a small boat design firm, Dodge Boating, Inc., based in Alabama, show the company's net worth to be close to $1.4 million. The combined tangible and intangible assets amount to $4,479,558, an amount that suggests that a takeover is inevitable.

The firm, however, can be purchased since the CEO expects to retire within the next two years.

The combined liabilities of the firm are somewhere near $1.1 million and are principally tied to the owner's own profits.

Serious restructuring of management would resolve the high upper-end salary, but any saving should probably be reinvested in the lower-level employees who may not feel great loyalty to new company owners.

After investing some earnest money to see the firm's audited records (this report works only with unaudited statements), future reports should target the long-range viability of this company, especially its ability to open its designs for multiple users, rather than one-time contractors.

FIGURE 15.8 A Comparison of a Traditional Abstract and an Executive Summary

Table of Contents

Because long reports are just that—long—readers can easily lose their way, miss the connections between ideas, or have to thumb through the entire document to find the information that pertains to them. Conscientious writers provide a table of contents that allows readers to scan the list of topics and turn immediately to the section(s) that concern them and their work.

Although it appears as front matter in a formal document, a table of contents is written last, because you will not know on which pages each section falls until you have completed the document. Fortunately, tables of contents are easy to prepare—they simply list the prefatory matter (excluding the memo/letter of authorization, transmittal, and title page), the introduction, the major and minor headings you have included throughout your document, and the references and appendixes. The table of contents in Figure 15.9 demonstrates these elements.

List of Illustrations (Optional)

Many reports contain numerous tables and figures to help readers understand complex information or see relationships between ideas (see Chapter 8). Some readers will review a report's graphics after reading the report, while others may turn to the graphics first as a way of getting an overview of information provided in certain sections. For reports with a number of graphics (usually more than three), writers provide a list of illustrations, which serves as a table of contents for graphics. In fact, the list of illustrations is constructed just like the table of contents: it is prepared at the end of the writing and revising processes and lists the figure number, title, and page number for each graphic (see Figure 15.10 on page 520).

Glossary (Optional)

In some reports, especially those written for readers who will need definitions of a number of terms, you should provide a glossary—a list of terms and their definitions in alphabetical order (see Figure 15.11 on page 520). The glossary is placed at the *beginning* of your report, rather than at the end, because readers frequently want to know the terms before they begin reading or at least want to know the kinds of terms you have included in the glossary. Be sure to follow other standard rules about defining terms (and documenting sources, if you use someone else's definition), discussed in Chapter 12 and the Appendix.

List of Symbols (Optional)

Special symbols that are meaningful only to members of a certain scientific or technological community often play an important role in workplace reports that are written for readers outside that community. To make sure these readers understand the report's message, writers provide a list of symbols, which operates like a glossary to define the meaning of the symbols (see Figure 15.12 on page 521).

Contents

prefatory material

scientific notation shows relationship of entries to each other

note parallelism

report proper

note parallelism

back matter

iii

FIGURE 15.9 A Table of Contents

Now, you are ready to present the report proper—the actual text of the introduction, body, conclusion(s), and recommendation(s).

The Introduction of the Formal Report

From your reading and work in other chapters, and especially from your understanding of the planning of workplace documents, you should be used to thinking of your report in terms of its subject, purpose, audience, scope and limitations,

tables are assigned
Roman numerals

tables grouped
together

figures are given
Arabic numerals

figures grouped
together

List of Illustrations

Table I: Revised Itemization and Value of Tangible Assets for 1999   2
Table II: Summary of Tangible Assets for Dodge Boating, Inc.   8

Figure 1: Materials Costs, Salaries, and Overhead (1997–1999)   4
Figure 2: Scheduled Plan of Action for Purchase Arrangements   6
Figure 3: Scheduled Plan of Action for Reinvesting Capital   18

iv

FIGURE 15.10   A List of Illustrations

alphabetical order

parallel forms for
definitions

definitions follow
formula:
term = group +
differentiating
qualities

Glossary

contribution margin   the difference between revenues and all variable costs associated with those revenues.

intangible asset   an asset that does not have physical substance, such as a property right or company goodwill.

operating income   the difference between revenues and the cost of service and administrative expenses.

tangible asset   a long-term asset that has physical substance, such as the fleet of boats and/or trailers.

v

FIGURE 15.11   A Glossary

List of Symbols

symbols/explanations

£   money in British currency

¢   money less than or over a full dollar

¥   money in Japanese currency

§   money from reinvestment

¶   money from capital gains

°   money from warehouse rentals

∞   money from design initiatives

μ   money from tax returns

√   money in Russian currency

vi

FIGURE 15.12   A List of Symbols

methods, definitions, and plan of organization. These topics now reappear as the introduction to a formal report (see Figure 15.13 on page 522). (See Strategy Review 15.3.) You may want to review Chapters 2, 4, and 5 (on planning documents, organizing, and drafting, respectively) to refresh your memory.

STRATEGY REVIEW 15.3

WRITING AND REVISING THE INTRODUCTION

Briefly, you should remember that the introduction should do all of the following:

- Orient your reader to the content and context of your report (subject).
- Clarify the intent of your report's message (purpose).
- Indicate which readers will find the information useful (audience).

(continued on page 523)

DODGE BOATING, INC.:
AN EXTENDED FEASIBILITY STUDY

1.0 Introduction

context/purpose

finding

audience

release of
information

This report presents a follow-up to an initial investigation (6 December 2001) into the feasibility of purchasing Dodge Boating, Inc., a small business located in eastern Alabama. The results of this in-depth investigation provide sound evidence that Dodge Boating, Inc., is an excellent investment opportunity for the clients of Coastal Corporate Investments, Inc. This report is provided for Coastal Corporate Investments' account executives to analyze; then, the information may be freely adapted and provided to Coastal Corporate Investments' clients who may want to invest in Dodge Boating, Inc.

methods

findings

methods

scope and
limitations

Based on analyses of audited statements, interviews with the owner/CEO Pamela Hawke, and interviews with design engineers, machinists, and technicians, this report shows that Dodge Boating, Inc., has enjoyed huge profits and has earned a significant, though small, place in the boat design market. The report includes analyses of the company's assets and liabilities, based on audited reports. Because of the boating industry's tremendous economic upswing in recent years, the researchers for this report can only speculate about the long-range potential of Dodge Boating. Nevertheless, the report does incorporate employees' views of growth in revenues and nontangible assets.

definitions

A glossary of terms is provided for Coastal Corporate Investments' clients who may want to read this report to determine their interest in investing in Dodge Boating.

plan of
organization

Following this introduction, the report addresses the financial details—assets and liabilities—of Dodge Boating, Inc., as of 15 June 1999. Then, the report addresses other issues critical to maintaining and even expanding the growth potential of the company: personnel issues, equipment issues, and location issues. The conclusions and recommendations are directly tied to these crucial details, which, if they can be resolved, should clearly indicate the enthusiasm our researchers feel for Dodge Boating, Inc.

F I G U R E 15.13   An Introduction for a Long/Formal Report

- Explain the kinds of information you have included and excluded from the report (scope and limitations).
- Indicate the methods and resources you used to generate information for the report (methods).
- Define any terms your reader may not already know or that you use in a special way in your report (definitions).
- Outline the remaining issues addressed in the report (plan of organization).

Depending on the length of your formal report, the introduction may consist of a single sentence for each element, several paragraphs, or several pages. In a short (three to five pages) report, a sentence for each element would be appropriate; a report of ten to twenty pages would have an introduction of several paragraphs, and a longer report might have a several-page introduction.

Pagination of Formal Reports

After the title page, the pages of the prefatory or front matter are counted and given page numbers using lowercase Roman numerals (i, ii, iii, iv, v, and so on), not Arabic numerals (1, 2, 3, and so on), which are used for the report proper. The lowercase Roman numerals indicate to readers that the pages are front matter, not part of the report proper.

Beginning with the introduction, pages should be numbered consecutively with Arabic numerals. The first page is counted, but not numbered, so the first page number appears on page 2. Your organization (or instructor) will tell you where the number should appear on a page—typically either in the top, right-hand corner or centered at the bottom of the page.

The Body of the Formal Report

The body of the report is the longest portion of the report and, consequently, consumes the most writing and revising time. Ironically, many readers will bypass the body if they can find all the information they need in the abstract, executive summary, introduction, conclusions, and/or recommendations. Don't be insulted if busy readers skip your report's body. Instead, you should consider it a compliment to your ability to present information quickly, persuasively, thoroughly, and ethically.

Nevertheless, the body of the report is an important aspect of your formal report because it may serve a number of purposes:

- Clarifying the details of points you make in the introduction and conclusion sections of the report
- Supporting the rationale of the arguments you present in the introduction, conclusion(s), and recommendation(s)
- Allowing you to provide statistics, examples, anecdotes, and other forms of supporting evidence (discussed in Chapter 5 on drafting information)
- Helping you explain causes, relationships, specific instructions, or consequences of particular actions or behaviors

Thus, in the body of the report, you may break down ideas into problems and solutions, describe the various parts of a mechanism and their functions, present numerous reasons why your organization should be awarded a contract for building a new civic center, or review the highlights of your investigations of San Diego as the new headquarters for your organization's West Coast operations. In short, the body of your report is the anchor of your document.

Figure 15.14 on pages 525–526 is an excerpt (report pages 2 and 3) from the body of a formal report; note the use of headings and subheadings, as well as graphics, that help the writer tell the whole story and let the reader see the organizational and topical scheme for the work. Note that unlike the introduction of your report, which may be titled "Introduction" (or may have no heading at all since readers expect the beginning of your report to be the introduction), the body of the report cannot use the heading "Body." Instead, you should provide headings and subheadings that identify the subject of major and minor points you address in the discussion section of the report.

The Conclusions of the Formal Report

Because so many report readers turn first to the conclusion(s) and recommendation(s) sections—they want to know what you have learned, based on your investigations—conclusions are rarely simple summaries of the report (see Chapter 5). You'll recall that the abstract summarizes information as part of the prefatory matter in a formal report, making it redundant to present yet another full-blown summary at the end of the report. Thus, the conclusions in a formal report more usefully allow you to summarize the report's contents *briefly* before moving on to do the following:

- Present recommendations and solutions
- Explain the significance of a particular situation
- Explain the consequences of a particular situation
- Offer a view of trends as they affect the organization
- Present predictions about the topic in light of the organization's future

	Dodge Boating, Inc.
	p. 2
major heading	**2.0 Assets**
	Dodge Boating's assets may be divided into tangible assets, such as cash, equipment, and furnishings, and intangible assets, such as its reputation, contracts, and client list. Although the tangible assets outweigh the value of the intangibles, the benefits of the intangibles should not be minimized for this company.
subheading	2.1 Tangible Assets
	Dodge Boating's tangible assets were grossly underreported in the initial investigation due, perhaps, to attempts to lower the tax value of the company. Further devaluing the initial investigation's summary of tangible assets was the omission of cash accounts. A revised itemization and value of tangible assets over the past three years is presented and then totaled in Table I:
table introduced	

Table I: Revised Itemization and Value of Tangible Assets for 1999

ASSET	1997	1998	1999
Cash accounts	$21,029	$41,294	$77,392
Accounts receivable	47,200	99,204	153,219
Supplies	1,120	2,140	5,389
Repair parts	3,295	4,295	6,228
Boats	59,203	193,576	593,232
Trailers	73,201	97,036	200,118
Forklifts	43,042	45,795	86,394
Office equipment (including computers)	32,449	49,036	52,493
Furnishings (including office and outside displays)	9,322	14,396	25,395
Totals	**$289,861**	**$546,772**	**$1,199,860**

2.2 Intangible Assets

The valuation of intangible assets is always difficult to determine because such assets do not carry a specific dollar figure. For our analysis, we used the Smythe Johnson formula, which has been shown to allow only small discrepancies and to provide more thorough readings of the true value of intangible assets.

(Margin labels: *table inserted into text*, *subheading*, *warning*)

FIGURE 15.14 Page 2 of a Long/Formal Report Continued from the Introduction (Figure 15.13)

Dodge Boating, Inc.
p. 3

third-level heading

2.2.1 Employee Issues

leading idea

Perhaps the greatest asset (or liability, for that matter) in any company is its employees. The personnel issues of Dodge Boating are at the heart of the company's success and may, ironically, pose a problem for a new owner. Inherent in the quality of work produced by these employees is their tremendous respect for and loyalty to Pamela Hawke. Many employees spoke of her awards in boat design, her lineage from a well-known boat designing family, and her keen sense of proportion in all the designs. . . .

support for
leading idea

third-level heading

2.2.2 Equipment Status

Dodge Boating has invested quite a bit of money in its equipment, with the latest figures showing $298,026 total investment in supplies, forklifts, trailers, and general drafting equipment and machinery. The equipment is all either new or in exceptionally good shape. These tangible values are enhanced by the innovative changes the teams have made in the equipment, with their additional modifications making standard equipment worth, perhaps, twice its original value. For instance, when the mast needs to be attached to the stern at a certain angle to make a design work, the designers, machinists, and technicians collaborate to design and make a piece of equipment that will hold the mast at exactly that angle. This kind of innovative spirit characterizes the work at Dodge Boating and makes it difficult to put a price on the intangible assets of the company.

major finding

other details

third-level heading

2.2.3 Location

graphic introduced

The location of Dodge Boating is both an asset and a liability (see map in appendix). Located on the Ipsiena River in eastern Alabama, the company currently uses the waterway as a testing site for some of its smaller boats. The site also allows clients to see the tests of their boats, while putting them in the proper "waterway" setting for demonstrations and purchases. The employees enjoy the view as they work because all offices and workshops face the river and have glass walls. The current owner bought the building from the town's Chamber of Commerce and then added the manufacturing portion of the company to the back of the lot.

Unfortunately, the company sits on an old EPA Superfund site, a contaminated area that makes the property unsuitable for additional building and, consequently, for the kind of expansion that would make the business grow. Numerous lawsuits have been filed and settled, but the possibility of future lawsuits is not out of the question, making long-range commitments to this site unwise.

A better site might be in the Princeton Industrial Park. Located twelve miles north of Dodge Boating's current site, the industrial park has water access and land available. Further, the employees of Dodge Boating would not have to move. . . .

FIGURE 15.14 Page 3 of a Long/Formal Report

conclusion

significance of
findings

Dodge Boating, Inc.
p. 25

7.0 Conclusions

Based on the financial information provided throughout this report, along with
evaluations of the intangible assets and liabilities of Dodge Boating, Inc., we
conclude that the company is a sound investment opportunity for clients of
Coastal Corporate Investments, Inc.

Further, because the owner/CEO of the company is interested in retirement, and
because the financial status of the company seems so sound, we believe that
several companies might consider the purchase of Dodge Boating, Inc., if we
do not move quickly on this opportunity. Given the expansion in the boating
industry at this time, there is little reason to believe that anything short of a
major economic recession will dent the profitability of the business.

FIGURE 15.15a   A Brief Conclusion for a Long/Formal Report

- Recommend a plan of action
- Pose questions for future research or investigations related to the issue at
  hand

In the conclusion, you should also offer your own interpretation of the facts
you have accumulated. Although your opinions may not be appropriate in other
segments of the report, your responsibilities as a report writer may include presenting your interpretation of events and situations in the conclusions. Consider
Figure 15.15a (above) and Figure 15.5b on page 528, which show two versions of
a formal report's conclusion that presents the findings of the report writer who
wants to help readers understand the consequences of the problems and solutions
she has described in the introduction and body of her report.

The Recommendations of the Formal Report

Because so many reports are problem-solution oriented, many writers include a
special section at the end of formal reports: *recommendations*. In this section, you
should present a plan of action that will help readers eliminate or at least reduce
the problem you described in the report (see Figure 15.16 and Strategy Review
15.4 on page 529).

Dodge Boating, Inc.
p. 25

conclusion

7.0 Conclusions

main finding

Based on the financial information provided throughout this report, along with evaluations of the intangible assets and liabilities of Dodge Boating, Inc., we conclude that the company is a sound investment opportunity for clients of Coastal Corporate Investments, Inc.

plan of action

Further, because the owner/CEO of the company is interested in retirement, and because the financial status of the company seems so sound, we believe that several companies might consider the purchase of Dodge Boating, Inc., if we do not move quickly on this opportunity. Given the expansion in the boating industry at this time, there is little reason to believe that anything short of a major economic recession will dent the profitability of the business.

In addition, we have reached a number of other conclusions about Dodge Boating, Inc.:

additional findings

1. Its history as a small, family-owned business is largely responsible for the loyalty its employees feel toward the company and the Hawke family.

2. Keeping workers will be difficult, given their lack of loyalty to new owners, whom they are likely to perceive as outsiders.

3. Ms. Hawke's pledge to help inspire loyalty in the new owners may help in the short run, but in the long run, we will have to find our own way to instill loyalty in these workers.

4. The collaborative atmosphere in which Dodge Boating's employees work is remarkable. Their time may often seem wasted, from a corporate view; yet, this "downtime"—time spent drinking coffee, getting snacks, and visiting with each other—seems to produce a cohesiveness among the workers that leads directly to their abilities to share ideas and solve problems collectively. Trying to modify this system with "time management" approaches would likely be disastrous.

final finding

The conclusions we have reached clearly suggest that Dodge Boating is its own company, and its employees are their own people. We suspect they would be highly resistant to corporate restructuring of their work areas, work ethics, teams, goals, or work strategies.

F I G U R E   15.15b An Extended Conclusion for a Long/Formal Report

recommendations

chronological
pattern for
recommended
plan of action

Dodge Boating, Inc.
p. 26

8.0 Recommendations

We recommend the following plan of action:

1. Approach owner/CEO Pamela Hawke with a bid on the company.
2. Include with the bid a proposal for Ms. Hawke to have a two-year, limited
   partnership and a redefined role with benefits.
3. Prepare a prospectus for Coastal Corporate Investments, Inc.'s clientele.
4. Arrange for tours of Dodge Boating, Inc., for Coastal Corporate Investments'
   account executives.
5. Extend tours to potential clients of Coastal Corporate Investments who
   might be interested in investing in the company. . . .

FIGURE 15.16 Recommendations from a Long/Formal Report

STRATEGY   REVIEW   15.4

BULLETED VERSUS NUMBERED LISTS FOR RECOMMENDATIONS

You may list recommendations in no particular order (as a bulleted list) if there is
no step-by-step procedure for initiating these solutions or if no one solution is to
be preferred over the others:

8.0 Recommendations

In addition to the standard business procedures and financial records that need to be
investigated more thoroughly, we recommend a number of philosophical approaches
that may be crucial to the successful acquisition of Dodge Boating, Inc.

Specifically, we recommend that a consortium of corporate representatives and Dodge
Boating's employees meet to discuss the following:

- The basis for Dodge Boating's success
- The employees' views of management
- The employees' expectations from management
- Management's expectations from employees

(continued)

- The role employees would like to play in the future of Dodge Boating
- The role managers would like to play in the future of Dodge Boating

Any cross-purposes should be negotiated during this initial meeting to determine how likely a buyout is to succeed. If managers can maintain the hands-off approach that the owners implemented so effectively in this company, there seems to be little reason for the company not to continue its success.

Alternativley, you may rank and number your recommendations according to some clearly explained pattern: as steps to be performed in a particular order, as a list of ideas arranged from most to least likely to work, or as a list of solutions ranging from most to least cost-effective (time-efficient, agreeable to employees, or some other criteria):

8.0 Recommendations

We recommend the following plan of action as steps for acquiring Dodge Boating, Inc.:

1. Approach owner/CEO Pamela Hawke with a bid on the company.
2. Include with the bid a proposal for Ms. Hawke to have a two-year, limited partnership and a redefined role with benefits.
3. Prepare a prospectus for Coastal Corporate Investments, Inc.'s clientele.
4. Arrange for tours of Dodge Boating, Inc., for Coastal Corporate Investments' account executives.
5. Extend tours to potential clients of Coastal Corporate Investments who might be interested in investing in the company.
6. Arrange seminars on investment opportunities in the boating industry.

Finally, we recommend that such procedures be undertaken as soon as possible. Given that the company is certain not to be on the market for long, our biggest advantage in acquiring this company is speed.

Be sure to clarify the basis on which you have ranked the recommendations in your list.

Optional Back Matter: References, Appendixes, and Indexes of the Formal Report

After writing the introduction, body, and conclusions/recommendations of a formal report, you may have to include a list of references—resources (books, journal articles, government publications, other reports, staff members, consultants, supervisors, and other people) from which you have gathered information for your report. You may also have to include an *appendix* containing all oversized or marginal data that certain (but not all) readers might want to consider about your topic. You may, of course, omit the references if you relied on no additional information other than your own experience and observations for the report. Similarly, you will not need an appendix if you do not have any additional, relevant information that is not presented in the text of your report.

References

As you conducted your research for your formal report, you should have kept thorough notes about the sources of your information (see Chapter 3). That list of references is critical to substantiating your facts. It means a great deal, for instance, whether information about the U.S. economy comes from the Bureau of Labor Statistics (BLS) or from a right- or left-wing interpretation of BLS data. Readers are also more likely to believe test results if you show they have been verified in research laboratories than if you seem to present them out of thin air.

Businesses rarely follow academic systems for Bibliographies—now more commonly referred to as "Works Cited," "Citations," or "References," because not all resources are books. Instead, many organizations have their own systems for documenting sources of information. Regardless of the system you use, almost every citation will include several critical elements that answer the following questions:

1. Who said it?
2. Where did they say it?
3. When did they say it?
4. How can I get a copy of what was said?

Thus, most citations manuals require you to include the following:

- Author(s)
- Medium of communication (title of book, interview, or electronic message)
- Place of communication (name of publishing firm and location of its headquarters, site of the interview, or type of message system)
- Date of the information's availability (date of publication, interview, or E-mail correspondence, for example)
- Page numbers (for published information)

Figure 15.17 and Strategy Review 15.5 on page 532 show how to set up a page of references. The Appendix at the end of this text provides more thorough coverage of the strategies for creating a documentation segment for workplace writing.

credit person
first—then list
"publication" data

alphabetical
arrangement

interview and
records

interview

Web site

book

interview and
records

interview

telephone
interview

REFERENCES

Dandeens, John Q., Certified Public Accountant. Personal Interview and
    Accounting Records. January 2, 1999. 322 Main Street, Bengal, Alabama.

Hawke, Pamela. Personal Interviews. January 3, 6, 18, and 30, 2001. Dodge
    Boating, Inc., plant. New Haven, Alabama.

httl.www/anmee.boat.com. Discussion provided on Web page. January 4, 2001.

Smith, Angela R., and Edgar B. Johnson. *Measuring Intangibles: An Economic
    Reality.* New York: Durwood Press, 1997. pp. 342–49.

Trothers, Benson, Attorney for Dodge Boating, Inc. Personal Interview and
    Records. January 4, 1998. 441 W. Newansone Street, Bengal, Alabama.

Vinson, Lamonte, Chief Engineer. Personal Interview. February 4, 2000. Dodge
    Boating, Inc., plant. New Haven, Alabama.

————. Telephone interview. 15 February 1999.

FIGURE 15.17 A Reference Page from a Long/Formal Report

STRATEGY REVIEW 15.5

DOCUMENTING SOURCES FOR THE FORMAL REPORT'S REFERENCE PAGE(S)

In Chapter 5 on drafting workplace documents, you were introduced to the various forms a particular citation might take on a reference page. For example, information cited from a book might look like this entry:

James, Arquette. *Business in the 90s: Staying Afloat.* New York: Norton, 1996.
pp. 23–62.

Information cited from an interview might look like this:

James, Arquette. Personal Interview. San Diego, CA: Mayor's Convention, March 17, 1997.

The Appendix at the end of this text will help you decide what kinds of information should be included in a reference list. Regardless of which documentation system your organization uses, you should follow that system rigorously in documenting your sources of information (see Figure 15-17).

Appendixes

At the drafting stage (see Chapter 5), you learned that some related information you uncover might be useful to a secondary group of readers, but not to the primary group. You may have accumulated complicated statistics, graphs, and equations that a few readers would like to see but that, if placed in the body of the report, would overwhelm the majority of readers. Or you may have an oversized map or set of blueprints that would be physically awkward to manage in the middle of the report. These items are best placed in an *appendix*, where they will not disrupt the reading, are easier to manage, and can be reviewed at any time during the reading process.

An appendix may also provide other relevant information or aids to understanding, such as the following:

- Useful addresses or phone numbers for resources (agencies, businesses, organizations, etc.) relevant to the report's discussion
- Additional reading materials for readers who want to follow up on information or learn more about a topic
- A copy of the survey, questionnaire, or other material used to generate information for the report
- a list of resources that provided background information that was not specifically cited in the body of the report

Important information and traditional graphics that help readers understand the information in the text should not be placed in the appendix, however. They should be incorporated into the text where the reader would find them most useful. No one likes having to flip back and forth through a document to find crucial information.

If only one kind of information is included as back matter, the final section is titled "Appendix." If the back matter includes several kinds of information—say, a map, a set of blueprints, a series of equations, and a list of addresses and phone numbers—then the heading is the plural "Appendixes," and each set of information is a separate appendix with its own letter or number and title:

Just as you do with graphics, you should refer to the appendixes in the text of your report wherever the references might be most useful for your readers.

Indexes

Writers sometimes include an index in a lengthy formal report so that readers can find information about specific topics. If you compare a table of contents and an index (see Figures 15.9 and 15.18), you will see that they have very different purposes and organizations. Although both provide page numbers so that readers can turn to a specific page for information, the table of contents lists the headings and subheadings in the order in which they appear in the document. An index lists subjects alphabetically and is not limited to the headings and subheadings (see Figure 15.18). Further, the table of contents lists each heading or subheading only once with no overlapping, but the index (if it is a truly useful one) will include cross-references that refer readers to related information. (See Strategy Review 15.6 on page 535.)

Index

alphabetical
arrangement
by topic

assets, 1+, 3, 4
   intangibles, 5
   tangibles, 4, 15–29

all page
references cited

benefits, 2

cross-reference
cited

employees, 2 *See also* loyalty

EPA, 3

equipment, 3, 5

location, 3, 10

loyalty, 2

salaries, 2, 25, 37

FIGURE 15.18 An Index for a Formal Report

STRATEGY REVIEW 15.6

INDEXING YOUR REPORT

Although a number of computer programs can be used to index reports, the task really requires *you* to make decisions about the logical connections between the report's subjects—connections that computer programs have not adequately mastered. Therefore, if you need to construct an index for your work, your best strategy is to follow these guidelines:

1. Highlight major concepts as you read through the work.
2. Make notecards with a major concept as each notecard's heading.
3. For each major concept (one per notecard), list each page number on which that word appears.
4. List related or substantive concepts, along with the page numbers where they appear in the document.
5. Ask yourself, "Where would I look in the index to find information about [blank]?" Make sure you have provided all cross-references.
6. Alphabetize your list.

THE WORLD OF WORKPLACE WRITING

Tables of Contents, Indexes, and Technological Possibilities

In a book on birds of North America, the table of contents might reveal that the book is organized by geography: Northeast, Northwest, Middle Atlantic area, Midwest, Southeast, and Southwest. Alternatively, it may be organized by terrain: forest birds, grassland birds, desert birds, swamp birds, shorebirds, and the like. Such an organization shows a hierarchy of information that depends on a careful classification of birds. In contrast, indexes list topics in strict alphabetical order.

Suppose you look out at your backyard and see a fully mature, but small, brown bird with a white head, almost like a miniature bald eagle. How would you go about finding this bird in your bird guide? You will find that neither the table of contents nor the index is particularly useful in this case. You will probably have to thumb through the entire section of birds in your geographic region.

Researchers and writers of *hypertext*—computerized programs that try to imitate how humans think and actually need information—will eventually make some kinds of tables of contents and indexes obsolete. Hypertext allows readers to find information according to associations they make between various topics and

(continued)

issues. Such associations are not necessarily from general to specific (as in tables of contents) and are rarely alphabetical (as in indexes). Instead, the hypertext may follow a pattern of related ideas or a progression of clarifications. In the bird guide example, a hypertext program would begin by asking you some questions:

1. Where did you observe the bird?

   Southeastern United States

2. What is the dominant color of the bird?

   Brown

3. How large is the bird?

   1–2 inches high   3–4 inches high
   2–3 inches high   4–5 inches high, and so on

4. Click on the bird that most resembles the bird you saw:

  **?**

Wood Thrush   Chipping Sparrow   None

The program may then allow you to acknowledge that "yes," this is exactly the bird you saw, or "no," it is not the bird you saw. If you answer "no," the program may ask for more specific features, such as head shape, beak shape, wing coloring, and so on to help identify the bird.

Such programs allow you to find information using very different thinking processes from those used with the traditional table of contents and index. The computer industry has an enormous need for professional writers who can describe how to use such systems, making the industry one of the richest employment prospects for professional writers.

Figure 15.19 on pages 537–551 presents the formal report, which is a follow-up to the short report that we have examined in separate figures earlier in the chapter. (The four middle sections of the report, which follow the same format as shown in other parts of the report, are excluded in Figure 15.19 to save space.) Note how the segments flow in a logical, reader-oriented fashion. Graphics are inserted into the text to help readers who need images and graphic displays at the site of the content—not clustered in the back of the report.

Business Opportunities & Investigations, Inc.

111 Gawain Street
Benson, AK 58392
(433) 542-9485

16 March 2002

Mr. Charles Richmond, President
Coastal Corporate Investments, Inc.
2332 Sudan Road
New Berne, AL 43627

Dear Mr. Richmond:

Our preliminary studies on the feasibility of a Dodge Boating, Inc., purchase indicated that the potential for growth and profitability seemed promising. Our more extensive review, however, suggests that we might have underestimated that promise.

Once we had the opportunity to examine the accounting books of the organization, we learned that Dodge Boating is uniquely positioned in the market to have a greater share of the market overall and to dominate the sales in some areas. Further investigation revealed sound environmental and fiscal planning, features that tremendously increase the attractiveness of this purchase.

We continue to appreciate the efforts of your staff—especially James Overton and Maria Sanchez—who have so graciously answered our questions about criteria and expectations.

Should you have additional questions about the purchase arrangement or about Dodge Boating itself, we will be happy to meet with you.

Sincerely,

April Tyndall

April Tyndall
Account Representative

encl: report

FIGURE 15.19 A Long/Formal Report, Letter of Transmittal Attached to the Cover

DODGE BOATING, INC.:
AN EXTENDED FEASIBILITY STUDY

Submitted to
Charles Richmond, President
Coastal Corporate Investments, Inc.

Prepared by

Business Opportunities & Investigations, Inc.

April Tyndall
Timothy Atkins
Pentros Abeynne

16 March 2002

This report describes the results of a follow-up evaluation of Dodge Boating, Inc. The original report (6 December 2001) suggested that investing in Dodge Boating would be a generally sound move, and additional studies make an even stronger case for the purchase. Based on extensive analyses, environmental statements, and tentative purchase agreements, this report concludes that the purchase of Dodge Boating should be an immediate priority for Coastal Investments, Inc.

F I G U R E   15.19   A Long/Formal Report, Cover/Title Page

Coastal Corporate Investments, Inc.

2332 Sudan Road
New Berne, AL 43627
(312) 447-3923
FAX: (312) 447-3838

17 January 2002

Ms. April Tyndall
Business Opportunities & Investigations, Inc.
111 Gawain Street
Benson, AK 58392

Dear Ms. Tyndall:

I read with great interest your initial investigation into the financial soundness of
Dodge Boating, Inc. I agree with you that the preliminary findings merit a closer
look, and I authorize you and your colleagues to conduct the more thorough study
you recommended.

I am anxious to see the results of the environmental study, of course, but I'm
even more anxious to learn about the holdings and debts of the company. We'd
also like to know what the employees' attitudes are toward a buyout. Purchasing
a company becomes more difficult if the employees are hostile or must be
replaced.

Please make full use of our staff at Coastal Corporate Investments to help you
gather information and report back to us as soon as possible.

Sincerely,

Charles Richmond

Charles Richmond,
President

FIGURE 15.19　A Long/Formal Report, Letter of Authorization (page i)
Bound into Report

Abstract

This report presents evaluations of audited financial statements, tangible and intangible assets, and the numerous positives and negatives of Dodge Boating, Inc. The researchers have investigated and evaluated the company's competitors, the growth potential of the company, and its financial statements for the past three years.

The total value of the business is approximately $5,312,000. The growth potential of the company looks sound, and profitability should continue. Positive points include the company's ability to sustain profits over a three-year period, its prime location, and the distribution of its revenue base. Negatives include the company's limited geographic area (small niche market), the firm's dependency on its owner, a lack of long-term contracts, and the presence of an old EPA Superfund site. Overall the firm appears to be solid financially, and we recommend that serious purchase negotiations begin with the owner.

This report is a limited business evaluation of Dodge Boating, Inc., of New Haven, Alabama. It is designed to introduce the feasibility of purchasing the company from its current owner and CEO Pamela Hawke, who has expressed an interest in selling the firm. The report is intended for the private use of Coastal Corporate Investments, and its contents are confidential.

ii

FIGURE 15.19 A Long/Formal Report, page ii

Contents

FIGURE 15.19 A Long/Formal Report, page iii

List of Illustrations

iv

FIGURE 15.19 A Long/Formal Report, page iv

Glossary

contribution margin   the difference between revenues and all variable costs associated with those revenues.

intangible asset   an asset that does not have physical substance, such as a property right or company goodwill.

operating income   the difference between revenues and the cost of service and administrative expenses.

tangible asset   a long-term asset that has physical substance, such as the fleet of boats and/or trailers.

v

FIGURE 15.19   A Long/Formal Report, page v

List of Symbols

£   money in British currency

¢   money less than or over a full dollar

¥   money in Japanese currency

§   money from reinvestment

¶   money from capital gains

°   money from warehouse rentals

∞   money from design initiatives

μ   money from tax returns

√   money in Russian currency

vi

F I G U R E 15.19 A Long/Formal Report, page vi

DODGE BOATING, INC.:
AN EXTENDED FEASIBILITY STUDY

1.0 Introduction

This report presents a follow-up to an initial investigation (6 December 2001) into the feasibility of purchasing Dodge Boating, Inc., a small business located in eastern Alabama. The results of this in-depth investigation provide sound evidence that Dodge Boating, Inc., is an excellent investment opportunity for the clients of Coastal Corporate Investments, Inc. This report is provided for Coastal Corporate Investments' account executives to analyze; then the information may be freely adapted and provided to Coastal Corporate Investments' clients who may want to invest in Dodge Boating, Inc.

Based on analyses of audited statements, interviews with the owner/CEO Pamela Hawke, and interviews with design engineers, machinists, and technicians, this report shows that Dodge Boating, Inc., has enjoyed huge profits and has earned a significant, though small, place in the boat design market. The report includes analyses of the company's assets and liabilities, based on audited reports. Because of the boating industry's tremendous economic upswing in recent years, the researchers for this report can only speculate about the long-range potential of Dodge Boating. Nevertheless, the report does incorporate employees' views of growth in revenues and nontangible assets.

A glossary of terms is provided for Coastal Corporate Investments' clients who may want to read this report to determine their interest in investing in Dodge Boating.

Following this introduction, the report addresses the financial details—assets and liabilities—of Dodge Boating, Inc., as of 15 June 1999. Then, the report addresses other issues critical to maintaining and even expanding the growth potential of the company: personnel issues, equipment issues, and location issues. The conclusions and recommendations are directly tied to these crucial details, which, if they can be resolved, should clearly indicate the enthusiasm our researchers feel for Dodge Boating, Inc.

2.0 Assets

Dodge Boating's assets may be divided into tangible assets, such as cash, equipment, and furnishings, and intangible assets, such as its reputation, contracts, and client list. Although the tangible assets outweigh the value of

FIGURE 15.19 A Long/Formal Report, page 1

Dodge Boating, Inc.
p. 2

the intangibles, the benefits of the intangibles should not be minimized for this company.

2.1 Tangible Assets

Dodge Boating's tangible assets were grossly underreported in the initial investigation due, perhaps, to attempts to lower the tax value of the company. Further devaluing the initial investigation's summary of tangible assets was the omission of cash accounts. A revised itemization and value of tangible assets over the past three years is presented and then totaled in Table I:

Table I: Revised Itemization and Value of Tangible Assets for 1999

ASSET	1997	1998	1999
Cash accounts	$21,029	$41,294	$77,392
Accounts receivable	47,200	99,204	153,219
Supplies	1,120	2,140	5,389
Repair parts	3,295	4,295	6,228
Boats	59,203	193,576	593,232
Trailers	73,201	97,036	200,118
Forklifts	43,042	45,795	86,394
Office equipment (including computers)	32,449	49,036	52,493
Furnishings (including office and outside displays)	9,322	14,396	25,395
Totals	**$289,861**	**$546,772**	**$1,199,860**

2.2 Intangible Assets

The valuation of intangible assets is always difficult to determine because such assets do not carry a specific dollar figure. For our analysis, we used the Smythe Johnson formula, which has been shown to allow only small discrepancies and to provide more thorough readings of the true value of intangible assets.

F I G U R E   15.19   A Long/Formal Report, page 2

Dodge Boating, Inc.
p. 3

2.2.1 Employee Issues

Perhaps the greatest asset (or liability, for that matter) in any company is its employees. The personnel issues of Dodge Boating are at the heart of the company's success and may, ironically, pose a problem for a new owner. Inherent in the quality of work produced by these employees is their tremendous respect for and loyalty to Pamela Hawke. Many employees spoke of her awards in boat design, her lineage from a well-known boat designing family, and her keen sense of proportion in all the designs. . . .

2.2.2 Equipment Status

Dodge Boating has invested quite a bit of money in its equipment, with the latest figures showing $298,026 total investment in supplies, forklifts, trailers, and general drafting equipment and machinery. The equipment is all either new or in exceptionally good shape. These tangible values are enhanced by the innovative changes the teams have made in the equipment, with their additional modifications making standard equipment worth, perhaps, twice its original value. For instance, when the mast needs to be attached to the stern at a certain angle to make a design work, the designers, machinists, and technicians collaborate to design and make a piece of equipment that will hold the mast at exactly that angle. This kind of innovative spirit characterizes the work at Dodge Boating and makes it difficult to put a price on the intangible assets of the company.

2.2.3 Location

The location of Dodge Boating is both an asset and a liability (see map in appendix). Located on the Ipsiena River in eastern Alabama, the company currently uses the waterway as a testing site for some of its smaller boats. The site also allows clients to see the tests of their boats, while putting them in the proper "waterway" setting for demonstrations and purchases. The employees enjoy the view as they work because all offices and workshops face the river and have glass walls. The current owner bought the building from the town's Chamber of Commerce and then added the manufacturing portion of the company to the back of the lot.

FIGURE 15.19 A Long/Formal Report, page 3

Dodge Boating, Inc.

p. 4

Unfortunately, the company sits on an old EPA Superfund site, a contaminated area that makes the property unsuitable for additional building and, consequently, for the kind of expansion that would make the business grow. Numerous lawsuits have been filed and settled, but the possibility of future lawsuits is not out of the question, making long-range commitments to this site unwise.

A better site might be in the Princeton Industrial Park. Located twelve miles north of Dodge Boating's current site, the industrial park has water access and land available. Further, the employees of Dodge Boating would not have to move. . . .

[Sections 3.0 through 6.0 Not Shown]

Dodge Boating, Inc.

p. 25

7.0 Conclusions

Based on the financial information provided throughout this report, along with evaluations of the intangible assets and liabilities of Dodge Boating, Inc., we conclude that the company is a sound investment opportunity for clients of Coastal Corporate Investments, Inc.

Further, because the owner/CEO of the company is interested in retirement, and because the financial status of the company seems so sound, we believe that several companies might consider the purchase of Dodge Boating, Inc., if we do not move quickly on this opportunity. Given the expansion in the boating industry at this time, there is little reason to believe that anything short of a major economic recession will dent the profitability of the business.

In addition, we have reached a number of other conclusions about Dodge Boating, Inc.:

1. Its history as a small, family-owned business is largely responsible for the loyalty its employees feel toward the company and the Hawke family.

F I G U R E   15.19   A Long/Formal Report, pages 4 (partial) and 25 (partial)

Dodge Boating, Inc.
p. 26

2. Keeping workers will be difficult, given their lack of loyalty to new owners, whom they are likely to perceive as outsiders.

3. Ms. Hawke's pledge to help inspire loyalty in the new owners may help in the short run, but in the long run, we will have to find our own way to instill loyalty in these workers.

4. The collaborative atmosphere in which Dodge Boating's employees work is remarkable. Their time may often seem wasted, from a corporate view; yet, this "downtime"—time spent drinking coffee, getting snacks, and visiting with each other—seems to produce a cohesiveness among the workers that leads directly to their abilities to share ideas and solve problems collectively. Trying to modify this system with "time management" approaches would likely be disastrous.

The conclusions we have reached clearly suggest that Dodge Boating is its own company, and its employees are their own people. We suspect they would be highly resistant to corporate restructuring of their work areas, work ethics, teams, goals, or work strategies.

8.0 Recommendations

We recommend the following plan of action as steps for acquiring Dodge Boating, Inc.:

1. Approach owner/CEO Pamela Hawke with a bid on the company.
2. Include with the bid a proposal for Ms. Hawke to have a two-year, limited partnership and a redefined role with benefits.
3. Prepare a prospectus for Coastal Corporate Investments, Inc.'s clientele.
4. Arrange for tours of Dodge Boating, Inc., for Coastal Corporate Investments' account executives.
5. Extend tours to potential clients of Coastal Corporate Investments who might be interested in investing in the company.
6. Arrange seminars on investment opportunities in the boating industry.

Finally, we recommend that such procedures be undertaken as soon as possible. Given that the company is certain not to be on the market for long, our biggest advantage in acquiring this company is speed.

FIGURE 15.19 A Long/Formal Report, page 26

REFERENCES

Dandeens, John Q., Certified Public Accountant. Personal Interview and Accounting Records. January 2, 1999. 322 Main Street, Bengal, Alabama.

Hawke, Pamela. Personal Interviews. January 3, 6, 18, and 30, 2001. Dodge Boating, Inc., plant. New Haven, Alabama.

httl.www/anmee. boat.com. Discussion provided on Web page. January 4, 2001.

Smith, Angela R., and Edgar B. Johnson. *Measuring Intangibles: An Economic Reality*. New York: Durwood Press, 1997. pp. 342–49.

Trothers, Benson, Attorney for Dodge Boating, Inc. Personal Interview and Records. January 4, 1998. 441 W. Newansone Street, Bengal, Alabama.

Vinson, Lamonte, Chief Engineer. Personal Interview. February 4, 2000. Dodge Boating, Inc., plant. New Haven, Alabama.

———. Telephone interview. 15 February 1999.

[Appendix Not Shown]

27

FIGURE 15.19   A Long/Formal Report, page 27

Index

assets, 1+, 3, 4
   intangibles, 5
   tangibles, 4, 15–29
benefits, 2
employees, 2 *See also* loyalty
EPA, 3
equipment, 3, 5
location, 3, 10
loyalty, 2
salaries, 2, 25, 37

29

FIGURE 15.19   A Long/Formal Report, page 29

Summary

In this chapter, you have been able to apply your understanding of the previous chapters' discussions of report purposes, topics, and patterns of organization to a discussion of report lengths and format.

Length depends on two critical issues: (1) How complex is my topic? and (2) How much do my readers know or need to know? These two issues underpin the writer's decisions about the length of a document, for some complex information can be better explained in short, abbreviated summaries, while other complex information may require pages and pages of explanations, details, examples, graphics, and summaries.

The format of both informal and formal reports is typically determined by a combination of your organization's idiosyncrasies and some standard elements of formatting workplace documents. Although informal reports may be formatted as letters, memos, or standard reports, long reports require special formatting features, such as front matter and back matter that are designed to help guide readers through the bulk of the report, while providing special places to which they can turn to find the information that most concerns them. For example, a cover page gives readers the primary topic of the report without their having to open the report itself. An abstract helps readers understand the big picture that is the basis or perhaps even the subject of the report. Readers may then turn to a table of contents that helps them find any special sections that are important for them to read.

In the workplace, reports serve to update information, predict trends, and resolve problems. As a workplace writer, you will have to investigate several aspects of the readers' relationship to the information in order to produce a useful report:

- What kinds of information do the readers need?
- How will the readers use the information provided?
- In what order should that information appear?
- What kinds of graphics will clarify or emphasize the appropriate information?
- What kinds of references and resources will the readers respect as credible sources of the information in the report?
- How can I verify the accuracy of the information presented?
- How can I verify the thoroughness of my research?

Finally, be sure to review the discussions of visual elements in Chapters 8 and 9—layout, design, and graphics—for your documents. These elements help readers find their way through long and often complex information. They also provide a break from reading and help direct the reader's attention to the most significant information on a page.

In the end, your readers' abilities to use the information you have provided for the purposes intended means you have succeeded as a communicator. You have provided valuable information for your organization's readers and also enhanced your own credibility as a thinker and writer.

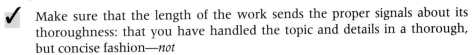

CHECKLIST

Length

✔ Make sure that the length of the work sends the proper signals about its thoroughness: that you have handled the topic and details in a thorough, but concise fashion—*not*

- that you have overindulged in writing and explaining, producing a report that is too long, or
- that you have underestimated readers' needs for thorough information, producing a report that is too short.

✔ To measure the appropriateness of the length of a report, focus on (1) what readers *already know* about the topic, (2) what readers *need to know* about the topic, and (3) how much readers *want to know* about the topic.

✔ Because workplace readers are busy people, your best bet is to ask yourself these questions:

- Can I explain all my reader needs to know in a one- to three-page letter or memo?
- Can I explain all my reader needs to know in a three- to ten-page short report?
- Will it take ten pages or more to thoroughly explain all my reader needs to know?

Format for Short/Informal Reports

✔ If your short/informal report will remain inside the organization, format it as a memo.

✔ If your short/informal report will go to readers outside the organization, format it as a letter.

✔ If your short/informal report will go both inside and outside the organization, or if it first addresses readers inside your organization but may then be passed on to readers outside your organization, adopt the standard report format.

Regardless of whether your readers are inside or outside your organization, if your report is longer than three pages, use the standard report format.

Format for Long/Formal Reports

 Be sure to include the appropriate prefatory matter for a formal report:
- Letter of transmittal
- Cover
- Letter of authorization (if available)
- Title page
- Abstract and/or executive summary
- Table of contents
- List of illustrations (if needed)
- Glossary (if needed)
- List of symbols (if needed)

 Be sure to include complete information in the introduction of your formal report:
- Subject
- Purpose
- Audience
- Scope and limitations
- Methods
- Definitions (optional)
- Plan of organization

 Be sure to develop the body of your report so that it does all of the following:
- Clarifies the details of points you make in the introduction and conclusion sections of the report
- Supports the rationale of the arguments you present in the introduction and conclusions
- Provides statistics, examples, anecdotes, and other forms of supporting evidence (discussed in Chapter 5 on drafting)
- Explains causes, relationships, specific instructions, or consequences of particular actions or attitudes
- Answers any other questions about your work

 Provide conclusions that do any or all of the following:
- Present recommendations and solutions
- Explain the significance of a particular situation

- Explain the consequences of a particular situation
- Offer a view of trends as they affect the organization
- Present predictions about the topic in light of the organization's future
- Recommend a plan of action
- Pose questions for future research or investigations related to the issue at hand

✔ Include a list of references—built from books, articles, data banks, company files, Internet sources, and people you have interviewed—to give credit to others for their ideas, help alleviate skepticism about the information you provide, and show readers where they can find the information you have used for your report.

✔ Place relevant, supplemental materials that may overwhelm readers in the appendix of your report. You may include any or all of the following:

- Complex equations that might confound some readers
- Additional reading sources on your topic
- Oversized articles, such as maps or blueprints
- Addresses or phone numbers of resources
- Copies of surveys or other instruments used to gather information

✔ Construct an index if your work is lengthy and if readers might need detailed information about specific topics in your report.

For All Reports

✔ Incorporate directly into the text any graphics that will help clarify or emphasize crucial elements in your report (see Chapters 8 and 9).

✔ Include headings and subheadings to help readers find the parts of your document that are most crucial for them to read, to highlight the organization of your work, and to give your readers a break from reading.

✔ Follow a standard documentation system, established by your organization or by the field in which you work, to list resources and references of information in the report.

✔ Review your report for thoroughness, accuracy, relevance, and organization. Read the report from your readers' perspectives.

✔ Proofread.

Individual Exercises

1. Consider each of the following audiences and topics for reports:

   a. High school principals: a policy concerning handguns on campus

   b. High school students: a description of the policies and plans for recruiting, training, and selecting members of the basketball team

   c. Parents: a policy concerning punishment of violent students in the high school

   d. Graduating seniors: how to prepare for graduation

   e. Traffic engineers: a plan to increase the number of lanes through a congested three-mile stretch in your town

   f. The mayor: a request to sponsor the rezoning of an area currently off-limits for retail outlets

   Using your imagination, discuss the information you would include and the approach you would take for each topic in each of the following: (a) a one- to three-page memo or letter; (b) a three- to eight-page report; and (c) a report of more than ten pages. Be prepared to defend your answers, indicating the critical issues you considered in forming your opinion. An example is provided for you:

   Example: Engineers: a notice encouraging them to enroll in safety regulation courses

   a. A one- to three-page memo explaining why safety regulation courses are important to engineers in our company and a list of courses offered at the local college during the next semester.

   b. A three- to eight-page informal report explaining why safety regulation courses are important to engineers in our company, a list of topics that need to be addressed in such courses, a list of courses offered at the local college during the next semester, a full description of those courses, and registration procedures for enrolling in the courses.

   c. A report of more than ten pages to engineers explaining why safety courses are important to engineers in our company, why traditional safety courses do not meet our engineers' needs, a proposal to establish our own safety courses, a cost and benefits analysis of initiating such a program, and a plan for evaluating the success of the courses.

2. Select one of the long (more than ten pages) reports you proposed to write in the previous exercise, and draft the following for it:

   a. A letter/memo of authorization from your reader, addressed to you, agreeing to let you investigate the topic and write a report on it

  b. A letter/memo of transmittal to your reader, which would accompany your completed report

  c. A title page, including an appropriate title and the other elements that are part of the standard title page of a formal report

  d. A list of terms you might need to define for a glossary (optional)

3. Evaluate the following introduction for a report. Does it meet all the readers' needs for information? How would you improve the introduction?

   The purpose of this report is to explain to my readers how a background in accounting is important to everybody. You just cannot get along these days without it. Of course, you don't have to be a banker or a CPA, but you do need to know the basics of debits, credits, assets, and liabilities. This report focuses on how to balance your checkbook and how to set up a savings account. Setting aside as little as 5 percent of each paycheck would make a real difference in your financial picture. This information comes from a brochure I picked up at the bank; your bank probably has similar literature for you. Of course, if you don't have a bank, that's what this report is about.

4. Determine whether the following excerpts from reports demonstrate formal or informal writing styles. Be prepared to explain your answers.

   a. During northeastern storms, the undertow tends to increase by 2 to 19 pounds, depending on the tide and the amount of rainfall. When the undertow exceeds a 15-pound pull, surfing, swimming, and all other in-water sports should cease. Because of the serious shortage of lifeguards, who should not be asked to put their lives on the line routinely for the sake of sports such as surfing and swimming, the chances of lone swimming accidents increase during northeastern storms. Our data show, in fact, that over the past seven years, northeastern storm undertows may have been responsible for as many as five deaths on the Outer Banks.

   b. Although I love those storms, I also have the good sense to stay out of the surf when they hit. Actually, the waves tend to increase both before and after the storms, making surfing ideal for as many as three or more days. But the undertow is bad only during specific times. If we had a system to measure the undertow levels for the surfers, they would probably still surf the high tides but would know when to be more careful because of the undertow levels. At the very least, they might adopt a buddy system and learn to avoid lone swimming exploits during those periods.

Collaborative Exercises

1. You and your colleagues have written a collaborative report introducing international students to the day-to-day routines of campus life at your college. Provide a glossary for these readers that defines the following terms:

registration	liberal arts
drop-add	Student Government Association
cutting a class	take-home exam
adviser	honor/judicial board

2. You and your colleagues have been asked to write a report about "who's who at our college." How would you investigate the role(s) of the following college professionals? After conducting your research, write a one- to three-page report for new students who also want to know who's who on your campus.

   a. Registrar

   b. Provost, chancellor, or president

   c. Dean

   d. Bursar

Extended Report Exercises—for Individual or Collaborative Projects

Long or Short Report

Describe your college library's policies regarding the following:

   a. Overdue books

   b. Lost books

   c. Unpaid fines

   d. Lost library card

   e. Interlibrary loan

   f. Computerized databases

Choose any or all of these topics and prepare a report for an appropriate audience. You will have to determine who that audience is and why they might be reading your report.

Short/Informal Report

Work through the planning, organizing, drafting, and revising stages as you write both of the following reports. Plan the graphics that might be useful for your readers.

   a. Write a brief report for full-time workers who want to enroll in one or two courses at your college; explain the steps they can take to manage their time so they can handle both school and a job.

b. Write a brief report for full-time students who want to take a part-time job; explain the steps they can take to manage their time so they can handle both school and a job.

For both groups of readers and both reports, explain what special considerations might make a difference in the advice you would offer. For example, would it matter whether your reader was a single mother or a father who travels quite a bit? Specify a *particular* audience for your work.

What kinds of information would be useful for both audiences? In other words, what topics that would be appropriate for full-time worker turned student would also be useful for full-time student turned worker?

Long/Formal Report

Increasingly, people are afraid to leave their homes unattended when they go out of town on vacation or for business. Hiring students to "house-sit" is common in college towns, but many homeowners and students don't know how to find each other. You and your colleagues have started a new company, "They're Out of Town," that provides house-sitters for homeowners. The idea has caught on, and you have been asked to explain your ideas—how your company works and the do's and don'ts of starting such a business—to a group of high-income investors who want to buy your business, possibly for millions of dollars. The investors want exclusive rights to your company's plans and procedures.

a. What assumptions can you make about your audience, based on the little bit of information you have about them?

b. Brainstorm with your colleagues about the kinds of topics that might be included in a long, formal report. Keep your readers and their needs in mind.

c. Narrow your topic for a fifteen-page report. What topics have you included and excluded from consideration? Why?

d. Use the planning worksheet on pages 50–51 in Chapter 2 to list your ideas and considerations for this report.

e. Draw on your knowledge and experience with drafting workplace documents to draft the report.

f. Consider the forms and placement of graphics in your formal report. Where do you need to simplify or emphasize information for your reader? Which graphic forms are most useful for your audience and your purpose?

g. Draft the additional front and back matter you will need for the formal report format.

   h. Revise your report on the basis of your readers' needs and expectations.

   i. Submit your report to your teacher, who is acting as a business broker for the investment group.

 ## ONGOING ASSIGNMENT

■ Using the newcomers' handbook you have been working on throughout the semester, create a formal or informal report (following your instructor's directions) that explains the purpose, the audience, and the message of the handbook. Devise a document that will explain how you gathered your information and indicate any suggestions you have for improving the organization's culture, based on input from your colleagues (coworkers or fellow students). In short, what areas of your organization's culture could stand some improvement? Writing for the chief manager or academic officer of your organization, present your findings, with the handbook as the attached appendix.

CHAPTER 16

Oral Communications in the Workplace

Just as the ability to write can enhance your success in an organization, the ability to speak before a small committee of colleagues or a large group of strangers might be important to your career. Although this text emphasizes written communication, rather than oral communication, many on-the-job writing assignments will also require you to present your findings orally.

In this chapter, you will learn the nuances that differentiate oral communication situations—typically depending on the size of the group and the purpose for the meeting. The chapter will also help you understand the kinds of decisions you will have to make about (1) preparing your presentation, (2) creating visual aids and other features that can make your presentation both clearer and more memorable, and (3) delivering the presentation. You will also learn to handle question-and-answer sessions knowledgeably and tactfully.

Differentiating between Types and Purposes of Presentations

Most oral communication situations are described according to the size of the audience, as in "small" and "large" group presentations. Knowing the size of the audience is important because that knowledge gives you the proper sense of the group before you walk into a speaking situation, helps you determine the kinds of visual aids that will be most useful, and suggests the amount of formality the situation requires.

Far more important, however, is knowing what interest, concern, issue, or topic brings these people together. Is this a mandatory meeting, arranged by management, or have some people come voluntarily because the topic has generated interest within the organization? Knowing whether the group wants to meet or finds such meetings tedious and unnecessary is critical in helping you determine the content and visual aspects of your presentation.

In the workplace, the following are some of the most common purposes for audiences to gather:

- To voice concerns over some issue that affects the organization's image, productivity, status, and/or employees
- To offer information about concerns, ideas, and solutions to problems
- To gather information about concerns, ideas, and solutions to problems

Most groups, therefore, band together as one of the following:

- A committee or board charged with representing a greater population of constituents: The board of trustees at your college or the policies committee of an organization, for example. *You can appeal to their sense of responsibility to those constituents.*

- A group of delegates representing individual constituencies: The U.S. Senate, charged with representing the citizens of individual states and the states' economic and social agendas, or a group representing members of various departments within an organization, for example. *You can appeal to their sense of responsibility toward their special constituencies in relation to the issue(s)—why the constituents care about the issue or how they are affected by it.*
- A group representing special interests: A group representing the concerns of senior citizens, women, or union workers, for example. *You can appeal to their special concerns in light of their perspectives on the issue.*
- A group voicing its own interests: A group of citizens who are concerned with school reform, the effects of a new industry on the local environment, or increases in utility rates, for example. *You can appeal to the factors that motivate their interest (fear, opportunity, cooperation, good citizenship, profit, etc.).*
- A group charged with distributing information to its constituents: Department representatives given information about a new product line with the understanding that they will relay that information to their coworkers, for example. *You can appeal to their own understanding as an avenue for helping others understand.*

In short, most groups band together either through *necessity* (as required by the members' job descriptions and duties), through *strength* (the idea of strength in numbers to voice concerns, address special needs, or educate the public), through *common interests* (as stockholders, citizens, or members of a profession), or as a matter of information exchange. As a speaker, you should draft an oral presentation that places your topic directly in the proper perspective for your listeners, allowing them to answer these questions:

- What should I do with this information?
- What should I think, do, or believe according to this information?
- What use is this information to me or my constituents?

As an entry-level worker, you will probably not be charged with addressing special interest groups; those assignments usually go to corporate spokespersons. But you may be asked to address the members of your profession at a professional conference, the stockholders at your organization's annual meeting, and (most often) the members of various committees and representative groups throughout your organization. Although information exchange is increasingly offered via computer networks (both inside and between organizations), on many occasions discussions are too complex, too heated, too confidential, or otherwise too sensitive to relay through computers. On those occasions, the presence of a speaker is still required.

Speakers cite the following as their most common purposes:

- To provide information that the audience needs, such as general announcements, updates on a project, details about new strategies or products, scheduling information, forecasts, or status reports

- To persuade the audience to act or believe a certain way, such as using a new sales technique, following a new policy, adopting a new plan, or considering alternative solutions to problems

In most cases, oral communications require the speaker to accomplish both functions: to provide information *and* to persuade the listeners of an important point.

Small/Informal Group Presentations

The gathering of a small group may be routine and scheduled, such as a monthly review of progress on a particular project, or it may be an emergency, such as a hurriedly called meeting of advisers when an organization faces a crisis. The topics for such meetings also range from routine updates and information exchanges to major problems that the group is asked to help resolve.

The participants in the small group meeting may come from a single department, such as the design department, or from every department in your organization, including the engineering, marketing, advertising, legal, management, manufacturing, and other departments. Knowing who will attend your small meeting will help you determine the kind and amount of information you must present.

Small/informal group presentations typically allow for a more open exchange than larger meetings do; thus, you should be prepared to offer a more detailed accounting of a situation, provide a wider set of alternatives and solutions, and answer a wider variety of questions in a small meeting. Your organization's culture will determine how docile or contentious such meetings typically are. In some organizations, for instance, new ideas and solutions presented in small group meetings are practically dissected for inspection, review, and challenges. In other organizations, ideas are examined more generally, with polite suggestions offered for modifications or clarifications. In either culture, however, as the presenter of a project or idea, you will have to determine the kinds of information needed, as well as the questions most likely to be raised.

Large Group Presentations

Large groups can have from twenty to two thousand participants and are often attended by both experts in the topic and general participants. In a general stockholders' meeting, for instance, some participants may be extremely savvy about the product/service and the financial implications of the organization's report, while others have only a general understanding of such matters. This wide range in the audience members' knowledge is the reason many speakers say addressing a large group is more difficult than speaking to a small group (contrary to what you might think, stage fright can affect speakers in any size group and is not associated primarily with large groups).

When addressing a large group, your best bet is to focus on the median knowledge range. What details do *most* of the participants already know? What information do most listeners need to know? What background information might help the majority of listeners?

Teleconferences and Videoconferences

Increasingly popular, thanks to current technology, are teleconferences and videoconferences, which allow any number of people to meet via technology, rather than having to travel. *Teleconferences* are audio-only meetings. They can be one-on-one telephone discussions, one-on-group discussions, or even group-on-group discussions. If you have ever talked over a speaker phone, you are familiar with the concept of teleconferencing.

Videoconferences are audio *and* visual meetings. Unlike television, which is one-way communication, videoconferences allow both sound and images to be communicated back and forth between a speaker/group and another speaker/group. If you are familiar with the concept of distance learning, for instance, you know that many contemporary classrooms are actually television screens that allow teachers to "meet" with students hundreds of miles away.

Because teleconferences and videoconferences require specialized oral communication skills, they are not covered in this chapter. Nevertheless, depending on the organization you join, you might need to learn more about these forms of oral presentations.

Preparing for the Presentation

Whether you are addressing a small committee or a large group, a key tip for succeeding as a speaker is preparation. The information in Chapter 2 on planning your workplace writing is also useful for planning oral presentations. But, before planning the content of your presentation, you must know what you hope to accomplish. Then, you must determine how much background knowledge the audience members have, the amount of information and details they need to understand your message completely, and the most likely—and ethical—means of accomplishing your purpose.

In essence, your role as the speaker/writer is to balance your topic or message with the audience's ability and need to understand and with your primary and secondary purposes or goals. Then, you must also consider the relationship between your audience and your purposes and goals, determining how the content of your message and the accomplishment of your goals will affect your audience. Next, you must consider how the success or failure of your purpose and goals will change the topic in future presentations and how your audience will either affect your purpose or be affected by it. Finally, you must consider the powers you hold as the speaker/writer who is trying to inform or persuade an audience. Pictorially, the relationship among the four elements may be represented as a rhombus, with no one element taking precedence over the others (see Figure 16.1).

Determining Your Message and Your Purpose

Although many speakers believe their purpose is to communicate some information, more than likely they want to do far more than just relay details. For instance, if you are asked to give a small committee report on the progress your group is making toward developing a new sailboat design, you want to do far more than just present the design, tests, and experiments your group has initiated. You want to instill confidence in your group; you want to convince the committee either that you are well on your way to success or that some obstacle (such

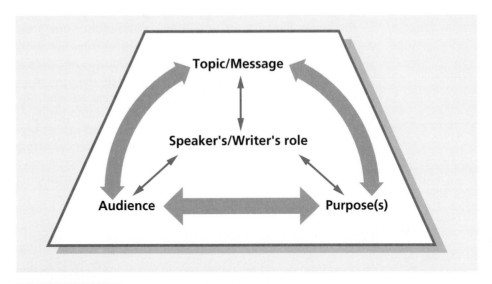

FIGURE 16.1 The Interplay of the Elements of Effective Oral Presentation

as budget restrictions, outdated testing equipment, or insufficient staffing) should be eliminated to advance the pace of your work. You should also make clear what that achievement will mean to your audience—increased profits or prestige in the industry, more time for other important projects, or a significant morale boost.

Accommodating the Audience

Once you have determined the primary message you need to convey and your primary (and secondary) purpose, you are ready to consider your audience. Successful speakers, for both small and large groups, have identified a few crucial points about audiences that help them plan the content of their messages:

- *Audiences have limited attention spans.* Many researchers have shown that the adult attention span is about fifteen to twenty minutes—assuming an interested audience and an informative presentation. If your presentation must go on longer than twenty minutes, you will have to incorporate some strategies, noted throughout this chapter, to enhance attention.

- *Audiences see better than they hear.* Effective visual presentations are crucial to helping audiences hear your message. Review information from Chapter 8 on graphics to determine which graphics help communicate particular kinds of information and how to construct those graphics. Then, read further in this chapter to learn how to use visuals to enhance your oral presentation.

- *Audiences need to know where your presentation is going.* Organization is just as crucial in oral presentations as in written ones, so make your presentation's organization clear to your listeners. First, tell listeners your major points at the beginning of your talk. Then, throughout your presentation, remind them of what you have already covered and what is coming next.

■ *Audiences appreciate a speaker who can finish on time or, even better, before the allotted time limit.* Just as you probably appreciate the professor who occasionally lets class out early, audiences appreciate speakers who can get to the point, cover their message, and sit down. At the same time, audiences can feel slighted when speakers gloss over information just to save a few minutes. The audience may wonder whether the speakers are trying to hide something, prevent discussion, or believe the audience is too simpleminded to understand the details of the topic. Finding the balance between thoroughness and brevity is a delicate matter.

Determining Your Own Role as Speaker/Writer

As with written documents, you should focus on the relationship you want to establish with your listeners as you plan your presentation. Most speakers, whether by plan or by accident, adopt one of the following roles:

- Authority
- Adviser
- Interpreter
- Messenger
- Expert

The speaker in the workplace holds a powerful position, especially when the speaker adopts the proper role for the message. You have probably observed speakers in situations where their own role contrasted dramatically with their message: the underling trying to deliver stringent new policy regulations, the CEO chastising employees for returning from lunch a little late, and the isolated newcomer freely (and, more than likely, incorrectly) interpreting the meaning of workplace ripples and fluctuations.

Recognizing that the role you occupy in an organization will have a significant effect on the role you can play with your audience, message, and purpose will help you plan the best strategy for delivering your message to that audience. Speaking is a powerful—and somewhat frightening—opportunity; savvy workers develop their oral presentation skills in order to serve their organizations as better communicators.

Drafting the Presentation

As you draft your presentation—with the knowledge that you will revise your ideas several times before the presentation gels—begin by jotting down your major message and your intended goal. Then, list the major points you want to make to support that message and goal. Although the elements of the oral presentation are discussed here in presentation order—that is, introduction, body, and conclusion—you need not feel tied to that order at the drafting stage. Just as you do when drafting a written communication, begin with the segment that feels most familiar and natural for you.

When you are ready to draft the *introduction*, which should be appropriate for your audience, reconsider your primary message and the goal of your presentation. The most effective introduction is a summary of why the group is meeting, the context or background for your message, and what your message is. You may briefly refer to your research and preparation for this talk as a means of generating confidence in your message and conclusions, but such references should be quick and to the point. An additional note: Do not open your talk with an apology—either for your abilities as an oral communicator or for your message's content. Audiences who are set up to believe you are a poor speaker or that your message is complex or poorly planned usually retain those beliefs through the end of your presentation.

The *body* of your presentation should be a list of the major factors, issues, or steps that contribute to and support your overall message. If your audience is likely to be skeptical about these points, you must explain why you included them in your discussion. But keep the details in perspective; do not present complicated facts and figures if audience members are unlikely to understand them. Rely, instead, on other attention-enhancing options such as visual aids, anecdotes, and comparisons (discussed below).

The *conclusion* of your presentation should not provide new information to your listeners. Instead, it should summarize your main points—quickly—and lead to any call for action that you deem necessary. For instance, you may ask audience members to sign up for committee responsibilities, invest more money, play a larger role in community affairs, or adopt a new policy. The conclusion, in other words, is where you are most likely to parlay the message of your presentation into the mechanism for achieving your goal.

Revising the Presentation

As you review the notes you have made about your major points and any additional information you want to include as support for those points, you should begin to consider how to revise your presentation for these factors:

- *Clarity:* Will all the major ideas and their support help your audience understand or will some issues confuse them?
- *Support:* Are all the elements of support going to prove your point(s) or raise more questions?
- *Interest:* Does your presentation have dull spots that might bore listeners?
- *Time limitations:* Do you present enough information to help your audience without going beyond your allotted time?

The following strategies can help you revise your presentation for these critical issues.

Revising for Clarity

Two of the primary issues affecting the clarity of a workplace presentation are context and organization:

- *Consider context:* Describe, briefly, the background or context of the situation you are discussing. Make sure that you use vocabulary and terminology your audience can understand. Carefully consider whether the circumstances of this presentation warrant the words you have selected. Finally, clarify the contribution each of your major points makes to your overall message. An effective technique is to use alliteration for your major points; that is, start each point with the same letter of the alphabet. For example, "In this presentation, we will consider the *r*ewards, the *r*esponsibilities, and the *r*ealities of instituting a college enhancement program for our employees."

- *Consider organization.* Clarify the organization of your talk, preferably by numbering your points as "point number one," "point number two," and so on. Such enumeration also shows that you do not assume listeners will know what's important in your presentation; you have gone to the effort to tell them. Also, show a clear relationship between the major points you make. Using transitions that explain relationships ("similarly," "on the other hand," "in the meantime," and "consequently," for instance) helps your audience follow the ideas you are trying to connect or dissect in your presentation.

Revising for Supporting Information

In revising for supporting information, make sure that the audience is convinced that you have made your point or proved your case:

- *Include relevant support.* Make sure listeners know that your ideas are not based on speculation, superstition, hearsay, or fluff. Specific, concrete reasons must exist for all of the points and suggestions you are making. Also, include the kinds of support that your listeners find convincing. It makes little sense, for instance, to quote a scientific study to support your idea if your audience believes all scientific studies are tainted by political bias and deception.

    At the same time, you should be careful not to overwhelm your audience with statistics and other complicated data. Percentages that add up to 100 percent and numbers that do not require too many divisions are more effective in speaking situations than more complex statistics.

Revising for Interest

In revising for interest, these guidelines can be helpful (see also Adding Special Touches to Your Presentations later in the chapter):

■ *Plan to use visuals that will enhance both the message you are trying to present and your audience's attention span.* Standard visual aids may not be enough in an oral presentation; use color, slides, video, and other dynamic options (discussed below) to enliven the presentation.

■ *Try to include the audience in the presentation as much as possible.* Refer to specific people, groups, or departments represented in the audience. Also explain why your message is important for that audience, again referring to specific people, groups, and departments as often as possible. When people understand why a message is significant to them, they are more likely to pay attention.

■ *Include relevant stories and anecdotes as often as possible.* Explaining how a new policy will work can be boring; explaining how it worked at other well-known companies and how individuals responded will add life to your presentation.

■ *Encourage audience participation, if appropriate.* You may want to instruct audience members to interrupt with questions at any time. Asking for volunteers to help you make a point and calling on audience members to provide examples or testimonials about major points are other ways to involve the audience in your presentation. You can also incorporate audience participation into your use of visual aids, using an assistant, for instance, to record responses or ideas on a flip chart.

Revising for Time Limitations

Few speaker flaws are as unforgivable as running over the allotted time limit. Even if the presentation is good, the speaker who goes past the deadline runs a very real chance of alienating the audience. To avoid such risks with your own presentations, try the following strategies:

■ *Determine the real length of your presentation.* With a stopwatch, time your presentation to determine how long it is. Then look for places to edit. If necessary, offer to meet with individuals or smaller groups to clarify details that may be time-consuming and irrelevant to the group as a whole.

■ *Look for shortcuts—strategies you can use to shorten the presentation time without shortchanging the information or the audience.* For instance, determine what information you can offer in a handout, rather than as part of your presentation. Distribute detailed statistics, lists of supporters, additional readings, and even sources of your information as handouts, either at the end of your talk or at the beginning so that you can refer to the materials at appropriate places in your presentation.

Also use lists for information whenever possible, but be sure not to overwhelm listeners with lists that quickly lose their cohesiveness. Make sure, in other words, that listeners can see the overall point you are trying to make with your list.

Finally, consider using visuals as a means of combining various sorts of information. (See Adding Visual Interest to Your Presentation later in the chapter; see also Chapter 8.)

Adding Special Touches to Your Presentations

To add life to your oral communications, personalize your presentations. Audiences should feel that you have prepared your talk especially for them, not that your talk is part of a repertoire you pull out of a drawer to present on any occasion. Make sure that your own voice comes through so that your presentation will not sound as though it could have been delivered by anybody.

Many speakers try to personalize their oral communications by adding jokes. You have probably heard speakers who begin with a joke and then try to make it relevant to the topic and occasion. This strategy rarely works; instead, the speaker has wasted time and must now regroup to get to the real point of the talk. In organizational presentations, jokes are a poor strategy for a number of reasons:

- They may signal that you do not take the topic or the occasion very seriously.
- They may confuse your audience.
- They may not be funny to your audience.
- They may offend your audience.
- They may be irrelevant to the topic of the presentation.

Most people, in fact, regard joke telling as a rather childish or naive ploy. The message the joke sends is that rather than trying to be enlightening or appropriate, the speaker has decided to try to entertain the audience. The place for jokes is a comedy club, where the audience is willing to pay for them. In most organizational situations, such an approach is simply inappropriate.

Unlike jokes, wit and humor, which arise directly out of the situation, rather than being manipulated to fit the context, can work quite well in organizational presentations. A joke requires a setup and a punch line, but wit and humor can take the form of asides, plays on words, or lively descriptions that add vitality to a presentation. Wit and humor that stem from the speaker's own experience are especially effective, as long as the humor is at no one else's expense.

In addition to offering a source of humor, personal experience may be used to invigorate a presentation in other ways. Audiences tend to respond to other people's experiences—consider the use of personal testimonials about products and services in advertising and infomercials. When you describe something that has happened to you or to someone you know, people are likely to find your story believable and convincing.

THE WORLD OF WORKPLACE WRITING

Incorporating Humor and Wit

Although tomes have been written about what's funny and how to be funny, even the novice humorist can incorporate some basic elements of wit into a presentation. First, you have to remember that funny things happen to all of us all the time; be aware of your surroundings and observe daily life carefully. When you *see, hear, read,* or *experience* something humorous, write it down on a notecard and save it for your oral presentations.

Second, be aware of how others use humor successfully. When you see or hear a humorous statement or technique, make a note of it and try practicing the strategy for your own presentations.

Third, be aware of what kinds of observations most people find humorous. You'll probably find that the best humor either pokes fun at the speaker or identifies an experience that is common to most people. Most humorists find their richest material in common experiences that are somehow incongruous with expectations or logic.

Several other sources of humor are also effective in oral presentations:

- *Humorous quotations:* For instance, the comedian George Jessel once said, "The human brain is a wonderful organ. It starts to work as soon as you are born and doesn't quit until you get up to deliver a speech."

- *Wild exaggerations:* These can be effective provided that the audience immediately recognizes the absurdity of the remark. When encouraging better college advising, more concerted efforts to be role models, and more attention to the overall well-being of students, a college president addressing the faculty announced, "The incoming freshman class totals a record 3,400 students—that's about 3,399 more teenagers than any adult should have to deal with! And while I feel sorry for you teachers, I'm sure those teenagers would feel especially sorry for *me*—I get to deal with about 6,799 more parents than anyone should have to cope with!"

- *Incongruities:* Juxtaposing ideas that do not logically go together or offering ridiculous solutions can be fruitful sources of humor. For example, a speaker announced that the primary issues facing his organization were "profits, productivity, morale, and the company softball team's abysmal record."

- *Plays on words:* Word plays are especially useful in titles of presentations and in the major points of a presentation where this technique is most likely to stand out. For example, one speaker announced that the title of her talk for the annual sales meeting was "Life on the Road: Cold Calls, Hot Prospects, and Lukewarm Coffee."

Incorporating humorous elements into a presentation requires timing and propriety—and practice. Make sure humor is appropriate for your topic and audi-

(continued)

ence; make sure you pause, gesture, or raise or lower your voice to differentiate the humor from the more serious elements of your talk. And, finally, practice your delivery (determining which words should be emphasized, what gestures should be used, and so on) with your colleagues or trusted advisers before risking humorous elements on your listeners.

A final way to personalize your message and make it more memorable is to tell a story. Most researchers find that people learn more from stories than they learn from data. Narratives that feature characters in situations similar to that of the audience can be very persuasive. If, for example, you are talking to a group of senior investors in your organization, you might add a story about a successful senior investor who supplemented her retirement income by investing $5,000 in the organization's stock ten years ago. Now her investment is worth a whopping $59,300!

Practicing the Presentation

As part of an interview for a highly visible, prestigious job, a man was to present an overview of his ideas for leading the organization into the next century. He summoned his best advisers, a group of his colleagues, and asked them to listen to him practice his speech. He won the job after he corrected a number of weaknesses that his advisers pointed out: he had mispronounced an important term throughout his speech; he had read too much; he kept his head down when offering significant points; and he took a cheap potshot at the predecessor in the position. After he revised his presentation and his delivery, he sounded like the highly successful executive he soon became.

Of all the strategies for planning and drafting your presentation, nothing will help more than practice. We have all seen speakers fumble for words, lose track of their thoughts, and read from their notes—all due to lack of practice. Not only is such a performance embarrassing for the speaker, but, truth to tell, it is just as embarrassing for the audience who must witness the humiliating display of poor preparation.

Although you should probably allot time for practice in proportion to the significance of the presentation (with more practice time being allotted for the more significant communication situations), even minor presentations before small committees demand a certain amount of practice. Practice before a mirror, with your colleague(s), or in front of a video camera. Be sure to evaluate or to ask for candid feedback on your performance, especially about these matters:

- Word usage and pronunciations
- The effectiveness of stories or comparisons
- The visibility, usefulness, appeal, and handling of visual aids
- The emphasis given to major points
- The clarity of the presentation

- The tone of the presentation
- The persuasiveness of each point and of the entire presentation
- Your comfort with the topic and details
- Your use of gestures and body language throughout the presentation

Adding Visual Interest to Your Presentation

Few additions to a well-prepared and well-rehearsed presentation can make more difference than effective visual aids. (See Strategy Review 16.1.) As in written documents (see Chapter 8), visual aids can add to an oral communication in several ways:

- Enhance the overall cohesiveness of your ideas
- Emphasize important points
- Simplify complex information
- Relieve the tedium of technical details
- Arouse or maintain the audience's interest

As you draft the presentation, mark special sections in your talk that can be enhanced with visual aids.

STRATEGY REVIEW 16.1

GENERAL PRINCIPLES FOR VISUAL AIDS

Whatever visual aids you use, follow these rules for making them an effective part of your presentation:

- Consider the ethics of the visual aids you are using. Misrepresentations and distortions in sizes can be particularly problematic in oral presentations.
- Use visual representations that are as professional as time and money allow.
- Use color and textual variations (such as boldface and italic type) to emphasize important information, focus audience attention, and enliven your visuals.
- Consider whether your visuals—especially photographs—send additional messages that you may not intend. A photograph of your organization's workers that includes only Caucasian or only male workers suggests your organization is not diverse. Is that an accurate portrayal? Also consider what is going on in the background of any photographs you use; catching a worker in an embarrassing pose is likely to detract from the message you are trying to send with your visual.

(continued)

- Follow rules about audience accommodations regarding the complexity of your graphics. A reader who cannot understand an exploded diagram will be unlikely to understand that diagram any better as a listener.

- Refer to your graphics as you talk, bringing them in at appropriate points in your presentation and explaining to the audience members what they should see in each graphic.

- Avoid standing between your audience and your visual. As you practice your presentation, make sure you stand to the side of your visual so that your audience can see both you and the visual.

- Maintain eye contact with your audience—not with your visual. Talking to the visual is silly and undermines your professionalism and your effectiveness.

- Use pointers or highlighters to direct your audience's attention to appropriate aspects of your graphics.

- Avoid leaving graphics on display after you move to another point. Turn off projectors or cover posters to refocus your audience's attention on you.

Some standard options for visual aids include flip charts and posters, overhead transparencies, slides, and models. More specialized options, such as videos, computer graphics, and other visual forms, are available for considerably more cost, time, and expertise. Nevertheless, they may be appropriate for important, polished presentations before specialized audiences. All of these options have special do's and don'ts for their most effective use.

Flip Charts and Posters

Flip charts and posters offer a primary advantage over some other visual aids: they are usually quick to produce, inexpensive, and may be prepared ahead of time or on the spot. Their disadvantage, however, is that they tend to look a bit unprofessional and often present only text (such as lists) and static pictures or illustrations. If you are presenting ideas before a committee that does not expect elaborate graphics, or if you are presenting your information before a knowledgeable audience—one that does not need elaborate graphics to understand your message—flip charts and posters may be an effective form of visual aid. Follow these guidelines when using these visual aids:

- Use flip charts and posters to record responses from your audience.

- Avoid turning your back to your audience or writing for long periods of time; learn to use a shorthand code that prevents your audience from getting restless. (You might want to assign an assistant to help you with the writing while you stay focused on the group.)

- Write large enough for all members of the audience to see.
- Use markers that are easily visible to all members of your audience.
- Avoid using flip charts and posters for groups larger than twenty people.
- If you intend to return to one visual on a flip chart or poster, either redraw it into your visual presentation at the proper place or mark the place for easy reference. No one likes to wait while a speaker thumbs through flip charts and posters to find the one that pertains to the current point.

Overhead Transparencies

Like flip charts and posters, overhead transparencies are quick to produce, inexpensive, and may be prepared ahead of time or on the spot. The primary advantage of overhead transparencies over flip charts and posters is that they may be projected to a larger audience. Many people also prefer overhead transparencies because they can use erasable markers on them; the speaker who draws on, highlights, or checks off items on a transparency while speaking will also enliven the presentation.

These guidelines will help you use transparencies effectively:

- Limit the amount of information you put on a transparency to six lines. Crowded information is annoying and hard to read.
- Include a heading or title on each transparency. A heading will help the audience focus on the importance of the information on the transparency.
- Use large lettering—preferably type that is at least ¼ inch tall—so your audience can read your text. Remember, too, that the larger the room and the larger the audience, the larger the type will have to be. Make sure that the people sitting in the back row can read your transparency.
- Use transparencies for more than just text. An occasional illustration, chart, cartoon, or table can enliven any presentation.
- Use frames for your transparencies. Then, you can make notes in the frame margins that will help you remember your points. Frames also help you keep your transparencies organized (be sure to number them), prevent them from developing static electricity and sticking together, and keep them from sliding off the projector.
- Use your word processor (or permanent markers) for text you intend to keep; use washable, color markers for notes, arrows, or underlining that you'll want to wash off.
- Check the projector before your presentation, making sure it has a bulb, a clean surface, and a sharp focus.

- Practice using transparencies as you practice your talk. You don't want to fumble for the next transparency or be surprised by what you put up. Remember, too, that the projector adds extra noise; practice speaking louder when the projector is on.

- Remove transparencies when you finish with them. Leaving them up can distract your audience members and keep them from moving on to your next point.

Slides

With enough time and a professional photographer, graphic illustrator, or versatile computer graphics software, you can use slides to produce an effective visual presentation. Because slides most frequently rely on text (lists) and photographs, you should make sure the message of your presentation lends itself to such graphic representations. With computer-generated graphics, such as those created by Power Point, you can also produce slides that incorporate illustrations, cartoons, charts, clip art, and other visuals that were once far beyond the range of slides' capabilities.

When creating slides for presentations, remember these tips:

- Make sure that photographs and illustrations reproduce clearly on the slide.

- Number all slides. Then, if the carousel spills, you'll know exactly where each slide goes.

- Arrange slides in the carousel before your presentation, making sure they are right side up. Your professionalism is jeopardized when slides appear backward or upside down.

- Check the slide projector to make sure it has a bulb, focuses sharply, and projects the distance you need for your presentation. Check the advance clicker to make sure it is working properly.

- Pace the presentation to allow about fifteen seconds to view each slide. To avoid monotony, however, you may occasionally orchestrate a brief series of "quick slides"—three or four slides that stay up for only seconds and hammer particularly crucial points. Be sure that these quick slides contain only one or two words or one central and easily recognizable image; otherwise, audience members will wonder what they've missed (or what you've tried to hide).

- Practice with your slides so you know when to click the advancer. Having to backtrack is annoying and disorienting to your audience. Similarly, advancing too quickly to a new slide also disorients your audience.

- Turn off the slide projector—or insert a blank slide—during periods of your presentation when you do not want the audience to be distracted by a slide you have already discussed.

■ Remember that the projector contributes extra noise. Talk louder when it is on.

Models

Just as fashion designers use real-life models to show off their new styles, architects, designers, product developers, and planners often use models of their plans or products to show off their ideas. For describing the layout of a city park, for instance, a new condominium development, or a new handheld computer, models are far superior to drawings that are limited to showing individual parts or one dimension of the concept.

When using models, these tips can help:

■ Make sure the model is either to scale (*actual size*) or is clearly marked as a proportion of the actual size (*model is twice as large as actual concept*).

■ Be sure the model is large enough for audience members to see—or that they are invited to investigate it before or after your presentation.

■ Determine whether audience members should see the model before your talk, during it, or afterward.

■ Determine whether audience members should be able to touch, hold, or use the model.

■ Make sure you are thoroughly familiar with the model and all its parts so that you can answer questions about it.

Videos

Some presentations work remarkably well by making their points with videos. For example, representatives of the National Hurricane Center (NHC) have ample footage of coastal and inland areas experiencing a hurricane. Equally impressive is the footage of the destruction that hurricanes can wreak. Members of the NHC can return to their video library whenever they want to issue warnings with supporting footage of hurricane damage.

If you are lucky, your organization already has a library of videos from which you can select appropriate footage. Many organizations even employ full-time videographers who create and edit videos for public relations, training, and a multitude of other organizational purposes. (Of course, you or your organization may also purchase videos from professional video companies, but such presentations often miss the most important points you want to make because they cannot include the specific context of your organization's culture.)

Creating a video is such time-consuming and specialized work—and so expensive—that few nonprofessionals attempt it. Further, most viewers are so accustomed to the high-quality productions of television and movies that in-house videos can seem embarrassingly amateurish. If, however, you do not have access to experts and need to create your own videos, consider the following pointers:

- Keep the video short.
- Minimize the dialogue.
- Pace the video to move reasonably fast.
- Show all you need to show in order for the audience to understand your message.
- Avoid collections of "talking heads"—various speakers talking, but doing nothing.
- Remember that background music and noise can enhance or detract from your message.
- Consider the crucial importance of editing for inappropriate pauses, distractions, emphasis, and so on.

Computer Graphics

Most computer graphics packages offer a number of options for visual presentations. Although you will probably use these packages to create overhead transparencies or slides, increasingly the computer itself is being used as a visual aid. Because such graphics can be projected onto a large screen, much as slides or overheads can be, you may want to consider hooking a computer into a computer projector and forgoing the huge posters, piles of transparencies, and bulky slide carousels that have long been popular in presentations.

Some highly specialized (and impressive) presentations can be created using computer graphics programs such as Astound, Persuasion, or the highly technical program, Director. Many of these programs create additional concerns for the oral presenter, however. In addition to the concerns listed above for other forms of visual representations, consider these points:

- Try not to overwhelm your message with the technology (Wow!) of your graphics presentation. Your message and goals should not become convoluted or be missed because the presentation technology mesmerized your audience.
- Carefully consider the timing of your message and the image(s) you create. You cannot, for instance, create a separate slide for every word in a list without allowing a couple of seconds (in some cases) for those images to come up on the screen. Think how tedious it would be for the audience to wait as you read a list, such as "marketing" (pause 2–3–4), "planning" (pause 2–3–4), "and delivering" (pause 2–3–4). Far better would be to use a single image that represents all three of these functions.
- Do consider the size of the display of your graphics, making sure audience members in the back row can see them.
- Do check all computer and projector equipment to make sure they run.

STRATEGY REVIEW 16.2

ORAL PRESENTATION PLANNING WORKSHEET

This worksheet will help you plan your presentation. After reading the entire chapter, you should be able to consider each option and use the worksheet to help you prepare your notes for your presentation. Be sure to complete the worksheet as thoroughly as possible before going on to draft your presentation.

Subject and Purpose

1. The primary subject of my presentation is ——————————————.

2. The primary purpose of my presentation is ——————————————.

3. The secondary purpose of my presentation is ——————————————.

Audience

1. I expect ————— number of people to attend.

2. These people are brought together by
   - their common interests,
   - their job descriptions, or
   - some other factor.

3. These people are
   - very eager to attend this meeting,
   - moderately eager to attend this meeting, or
   - not eager at all to attend this meeting.

4. These people are likely to respond to my subject
   - positively,
   - neutrally, or
   - negatively.

5. These people already know
   - a great deal about the subject,
   - a moderate amount about the subject, or
   - little to nothing about the subject.

6. These people need to know
   - all the relevant details about the subject or
   - an overview of the subject.

(continued)

Content

1. The most significant points I need to make are

   a.

   b.

   c.

2. The details I need to provide are

   a. (point a)
      1.
      2.
      3.

   b. (point b)
      1.
      2.
      3.

3. The best way to present my points are through

   - examples,
   - stories,
   - personal experience,
   - statistics,
   - financial data, and/or
   - visual aids.

4. The best way to organize my presentation is

   - directly—with the most important point first—or
   - indirectly—with the ideas building to an overwhelming conclusion.

Visual Aids

1. To clarify complex information, I need to add a visual when I make the point about _____

   _____.

2. To emphasize important information, I need to add a visual when I make the point about _____

   _____.

3. To summarize information, I need to add a visual when I make the point about _____

   _____.

4. To maintain the audience's attention, I need to add a visual when _____

   _____.

5. The kinds of information I need to present lend themselves most naturally to
   - photographs, illustrations, or models of concepts,
   - charts and graphs of data, or
   - motion pictures of processes.

6. I can best represent my points and involve my audience directly by using
   - flip charts and posters,
   - overhead transparencies,
   - slides,
   - models,
   - video presentations, or
   - computer-generated graphics.

Conclusion

1. At the conclusion of my presentation, I want audience members to know

   _____.

2. At the conclusion of my presentation, I want audience member to do

   _____.

3. At the conclusion of my presentation, I want audience members to believe

   _____.

4. At the conclusion of my presentation, I want audience members to see me as

   _____.

Delivering the Presentation

When it comes to delivering the presentation, the uppermost issue for even the most well-seasoned speaker is stage fright or speaker anxiety (commonly betrayed by nervous mannerisms such as fidgeting, rocking, and failing to maintain eye contact with the audience). Everyone feels it—even with years of practice standing before various groups. The good news is that you can use speaker anxiety to work for you, rather than against you, by rechanneling the energy into alertness and focus.

Your goal as a speaker is to build credibility. Therefore, you have little reason to fear anxiety as long as it does not undermine your credibility. Instead, use that heightened emotion to focus on what your presentation can accomplish in terms of your organization's mission, your audience's need for information, and your purpose.

In addition to anxiety, of course, some other aspects of delivering an oral presentation deserve attention. Just as gourmet food merits a fine presentation, so do your ideas in an oral communication. Making your ideas palatable requires attention to details that may be far removed from the actual content and message of your talk. Thus, these standard do's and don'ts are considered basic, regardless of the size and formality of the group to which you are speaking:

- *Adjust the time and place of the meeting according to when and where your listeners are likely to be at their best.* Late afternoon meetings—especially on Friday—are often deadly because workers are tired or distracted by their plans for the weekend (especially if their weekend begins the second your presentation is over). Similarly, early Monday morning meetings are difficult for many audience members who are not quite back into the work routine after their weekends. Also beware of rooms that are too large or too small for the group, too hot or too cold, or too noisy or too dark—poor room selection can sabotage even the best presentation.

- *Arrive early to get a feel for the room in which you are speaking, adjust the temperature and lighting, and check all equipment before you begin.* Few things are more disconcerting for a speaker and for an audience than to encounter surprises during a talk. Knowing the size and shape of a room gives you a feel for how the audience will be seated—and whether you want to change the seating arrangement. A room that is too hot or cold, or too bright or too dark, can require some adjustments before the listeners arrive. A burned-out bulb or faulty wiring can sabotage your plans to present visuals; make sure all equipment is working properly before your listeners arrive.

- *Expect a certain amount of stage fright.* As this section has pointed out, everyone feels anxious about giving speeches; remember that and do not be caught offguard when you experience a little shortness of breath and a few butterflies before you speak and as you begin your presentation. Relax, take a few deep breaths, and take a moment or two to collect your thoughts—and your proper speaking voice—before going on with your presentation.

- *Concentrate on lowering the pitch of your voice.* A high, shrill voice betrays your lack of control and confidence and makes it hard for the listeners to focus on your message. A lower pitch is more audible and more pleasing to most listeners.

- *Determine beforehand whether you need to use a microphone.* Just because one is available does not mean you should use it. Determine whether the size of the audience and the size of the facility in which you are speaking will make it hard for listeners to hear you. Be sure to practice using a microphone, too; some are more sensitive to the sound of your breathing than others, for instance. Hold the microphone so that listeners can hear your words clearly.

- *Set a proper pace for your talk.* If you begin talking too rapidly, you'll soon run out of breath. Slow down. If you normally speak extremely slowly, though, you may want to speed up your delivery so you don't bore your audience.

- *Set the proper tone for your presentation at the outset.* If you have a serious message to deliver, do not sabotage it by making witty, irrelevant, or misleading comments. If your message is positive and uplifting, do not undermine it by sounding peevish and sour.

- *Do not read your notes—much less your entire talk.* With proper practice, you should be able to talk from a speaking outline—a list of your major points written out on notecards—or, better yet, from your visual aids. Reading is immensely boring to most groups and suggests that you don't really know what you are talking about; after all, almost anyone can read before a group. Memorization is a risky substitute for notecards or visual aids unless you are a seasoned performer who is used to memorizing a lot of text.

- *Make eye contact with your audience members.* In spite of the old suggestion that you should look just above the heads of your listeners, unless you are in a very large group your listeners will know that you are avoiding eye contact with them. Instead, select a representative from the left, another from the center, and a third from the right to focus on; then, sweep the remainder of the crowd.

- *Do not underestimate the value of a well-placed pause, but be careful not to overuse pauses.* A pause can emphasize your most important remarks as long as it is planned and not the result of losing your concentration. Pauses also help you signal that you are moving to a new point.

- *Determine what gestures are natural for you and use them in your presentation.* Holding your arms by your side makes you look stiff and unnatural. Effective gestures can help you send additional messages about your topic—that certain points are crucial or that certain statements are intended to amuse the audience. Avoid empty or nervous mannerisms, such as rocking while you talk or draping yourself over the podium. Good posture sends the message of self-confidence.

- *Adopt a pleasant expression.* Regardless of the message you have to send, audiences are more receptive to people who smile and present themselves in a positive light.

- *Dress appropriately for the occasion.* Many speakers have favorite "performance" attire that makes them feel confident or upbeat. Research shows that conservative clothing lends more weight to speakers than brighter, more trendy fashions do. Make necessary adjustments in your appearance to garner the attention you want.

Handling Question-and-Answer Sessions

At the end of your presentation, regardless of how well you have tried to cover each issue, some audience members are likely to have questions. Your ability to handle these questions will further reveal your knowledge of your topic and thus enhance your credibility as a speaker.

Just as you prepare and practice for the talk itself, you should also prepare and practice for the question-and-answer session. Although you may not know the specific questions you will be asked, you can still prepare by knowing that most questions will ask for one or more of the following:

- *Clarification* of some point you made in the presentation: "Could you explain that again?" Practice by preparing alternative explanations and additional examples, anecdotes, or illustrations of your primary points.

- *Illumination* of some point you made in the presentation: "Does that mean that . . . ?" Practice by breaking down your major points into their simplest components.

- *Qualification* of some point you made in the presentation: "Does that always happen? Even when . . . ?" Practice by being sure you have considered cases in which your topic (problem, solution, or idea) will not work as you have described.

- *Speculation* about some point you made in the presentation: "What's likely to happen when . . . ?" Practice by considering the impact of your topic on other aspects of the organization's goals or daily routines. Also consider outside events (such as economic windfalls, higher taxes, or globalization) that might affect your topic.

- *Comparison* of some point you made in the presentation: "Is that the same as . . . ?" or "How does this differ from . . . ?" Practice by considering the kinds of comparisons your audience could make between your topic and other issues in the organization. Be able to describe similarities and differences in ways the audience will understand, but also take care not to confuse listeners who often hear "exactly like" when you mean "similar to."

Knowing the forms of questions the audience is likely to ask will help you prepare for the question-and-answer session. To make you even more comfortable, you may want to plant a question with one or more audience members. By doing so, you will know at least the first one or two questions you will be asked and can relax a little while you reemphasize key points. Some other guidelines can also help you respond and can make the question-and-answer session productive for all listeners:

1. Maintain your composure throughout the session.

   - Do not get rattled by questions to which you do not know the answer. Offer to find out for the questioner.

   - Do not be offended by hostile questioners. The calmer you remain, the less likely you are to end up looking foolish, testy, defensive, or even conspiratorial.

   - Do not be condescending or sarcastic with questioners. Even if you have to break down your major points into their simplest elements, your questioners have a right to understand your message. At the same time, if you sense that everyone else in the group understands and is bored with the minutiae you have to offer to explain your point, offer to meet with the questioner after the presentation—but only after you have tried to explain the answer once or twice before the group.

- ■ Do not become impatient with a questioner who repeats a question that has already been asked and answered. Try, briefly, to answer the question again—perhaps using different words or different examples. If such repetition is continuous, however, politely explain that the question has already been asked and answered. Then, turn to another questioner.

2. Unless you are in a small committee meeting, repeat each question you are asked to make sure you heard the question correctly and to make sure all others heard the question, too.

3. If you do not understand the question, ask the questioner to rephrase it—or rephrase it yourself and then ask the questioner if your interpretation is correct.

4. Do not abandon your responsibility as an answerer/speaker, but also acknowledge the expertise of others in the meeting/speaking situation who may be better equipped to answer certain kinds of questions than you are.

5. Be sure to clarify whether the answer you are providing is fact or speculation.

6. Do not let one audience member monopolize the session; ask for questions from other members.

7. Be aware of time limitations, but seek a balance between how many questions your listeners actually have and how long you can reasonably expect to keep their attention—or keep them away from their other work. Just as frustrating as long-winded presentations are long-winded question-and-answer sessions. When you sense a lull in the questions, disband the group but offer to be available for individual questions.

S T R A T E G Y   R E V I E W   1 6 . 3

EVALUATING YOUR PRESENTATION

In special situations, such as training sessions, your audience may be given the opportunity to evaluate your performance and effectiveness as a speaker. As useful as such evaluations are, they are rarely possible if you speak before a committee or small group. Besides, if people comment on your performance in such groups, it is usually positive; although they may criticize your message, they will rarely criticize your delivery.

(continued)

Nevertheless, you can determine your effectiveness by evaluating your presentation yourself. As soon as possible after your presentation, answer the following questions:

1. *What kinds of questions were asked during the question-and-answer session? Were these the same questions I expected to be asked? Did they ask for extension of ideas or rehashings?* Questions asking for extension of ideas suggest you have prompted the listeners to think carefully about your message; rehashings suggest you were unclear.

2. *How much movement went on in the audience as I talked?* Twitching in seats suggests the audience members are bored and are trying to stay awake—or that your message has made them uncomfortable. Nodding their heads, taking notes, moving to the edge of their seats, and responding appropriately (laughing, smiling, clapping, or looking disgusted) suggest you have the agreement and attention of your listeners. No movement suggests your audience is either hanging on your every word—or asleep.

3. *How much talking or whispering went on in the audience as I talked?* Continued, isolated pockets of whisperers may signal that those listeners are distracted, bored, or taking issue with your points. Encouraging audience participation can reduce the amount of whispering and give audience members a chance to offer their insights to all listeners.

    Brief whispers, though, may signal the audience member's agreement and that they are exchanging examples from their own experiences. Again, you may want to encourage audience members to discuss their own experiences before the group.

4. *Did I get the appropriate response at critical points in my presentation?* Laughter at humorous remarks reassures you that your point was well made. Laughter at inappropriate times, however, signals distrust or disbelief. Most telling, of course, is the response you get during the concluding "action" stage: Did listeners agree to vote the way you wanted, provide the resources you wanted, or otherwise signal their agreement with your conclusions?

5. *If I got the wrong response, what could I have done differently to present my message and persuade my audience?* Speakers often get good insights for improving content preparation from the question-and-answer session. If you feel the listeners asked questions that should have been clear from your presentation, look at your content more carefully: Should you have provided more information, more examples, more visual aids? If listeners seemed bored or nonplused by your message, consider what you could have done to enliven or clarify the presentation: Changed the pace or the time or place of the meeting? Used more or fewer visual aids? Added more narrative elements or examples? If audience members seemed disengaged during your presentation, could you have found ways to incorporate their ideas, experiences, or questions during the presentation?

Summary

In this chapter, you have had an opportunity to learn more about the oral presentations you will most likely be asked to make in the workplace. Whether your presentation is before a large group or a small committee, you must attend to matters of audience analysis while balancing your topic and purpose with any secondary motivations or accomplishments you hope to gain.

As you plan your presentation, be especially aware of time and budget constraints that will affect how much information you can present and in what visual forms. Also consider the span of attention your audience is able to devote to your message. Determine the ethical pitfalls you might face in drafting, polishing, and delivering your presentation and in your visual aids; as you practice your presentation and your responses to likely questions and as you construct your visual aids, be sure to avoid such pitfalls.

As you draft and deliver your presentation, be aware of particular techniques you can use to enliven it. In particular, consider the usefulness and appropriateness of pace changes, audience participation, wit, visual aids, and movement.

Finally, as with any communication, be prepared to draft, refine, and polish the content of your message. Practice your presentation and your references to visual aids with a friend or colleague, or in front of a video camera. Then, at the end of each practice session and at the end of your presentation, evaluate your performance so you can improve as a speaker.

CHECKLIST

✓ Determine ahead of time the size of the group you are going to address. Then, you will know more about the seating arrangement, the kinds of visual aids and handouts that will be most appropriate, and the level of formality of the situation.

✓ Determine why your audience has gotten together. Do the members share a common interest? Do their jobs demand their attendance? Do they want to get some information from you? Do they want to give some information to you?

✓ As you draft your presentation, be prepared to answer these questions for your audience:
  - What should I do with this information?
  - What should I think, do, or believe according to this information?
  - What use is this information to me or my constituents?

✓ Be prepared to provide more depth to your topic for small group presentations than for larger groups.

✔ For large group presentations, be prepared to provide overviews and a low to median level of information.

✔ To plan your presentation, consider what you hope to accomplish, what you know about your audience, and what kinds of ethical challenges you face.

✔ Draft your presentation, just as you would any other communication, with the intent of revising and polishing it.

✔ Revise your presentation for clarity, support, interest, and time limitations.

✔ Add special touches—personalizations, wit or humor, experiences, and testimonials—to enliven your presentation.

✔ Practice the presentation carefully and repeatedly. Practice with colleagues, friends, or in front of a mirror or video camera. Evaluate your presentation critically.

✔ Incorporate visual aids in your presentation to add some life and to serve the standard purpose(s) of graphics:

■ Enhance the overall cohesiveness of your ideas.

■ Emphasize important points.

■ Simplify complex information.

■ Relieve the tedium of technical details.

■ Arouse and maintain the audience's interest.

✔ Select appropriate visual aids depending on your audience' s size and level of sophistication; the significance and formality of your presentation; the budget, time, and expertise of your organization's graphics/illustrations department; and the type and amount of visual aids you need to present. Choose from the following visual aid options:

■ Flip charts and posters

■ Overhead transparencies

■ Slides

■ Models

■ Videos

■ Computer graphics

✔ Control the speaking situation—room selection (size, temperature, arrangement, and so on); use of microphones; pitch, pace, and tone of your talk; and working quality of your equipment (overhead projectors, slide projectors, computer projectors)—before you begin your presentation.

✔ Adopt natural expressions and gestures throughout your talk.

Prepare for question-and-answer sessions with colleagues and friends.

 Maintain your composure throughout the question-and-answer session, answering each question with clarity and respect.

EXERCISES

Individual Exercises

1. Describe a speaker, perhaps a professor, religious leader, or politician, whom you found effective.
   a. What was the person's primary message?
   b. What was the person most likely trying to accomplish?
   c. What was the person's attitude toward the message?
   d. What assumptions did the person obviously make about you or the audience? How appropriate were those assumptions?
   e. What attitude did the speaker take toward the audience?
   f. What visual aids (if any) did the speaker use?
   g. What facts, details, or statistics did the person offer to prove points? How convincing were those elements of proof? How certain are you that those elements were ethically used?
   h. What characteristics of the person's delivery were most noticeable? Which were most effective?
   i. How did the speaker handle questions from the audience?
   j. What weaknesses did you note in the presentation? How would you recommend that the speaker improve on those weaknesses?
   k. How was the speaker dressed? What did the speaker's attire lend to the atmosphere of the presentation? To the speaker's credibility?

2. Now choose a particularly ineffective speaker you have heard. Answer the questions in exercise 1.

3. During the evening news or during an interview/investigative television show (such as *60 Minutes, 20/20,* or *Dateline*), determine how effective the speaker and/or the interviewer was. Did the person seem well prepared? Did the person establish the background information you needed to understand the context? Did the person provide facts, statistics, or examples that helped you understand the message?

Collaborative Writing Exercises

1. With a partner or a group, attend an on-campus lecture and evaluate the presentation:

- What assumptions did the speaker make about the audience? Were those assumptions appropriate for the majority of the audience?

- How well organized was the presentation? Could you follow it point by point?

- How well drawn were the examples and details used to explain the speaker's points?

- What sorts of visual aids (if any) did the speaker use? Were they effective? If so, explain why; if not, explain why not.

- Did the physical features of the presentation area (room, auditorium, lecture hall, etc.) accommodate the crowd, the visual aids, and the general purpose of the presentation?

In a two- to three-page analysis, evaluate the speaker's presentation for another group who is thinking of engaging this speaker for a discussion of the speaker's topic. Finally, in a separate one- to two-page analysis, evaluate the speaker's presentation for the speaker. How would your information—and your rhetorical concerns for tactfulness (perhaps) and clarity—change because of the difference in audience and purpose?

2. With a partner or team members, evaluate the credibility of one of the following:

- A local or national politician

- A well-known religious leader

- A television spokesperson

- An international figure

- A well-known movie star/rock star/celebrity

In what situations would this person be an inappropriate spokesperson? What, in particular, has this person done to enhance or erode his or her credibility? How might that credibility change? If you were the person's image consultant, what would you suggest the person do to improve or maintain her or his current image?

➡ ONGOING ASSIGNMENT

- Prepare a presentation for your class on what newcomers should know about your organization's culture (your instructor will tell you how much time is allotted for your presentation). Assume, first of all, that your classmates are the newcomers. Next, develop a list of major points you want to communicate, along with specific details and examples that might be useful. Then, prepare visual aids to accompany your presentation. Present your findings to the class; finally, entertain questions from these "newcomers."

Brief Usage Guidebook for Grammar, Punctuation, and Mechanics

This guidebook should serve as a brief reference for basic rules of grammar and usage. For comprehensive treatment of mechanical and grammatical styles, consult professional association guidebooks and full-length reference texts.

Complete Sentences

Sentences make complete statements by using three basic structures. A **simple sentence** contains a single **independent clause** with a core subject and verb, often with various modifiers:

> **Simple:** The new technology (*subject*) has revolutionized (*verb*) our indexing system.

A **compound sentence** contains two or more independent clauses connected by a coordinate conjunction such as *and, but, nor:*

> **Compound:** Technology has revolutionized our indexing system, *but* many patrons are afraid of that system.

A **complex sentence** contains an independent clause and at least one **dependent clause**—a statement attached to an independent sentence with a connecting word such as *which, whom, that, after, although:*

> **Complex:** The technology *that revolutionized the indexing system* takes only seconds to learn.

In addition to these basics, a **compound/complex** sentence is a combination structure involving both a compound sentence (with two or more independent clauses) and a complex sentence (with at least one dependent clause):

> **Compound/complex:** The technology, *which revolutionized our indexing system*, allows patrons to call up books, articles, music, and even movies, *but* many patrons are afraid of the new system.

593

Sentences may also contain **verbal phrases** serving as components. These include **infinitive phrases** serving as nouns and using a base verb form frequently preceded by an infinitive marker, *to*; **gerundive phrases** serving as nouns and using the verb form plus an *-ing* ending; and **participial phrases** serving as adjective modifiers and using the verb form plus an *-ing* ending:

> ***Infinitive phrase:*** Some managers' directives are hard *to understand.*
>
> ***Gerundive phrase:*** *Understanding managers' directives* can be difficult.
>
> ***Participial phrase:*** The new directives *emanating from upper-level management* are absurd.

These verb-form constructions, which are commonly used as nouns or modifiers within sentences, cause problems if they are left by themselves without a main verb; they cannot stand alone as complete statements or sentences.

A. *Editing Fragments*

A sentence is complete when it has a core subject and is capable of standing by itself as an independent statement. To avoid writing an incomplete thought punctuated as if it were an independent sentence, check your sentences to be sure they are complete:

1. Find a main verb, expressing action or status. *Disqualify verbals* and verbal phrases like those in italic type at the top of this page.
2. Locate a subject for the verb. The subject will be a noun, a pronoun, or an infinitive or gerundive phrase serving as a noun.
3. Look for connecting words (e.g., *which, whom, that, after, although*) that may signal a statement that has the form of a dependent clause, but cannot stand by itself unless it is properly linked to a simple or compound sentence (see the definition of a complex sentence on page 593).

If you find a fragment, use one of these techniques to eliminate it:

1. Revise subordinate clauses by converting them to a simple independent clause (eliminating the connecting word), or join dependent clauses to form a complex sentence (see page 593).
2. Revise phrases to include them as a component of a sentence.
3. Revise any repeating structures to incorporate them into one of the basic sentence structures described on page 593.

B. *Editing Comma Splices and Fused Sentences*

Sentences of explanation with expanded examples or sentences with transitional words such as *therefore, consequently, so,* or *for example* may signal a **comma splice** (two sentences insufficiently connected with a simple comma) or a **fused sentence** (two sentences with no boundary between them). When complete sentences are strung together and are not bounded by proper connecting words or punctuation, they don't form any of the basic structures because their boundaries or connections are missing:

> **Fused sentence:**   Technology offers new options for our patrons yet they are afraid of those systems.

> **Comma splice:**   Technology can intimidate some patrons, therefore many insist on using tedious, outdated methods of research.

These errors can be corrected in several ways:

> **Make two sentences:**   Technology offers new options for our patrons. Yet, they are afraid of those systems.

> **Use a semicolon to separate the clauses:**   Technology offers new options for our patrons; nevertheless, they are afraid of those systems.

> **Separate clauses with a comma and coordinating conjunction:**   Technology offers new options for our patrons, yet they are afraid of those systems.

> **Make one clause dependent to create a complex sentence:**   Although technology offers new options for our patrons, they are afraid of those systems.

Sentence Parts

Sentences are formed of words classified as the traditional **parts of speech**—the types of words that make up sentences. The subject of a sentence is either a **noun** (a naming word), a **pronoun** (words like *he* or *she*), or a verbal phrase serving as a noun. The action or assertion of the sentence is conveyed by a **verb.** Words that describe or qualify these key words are **modifiers,** either **adjectives,** which qualify a noun or pronoun, or **adverbs,** which qualify verbs or adjectives. Connecting words that link sentences or clauses are **conjunctions** (e.g., *and, or, but, whereas, nevertheless*), while connecting words that link nouns and adjectives are **prepositions** (e.g., *in, out, to, of, with*).

C. *Editing the Forms of Pronouns and Nouns*

Nouns and pronouns function in sentences not only as **subjects,** but also as direct or indirect **objects** of action from the verb, as in this example: *She* (subject) *gives* (verb) *me* (indirect object) *hives* (direct object). Nouns and pronouns can also function as objects for a preposition, as in this example: *An idea* (subject) *came* (verb) *to* (preposition) *her* (object of the preposition). These sentence functions never affect the form of nouns, which does not change unless an *'s* is added to show possession.

Most personal pronouns and the relative pronoun *who* change form, however, depending on whether they are used in a sentence as subjects or objects; therefore, these forms require you to make some editing decisions:

Subject Form	*Object Form*
I, we, he/she, they	*me, us, him/her, them*
who, whoever	*whom, whomever*

In most sentences native speakers have little or no problem in choosing these forms. Here are some guidelines for editing when the subject or object form may seem uncertain:

1. *Use the subjective form for pronouns with the linking verb* **be.** A sentence using the linking verb *be* (*am, are, is, was, were*) sets up a kind of equation, in which the subject on one side is equal to the completing word on the other side of the verb, as in these sentences:

   I am the author.   The author is I.   It is I.   Not "The author is me."
   She was the patient.   The patient was she.   It was she.   Not "The patient was her."

   In conversation, you may have heard the unacceptable object forms, but formal language usage requires that the subject form be used. Because the object form may sound more "natural" to some people, however, this kind of construction is best avoided, either by putting the pronoun first or by rewriting the sentence to avoid a linking verb construction.

2. *Use the objective form for pronouns functioning as the subject of an infinitive.* When a personal pronoun follows a verb and precedes an infinitive—a position that makes it the subject of an infinitive verbal used as a noun—the objective form is used: "She helped *us to reach* our goal" or "She helped *us reach* our goal." This distinctive formation seldom gives trouble in editing.

3. *In compound constructions, use pronouns according to their sentence functions.* Writers sometimes lose sight of basic sentence relationships if the subject or object is doubled or tripled in a compound construction with *and* and *or*. Sometimes writers will need to edit:

   Wrong forms: *Fred and me* (subjects) *quietly went out.*

   They had to leave with you and I. (objects of the preposition *with*)

   With the compound subject or object dropped out, the sentence positions make the right form obvious:

   Edited: *I quietly went out.   Fred and I quietly went out.*

   They had to leave with me.   They had to leave with you and me.

   To edit such sentences, mentally drop out the compound, and choose the form that would be normal with a singular subject or object.

4. *In questions and clauses, choose the form* **who** *or* **whom** *that fits in a normal statement.* Because sentences in question form reverse normal sentence order, writers can lose sight of the subject or object form of *who, whoever, whom, whomever* that would be more obvious in a normal sentence.

   Uncertain: *Who/whom should we ask to dinner?*

   As a clue to editing such sentences, *answer* the question using a pronoun: We should ask *him or her.*

The process of decision making is this: (a) Reverse the question order: We should ask *who/whom*? Then (b) substitute a personal pronoun: We should ask *him or her*. (c) Restore the order and choose the *who/whom* form that matches:

Correct: *Whom* should we ask?

5. *In clauses with* **whoever** *or* **whomever,** *choose the form that fits the pronoun's role in the clause.* With forms of *whoever/whomever,* the questionable element is usually in a dependent clause:

Uncertain: I will dance with *whoever/whomever asks me.*

Here the clause—*whoever/whomever asks me*—must function with its own subject, verb, and object, even though as a whole the clause also serves as an object of the preposition (*with*). Edit such sentences by (a) substituting the pronoun *who/whom,* and ask it in a question: *Who/whom asks me?* Then (b) choose the form normally used in the question: *Who asks me?* which shows the correct choice:

Edited: I will dance with *whoever asks me.*

6. *Use possessive forms of nouns and pronouns before a gerund.* Possessive forms for nouns are regularly formed by adding *'s* as an ending. Pronouns have distinct possessive forms: *mine, ours, yours, hers, theirs,* which are used as the completing word on the other side of the linking verb *be* (*am, are, is, was, were*), as in *These are ours.* The possessive pronouns *my, our, your, his, her, its, their* are used to modify nouns (He disliked *my talk*) and also to modify noun phrases with *-ing* gerunds:

> He (subject) *disliked* (verb) *my* (possessive modifier) *talking* (gerund) loudly.
>
> He (subject) *disliked* (verb) *Alice's* (possessive modifier) *talking* (gerund) loudly.

Editing is often needed to avoid incorrect use of the subjective form with a gerund:

> He disliked ~~me~~ *my talking* loudly. He also disliked ~~Alice~~ *Alice's talking* loudly.

D. *Editing Verb Forms and Tenses*

Standard verb forms cause little problem for native speakers, although some irregular verb forms are not always familiar, and some verbs have alternate forms (e.g., *burn,* with alternative past and participle forms *burned* or *burnt*). Writers need to consult a dictionary to be sure of irregular forms.

Verb **tenses** express when actions or statuses occur—usually described as present, past, and future. Some special uses of present tenses include expressing historical or literary events as if continually present (Bogart *says,* "I was misinformed.") or future intentions with time expressions (I *go* off to college *tomorrow.*) Beyond the simple present and past tense forms, other tenses are formed with **auxiliary** or helping verbs, especially *be, have,* and *will* in combination with the past participle *-ed* forms and the present participle *-ing* forms for progressive, ongoing tenses.

1. *Tense sequences for two closely related events.* While tenses are familiar to native speakers and cause few editing problems in themselves, an editing decision is sometimes needed to clarify which tense or time sequence is appropriate when two closely related events are described in adjoining sentences or as parts of the same sentence. When two closely related events are being described together, use these guidelines:

   a. If both events occurred in the past, you can use a simple past tense for the first event and any of the past tenses for the second:

   > They *liked* what they *saw.*

   > They *considered* what they *had done* (or *had been doing*).

   b. If one event happened before the other, you can use past perfect tense for the event that occurred first and simple past tense for the event that occurred later:

   > She *had considered* the matter settled before she *saw* the outcome of the action.

   c. If one event happened in the past and the other is a recognized fact or condition, you can use simple past tense for the first event and simple present tense for the recognized fact:

   > The researchers *discovered* that people *do not always trust* each other.

2. *Conditional events with subjunctive verb forms.* Hypothetical or unreal statements about the future conventionally use **subjunctive** mood forms of the verb, which often look like past tense forms: If I *did* that, or if I *had done* it, I would be dead.

   a. Note that the *would* or *could* form (a modal helping verb with a form of *be*) occurs only in the main clause expressing the result of an unreal situation, but *not* in the conditional *if* clause.

   > **Revised:** If he ~~would have~~ had been alert, he would have avoided the issue.

   b. In wished and hypothetical expressions, the correct past subjunctive form with *I, he, she,* or *it* is *were*, not *was.*

   > **Revised:** I wish that I ~~was~~ were in New Orleans. If I ~~was~~ were there, I'd be happy.

E. *Choosing Verbs in the Active versus Passive Voice*

Verbs in the **active voice** name the subject of the clause as actor or protagonist of the act or assertion that the verb expresses; when the verb is transitive, anything acted upon becomes the object of the verb:

> **Active:** *The administrator* (subject) *reviewed* (active verb) *the college honor code* (object).

Active voice is the clearer and simpler mode for making direct statements and is preferable for most general exposition.

Verbs in the **passive voice** are useful to emphasize the object acted on and also to avoid the active voice's emphasis on the actor. Passive verbs are formed with the past participle verb form and a form of *to be*, with the original subject relegated to a *by* phrase:

Passive: The college honor code *was reviewed* by the administrator.

If the *by* phrase is dropped, the object of the verb gets even more emphasis and the actor is eliminated from view:

Passive: The college honor code *was reviewed*.

Because the passive voice leaves the actor less specific and is sometimes wordy, many readers strongly object to its frequent use. Nevertheless, some writers use passive voice to focus on the material acted on rather than on the actors. If passive voice becomes a deliberate way to avoid responsibility for a statement or to give a false impression of objectivity, however, its use becomes irresponsible.

F. *Editing Some Troublesome Verb Forms*

1. *Verbs frequently confused—transitive and intransitive forms.* Some verbs with similar sounds and related meaning are commonly confused and given incorrect roles in a sentence. A **transitive verb** takes a direct object:

   The USDA (subject) *sets* (transitive verb) *standards* (object) for meat quality.

   An **intransitive verb** takes no action on any object:

   The judge (subject) *sits* (intransitive verb with no object).

   The transitive verb *set* is incorrect in such a sentence.
   Similarly, the transitive verb *lay* takes an object (A decorator *lays* an elegant place setting), but the intransitive verb *lie* takes no object (Here the rumor *lies*); in the latter sentence, the transitive *lay* is incorrect.
   The transitive verb *raise* takes an object (Legislators *raise* taxes), but the intransitive verb *rise* takes no object (Taxes *rise*); in the latter sentence, the transitive *raise* is incorrect.

2. *The split infinitive.* The infinitive—the base verb form—is frequently preceded by an infinitive marker *to*. Some readers are disturbed by any verbal modifier that "splits" the marker (*to*) from the base form (*challenge*):

   Split: The legal staff's job is *to* rigorously and promptly *review* all contractual elements.

   Revised: The legal staff's job is *to review* all contractual elements rigorously and promptly.

   However, the split formation may often prevent more awkward phrasing in a sentence full of complex modifiers (see Editing Modifiers: Placement and Misplacement below).

G. *Subject–Verb Agreement*

A verb must agree with or match its subject in **number;** that is, either both must be singular or both must be plural. This normal pattern is a problem only with third-person subjects (*he, she, it, they*) and with verbs that require the *-s* form, and even then only in certain confusing situations when extra caution and remedial action are required.

1. *Third-person subjects must agree in number with verbs, even if long phrases separate the subject and the verb.* If visualizing the normal pattern of agreement is hard because a long phrase or clause separates subject and verb, mentally removing the distracting sentence elements will reveal the correct form:

   (For determined players) a *goal* (if they want to make the professional teams) *is* (steady and reliable) *improvement* (based on their college careers).

2. *Compound subjects linked by* **and** *are ordinarily plural and must agree with a plural verb.* A subject with several parts joined by *and* becomes plural:

   Sage, rosemary, parsley, *and* thyme *are* basic spices.

   Note that the combination would be singular only if the elements become a single unit:

   "Parsley, Sage, Rosemary, and Thyme" *was* a lyric in a popular song in the 1960s.

3. *Verbs with compound subjects linked by* **or** *and* **nor** *must agree with the nearest element.* Agreement with a multiple-part subject joined with *or* is clear when both are singular or both plural:

   Either Harry *or* Joe *has* a chance to win. Neither they *nor* the other opponents *know* the odds.

   When the elements joined by *or* do not match in number or person, the "nearest element" rule is used to produce a verb that sounds most agreeable for the grouping:

   Either he *or* I *have* a chance to win. Neither they *nor* he *knows* the odds today.

4. *A linking verb must agree with the subject rather than the complementing element of its sentence.* With linking verbs (*be, seem, become*), a sentence forms an "equation" of equal parts; but if the parts differ in number, the subject determines whether the verb is singular or plural:

   His *downfall* (subject) *is* too many cigarettes.

   One (subject) of my rules *is* returning messages promptly.

5. *A phrase or clause functioning as a complete subject serves as a singular subject with a singular verb.* A noun phrase—a gerundive or infinitive—as well as a dependent noun clause, can function as a single unit to form a singular subject:

   Living happily and living well *is* the best revenge. That I am happy *is* no guarantee of success.

6. *Singular verbs are used with nouns and pronouns that convey a group sense, even if the noun appears plural.* A number of noun or pronoun forms convey a group sense that is considered singular in agreement with a singular verb.

    a. Indefinite pronouns (*every, any, each*) agree with singular verbs (see H-4 below):

        Anybody who *comes* here is welcome.

    b. Collective nouns (*group, crowd, bunch, team,* and the like) agree with singular verbs:

        The audience *was* ready to applaud.

    c. Plural-form nouns that have a singular sense agree with singular verbs. Nouns such as *news, politics, economics,* and *mathematics* are generally considered singular:

        Physics *is* basic to many other sciences.

H. *Pronouns and Antecedents: Reference and Agreement*

A pronoun renames and refers to a noun or indefinite pronoun located somewhere nearby in the same or a neighboring sentence; every pronoun needs an **antecedent** to which it refers clearly in order to get a specific meaning.

    To make the reference clear, observe these rules:

1. *Keep pronouns close to their antecedents.* Too many nouns between a pronoun and its antecedent can be confusing:

    News reporters or city editors when dealing with angry readers or troubled sources must keep *their* (*whose?*) tempers.

    Rewriting to close the gap will help:

    News reporters or city editors must keep *their* tempers when . . . .

2. *Keep pronouns referenced to specific things or persons.* Avoid using vague pronoun constructions such as *you know, they say,* and *it figures,* and be sure that *this, that, which,* and *it* refer to specific nouns. Check for sentences with vague or implied antecedents:

    In a thunderstorm it (*?*) creates a lightning discharge.

    Rewrite to make a specific antecedent:

    If an electric *charge* builds during a thunderstorm, *it* creates lightning.

To make an accurate reference, a pronoun must **agree** with the number, person, and gender of its antecedent. Some sentence situations may make this agreement unclear and may require some corrective action. Here are some of these situations:

3. *Agreement when there is a compound antecedent.* When two or more antecedent nouns are joined by *and,* the pronoun should be plural; it should be singular if the nouns are joined by either *or* or *nor:*

    Singular: Either the clerks or the bailiff, whichever *is* willing to assume responsibility, should handle the situation.

> ***Plural:***   Both the clerks and the bailiffs, who *are* responsible for the situation, should be involved in the decision.

4. *Agreement when the antecedent is a common indefinite pronoun.* The pronoun should be singular when referring to the following indefinite antecedents:

each	anyone	everyone
either	anybody	everybody
neither	someone	no one
one	somebody	person

5. *Avoid gender bias with indefinite pronouns.* **Choosing an appropriate gender** for the personal pronoun referring to one of these indefinite pronouns is no problem when the antecedent is limited to an all-male or all-female group (e.g., The nuns took turns singing; each took *her* turn singing). In most other cases, however, these singular indefinite antecedents create an editing decision for the writer, who must either use the somewhat awkward *he or she* construction or rewrite the sentence. Commonly used rewriting options include these:

> ***Plural constructions:***   They *all* took *their* turns telling stories.

> ***Passive voice, de-emphasizing the actors:***   Stories were told throughout the night.

Sentence Structure

I. *Editing Modifiers: Placement and Misplacement*

In general, modifiers are clearest when they are placed *immediately before or after the word they modify*, but in placing them, the writer must also avoid breaking up the basic integrity of the sentence. In certain situations, especially with lengthy modifiers, they must be placed carefully to prevent confusion.

1. *Reposition a lengthy modifier that splits a subject and its verb or splits a verb and its object or complement.* Usually, a lengthy modifying phrase or clause will be less disruptive if moved to the beginning or end of the main statement:

> ***Confusing:***   Parents are, because of their habitual and healthy skepticism, often hesitant to leave their children in day care.

> ***Repositioned:***   Because of their habitual and healthy skepticism, parents are often hesitant to leave their children in day care.

2. *Use care with limiting modifiers.* **Limiting modifiers** such as *only, almost, nearly, even,* and *simply* can change the meaning significantly and must be placed with special care. Notice the different meanings:

> *Nearly* all of our $1.2 million in profits came from Easter decorations.

> All of our *nearly* $1.2 million in profits came from Easter decorations.

3. *Reposition modifiers that describe two elements simultaneously.* In certain phrasings a modifier's placement between two elements can create ambiguity:

The council members who argued *vehemently* spoke of their concerns.

Repositioning the modifier will clarify the meaning: either "The council members who *vehemently* argued . . ." or ". . . spoke *vehemently* of their concerns."

4. *Correct "dangling" modifiers.* A modifier "dangles" when the word it modifies is not clearly visible in the sentence. This problem can happen *either* when a long introductory phrase or clause is not followed up with a word it can modify, *or* when a sentence with a passive verb provides no mention of the performer of the action. Correct the problem by rewriting the sentence to provide a word that can be clearly modified.

Dangling: After daring the officer to do anything, a six-pack of beer was opened.

Corrected: After daring the officer to do anything, he opened a six-pack of beer.

J. *Maintaining Parallelism*

Words, phrases, and clauses that are paired together or compared must share an equivalent or parallel grammatical form to achieve sentence clarity and consistency. This principle operates within sentences whenever coordinate or correlative conjunctions are used or whenever comparisons or contrasts are made.

1. *Use parallel words, phrases, and clauses with coordinate and correlative conjunctions.* When elements are joined or paired by coordinate conjunctions (*and, but, for, or, nor, so, yet*) or when they are contrasted with correlative conjunctions (*either/or, neither/nor, both/and, not only/but also*), the linked elements must be the same kind of grammatical unit:

Adjectives: ***Not Parallel:***   A good boss must be both focused and a good listener.

   Parallel: A good boss must be able to focus and eager to listen.

Phrases: ***Not Parallel:***   The line workers need split-second timing yet to work carefully.

   Parallel: The line workers need to work quickly yet carefully.

2. *Use parallel structures with compared and contrasted elements.* Elements are contrasted or compared using such expressions as *rather than, on the other hand, like, unlike,* or *just as/so too.* The compared elements must share an equivalent grammatical form.

Not parallel: The Samson Group wanted to pursue contracts that were marginally profitable rather than as a get-rich-quick operation.

Parallel: The Samson Group wanted to pursue contracts that were marginally, rather than tremendously, profitable.

3. *Use parallel grammatical forms for entries in a list or outline.* To emphasize the logical connections among items in outlines and lists, make sure the elements are of equivalent grammatical form:

Not parallel: Items needing attention:

- survey of Mennis acreage
- making roadway changes
- revise view of rotunda
- how to reposition the dome

Parallel: Items needing attention:

- survey Mennis acreage
- make roadway changes
- revise view of rotunda
- reposition the dome

K. *Coordination and Subordination Decisions*

Writers combine phrases and clauses to establish two basic relationships: elements can have a **coordinate** connection, which emphasizes a balance or equality between the elements, or a **subordinate** or **dependent** connection, which emphasizes that the elements are unequal and that one has a dependent link to the other. Phrases and clauses are often logically linked with connecting words—**conjunctions** and **conjunctive adverbs**—that require writers to consider carefully the kind of connection they wish to establish.

1. *Choose the right connection for coordinate structures.* Connecting words for a coordinate, or balanced, relationship include **coordinating conjunctions** (*and, but, or, no, so, for, yet*), **correlative conjunctions** (*either/neither, neither/nor, both/and, not only/but, whether/or, not only/but also*), and many **conjunctive adverbs** (*however, nevertheless, accordingly, also, besides, afterward, then, indeed, otherwise*). These words show relationships of contrast, consequence, sequence, and emphasis.

    After deciding on the desired relationship between sentence parts, select a *single set of connecting words* and avoid a mixture of words that may cancel out the meaning:

    Mixed: They were *both* competitive, *besides* Madge had more common sense. (The mixed connecting words show similarity and contrast at the same time.)

    Balanced: They were *both* competitive, *but* Madge had more common sense. They were competitive; *however,* Madge had more common sense.

2. *Choose a subordinating conjunction for a dependent relationship.* An array of subordinating conjunctions can be used to establish various relationships, including conditional relationships, or relations of contrast, cause and effect, time and place, or purpose and outcome:

    Contrast: *though, although, as if, even though*
    Cause: *since, because*
    Purpose: *that, in order that, so that*
    Condition: *if, unless, even if, provided that*
    Time: *whenever, when, while, as, since, once, until*
    Place: *where, wherever*

    Choose a single subordinating conjunction, and avoid combinations that are contradictory or confusing.

> **Mixed:** *Because* she was in labor, *so* she went to the hospital. (A relation of cause and effect is confusingly combined with one of purpose or outcome.)
>
> **Clear:** *Because* she was in labor, she went to the hospital. (cause and effect)

Punctuation to Mark Sentence Structure

L. *End Punctuation*

1. *Periods.* Periods are used to mark the end of a sentence. A period is always placed inside a quotation that ends a sentence, but is placed inside a parenthesis only if the parenthetical remark is a complete sentence. Periods are used with most standard abbreviations—Mr., Mrs., Ave., Dr., and also with Ms. (though it is not an abbreviation). A period is *not* used with acronyms or acronym abbreviations—CIA, NATO, NASA, NPR, FDIC.

2. *Question marks.* A question mark is placed at the end of a direct question and after a quoted question within quotation marks. However, an indirect question uses no question mark: "He asked why we should do it."

3. *Exclamation marks.* Exclamation marks normally are not used in informative workplace writing except after a direct exclamatory quotation within quotation marks. The overuse of exclamation marks conveys a breathless, somewhat frivolous tone to writing.

M. *Semicolons*

1. *Use a semicolon, not a comma, to link independent clauses.* Semicolons can link clauses that are intended to be closely related; commas cannot do this without creating the comma splice error (see Editing Comma Splices and Fused Sentences above). Whether clauses are separated into sentences with periods or are linked with a semicolon depends on your intention about their relationship and also on the tone and timing if the two clauses were spoken. Thus, in the following examples, you might hear a difference in the relationship of the parts:

> You should include a letter of application with your résumé; it tells the reader how to read your résumé.
>
> You should include a letter of application with your résumé. It tells the reader how to read your résumé.

Similarly, independent clauses can be linked by semicolons—not by commas— immediately before the following conjunctions and conjunctive expressions: *however, therefore, moreover, nevertheless, furthermore, instead, consequently, accordingly, of course, for example.*

> You should include a letter of application with your résumé to show your reader how to interpret the résumé; furthermore, it allows you to specify what you can do for the organization to which you are applying.

2. *Use a semicolon to join a series of clauses or phrases that require internal commas.*

> The newest offices for the Merchants Association will be in Wilshire, Kansas; Pohoton, New Jersey; and Fairbanks, Alaska.

> Semicolons are placed outside end quotation marks.

N. *Commas*

The purpose of commas is to avoid confusion within a sentence by setting off or separating words, phrases, or clauses. When commas are used incorrectly to join totally independent sentences, they create the comma splice error (see Editing Comma Splices and Fused Sentences above). The key uses of commas can be described under the following categories.

1. *A comma is required before a coordinating conjunction* (and, or, but) *joining independent clauses.* Using a comma with a coordinating conjunction is a common way to join dependent clauses:

   > We can walk away from trouble, *or* we can face and overcome it.

   > I like to hike, *but* I always regret it afterward.

2. *Commas are used to separate items in a series.* A string of three or more related items in a phrase needs separating commas. Some writers omit the final comma before the *and* that precedes the last item in the series:

   > *The flag was green, white, and gold.*   or   *The flag was green, white and gold.*

   When two or more adjectives in a series are *completely interchangeable* without influencing meaning or conventional order, commas may be used to separate them:

   > He's a tired, sleepy, grouchy boy.

   But note: It's a bright red flower. (When order is critical to meaning, no comma is used.)

3. *Commas set off introductory and transitional expressions and phrases.* Commas are used after words, phrases, or clauses that begin a sentence:

   > Yes, it's time to go. As we speak, the show is starting.

   Commas are also used to set off interrupting or contrasting modifiers in mid-sentence:

   > The horse started bucking, even without its saddle, as we approached.

4. *Commas must set off nonessential or interrupting units.* Commas are often used to set apart clauses or phrases that are **nonessential**, that is, not limiting to a basic sentence's meaning. Such units (also called nonrestrictive) do not restrict meaning but merely add more information. Commas are *not* correctly used

with any essential (restrictive) clause or phrase that limits meaning with an important modifier.

Essential modifier: The reports *that were written yesterday* tallied the
accounts to date. (The modifying clause means we're limiting
discussion to yesterday's reports; any reports written before or after
yesterday are not under discussion.)

Nonessential: The reports, *which were written yesterday*, tallied the
accounts to date. (Here we're discussing the subject of the reports,
which, incidentally, were written yesterday.)

Because the nonessential information is seen as an interruption of the basic statement, it is set off or surrounded by commas. If on rereading, however, you decide that the information is essential and restricts the intended meaning, you should signal this importance by eliminating any commas around the clause or phrase.

O. *Colons and Dashes*

1. *Colons.* Colons are used after a complete sentence to announce a list (or another statement) that is separate from the announcing sentence:

> Ingredients to make red clam sauce include the following: clams, fresh tomatoes, kalamata olives, capers, fresh basil, garlic, olive oil, and oregano.

> You can use these ingredients to make red clam sauce: clams, fresh tomatoes, kalamata olives, capers, fresh basil, garlic, olive oil, and oregano.

A colon should follow a complete sentence, *not* a fragment that lacks critical parts:

Incorrect: The reports are: progress, problem/solution, and feasibility.

Correct this error by completing the sentence before the colon:

Correct: These reports were sent to the district office: progress, problem/solution, and feasibility.

2. *Dashes.* Dashes are also used, though more informally than colons, to announce a list (or another statement) that is separate from or an interruption of an opening statement.

  Dashes are also used to set off and emphasize a statement added to a complete sentence. The added statement is usually itself a complete sentence but may be a phrase or clause:

> We submitted the proposal—we stayed up all night to complete it—by the 8:00 A.M. deadline.

Emphatic interruptions with dashes should be used sparingly in most workplace writing. A dash is indicated on a typewriter or computer by a double hyphen.

Other Punctuation for Quotations and Word Forms

P. *Apostrophes*

Apostrophes are used to mark certain plural forms, show possession, and show the omission of letters in contractions.

1. *Personal pronouns.* Apostrophes should *never* be used to show possession with personal pronouns, which have their own forms in the possessive case: *your, yours* (e.g., your book; the book is yours), *its, whose, our, ours.* These forms must be systematically distinguished from nonpossessive pronouns, which use apostrophes in contractions with *to be* verbs: *it's* (it is), *who's* (who is), *you're* (you are).

2. **Contractions.** Although formal workplace writing has conventionally avoided using contraction forms (*can't, won't, it's*), much everyday writing uses a contraction style. To help decide whether to use contractions, check writing similar in tone that is addressed to audiences like those for which you are writing.

3. *Possession with multiple nouns.* When a pair or cluster of words functions as a single unit, or when joint possession is indicated, add an *'s* to the last word: *John and Susan's report; brother-in-law's job.* If possession is individual to each person named, each gets an *'s: Both John's and Susan's reports are late.*

4. *Certain plurals.* An *'s* is used to pluralize named letters, numerals, or words identified as words: *dot your i's, three 2's, two and's. Never* use apostrophes to form regular plurals of nouns.

Q. *Quotations and Quotation Marks*

Opening and closing double quotation marks are used to enclose and set off **direct quotations** from the rest of the sentence or paragraph where they appear. If a quotation runs beyond four lines of type in your document, it is better to set it off as a **block extract quotation**—a subsidiary paragraph with margins usually indented from the main text. In dialogue sequences, a new paragraph conventionally is used to indicate each change of speaker.

When you place anything within quotation marks or in a block, you are representing that these words are *exactly* the same as the original. If the exact wording of the original cannot be guaranteed, a writer should create an **indirect quotation,** a statement introduced by a *that . . .* clause: *I thought he said that things were looking good.*

Punctuation to accompany quotation marks requires some editing:

1. *Quotation marks are used to enclose titles of short works such as chapters, stories, poems, and articles.* Titles of short works are enclosed in quotation marks, and titles of longer works such as books or periodicals are italicized:

> A limerick called "Get Shorty" appeared in "Notes and Comments" in yesterday's *USA Today.*

2. *Commas enclosing explanatory remarks fall outside quotation marks:*

> Pleaded Rabbit, "Won't you help me?" He was thinking, "I might as well ask."

3. *At the end of a quotation, place all commas and periods inside quotation marks, as well as any question or exclamation marks belonging to the quotation itself.*

> "I will not," said Fox, "and why should I?"
> Rabbit replied, "You'll see. I might have a deal for you."

4. *Colons, semicolons, and citation notes or parentheses are placed outside the quotation marks.*

> This is how they worded their "terms": "Get lost"; "Stuff it!"; "Take off, Charlie!" (Jones, 27).

5. *Question or exclamation marks fall outside quotation marks when not applied to the quotation itself.*

> Is it polite to say, "I want some!"? I just hate an answer like, "Why should you?"!

6. *Single quotation marks (' ') are used to set off quotations (or titles) within larger quotations.*

> "At best," he said, "you might hear 'I'm not sure' for an answer. If so, you can pester her by singing the song 'Maybe' from the show *Annie*."

R. *Parentheses, Brackets, Ellipses, and Slashes*

The key functions of parentheses, brackets, and ellipses are to show insertions of nonessential information or gaps and editorial insertions in quotations.

1. *Parentheses set apart nonessential information, dates, or inserted comments within sentences.*

> I commented politely on the dinner (*I didn't like it much*) and went on talking to him.
> The war leader Tecumseh (*1768?–1813*) tried to rally tribes against Yankee invaders.

2. *Parentheses are conventionally used to enclose numbered or lettered items within sentences.*

> We asked them (1) to stop the merger, (2) to inform stockholders, and (3) to change policy.

3. *Brackets are used to enclose a writer's words inserted into quoted material to help with clarity or sentence structure.*

> Lincoln's "[f]our score and seven years ago [1776]" called up the . . . and Jefferson's statement that "all [people] are created equal . . . ."

4. *Brackets are used around a parenthetical comment placed inside a larger one.*

> Lincoln's way of dating the Revolution (*four score and seven years before his speech* [*1863*]) is a resounding turn of rhetoric that nearly overwhelms his meaning.

5. *Ellipses are used to show a break in continuity.* Three spaced periods (. . .) make an ellipsis, which is used to show that words or sentences have been deliberately deleted from a quoted source. Use them to show words deleted from the middle or the end of a sentence. At the end of the sentence, add another period at the place it would normally go around quoted punctuation or citations:

> "Four score and seven years ago, our fathers brought forth a new nation . . . dedicated to the proposition that all men are created equal," said Lincoln. (Three periods mark the gap.)
>
> Lincoln said that our nation was "conceived in liberty. . . ." (A fourth period ends the sentence.)
>
> The phrase was "[f]our score and seven years ago . . ." (Lincoln works, 337). (The period falls outside a citation.)

Note: An ellipsis is *not* used to indicate words omitted from the beginning of a sentence, *nor* those omitted from a sentence ending with a period that also ends the writer's own sentence:

> Lincoln said, "our fathers brought forth a new nation . . . dedicated to the proposition that all men are created equal."

6. *Slashes are used to show choices and fractions and to separate lines of poetry quoted within sentences or paragraphs.*

> "You're either the problem or the solution" is a logically false either/or choice.
>
> The measurement falls 9/16 inches short of three feet.
>
> Shelley's "Skylark" begins, "Hail to thee blithe spirit / Bird thou never wert."

Mechanics

S. *Italic Type*

Italic type is indicated by slanted type in typography and by an underline on most typewriters or word processors. In sentences italic type may be used to call attention to a word or letter. On special occasions, a few words in a sentence may need emphasis to convey the meaning:

> When responding to a car fire, you must wear *all* turnout gear.

Overuse of italic type devalues such emphasis and makes writing appear overexcited and unconvincing. Most writing for technical communities makes very sparing use of italic type for emphasis.

Italic type has three main mechanical uses.

1. Italic type is used to identify key technical terms or numerals that will be defined or referred to as words or numerals:

   > The term *reconfiguration* will be further labeled as types *1* and *2*.

2. Italic type is used to identify foreign words or expressions not yet assimilated into English, such as the Latin expression *post hoc* (after the fact). Note that many terms that originally were foreign have been assimilated and are no longer put in italic type, such as the Latin expression alter ego (someone's stand-in). For any given word, your dictionary or the style sheet for your organization is the final arbiter.

3. Italic type is a key element in bibliographical conventions. Both in text and in reference listings, italic type is used for the titles of the following:

   - Books, journals, and government publications
   - Laws and statutes
   - Individually named transport craft, such as ships, trains, and aircraft
   - Newspapers, magazines, and periodicals

   With newspapers it is conventional not to italicize the word *the*, even if it is part of the paper's title. With academic journals of all kinds, it is best to consult a bibliography from your discipline to determine how titles are rendered.

T. *Abbreviations and Acronyms*

In using abbreviations, especially for the names of professional or news journals, you need to be extremely careful that the readers in your audience know what the abbreviations stand for. When in doubt, spell out the full name at the first mention. For **acronyms**—pronounceable abbreviations formed by the initials for the names of agencies, groups, job titles, and the like—it is essential to write out the full name at the first occurrence. In formal workplace writing, use as few abbreviations as possible.

Use of abbreviations such as i.e. (that is), e.g. (for example), N.B. (note well), and et al. (and others) in citation and references should follow the style guidelines of your organization or professional group. The abbreviation *etc.* (et cetera—and so on) is so vague that its use is considered confusing and unprofessional unless limited to very obvious sequences: *They started counting, 1, 2, 3, 4, etc.*

1. *Follow conventions for standard titles and times.* Standard titles of address—*Mr., Mrs., Ms., Dr.*—are used only before the proper name and not by themselves: *Dr. Florence Nightingale,* but not *She is a Dr.* Certain abbreviated titles (*Jr., Sr.*) or honors are conventionally used *after* a proper name or title, preceded by a comma. For academic degrees, such as *B.A., M.D., Ph.D.,* and *M.A.,* and the term *Esq.,* the abbreviation is used *without* an abbreviated title of address before the name:

   > *Florence Nightingale, M.D.*   or   *Dr. Florence Nightingale*
   > *James Callahan, Esq.*   or   *Mr. James Callahan*
   > But not   *Dr. Florence Nightingale, M.D.*   or   *Mr. James Callahan, Esq.*

Time, prior to noon or after, is indicated with A.M. or P.M., either in capital or lowercase letters, or sometimes in small capitals, depending on the publishing style: 6:50 A.M. (or a.m.).

2. *Abbreviations for numbers, times, units, money, and titles are used* **only** *with specifics.* None of the standard unit or title abbreviations should be used alone or for generic names; these should always be included with the specific items in specific contexts:

> They will deliver exactly $27.50 at 6:15 A.M. at No. 10 Downing Street.
> Not *Be there in the A.M. with a large No. of $.*

3. *For addresses and company abbreviations, consult professional references and letterheads.* Formal addresses tend to minimize abbreviations for streets and companies, while listings and databanks use them extensively. *The Staybrite Company, 150 Bleecker Road* may appear in formal addresses, while summarized listings may abbreviate the address as *Staybrite Co., 150 Bleecker Rd.*

U. *Capitalization and Numbers*

In addition to designating the beginning of each sentence, capital letters are used in titles for words of significance. The first and last words, including articles, and prepositions of five letters or more are capitalized; short prepositions and the articles *a, an,* and *the* are otherwise *not* capitalized in titles.

1. *Proper noun capitalization.* Capital letters are conventionally used for any noun that refers to a *particular* person, place, or object that has been given an individual (proper) name or title. Such nouns include the following:

   a. Names of people or groups of people.
   b. Religions, religious titles, and nationalities.
   c. Languages, places (including those in addresses), and regions. Capitalize *the South* (a region) but *not* a compass heading as in *we headed south.*
   d. Adjectives formed from proper nouns (*French perfume*) and titles of distinction that are part of proper nouns.
   e. Names of days, months, holidays, historical events, and periods.
   f. Particular objects (*Hope Diamond*) and brand-name products.
   g. Abbreviations for words that are themselves capitalized.
   h. Acronyms for companies and agencies and established abbreviations.

2. *Editing decisions with numbers.* In written sentences, numbers that begin sentences and numbers that can be expressed in one or two words (seventy-six, three-fourths) are normally written out. When time is expressed with the term *o'clock,* the number is written out (ten o'clock but 10 A.M.). As you proofread, it's important to be sure that short numbers have been treated consistently throughout the document.

   Treatment of numbers and abbreviations must conform to the standards set by an organization or by professional or business journals that you or your audience refers to regularly.

A P P E N D I X

Citing and Documenting Sources in Workplace Documents

Citing Sources

When you refer to various references in the text, you must document those sources. You have three options for documenting sources:

1. *Footnotes:* A rather old-fashioned method in which superscript numbers are added after borrowed material and the sources are listed at the bottom of each page with corresponding superscript numbers (see Figure A.1). Even though the sources are cited at the bottom of each page, you must still construct a Works Cited list, which serves as a final resource for readers who want to see the complete list of sources for your document.

In technical communication, humanism has taken its grandest swipes at the very subject of the profession: technology. Recognizing the dangers of losing sight of the many, humanism most eloquently supports the mission of the profession: information exchange. *Humanistic Aspects of Technical Communication* argues a humanistic center for the profession that includes the sense of humanism (and its roots for technical communication) in the ancient eras and leading into the modern era.[1] In "A Humanistic Rationale for Technical Writing," Carolyn Miller argues that humanism precludes the certainties of positivist science and technology that have infringed on the flexibility of language,[2] a view that has led professional communicators to put aside the traditional view that there can be "one meaning [and] . . . only one meaning"[3] to communicate clearly. The humanist perspective is the alternative to this kind of positivism, recognizing that language and interpretation are defiantly complex and irreducible to formulaic notions of expression and communication.

---

[1] Paul Dombrowski, *Humanistic Aspects of Technical Communication*. Amityville, NY: Baywood, 1994.
[2] Carolyn Miller, "A Humanistic Rationale for Technical Communication." *College English* 40 (1979): 610–17.
[3] Britton, Earl. "What Is Technical Writing? A Redefinition." *College Composition and Communication* 16 (1965): 115. Rpt. in *The Teaching of Technical Writing*. Ed. by Donald H. Cunningham and Herman A. Estrin. Urbana, IL: National Council of Teachers of English, 1975, p. 13.

FIGURE A.1   Text Using Footnotes to Document Sources

In technical communication, humanism has taken its grandest swipes at the very subject of the profession: technology. Recognizing the dangers of losing sight of the many, humanism most eloquently supports the mission of the profession: information exchange. *Humanistic Aspects of Technical Communication* argues a humanistic center for the profession that includes the sense of humanism (and its roots for technical communication) in the ancient eras and leading into the modern era [1]. In "A Humanistic Rationale for Technical Writing," Carolyn Miller argues that humanism precludes the certainties of positivist science and technology that have infringed on the flexibility of language [2], a view that has led professional communicators to put aside the traditional view that there can be "one meaning [and] . . . only one meaning" to communicate clearly [3]. The humanist perspective is the alternative to this kind of positivism, recognizing that language and interpretation are defiantly complex and irreducible to formulaic notions of expression and communication.

F I G U R E A.2 Text Using Numerical Citations to Document Sources

2. *Numerical citations:* A system in which bracketed numbers are added after borrowed material to indicate the corresponding citation in the Works Cited list (see Figure A.2).

3. *Parenthetical citations:* A system in which the *name of the author* and *the page number(s)* or the *author* and *year* of the work and *page number(s)* (depending on the style manual you follow) of the borrowed work are added in parentheses after the information in the text (see Figure A.3).

If your organization or discipline does not offer specific guidelines for citing material, you may follow any of these systems, provided you are consistent throughout your document.

Documenting Sources

There are three essential purposes for documenting sources in any work that you create on the job:

1. to give credit for ideas and research to others
2. to help alleviate suspicion or skepticism about your facts
3. to help readers find the original sources of information

Consequently, the most important features of documentation are

1. *complete* information that will help the reader locate the source
2. *accurate* information that will prevent confusion
3. *consistent* formatting of the information so readers will know where to look for various bits of information (pages, dates, etc.) within any given citation

In technical communication, humanism has taken its grandest swipes at the very subject of the profession: technology. Recognizing the dangers of losing sight of the many, humanism most eloquently supports the mission of the profession: information exchange. *Humanistic Aspects of Technical Communication* (Dombrowski 1994) argues a humanistic center for the profession that includes the sense of humanism (and its roots for technical communication) in the ancient eras and leading into the modern era. In "A Humanistic Rationale for Technical Writing," Carolyn Miller (1980) argues that humanism precludes the certainties of positivist science and technology that have infringed on the flexibility of language, a view that has led professional communicators to put aside the traditional view that there can be "one meaning [and] . . . only one meaning" to communicate clearly (Britton 1965, p. 114). The humanist perspective is the alternative to this kind of positivism, recognizing that language and interpretation are defiantly complex and irreducible to formulaic notions of expression and communication.

FIGURE A.3 Text Using Parenthetical Citations to Document Sources

---

The following examples are some of the most often used resources in workplace documents.

1. author
   title
   place of publication
   publisher
   date of publication

2. authors
   title
   place of publication
   publisher
   date of publication

3. corporation/author
   title
   place of publication
   publisher
   date of publication

4. editor
   title
   place of publication
   publisher
   date

5. author
   title
   editor
   place of publication
   publisher
   date

6. title
   date
   place/publisher
   medium
   vendor
   date of access

Books

A Book by a Single Author

1 Picairn, Peter J. *Management Principles: On Our Own.* New York: Michaelson, 1999.

A Book by Two or More Authors

2 Langworthy, Lacey, and Sherrie Small. *Communicating Principles of Learning.* Needham Heights, NJ: Farnsworth, 2001.

A Book by a Corporate Author

3 Boston Stockbrokers' Association. *Investing in Your Own Venture.* Boston: Simon, 1999.

A Book by an Editor (when you are citing the entire book)

4 Price, Raymond, ed. *A View of Tomorrow's Business.* Los Angeles: Rosemund, 1998.

A Book by an Author and an Editor

5 Marshall, Dianne. *Melrose Money.* Ed. Melissa Graves New York: Turner, 1998.

Original Work Stored on CD-ROM

6 *Company Report.* 4 November 1988. New York: Erskine, Inc. CD-ROM. Erskine, Inc. 30 November 1998.

Online Database Storing Published Work

7. author
   title
   [publication information]
   medium
   vendor/source
   date of access

7 Vitale, Jackson. "The Cost of Crisis." *Quarterly Review* June/July 1997: 33–67. *ProQuest*. On-line. 5 October 1999.

Electronic Journals

8. author
   title
   [publication information]
   medium
   vendor
   date of access

8 Vereen-Benson, Taylor. "Assessing Damage." *Pique* 3.2 (1999): n. pag. On-line. Internet. 3 October 1999.

Electronic Mail

9. author
   title/subject
   form/medium to recipient
   date

9 Camden, Suzanne. "Job Description." E-mail to Karen Beardslee. 7 April 2001.

Alternative Resources

In-house Reports

1. author(s)
   title
   city
   publisher
   date
   page(s)

1 Maier, Johnson, Betty McCall, and Timothy Ginnes. *The Quarterly Review.* New York: Erskine, Inc., 12 January 1998: 12–13.

Graphics

2. title of graphic
   type of graphic
   larger work's title
   [publication information]

2 "The Costs of the Benton Buyout." Chart. In *Acquiring the Benton Group: A Look at Stability Effects.* New York: Erskine, Inc., 2 December 1998: 22.

Letters

3. author
   medium/recipient
   date
   [corporate information]

3 Geronne, Ben: Letter to Pearson McCullah. 3 May 1999. New York: Erskine, Inc.

Interviews

4. interviewee
   medium
   date
   [corporate
      information/place]

4 Warsaw, Lilah. Telephone interview. 30 June 1998.
   Warsaw, Lilah. Personal interview. 30 July 1997. Portland, OR: Finesco, Inc.

Speeches or Seminars

5. speaker
   title/subject
   place of presentation
   group/audience
   date

5 McClain, Patrick. "Getting the Client On-line." Boston: Association of Marketing Researchers. 4 May 1998.
   McClain, Patrick. "Getting the Client On-line." Boise, ID: Erskine in-house seminar. 15 June 1999.

1. author
   title of work used
   title of entire work
   editor
   place of publication
   publisher
   date
   page(s) of work used

Works within Larger Works

1 A Work within an Anthology

Jeeves, Gerard. "When the Money Ends." *Imagining the Worst.* Ed. Marissa Thompson. Chapel Hill, NC: Algorithm, 2001, 292–93.

2. author
   title of article
   newspaper
   date of publication
   edition
   section:page(s)

3. title of article
   newspaper
   date of publication
   edition
   section:page(s)

4. title of article
   newspaper
   town
   date
   edition
   section:page(s)

5. author
   title of article
   title of publication
   date
   page(s)

6. author
   title of article
   title of publication
   date
   page(s)

7. author
   title of article
   title of publication
   volume number
   date
   page(s)

8. author
   title of article
   title of publication
   volume: issue number
   date
   page(s)

1. overall place of origination
   specific government group
   most specific government
      group
   title of work
   place of publication
   publisher
   date

1. author
   title of work
   title of larger work
   volume
   date of publication
   pages
   database title
   medium
   vendor
   date of access

An Article from a Daily Newspaper

2 Jackson, Diane. "Farming for Cash Crops." *The Washington Post* 22
September 1999, morning ed., sec. 2:8.

If the article is unsigned

3 "Farming for Cash Crops." *The Washington Post* 22 September 1999, morning
ed., sec. 2:8.

If the newspaper's name does not disclose its location

4 "Farming for Cash Crops." *The Daily Reader* (Jackson, MS) 22 September
1999, morning ed., sec. 2:8.

An Article from a Monthly or Bimonthly Magazine

5 Snosher, Kallie. "The Murovian Deal: Corporate America on its Back."
Atlantic October 1999: 35–45.

An Article from a Weekly or Biweekly Magazine

6 Nordstrom, Merle. "In This Cultural Time." *New Yorker* 14 Feb. 1999: 33–41.

An Article from a Journal with Continuous Pagination from Issue to Issue

7 Sample, Betty. "Documenting Workplace Writing." *Technical Communication
Quarterly* 5 (1998): 223–35.

An Article from a Journal That Paginates Each Issue Separately

8 Mercer, Daylon. "Downsizing the Corporate Structure." *Management* 15.6
(1996): 33–67.

Government Documents

1 United States. Cong. House. Committee on Foreign Affairs. *Aid to Israel:
A Report on the Bush Administration.* Washington: GPO, 1994.

CD-ROMs and Online Resources

Printed/Published Work Stored on CD-ROM

1 Markel, Myron. "Getting it in Print." *Publication Quarterly* 39 (1999): 33–56.
Publisher's International Bibliography. CD-ROM. Basic. March 1999.

Preparing the List of Works Cited

After completing your document, you are ready to prepare the list of Works Cited,
a comprehensive list of all resources used in your work. If your discipline uses a
specific style manual, such as the MLA (Modern Language Association) Manual of

Works Cited

Boston Stockbrokers' Association. *Investing in Your Own Venture.* Boston: Simon, 1999.

Jeeves, Gerard. "When the Money Ends." *Imagining the Worst.* Ed. Marissa Thompson. Chapel Hill, NC: Algorithm, 2001, 292–93.

United States. Cong. House. Committee on Foreign Affairs. *Aid to Israel: A Report on the Bush Administration.* Washington: GPO, 1994.

Vitale, Jackson. "The Cost of Crisis." *Quarterly Review* June/July 1997: 33–67. On-line. *ProQuest.* 5 October 1999.

FIGURE A.4   A Sample Alphabetical Listing

Style or the APA (American Psychological Association) style manual, by all means follow that guide in preparing your Works Cited. Many workplace organizations prepare their own style manuals to standardize documentation of resources. If yours does, be sure to follow its format.

If, however, neither your discipline nor your workplace organization has a style manual, you should determine from the outset whether you intend to list works alphabetically or by correlating reference numbers in the text to numbered entries in your Works Cited list. If you have used footnotes throughout your work, you should use an alphabetical list, as shown in Figure A.4. If you have used numerical references in the text, you should use a numbered list, as shown in Figure A.5.

Works Cited

1. Marshall, Dianne. *Melrose Money.* Ed. Melissa Graves. New York: Turner, 1998.
2. Markel, Myron. "Getting it in Print." *Publication Quarterly* 39 (1999): 33–56. *Publisher's International Bibliography.* CD-ROM. Basic. March 1999.
3. "Farming for Cash Crops." *The Daily Reader* (Jackson, MS) 22 September 1999, morning ed., sec. 2:8.
4. Geronne, Ben: Letter to Pearson McCullah. 3 May 1999. Erskine, Inc., New York.
5. Warsaw, Lilah. Telephone interview. 30 June 1998.
6. Camden, Suzanne. "Job Description." E-mail to Karen Beardslee. 7 April 2001.

FIGURE A.5   A Sample Numerical Listing

Index

619

621

622

STRATEGY REVIEW BOXES